The Hegel Reader

Blackwell Readers

In a number of disciplines, across a number of decades, and in a number of languages, writers and texts have emerged which require the attention of students and scholars around the world. United only by a concern with radical ideas, *Blackwell Readers* collect and introduce the works of pre-eminent theorists. Often translating works for the first time (Levinas, Irigaray, Lyotard, Blanchot, Kristeva), or presenting material previously inaccessible (C. L. R. James, Fanon, Elias), each volume in the series introduces and represents work which is now fundamental to study in the humanities and social sciences.

The Hegel Reader

Edited by

Stephen Houlgate

Copyright © Blackwell Publishers Ltd, 1998
Introduction and editorial apparatus copyright © Stephen Houlgate, 1998

First published 1998

2 4 6 8 10 9 7 5 3 1

Blackwell Publishers Ltd
108 Cowley Road
Oxford OX4 1JF
UK

Blackwell Publishers Inc.
Commerce Place
350 Main Street
Malden, Massachusetts 02148
USA

British Library Cataloguing in Publication Data

A CIP catalogue record for this book is available from the British Library.

Library of Congress Cataloging-in-Publication Data

Hegel, Georg Wilhelm Friedrich, 1770–1831.
[Selections. English. 1998]
The Hegel reader / edited by Stephen Houlgate.
p.   cm. — (Blackwell readers)
Includes bibliographical references and index.
ISBN 0–631–20346–X (hardcover : alk. paper)
ISBN 0–631–20347–8 (pbk. : alk. paper)
1. Philosophy.   I. Houlgate, Stephen.   II. Title.   III. Series.
B2908.H68   1998
193—ddc21

97–41251
CIP

Typeset in 10½ on 12½ pt Plantin
by Graphicraft Limited, Hong Kong
Printed in Great Britain by MPG Books Ltd, Bodmin, Cornwall

This book is printed on acid-free paper

In Memory of Duncan Forbes (1922–1994)

Contents

Part IV Philosophy of Nature and Philosophy of Subjective Spirit

Part V Philosophy of Objective Spirit: Philosophy of Right and Philosophy of History

Part VI Philosophy of Absolute Spirit: Aesthetics, Philosophy of Religion and History of Philosophy

Preface

For many Hegel is one of the subtlest and most perceptive philosophers in the Western tradition: the one who has provided the most acute and penetrating analyses we have of tragedy, of the essential historicity of human life and of the complex blend of freedom and alienation that characterizes modern civil society. For others Hegel is simply the standard bearer for the (allegedly totalitarian) Prussian state, the one who subordinates all difference and diversity to the 'logic of the same' or who advocates the mind-befuddling 'mystery method' of dialectic. My own judgement, based on twenty years of studying and teaching Hegel in both Britain and the USA, is that he is, without doubt, the subtlest and most perceptive of philosophers. The richness and originality of his *Phenomenology of Spirit* and *Science of Logic* are, in my view, matched only by Kant's *Critique of Pure Reason* and Heidegger's *Being and Time*, and his *Philosophy of Right* stands with Plato's *Republic* as one of the most profound texts in political philosophy ever written. One must also recognize, however, that hostile prejudice against Hegel (promoted by such figures as Schopenhauer and Karl Popper) still holds sway in the minds of many today. The purpose of *The Hegel Reader* is to counter such prejudice by making as much of Hegel's work as possible available in one book, so affording a wide range of readers, who might otherwise neglect Hegel, an opportunity to discover for themselves just how rich and subtle a thinker he actually is.

The Hegel Reader is the most comprehensive collection of Hegel's writings currently available in English. It includes four important early pieces, as well as selections from the *Phenomenology of Spirit*, the *Science of Logic*, the *Encyclopaedia Logic*, the *Philosophy of Nature*, the *Philosophy of Subjective Spirit*, the *Philosophy of Right*, the *Philosophy of History*, the *Aesthetics*, the *Philosophy of Religion* and the *Lectures on the History of Philosophy*. The book has been divided into six parts, each of which begins with a short introduction indicating how the selections that follow relate to Hegel's overall philosophical project and drawing attention to particularly significant or influential ideas in those selections. There is also a general introduction at the beginning of the book which describes Hegel's considerable influence on subsequent philosophy, offers a brief account of his life, and introduces the reader to the central themes of his mature philosophy through a comparison with the theoretical philosophy of Kant. At the end of the book I have included an extensive bibliography which lists the main German editions of Hegel's works, most of the currently available English translations of his texts, as well as a selection of important secondary works.

Books are never produced in a vacuum, and this one in particular owes its existence to an atmosphere of support and encouragement that has sustained me throughout many years of often arduous and demanding work on Hegel's texts. I have benefited especially from conversations about Hegel and related issues with several friends, students and colleagues. Those I would particularly like to thank for their enduring support and friendship are Michael Baur, Tom Brugger, John Burbidge, Kathleen Dow, Joseph Flay, Wendell Kisner, David Kolb, John McCumber, Ron Nahser, Mary O'Neill, John Protevi, Paul Schafer, Sally Sedgwick, Robert Stern and Robert Williams. When I was an undergraduate at Cambridge in the 1970s, my interest in Hegel was initially stimulated by my supervisor, Nicholas Boyle, and by the exhilarating lectures given by Duncan Forbes. Forbes was deeply committed to Hegel's vision of social and political life and devoted himself for thirty years to the task of rendering the subtlety of that vision intelligible to his students. In gratitude for the energetic encouragement and sound advice which he always gave me, from our first meeting to the time of his death, I dedicate this volume to him.

Steve Smith and Nathalie Manners of Blackwell deserve my thanks for inviting me to edit *The Hegel Reader*, and I should also like to thank Will McNeill for his enthusiastic support for my original proposal. Lastly, and most importantly, I owe my greatest debt of gratitude to my wife, Mary, for her loving companionship throughout the gestation of this *Reader* and to my children, Mark, Michael, Margaret and Christopher, for their good-humoured indulgence (and frequent, much needed distraction).

Stephen Houlgate
July 1997

Acknowledgements

For permission to publish copyright material in this book grateful acknowledgement is made to the following:

Cambridge University Press: for extracts from *Elements of the Philosophy of Right*, by G. W. F. Hegel, edited by A. W. Wood, translated by H. B. Nisbet (1991); and for extracts from *Lectures on the Philosophy of World History*, by G. W. F. Hegel, translated by H. B. Nisbet (1975). Reprinted by permission of the translator and publisher.

Hackett Publishing Company: for selections from *The Encyclopaedia Logic*, by G. W. F. Hegel, translated by T. F. Geraets, W. A. Suchting, and H. S. Harris (1991), © 1991. All rights reserved. Reprinted by permission of the publisher.

Oxford University Press: for selections from *Aesthetics: Lectures on Fine Art*, by G. W. F. Hegel, translated by T. M. Knox (1975); for selections from *Introduction to the Lectures on the History of Philosophy*, by G. W. F. Hegel, translated by T. M. Knox and A. V. Miller (1985); for selections from *Phenomenology of Spirit*, by G. W. F. Hegel, translated by A. V. Miller (1977); for selections from *Philosophy of Mind*, by G. W. F. Hegel, translated by A. V. Miller (1971); for selections from *Philosophy of Nature*, by G. W. F. Hegel, translated by A. V. Miller (1970); and a selection (translated by H. S. Harris) from *Hegel's Development: Towards the Sunlight. 1770–1801*, by H. S. Harris (1972). Reprinted by permission of the publisher.

Routledge Ltd: for selections from *Science of Logic*, by G. W. F. Hegel, translated by A. V. Miller, foreword by J. N. Findlay (Humanities Press International/George Allen & Unwin). Reprinted by permission of the publisher.

University of California Press and Felix Meiner Verlag: for selections from *Lectures on the Philosophy of Religion, Part 1 and 3*, by G. W. F. Hegel, edited/translated by Peter Hodgson (Berkeley: University of California Press, 1984–7), English edition copyright © 1984 The Regents of the University of California, German edition copyright © Felix Meiner Verlag, Hamburg, 1983, 1984.

General Introduction

Georg Wilhelm Friedrich Hegel (1770–1831) has been one of the most influential philosophers since Kant. His thought has left its mark on the existentialism of Kierkegaard and the historical materialism of Marx and Engels, as well as on British Idealism, American pragmatism, Frankfurt School social philosophy, Heidegger's 'history of Being', Gadamerian hermeneutics and Derridean deconstruction. The work of aesthetic theorists, such as Benedetto Croce and Peter Szondi, would be inconceivable without Hegel's influence, as would the thought of theologians, such as Karl Barth and Eberhard Jüngel. Even such notorious critics of Hegel as Nietzsche and Bertrand Russell acknowledge a debt to their German Idealist forebear – Nietzsche praising 'the astonishing stroke of *Hegel*, who . . . dared to teach that species concepts develop *out of each other*', and Russell declaring his own early *Essay on the Foundations of Geometry* to be the work of a 'full-fledged Hegelian'.[1]

Hegel's legacy to subsequent generations has not been a simple or unified one, but encompasses a broad array of different ideas. In the view of T. W. Adorno, Hegel challenged the naïve, positivistic belief that experience renders 'something immediately present, . . . free, as it were, of any admixture of thought', and showed that there is in fact nothing in our experience that is not *mediated* in some way by reflection and understanding.[2] In the view of Charles Taylor, Hegel's achievement is to have undermined the idea that human consciousness can be understood in the abstract and to have insisted that we 'situate subjectivity by relating it to our life as embodied and social beings'.[3] Taylor claims that Hegel also discerned the two great disruptive forces which threaten the modern state: the force of private interest, which threatens to polarize society between rich and poor and dissolve the bonds of the state, and the opposed attempt to overcome such divisions by sweeping away all differentiation in the name of the general will. He does not think that Hegel's proposals for containing these two forces succeed, but he believes that Hegel offers the most profound analysis of those forces that we have.[4] In the view of the theologian, Eberhard Jüngel, Hegel's achievement is to have overcome the abstract Enlightenment conception of God as the *ens realissimum* and to have given philosophical expression to the theological truth that negation, finitude and death are essential moments of divine life itself.[5] This view finds a secular echo in the work of Jacques Derrida, who argues that Hegel's revolution consisted 'in taking the negative *seriously*', perhaps too seriously.[6] For many modern thinkers – both theological and secular – Hegel's most significant insight is thus contained in this famous statement from the *Phenomenology of Spirit*: 'the life of Spirit is not the life that shrinks from death and keeps itself untouched by devastation, but rather the life that endures it and maintains itself in it. It wins its truth only when, in utter dismemberment, it finds itself'.[7]

For others in the nineteenth and twentieth centuries, Hegel's most profound insights have been held to lie in his theory of tragedy, or his analysis of desire and recognition in the master/slave relation, or his dialectical account of difference, opposition and contradiction. And, of course, for philosophers such as Marx, Heidegger and Gadamer, Hegel's most important contribution to modern thought is to have demonstrated that human life is irreducibly *historical*. After Hegel, so these thinkers argue, we must not only be acutely aware of our own historical position when examining a given phenomenon, but any understanding of such a phenomenon – of society, philosophy or art – must always conceive of it as itself developing historically.

Hegel's contribution to philosophy has not always been regarded as wholly positive, however. Karl Popper famously – and ignorantly – accused Hegel of setting out 'to deceive and bewitch others' with his 'mystery method' of dialectic.[8] Bertrand Russell claimed – just as ignorantly – that Hegel's doctrine of the state 'justifies every internal tyranny and every external aggression that can possibly be imagined'.[9] And Gilles Deleuze – blinded largely by Nietzsche – saw in Hegelian dialectic the ultimate denial of life: the thought of 'the theoretical man, reacting against life, claiming to judge life', of 'the priest who subjects life to the labour of the negative', and of 'the slave, expressing reactive life in itself'.[10] In spite of their rejection of Hegel, however, none of these philosophers denies his enormous significance and influence for modern thought. Indeed, so important does Deleuze consider Hegel to be that he associates what he regards as the two principal advances of recent philosophy – the post-Heideggerian emphasis on difference and the discovery of the power of repetition – specifically and explicitly with a 'generalised anti-*Hegelianism*'.[11]

As I noted above, therefore, there has clearly been no simple, unified Hegelian legacy. Nevertheless, so extensive has been the influence of Hegelian ideas, that, if one is to understand the major intellectual developments of the nineteenth and twentieth centuries, one has to come to grips with Hegel. This, however, is by no means an easily accomplished task. Hegel's texts and lectures are difficult to read – at times formidably so. Furthermore, they are invariably long and in certain cases (most notably that of the English translation of the *Lectures on Aesthetics*) only available in expensive hard-back editions. This means that, specialists apart, those proposing to study Hegel at first hand are unlikely to be able to explore more than one or two parts of his philosophical system – probably his *Phenomenology of Spirit* or his *Philosophy of History* – and will very likely remain unfamiliar with the *Philosophy of Nature* or the *Aesthetics*. Alternatively, if they are introduced to Hegel's theory of tragedy (through a few photocopied pages from the *Aesthetics* or through A. C. Bradley's well-known essay), they are unlikely to consider how that theory fits into Hegel's *Aesthetics* as a whole, or how it relates to his analysis of finitude in the *Science of Logic* and Christianity in the *Lectures on the Philosophy of Religion*. Students of Hegel are thus almost always in the position of having to pass judgement on what they have read without having studied more than a fraction of Hegel's system as a whole.

The aim of this collection is to remedy this situation by bringing together in one volume a wide selection of passages from Hegel's writings and lectures which reflect the whole range of his mature thought. Individual passages do not become easier in themselves by being included in an anthology. Hegel's thought is difficult however it is presented. But an anthology does at least allow selected passages from several different works to be read and understood together. It thus removes the additional difficulty which is often imposed on the various parts of Hegel's system by their artificial isolation from one another – isolation that is all-too-often made unavoidable by the inability of willing readers to afford the cost of Hegel's voluminous works or by the pressures of time in a course on nineteenth-century philosophy.

Several principles guided the choice of passages for this collection. First of all, I have endeavoured to be as comprehensive as is possible within the confines of one book. The reader will thus find passages here from every part of Hegel's mature system, together with four pieces which belong among Hegel's so-called 'early writings'. Secondly, I have included passages which are not only particularly important within Hegel's own system, but which also have special relevance for post-Hegelian thinkers. These include, for example: from the *Phenomenology*, the dialectic of master and slave (important for Marx, Kojève and Sartre) and the analysis of the unhappy consciousness (important for Feuerbach and Kierkegaard); the account of difference, opposition and contradiction from the *Science of Logic* (important for Deleuze, Derrida and, to a degree, Bertrand Russell); the analysis of time in the *Philosophy of Nature* (crucial for Heidegger); the account of language and memory in the *Philosophy of Subjective Spirit* (important for Derrida and Paul de Man); the critique of civil society and of the emergence of poverty (important for Marx); and the account of tragedy in the *Aesthetics* (which has been central for later writers on tragedy from Nietzsche to Martha Nussbaum). Thirdly, I have preferred, where possible, to include Hegel's most thorough account of a given subject-matter. The passages in which Hegel sets out his dialectical logic and political philosophy are thus taken, not from the more simplified *Encyclopaedia*, but from the much more detailed *Science of Logic* and *Philosophy of Right*. Fourthly, I have chosen numerous passages which deal with related themes and which should thus illuminate one other. Such passages include, for example, the early essay on love and the remarks on love from the *Philosophy of Right*; the opening of the *Phenomenology* on the immediacy of sense-certainty and the opening of the *Science of Logic* on the immediacy of simple being; and the discussions of death in the master/slave dialectic, in the section on the organism in the *Philosophy of Nature*, and in the account of Christ's crucifixion and resurrection in the *Lectures on the Philosophy of Religion*. Many interconnections between different passages are indicated in the index, but others, not anticipated by me, will no doubt be discovered by future readers of this book.[12]

II

Hegel was born in Stuttgart on 27 August 1770, the first child of a minor financial official at the court of the Duke of Württemberg. As a schoolboy he read widely in the works of both classical and modern authors, including Homer, Sophocles, Euripides, Shakespeare, Klopstock, Goethe and Schiller. From 1785 he also kept a diary in Latin.[13] In October 1788 he matriculated at the University of Tübingen to study theology and, during his five years there, became friends with Friedrich Hölderlin – his exact contemporary – and Friedrich Wilhelm Joseph von Schelling, who was four and a half years his junior. The three friends shared an enthusiasm for Plato, Lessing, Rousseau and Jacobi's letters *On the Doctrine of Spinoza*, and especially for the two great revolutions of the time: the political revolution started in France in 1789 and the intellectual revolution inaugurated in Germany in the early 1780s by the philosophy of Immanuel Kant.[14] The focus of attention was particularly Kant's moral philosophy and philosophy of religion. According to Dieter Henrich, this was because Kant's practical philosophy was seen as providing a profound critique of the stifling theological orthodoxy prevalent in Tübingen at that time. For the best of the critical students, indeed, enlightened religion was equated specifically with *Kantian* moral theology.[15]

In 1793 Hegel finished his studies, left Tübingen and took up a post as a house-tutor in Berne, Switzerland. His continuing commitment to a radical Kantian critique of contemporary religion and politics is evident from a letter he wrote to Schelling in April, 1795:

> From the Kantian system and its highest completion I expect a revolution in Germany. It will proceed from principles that are present and that only need to be elaborated generally and applied to all hitherto existing knowledge. . . . I believe that there is no better sign of the times than this, that mankind is being

presented as so worthy of respect in itself. It is proof that the aura of prestige surrounding the heads of the oppressors and gods of this earth is disappearing. The philosophers are proving the dignity of man. The peoples will learn to feel it.[16]

Hegel later read Schiller's letters *On the Aesthetic Education of Man* with great enthusiasm and learned much from Schiller regarding the role that aesthetic experience can play in teaching people to develop this feeling for human dignity.

Hegel felt socially and intellectually isolated during his years in Switzerland, but in 1797 his situation improved dramatically when he moved to his second position as a house-tutor, this time in Frankfurt-am-Main. Here Hegel was able to rejoin his friend Hölderlin and, together with other likeminded friends, enjoy conversations about poetry, politics and philosophy (and also visit the theatre, opera and balls). Under the influence of Hölderlin, Hegel turned his back on what Otto Pöggeler calls 'the moralism and Kantianism of his Berne works' and developed a new, more sophisticated conception of religion based on the concepts of 'love' and 'life'.[17] Hegel's conception of life as 'the union of union and nonunion', set out in the *Fragment of a System* of 1800, has been seen by many as a particularly important turning point in his career, because, more than any previous idea of Hegel's, it prepared the way for his mature understanding of speculative reason as 'the unity of . . . determinations in their opposition'.[18]

In 1801 Hegel left Frankfurt to join Schelling in Jena, which not long before had been home to both Fichte and the circle of Romantics around Friedrich Schlegel. Though Hegel did not become an 'extraordinary professor' at the University of Jena until 1805, he held lectures throughout his years there and in them set out the first version of his philosophical system. Besides giving these lectures (on logic and metaphysics, philosophy of nature and philosophy of spirit), Hegel published his first book in 1801, the so-called *Difference* essay, in which he defended Schelling's system against that of Fichte and thereby helped to widen the personal rift between Schelling and Fichte themselves.[19]

In 1807 Hegel published the work which marks the beginning of his philosophical maturity – the *Phenomenology of Spirit*. In this work, which in some ways is prefigured by Schelling's *System of Transcendental Idealism* (1800) but which also departs radically from everything Schelling or Fichte had attempted before, Hegel provides an account of the development of consciousness from the standpoint of immediate sense-certainty to the standpoint of absolute knowing or philosophy itself. Hegel's manuscript was famously completed shortly before the French defeated the Prussians at the Battle of Jena in October 1806, and Hegel had to send his text to his publisher in Bamberg through French lines. 'Should a part of the manuscript be lost,' he wrote in some anxiety to his friend, Immanuel Niethammer, 'I would scarcely know what to do. I would be able to reproduce it only with difficulty.'[20]

February 1807 saw the birth of Hegel's illegitimate son, Ludwig Fischer, to Christiana Burkhardt, the wife of Hegel's landlord in Jena. Hegel then left Jena in March 1807 to become editor of a newspaper in Bamberg. After a year and a half, however, he moved to Nuremberg to become rector of the Aegidiengymnasium. During his years at Nuremberg he wrote the second great work of his philosophical maturity, the monumental *Science of Logic*, and – incredibly – taught speculative logic to the young boys at his school (though, thankfully, not from the *Science of Logic* itself). In 1811 he married Marie von Tucher with whom he had a daughter, Susanna, who died, barely a month old, in August 1812, and two sons, Karl (born 1813) and Immanuel (born 1814).

Hegel and his wife were deeply saddened by the loss of Susanna, but Hegel reports her death to Niethammer without a hint of bitterness. Indeed, the first thing he writes of is the joy – still fresh in his mind – of her birth.[21] Many years later in 1831, in a letter to a friend, Heinrich Beer, who had just lost a son, Hegel shows that he still views death with a characteristic blend of sober acceptance and joyous, open-hearted affirmation of life. 'Your joy has now passed,' he writes to Beer,

> yet there remains with you the feeling of that happiness, your memory of the dear boy, of his joys, his hours of happiness, his love for you and for his mother, his childlike sensibility, his good-naturedness and friendliness towards everyone. Do not be ungrateful for the satisfaction and the happiness you have had; keep its memory alive and steadily before your gaze over against your loss of his presence. In this way your son and your joy in having had him will not be lost to you.[22]

Death cannot destroy life, in Hegel's view, as long as we keep the life that has been lived before our mind, steadily and joyously.

In 1816 Hegel took up a professorship in Heidelberg, where he first became friends with Friedrich Creuzer, whose *Symbolik und Mythologie der alten Völker, besonders der Griechen* (1810ff) would later prompt him to adopt his tripartite division of art into symbolic, classical and romantic art-forms.[23] Hegel lectured on aesthetics for the first time at Heidelberg and also gave lectures on the history of philosophy, logic and metaphysics, anthropology and psychology, natural law and political science, and on the *Encyclopaedia of the Philosophical Sciences*, the first edition of which was published in 1817.

Hegel reached the height of his fame and influence during his years in Berlin from 1818 to 1831. Here he published the *Elements of the Philosophy of Right* (1820) and two further editions of the *Encyclopaedia* (1827 and 1830), edited the official 'organ' of Hegelianism, the *Yearbooks for Scientific Criticism*, and gave the great series of lectures with which we are familiar today. By the time Hegel died in 1831, he had become the most famous philosopher in Germany. He had been appointed rector of the University of Berlin in 1829, had been awarded the Red Eagle (Third Class) by King Friedrich Wilhelm

III of Prussia in 1831, and had become well acquainted with many of the literary and philosophical luminaries of the time.

After his death, Hegel's philosophy was soon eclipsed in university circles in Germany by the rise of science and the discipline of professional history. But it continued to exercise profound influence on a whole generation of German writers and philosophers outside the academic mainstream, from Young Hegelians, such as Feuerbach and D. F. Strauss, to Marx, Engels and Nietzsche. Indeed, the mark his thought left on these writers, as well as on Kierkegaard, Heidegger, Sartre, Gadamer, Adorno, Habermas and Derrida, made Hegel one of the most widely influential post-Kantian philosophers of all.

III

Hegel's personal development takes him from an early concern with Kant's practical philosophy and the revitalization of religion, via an engagement with Schiller's aesthetic theory, Hölderlin's conception of love and Schelling's philosophy of the Absolute, to his mature philosophical system. Once he reaches his philosophical maturity, however, Hegel comes to understand his thought as a radicalization of Kant's *theoretical*, rather than practical, philosophy – in particular, as a radicalization of Kant's theoretical critique of metaphysics. He understands the systematic starting-point of his mature system to be his own *Phenomenology of Spirit*, which leads to the *Science of Logic* and then on to the *Philosophy of Nature* and *Philosophy of Spirit*. But he understands the *historical* source of his mature thought to lie in Kant's *Critique of Pure Reason* (1781), from which paths lead either to the *Phenomenology* or directly to the *Science of Logic*. For the remainder of this introduction I will thus focus specifically on the ways in which Hegel's philosophy carries forward and transforms the project of Kant's first *Critique*.

In the *Encyclopaedia* (1830), prior to his discussion of Kant, Hegel points to what he regards as the main characteristics of metaphysical thinking. Metaphysics, he tells us, assumes first of all that the true nature of things is knowable through thought alone. Secondly, it assumes that thought proceeds by stating in judgements that certain concepts or predicates apply (or do not apply) to what there is – that is, that God 'exists', or that monads are 'simple substances'. Thirdly, metaphysics assumes that the predicates with which it operates are mutually exclusive – that is, that the soul is either simple or compound, that space is either infinitely divisible or not, and so on. Hegel claims that such metaphysical thinking is to be found in the work of philosophers, such as the Scholastics, Wolff and Leibniz, but that it is also the perennial way 'in which the *mere understanding views* the objects of reason'.[24]

The significance of Kant, in Hegel's view, is that he asks how metaphysicians can be sure that the true nature of things is indeed captured by the pure, a priori concepts they employ. Metaphysicians take it for granted that the world can be properly understood by means of concepts such as sub-stance and causality, but how do they know that those concepts actually have 'value and validity'? How do they know that what there is, is actually 'substance' and is governed by 'causality'? The merit of Kant's theoretical philosophy, for Hegel, is thus that, for the first time, it 'subjects to investigation the validity of the *concepts of the understanding* that are used in metaphysics' and requires metaphysicians to justify, rather than simply take for granted, their conviction that a priori concepts tell us about things.[25]

As Hegel points out, Kant believes that this conviction can in fact only be justified under certain conditions. According to Kant, we can only justify the conviction that a priori concepts tell us about things, if we can show that things or objects themselves have to *conform* to those concepts. This is Kant's well-known 'Copernican' revolution. 'Hitherto,' he writes in the preface to the second edition (1787) of the *Critique of Pure Reason*,

> it has been assumed that all our knowledge must conform to objects. But all attempts to extend our knowledge of objects . . . a priori, by means of concepts, have, on this assumption, ended in failure. We must therefore make trial whether we may not have more success in the tasks of metaphysics, if we suppose that objects must conform to our knowledge.[26]

Kant thinks that we can show that objects have to conform to our a priori concepts, if we can demonstrate that such concepts are the very *conditions* of objects. For if our concepts are the conditions of objects, they must make objects possible in the first place; and, if concepts make objects possible in the first place, then objects cannot but conform to them. In that case, our concepts will obviously tell us something about objects, and metaphysical knowledge of objects through such concepts will thus be possible. Kant insists, however, that we can only demonstrate that our concepts make possible objects as *we* experience them; we cannot prove that our concepts make possible objects as they are in themselves. We cannot prove, therefore, that our a priori concepts tell us anything about objects as they are in themselves. All we can prove is that such concepts necessarily tell us about objects of experience – because our concepts are the very conditions which enable there to be objects of experience at all. As Kant himself puts it,

> the objective validity of the categories as a priori concepts rests . . . on the fact that, so far as the form of thought is concerned, through them alone does experience become possible. They relate of necessity and a priori to objects of experience, for the reason that only by means of them can any object whatsoever of experience be thought.[27]

The concepts or categories of the understanding make objects of experience possible, in Kant's view, because they allow us to understand what we intuit in space and time as something unified and as something actually existing or occurring. Kant thinks that spatio-temporal intuitions do not come already unified in themselves, but have to be unified or 'synthesized' by our imagination and understanding in various ways. The specific categories which allow us to think of what we intuit as unified are the categories of quantity: unity, plurality and totality. It is thus only by virtue of these categories that what we intuit can be gathered together and understood as *one* thing, *many* things or *all* things. Without these categories, Kant believes, we could not understand what we see as exhibiting any such unity at all.[28]

Kant thinks, further, that all intuition or perception is successive – that I always perceive this, *then* this, *then* this – but that there is nothing in the succession of my perceptions as such which indicates whether I am actually perceiving the successive stages of an event or am simply perceiving the coexisting states of an object one after another. All that is given to me is a *succession* of perceptions. If these successive perceptions are to count as perceptions of an objective event, Kant maintains, they have to be understood in a certain way. In particular, the order in which they enter my consciousness must be understood to be irreversible. That is to say, we must understand one state as having to precede another in our perception, and as not being able to succeed it. This, indeed, is all that it means for beings such as us to perceive an event: to perceive an event is simply to understand perceived states as *having* to enter consciousness in a definite, irreversible order, the order of occurrence. (To say that what I perceive are coexisting states of things, by contrast, is to say that the perceived states can enter consciousness in many different ways. I can see the top of the house first and then the bottom, for example, or vice versa.) Now, in Kant's view, I can only understand perceived states as *having* to enter consciousness in a definite, irreversible order, if I understand them to be determined or *caused* to come in the order they do. That means that I can only understand what I perceive to be an objective event, if I understand what I perceive to be governed by causality. An event, for Kant, is thus nothing but a series of perceived states which are understood as having to follow in a certain order due to some prior cause.[29]

Kant's central claim, therefore, is that experience would not be possible for us, if we did not think in terms of certain *concepts*. For what we intuit or perceive can only be encountered as a unified object or event, if it is understood as a quantitative unity and as belonging in a causally determined sequence. This follows necessarily, he maintains, from the nature of human intuition and understanding. On the basis of this insight into the conditions of experience, Kant argues, various metaphysical judgements can then be derived. For example, we can judge a priori – with metaphysical certainty – that everything we can experience must be quantifiable (the principle of the axioms of intuition) and that every event must have a cause (the principle of the second analogy). These metaphysical judgements are based not on any privileged insight into 'being', but on an analysis of our experience of objects and events and of its necessary conditions. Those judgements can thus only be known to be true of objects of experience. Since Kant can envisage no other justification for metaphysical judgements than the one he provides, he insists that philosophers abandon all pretension to direct insight into being and base their a priori claims about objects solely on the transcendental analysis of experience and cognition presented in the *Critique of Pure Reason*. That is to say, in Kant's view, 'the proud name of an Ontology that presumptuously claims to supply, in systematic doctrinal form, synthetic a priori knowledge of things in general . . . must . . . give place to the modest title of a mere Analytic of pure understanding'.[30]

According to the mature Hegel, Kant's transcendental analysis draws attention to a vitally important insight: namely, that the *categories* of our thought and understanding are what enable us to conceive of a realm of objectivity. Without these categories we would be unable to frame the thought that there is such a thing as a unified, objective world at all. With those categories, however, what we see can be thought not just to be the space of our subjective imagination, but to be an objective space within which we ourselves are located. As Hegel puts it in the *Encyclopaedia*, 'the thought-determinations or *concepts of the understanding* make up *the objectivity* of the cognitions of experience'.[31]

In Hegel's view, therefore, Kant alerts us to the fact that, if we wish to understand what it means to be *objective*, we must examine and learn to understand what is contained in our own a priori concepts or *categories* (such as quantity, substance and causality) – categories through which alone we can conceive of what we see *as* objective. There is much in Kant's critical philosophy with which Hegel does not agree. But Hegel acknowledges that the critical philosophy involves 'the correct insight that the forms of thinking themselves' – the *categories* – 'must be made the object of cognition'.[32] By maintaining in this way that the meaning of 'objectivity' can only be discerned by analysing the categories of thought, Kant, in Hegel's view, 'turned metaphysics into logic'.[33] The principal object of cognition for pre-Kantian metaphysics, such as that of Spinoza and Leibniz, was being, substance or God, not thought and its numerous categories as such. With Kant, however, metaphysics turns into logic because the principal object of cognition is nothing other than the necessary structure of *thought* itself (within which the necessary structure of objectivity is to be found).

Hegel conceives of his own *Science of Logic* as an unequivocally post-Kantian metaphysics, precisely because its task is to present an exhaustive account of the basic categories of thought as such and *within* those categories alone to discern the meaning and structure of objectivity. Yet, a cursory comparison of Hegel's *Science of Logic* and Kant's *Critique of Pure Reason* reveals them to be clearly very different works. If the *Logic* is supposed to be a post-Kantian metaphysics, why does it appear to be such an *un*-Kantian text? There are several reasons for this.

First of all, Hegel thinks that philosophy needs to examine much more rigorously and critically than Kant does *how* the categories should actually be conceived, and he seeks to carry out this task in the *Science of Logic*. Kant asserts in the *Critique of Pure Reason* that categories only have real 'sense' or meaning when they are 'made sensible', that is to say, when they are 'schematized' or understood in temporal terms. We can thus only understand fully what is meant by substance and causality when they are taken to involve permanence and irreversible time-order, respectively.[34] Nevertheless, Kant recognizes that these categories have a logical meaning, too, apart from their temporal connotation. 'Substance, for instance, when the sensible determination of permanence is omitted, would mean simply a something which can be thought only as subject, never as predicate of something else'; and a cause, considered in abstraction from time, is simply something which acts as the ground of a given consequence.[35] Kant derives the categories from what he sees as the different forms – or 'logical functions' – of judgement. As he puts it, categories are 'concepts of an object in general, by means of which the intuition of an object is regarded as determined in respect of one of the logical functions of judgement'.[36] What this means is less complex than Kant's intimidating language suggests. Kant begins from the fact that human beings judge in certain ways. For example, we judge that this *subject* is to be understood through this *predicate* (S is P); or we judge that *if* such and such is the case, *then* such and such will follow (if A, then B). He then constructs the categories through the introduction of the thought of an 'object' – the thought of 'something' – and by conceiving of that object as determined in terms of one these ways of judging. The category of substance is thus the thought of something determined as subject rather than predicate, and the category of cause is the thought of something determined as ground rather than consequent (as 'if' rather than 'then'). Whereas judgement forms are general ways in which we connect concepts, categories are employed to understand what we *intuit* to be an object or 'something determinate'.

Kant thus bases his conception of the categories firmly on the fact that understanding is above all the faculty of *judgement*. This is why he understands substance (with Aristotle) to be that *subject* which can never be a *predicate* of something else, rather than (with Spinoza) as 'what is in itself and is conceived through itself'.[37] From Hegel's point of view, however, Kant does not properly justify the claim that understanding is equivalent to judging or that concepts are essentially predicates of possible judgements. He simply takes it for granted that this is the case and derives his conception of the categories from that assumed 'fact' of understanding. For Hegel, however, a truly *critical* philosophy ought not to make such an assumption about thinking, but ought to consider much more closely whether understanding is fundamentally the activity of judging and indeed 'whether the form of the judgement could be the form of truth'.[38] Furthermore, a truly critical philosophy should not derive the *categories* from any mere assumption that understanding is equivalent to judging. Indeed, in Hegel's view, a truly critical philosophy should not take anything for granted at all about thought and its categories, except the quite minimal thought that thought *is*.

A critical philosophy should thus not assume that understanding involves judgement, syllogistic reasoning, or any particular conception of the categories, but should seek to derive all the rules and categories of thought from the ultimately indeterminate thought of thought's own simple being.[39]

Hegel's *Logic* thus appears to be such an un-Kantian text because it seeks to determine *from scratch* that which Kant derives from the presupposed activity of judgement: namely, an understanding of how the categories are to be conceived. Furthermore, Hegel's *Logic* provides a much more extensive analysis than Kant of the logical form of the categories before he proceeds (in the *Philosophy of Nature*) to consider the issue of the temporal (and spatial) form that categories, such as causality, should take. What needs to be remembered, however, is that Hegel departs from Kant in the *Logic* because he thinks that philosophy should become *more* critical, not less critical, than Kant has made it. Kant inaugurated the modern era of philosophical critique. In Hegel's view, however, 'Kant's philosophy took the easy way in its *finding* of the categories', because he simply derived them from what he *assumed* thought to be.[40] A thoroughly critical philosophy, by contrast, may not assume anything about thought, but must *discover* what it is to think starting from nothing but the simple, indeterminate *being* of thought itself. Hegel's apparently un-Kantian *Science of Logic* is thus the product of what he sees as the intensification and radicalization of Kant's critical project, not of its reversal.

The second obvious difference between Hegel's philosophy and that of Kant is that Hegel understands his logical study of the categories to be also an ontology in the strongest possible sense. Hegel agrees with Kant that our categories contain the meaning and structure of objectivity; but, against Kant, he thinks that the categories contain the structure not just of objectivity *for us*, but of objectivity *as such*. That is to say, what is to be found in the categories is not just the objective structure of *our* world, but the objective structure of being itself. As Hegel puts it, 'the absolute truth of being is the known Concept and the Concept as such is the absolute truth of being'.[41] Hegel's post-Kantian examination of what it is to *think*, is thus at one and the same time and in one and the same respect a pre-Kantian, quasi-Spinozan examination of what it is to *be*. Once again, however, Hegel departs from Kant because he wishes to be more critical, not less critical, than Kant himself. In other words, he proceeds through Kant, and because of Kant, to his new 'Spinozism'.

Kant argues that the role of the categories is to enable us to understand what we intuit to be unified and objective. Through the categories, therefore, we understand what we intuit to be an *object of experience*. But intuition, for Kant, only shows us the way things appear in the a priori forms of our own intuiting. It does not show us what things are like in themselves. Experience – which takes its material content from intuition – is thus not experience of things in themselves, but experience of things as they appear to us in space and time. This means that the role of the categories, for Kant, is quite restricted. For, in so far as they allow us to understand what we intuit to be objective, all they do is enable us to conceive of the *appearance* of things in space and time as constituting an objective world. In judging what we see to have been caused by something else, we are thus not understanding things as they are in themselves, but we are simply understanding – indeed, interpreting – the spatio-temporal appearance of things in a certain way. This is why metaphysical judgements that are based on our understanding, such as the judgement that 'every event has a cause', cannot be regarded as providing knowledge of being as such (in the manner of Spinoza's *Ethics*).

From Hegel's point of view, however, Kant's denial that experience discloses what there truly *is*, rests on contrasting the appearance of a thing with the quite empty idea of the thing as it is purely 'in itself'. According to Hegel, this concept of the thing 'in itself' 'expresses the object, inasmuch as *abstraction* is made of all that it is for consciousness'. Thus, 'it is easy to see what is left, namely, what is *completely abstract*, or totally *empty*'.[42] Kant's denial that experience discloses what ultimately is, thus does not stem from any sober and modest assessment of the intrinsic limits of human cognition, but from clinging *uncritically* to an utter abstraction. Hegel's derivation of the categories in the *Logic* proves Kant's conception of the thing in itself to be an abstraction, by demonstrating that what something is in itself has actually to be conceived as inseparable from its relations to other things and from the way it appears. If one takes heed of Hegel's analysis – which is a thoroughly critical analysis because it takes nothing for granted about thought – then there is in fact no good reason to contrast the appearance of a thing with what it is in itself, as Kant does. Appearance, rather, must be understood as *manifesting* what the thing is in itself, and experience must thus be understood as the experience of what there ultimately *is*. Neither is there any good reason to contrast objectivity as it is understood through our categories with the true nature of things in themselves. Our understanding and its categories must, rather, be regarded as disclosing the intelligible, objective structure that things in themselves must have. For Hegel, therefore, 'the true objectivity of thinking consists in this: that thoughts are not merely our thoughts, but at the same time the *In-itself* of things and of whatever else is objective'.[43]

From Hegel's point of view, there is nothing presumptuous about this claim that we are able to understand the nature of being as such: because the idea that understanding is anything *less* than the understanding of being itself is merely the product of an unwarranted and untenable *abstraction* on our part. Hegel's return to the Spinozan position that thought can understand the very nature of being itself is thus not the result of failing to acknowledge Kant's sober and modest restriction of our understanding. It is, rather, the result of challenging the uncritically assumed abstraction – the abstract thought of the thing 'in itself' – which underlies Kant's apparent epistemic sobriety and modesty.

The third way in which Hegel departs from Kant in his *Science of Logic* is by claiming that the categories (and structures of being which they disclose) are *dialectical*. This also represents a significant difference between Hegel's post-Kantian metaphysics and the pre-Kantian metaphysics of Parmenides, Plato and Spinoza. Indeed, from the perspective of Hegel's *Logic*, there is actually a deep affinity between Kant and the metaphysicians whose pretensions he wishes to curb, in so far as all fall short of a proper dialectical grasp of the categories.

The principle of dialectic, according to Hegel, is that categories turn through themselves into their opposites.[44] The thought of 'being' turns into the thought of 'nothing', the thought of 'something' turns into the thought of what is 'other', the thought of finitude turns into the thought of infinity, and so on. Through this dialectic, in Hegel's view, thought is required to give up its one-sided conception of being as sheer being, of finitude as sheer finitude and, indeed, of being in itself as sheer being *in itself*, and is required to recognize that determinations which have previously been thought to be simply opposed to one another are in fact inseparable. When thought apprehends the 'unity of the determinations in their opposition' and so comes to a new, concrete conception of being, something and finitude, it comes to be not only dialectical but *speculative*.[45]

The idea that being unites opposite determinations within itself is, of course, already to be found in the notoriously cryptic fragments of Heraclitus. 'God,' Heraclitus says, 'is day night, winter summer, war peace, satiety hunger'. It is also implied in Anaxagoras' remark that 'the things in the one world-order are not separated one from the other nor cut off with an axe, neither the hot from the cold nor the cold from the hot'.[46] The dominant voice in the metaphysical tradition, however, has been not that of Heraclitus, but that of Parmenides, for whom one opposition at least – that between 'being' and 'nothing' – is absolute and unbridgeable. 'Being', for Parmenides, has no association whatsoever with 'nothing' or 'non-being', and 'nothing' has no association whatsoever with 'being'. Being thus simply *is*, and does not arise from, pass into, or in any way involve, non-being. Equally, nothing simply is *not* and cannot in any way be said to be. 'What is there to be said and thought must needs be: for it is there for being, but nothing is not.'[47]

Plato appears to take a Heraclitean/Hegelian view of opposites, when he has Socrates comment in the *Phaedo* on the close connection between 'pleasant' and its 'supposed opposite, painful'. 'The pair of them refuse to visit a person together,' Socrates says, 'yet if anybody pursues one of them and catches it, he's always pretty well bound to catch the other as well, as if the two of them were attached to a single head.'[48] Later in the dialogue, however, Plato reveals a more clearly Parmenidean conception of opposites. The concepts he considers are not those of 'being' and 'nothing' as such. Nevertheless, his position is recognizably Parmenidean, in so far as he argues that opposites simply *are* what they are and exclude what they are *not*, that is, exclude their opposites.

An individual, for Plato, can certainly take on a quality or 'form' that is opposed to one he or she currently exhibits: the individual can pass from being beautiful to being ugly, from being just to being unjust, or from enjoying pleasure to being in pain. But what it is to *be* beautiful, ugly, just or unjust cannot itself change into its opposite because it is fixed and immutable. That is to say, beauty itself cannot turn into – or turn out to be – ugliness, and justice itself cannot turn into – or turn out to be – injustice. Beauty is one thing and ugliness is something else, and the two will always remain simply opposed to one another, even though the one can give way to the other in an individual. Thus, whereas Hegel says of the opposites, being and nothing, that 'each sublates itself in itself and is in its own self the opposite of itself', Plato says of every opposite that 'the opposite itself could never come to be opposite to itself'.[49] Beauty is beauty and is quite simply opposed to ugliness, therefore, just as, for Parmenides, being is being and is quite simply opposed to nothing.

In Plato's *Sophist* the Stranger seems to move closer to Hegel, when he admits that it is necessary 'to put the speech of our father Parmenides to the torture and force it to say that "that which is not" is in some respect, and again, in turn, "that which is" is not in some point'.[50] But the Stranger only 'tortures' Parmenides' speech to a certain degree, because he asserts that being, non-being and other genera only 'mix together with one another' in certain non-contradictory ways when specific conditions are taken into account. 'That which is not' only *is* to the extent that it is spoken of, and 'that which is' only *is not* to the extent that it is thought to be *other than* forms such as 'sameness' and 'otherness'. This does not mean, however, that 'being', 'nothing', 'sameness' and 'otherness' turn into their opposites purely by virtue of what they are in themselves without regard to the conditions imposed on them by our thought and speech. Indeed, as Gadamer notes, the Stranger specifically rejects what will prove to be Hegel's position that opposites turn into one another simply by being what they are.

> To show that 'the same' [is] other in some way *no matter what*, and 'the other' the same, and the big small, and the similar dissimilar, and in this way to take pleasure in always putting forward the contraries in one's speeches, this is not a simply true examination, and it shows as well that it is the fresh offspring of someone who just now is getting his hands on 'the things which are'.[51]

For all his sophistication, therefore, Plato – at least as represented by the Stranger – remains tied to the Parmenidean assumption that opposites do not pass over into one another through themselves alone and so do not include one another *within* themselves.

The influence of Parmenides continues to be seen centuries later in Spinoza's conception of a thing's essence or *conatus* as that through which a thing is what it is. For, according to Spinoza, there is nothing whatsoever in what a thing is which can destroy it and so cause it to pass from being into non-being. 'While we attend only to the thing itself, and not to external causes,' Spinoza maintains, 'we shall not be able to find anything in it which can destroy it.'[52] The possibility of a thing's non-being is thus not immanent within the very being of the thing itself, and the possibility of death is not immanent in life. Rather, both non-being and death come upon things from the outside. It is true that Spinoza speaks of things, whereas Parmenides speaks of being as such. Nevertheless, Spinoza's position remains indebted to that of Parmenides, in that neither understands 'that which is' to have the seeds of its own negation immanent within itself. For Hegel, by contrast, all things have the 'germ of decease' within themselves: 'the hour of their birth is the hour of their death'.[53] And this is due not just to the external relations in which things stand, but to the fact that being as such turns dialectically into non-being *through itself*.

The idea that a relation to non-being and death is not just imposed on things from the outside, but is constitutive of what it is to be in the first place, is explored in different ways in the twentieth century by, amongst others, Heidegger and Derrida. Both thinkers distance themselves from Hegel in some ways, but Heidegger's analysis of being-towards-death as integral to *Dasein* in *Being and Time* and Derrida's claim in *Speech and Phenomena* that 'the statement "I am alive" . . . requires the possibility that I be dead' clearly continue Hegel's deconstruction of the age-old Parmenidean opposition between being and non-being that has dominated much of the metaphysical tradition.[54] Indeed, one of the main differences between twentieth-century analytic and continental philosophy is precisely that continental philosophers have sought to develop further, rather than simply counter, Hegel's dialectical revolution in ontology.

Kant does not look like a particularly Parmenidean thinker, since he is concerned less with being and non-being and more with the conditions of experience. Nevertheless, Parmenides has clearly left his mark on Kant's thought, too. This is especially evident in Kant's conception of the relation between 'reality' and 'negation' in his discussion of the Transcendental Ideal in the *Critique of Pure Reason*. Kant recognizes there that things are distinguished from one another through limitation and negation, but he denies that reality as such is in itself *originally* negative. Reality as such, for Kant, is in itself purely affirmative, and limitation and negation have to be *introduced* into reality for different things to be possible. 'All concepts of negations are thus derivative,' Kant says, 'it is the realities which contain the data, and, so to speak, the material or transcendental content, for the possibility and complete determination of all things'.[55] Indeed, it is precisely the fact that one can separate the concept of reality from that of negation in this way that allows Kant to generate his conception of God as the *ens realissimum* or 'most real being' in which there is no intrinsic negation or limitation. For Hegel, by contrast, reality is originally negative in itself. 'Reality is quality, determinate being,' Hegel maintains, 'consequently, it contains the moment of the negative and is through this alone the determinate being that it is.'[56]

Accordingly, God for Hegel cannot just be understood as the most real being, because 'negation itself is found in God'. Hegel's God – who is the God of Christianity – thus does not remain aloof from the world, pure in himself, but becomes incarnate in and as finite human beings who love one another 'even unto death'.[57]

In his *Logic*, Hegel not only shows being and nothing to be dialectically related to one another, but also other concepts, such as quality and quantity, being-in-itself and being-in-relation-to-others, identity and difference, and positivity and negativity. (Indeed, in his philosophy of nature and philosophy of spirit he explores many other dialectical relations, for example, between organic life and death, choice and dependency, freedom and necessity.) In those cases where Kant addresses the same concepts as Hegel, however, he holds to a resolutely non-dialectical conception of them. A qualitative concept, such as 'straight', for example, does not intrinsically imply any quantitative concept, for Kant (which is why he considers the judgement that a straight line between two points is the shortest to be a synthetic judgement). Similarly, as far as Kant is concerned, 'a thing in itself cannot be known through mere relations'.[58] Hegel's dialectical conception of the categories thus appears to mark him out as a definitively un-Kantian thinker. The relation between the two philosophers is not, however, as straightforward as it seems, because once again Hegel departs from Kant (and from his other Parmenidean predecessors) for what he takes to be ultimately Kantian reasons.

Hegel conceives of opposed concepts as dialectically interrelated because he believes he is required to by his philosophical method. He believes that a truly *critical* philosophy is one that takes nothing for granted about thought or being and that lets the categories of thought and the determinations of being emerge freely and immanently from an initial indeterminate starting-point. He also believes that this approach shows the categories of thought and the basic determinations of being to be necessarily dialectical. Hegel's dialectical – and *non*-Kantian – conception of fundamental categories, such as reality and negation, finitude and infinity, quality and quantity, thus stems, paradoxically, from his desire to be even more *critical* than Kant himself by assuming less to begin with about what it means to think.

For all its obvious differences from Kant's thought, therefore, Hegel's philosophy should be understood as a radicalization, not a reversal, of Kant's critical project. For Hegel, to be genuinely critical means not just to question the validity of the metaphysical claims that have been made about the world, but to question *all* determinate assumptions about thought and being and to seek to discover from scratch what it is to think and what it is to be. To be critical thus means not assuming in advance that contradiction is a sign of error, or that understanding is basically judgement, or that being is something determinate, but suspending all such presuppositions and starting out from the simple, and quite indeterminate, thought of being as such. In other words, philosophy or 'science', for Hegel, 'should be preceded by *universal doubt*, i.e., by total *presuppositionlessness*'.[59] Contrary to what Heidegger claims, therefore, Hegel cannot be determining the nature of time, or the I, or anything else, 'in accordance with a predetermined idea of being'. Nor, as Derrida asserts, can Hegel be thinking from 'within the horizon of absolute knowledge'.[60] Hegel cannot assume in advance that being will have any particular overall structure or that the categories will turn out to be moments of the Absolute, because that would violate the very idea of a thoroughly critical, presuppositionless philosophy.[61]

Thus, even though he states in the preface to the *Phenomenology* that 'the true is the whole', Hegel cannot start out from any preconceived idea of the whole. All he can do is start, in the *Science of Logic*, with the simple, indeterminate concept of being (or, in the *Phenomenology*, with the simple, immediate consciousness of being), let this 'move spontaneously of its own nature' and 'contemplate this movement'.[62] Hegel believes that a whole does indeed *emerge* through the movement which the philosopher describes, but he insists equally that such a whole may not be taken for granted at the start. The form of thought which does start out from a prior conception of the whole is not fully self-critical, philosophical reason, but abstract understanding. 'Instead of entering into the immanent content of the thing,' Hegel says, '[the understanding] is forever surveying the whole and standing above the particular existence of which it is speaking.' By contrast, 'scientific cognition', or philosophy, 'forgets about that general survey', immerses itself in 'the life of its object' and traces its specific immanent development.[63] Philosophy, for Hegel, thus demands above all else the willingness to attend to *specific* concepts (or forms of consciousness), to understand their *specific* dialectical character in relation to one another, and in this way alone to build up a conception of the whole.

In my view, Hegel remains true to his method throughout his philosophical system – in his phenomenological analysis of consciousness, his philosophical analysis of the concept of being, and his further philosophical analyses of the concepts of space, time and matter in the *Philosophy of Nature* and of freedom, history, art, religion and philosophy in the *Philosophy of Spirit*. In each part of his system, Hegel shows how specific determinations develop immanently into other determinations, and he does so without reference to any presupposed whole or Absolute in which contradictions are to be resolved. The task facing the reader of Hegel's texts and lectures is thus to try to understand why *in each specific case* a concept (or form of consciousness) develops as it does. Why does the thought of 'determinate being' turn into the thought of 'something'? Why does the thought of 'identity' turn into the thought of 'difference'? Why does the concept of space turn into that of time? And why does the freedom of morality lead to that of ethical life? It is only by comprehending these specific transitions, and their interconnections with one another, that a grasp of Hegel's whole system can be built up. Hegel's system does certainly form an integrated whole, but that whole is nothing beyond the interrelatedness of its manifold parts. Consequently, there is no short cut to the whole 'itself'. There is nothing but the long and difficult, at times tortuous, at times exhilarating, path through the details.

No collection can do justice to the enormous range of Hegel's ideas. My hope, however, is that the passages selected here will enable the reader to see that Hegel is not simply the hubristic thinker of popular caricature who made sweeping, incomprehensible claims about the Absolute, but that he is a rigorous and critical philosopher who provides subtle analyses of a multiplicity of different specific forms of being, nature and human life. Hegel is without doubt one of the most difficult of all philosophers. But there is also no doubt that, if he is read with due patience and attentiveness, he can be one of the most rewarding.

Notes

1 F. Nietzsche, *The Gay Science*, translated, with commentary by W. Kaufmann (New York: Vintage Books, 1974), p. 305 (§ 357), and B. Russell, *My Philosophical Development* (London: Allen and Unwin, 1959), p. 42.

2 T. W. Adorno, *Hegel: Three Studies*, translated by S. W. Nicholsen, with an introduction by S. W. Nicholsen and J. J. Shapiro (Cambridge, Mass.: MIT Press, 1993), pp. 57, 59.

3 C. Taylor, *Hegel and Modern Society* (Cambridge: Cambridge University Press, 1979), p. 167.

4 Taylor, *Hegel and Modern Society*, p. 131.

5 E. Jüngel, *Gott als Geheimnis der Welt* (Tübingen: J. C. B. Mohr, 1977), p. 100.

6 J. Derrida, *Writing and Difference*, translated with an introduction and additional notes by A. Bass (London: Routledge and Kegan Paul, 1978), p. 259.

7 G. W. F. Hegel, *Phenomenology of Spirit*, translated by A. V. Miller, with analysis of the text and foreword by J. N. Findlay (Oxford: Oxford University Press, 1977), p. 19. See below, p. 59.

8 K. R. Popper, *The Open Society and its Enemies* (1945), 2 vols (London: Routledge, 1966), 2: 28.

9 B. Russell, *History of Western Philosophy* (1946) (London: Allen and Unwin, 1961), p. 711.

10 G. Deleuze, *Nietzsche and Philosophy*, translated by H. Tomlinson (New York: Columbia University Press, 1983), p. 196.

11 G. Deleuze, *Difference and Repetition*, translated by P. Patton (London: Athlone Press, 1994), p. xix (my italics).

12 Selected passages from Hegel's works can also be found in *Hegel. Selections*, edited by J. Loewenberg (New York: Charles Scribner's Sons, 1929), *The Philosophy of Hegel*, edited with an introduction by C. J. Friedrich (New York: Random House, 1953), *Hegel: The Essential Writings*, edited and with introductions by F. G. Weiss, foreword by J. N. Findlay (New York: Harper and Row, 1974), and *Hegel. Selections*, edited, with introduction, notes and bibliography by M. J. Inwood (New York: Macmillan, 1989). Loewenberg's collection contains parts of the *Phenomenology*, but only introductory material from the *Aesthetics* and *Lectures on the Philosophy of World History*. Passages relating to Hegel's logic and political philosophy are taken primarily from the *Encyclopaedia*. Friedrich's collection concentrates mainly on Hegel's *Philosophy*

of History, *Philosophy of Right*, *Aesthetics* and *Phenomenology*, but also includes some of Hegel's political essays. Weiss's collection includes passages from the *Phenomenology* and *Philosophy of Right*, but only has the introductions from the *Philosophy of Nature* and the *Philosophy of Spirit*. There is nothing from the lectures on aesthetics, philosophy of religion or the history of philosophy, but only the closing section of the *Encyclopaedia* on 'absolute mind (or spirit)'. Inwood's collection is the most comprehensive of the four, but, like that of Loewenberg and in contrast to the present collection, it also draws more on the *Encyclopaedia* and less on the *Science of Logic*, the *Philosophy of Right* and the main text of Hegel's lectures on aesthetics and philosophy of religion. Inwood includes passages from Hegel's early essay, *The Positivity of the Christian Religion*, but he does not include Hegel's account of the unhappy consciousness from the *Phenomenology*, his account of the organism and of language and memory from the *Philosophy of Nature* and *Philosophy of Spirit*, or his account of tragedy and comedy from the *Aesthetics*.

13 C. Helferich, *G. W. Fr. Hegel* (Stuttgart: J. B. Metzler, 1979), pp. 12–13.
14 *Hegel. Einführung in seine Philosophie*, edited by O. Pöggeler (Freiburg/Munich: Karl Alber, 1977), p. 11.
15 D. Henrich, *Hegel im Kontext* (Frankfurt: Suhrkamp Verlag, 1967), p. 53.
16 *Hegel: The Letters*, translated by C. Butler and C. Seiler, commentary by C. Butler (Bloomington: Indiana University Press, 1984), p. 35.
17 *Hegel. Einführung in seine Philosophie*, p. 14.
18 See G. W. F. Hegel, *Early Theological Writings*, translated by T. M. Knox, with an introduction, and fragments translated by R. Kroner (Chicago: University of Chicago Press, 1948), p. 312, and Hegel, *The Encyclopaedia Logic. Part 1 of the Encyclopaedia of the Philosophical Sciences with the Zusätze*, translated by T. F. Geraets, W. A. Suchting and H. S. Harris (Indianapolis: Hackett Publishing, 1991), p. 131 (§ 82). See also below, p. 172.
19 G. W. F. Hegel, *The Difference between Fichte's and Schelling's System of Philosophy*, translated by H. S. Harris and W. Cerf (Albany: SUNY Press, 1977). See below, pp. 40–3.
20 *Hegel: The Letters*, p. 114.
21 *Hegel: The Letters*, p. 270.
22 *Hegel: The Letters*, p. 271.
23 See M. Donougho, 'Hegel and Creuzer: or, Did Hegel Believe in Myth?' in *New Perspectives on Hegel's Philosophy of Religion*, edited by D. Kolb (Albany: SUNY Press, 1992), p. 69, and Helferich, *G. W. Fr. Hegel*, p. 61.
24 Hegel, *The Encyclopaedia Logic*, pp. 65–6 (§§ 26–8). See below, pp. 143–4.
25 Hegel, *The Encyclopaedia Logic*, pp. 81–2 (§ 41 and Additions). See below, pp. 153–5.
26 I. Kant, *Critique of Pure Reason*, translated by N. Kemp Smith (London: Macmillan, 1929), p. 22 (B xvi).
27 Kant, *Critique of Pure Reason*, p. 126 (B 126).
28 See Kant, *Critique of Pure Reason*, pp. 197–201 (B 202–7).
29 See Kant, *Critique of Pure Reason*, pp. 218–33 (B 232–56).
30 Kant, *Critique of Pure Reason*, p. 264 (B 303).
31 Hegel, *The Encyclopaedia Logic*, p. 81 (§ 40). See below, p. 153.
32 Hegel, *The Encyclopaedia Logic*, p. 82 (§ 41 Addition 1). See below, p. 153.
33 G. W. F. Hegel, *Science of Logic*, translated by A. V. Miller, foreword by J. N. Findlay (Atlantic Highlands, NJ: Humanities Press International, 1989), p. 51.
34 Kant, *Critique of Pure Reason*, pp. 260, 184–5 (B 299, 183–4).
35 Kant, *Critique of Pure Reason*, pp. 187, 117 (B 186, 112).

36 Kant, *Critique of Pure Reason*, p. 128 (B 128).

37 B. de Spinoza, *A Spinoza Reader: The Ethics and Other Works*, edited and translated by E. Curley (Princeton: Princeton University Press, 1994), p. 85 (*Ethics*, I D3).

38 Hegel, *The Encyclopaedia Logic*, p. 66 (§ 28). See below, p. 144.

39 Hegel, *Science of Logic*, p. 43: 'Logic, on the contrary, cannot presuppose any of these forms of reflection and laws of thinking, for these constitute part of its own content and have first to be established within the science.'

40 Hegel, *The Encyclopaedia Logic*, p. 84 (§ 42). See below, p. 155.

41 Hegel, *Science of Logic*, p. 49. See below, p. 175.

42 Hegel, *The Encyclopaedia Logic*, p. 87 (§ 44), and *Science of Logic*, p. 121. See below, pp. 156, 201.

43 Hegel, *The Encyclopaedia Logic*, p. 83 (§ 41 Addition 2). See below, p. 155.

44 Hegel, *The Encyclopaedia Logic*, p. 128 (§ 81). See below, p. 170.

45 Hegel, *The Encyclopaedia Logic*, p. 131 (§ 82). See below, p. 172.

46 *The Presocratic Philosophers* (1957), edited by G. S. Kirk, J. E. Raven and M. Schofield (Cambridge: Cambridge University Press, 1983), pp. 190, 371.

47 *The Presocratic Philosophers*, p. 247.

48 Plato, *Phaedo*, translated and edited by D. Gallop (Oxford: Oxford University Press, 1993), p. 4 (60b).

49 Hegel, *Science of Logic*, p. 106 (see below, p. 193); Plato, *Phaedo*, p. 60 (103b).

50 Plato, *Sophist*, translated and with commentary by S. Benardete (Chicago: University of Chicago Press, 1986), p. 33 (241d).

51 Plato, *Sophist*, pp. 56–7 (259a–d) (my italics). See also H.-G. Gadamer, *Hegel's Dialectic: Five Hermeneutical Studies*, translated and with an introduction by P. C. Smith (New Haven: Yale University Press, 1976), p. 22.

52 Spinoza, *A Spinoza Reader*, p. 159 (*Ethics*, III P4 Dem).

53 Hegel, *Science of Logic*, p. 129. See below, p. 204.

54 J. Derrida, *Speech and Phenomena*, translated, with an introduction, by D. B. Allison, preface by N. Garver (Evanston, Ill.: Northwestern University Press, 1973), pp. 96–7.

55 Kant, *Critique of Pure Reason*, p. 490 (B 603).

56 Hegel, *Science of Logic*, p. 112.

57 G. W. F. Hegel, *Lectures on the Philosophy of Religion* (One Volume Edition: The Lectures of 1827), edited by P. C. Hodgson, translated by R. F. Brown, P. C. Hodgson and J. M. Stewart, with the assistance of H. S. Harris (Berkeley: University of California Press, 1988), p. 465. See below, p. 498.

58 Kant, *Critique of Pure Reason*, pp. 53, 87 (B 16, 67).

59 Hegel, *The Encyclopaedia Logic*, p. 124 (§ 78). See below, p. 168.

60 M. Heidegger, *Hegel's Phenomenology of Spirit*, translated by P. Emad and K. Maly (Bloomington: Indiana University Press, 1988), p. 82; J. Derrida, *The Gift of Death*, translated by D. Wills (Chicago: University of Chicago Press, 1995), p. 83.

61 On the *uncritical* mode of thought that 'relies on truths which are taken for granted and which it sees no need to re-examine', see Hegel, *Phenomenology of Spirit*, pp. 41, 47. See below, pp. 68, 71.

62 Hegel, *Phenomenology of Spirit*, pp. 11, 36. See below, pp. 53, 64.

63 See Hegel, *Phenomenology of Spirit*, p. 32. See below, p. 62.

Part I
Early Writings

Introduction

Prior to the publication of the *Phenomenology of Spirit* in 1807, Hegel produced numerous essays, fragments and lectures on an impressive range of topics. From his days as a student at the Tübingen Theological Seminary or *Stift* (1788–93), through his years as a house-tutor in Berne and Frankfurt (1793–1800), to the period he spent lecturing in Jena (1801–7), Hegel wrote or lectured with great insight and sophistication on philosophy, logic, history, art, religion, mythology, politics and economics, drawing in the course of his studies on the work of, amongst others, Plato, Kant, Fichte, Hölderlin, Schelling, Schiller, Rousseau and Adam Smith. Hegel's early work remained largely unknown until it was rediscovered by Wilhelm Dilthey at the beginning of the twentieth century. Now, however, in the view of many commentators, even if Hegel had died in 1805 and never produced the texts and lectures of his philosophical maturity, he would still count as a significant representative of German Idealism on the strength of his early work alone.

The most comprehensive and informative account of Hegel's early writings (including the difficult lectures of the Jena period) is provided by H. S. Harris in the two volumes of his magisterial *Hegel's Development*.[1] As anyone will see from reading Harris's work, the passages that I have selected represent a very small part of Hegel's early output. The four pieces reproduced here do, however, belong amongst the most important of Hegel's early writings and reward careful consideration both for their own sake and for the fruitful points of comparison with Hegel's mature philosophy which they afford.

The authorship of the first piece – the *Earliest System-Programme of German Idealism* (1796 or 1797) – is disputed. The text is preserved in Hegel's handwriting, but it has been attributed in turn to Hegel, Hölderlin and Schelling. Research by Harris and Otto Pöggeler suggests, however, that Hegel is the most likely author and it is included here under that assumption. Beginning from Kant's 'practical postulates', Hegel first proposes a new physics 'from a moral point of view' and then advocates challenging the 'machine state', uprooting all superstition and prosecuting the priesthood in the name of reason and the 'absolute freedom of all spirits'.[2] Hegel also suggests – perhaps under the influence of Schiller – that the highest act of reason is actually a creative, *aesthetic* act and that the 'Ideas' of practical reason have to be presented in the aesthetico-religious form of a mythology, if they are to be made sensuous or 'sensible' (*sinnlich*) and to have 'interest for the people'. The later Hegel will regard the state as fulfilling, rather than restricting, human freedom, but he will remain committed to promoting the idea of freedom throughout his life and he will continue to insist on the role that art and religion must play in rendering reason concrete for all.

The other three pieces selected here are without doubt by Hegel and document the development of his thought on one of the most important philosophical topics: the relation between unity and difference. In the fragment on *Love* (Frankfurt, 1797–8), which shows the strong influence of his friend, Hölderlin, Hegel declares love to be 'true union' and states that such union 'excludes all oppositions'.[3] In love, Hegel says, 'the separate does still remain, but as something united and no longer as something separate'.[4] All *distinction* between lovers is thus 'annulled' and their union is 'free from all inner division'.[5] Division can enter into and disrupt the union of love, however, because lovers are not only lovers but are also potential owners of private – and so exclusive – property.

In his mature philosophy, Hegel continues to insist that love is of central importance in human life and that love is the *union* of two people. At the same time, however, the mature Hegel places greater emphasis on the fact that love is the union or identity of two *different* people. This change of emphasis is a subtle one, but it is none the less real. In 1797 the main idea is that love simply *annuls* the distinction between lovers. By contrast, in the 1827 *Lectures on the Philosophy of Religion*, the main idea is that 'love is *both* a distinguishing *and* the sublation of the distinction'. Love is thus conceived by the later Hegel (in the words of the *Philosophy of Right*) as 'the most immense contradiction', because it is understood as the union in which difference is not just eliminated but preserved – the union in which 'I have my self-consciousness . . . in the *other*'.[6]

Hegel moves towards this more complex conception of union in the passage entitled *Fragment of a System* (Frankfurt, 1800). Here the focus is not on love, but on life. Nevertheless, Hegel's path towards his later conception of love (and spirit) as unity-in-difference is clearly opened up by his famous and much-quoted claim that 'life is the union of union and nonunion'.[7] Life does not exclude opposition on this view, therefore, but rather includes 'death, opposition, and understanding' within itself.

A similar note is struck in the section included here from the *Difference* essay, 'The Need of Philosophy' (Jena, 1801), in which Hegel writes that, although reason seeks to overcome fixed oppositions, necessary division (or 'dichotomy') is nevertheless one factor in life.[8] Despite preparing the way for Hegel's mature thought in this way, however, this passage clearly falls short philosophically of that mature thought itself, because in it Hegel espouses the Schellingian idea (prefigured by Hölderlin) that reason frees consciousness from limitations and fixed oppositions by *presupposing* the thought of 'unlimitedness' or 'original identity'.[9] In his mature thought Hegel insists that no such presupposition may be made, but that all finite determinations have to be shown to 'pass into their opposites' and so undermine their fixity *through their very own finitude*.[10] Hegel thus does not presuppose absolute knowing in the *Phenomenology of Spirit* in order to show up the limitations of ordinary consciousness; nor does he presuppose an 'original identity' or the absolute Idea in the *Science of Logic* as a standard by which to criticize other categories. Hegel's mature thought leads *to* absolute knowing and the absolute Idea through a wholly immanent critique of ordinary consciousness and of the immediate and reflexive categories of thought themselves. If Hegel is to be criticized for presupposing the Absolute in his critique of the oppositions of consciousness or the understanding, then this critique must be levelled, not at the mature texts and lectures, but at early texts such as the *Difference* essay which were written under the influence of Schelling and Hölderlin.

The passages in Part I are taken from the following sources: (1) *Earliest System-Programme* from: H. S. Harris, *Hegel's Development. Towards the Sunlight. 1770–1801* (Oxford: Clarendon Press, 1972), pp. 510–12; (2) *Love* from: G. W. F. Hegel, *Early Theological Writings*, translated by T. M. Knox, with an introduction, and fragments translated by R. Kroner (Chicago: University of Chicago Press, 1948), pp. 302–8 (fragment translated by T. M. Knox); (3) *Fragment of a System* from: Hegel, *Early Theological Writings*, pp. 309–19 (fragment translated by R. Kroner); (4) 'The Need of Philosophy' from: G. W. F. Hegel, *The Difference between Fichte's and Schelling's System of Philosophy*, translated by H. S. Harris and W. Cerf (Albany: SUNY Press, 1977), pp. 89–94. (The *Difference* essay was the only one of these pieces published during Hegel's life-time.) For the German text of these passages, see G. W. F. Hegel, *Werke in zwanzig Bänden*, edited by E. Moldenhauer and K. M. Michel, 20 vols and Index (Frankfurt: Suhrkamp Verlag, 1969ff), vol. 1 (pp. 234–6, 244–50, 419–27) and vol. 2 (pp. 20–5).

Notes

1 H. S. Harris, *Hegel's Development: Towards the Sunlight. 1770–1801* (Oxford: Clarendon Press, 1972), and *Hegel's Development: Night Thoughts (Jena 1801–1806)* (Oxford: Clarendon Press, 1983).
2 H. S. Harris, *Hegel's Development: Towards the Sunlight. 1770–1801*, p. 512. See below, p. 28.
3 Hegel, *Early Theological Writings*, p. 304. See below, p. 31.
4 Hegel, *Early Theological Writings*, p. 305. See below, p. 31.
5 Hegel, *Early Theological Writings*, p. 307. See below, pp. 32–3.
6 Hegel, *Lectures on the Philosophy of Religion*, p. 418 (my italics), and G. W. F. Hegel, *Elements of the Philosophy of Right*, edited by A. W. Wood, translated by H. B. Nisbet (Cambridge: Cambridge University Press, 1991), p. 199 (§ 158 Addition). See below, pp. 360, 489.
7 Hegel, *Early Theological Writings*, p. 312. See below, p. 36.
8 Hegel, *The Difference between Fichte's and Schelling's System of Philosophy*, p. 91. See below, p. 41.
9 Hegel, *The Difference between Fichte's and Schelling's System of Philosophy*, pp. 91, 93. See below, pp. 41, 43.
10 See e.g. Hegel, *The Encyclopaedia Logic*, p. 128 (§ 81). See below, p. 170.

1

The Earliest
System-Programme of
German Idealism

. . . an *Ethics*.[1] Since the whole of metaphysics falls for the future within *moral theory* – of which Kant with his pair of practical postulates has given only an *example*, and not *exhausted* it, this Ethics will be nothing less than a complete system of all Ideas [*Ideen*] or of all practical postulates (which is the same thing). The first Idea is, of course, the presentation [*Vorstellung*] *of my* self as an absolutely free entity [*Wesen*]. Along with the free, self-conscious essence there stands forth – out of nothing – an entire *world* – the one true and thinkable creation out of nothing. – Here I shall descend into the realms of physics; the question is this: how must a world be constituted for a moral entity? I would like to give wings once more to our backward physics, that advances laboriously by experiments.

Thus – if philosophy supplies the Ideas, and experience the data, we may at last come to have in essentials the physics that I look forward to for later times. It does not appear that our present-day physics can satisfy a creative spirit such as ours is or ought to be.

From nature I come to the *work of man*. The Idea of mankind [being] premised – I shall prove that it gives us no Idea of the *State*, since the State is a mechanical thing, any more than it gives us an Idea of a *machine*. Only something that is an objective [*Gegenstand*] of *freedom* is called an *Idea*. So we must go even beyond the State! – for every State must treat free men as cogs in a machine; and this it ought not to do; so it must *stop*. It is self-evident that in this sphere all the Ideas, of perpetual peace etc., are only *subordinate* Ideas under a higher one. At the same time I shall here lay down the principles for a *history of mankind*, and strip the whole wretched human work of State, constitution, government, legal system – naked to the skin. Finally come the Ideas of a moral world, divinity, immortality – uprooting of all superstition, the prosecution of the priesthood which of late poses as rational, at the bar of Reason itself. – Absolute freedom of all spirits who bear the intellectual world in themselves, and cannot seek either God or immortality outside themselves.

Last of all the Idea that unites all the rest, the Idea of *beauty* taking the word in its higher Platonic sense. I am now convinced that the highest act of Reason, the one through which it encompasses all Ideas, is an aesthetic act, and that *truth and goodness only become sisters in beauty* – the philosopher must possess just as much aesthetic power as the poet. Men without aesthetic sense is what the philosophers-of-the-letter of our times [*unsre Buchstaben-philosophen*] are. The philosophy of the spirit is an aesthetic philosophy. One cannot be creative [*geistreich*] in any way, even about history one cannot argue creatively – without aesthetic sense. Here it ought to become clear what it is that men lack, who understand no ideas – and who confess honestly enough that they find everything obscure as soon as it goes beyond the table of contents and the index.

Poetry gains thereby a higher dignity, she becomes at the end once more, what she was in the beginning – the *teacher of mankind*; for there is no philosophy, no history left, the maker's art alone will survive all other sciences and arts.

At the same time we are told so often that the great mob must have a *religion of the senses*. But not only does the great mob need it, the philosopher needs it too. Monotheism of Reason and heart, polytheism of the imagination and of art, this is what we need.

Here I shall discuss particularly an idea which, as far as I know, has never occurred to anyone else – we must have a new mythology, but this mythology must be in the service of the Ideas, it must be a mythology of *Reason*.

Until we express the Ideas aesthetically, i.e. mythologically, they have no interest for the *people*, and conversely until mythology is rational the philosopher must be ashamed of it. Thus in the end enlightened and unenlightened must clasp hands, mythology must become philosophical in order to make the people rational, and philosophy must become mythological in order to make the philosophers sensible [*sinnlich*]. Then reigns eternal unity among us. No more the look of scorn [of the enlightened philosopher looking down on the mob], no more the blind trembling of the people before its wise men and priests. Then first awaits us *equal* development of *all* powers, of what is peculiar to each and what is common to all. No power shall any longer be suppressed for universal freedom and equality of spirits will reign! – A higher spirit sent from heaven must found this new religion among us, it will be the last and greatest work of mankind.

Notes

1   The first sentence is fragmentary in Hegel's manuscript. Occasional words and phrases in square brackets in this passage have been added by the translator, H. S. Harris. [s.h.]

2

Love

[. . .] But the wider this whole [i.e., either the Jewish people or Christendom] extends,[1] the more an equality of rights is transposed into an equality of dependence (as happens when the believer in cosmopolitanism comprises in his whole the entire human race), the less is dominion over objects granted to any one individual, and the less of the ruling Being's favour does he enjoy. Hence each individual loses more and more of his worth, his pretensions, and his independence. This must happen, because his worth was his share in dominion [over objects]; for a man without the pride of being the center of things the end [*Zweck*] of his collective whole is supreme, and being, like all other individuals, so small a part of that, he despises himself.

[Here there is no living union between the individual and his world; the object, severed from the subject, is dead; and the only love possible is a sort of relationship between the living subject and the dead objects by which he is surrounded.] Since something dead here forms one term of the love relationship, love is girt by matter alone, and this matter is quite indifferent to it. Love's essence at this level, then, is that the individual in his innermost nature is something opposed [to objectivity]; he is an independent unit for whom everything else is a world external to him. That world is as eternal as he is, and, while the objects by which he is confronted change, they are never absent; they are there, and his God is there, as surely as he is here; this is the ground of his tranquillity in face of loss and his sure confidence that his loss will be compensated, because compensation here is possible. This attitude makes matter something absolute in man's eyes; but, of course, if he never existed, then nothing would exist for him, and what necessity was there for his existence? That he might exist is intelligible enough, because beyond that collection of restricted experiences which make up his consciousness there is nothing whatever; the eternal and self-complete unification [with the object] is lacking. But the individual cannot bear to think himself in this nullity. He exists only as something opposed [to the object], and one of a pair of opposites is reciprocally condition and conditioned. Thus his thought of self must transcend his own consciousness, for there is no determinant without something determined, and vice versa.

In fact, nothing is unconditioned; nothing carries the root of its own being in itself. [Subject and object, man and matter,] each is only *relatively* necessary; the one exists only for the other, and hence exists for itself[2] only on the strength of a power outside itself; the one shares in the other only through that power's favour and grace. Nowhere is any independent existence to be found except in an alien Being; it is this Being which presents man with everything. This is the Being which man has to thank for himself and for immortality, blessings for which he begs with fear and trembling.

True union, or love proper, exists only between living beings who are alike in power and thus in one another's eyes living beings from every point of view; in no respect is either dead for the other. This genuine love excludes all oppositions. It is not the understanding, whose relations always leave the manifold of related terms as a manifold and whose unity is always a unity of opposites [left as opposites]. It is not reason either, because reason sharply opposes its determining power to what is determined. Love neither restricts nor is restricted; it is not finite at all. It is a feeling, yet not a single feeling [among other single feelings]. A single feeling is only a part and not the whole of life; the life present in a single feeling dissolves its barriers and drives on till it disperses itself in the manifold of feelings with a view to finding itself in the entirety of this manifold. This whole life is not contained in love in the same way as it is in this sum of many particular and isolated feelings; in love, life is present as a duplicate of itself and as a single and unified self. Here life has run through the circle of development from an immature to a completely mature unity: when the unity was immature, there still stood over against it the world and the possibility of a cleavage between itself and the world; as development proceeded, reflection produced more and more oppositions (unified by satisfied impulses) until it set the whole of man's life in opposition [to objectivity]; finally, love completely destroys objectivity and thereby annuls and transcends reflection, deprives man's opposite of all foreign character, and discovers life itself without any further defect. In love the separate [*das Getrennte*] does still remain, but as something united and no longer as something separate; life [in the subject] senses life [in the object].

Since love is a sensing of something living, lovers can be distinct only in so far as they are mortal and do not look upon this possibility of separation as if there were really a separation or as if reality were a sort of conjunction between possibility and existence. In the lovers there is no matter; they are a living whole. To say that the lovers have an independence and a living principle peculiar to each of themselves means only that they may die [and may be separated by death]. To say that salt and other minerals are part of the makeup of a plant and that these carry in themselves their own laws governing their operation is the judgement of external reflection and means no more than that the plant may rot. But love strives to annul even this distinction [between the lover as lover and the lover as physical organism], to annul this possibility [of separation] as a mere abstract possibility, to unite [with itself] even the mortal element [within the lover] and to make it immortal.

If the separable element persists in either of the lovers as something peculiarly his own before their union is complete, it creates a difficulty for them. There is a sort of antagonism between complete surrender or the only possible cancellation of opposition (i.e., its cancellation in complete union) and a still subsisting independence. Union feels the latter as a hindrance; love is indignant if part of the individual is severed and held back as a private property. This raging of love against [exclusive] individuality is shame. Shame is not a reaction of the mortal body, not an expression of the freedom to maintain one's life, to subsist. The hostility in a loveless assault does injury to the loving heart itself, and the shame of this now injured heart becomes the rage which defends only its right, its property. If shame, instead of being an effect of love, an effect which only takes an indignant form after encountering something hostile, were something itself by nature hostile which wanted to defend an assailable property of its own, then we would have to say that shame is most of all characteristic of tyrants, or of girls who will not yield their charms except for money, or of vain women who want to fascinate. None of these love; their defence of their mortal body is the opposite of indignation about it; they ascribe an intrinsic worth to it and are shameless.

A pure heart is not ashamed of love; but it is ashamed if its love is incomplete; it upbraids itself if there is some hostile power which hinders love's culmination. Shame enters only through the recollection of the body, through the presence of an [exclusive] personality or the sensing of an [exclusive] individuality. It is not a fear *for* what is mortal, for what is merely one's own, but rather a fear *of* it, a fear which vanishes as the separable element in the lover is diminished by his love. Love is stronger than fear. It has no fear of its fear, but, led by its fear, it cancels separation, apprehensive as it is of finding opposition which may resist it or be a fixed barrier against it. It is a mutual giving and taking; through shyness its gifts may be disdained; through shyness an opponent may not yield to its receiving; but it still tries whether hope has not deceived it, whether it still finds itself everywhere. The lover who takes is not thereby made richer than the other; he is enriched indeed, but only so much as the other is. So too the giver does not make himself poorer; by giving to the other he has at the same time and to the same extent enhanced his own treasure (compare Juliet in *Romeo and Juliet* [ii.2.133–5: 'My bounty is as boundless as the sea, My love as deep;] the more I give to thee, The more I have').[3] This wealth of life love acquires in the exchange of every thought, every variety of inner experience, for it seeks out differences and devises unifications ad infinitum; it turns to the whole manifold of nature in order to drink love out of every life. What in the first instance is most the individual's own is united into the whole in the lovers' touch and contact; consciousness of a separate self disappears, and all distinction between the lovers is annulled. The mortal element, the body, has lost the character of separability, and a living child, a seed of immortality, of the eternally self-developing and self-generating [race], has come into existence. What has been united [in the child] is not divided again; [in love and through love] God has acted and created.

This unity [the child], however, is only a point, [an undifferentiated unity,] a seed; the lovers cannot so contribute to it as to give it a manifold in itself at the start. Their union is free from all inner division; in it there is no working on an opposite. Everything which gives the newly begotten child a manifold life and a specific existence, it must draw into itself, set over against itself, and unify with itself. The seed breaks free from its original unity, turns ever more and more to opposition, and begins to develop. Each stage of its development is a separation, and its aim in each is to regain for itself the full riches of life [enjoyed by the parents]. Thus the process is: unity, separated opposites, reunion. After their union the lovers separate again, but in the child their union has become unseparated.

This union in love is complete; but it can remain so only as long as the separate lovers are opposed solely in the sense that the one loves and the other is loved, i.e., that each separate lover is one organ in a living whole. Yet the lovers are in connection with much that is dead; external objects belong to each of them. This means that a lover stands in relation to things opposed to him in his own eyes as objects and opposites; this is why lovers are capable of a multiplex opposition in the course of their multiplex acquisition and possession of property and rights. The dead object in the power of one of the lovers is opposed to both of them, and a union in respect of it seems to be possible only if it comes under the dominion of both. The one who sees the other in possession of a property must sense in the other the separate individuality which has willed this possession. He cannot himself annul the exclusive dominion of the other, for this once again would be an opposition to the other's power, since no relation to an object is possible except mastery over it; he would be opposing a mastery to the other's dominion and would be cancelling one of the other's relationships, namely, his exclusion of others from his property. Since possession and property make up such an important part of men's life, cares, and thoughts, even lovers cannot refrain from reflection on this aspect of their relations. Even if the use of the property is common to both, the right to its possession would remain undecided, and the thought of this right would never be forgotten, because everything which men possess has the legal form of property. But if the possessor gives the other the same right of possession as he has himself, community of goods is still only the right of one or other of the two to the thing.

Notes

1 All English material in square brackets has been added by the translator, T. M. Knox. [S.H.]
2 Knox's translation has 'in and for itself', but the German text only has 'für sich'. [S.H.]
3 Knox gives the reference as 'ii.1.175–7'. [S.H.]

3

Fragment of a System

Absolute opposition holds good [in the realm of the dead.][1] One kind of opposition is to be found in the multiplicity of living beings. Living beings must be regarded as organizations. The multiplicity of life has to be thought of as being divided against itself; one part of this multiplicity (a part which is itself an infinite multiplicity because it is alive) is to be regarded purely as something related, as having its being purely in union; the second part, also an infinite multiplicity, is to be regarded as solely in opposition, as having its being solely through a separation from the first. Therefore the first part [the unity] can also be defined as having its being only by means of separation from the second one. The unity is called an organization or an individual. It is self-evident that this life, whose manifold is regarded purely as being related and whose very existence is exactly this relation, can also be regarded as being differentiated in itself, as a mere multiplicity, because the relation between the separated is not more intrinsic to it than the separation between that which is related. On the other hand, it must also be considered as capable of entering into relation with what is excluded from it, as capable of losing its individuality or being linked with what has been excluded. Similarly, the manifold itself, excluded from an organic whole and existing only as thus opposed [to it], must nevertheless be conceived, in itself and in abstraction from that organization, not only as absolutely manifold, yet at the same time itself internally related, but also as connected with the living whole which is excluded from it.

The concept of individuality includes opposition to infinite variety and also inner association with it. A human being is an individual life in so far as he is to be distinguished from all the elements and from the infinity of individual beings outside himself. But he is only an individual life in so far as he is at one with all the elements, with the infinity of lives outside himself. He exists only inasmuch as the totality of life is divided into parts, he himself being one part and all the rest the other part; and again he exists only inasmuch as he is no part at all and inasmuch as nothing is separated from him. If we presuppose life undivided as fixed, then we can regard living beings as expressions or manifestations of that life. Precisely because these manifestations are posited, the infinite multiplicity of living beings is posited simultaneously, but reflection then crystallizes this multiplicity into stable, subsistent and fixed points, i.e., into individuals.

If on the contrary we presuppose individual lives, namely, ourselves, as the spectators, then that life which is posited outside our own restricted spheres is an infinite life with an infinite variety, infinite oppositions, infinite relations; as a multiplicity, it is an infinite multiplicity of organizations or individuals, and as a unity it is one unique organized whole, divided and unified in itself – Nature. Nature is a positing of life, for reflection has applied to life its concepts of relation and separation, of the self-subsistent particular (something restricted) and the unifying universal (something unrestricted), and by positing these has turned life into nature.

Now because life, as an infinity of living beings or as an infinity of figures, is thus, as nature, an infinitely finite, an unrestricted restrictedness, and because this union and this separation of the finite and the infinite are within nature, nature is not itself life but is only a life crystallized by reflection, even though it be treated by reflection in the worthiest manner. Therefore life in thinking and in contemplating nature still senses (or however else one may describe the mode of apprehension involved) this contradiction, this one opposition which still exists between itself and the infinite life; or, in other words, reason still recognizes the one-sidedness of this mode of treating life and of this mode of positing [concepts]. Out of the mortal and perishable figure, out of what is self-opposed and self-antagonistic, this thinking life raises that living being, which would be free from transience; raises a relation between the multiplex elements which is not dead or killing, a relation which is not a [bare] unity, a conceptual abstraction, but is all-living and all-powerful infinite life; and this life it calls God. In this process it is no longer [merely] thinking or contemplating, because its object does not carry in itself anything reflected, anything dead.

This self-elevation of man, not from the finite to the infinite (for these terms are only products of mere reflection, and as such their separation is absolute), but from finite life to infinite life, is religion. We may call infinite life a spirit in contrast with the abstract multiplicity, for spirit is the living unity of the manifold if it is contrasted with the manifold as spirit's configuration and not as a mere dead multiplicity; contrasted with the latter, spirit would be nothing but a bare unity which is called law and is something purely conceptual and not a living being. The spirit is an animating law in union with the manifold which is then itself animated. When man takes this animated manifold as a multiplicity of many individuals, yet as connected with the animating spirit, then these single lives become organs, and the infinite whole becomes an infinite totality of life. When he takes the infinite life as the spirit of the whole and at the same time as a living [being] outside himself (since he himself is restricted), and when he puts himself at the same time outside his restricted self in rising toward the living being and intimately uniting himself with him, then he worships God.

Although the manifold is here no longer regarded as isolated but is rather explicitly conceived as related to the living spirit, as animated, as organ, still something remains excluded, namely, the dead, so that a certain imperfection and opposition persists. In other words, when the manifold is conceived as an organ only, opposition itself is excluded; but life cannot be regarded as union or relation alone but must be regarded as opposition as well. If I say that life is the union of opposition and relation, this union may be isolated again, and it may be argued that union is opposed to non-union. Consequently, I would have to say: Life is the union of union and non-union. In other words, every expression whatsoever is a product of reflection, and therefore it is possible to demonstrate in the case of every expression that, when reflection propounds it, another expression, not propounded, is excluded. Reflection is thus driven on and on without rest; but this process must be checked once and for all by keeping in mind that, for example, what has been called a union of synthesis and antithesis is not something propounded by the understanding or by reflection but has a character of its own, namely, that of being a reality beyond all reflection. Within the living whole there are posited at the same time death, opposition, and understanding, because there is posited a manifold that is alive itself and that, as alive, can posit itself as a whole. By so doing, it is at the same time a part, i.e., something for which there is something dead and which itself is something dead for other such parts. This partial character of the living being is transcended in religion; finite life rises to infinite life. It is only because the finite is itself life that it carries in itself the possibility of raising itself to infinite life.

Philosophy therefore has to stop short of religion because it is a process of thinking and, as such a process, implies an opposition with non-thinking [processes] as well as the opposition between the thinking mind and the object of thought. Philosophy has to disclose the finiteness in all finite things and require their integration by means of reason. In particular, it has to recognize the illusions generated by its own infinite and thus to place the true infinite outside its confines.

The elevation of the finite to the infinite is only characterized as the elevation of finite life to infinite life, as religion, in virtue of the fact that it does not posit the reality of the infinite as a reality created by reflection, be it objective or subjective, i.e., it has not simply added to the restricted that which restricts. If it had done so, the latter would be recognized again as something posited by reflection and thereby itself restricted and would now again seek what restricts it and would postulate a continuation in such a way *ad infinitum*. Even this activity of reason is an elevation to the infinite, but this infinite is a [false one.][2]

. . . , objective centre.[3] For all nations this centre was the temple facing the east, and to the worshippers of an invisible God it was nothing but this shapeless special room, nothing but a place. But this mere opposite, this purely objective and merely spatial centre, must not necessarily remain in this imperfection of entire objectivity. It can itself, as being self-sustained, revert to its own subjectivity by becoming configurated. Divine emotion, the infinite sensed by the finite, is not integrated until reflection is added and dwells upon it. But the relation of reflection to emotion is only the recognition of it as something subjective, is only consciousness of feeling, in which reflection reflects on emotion but each is separate from the other. The pure spatial objectivity provides the unifying centre for many, and the objectivity configurated is at the same time what it ought to be, namely, not an actual but only a potential objectivity because subjectivity is now linked with it. This objectivity configurated may be thought as an actual objectivity, but this is not necessary, because it is certainly not pure [or abstract] objectivity.

And thus, just as the antinomy of time was posited above[4] as necessary, namely, the antinomy between a moment and the time needed by life [for its actuality], so now the objective antinomy with respect to the thing confronting us is posited. The infinite being, filling the immeasurability of space, exists at the same time in a definite space, as is said, for instance, in the verse:[5]

> He whom all heavens' heaven ne'er contained
> Lies now in Mary's womb.

In the religious life both man's relation to objects and also his action were interpreted [above] as a preservation of the objects in life or as an animation of them, but man was also reminded of his destiny, which demands of him that he admit the existence of the objective as objective or even that he make the living being itself into an object. It may be that this objectification would last only for a moment and that life would withdraw again from the object, free itself from it, and would leave the oppressed to its own life and to its resuscitation. But it is necessary that life should also put itself into a permanent relation with objects and thus maintain their objectivity even up to the point of completely destroying them.

Even in all the increased religious union disclosed by the above-mentioned acts of integration [in worship] hypocrisy may still exist, namely, owing to one's retention of a particular property for one's self. If he kept things firmly in his own grasp, man would not yet have fulfilled the negative prerequisites of religion, i.e., would not yet be free from absolute objectivity and would not yet have risen above finite life. He would still be unable to unite himself with the infinite life because he would have kept something for himself; he would still be in a state of mastering things or caught in a dependence upon them. This is the reason why he gives up only part of his property as a sacrifice, for it is his fate to possess property, and this fate is necessary and can never be discarded. In God's sight man destroys part of his property [on the altar]. The rest he destroys to some extent by taking away as far as possible its character as private property and sharing it with his friends. The destruction of property [on the altar] is an additional negation of private ownership because such destruction is useless and superfluous. Only through this uselessness of destroying, through this destroying for destroying's sake, does he make good the destruction which he causes for his own particular purposes. At the same time he has consummated the objectivity of the objects by a destruction unrelated to his own purposes, by that complete negation of relations which is called death. This aimless destruction for destruction's sake sometimes happens, even if the necessity of a purposive destruction of objects remains, and it proves to be the only religious relation to absolute objects.

It only needs to be briefly mentioned that the remaining external surroundings, as necessary confines, should not so much entertain [the devout] by their useless beauty as hint at something else by purposive embellishment, and further that it is the essence of worship to cancel the intuitive or thoughtful contemplation of an objective God, or rather to blend this attitude with the joyful subjectivity of living beings, of song, or of motions of the body, a sort of subjective expression which like the solemn oration can become objective and beautiful by rules, namely: dance; or offer words with a manifold of observances, the due ordering of offerings, sacrifices, and so on. Moreover, this variety of expressions, and of those whose expressions they are, demands unity and order which come alive in someone who orders and commands, i.e., a priest, who himself has a separate position of his own if man's external life has been split into separate compartments for the fulfilment of his many needs. There is no need to mention other consequences and the means of completely realizing them.

This more perfect union in the realm of religion is not absolutely necessary because it consists in such an elevation of finite life to infinite life that as little as possible of the finite and restricted, i.e., of the merely objective or merely subjective, remains, and that every opposition springing from this elevation and integration is reintegrated. Religion is *any* elevation of the finite to the infinite, when the infinite is conceived as a definite form of life. Some such elevation is necessary because the finite depends on the infinite. But the stage of opposition and unification on which the determinate nature of one generation of men persists is accidental in respect to indeterminate nature. The most perfect integration [or completion] is possible in the case of peoples whose life is as little as possible separated and disintegrated, i.e., in the case of happy peoples. Unhappy peoples cannot reach that stage, but they, living in a state of separation, must take anxious care for the preservation of one member [of the whole], i.e., for their own independence. They are not permitted to abandon the quest for this independence; their highest pride must be to cling to separation and maintain the existence of the unit [whose independence is in question].[6]

One may consider this situation from the side of subjectivity as independence, or from the other side as an alien, remote, inaccessible object. Both seem to be compatible with one another, although it is necessary that, the stronger the separation is, the purer must the Ego be and the further must the object be removed from and above man. The greater and the more isolated the inner sphere, the greater and the more isolated is the outer sphere also, and if the latter is regarded as the self-subsistent, the more subjugated man must appear. But it is precisely this being mastered by the immeasurably great object which is steadily retained as man's relation to the object; it does not matter what mode of consciousness man prefers, whether that of fearing a God who, being infinite and beyond the heaven of heavens, exalted above all connection and all relationship, hovers all-powerful above all nature; or that of placing himself as pure Ego above the ruins of this body and the shining suns, above the countless myriads of heavenly spheres, above the ever new solar systems as numerous as ye all are, ye shining suns.

When the separation is infinite, it does not matter which remains fixed, the subject or the object; but in either case the opposition persists, the opposition of the absolutely finite to the absolutely infinite. In either case the elevation of finite to infinite life would be only an elevation over finite life; the infinite would only be the completely integrated in so far as it was opposed to the totality, i.e., to the infinity of the finite. The opposition would not be overcome in a beautiful union; the union would be frustrated, and opposition would be a hovering of the Ego over all nature, a dependence upon, or rather a relation to, a Being beyond all nature. This religion can be sublime and awful, but it cannot be beautifully humane. And hence the blessedness enjoyed by the Ego which opposes itself to everything and has thus brought everything under its feet is a phenomenon of the time, at bottom equivalent to the phenomenon of dependence on an absolutely alien being which cannot become man, or if it did become man (namely, at a point in time) would, even in this union [between eternal and temporal, infinite and finite], remain something absolutely specialized, i.e., would remain just an absolute unit. Nevertheless, this blessedness may be man's worthiest and noblest achievement if the union [of the eternal] with the temporal were ignoble and ignominious.

Notes

1 The first sentence is fragmentary in Hegel's manuscript and has been completed by the translator, Richard Kroner. All material in square brackets has been added by the translator. [S.H.]

2 Hegel's manuscript breaks off here. The concluding sentence has been completed by the translator. Twelve manuscript sheets are missing between this paragraph and the one that begins '. . . , objective centre'. [S.H.]

3 The first sentence of this paragraph is fragmentary in Hegel's manuscript. [S.H.]

4 i.e., in the part of the manuscript which is lost. [Translator's note.]

5 Taken, with a slight change, from a hymn by Martin Luther, beginning 'Gelobet seist Du, Jesu Christ'. [Translator's note.]

6 This contrast between happy and unhappy peoples may refer to that between the Greeks and the Israelites. [Translator's note.]

4

The Difference Between Fichte's and Schelling's System of Philosophy: The Need of Philosophy

If we look more closely at the particular form worn by a philosophy we see that it arises, on the one hand, from the living originality of the spirit whose work and spontaneity have re-established and shaped the harmony that has been rent; and on the other hand, from the particular form of the dichotomy from which the system emerges. Dichotomy is the source of *the need of philosophy*; and as the culture of the era, it is the unfree and given aspect of the whole configuration. In [any][1] culture, the appearance of the Absolute has become isolated from the Absolute and fixated into independence. But at the same time the appearance cannot disown its origin, and must aim to constitute the manifold of its limitations into one whole. The intellect [*Verstand*], as the capacity to set limits, erects a building and places it between man and the Absolute, linking everything that man thinks worthy and holy to this building, fortifying it through all the powers of nature and talent and expanding it *ad infinitum*. The entire totality of limitations is to be found in it, but not the Absolute itself. [The Absolute is] lost in the parts, where it drives the intellect in its ceaseless development of manifoldness. But in its striving to enlarge itself into the Absolute, the intellect only reproduces itself *ad infinitum* and so mocks itself. Reason [*Vernunft*] reaches the Absolute only in stepping out of this manifold of parts. The more stable and splendid the edifice of the intellect is, the more restless becomes the striving of the life that is caught up in it as a part to get out of it, and raise itself to freedom. When life as Reason steps away into the distance, the totality of limitations is at the same time nullified, and connected with the Absolute in this nullification, and hence conceived and posited as mere appearance. The split between the Absolute and the totality of limitations vanishes.

The intellect copies Reason's absolute positing and through the form [of absolute positing] it gives itself the semblance of Reason even though the posits are in themselves opposites, and hence finite. The semblance grows that much stronger when intellect transforms and fixes Reason's negating activity [as distinct from its positing activity] into a product. The infinite, in so far as it gets opposed to the finite, is a thing of this kind, i.e., it is something rational as posited by the intellect. Taken by itself, as something rational, it merely expresses the negating of the finite. By fixing it, the intellect sets it up in absolute opposition to the finite; and reflection which had risen to the plane of Reason when it suspended the finite, now lowers itself again to being intellect because it has fixed Reason's activity into [an activity of] opposition. Moreover, reflection still pretends to be rational even in its relapse.

The cultures of various times have established opposites of this kind, which were supposed to be products of Reason and absolutes, in various ways, and the intellect has laboured over them as such. Antitheses such as spirit and matter, soul and body, faith and intellect, freedom and necessity, etc. used to be important; and in more limited spheres they appeared in a variety of other guises. The whole weight of human interests hung upon them. With the progress of culture they have passed over into such forms as the antithesis of Reason and sensibility, intelligence and nature and, with respect to the universal concept, of absolute subjectivity and absolute objectivity.

The sole interest of Reason is to suspend such rigid antitheses. But this does not mean that Reason is altogether opposed to opposition and limitation. For the necessary dichotomy is One factor in life.[2] Life eternally forms itself by setting up oppositions, and totality at the highest pitch of living energy [*in der höchsten Lebendigkeit*] is only possible through its own re-establishment out of the deepest fission. What Reason opposes, rather, is just the absolute fixity which the intellect gives to the dichotomy; and it does so all the more if the absolute opposites themselves originated in Reason.

When the might of union vanishes from the life of men and the antitheses lose their living connection and reciprocity and gain independence, the need of philosophy arises. From this point of view the need is contingent. But with respect to the given dichotomy the need is the necessary attempt to suspend the rigidified opposition between subjectivity and objectivity; to comprehend the achieved existence [*das Gewordensein*] of the intellectual and real world as a becoming. Its being as a product must be comprehended as a producing. In the infinite activity of becoming and producing, Reason has united what was sundered and it has reduced the absolute dichotomy to a relative one, one that is conditioned by the original identity. When, where and in what forms such self-reproductions of Reason occur as philosophies is contingent. This contingency must be comprehended on the basis of the Absolute positing itself as an objective totality. The contingency is temporal in so far as the objectivity of the Absolute is intuited as a going forth in time. But in so far as it makes its appearance as spatial compresence, the dichotomy is a matter of regional climate. In the form of fixed reflection, as a world of thinking and thought essence in antithesis to a world of actuality, this dichotomy falls into the Northwest.[3]

As culture grows and spreads, and the development of those outward expressions of life into which dichotomy can entwine itself becomes more manifold, the power of dichotomy becomes greater, its regional sanctity is more firmly established and the strivings of life to give birth once more to its harmony become more meaningless, more alien to the cultural whole. Such few attempts as there have been on behalf of the cultural whole against more recent culture, like the more significant beautiful embodiments of far away or long ago, have only been able to arouse that modicum of attention which remains possible when the more profound, serious connection of living art [to culture as a living whole] can no longer be understood. The entire system of relations constituting life has become detached from art, and thus the concept of art's all-embracing coherence has been lost, and transformed into the concept either of superstition or of entertainment. The highest aesthetic perfection, as it evolves in a determinate religion in which man lifts himself above all dichotomy and sees both the freedom of the subject and the necessity of the object vanish in the kingdom of grace, could only be energized up to a certain stage of culture, and within general or mob barbarism. As it progressed, civilization has split away from it [i.e., this aesthetic religious perfection], and juxtaposed it to itself or vice versa. Because the intellect has grown sure of itself, both [intellect and the aesthetic religious perfection] have come to enjoy a measure of mutual peace by separating into realms that are completely set apart from one another. What happens in one has no significance in the other.

However, the intellect can also be directly attacked by Reason in its own realm. These attempts to nullify the dichotomy, and hence the absoluteness of intellect, through reflection itself are easier to understand. Dichotomy felt itself attacked, and so turned with hate and fury against Reason, until the realm of the intellect rose to such power that it could regard itself as secure from Reason. – But just as we often say of virtue that the greatest witness for its reality is the semblance that hypocrisy borrows from it, so intellect cannot keep Reason off. It seeks to protect itself against the feeling of its inner emptiness, and from the secret fear that plagues anything limited, by whitewashing its particularities with a semblance of Reason. The contempt for Reason shows itself most strongly, not in Reason's being freely scorned and abused, but by the boasting of the limited that it has mastered philosophy and lives in amity with it. Philosophy must refuse friendship with these false attempts that boast insincerely of having nullified the particularities, but which issue from limitation, and use philosophy as a means to save and secure these limitations.

In the struggle of the intellect with Reason the intellect has strength only to the degree that Reason forsakes itself. Its success in the struggle therefore depends upon Reason itself, and upon the authenticity of the need for the reconstitution of totality, the need from which Reason emerges.

The need of philosophy can be called the *presupposition* of philosophy if philosophy, which begins with itself, has to be furnished with some sort of vestibule; and there has been much talk nowadays about an absolute presupposition.[4] What is called the presupposition of philosophy is nothing else but the need that has come to utterance. Once uttered, the need is posited for reflection, so that [because of the very nature of reflection] there must be two presuppositions.

One is the Absolute itself. It is the goal that is being sought; but it is already present, or how otherwise could it be sought? Reason produces it, merely by freeing consciousness from its limitations. This suspension of the limitations is conditioned by the presupposed unlimitedness.

The other presupposition may be taken to be that consciousness has stepped out of the totality, that is, it may be taken to be the split into being and not-being, concept and being, finitude and infinity. From the standpoint of the dichotomy, the absolute synthesis is a beyond, it is the undetermined and the shapeless as opposed to the determinacies of the dichotomy. The Absolute is the night, and the light is younger than it; and the distinction between them, like the emergence of the light out of the night, is an absolute difference – the nothing is the first out of which all being, all the manifoldness of the finite has emerged. But the task of philosophy consists in uniting these presuppositions: to posit being in non-being, as becoming; to posit dichotomy in the Absolute, as its appearance; to posit the finite in the infinite, as life.

Still, it is clumsy to express the need of philosophy as a presupposition of philosophy, for the need acquires in this way a reflective form. This reflective form appears as contradictory propositions [. . .]. One may require of propositions that they be justified. But the justification of these propositions as presuppositions is still not supposed to be philosophy itself, so that the founding and grounding gets going before, and outside of, philosophy.

Notes

1 English material in square brackets has been added by the translators, H. S. Harris and W. Cerf. [S.H.]
2 Hegel capitalized 'Ein'. The 'Other' factor is 'union' or 'identity' (with the Absolute). [Translator's note.]
3 The reference here is to Descartes. [Translator's note.]
4 Hegel is principally thinking of Reinhold with his 'founding and grounding' and his 'arch-truth'. [Translator's note.]

Part II
Phenomenology of Spirit

Introduction

Hegel's mature philosophy begins – historically and systematically – with the *Phenomenology of Spirit* which was published in 1807. That is to say, the *Phenomenology* inaugurates the period of Hegel's philosophical maturity and also serves as the introduction to his developed philosophical system. The specific task of the *Phenomenology* is to show that the standpoint of speculative philosophy is made necessary by the unresolved tensions and contradictions within ordinary, non-philosophical consciousness itself – within what Hegel calls 'natural consciousness'. Hegel's aim is thus not just to take the standpoint of speculative philosophy for granted, but to start from the assumptions of natural consciousness and, from those very assumptions, to justify the philosophical point of view. He seeks to fulfil this aim by considering a series of 'shapes' of consciousness – including sense-certainty and perception (with their natural assumptions about objects), the various forms of self-consciousness, and ethical, moral and religious spirit – and demonstrating that the structure of any shape of consciousness requires it to *turn into* a different shape if it is actually to achieve the level of consciousness which it claims for itself. He thus shows that sense-certainty must become concrete perception, not just immediate certainty, if it is to be genuinely *certain* of what it confronts, and that moral consciousness must pass (through forgiveness) into religious consciousness, if it is to be genuinely *moral*. The ultimate conclusion to which Hegel's analysis leads is that, if consciousness or spirit as a whole is to achieve the knowledge which it claims for itself, it must give up the idea that being or 'truth' is something *other* than itself to which it stands in relation, and must conceive of the very nature of being as determinable from *within* thought itself. The shape of consciousness which gives up 'the antithesis of being and knowing' in this way, and which looks for the form of being in thought itself, is speculative philosophy or 'absolute knowing'.[1]

Hegel calls his study of natural consciousness a 'phenomenology' or 'logic of appearance' (borrowing the word from J. H. Lambert and Kant) for two reasons. On the one hand, Hegel's study shows how true knowledge – philosophy – gradually and necessarily *appears* or 'comes on the scene'. On the other hand, Hegel demonstrates the necessity of philosophy by considering, not what natural consciousness *is*, but what natural consciousness takes itself and its objects to be, that is, the way consciousness and its objects *appear* to consciousness itself.[2] It is especially important to bear this second point in mind, if we are to understand the precise difference between phenomenology and philosophy.

In spite of what some of its critics have charged, Hegel's phenomenology is clearly the product of rigorous, disciplined *thought*, not the product of poetic imagination or quasi-religious enthusiasm. The structure of each shape of consciousness is made intelligible through precise 'abstract determinations' or concepts, such as 'being in itself' and 'being for itself', not by means of poetic or religious images.[3] Furthermore, the phenomenological study of consciousness is clearly *scientific* in Hegel's sense, since it is a strictly immanent study which renders explicit what is implicit in what consciousness takes itself to be and in so doing shows how one shape of consciousness turns dialectically and necessarily into another.[4] Nevertheless, the thought at work in Hegel's study of consciousness is specifically *phenomenological*, not *philosophical* thought. This is because such thought does not yet claim to be able to discover the true nature of *being* purely from within itself and so does not set out to determine purely from within itself what consciousness truly *is*. All that phenomenological thought sets out to do is consider what consciousness itself ordinarily *takes itself* (and its object) to be, and think through the tensions and contradictions that are inherent in the manifold ways in which consciousness and its objects appear to consciousness (and that finally lead it to become philosophical). Phenomenology anticipates speculative philosophy by discovering that consciousness develops dialectically (this, indeed, is what most obviously distinguishes Hegel's phenomenology from that of Husserl). But phenomenology is still not philosophy proper. It is simply the discipline that shows that philosophy is needed to fulfil the claims made for itself by non-philosophical consciousness – the discipline that constitutes the ladder to philosophy.

Hegel's *Phenomenology* has exercised an enormous influence on subsequent philosophers, social theorists and theologians, and the passages selected here belong among the most influential parts of the book. The selections from the Preface contain noteworthy remarks on immanent, scientific method, on the 'labour of the negative' and on the speculative sentence (which is characteristic of both phenomenology and philosophy proper, even though Hegel refers to it specifically as the 'philosophical' sentence).[5] The Introduction, in which the distinctive character of phenomenological method is explained, is reproduced here in full, as is the opening section on sense-certainty, in which Hegel exposes (in a proto-Wittgensteinian manner) the essential indeterminacy of all claims by consciousness to be immediately certain of *this, here, now*.

I have included the whole of Hegel's analysis of self-consciousness in order to show phenomenological thought 'at work' throughout a complete section of the text and also because so much important material is contained in that analysis. This section includes Hegel's condensed, but seminal remarks on life, desire and recognition, as well as the famous dialectic of master and slave (or 'lordship and bondage'), which clearly left its mark on Marx's analysis of alienated consumption and production in capitalism (despite the surprising absence of direct reference to it in Marx's writings) and which, through the influential interpretation offered by Alexandre Kojève, came to represent the cornerstone of Hegel's philosophy for a whole generation of French thinkers from Bataille to Sartre to Derrida. The section also contains Hegel's subtle accounts of stoicism and scepticism, and his long and complex analysis of the unhappy consciousness in its alienation from its own essence – an analysis which finds its clearest echo in the writings of Feuerbach and Kierkegaard. The selections from the *Phenomenology* conclude with Hegel's abstract but penetrating account of the French Revolution and its 'fury of destruction',[6] and with his brief review of the transition from phenomenology to 'absolute knowing' or philosophy proper.

The passages in Part II are taken from G. W. F. Hegel, *Phenomenology of Spirit*, translated by A. V. Miller, with analysis of the text and foreword by J. N. Findlay (Oxford: Oxford University Press, 1977). For the German text of these passages, see G. W. F. Hegel, *Werke in zwanzig Bänden*, edited by E. Moldenhauer and K. M. Michel, 20 vols and Index (Frankfurt: Suhrkamp Verlag, 1969ff), vol. 3.

Notes

1 Hegel, *Phenomenology of Spirit*, p. 22. See below, p. 61.
2 Hegel, *Phenomenology of Spirit*, pp. 48, 53. See below, pp. 72, 75.
3 Hegel, *Phenomenology of Spirit*, pp. 35, 52. See below, pp. 64, 75.
4 Hegel, *Phenomenology of Spirit*, pp. 55–6, 493. See below, pp. 77–8, 122.
5 Hegel, *Phenomenology of Spirit*, p. 39. See below, p. 67.
6 Hegel, *Phenomenology of Spirit*, p. 359. See below, p. 116.

5

Phenomenology of Spirit: Preface

11. Besides, it is not difficult to see that ours is a birth-time and a period of transition to a new era. Spirit [*Geist*] has broken with the world it has hitherto inhabited and imagined, and is of a mind to submerge it in the past, and in the labour of its own transformation. Spirit is indeed never at rest but always engaged in moving forward. But just as the first breath drawn by a child after its long, quiet nourishment breaks the gradualness of merely quantitative growth – there is a qualitative leap, and the child is born – so likewise the Spirit in its formation matures slowly and quietly into its new shape, dissolving bit by bit the structure of its previous world, whose tottering state is only hinted at by isolated symptoms. The frivolity and boredom which unsettle the established order, the vague foreboding of something unknown, these are the heralds of approaching change. The gradual crumbling that left unaltered the face of the whole is cut short by a sunburst which, in one flash, illuminates the features of the new world.

12. But this new world is no more a complete actuality than is a new-born child; it is essential to bear this in mind. It comes on the scene for the first time in its immediacy or its Notion [*Begriff*].[1] Just as little as a building is finished when its foundation has been laid, so little is the achieved Notion of the whole the whole itself. When we wish to see an oak with its massive trunk and spreading branches and foliage, we are not content to be shown an acorn instead. So too, Science, the crown of a world of Spirit, is not complete in its beginnings. The onset of the new spirit is the product of a widespread upheaval in various forms of culture, the prize at the end of a complicated, tortuous path and of just as variegated and strenuous an effort. It is the whole which, having traversed its content in time and space, has returned into itself, and is the resultant *simple Notion* of the whole. But the actuality of this simple whole consists in those various shapes and forms which have become its moments, and which will now develop and take shape afresh, this time in their new element, in their newly acquired meaning.

13. While the initial appearance of the new world is, to begin with, only the whole veiled in its *simplicity*, or the general foundation of the whole, the

wealth of previous existence is still present to consciousness in memory. Consciousness misses in the newly emerging shape its former range and specificity of content, and even more the articulation of form whereby distinctions are securely defined, and stand arrayed in their fixed relations. Without such articulation, Science lacks universal intelligibility, and gives the appearance of being the esoteric possession of a few individuals: an esoteric possession, since it is as yet present only in its Notion or in its inwardness; of a few individuals, since its undiffused manifestation makes its existence something singular. Only what is completely determined is at once exoteric, comprehensible, and capable of being learned and appropriated by all. The intelligible form of Science is the way open and equally accessible to everyone, and consciousness as it approaches Science justly demands that it be able to attain to rational knowledge by way of the ordinary understanding [*Verstand*]; for the understanding is thought, the pure 'I' as such; and what is intelligible is what is already familiar and common to Science and the unscientific consciousness alike, the latter through its having afforded direct access to the former.

14. Science in its early stages, when it has attained neither to completeness of detail nor perfection of form, is vulnerable to criticism. But it would be as unjust for such criticism to strike at the very heart of Science, as it is untenable to refuse to honour the demand for its further development. This polarization seems to be the Gordian knot with which scientific culture is at present struggling, and which it still does not properly understand. One side boasts of its wealth of material and intelligibility, the other side at least scorns this intelligibility, and flaunts its immediate rationality and divinity. Even if the former side is reduced to silence, whether by the force of truth alone or by the blustering of the other, and even if, in respect of fundamentals, it feels itself outmatched, it is by no means satisfied regarding the said demands; for they are justified, but not fulfilled. Its silence stems only half from the triumph of its opponent, and half from the boredom and indifference which tend to result from the continual awakening of expectations through unfulfilled promises.

15. As for content, the other side make it easy enough for themselves at times to display a great expanse of it. They appropriate a lot of already familiar and well-ordered material; by focusing on rare and exotic instances they give the impression that they have hold of everything else which scientific knowledge had already embraced in its scope, and that they are also in command of such material as is as yet unordered. It thus appears that everything has been subjected to the absolute Idea, which therefore seems to be cognized in everything and to have matured into an expanded science. But a closer inspection shows that this expansion has not come about through one and the same principle having spontaneously assumed different shapes, but rather through the shapeless repetition of one and the same formula, only externally applied to diverse materials, thereby obtaining merely a boring show of diversity. The Idea, which is of course true enough on its

own account, remains in effect always in its primitive condition, if its development involves nothing more than this sort of repetition of the same formula.
When the knowing subject goes around applying this single inert form to
whatever it encounters, and dipping the material into this placid element
from outside, this is no more the fulfilment of what is needed, i.e. a self-
originating, self-differentiating wealth of shapes, than any arbitrary insights
into the content. Rather it is a monochromatic formalism which only arrives
at the differentiation of its material since this has been already provided and
is by now familiar.

16. Yet this formalism maintains that such monotony and abstract universality are the Absolute, and we are assured that dissatisfaction with it indicates the inability to master the absolute standpoint and to keep hold of it.
Time was when the bare possibility of imagining something differently was
sufficient to refute an idea, and this bare possibility, this general thought,
also had the entire positive value of an actual cognition. Nowadays we see
all value ascribed to the universal Idea in this non-actual form, and the
undoing of all distinct, determinate entities (or rather the hurling of them all
into the abyss of vacuity without further development or any justification) is
allowed to pass muster as the speculative mode of treatment. Dealing with
something from the perspective of the Absolute consists merely in declaring
that, although one has been speaking of it just now as something definite,
yet in the Absolute, the A = A, there is nothing of the kind, for there all is
one. To pit this single insight, that in the Absolute everything is the same,
against the full body of articulated cognition, which at least seeks and
demands such fulfilment, to palm off its Absolute as the night in which, as
the saying goes, all cows are black – this is cognition naïvely reduced to
vacuity.[2] The formalism which recent philosophy denounces and despises,
only to see it reappear in its midst, will not vanish from Science, however
much its inadequacy may be recognized and felt, till the cognizing of absolute actuality has become entirely clear as to its own nature. Since the
presentation of a general idea in outline, before any attempt to follow it out
in detail, makes the latter attempt easier to grasp, it may be useful at this
point to give a rough idea of it, at the same time taking the opportunity to
get rid of certain habits of thought which impede philosophical cognition.

17. In my view, which can be justified only by the exposition of the
system itself, everything turns on grasping and expressing the True, not only
as *Substance*, but equally as *Subject*. At the same time, it is to be observed
that substantiality embraces the universal, or the *immediacy of knowledge*
itself, as well as that which is *being* or immediacy *for* knowledge. If the
conception of God as the one Substance shocked the age in which it was
proclaimed,[3] the reason for this was on the one hand an instinctive awareness that, in this definition, self-consciousness was only submerged and not
preserved. On the other hand, the opposite view, which clings to thought as
thought, to *universality* as such, is the very same simplicity, is undifferentiated,
unmoved substantiality. And if, thirdly, thought does unite itself with the

being of Substance, and apprehends immediacy or intuition as thinking, the question is still whether this intellectual intuition does not again fall back into inert simplicity, and does not depict actuality itself in a non-actual manner.

18. Further, the living Substance is being which is in truth *Subject*, or, what is the same, is in truth actual only in so far as it is the movement of positing itself, or is the mediation of its self-othering with itself. This Substance is, as Subject, pure, *simple negativity*, and is for this very reason the bifurcation of the simple; it is the doubling which sets up opposition, and then again the negation of this indifferent diversity and of its antithesis [the immediate simplicity]. Only this self-*restoring* sameness, or this reflection in otherness within itself – not an *original* or *immediate* unity as such – is the True. It is the process of its own becoming, the circle that presupposes its end as its goal, having its end also as its beginning; and only by being worked out to its end, is it actual.

19. Thus the life of God and divine cognition may well be spoken of as a disporting of Love with itself,[4] but this idea sinks into mere edification, and even insipidity, if it lacks the seriousness, the suffering, the patience, and the labour of the negative. *In itself*, that life is indeed one of untroubled equality and unity with itself, for which otherness and alienation, and the overcoming of alienation, are not serious matters. But this *in-itself* is abstract universality, in which the nature of the divine life *to be for itself*, and so too the self-movement of the form, are altogether left out of account. If the form is declared to be the same as the essence, then it is *ipso facto* a mistake to suppose that cognition can be satisfied with the in-itself or the essence, but can get along without the form – that the absolute principle or absolute intuition makes the working-out of the former, or the development of the latter, superfluous. Just because the form is as essential to the essence as the essence is to itself, the divine essence is not to be conceived and expressed merely as essence, i.e. as immediate substance or pure self-contemplation of the divine, but likewise as *form*, and in the whole wealth of the developed form. Only then is it conceived and expressed as an actuality.

20. The True is the whole. But the whole is nothing other than the essence consummating itself through its development. Of the Absolute it must be said that it is essentially a *result*, that only in the *end* is it what it truly is; and that precisely in this consists its nature, viz. to be actual, subject, the spontaneous becoming of itself. Though it may seem contradictory that the Absolute should be conceived essentially as a result, it needs little pondering to set this show of contradiction in its true light. The beginning, the principle, or the Absolute, as at first immediately enunciated, is only the universal. Just as when I say 'all animals', this expression cannot pass for a zoology, so it is equally plain that the words, 'the Divine', 'the Absolute', 'the Eternal', etc., do not express what is contained in them; and only such words, in fact, do express the intuition as something immediate. Whatever is more than such a word, even the transition to a mere proposition,

contains a *becoming-other* that has to be taken back, or is a mediation. But it is just this that is rejected with horror, as if absolute cognition were being surrendered when more is made of mediation than in simply saying that it is nothing absolute, and is completely absent in the Absolute.

21. But this abhorrence in fact stems from ignorance of the nature of mediation, and of absolute cognition itself. For mediation is nothing beyond self-moving selfsameness, or is reflection into self, the moment of the 'I' which is for itself pure negativity or, when reduced to its pure abstraction, *simple becoming*. The 'I', or becoming in general, this mediation, on account of its simple nature, is just immediacy in the process of becoming, and is the immediate itself. Reason is, therefore, misunderstood when reflection is excluded from the True, and is not grasped as a positive moment of the Absolute. It is reflection that makes the True a result, but it is equally reflection that overcomes the antithesis between the process of its becoming and the result, for this becoming is also simple, and therefore not different from the form of the True which shows itself as *simple* in its result; the process of becoming is rather just this return into simplicity. Though the embryo is indeed *in itself* a human being, it is not so *for itself*; this it only is as cultivated Reason, which has *made* itself into what it is *in itself*. And that is when it for the first time is actual. But this result is itself a simple immediacy, for it is self-conscious freedom at peace with itself, which has not set the antithesis on one side and left it lying there, but has been reconciled with it.

22. What has just been said can also be expressed by saying that Reason is *purposive activity*. The exaltation of a supposed Nature over a misconceived thinking, and especially the rejection of external teleology, has brought the form of purpose in general into discredit. Still, in the sense in which Aristotle, too, defines Nature as purposive activity, purpose is what is immediate and *at rest*, the unmoved which is also *self-moving*, and as such is Subject. Its power to move, taken abstractly, is *being-for-self* or pure negativity. The result is the same as the beginning, only because the *beginning* is the *purpose*; in other words, the actual is the same as its Notion only because the immediate, as purpose, contains the self or pure actuality within itself. The realized purpose, or the existent actuality, is movement and unfolded becoming; but it is just this unrest that is the self; and the self is like that immediacy and simplicity of the beginning because it is the result, that which has returned into itself, the latter being similarly just the self. And the self is the sameness and simplicity that relates itself to itself.

23. The need to represent the Absolute as *Subject* has found expression in the propositions: *God is the eternal, the moral world-order, love*, and so on. In such propositions the True is only posited *immediately* as Subject, but is not presented as the movement of reflecting itself into itself. In a proposition of this kind one begins with the word 'God'. This by itself is a meaningless sound, a mere name; it is only the predicate that says *what God is*, gives Him content and meaning. Only in the end of the proposition does the

empty beginning become actual knowledge. This being so, it is not clear why one does not speak merely of the eternal, of the moral world-order, and so on, or, as the ancients did, of pure notions like 'being', 'the One', and so on, in short, of that which gives the meaning without adding the *meaningless* sound as well. But it is just this word that indicates that what is posited is not a being [i.e. something that merely *is*], or essence, or a universal in general, but rather something that is reflected into itself, a Subject. But at the same time this is only anticipated. The Subject is assumed as a fixed point to which, as their support, the predicates are affixed by a movement belonging to the knower of this Subject, and which is not regarded as belonging to the fixed point itself; yet it is only through this movement that the content could be represented as Subject. The way in which this movement has been brought about is such that it cannot belong to the fixed point; yet, after this point has been presupposed, the nature of the movement cannot really be other than what it is, it can only be external. Hence, the mere anticipation that the Absolute is Subject is not only *not* the actuality of this Notion, but it even makes the actuality impossible; for the anticipation posits the subject as an inert point, whereas the actuality is self-movement.

24. Among the various consequences that follow from what has just been said, this one in particular can be stressed, that knowledge is only actual, and can only be expounded, as Science or as *system*; and furthermore, that a so-called basic proposition or principle of philosophy, if true, is also false, just because it is *only* a principle. It is, therefore, easy to refute it. The refutation consists in pointing out its defect; and it is defective because it is only the universal or principle, is only the beginning. If the refutation is thorough, it is derived and developed from the principle itself, not accomplished by counter-assertions and random thoughts from outside. The refutation would, therefore, properly consist in the further development of the principle, and in thus remedying the defectiveness, if it did not mistakenly pay attention solely to its *negative* action, without awareness of its progress and result on their *positive* side too – The genuinely *positive* exposition of the beginning is thus also, conversely, just as much a negative attitude towards it, viz. towards its initially one-sided form of being *immediate* or *purpose*. It can therefore be taken equally well as a refutation of the principle that constitutes the *basis* of the system, but it is more correct to regard it as a demonstration that the *basis* or principle of the system is, in fact, only its *beginning*.

25. That the True is actual only as system, or that Substance is essentially Subject, is expressed in the representation of the Absolute as *Spirit* – the most sublime Notion and the one which belongs to the modern age and its religion. The spiritual alone is the *actual*; it is essence, or that which has *being in itself*; it is that which *relates itself to itself* and is *determinate*, it is *other-being* and *being-for-self*, and in this determinateness, or in its self-externality, abides within itself; in other words, it is *in and for itself*. – But this being-in-and-for-itself is at first only for us, or *in itself*, it is spiritual *Substance*. It

must also be this *for itself*, it must be the knowledge of the spiritual, and the knowledge of itself as Spirit, i.e. it must be an *object* to itself, but just as immediately a sublated object, reflected into itself. It is *for itself* only for *us*, in so far as its spiritual content is generated by itself. But in so far as it is also for itself for its own self, this self-generation, the pure Notion, is for it the objective element in which it has its existence, and it is in this way, in its existence for itself, an object reflected into itself. The Spirit that, so developed, knows itself as Spirit, is *Science*; Science is its actuality and the realm which it builds for itself in its own element.

26. *Pure* self-recognition in absolute otherness, this Aether *as such*, is the ground and soil of Science or *knowledge in general*. The beginning of philosophy presupposes or requires that consciousness should dwell in this *element*. But this element itself achieves its own perfection and transparency only through the movement of its becoming. It is pure spirituality as the *universal* that has the form of simple immediacy. This simple being in its *existential* form is the soil [of Science], it is thinking which has its being in Spirit alone. Because this element, this immediacy of Spirit, is the very substance of Spirit, it is the *transfigured essence*, reflection which is itself simple, and which is for itself immediacy as such, *being* that is reflected into itself. Science on its part requires that self-consciousness should have raised itself into this Aether in order to be able to live – and [actually] to live – with Science and in Science. Conversely, the individual has the right to demand that Science should at least provide him with the ladder to this standpoint, should show him this standpoint within himself. His right is based on his absolute independence, which he is conscious of possessing in every phase of his knowledge; for in each one, whether recognized by Science or not, and whatever the content may be, the individual is the absolute form, i.e. he is the *immediate certainty* of himself and, if this expression be preferred, he is therefore unconditioned *being*. The standpoint of consciousness which knows objects in their antithesis to itself, and itself in antithesis to them, is for Science the antithesis of its own standpoint. The situation in which consciousness knows itself to be at home is for Science one marked by the absence of Spirit. Conversely, the element of Science is for consciousness a remote beyond in which it no longer possesses itself. Each of these two aspects [of self-conscious Spirit] appears to the other as the inversion of truth. When natural consciousness entrusts itself straightway to Science, it makes an attempt, induced by it knows not what, to walk on its head too, just this once; the compulsion to assume this unwonted posture and to go about in it is a violence it is expected to do to itself, all unprepared and seemingly without necessity. Let Science be in its own self what it may, relatively to immediate self-consciousness it presents itself in an inverted posture; or, because this self-consciousness has the principle of its actual existence in the certainty of itself, Science appears to it not to be actual, since self-consciousness exists on its own account outside of Science. Science must therefore unite this element of self-certainty with itself, or rather

show *that* and *how* this element belongs to it. So long as Science lacks this *actual* dimension, it is only the content as the *in-itself*, the *purpose* that is as yet still something *inward*, not yet Spirit, but only spiritual Substance. This *in-itself* has to express itself outwardly and become *for itself*, and this means simply that it has to posit self-consciousness as one with itself.

27. It is this coming-to-be of *Science as such* or of *knowledge*, that is described in this *Phenomenology* of Spirit. Knowledge in its first phase, or *immediate Spirit*, is the non-spiritual, i.e. *sense-consciousness*. In order to become genuine knowledge, to beget the element of Science which is the pure Notion of Science itself, it must travel a long way and work its passage. This process of coming-to-be (considering the content and patterns it will display therein) will not be what is commonly understood by an initiation of the unscientific consciousness into Science; it will also be quite different from the 'foundation' of Science; least of all will it be like the rapturous enthusiasm which, like a shot from a pistol, begins straight away with absolute knowledge, and makes short work of other standpoints by declaring that it takes no notice of them.

28. The task of leading the individual from his uneducated standpoint to knowledge had to be seen in its universal sense, just as it was the universal individual, self-conscious Spirit, whose formative education had to be studied. As regards the relation between them, every moment, as it gains concrete form and a shape of its own, displays itself in the universal individual. The single individual is incomplete Spirit, a concrete shape in whose whole existence *one* determinateness predominates, the others being present only in blurred outline. In a Spirit that is more advanced than another, the lower concrete existence has been reduced to an inconspicuous moment; what used to be the important thing is now but a trace; its pattern is shrouded to become a mere shadowy outline. The individual whose substance is the more advanced Spirit runs through this past just as one who takes up a higher science goes through the preparatory studies he has long since absorbed, in order to bring their content to mind: he recalls them to the inward eye, but has no lasting interest in them. The single individual must also pass through the formative stages of universal Spirit so far as their content is concerned, but as shapes which Spirit has already left behind, as stages on a way that has been made level with toil. Thus, as far as factual information is concerned, we find that what in former ages engaged the attention of men of mature mind, has been reduced to the level of facts, exercises, and even games for children; and, in the child's progress through school, we shall recognize the history of the cultural development of the world traced, as it were, in a silhouette. This past existence is the already acquired property of universal Spirit which constitutes the Substance of the individual, and hence appears externally to him as his inorganic nature. In this respect formative education, regarded from the side of the individual, consists in his acquiring what thus lies at hand, devouring his inorganic nature, and taking possession of it for himself. But, regarded from the side of universal Spirit as substance, this

is nothing but its own acquisition of self-consciousness, the bringing-about of its own becoming and reflection into itself.

29. Science sets forth this formative process in all its detail and necessity, exposing the mature configuration of everything which has already been reduced to a moment and property of Spirit. The goal is Spirit's insight into what knowing is. Impatience demands the impossible, to wit, the attainment of the end without the means. But the *length* of this path has to be endured, because, for one thing, each moment is necessary; and further, each moment has to be *lingered* over, because each is itself a complete individual shape, and one is only viewed in absolute perspective when its determinateness is regarded as a concrete whole, or the whole is regarded as uniquely qualified by that determination. Since the Substance of the individual, the World-Spirit itself, has had the patience to pass through these shapes over the long passage of time, and to take upon itself the enormous labour of world-history, in which it embodied in each shape as much of its entire content as that shape was capable of holding, and since it could not have attained consciousness of itself by any lesser effort, the individual certainly cannot by the nature of the case comprehend his own substance more easily. Yet, at the same time, he does have less trouble, since all this has already been *implicitly* accomplished; the content is already the actuality reduced to a possibility, its immediacy overcome, and the embodied shape reduced to abbreviated, simple determinations of thought. It is no longer existence in the form of *being-in-itself* – neither still in the original form [of an abstract concept], nor submerged in existence – but is now the *recollected in-itself*, ready for conversion into the form of *being-for-self*. How this is done must now be described more precisely.

30. We take up the movement of the whole from the point where the sublation of *existence* as such is no longer necessary; what remains to be done, and what requires a higher level of cultural reorientation, is to represent and to get acquainted with these forms. The existence that has been taken back into the Substance has only been *immediately* transposed into the element of the self through that first negation. Hence this acquired property still has the same character of uncomprehended immediacy, of passive indifference, as existence itself; existence has thus merely passed over into *figurative representation* [*Vorstellung*]. At the same time it is thus something *familiar*, something which the existent Spirit is finished and done with, so that it is no longer active or really interested in it. Although the activity that has finished with existence is itself only the movement of the particular Spirit, the Spirit that does not comprehend itself, [genuine] knowing, on the other hand, is directed against the representation thus formed, against this [mere] familiarity; knowing is the activity of the *universal self*, the concern of *thinking*.

31. Quite generally, the familiar, just because it is familiar, is not cognitively understood.[5] The commonest way in which we deceive either ourselves or others about understanding is by assuming something as familiar, and accepting it on that account; with all its pros and cons, such knowing never gets

anywhere, and it knows not why. Subject and object, God, Nature, Understanding, sensibility, and so on, are uncritically taken for granted as familiar, established as valid, and made into fixed points for starting and stopping. While these remain unmoved, the knowing activity goes back and forth between them, thus moving only on their surface. Apprehending and testing likewise consist in seeing whether everybody's impression of the matter coincides with what is asserted about these fixed points, whether it seems that way to him or not.

32. The *analysis* of an idea, as it used to be carried out, was, in fact, nothing else than ridding it of the form in which it had become familiar. To break an idea up into its original elements is to return to its moments, which at least do not have the form of the given idea, but rather constitute the immediate property of the self. This analysis, to be sure, only arrives at *thoughts* which are themselves familiar, fixed, and inert determinations. But what is thus *separated* and non-actual is an essential moment; for it is only because the concrete does divide itself, and make itself into something non-actual, that it is self-moving. The activity of dissolution is the power and work of the *Understanding*, the most astonishing and mightiest of powers, or rather the absolute power. The circle that remains self-enclosed and, like substance, holds its moments together, is an immediate relationship, one therefore which has nothing astonishing about it. But that an accident as such, detached from what circumscribes it, what is bound and is actual only in its context with others, should attain an existence of its own and a separate freedom – this is the tremendous power of the negative; it is the energy of thought, of the pure 'I'. Death, if that is what we want to call this non-actuality, is of all things the most dreadful, and to hold fast what is dead requires the greatest strength. Lacking strength, Beauty hates the Understanding for asking of her what it cannot do. But the life of Spirit is not the life that shrinks from death and keeps itself untouched by devastation, but rather the life that endures it and maintains itself in it. It wins its truth only when, in utter dismemberment, it finds itself. It is this power, not as something positive, which closes its eyes to the negative, as when we say of something that it is nothing or is false, and then, having done with it, turn away and pass on to something else; on the contrary, Spirit is this power only by looking the negative in the face, and tarrying with it. This tarrying with the negative is the magical power that converts it into being. This power is identical with what we earlier called the Subject, which by giving determinateness an existence in its own element supersedes abstract immediacy, i.e. the immediacy which barely is, and thus is authentic substance: that being or immediacy whose mediation is not outside of it but which is this mediation itself.

33. The fact that the object represented becomes the property of pure self-consciousness, its elevation to universality in general, is only one aspect of formative education, not its fulfilment – The manner of study in ancient times differed from that of the modern age in that the former was the

proper and complete formation of the natural consciousness. Putting itself to the test at every point of its existence, and philosophizing about everything it came across, it made itself into a universality that was active through and through. In modern times, however, the individual finds the abstract form ready-made; the effort to grasp and appropriate it is more the direct driving-forth of what is within and the truncated generation of the universal than it is the emergence of the latter from the concrete variety of existence. Hence the task nowadays consists not so much in purging the individual of an immediate, sensuous mode of apprehension, and making him into a substance that is an object of thought and that thinks, but rather in just the opposite, in freeing determinate thoughts from their fixity so as to give actuality to the universal, and impart to it spiritual life. But it is far harder to bring fixed thoughts into a fluid state than to do so with sensuous existence. The reason for this was given above: fixed thoughts have the 'I', the power of the negative, or pure actuality, for the substance and element of their existence, whereas sensuous determinations have only powerless, abstract immediacy, or being as such. Thoughts become fluid when pure thinking, this inner *immediacy*, recognizes itself as a moment, or when the pure certainty of self abstracts from itself – not by leaving itself out, or setting itself aside, but by giving up the *fixity* of its self-positing, by giving up not only the fixity of the pure concrete, which the 'I' itself is, in contrast with its differentiated content, but also the fixity of the differentiated moments which, posited in the element of pure thinking, share the unconditioned nature of the 'I'. Through this movement the pure thoughts become *Notions*, and are only now what they are in truth, self-movements, circles, spiritual essences, which is what their substance is.

34. This movement of pure essences constitutes the nature of scientific method in general. Regarded as the connectedness of their content it is the necessary expansion of that content into an organic whole. Through this movement the path by which the Notion of knowledge is reached becomes likewise a necessary and complete process of becoming; so that this preparatory path ceases to be a casual philosophizing that fastens on to this or that object, relationship, or thought that happens to pop up in the imperfect consciousness, or tries to base the truth on the pros and cons, the inferences and consequences, of rigidly defined thoughts. Instead, this pathway, through the movement of the Notion, will encompass the entire sphere of secular consciousness in its necessary development.

35. Further, an exposition of this kind constitutes the *first* part of Science, because the existence of Spirit *qua* primary is nothing but the immediate or the beginning – but not yet its return into itself. The *element of immediate existence* is therefore what distinguishes this part of Science from the others. The statement of this distinction leads us into a discussion of some fixed ideas which usually crop up in this connection.

36. The immediate existence of Spirit, *consciousness*, contains the two moments of knowing and the objectivity negative to knowing. Since it is in

this element [of consciousness] that Spirit develops itself and explicates its moments, these moments contain that antithesis, and they all appear as shapes of consciousness. The Science of this pathway is the Science of the *experience* which consciousness goes through; the substance and its movement are viewed as the object of consciousness. Consciousness knows and comprehends only what falls within its experience; for what is contained in this is nothing but spiritual substance, and this, too, as *object* of the self. But Spirit becomes object because it is just this movement of becoming an *other to itself*, i.e. becoming an *object to itself*, and of suspending this otherness. And experience is the name we give to just this movement, in which the immediate, the unexperienced, i.e. the abstract, whether it be of sensuous [but still unsensed] being, or only thought of as simple, becomes alienated from itself and then returns to itself from this alienation, and is only then revealed for the first time in its actuality and truth, just as it then has become a property of consciousness also.

37. The disparity which exists in consciousness between the 'I' and the substance which is its object is the distinction between them, the *negative* in general. This can be regarded as the *defect* of both, though it is their soul, or that which moves them. That is why some of the ancients conceived the *void* as the principle of motion, for they rightly saw the moving principle as the *negative*, though they did not as yet grasp that the negative is the self. Now, although this negative appears at first as a disparity between the 'I' and its object, it is just as much the disparity of the substance with itself. Thus what seems to happen outside of it, to be an activity directed against it, is really its own doing, and Substance shows itself to be essentially Subject. When it has shown this completely, Spirit has made its existence identical with its essence; it has itself for its object just as it is, and the abstract element of immediacy, and of the separation of knowing and truth, is overcome. Being is then absolutely mediated; it is a substantial content which is just as immediately the property of the 'I', it is self-like or the Notion.

With this, the Phenomenology of Spirit is concluded. What Spirit prepares for itself in it, is the element of [true] knowing. In this element the moments of Spirit now spread themselves out in that *form of simplicity* which knows its object as its own self. They no longer fall apart into the antithesis of being and knowing, but remain in the simple oneness of knowing; they are the True in the form of the True, and their difference is only the difference of content. Their movement, which organizes itself in this element into a whole, is *Logic* or *speculative philosophy*. [. . .]

53. Science dare only organize itself by the life of the Notion itself. The determinateness, which is taken from the schema and externally attached to an existent thing, is, in Science, the self-moving soul of the realized content. The movement of a being that immediately is, consists partly in becoming an other than itself, and thus becoming its own immanent content; partly in taking back into itself this unfolding [of its content] or this existence of it, i.e. in making *itself* into a moment, and simplifying itself into something

determinate. In the former movement, *negativity* is the differentiating and positing of *existence*; in this return into self, it is the becoming of the *determinate simplicity*. It is in this way that the content shows that its determinateness is not received from something else, nor externally attached to it, but that it determines itself, and ranges itself as a moment having its own place in the whole. The Understanding, in its pigeon-holing process, keeps the necessity and Notion of the content to itself – all that constitutes the concreteness, the actuality, the living movement of the reality which it arranges. Or rather, it does not keep this to itself, since it does not recognize it; for, if it had this insight, it would surely give some sign of it. It does not even recognize the need for it, else it would drop its schematizing, or at least realize that it can never hope to learn more in this fashion than one can learn from a table of contents. A table of contents is all that it offers, the content itself it does not offer at all.

Even when the specific determinateness – say one like Magnetism, for example, – is in itself concrete or real, the Understanding degrades it into something lifeless, merely predicating it of another existent thing, rather than cognizing it as the immanent life of the thing, or cognizing its native and unique way of generating and expressing itself in that thing. The formal Understanding leaves it to others to add this principal feature. Instead of entering into the immanent content of the thing, it is forever surveying the whole and standing above the particular existence of which it is speaking, i.e. it does not see it at all. Scientific cognition, on the contrary, demands surrender to the life of the object, or, what amounts to the same thing, confronting and expressing its inner necessity. Thus, absorbed in its object, scientific cognition forgets about that general survey, which is merely the reflection of the cognitive process away from the content and back into itself. Yet, immersed in the material, and advancing with its movement, scientific cognition does come back to itself, but not before its filling or content is taken back into itself, is simplified into a determinateness, and has reduced itself to *one* aspect of its own existence and passed over into its higher truth. Through this process the simple, self-surveying whole itself emerges from the wealth in which its reflection seemed to be lost.

54. In general, because, as we put it above, substance is in itself or implicitly Subject, all content is its own reflection into itself. The subsistence or substance of anything that exists is its self-identity; for a failure of self-identity would be its dissolution. Self-identity, however, is pure abstraction; but this is *thinking*. When I say 'quality', I am saying simple determinateness; it is by quality that one existence is distinguished from another, or is an existence; it is for itself, or it subsists through this simple oneness with itself. But it is thereby essentially a *thought*. Comprehended in this is the fact that Being is Thought; and this is the source of that insight which usually eludes the usual superficial [*begrifflos*] talk about the identity of Thought and Being. – Now, since the subsistence of an existent thing is a self-identity or pure abstraction, it is the abstraction of itself from itself, or it is itself its lack

of self-identity and its dissolution – its own inwardness and withdrawal into itself – its own becoming. Because this is the nature of what is, and in so far as what is has this nature for [our] knowing, this knowing is not an activity that deals with the content as something alien, is not a reflection into itself away from the content. Science is not that idealism which replaced the dogmatism of assertion with a dogmatism of assurance, or a dogmatism of self-certainty. On the contrary, since [our] knowing sees the content return into its own inwardness, its activity is totally absorbed in the content, for it is the immanent self of the content; yet it has at the same time returned into itself, for it is pure self-identity in otherness. Thus it is the cunning which, while seeming to abstain from activity, looks on and watches how determinateness, with its concrete life, just where it fancies it is pursuing its own self-preservation and particular interest, is in fact doing the very opposite, is an activity that results in its own dissolution, and makes itself a moment of the whole.

55. Above we indicated the significance of the *Understanding* in reference to the self-consciousness of substance;[6] we can now see clearly from what has been said its significance in reference to the determination of substance as being. Existence is Quality, self-identical determinateness, or determinate simplicity, determinate thought; this is the Understanding of existence [i.e. the nature of existence from the standpoint of the Understanding]. Hence, it is *Noûs*, as Anaxagoras first recognized the essence of things to be. Those who came after him grasped the nature of existence more definitely as *Eidos* or *Idea*, determinate Universality, Species or Kind. It might seem as if the term *Species* or *Kind* is too commonplace, too inadequate, for Ideas such as the Beautiful, the Holy, and the Eternal that are currently in fashion. But as a matter of fact Idea expresses neither more nor less than Species or Kind. But nowadays an expression which exactly designates a Notion is often spurned in favour of one which, if only because it is of foreign extraction, shrouds the Notion in a fog, and hence sounds more edifying.

Precisely because existence is defined as Species, it is a simple thought; *Noûs*, simplicity, is substance. On account of its simplicity or self-identity it appears fixed and enduring. But this self-identity is no less negativity; therefore its fixed existence passes over into its dissolution. The determinateness seems at first to be due entirely to the fact that it is related to an *other*, and its movement seems imposed on it by an alien power; but having its otherness within itself, and being self-moving, is just what is involved in the *simplicity* of thinking itself; for this simple thinking is the self-moving and self-differentiating thought, it is its own inwardness, it is the pure Notion. Thus common understanding, too, is a becoming, and, as this becoming, it is *reason*ableness.

56. It is in this nature of what is to be in its being its own Notion, that *logical necessity* in general consists. This alone is the rational element and the rhythm of the organic whole; it is as much *knowledge* of the content, as the content is the Notion and essence – in other words, it alone is *speculative philosophy*. The self-moving concrete shape makes itself into a simple

determinateness; in so doing it raises itself to logical form, and exists in its essentiality; its concrete existence is just this movement, and is directly a logical existence. It is for this reason unnecessary to clothe the content in an external [logical] formalism; the content is in its very nature the transition into such formalism, but a formalism which ceases to be external, since the form is the innate development of the concrete content itself.

57. This nature of scientific method, which consists partly in not being separate from the content, and partly in spontaneously determining the rhythm of its movement, has, as already remarked, its proper exposition in speculative philosophy. Of course, what has been said here does express the Notion, but cannot count for more than an anticipatory assurance. Its truth does not lie in this partly narrative exposition, and is therefore just as little refuted by asserting the contrary, by calling to mind and recounting conventional ideas, as if they were established and familiar truths, or by dishing up something new with the assurance that it comes from the shrine of inner divine intuition. A reception of this kind is usually the first reaction on the part of knowing to something unfamiliar; it resists it in order to save its own freedom and its own insight, its own authority, from the alien authority (for this is the guise in which what is newly encountered first appears), and to get rid of the appearance that something has been learned and of the sort of shame this is supposed to involve. Similarly, when the unfamiliar is greeted with applause, the reaction is of the same kind, and consists in what in another sphere would take the form of ultra-revolutionary speech and action.

58. What, therefore, is important in the *study* of *Science*, is that one should take on oneself the strenuous effort of the Notion.[7] This requires attention to the Notion as such, to the simple determinations, e.g. of Being-in-itself, Being-for-itself, Self-identity, etc.; for these are pure self-movements such as could be called souls if their Notion did not designate something higher than soul. The habit of picture-thinking, when it is interrupted by the Notion, finds it just as irksome as does formalistic thinking that argues back and forth in thoughts that have no actuality. That habit should be called material thinking, a contingent consciousness that is absorbed only in material stuff, and therefore finds it hard work to lift the [thinking] self clear of such matter, and to be with itself alone. At the opposite extreme, argumentation is freedom from all content, and a sense of vanity towards it. What is looked for here is the effort to give up this freedom, and, instead of being the arbitrarily moving principle of the content, to sink this freedom in the content, letting it move spontaneously of its own nature, by the self as its own self, and then to contemplate this movement. This refusal to intrude into the immanent rhythm of the Notion, either arbitrarily or with wisdom obtained from elsewhere, constitutes a restraint which is itself an essential moment of the Notion.

59. There are two aspects of the procedure of argumentation to which speculative [*begreifende*] thinking is opposed and which call for further notice. First, such reasoning adopts a negative attitude towards the content

it apprehends; it knows how to refute it and destroy it. That something is *not* the case, is a merely negative insight, a dead end which does not lead to a new content beyond itself. In order to have a content once again, something new must be taken over from elsewhere. Argumentation is reflection into the empty 'I', the vanity of its own knowing. – This vanity, however, expresses not only the vanity of this content, but also the futility of this insight itself; for this insight is the negative that fails to see the positive within itself. Because this reflection does not get its very negativity as its content, it is never at the heart of the matter, but always beyond it. For this reason it imagines that by establishing the void it is always ahead of any insight rich in content. On the other hand, in speculative [*begreifenden*] thinking, as we have already shown, the negative belongs to the content itself, and is the *positive*, both as the *immanent* movement and determination of the content, and as the whole of this process. Looked at as a result, what emerges from this process is the *determinate* negative which is consequently a positive content as well.

60. But in view of the fact that such thinking has a content, whether of picture-thoughts or abstract thoughts or a mixture of both, argumentation has another side which makes comprehension difficult for it. The remarkable nature of this other side is closely linked with the above-mentioned essence of the Idea, or rather it expresses the Idea in the way that it appears as the movement which is thinking apprehension. For whereas, in its negative behaviour, which we have just discussed, ratiocinative thinking is itself the self into which the content returns, in its positive cognition, on the other hand, the self is a *Subject* to which the content is related as Accident and Predicate. This Subject constitutes the basis to which the content is attached, and upon which the movement runs back and forth. Speculative [*begreifendes*] thinking behaves in a different way. Since the Notion is the object's own self, which presents itself as the *coming-to-be of the object*, it is not a passive Subject inertly supporting the Accidents; it is, on the contrary, the self-moving Notion which takes its determinations back into itself. In this movement the passive Subject itself perishes; it enters into the differences and the content, and constitutes the determinateness, i.e. the differentiated content and its movement, instead of remaining inertly over against it. The solid ground which argumentation has in the passive Subject is therefore shaken, and only this movement itself becomes the object. The Subject that fills its content ceases to go beyond it, and cannot have any further Predicates or accidental properties. Conversely, the dispersion of the content is thereby bound together under the self; it is not the universal which, free from the Subject, could belong to several others. Thus the content is, in fact, no longer a Predicate of the Subject, but is the Substance, the essence and the Notion of what is under discussion. Picture-thinking, whose nature it is to run through the Accidents or Predicates and which, because they are nothing more than Predicates and Accidents, rightly goes beyond them, is checked in its progress, since that which has the form of a Predicate in a proposition

is the Substance itself. It suffers, as we might put it, a counter-thrust. Starting from the Subject as though this were a permanent ground, it finds that, since the Predicate is really the Substance, the Subject has passed over into the Predicate, and, by this very fact, has been sublated; and, since in this way what seems to be the Predicate has become the whole and the independent mass, thinking cannot roam at will, but is impeded by this weight.

Usually, the Subject is first made the basis, as the *objective*, fixed self; thence the necessary movement to the multiplicity of determinations or Predicates proceeds. Here, that Subject is replaced by the knowing 'I' itself, which links the Predicates with the Subject holding them. But, since that first Subject enters into the determinations themselves and is their soul, the second Subject, viz. the knowing 'I', still finds in the Predicate what it thought it had finished with and got away from, and from which it hoped to return into itself; and, instead of being able to function as the determining agent in the movement of predication, arguing back and forth whether to attach this or that Predicate, it is really still occupied with the self of the content, having to remain associated with it, instead of being for itself.

61. Formally, what has been said can be expressed thus: the general nature of the judgement or proposition, which involves the distinction of Subject and Predicate, is destroyed by the speculative proposition, and the proposition of identity which the former becomes contains the counter-thrust against that subject–predicate relationship. – This conflict between the general form of a proposition and the unity of the Notion which destroys it is similar to the conflict that occurs in rhythm between metre and accent. Rhythm results from the floating centre and the unification of the two. So, too, in the philosophical proposition the identification of Subject and Predicate is not meant to destroy the difference between them, which the form of the proposition expresses; their unity, rather, is meant to emerge as a harmony. The form of the proposition is the appearance of the determinate sense, or the accent that distinguishes its fulfilment; but that the predicate expresses the Substance, and that the Subject itself falls into the universal, this is the *unity* in which the accent dies away.

62. To illustrate what has been said: in the proposition 'God is being', the Predicate is 'being'; it has the significance of something substantial in which the Subject is dissolved. 'Being' is here meant to be not a Predicate, but rather the essence; it seems, consequently, that God ceases to be what he is from his position in the proposition, viz. a fixed Subject. Here thinking, instead of making progress in the transition from Subject to Predicate, in reality feels itself checked by the loss of the Subject, and, missing it, is thrown back on to the thought of the Subject. Or, since the Predicate itself has been expressed as a Subject, as *the* being or *essence* which exhausts the nature of the Subject, thinking finds the Subject immediately in the Predicate; and now, having returned into itself in the Predicate, instead of being in a position where it has freedom for argument, it is still absorbed in the content, or at least is faced with the demand that it should be. Similarly,

too, when one says: 'the *actual* is the *universal*', the actual as subject disappears in its predicate. The universal is not meant to have merely the significance of a predicate, as if the proposition asserted only that the actual is universal; on the contrary, the universal is meant to express the essence of the actual. – Thinking therefore loses the firm objective basis it had in the subject when, in the predicate, it is thrown back on to the subject, and when, in the predicate, it does not return into itself, but into the subject of the content.

63. This abnormal inhibition of thought is in large measure the source of the complaints regarding the unintelligibility of philosophical writings from individuals who otherwise possess the educational requirements for understanding them. Here we see the reason behind one particular complaint so often made against them: that so much has to be read over and over before it can be understood – a complaint whose burden is presumed to be quite outrageous, and, if justified, to admit of no defence. It is clear from the above what this amounts to. The philosophical proposition, since it *is* a proposition, leads one to believe that the usual subject–predicate relation obtains, as well as the usual attitude towards knowing. But the philosophical content destroys this attitude and this opinion. We learn by experience that we meant something other than we meant to mean; and this correction of our meaning compels our knowing to go back to the proposition, and understand it in some other way.

64. One difficulty which should be avoided comes from mixing up the speculative with the ratiocinative methods, so that what is said of the Subject at one time signifies its Notion, at another time merely its Predicate or accidental property. The one method interferes with the other, and only a philosophical exposition that rigidly excludes the usual way of relating the parts of a proposition could achieve the goal of plasticity.

65. As a matter of fact, non-speculative thinking also has its valid rights which are disregarded in the speculative way of stating a proposition. The sublation of the form of the proposition must not happen only in an *immediate* manner, through the mere content of the proposition. On the contrary, this opposite movement must find explicit expression; it must not just be the inward inhibition mentioned above. This return of the Notion into itself must be *set forth*. This movement which constitutes what formerly the proof was supposed to accomplish, is the dialectical movement of the proposition itself. This alone is the speculative *in act*, and only the expression of this movement is a speculative exposition. As a proposition, the speculative is only the *internal* inhibition and the non-*existential* return of the essence into itself. Hence we often find philosophical expositions referring us to this *inner* intuition; and in this way they evade the systematic exposition of the dialectical movement of the proposition which we have demanded. – The *proposition* should express *what* the True is; but essentially the True is Subject. As such it is merely the dialectical movement, this course that generates itself, going forth from, and returning to, itself. In non-speculative cognition

proof constitutes this side of expressed inwardness. But once the dialectic has been separated from proof, the notion of philosophical demonstration has been lost.

66. Here we should bear in mind that the dialectical movement likewise has propositions for its parts or elements; the difficulty just indicated seems, therefore, to recur perpetually, and to be inherent in the very nature of philosophical exposition. This is like what happens in ordinary proof, where the reasons given are themselves in need of further reasons, and so on *ad infinitum*. This pattern of giving reasons and stating conditions belongs to that method of proof which differs from the dialectical movement, and belongs therefore to external cognition. As regards the dialectical movement itself, its element is the one Notion; it thus has a content which is, in its own self, Subject through and through. Thus no content occurs which functions as an underlying subject, nor receives its meaning as a predicate; the proposition as it stands is merely an empty form.

Apart from the self that is sensuously intuited or represented, it is above all the name as name that designates the pure Subject, the empty unit without thought-content. For this reason it may be expedient, e.g., to avoid the name 'God', since this word is not immediately also a Notion, but rather the proper name, the fixed point of rest of the underlying Subject; whereas, on the other hand, e.g. 'Being' or 'the One', 'Singularity', 'the Subject', etc. themselves at once suggest concepts. Even if speculative truths are affirmed of this subject, their content lacks the immanent Notion, because it is present merely in the form of a passive subject, with the result that such truths readily assume the form of mere edification. From this side, too, the habit of expressing the speculative predicate in the form of a proposition, and not as Notion and essence, creates a difficulty that can be increased or diminished through the very way in which philosophy is expounded. In keeping with our insight into the nature of speculation, the exposition should preserve the dialectical form, and should admit nothing except in so far as it is comprehended [in terms of the Notion], and is the Notion.

67. The study of philosophy is as much hindered by the conceit that will not argue, as it is by the argumentative approach. This conceit relies on truths which are taken for granted and which it sees no need to re-examine; it just lays them down, and believes it is entitled to assert them, as well as to judge and pass sentence by appealing to them. In view of this, it is especially necessary that philosophizing should again be made a serious business. In the case of all other sciences, arts, skills, and crafts, everyone is convinced that a complex and laborious programme of learning and practice is necessary for competence. Yet when it comes to philosophy, there seems to be a currently prevailing prejudice to the effect that, although not everyone who has eyes and fingers, and is given leather and last, is at once in a position to make shoes, everyone nevertheless immediately understands how to philosophize, and how to evaluate philosophy, since he possesses the criterion for doing so in his natural reason – as if he did not likewise possess the

measure for a shoe in his own foot. It seems that philosophical competence consists precisely in an absence of information and study, as though philosophy left off where they began. Philosophy is frequently taken to be a purely formal kind of knowledge, void of content, and the insight is sadly lacking that, whatever truth there may be in the content of any discipline or science, it can only deserve the name if such truth has been engendered by philosophy. Let the other sciences try to argue as much as they like without philosophy – without it they can have in them neither life, Spirit, nor truth. [. . .]

Notes

1 Miller translates the word 'Begriff' throughout the *Phenomenology* as 'Notion'. The word can, however, also be translated as 'Concept'. The paragraph numbers in all the passages from the *Phenomenology* collected here have been supplied by the translator, A. V. Miller, and are not found in the original German text. English material in square brackets in all the passages selected has been added by the translator. [s.h.]
2 This is usually understood to be a critique of Schelling or of his followers. [s.h.]
3 A reference to Spinoza. [s.h.]
4 'ein Spielen der Liebe mit sich selbst'. [s.h.]
5 'Das Bekannte überhaupt ist darum, weil es bekannt ist, nicht erkannt'. [s.h.]
6 See above p. 59 (§ 32). [s.h.]
7 i.e., the strenuous effort required to think in terms of the Notion. [Translator's note.]

6

Phenomenology of Spirit: Introduction

Modern
Critical
Turn

73. It is a natural assumption that in philosophy, before we start to deal with its proper subject-matter, viz. the actual cognition of what truly is, one must first of all come to an understanding about cognition, which is regarded either as the instrument to get hold of the Absolute, or as the medium through which one discovers it.[1] A certain uneasiness seems justified, partly because there are different types of cognition, and one of them might be more appropriate than another for the attainment of this goal, so that we could make a bad choice of means; and partly because cognition is a faculty of a definite kind and scope, and thus, without a more precise definition of its nature and limits, we might grasp clouds of error instead of the heaven of truth. This feeling of uneasiness is surely bound to be transformed into the conviction that the whole project of securing for consciousness through cognition what exists in itself is absurd, and that there is a boundary between cognition and the Absolute that completely separates them. For, if cognition is the instrument for getting hold of absolute being, it is obvious that the use of an instrument on a thing certainly does not let it be what it is for itself, but rather sets out to reshape and alter it. If, on the other hand, cognition is not an instrument of our activity but a more or less passive medium through which the light of truth reaches us, then again we do not receive the truth as it is in itself, but only as it exists through and in this medium. Either way we employ a means which immediately brings about the opposite of its own end; or rather, what is really absurd is that we should make use of a means at all.

It would seem, to be sure, that this evil could be remedied through an acquaintance with the way in which the *instrument* works; for this would enable us to eliminate from the representation of the Absolute which we have gained through it whatever is due to the instrument, and thus get the truth in its purity. But this 'improvement' would in fact only bring us back to where we were before. If we remove from a reshaped thing what the instrument has done to it, then the thing – here the Absolute – becomes for us exactly what it was before this [accordingly] superfluous effort. On the other hand, if the Absolute is supposed merely to be brought nearer to us through this instrument, without anything in it being altered, like a bird caught by a lime-twig, it would surely laugh our little ruse to scorn, if it were not with us, in and for itself, all along, and of its own volition. For a ruse is just what cognition would be in such a case, since it would, with its manifold exertions, be giving itself the air of doing something quite different from creating a merely immediate and therefore effortless relationship. Or, if by testing cognition, which we conceive of as a *medium*, we get to know the law of its refraction, it is again useless to subtract this from the end result. For it is not the refraction of the ray, but the ray itself whereby truth reaches us, that is cognition; and if this were removed, all that would be indicated would be a pure direction or a blank space.

74. Meanwhile, if the fear of falling into error sets up a mistrust of Science, which in the absence of such scruples gets on with the work itself, and actually cognizes something, it is hard to see why we should not turn round and mistrust this very mistrust. Should we not be concerned as to whether this fear of error is not just the error itself? Indeed, this fear takes something – a great deal in fact – for granted as truth, supporting its scruples and inferences on what is itself in need of prior scrutiny to see if it is true. To be specific, it takes for granted certain ideas about cognition as an *instrument* and as a *medium*, and assumes that there is a *difference between ourselves and this cognition*. Above all, it presupposes that the Absolute stands on one side and cognition on the other, independent and separated from it, and yet is something real; or in other words, it presupposes that cognition which, since it is excluded from the Absolute, is surely outside of the truth as well, is nevertheless true, an assumption whereby what calls itself fear of error reveals itself rather as fear of the truth.

75. This conclusion stems from the fact that the Absolute alone is true, or the truth alone is absolute. One may set this aside on the grounds that there is a type of cognition which, though it does not cognize the Absolute as Science aims to, is still true, and that cognition in general, though it be incapable of grasping the Absolute, is still capable of grasping other kinds of truth. But we gradually come to see that this kind of talk which goes back and forth only leads to a hazy distinction between an absolute truth and some other kind of truth, and that words like 'absolute', 'cognition', etc. presuppose a meaning which has yet to be ascertained.

76. Instead of troubling ourselves with such useless ideas and locutions about cognition as 'an instrument for getting hold of the Absolute', or as 'a medium through which we view the truth' (relationships which surely, in the end, are what all these ideas of a cognition cut off from the Absolute, and an Absolute separated from cognition, amount to); instead of putting up with excuses which create the incapacity of Science by assuming relationships of this kind in order to be exempt from the hard work of Science, while at the same time giving the impression of working seriously and zealously; instead of bothering to refute all these ideas, we could reject them out

of hand as adventitious and arbitrary, and the words associated with them like 'absolute', 'cognition', 'objective' and 'subjective', and countless others whose meaning is assumed to be generally familiar, could even be regarded as so much deception. For to give the impression that their meaning is generally well known, or that their Notion is comprehended, looks more like an attempt to avoid the main problem, which is precisely to provide this Notion. We could, with better justification, simply spare ourselves the trouble of paying any attention whatever to such ideas and locutions; for they are intended to ward off Science itself, and constitute merely an empty appearance of knowing, which vanishes immediately as soon as Science comes on the scene. But Science, just because it comes on the scene, is itself an appearance: in coming on the scene it is not yet Science in its developed and unfolded truth. In this connection it makes no difference whether we think of Science as the appearance because it comes on the scene alongside another mode of knowledge, or whether we call that other untrue knowledge its appearance.[2] In any case Science must liberate itself from this semblance, and it can do so only by turning against it. For, when confronted with a knowledge that is without truth, Science can neither merely reject it as an ordinary way of looking at things, while assuring us that its Science is a quite different sort of cognition for which that ordinary knowledge is of no account whatever; nor can it appeal to the vulgar view for the intimations it gives us of something better to come. By the former *assurance*, Science would be declaring its power to lie simply in its *being*; but the untrue knowledge likewise appeals to the fact that *it is*, and *assures* us that for it Science is of no account. One bare assurance is worth just as much as another. Still less can Science appeal to whatever intimations of something better it may detect in the cognition that is without truth, to the signs which point in the direction of Science. For one thing, it would only be appealing again to what merely *is*; and for another, it would only be appealing to itself, and to itself in the mode in which it exists in the cognition that is without truth. In other words, it would be appealing to an inferior form of its being, to the way it appears, rather than to what it is in and for itself. It is for this reason that an exposition of how knowledge makes its appearance will here be undertaken.

77. Now, because it has only phenomenal knowledge for its object, this exposition seems not to be Science, free and self-moving in its own peculiar shape; yet from this standpoint it can be regarded as the path of the natural consciousness which presses forward to true knowledge; or as the way of the Soul which journeys through the series of its own configurations as though they were the stations appointed for it by its own nature,[3] so that it may purify itself for the life of the Spirit, and achieve finally, through a completed experience of itself, the awareness of what it really is in itself.

78. Natural consciousness will show itself to be only the Notion of knowledge, or in other words, not to be real knowledge. But since it directly takes itself to be real knowledge, this path has a negative significance for it, and

what is in fact the realization of the Notion, counts for it rather as the loss of its own self; for it does lose its truth on this path. The road can therefore be regarded as the pathway of *doubt*, or more precisely as the way of despair. For what happens on it is not what is ordinarily understood when the word 'doubt' is used: shilly-shallying about this or that presumed truth, followed by a return to that truth again, after the doubt has been appropriately dispelled – so that at the end of the process the matter is taken to be what it was in the first place. On the contrary, this path is the conscious insight into the untruth of phenomenal knowledge, for which the supreme reality is what is in truth only the unrealized Notion. Therefore this thoroughgoing scepticism is also not the scepticism with which an earnest zeal for truth and Science fancies it has prepared and equipped itself in their service: the *resolve*, in Science, not to give oneself over to the thoughts of others, upon mere authority, but to examine everything for oneself and follow only one's own conviction, or better still, to produce everything oneself, and accept only one's own deed as what is true.

The series of configurations which consciousness goes through along this road is, in reality, the detailed history of the *education* of consciousness itself to the standpoint of Science. That zealous resolve represents this education simplistically as something directly over and done with in the making of the resolution; but the way of the Soul is the actual fulfilment of the resolution, in contrast to the untruth of that view. Now, following one's own conviction is, of course, more than giving oneself over to authority; but changing an opinion accepted on authority into an opinion held out of personal convic-tion, does not necessarily alter the content of the opinion, or replace error with truth. The only difference between being caught up in a system of opinions and prejudices based on personal conviction, and being caught up in one based on the authority of others, lies in the added conceit that is innate in the former position. The scepticism that is directed against the whole range of phenomenal consciousness, on the other hand, renders the Spirit for the first time competent to examine what truth is. For it brings about a state of despair about all the so-called natural ideas, thoughts, and opinions, regardless of whether they are called one's own or someone else's, ideas with which the consciousness that sets about the examination [of truth] *straight away* is still filled and hampered, so that it is, in fact, incapable of carrying out what it wants to undertake.

79. The necessary progression and interconnection of the forms of the unreal consciousness will by itself bring to pass the *completion* of the series. To make this more intelligible, it may be remarked, in a preliminary and general way, that the exposition of the untrue consciousness in its untruth is not a merely *negative* procedure. The natural consciousness itself normally takes this one-sided view of it; and a knowledge which makes this one-sidedness its very essence is itself one of the patterns of incomplete con-sciousness which occurs on the road itself, and will manifest itself in due course. This is just the scepticism which only ever sees pure nothingness in

its result and abstracts from the fact that this nothingness is specifically
the nothingness of that *from which it results*. For it is only when it is taken as
the result of that from which it emerges, that it is, in fact, the true result; in
that case it is itself a *determinate* nothingness, one which has a *content*. The
scepticism that ends up with the bare abstraction of nothingness or emptiness cannot get any further from there, but must wait to see whether something new comes along and what it is, in order to throw it too into the same
empty abyss. But when, on the other hand, the result is conceived as it is in
truth, namely, as a *determinate* negation, a new form has thereby immediately arisen, and in the negation the transition is made through which the
progress through the complete series of forms comes about of itself.

80. But the *goal* is as necessarily fixed for knowledge as the serial progression; it is the point where knowledge no longer needs to go beyond itself,
where knowledge finds itself, where Notion corresponds to object and object
to Notion. Hence the progress towards this goal is also unhalting, and short
of it no satisfaction is to be found at any of the stations on the way. Whatever is confined within the limits of a natural life cannot by its own efforts
go beyond its immediate existence; but it is driven beyond it by something
else, and this uprooting entails its death. Consciousness, however, is explicitly the *Notion* of itself. Hence it is something that goes beyond limits, and
since these limits are its own, it is something that goes beyond itself. With
the positing of a single particular the beyond is also established for consciousness, even if it is only *alongside* the limited object as in the case of
spatial intuition. Thus consciousness suffers this violence at its own hands:
it spoils its own limited satisfaction. When consciousness feels this violence,
its anxiety may well make it retreat from the truth, and strive to hold on to
what it is in danger of losing. But it can find no peace. If it wishes to remain
in a state of unthinking inertia, then thought troubles its thoughtlessness,
and its own unrest disturbs its inertia. Or, if it entrenches itself in sentimentality, which assures us that it finds everything to be *good in its kind*, then
this assurance likewise suffers violence at the hands of Reason, for, precisely
in so far as something is merely a kind, Reason finds it *not* to be good. Or,
again, its fear of the truth may lead consciousness to hide, from itself and
others, behind the pretension that its burning zeal for truth makes it difficult or even impossible to find any other truth but the unique truth of vanity
– that of being at any rate cleverer than any thoughts that one gets by
oneself or from others. This conceit which understands how to belittle every
truth, in order to turn back into itself and gloat over its own understanding,
which knows how to dissolve every thought and always find the same barren
Ego instead of any content – this is a satisfaction which we must leave to
itself, for it flees from the universal, and seeks only to be for itself.

81. In addition to these preliminary general remarks about the manner
and the necessity of the progression, it may be useful to say something
about the *method of carrying out the inquiry*. If this exposition is viewed as a
way of *relating Science* to *phenomenal* knowledge, and as an investigation and

examination of the reality of cognition, it would seem that it cannot take place without some presupposition which can serve as its underlying *criterion*. For an examination consists in applying an accepted standard, and in determining whether something is right or wrong on the basis of the resulting agreement or disagreement of the thing examined; thus the standard as such (and Science likewise if it were the criterion) is accepted as the *essence* or as the *in-itself*. But here, where Science has just begun to come on the scene, neither Science nor anything else has yet justified itself as the essence or the in-itself; and without something of the sort it seems that no examination can take place.

82. This contradiction and its removal will become more definite if we call to mind the abstract determinations of truth and knowledge as they occur in consciousness. Consciousness simultaneously *distinguishes* itself from something, and at the same time *relates* itself to it, or, as it is said, this something exists *for* consciousness; and the determinate aspect of this *relating*, or of the *being* of something for a consciousness, is *knowing*. But we distinguish this being-for-another from *being-in-itself*; whatever is related to knowledge or knowing is also distinguished from it, and posited as existing outside of this relationship; this *being-in-itself* is called *truth*. Just what might be involved in these determinations is of no further concern to us here. Since our object is phenomenal knowledge, its determinations too will at first be taken directly as they present themselves; and they do present themselves very much as we have already apprehended them.

83. Now, if we inquire into the truth of knowledge, it seems that we are asking what knowledge is *in itself*. Yet in this inquiry knowledge is *our* object, something that exists *for us*; and the *in-itself* that would supposedly result from it would rather be the being of knowledge *for us*. What we asserted to be its essence would be not so much its truth but rather just our knowledge of it. The essence or criterion would lie within ourselves, and that which was to be compared with it and about which a decision would be reached through this comparison would not necessarily have to recognize the validity of such a standard.

84. But the dissociation, or this semblance of dissociation and presupposition, is overcome by the nature of the object we are investigating. Consciousness provides its own criterion from within itself, so that the investigation becomes a comparison of consciousness with itself; for the distinction made above falls within it. In consciousness one thing exists *for* another, i.e. consciousness regularly contains the determinateness of the moment of knowledge; at the same time, this other is to consciousness not merely *for it*, but is also outside of this relationship, or exists *in itself*: the moment of truth. Thus in what consciousness affirms from within itself as *being-in-itself* or the *True* we have the standard which consciousness itself sets up by which to measure what it knows. If we designate *knowledge* as the Notion, but the essence or the *True* as what exists, or the *object*, then the examination consists in seeing whether the Notion corresponds to the object. But if we call

the *essence* or in-itself of the *object* the *Notion*, and on the other hand understand by the *object* the Notion itself as *object*, viz. as it exists *for an other*, then
the examination consists in seeing whether the object corresponds to its
Notion. It is evident, of course, that the two procedures are the same. But
the essential point to bear in mind throughout the whole investigation is that
these two moments, 'Notion' and 'object', 'being-for-another' and 'being-in-
itself', both fall *within* that knowledge which we are investigating. Consequently, we do not need to import criteria, or to make use of our own bright
ideas and thoughts during the course of the inquiry; it is precisely when we
leave these aside that we succeed in contemplating the matter in hand as it
is *in and for itself*.

85. But not only is a contribution by us superfluous, since Notion and
object, the criterion and what is to be tested, are present in consciousness
itself, but we are also spared the trouble of comparing the two and really
testing them, so that, since what consciousness examines is its own self, all
that is left for us to do is simply to look on. For consciousness is, on the one
hand, consciousness of the object, and on the other, consciousness of itself;
consciousness of what for it is the True, and consciousness of its knowledge
of the truth. Since both are *for* the same consciousness, this consciousness is
itself their comparison; it is for this same consciousness to know whether
its knowledge of the object corresponds to the object or not. The object, it
is true, seems only to be for consciousness in the way that consciousness
knows it; it seems that consciousness cannot, as it were, get behind the
object as it exists for consciousness so as to examine what the object is *in
itself*, and hence, too, cannot test its own knowledge by that standard. But
the distinction between the in-itself and knowledge is already present in the
very fact that consciousness knows an object at all. Something is *for it* the
in-itself; and knowledge, or the being of the object for consciousness, is, *for
it*, another moment. Upon this distinction, which is present as a fact, the
examination rests. If the comparison shows that these two moments do not
correspond to one another, it would seem that consciousness must alter its
knowledge to make it conform to the object. But, in fact, in the alteration of
the knowledge, the object itself alters for it too, for the knowledge that was
present was essentially a knowledge of the object: as the knowledge changes,
so too does the object, for it essentially belonged to this knowledge. Hence
it comes to pass for consciousness that what it previously took to be the *in-
itself* is not an *in-itself*, or that it was only an in-itself *for consciousness*. Since
consciousness thus finds that its knowledge does not correspond to its
object, the object itself does not stand the test; in other words, the criterion
for testing is altered when that for which it was to have been the criterion
fails to pass the test; and the testing is not only a testing of what we know,
but also a testing of the criterion of what knowing is.

86. *Inasmuch as the new true object issues from it*, this *dialectical* movement
which consciousness exercises on itself and which affects both its knowledge and its object, is precisely what is called *experience* [*Erfahrung*]. In this

connection there is a moment in the process just mentioned which must be brought out more clearly, for through it a new light will be thrown on the exposition which follows. Consciousness knows *something*; this object is the essence or the *in-itself*; but it is also for consciousness the in-itself. This is where the ambiguity of this truth enters. We see that consciousness now has two objects: one is the first *in-itself*, the second is the *being-for-consciousness of this in-itself*. The latter appears at first sight to be merely the reflection of consciousness into itself, i.e. what consciousness has in mind is not an object, but only its knowledge of that first object. But, as was shown previously, the first object, in being known, is altered for consciousness; it ceases to be the in-itself, and becomes something that is the *in-itself* only *for consciousness*. And this then is the True: the being-for-consciousness of this in-itself. Or, in other words, this is the *essence*, or the *object* of consciousness. This new object contains the nothingness of the first, it is what experience has made of it.

87. This exposition of the course of experience contains a moment in virtue of which it does not seem to agree with what is ordinarily understood by experience. This is the moment of transition from the first object and the knowledge of it, to the other object, which experience is said to be about. Our account implied that our knowledge of the first object, or the being-*for*-consciousness of the first in-itself, itself becomes the second object. It usually seems to be the case, on the contrary, that our experience of the untruth of our first notion comes by way of a second object which we come upon by chance and externally, so that our part in all this is simply the pure *apprehension* of what is in and for itself. From the present viewpoint, however, the new object shows itself to have come about through a *reversal of consciousness itself*. This way of looking at the matter is something contributed by *us*, by means of which the succession of experiences through which consciousness passes is raised into a scientific progression – but it is not known to the consciousness that we are observing. But, as a matter of fact, we have here the same situation as the one discussed in regard to the relation between our exposition and scepticism, viz. that in every case the result of an untrue mode of knowledge must not be allowed to run away into an empty nothing, but must necessarily be grasped as the nothing *of that from which it results* – a result which contains what was true in the preceding knowledge. It shows up here like this: since what first appeared as the object sinks for consciousness to the level of its way of knowing it, and since the in-itself becomes a *being-for-consciousness* of the in-itself, the latter is now the new object. Herewith a new pattern of consciousness comes on the scene as well, for which the essence is something different from what it was at the preceding stage. It is this fact that guides the entire series of the patterns of consciousness in their necessary sequence. But it is just this necessity itself, or the *origination* of the new object, that presents itself to consciousness without its understanding how this happens, which proceeds for us, as it were, behind the back of consciousness. Thus in the movement of consciousness there occurs a moment of *being-in-itself* or *being-for-us* which is not present to the consciousness

comprehended in the experience itself. The *content*, however, of what presents itself to us does exist *for it*; we comprehend only the formal aspect of that content, or its pure origination. *For it*, what has thus arisen exists only as an object; *for us*, it appears at the same time as movement and a process of becoming.

88. Because of this necessity, the way to Science is itself already *Science*, and hence, in virtue of its content, is the Science of the *experience of consciousness*.

89. The experience of itself which consciousness goes through can, in accordance with its Notion, comprehend nothing less than the entire system of consciousness, or the entire realm of the truth of Spirit. For this reason, the moments of this truth are exhibited in their own proper determinateness, viz. as being not abstract moments, but as they are for consciousness, or as consciousness itself stands forth in its relation to them. Thus the moments of the whole are *patterns of consciousness*. In pressing forward to its true existence, consciousness will arrive at a point at which it gets rid of its semblance of being burdened with something alien, with what is only for it, and some sort of 'other', at a point where appearance becomes identical with essence, so that its exposition will coincide at just this point with the authentic Science of Spirit. And finally, when consciousness itself grasps this its own essence, it will signify [*bezeichnen*] the nature of absolute knowledge itself.

Notes

1   Compare with Kant, *Critique of Pure Reason*, p. 46 (B7): 'Now it does indeed seem natural that . . .' [S.H.]
2   Miller's translation has 'manifestation'. The German word is 'Erscheinen'. [S.H.]
3   An allusion perhaps to the Stations of the Cross. [Translator's note.]

7

Phenomenology of Spirit: Consciousness

Sense-certainty: Or the 'This' and 'Meaning' [*Meinen*]

90. The knowledge or knowing which is at the start or is immediately our object cannot be anything else but immediate knowledge itself, a knowledge of the immediate or of what simply *is*. Our approach to the object must also be *immediate* or *receptive*; we must alter nothing in the object as it presents itself. In *ap*prehending it, we must refrain from trying to *com*prehend it.

91. Because of its concrete content, sense-certainty immediately appears as the *richest* kind of knowledge, indeed a knowledge of infinite wealth for which no bounds can be found, either when we *reach out* into space and time in which it is dispersed, or when we take a bit of this wealth, and by division *enter into* it. Moreover, sense-certainty appears to be the *truest* knowledge; for it has not as yet omitted anything from the object, but has the object before it in its perfect entirety. But, in the event, this very *certainty* proves itself to be the most abstract and poorest *truth*. All that it says about what it knows is just that it *is*; and its truth contains nothing but the sheer *being* of the thing [*Sache*]. Consciousness, for its part, is in this certainty only as a pure 'I'; or I am in it only as a pure 'This', and the object similarly only as a pure 'This'. I, *this* particular I, am certain of *this* particular thing, not because I, *qua* consciousness, in knowing it have developed myself or thought about it in various ways; and also not because *the thing* of which I am certain, in virtue of a host of distinct qualities, would be in its own self a rich complex of connections, or related in various ways to other things. Neither of these has anything to do with the truth of sense-certainty: here neither I nor the thing has the significance of a complex process of mediation; the 'I' does not have the significance of a manifold imagining or thinking; nor does the 'thing' signify something that has a host of qualities. On the contrary, the thing *is*, and it *is*, merely because it *is*. It *is*; this is the essential point for sense-knowledge, and this pure *being*, or this simple immediacy, constitutes its *truth*. Similarly, certainty as a *connection* is an *immediate* pure connection: consciousness is 'I', nothing more, a pure 'This'; the singular consciousness knows a pure 'This', or the single item.

92. But when we look carefully at this *pure being* which constitutes the essence of this certainty, and which this certainty pronounces to be its truth, we see that much more is involved. An actual sense-certainty is not merely this pure immediacy, but an *instance* of it. Among the countless differences cropping up here we find in every case that the crucial one is that, in sense-certainty, pure being at once splits up into what we have called the two 'Thises', one 'This' as 'I', and the other 'This' as object. When *we* reflect on this difference, we find that neither one nor the other is only *immediately* present in sense-certainty, but each is at the same time *mediated*: I have this certainty *through* something else, viz. the thing; and it, similarly, is in sense-certainty *through* something else, viz. through the 'I'.

93. It is not just we who make this distinction between essence and instance, between immediacy and mediation; on the contrary, we find it within sense-certainty itself, and it is to be taken up in the form in which it is present there, not as we have just defined it. One of the terms is posited in sense-certainty in the form of a simple, immediate being, or as the essence, the *object*; the other, however, is posited as what is unessential and mediated, something which in sense-certainty is not *in itself* but through [the mediation of] an other, the 'I', a *knowing* which knows the object only because the *object* is, while the knowing may either be or not be. But the object *is*: it is what is true, or it is the essence. It is, regardless of whether it is known or not; and it remains, even if it is not known, whereas there is no knowledge if the object is not there.

94. The question must therefore be considered whether in sense-certainty itself the object is in fact the kind of essence that sense-certainty proclaims it to be; whether this notion of it as the essence corresponds to the way it is present in sense-certainty. To this end, we have not to reflect on it and ponder what it might be in truth, but only to consider the way in which it is present in sense-certainty.

95. It is, then, sense-certainty itself that must be asked: 'What is the *This*?' If we take the 'This' in the twofold shape of its being, as 'Now' and as 'Here', the dialectic it has in it will receive a form as intelligible as the 'This' itself is. To the question: 'What is Now?', let us answer, e.g. 'Now is Night.' In order to test the truth of this sense-certainty a simple experiment will suffice. We write down this truth; a truth cannot lose anything by being written down, any more than it can lose anything through our preserving it. If *now, this noon*, we look again at the written truth we shall have to say that it has become stale.

96. The Now that is Night is *preserved*, i.e. it is treated as what it professes to be, as something that *is*; but it proves itself to be, on the contrary, something that is *not*. The Now does indeed preserve itself, but as something that is *not* Night; equally, it preserves itself in face of the Day that it now is, as something that also is not Day, in other words, as a *negative* in general. This self-preserving Now is, therefore, not immediate but mediated; for it is determined as a permanent and self-preserving Now *through* the fact that

something else, viz. Day and Night, is *not*. As so determined, it is still just as simply Now as before, and in this simplicity is indifferent to what happens in it; just as little as Night and Day are its being, just as much also is it Day and Night; it is not in the least affected by this its other-being. A simple thing of this kind which *is* through negation, which is neither This nor That, a *not- This*, and is with equal indifference This as well as That – such a thing we call a *universal*. So it is in fact the universal that is the true [content] of sense-certainty.

97. It is as a universal too that we *utter* what the sensuous [content] is. What we say is: 'This', i.e. the *universal* This; or, 'it is', i.e. *Being in general*. Of course, we do not *envisage* the universal This or Being in general, but we *utter* the universal; in other words, we do not strictly say what in this sense-certainty we *mean* to say. But language, as we see, is the more truthful; in it, we ourselves directly refute what we *mean* to say, and since the universal is the true [content] of sense-certainty and language expresses this true [content] alone, it is just not possible for us ever to say, or express in words, a sensuous being that we *mean*.

98. The same will be the case with the other form of the 'This', with 'Here'. 'Here' is, e.g., the tree. If I turn round, this truth has vanished and is converted into its opposite: 'No tree is here, but a house instead.' 'Here' itself does not vanish; on the contrary, it abides constant in the vanishing of the house, the tree, etc., and is indifferently house or tree. Again, therefore, the 'This' shows itself to be a *mediated simplicity*, or a *universality*.

99. *Pure being* remains, therefore, as the essence of this sense-certainty, since sense-certainty has demonstrated in its own self that the truth of its object is the universal. But this pure being is not an immediacy, but something to which negation and mediation are essential; consequently, it is not what we *mean* by 'being', but is 'being' defined as an abstraction, or as the pure universal; and our 'meaning', for which the true [content] of sense-certainty is *not* the universal, is all that is left over in face of this empty or indifferent Now and Here.

100. When we compare the relation in which knowing and the object first came on the scene, with the relation in which they now stand in this result, we find that it is reversed. The object, which was supposed to be the essential element in sense-certainty, is now the unessential element; for the universal which the object has come to be is no longer what the object was supposed essentially to be for sense-certainty. On the contrary, the certainty is now to be found in the opposite element, viz. in knowing, which previously was the unessential element. Its truth is in the object as *my* object, or in its being mine [*Meinen*]; it is, because *I* know it. Sense-certainty, then, though indeed expelled from the object, is not yet thereby overcome, but only driven back into the 'I'. We have now to see what experience shows us about its reality in the 'I'.

101. The force of its truth thus lies now in the 'I', in the immediacy of my *seeing, hearing*, and so on; the vanishing of the single Now and Here that

we mean is prevented by the fact that *I* hold them fast. 'Now' is day because I see it; 'Here' is a tree for the same reason. But in this relationship sense-certainty experiences the same dialectic acting upon itself as in the previous one. I, *this* 'I', see the tree and assert that 'Here' is a tree; but another 'I' sees the house and maintains that 'Here' is not a tree but a house instead. Both truths have the same authentication, viz. the immediacy of seeing, and the certainty and assurance that both have about their knowing; but the one truth vanishes in the other.

102. What does not disappear in all this is the 'I' as *universal*, whose seeing is neither a seeing of the tree nor of this house, but is a simple seeing which, though mediated by the negation of this house, etc., is all the same simple and indifferent to whatever happens in it, to the house, the tree, etc. The 'I' is merely universal like 'Now', 'Here', or 'This' in general; I do indeed *mean* a single 'I', but I can no more say what I *mean* in the case of 'I' than I can in the case of 'Now' and 'Here'. When I say 'this Here', 'this Now', or a 'single item', I am saying all Thises, Heres, Nows, all single items. Similarly, when I say 'I', this singular 'I', I say in general all 'Is'; everyone is what I say, everyone is 'I', this singular 'I'. When Science is faced with the demand – as if it were an acid test it could not pass – that it should deduce, construct, find a priori, or however it is put, something called 'this thing' or 'this one man', it is reasonable that the demand should *say* which 'this thing', or which 'this particular man' is *meant*; but it is impossible to say this.

C

103. Sense-certainty thus comes to know by experience that its essence is neither in the object nor in the 'I', and that its immediacy is neither an immediacy of the one nor of the other; for in both, what I *mean* is rather something unessential, and the object and the 'I' are universals in which that 'Now' and 'Here' and 'I' which I *mean* do not have a continuing being, or *are* not. Thus we reach the stage where we have to posit the *whole* of sense-certainty itself as its *essence*, and no longer only one of its moments, as happened in the two cases where first the object confronting the 'I', and then the 'I', were supposed to be its reality. Thus it is only sense-certainty as a *whole* which stands firm within itself as *immediacy* and by so doing excludes from itself all the opposition which has hitherto obtained.

104. This pure immediacy, therefore, no longer has any concern with the otherness of the 'Here', as a tree which passes over into a 'Here' that is not a tree, or with the otherness of the 'Now' as day which changes into a 'Now' that is night, or with another 'I' for which something else is object. Its truth preserves itself as a relation that remains self-identical, and which makes no distinction of what is essential and what is unessential, between the 'I' and the object, a relation therefore into which also no distinction whatever can penetrate. I, *this* 'I', assert then the 'Here' as a tree, and do not turn round so that the Here would become for me *not* a tree; also, I take no notice of the fact that another 'I' sees the Here as *not* a tree, or that I myself at another time take the Here as not-tree, the Now as not-day. On the contrary, I am

a pure [act of] intuiting; I, for my part, stick to the fact that the Now is day, or that the Here is a tree; also I do not compare Here and Now themselves with one another, but stick firmly to *one* immediate relation: the Now is day.

105. Since, then, this certainty will no longer come forth to *us* when we direct its attention to a Now that is night, or to an 'I' to whom it is night, we will approach *it* and have the Now that is asserted pointed out to us. We must have it *pointed out* to us;[1] for the truth of this immediate relation is the truth of *this* 'I' which confines itself to one 'Now' or one 'Here'. Were we to examine this truth *afterwards*, or stand *at a distance* from it, it would lose its significance entirely; for that would do away with the immediacy which is essential to it. We must therefore enter the same point of time or space, have the truth pointed out to us, i.e. have ourselves turned into the same singular 'I' as the one who knows with certainty.[2] Let us, then, see how that immediate is constituted that is pointed out to us.

106. The Now is pointed to, *this* Now. 'Now'; it has already ceased to be in the act of pointing to it. The Now that *is*, is another Now than the one pointed to, and we see that the Now is just this: to be no more just when it is. The Now, as it is pointed out to us, is Now that *has been*, and this is its truth; it has not the truth of *being*. Yet this much is true, that it has been. But what essentially *has been* [*gewesen ist*] is, in fact, not an essence that *is* [*kein Wesen*]; *it is not*, and it was with *being* that we were concerned.

107. In this pointing-out, then, we see merely a movement which takes the following course: (1) I point out the 'Now', and it is asserted to be the truth. I point it out, however, as something that *has been*, or as something that has been superseded; I set aside the first truth. (2) I now assert as the second truth that it *has been*, that it is superseded. (3) But what has been, *is not*; I set aside the second truth, its *having been*, its supersession, and thereby negate the negation of the 'Now', and thus return to the first assertion, that the '*Now*' *is*. The 'Now', and pointing out the 'Now', are thus so constituted that neither the one nor the other is something immediate and simple, but a movement which contains various moments. A *This* is posited; but it is rather an *other* that is posited, or the This is superseded: and this *otherness*, or the setting-aside of the first, is itself *in turn set aside*, and so has returned into the first. However, this first, thus reflected into itself, is not exactly the same as it was to begin with, viz. something *immediate*; on the contrary, it is *something that is reflected into itself*, or a *simple* entity which, in its otherness, remains what it is: a Now which is an absolute plurality of Nows. And this is the true, the genuine Now, the Now as a simple day which contains within it many Nows – hours. A Now of this sort, an hour, similarly is many minutes, and this Now is likewise many Nows, and so on. The pointing-out of the Now is thus itself the movement which expresses what the Now is in truth, viz. a result, or a plurality of Nows all taken together; and the pointing-out is the experience of learning that Now is a *universal*.

108. The *Here pointed out*, to which I hold fast, is similarly a *this* Here which, in fact, is *not* this Here, but a Before and Behind, an Above and

Below, a Right and Left. The Above is itself similarly this manifold otherness of above, below, etc. The Here, which was supposed to have been pointed out, vanishes in other Heres, but these likewise vanish. What is pointed out, held fast, and abides, is a *negative* This, which *is* negative only when the Heres are taken as they should be, but, in being so taken, they supersede themselves; what abides is a simple complex of many Heres. The Here that is *meant* would be the point; but it *is* not: on the contrary, when it is pointed out as something that *is*, the pointing-out shows itself to be not an immediate knowing [of the point], but a movement from the Here that is *meant* through many Heres into the universal Here which is a simple plurality of Heres, just as the day is a simple plurality of Nows.

109. It is clear that the dialectic of sense-certainty is nothing else but the simple history of its movement or of its experience, and sense-certainty itself is nothing else but just this history. That is why the natural consciousness, too, is always reaching this result, learning from experience what is true in it; but equally it is always forgetting it and starting the movement all over again. It is therefore astonishing when, in face of this experience, it is asserted as universal experience and put forward, too, as a philosophical proposition, even as the outcome of Scepticism, that the reality or being of external things taken as Thises or sense-objects has absolute truth for consciousness. To make such an assertion is not to know what one is saying, to be unaware that one is saying the opposite of what one wants to say. The truth for consciousness of a This of sense is supposed to be universal experience; but the very opposite is universal experience. Every consciousness itself supersedes such a truth, as e.g. Here is a tree, or, Now is noon, and proclaims the opposite: Here is *not* a tree, but a house; and similarly, it immediately again supersedes the assertion which set aside the first so far as it is also just such an assertion of a sensuous This. And what consciousness will learn from experience in all sense-certainty is, in truth, only what we have seen viz. the This as a *universal*, the very opposite of what that assertion affirmed to be universal experience.

With this appeal to universal experience we may be permitted to anticipate how the case stands in the practical sphere. In this respect we can tell those who assert the truth and certainty of the reality of sense-objects that they should go back to the most elementary school of wisdom, viz. the ancient Eleusinian Mysteries of Ceres and Bacchus, and that they have still to learn the secret meaning of the eating of bread and the drinking of wine. For he who is initiated into these Mysteries not only comes to doubt the being of sensuous things, but to despair of it; in part he brings about the nothingness of such things himself in his dealings with them, and in part he sees them reduce themselves to nothingness. Even the animals are not shut out from this wisdom but, on the contrary, show themselves to be most profoundly initiated into it; for they do not just stand idly in front of sensuous things as if these possessed intrinsic being, but, despairing of their reality, and completely assured of their nothingness, they fall to without ceremony and eat them up. And all Nature, like the animals, celebrates these open Mysteries which teach the truth about sensuous things.

110. But, just as our previous remarks would suggest, those who put forward such an assertion also themselves say the direct opposite of what they mean: a phenomenon which is perhaps best calculated to induce them to reflect on the nature of sense-certainty. They speak of the existence of *external* objects, which can be more precisely defined as *actual*, absolutely *singular, wholly personal, individual* things, each of them absolutely unlike anything else; this existence, they say, has absolute certainty and truth. They *mean* 'this' bit of paper on which I am writing – or rather have written – 'this'; but what they mean is not what they say. If they actually wanted to *say* 'this' bit of paper which they mean, if they wanted to *say* it, then this is impossible, because the sensuous This that is meant *cannot be reached* by language, which belongs to consciousness, i.e. to that which is inherently universal. In the actual attempt to say it, it would therefore crumble away; those who started to describe it would not be able to complete the description, but would be compelled to leave it to others, who would themselves finally have to admit to speaking about something which *is not*. They certainly mean, then, *this* bit of paper here which is quite different from the bit mentioned above; but they say 'actual *things*', '*external* or *sensuous objects*', '*absolutely singular entities*' [*Wesen*] and so on; i.e. they say of them only what is *universal*. Consequently, what is called the unutterable is nothing else than the untrue, the irrational, what is merely meant [but is not actually expressed].

If nothing more is said of something than that it is 'an actual thing', an 'external object', its description is only the most abstract of generalities and in fact expresses its sameness with everything rather than its distinctiveness. When I say: 'a single thing', I am really saying what it is from a wholly universal point of view, for everything is a single thing; and likewise 'this thing' is anything you like. If we describe it more exactly as 'this bit of paper', then each and every bit of paper is 'this bit of paper', and I have only uttered the universal all the time. But if I want to help out language – which has the divine nature of directly reversing the meaning of what is said, of making it into something else, and thus not letting what is meant *get into words* at all – by *pointing out* this bit of paper, experience teaches me what the truth of sense-certainty in fact is: I point it out as a 'Here', which is a Here of other Heres, or is in its own self a 'simple togetherness of many Heres'; i.e. it is a universal. I take it up then as it is in truth, and instead of knowing something immediate I take the truth of it, or *perceive* it.[3]

Notes

1   Miller's translation has 'let ourselves point to the Now that is asserted. We must let ourselves *point to it*'. The German text, however, is: '[wir] lassen uns das Jetzt zeigen,

das behauptet wird. *Zeigen* müssen wir es uns lassen'. Hegel is here using a construction with the word 'lassen', which corresponds in English to the expression 'to have something done' (e.g. 'ein Haus bauen lassen', 'to have a house built'). [S.H.]

2   Miller's translation has 'point them out to ourselves, i.e. make ourselves into the same singular "I" which is'. The German text is '[wir müssen] sie uns zeigen, d.h. uns zu demselben diesen Ich, welches das gewiß Wissende ist, machen lassen'. The word 'sie' in this sentence refers to 'die Wahrheit' (the truth) in the previous sentences. [S.H.]

3   The German for 'to perceive' is 'wahrnehmen' which means literally 'to take truly'. [Translator's note.]

8

Phenomenology of Spirit: Self-consciousness

The Truth of Self-certainty

166. In the previous modes of certainty what is true for consciousness is something other than itself. But the Notion of this truth vanishes in the experience of it. What the object immediately was *in itself* – mere being in sense-certainty, the concrete thing of perception, and for the Understanding, a Force – proves to be in truth, not this at all; instead, this *in-itself* turns out to be a mode in which the object is only for an other. The Notion of the object is superseded in the actual object, or the first, immediate presentation of the object is superseded in experience: certainty gives place to truth. But now there has arisen what did not emerge in these previous relationships, viz. a certainty which is identical with its truth; for the certainty is to itself its own object, and consciousness is to itself the truth. In this there is indeed an otherness; that is to say, consciousness makes a distinction, but one which at the same time is for consciousness *not* a distinction. If we give the name of *Notion* to the movement of knowing, and the name of *object* to knowing as a passive unity, or as the 'I', then we see that not only for *us*, but for knowing itself, the object corresponds to the Notion. Or alternatively, if we call Notion what the object is *in itself*, but call the object what *it* is *qua* object or *for an other*, then it is clear that being-*in-itself* and being-*for-an-other* are one and the same. For the *in-itself* is consciousness; but equally it is that *for which* an other (the *in-itself*) is; and it is *for* consciousness that the in-itself of the object, and the being of the object for an other, are one and the same; the 'I' is the *content* of the connection and the connecting itself. Opposed to an other, the 'I' is its own self, and at the same time it overarches this other which, for the 'I', is equally only the 'I' itself.

167. With self-consciousness, then, we have therefore entered the native realm of truth. We have now to see how the shape of self-consciousness first makes its appearance. If we consider this new shape of knowing, the knowing of itself, in relation to that which preceded, viz. the knowing of an other, then we see that though this other has indeed vanished, its moments have at

the same time no less been preserved, and the loss consists in this, that here they are present as they are in themselves. The [mere] *being* of what is merely 'meant', the *singleness* and the *universality* opposed to it of perception, as also the *empty inner being* of the Understanding, these are no longer essences, but are moments of self-consciousness, i.e. abstractions or distinctions which at the same time have no reality *for* consciousness itself, and are purely vanishing essences. Thus it seems that only the principal moment itself has been lost, viz. the *simple self-subsistent existence* for consciousness. But in point of fact self-consciousness is the reflection out of the being of the world of sense and perception, and is essentially the return from otherness. As self-consciousness, it is movement; but in so far as what it distinguishes from itself is *only itself as* itself, the difference, as an otherness, is *immediately superseded* for it; the difference *is not*, and *it* [self-consciousness] is only the motionless tautology of: 'I am I'; in so far as for it the difference does not have the form of *being*, it is *not* self-consciousness.[1] Hence otherness is for it in the form of *a being*, or as a *distinct moment*; but there is also for consciousness the unity of itself with this difference as a *second distinct moment*. With that first moment, self-consciousness is in the form of *consciousness*, and the whole expanse of the sensuous world is preserved for it, but at the same time only as connected with the second moment, the unity of self-consciousness with itself; and hence the sensuous world is for it an enduring existence which, however, is only *appearance*, or a difference which, *in itself*, is no difference. This antithesis of its appearance and its truth has, however, for its essence only the truth, viz. the unity of self-consciousness with itself; this unity must become essential to self-consciousness, i.e. self-consciousness is *Desire* in general. Consciousness, as self-consciousness, henceforth has a double object: one is the immediate object, that of sense-certainty and perception, which however *for self-consciousness* has the character of a *negative*; and the second, viz. *itself*, which is the true *essence*, and is present in the first instance only as opposed to the first object. In this sphere, self-consciousness exhibits itself as the movement in which this antithesis is removed, and the identity of itself with itself becomes explicit for it.

168. But *for us*, or *in itself*, the object which for self-consciousness is the negative element has, on its side, returned into itself, just as on the other side consciousness has done. Through this reflection into itself the object has become Life. What self-consciousness distinguishes from itself as having *being*, also has in it, in so far as it is posited as being, not merely the character of sense-certainty and perception, but it is being that is reflected into itself, and the object of immediate desire is a *living thing*. For the *in-itself*, or the *universal* result of the relation of the Understanding to the inwardness of things, is the distinguishing of what is *not* to be distinguished, or the *unity* of what is distinguished. But this unity is, as we have seen, just as much its repulsion from itself; and this Notion sunders itself into the antithesis of self-consciousness and life: the former is the unity *for which* the infinite unity of the differences is; the latter, however, *is* only this unity itself, so that it is

not at the same time *for itself*. To the extent, then, that consciousness is independent, so too is its object, but only *implicitly*. Self-consciousness which is simply *for itself* and directly characterizes its object as a negative element, or is primarily *desire*, will therefore, on the contrary, learn through experience that the object is independent.

169. The determination of Life as it has issued from the Notion, or the general result with which we enter this sphere, is sufficient to characterize it without having further to develop its nature. Its sphere is completely determined in the following moments. *Essence* is infinity as the *supersession* of all distinctions, the pure movement of axial rotation, its self-repose being an absolutely restless infinity; *independence* itself, in which the differences of the movement are resolved, the simple essence of Time which, in this equality with itself, has the stable shape of Space. The differences, however, are just as much present as *differences* in this simple universal medium; for this universal flux has its negative nature only in being the supersession of them; but it cannot supersede the different moments if they do not have an enduring existence [*Bestehen*]. It is this very flux, as a self-identical independence which is itself an *enduring existence*, in which, therefore, they are present as distinct members and parts existing on their own account. *Being* no longer has the significance of *abstract* being, nor has their pure essentiality the significance of *abstract* universality; on the contrary, their being is precisely that simple fluid substance of pure movement within itself. The *difference*, however, *qua* difference, of these members with respect to one another consists in general in no other *determinateness* than that of the moments of infinity or of the pure movement itself.

170. The independent members are *for themselves*; but this *being-for-self* is really no less immediately their reflection into the unity than this unity is the splitting-up into independent shapes. The unity is divided within itself because it is an absolutely negative or infinite unity; and because it is what *subsists*, the difference, too, has independence only in *it*. This independence of the shape appears as something *determinate, for an other*, for the shape is divided within itself; and the supersession of this dividedness accordingly takes place through an other. But this supersession is just as much within the shape itself, for it is just that flux that is the substance of the independent shapes. This substance, however, is infinite, and hence the shape in its very subsistence is a dividedness within itself, or the supersession of its being-for-self.

171. If we distinguish more exactly the moments contained here, we see that we have, as the first moment, the subsistence of the independent shapes, or the suppression of what diremption is in itself, viz. that the shapes have no being in themselves, no enduring existence. The second moment, however is the subjection of that existence to the infinity of the difference. In the first moment there is the existent shape; as being *for itself*, or being in its determinateness infinite substance, it comes forward in antithesis to the *universal* substance, disowns this fluent continuity with it and asserts that it

is not dissolved in this universal element, but on the contrary preserves itself by separating itself from this its inorganic nature, and by consuming it. Life in the universal fluid medium, a *passive* separating-out of the shapes becomes, just by so doing, a movement of those shapes or becomes Life as a *process*. The simple universal fluid medium is the *in-itself*, and the difference of the shapes is the *other*. But this fluid medium itself becomes the *other* through this difference; for now it is *for the difference* which exists in and for itself, and consequently is the ceaseless movement by which this passive medium is consumed: Life as a *living thing*.

This *inversion*, however, is for that reason again an invertedness *in its own self*. What is consumed is the essence: the individuality which maintains itself at the expense of the universal, and which gives itself the feeling of its unity with itself, just by so doing supersedes its antithesis to the other by means of which it exists for itself. Its self-given unity with itself is just that *fluidity* of the differences or their *general dissolution*. But, conversely, the supersession of individual existence is equally the production of it. For since the *essence* of the individual shape – universal Life – and what exists for itself is in itself simple substance, when this substance places the *other* within itself it supersedes this its *simplicity* or its essence, i.e. it divides it, and this dividedness of the differenceless fluid medium is just what establishes individuality. Thus the simple substance of Life is the splitting-up of itself into shapes and at the same time the dissolution of these existent differences; and the dissolution of the splitting-up is just as much a splitting-up and a forming of members. With this, the two sides of the whole movement which before were distinguished, viz. the passive separatedness of the shapes in the general medium of independence, and the process of Life, collapse into one another. The latter is just as much an imparting of shape as a supersession of it; and the other, the imparting of shape, is just as much a supersession as an articulation of shape. The fluid element is itself only the *abstraction* of essence, or it is *actual* only as shape; and its articulation of itself is again a splitting-up of what is articulated into form or a dissolution of it. It is the whole round of this activity that constitutes Life: not what was expressed at the outset, the immediate continuity and compactness of its essence, nor the enduring form, the discrete moment existing for itself; nor the pure process of these; nor yet the simple taking-together of these moments. Life consists rather in being the self-developing whole which dissolves its development and in this movement simply preserves itself.

172. Since we started from the first immediate unity and returned through the moments of formation and of process to the unity of both these moments, and thus back again to the original simple substance, this *reflected* unity is different from the first. Contrasted with that *immediate* unity, or that unity expressed as a [mere] *being*, this second is the *universal* unity which contains all these moments as superseded within itself. It is the simple genus which, in the movement of Life itself, does not *exist for itself qua* this *simple* determination; on the contrary, in this *result*, Life points to something other than itself, viz. to consciousness, for which Life exists as this unity, or as genus.

173. This other Life, however, for which the genus as such exists, and which is genus for itself[2] viz. self-consciousness, exists in the first instance for itself[3] only as this simple essence, and has itself as pure 'I' for object. In the course of its experience which we are now to consider, this abstract object will enrich itself for the 'I' and undergo the unfolding which we have seen in the sphere of Life.

174. The simple 'I' is this genus or the simple universal, for which the differences are *not* differences only by its being the *negative essence* of the shaped independent moments; and self-consciousness is thus certain of itself only by superseding this other that presents itself to self-consciousness as an independent life; self-consciousness is Desire. Certain of the nothingness of this other, it explicitly affirms that this nothingness is *for it* the truth of the other; it destroys the independent object and thereby gives itself the certainty of itself as a *true* certainty, a certainty which has become explicit for self-consciousness itself *in an objective manner*.

175. In this satisfaction, however, experience makes it aware that the object has its own independence. Desire and the self-certainty obtained in its gratification, are conditioned by the object, for self-certainty comes from superseding this other: in order that this supersession can take place, there must be this other. Thus self-consciousness, by its negative relation to the object, is unable to supersede it; it is really because of that relation that it produces the object again, and the desire as well. It is in fact something other than self-consciousness that is the essence of Desire; and through this experience self-consciousness has itself realized this truth. But at the same time it is no less absolutely *for itself*, and it is so only by superseding the object; and it must experience its satisfaction, for it is the truth. On account of the independence of the object, therefore, it can achieve satisfaction only when the object itself effects the negation within itself; and it must carry out this negation of itself in itself, for it is *in itself* the negative, and must be *for* the other what it *is*. Since the object is in its own self negation, and in being so is at the same time independent, it is consciousness. In the sphere of Life, which is the object of Desire, *negation* is present either *in an other*, viz. in Desire, or as a *determinateness* opposed to another indifferent form, or as the inorganic universal nature of Life. But this universal independent nature in which negation is present as absolute negation, is the genus as such, or the genus as *self-consciousness. Self-consciousness achieves its satisfaction only in another self-consciousness.*

176. The notion of self-consciousness is only completed in these three moments: (a) The pure undifferentiated 'I' is its first immediate object. (b) But this immediacy is itself an absolute mediation, it *is* only as a supersession of the independent object, in other words, it is Desire. The satisfaction of Desire is, it is true, the reflection of self-consciousness into itself, or the certainty that has become truth. (c) But the truth of this certainty is really a double reflection, the duplication of self-consciousness. Consciousness has for its object one which, of its own self, posits its otherness or difference as a nothingness, and in so doing is independent. The differentiated, merely

living, shape does indeed also supersede its independence in the process of Life, but it ceases with its distinctive difference to be what it is. The object of self-consciousness, however, is equally independent in this negativity of itself; and thus it is *for itself* a genus, a universal fluid element in the peculiarity of its own separate being; it is a living self-consciousness.

177. A self-consciousness exists *for a self-consciousness*. Only so is it in fact self-consciousness; for only in this way does the unity of itself in its otherness become explicit for it. The 'I' which is the object of its Notion is in fact not 'object'; the object of Desire, however, is only independent, for it is the universal indestructible substance, the fluid self-identical essence. A self-consciousness, in being an object, is just as much 'I' as 'object'. With this, we already have before us the Notion of *Spirit*. What still lies ahead for consciousness is the experience of what Spirit is ─ this absolute substance which is the unity of the different independent self-consciousnesses which, in their opposition, enjoy perfect freedom and independence: 'I' that is 'We' and 'We' that is 'I'. It is in self-consciousness, in the Notion of Spirit, that consciousness first finds its turning-point, where it leaves behind it the colourful show of the sensuous here-and-now and the nightlike void of the supersensible beyond, and steps out into the spiritual daylight of the present.

A. Independence and Dependence of Self-consciousness: Lordship and Bondage

178. Self-consciousness exists in and for itself when, and by the fact that, it so exists for another; that is, it exists only in being acknowledged [*als ein Anerkanntes*]. The Notion of this its unity in its duplication embraces many and varied meanings. Its moments, then, must on the one hand be held strictly apart, and on the other hand must in this differentiation at the same time also be taken and known as not distinct, or in their opposite significance. The twofold significance of the distinct moments has in the nature of self-consciousness to be infinite, or directly the opposite of the determinateness in which it is posited. The detailed exposition of the Notion of this spiritual unity in its duplication will present us with the process of Recognition [*Anerkennen*].

179. Self-consciousness is faced by another self-consciousness; it has come *out of itself*. This has a twofold significance: first, it has lost itself, for it finds itself as an *other* being; secondly, in doing so it has superseded the other, for it does not see the other as an essential being, but in the other sees its own self.

180. It must supersede this otherness of itself. This is the supersession of the first ambiguity, and is therefore itself a second ambiguity. First, it must proceed to supersede the *other* independent being in order thereby to become certain of *itself* as the essential being; secondly, in so doing it proceeds to supersede its *own* self, for this other is itself.

181. This ambiguous supersession of its ambiguous otherness is equally an ambiguous return *into itself*. For first, through the supersession, it receives back its own self, because, by superseding *its* otherness, it again becomes equal to itself; but secondly, it equally gives the other self-consciousness back again to itself,[4] for it saw itself in the other, but supersedes this being of itself in the other and thus lets the other again go free.

182. Now, this movement of self-consciousness in relation to another self-consciousness has in this way been represented as the action of *one* self-consciousness, but this action of the one has itself the double significance of being both its own action and the action of the other as well. For the other is equally independent and self-contained, and there is nothing in it of which it is not itself the origin. The first does not have the object before it merely as it exists primarily for desire, but as something that has an independent existence of its own, which, therefore, it cannot utilize for its own purposes, if that object does not of its own accord do what the first does to it. Thus the movement is simply the double movement of the two self-consciousnesses. Each sees the *other* do the same as it does; each does itself what it demands of the other, and therefore also does what it does only in so far as the other does the same. Action by one side only would be useless because what is to happen can only be brought about by both.

183. Thus the action has a double significance not only because it is directed against itself as well as against the other, but also because it is indivisibly the action of one as well as of the other.

184. In this movement we see repeated the process which presented itself as the play of Forces,[5] but repeated now in consciousness. What in that process was *for us*, is true here of the extremes themselves. The middle term is self-consciousness which splits into the extremes; and each extreme is this exchanging of its own determinateness and an absolute transition into the opposite. Although, as consciousness, it does indeed come *out of itself*, yet, though out of itself, it is at the same time kept back within itself, is *for itself*, and the self outside it, is for *it*. It is aware that it at once is, and is not, another consciousness, and equally that this other is *for itself* only when it supersedes itself as being for itself, and is for itself only in the being-for-self of the other. Each is for the other the middle term, through which each mediates itself with itself and unites with itself; and each is for itself, and for the other, an immediate being to its own account, which at the same time is such only through this mediation. They *recognize* themselves as *mutually recognizing* one another.

185. We have now to see how the process of this pure Notion of recognition, of the duplicating of self-consciousness in its oneness, appears to self-consciousness. At first, it will exhibit the side of the inequality of the two, or the splitting-up of the middle term into the extremes which, as extremes, are opposed to one another, one being only *recognized*, the other only *recognizing*.

186. Self-consciousness is, to begin with, simple being-for-self, self-equal through the exclusion from itself of everything else. For it, its essence and

absolute object is 'I'; and in this immediacy, or in this [mere] being, of its
being-for-self, it is an *individual*. What is 'other' for it is an unessential,
negatively characterized object. But the 'other' is also a self-consciousness;
one individual is confronted by another individual. Appearing thus immediately on the scene, they are for one another like ordinary objects, *independent*
shapes, individuals submerged in the being [or immediacy] of *Life* – for the
object in its immediacy is here determined as Life. They are, *for each other*,
shapes of consciousness which have not yet accomplished the movement of
absolute abstraction, of rooting-out all immediate being, and of being merely
the purely negative being of self-identical consciousness; in other words,
they have not as yet exposed themselves to each other in the form of pure
being-for-self, or as self-consciousnesses. Each is indeed certain of its own
self, but not of the other, and therefore its own self-certainty still has no
truth. For it would have truth only if its own being-for-self had confronted
it as an independent object, or, what is the same thing, if the object had
presented itself as this pure self-certainty. But according to the Notion of
recognition this is possible only when each is for the other what the other is
for it, only when each in its own self through its own action, and again through
the action of the other, achieves this pure abstraction of being-for-self.

187. The presentation of itself, however, as the pure abstraction of self-
consciousness consists in showing itself as the pure negation of its objective
mode, or in showing that it is not attached to any specific *existence*, not to
the individuality common to existence as such, that it is not attached to life.
This presentation is a twofold action: action on the part of the other, and
action on its own part. In so far as it is the action of the *other*, each seeks the
death of the other. But in doing so, the second kind of action, action on its
own part, is also involved; for the former involves the staking of its own life.
Thus the relation of the two self-conscious individuals is such that they
prove themselves and each other through a life-and-death struggle. They
must engage in this struggle, for they must raise their certainty of being *for
themselves* to truth, both in the case of the other and in their own case. And
it is only through staking one's life that freedom is won; only thus is it
proved that for self-consciousness, its essential being is not [just] being, not
the *immediate* form in which it appears, not its submergence in the expanse
of life, but rather that there is nothing present in it which could not be
regarded as a vanishing moment, that it is only pure *being-for-self*. The
individual who has not risked his life may well be recognized as a *person*, but
he has not attained to the truth of this recognition as an independent self-
consciousness. Similarly, just as each stakes his own life, so each must seek
the other's death, for it values the other no more than itself; its essential
being is present to it in the form of an 'other', it is outside of itself and must
rid itself of its self-externality. The other is an *immediate* consciousness
entangled in a variety of relationships, and it must regard its otherness as a
pure being-for-self or as an absolute negation.

188. This trial by death, however, does away with the truth which was
supposed to issue from it, and so, too, with the certainty of self generally.

For just as life is the *natural* setting of consciousness, independence without absolute negativity, so death is the *natural* negation of consciousness, negation without independence, which thus remains without the required significance of recognition. Death certainly shows that each staked his life and held it of no account, both in himself and in the other; but that is not for those who survived this struggle. They put an end to their consciousness in its alien setting of natural existence, that is to say, they put an end to themselves, and are done away with as *extremes* wanting to be *for themselves*, or to have an existence of their own. But with this there vanishes from their interplay the essential moment of splitting into extremes with opposite characteristics; and the middle term collapses into a lifeless unity which is split into lifeless, merely immediate, unopposed extremes; and the two do not reciprocally give and receive one another back from each other consciously, but leave each other free only indifferently, like things. Their act is an abstract negation, not the negation coming from consciousness, which supersedes in such a way as to preserve and maintain what is superseded, and consequently survives its own supersession.

189. In this experience, self-consciousness learns that life is as essential to it as pure self-consciousness. In immediate self-consciousness the simple 'I' is the absolute object which, however, for us or in itself is absolute mediation, and has as its essential moment lasting independence.[6] The dissolution of that simple unity is the result of the first experience; through this there is posited a pure self-consciousness, and a consciousness which is not purely for itself but for another, i.e. is a merely *immediate* consciousness, or consciousness in the form of *thinghood*. Both moments are essential. Since to begin with they are unequal and opposed, and their reflection into a unity has not yet been achieved, they exist as two opposed shapes of consciousness; one is the independent consciousness whose essential nature is to be for itself, the other is the dependent consciousness whose essential nature is simply to live or to be for another. The former is lord [*Herr*], the other is bondsman [*Knecht*].

190. The lord is the consciousness that exists *for itself*, but no longer merely the Notion of such a consciousness. Rather, it is a consciousness existing *for itself* which is mediated with itself through another consciousness, i.e. through a consciousness whose nature it is to be bound up with an existence that is independent, or thinghood in general. The lord puts himself into relation with both of these moments, to a *thing* as such, the object of desire, and to the consciousness for which thinghood is the essential characteristic. And since he is (a) *qua* the Notion of self-consciousness an immediate relation of *being-for-self*, but (b) is now at the same time mediation, or a being-for-self which is for itself only through another, he is related (a) immediately to both, and (b) mediately to each through the other. The lord relates himself mediately to the bondsman through a being [a thing] that is independent, for it is just this which holds the bondsman in bondage; it is his chain from which he could not break free in the struggle, thus proving himself to be dependent, to possess his independence in thinghood.

But the lord is the power over this thing, for he proved in the struggle that it is something merely negative; since he is the power over this thing and this again is the power over the other [the bondsman], it follows that he holds the other in subjection. Equally, the lord relates himself mediately to the thing through the bondsman; the bondsman, *qua* self-consciousness in general, also relates himself negatively to the thing, and takes away its independence; but at the same time the thing is independent *vis-à-vis* the bondsman, whose negating of it, therefore, cannot go to the length of being altogether done with it to the point of annihilation; in other words, he only *works* on it. For the lord, on the other hand, the *immediate* relation becomes through this mediation the sheer negation of the thing, or the enjoyment of it. What desire failed to achieve, he succeeds in doing, viz. to have done with the thing altogether, and to achieve satisfaction in the enjoyment of it. Desire failed to do this because of the thing's independence; but the lord, who has interposed the bondsman between it and himself, takes to himself only the dependent aspect of the thing and has the pure enjoyment of it. The aspect of its independence he leaves to the bondsman, who works on it.

191. In both of these moments the lord achieves his recognition through another consciousness; for in them, that other consciousness is expressly something unessential, both by its working on the thing, and by its dependence on a specific existence. In neither case can it be lord over the being of the thing and achieve absolute negation of it. Here, therefore, is present this moment of recognition, viz. that the other consciousness sets aside its own being-for-self, and in so doing itself does what the first does to it. Similarly, the other moment too is present, that this action of the second is the first's own action; for what the bondsman does is really the action of the lord. The latter's essential nature is to exist only for himself; he is the sheer negative power for whom the thing is nothing. Thus he is the pure, essential action in this relationship, while the action of the bondsman is impure and unessential. But for recognition proper the moment is lacking, that what the lord does to the other he also does to himself, and what the bondsman does to himself he should also do to the other. The outcome is a recognition that is one-sided and unequal.

192. In this recognition the unessential consciousness is for the lord the object, which constitutes the *truth* of his certainty of himself. But it is clear that this object does not correspond to its Notion, but rather that the object in which the lord has achieved his lordship has in reality turned out to be something quite different from an independent consciousness. What now really confronts him is not an independent consciousness, but a dependent one. He is, therefore, not certain of *being-for-self* as the truth of himself. On the contrary, his truth is in reality the unessential consciousness and its unessential action.

193. The *truth* of the independent consciousness is accordingly the servile consciousness of the bondsman. This, it is true, appears at first *outside* of itself and not as the truth of self-consciousness. But just as lordship showed

that its essential nature is the reverse of what it wants to be, so too servitude in its consummation will really turn into the opposite of what it immediately is; as a consciousness forced back into itself, it will withdraw into itself and be transformed into a truly independent consciousness.

194. We have seen what servitude is only in relation to lordship. But it is a self-consciousness, and we have now to consider what as such it is in and for itself. To begin with, servitude has the lord for its essential reality; hence the *truth* for it is the independent consciousness that is *for itself*. However, servitude is not yet aware that this truth is implicit in it. But it does in fact contain within itself this truth of pure negativity and being-for-self, for it has experienced this its own essential nature. For this consciousness has been fearful, not of this or that particular thing or just at odd moments, but its whole being has been seized with dread; for it has experienced the fear of death, the absolute Lord. In that experience it has been quite unmanned, has trembled in every fibre of its being, and everything solid and stable has been shaken to its foundations. But this pure universal movement, the absolute melting-away of everything stable, is the simple, essential nature of self-consciousness, absolute negativity, *pure being-for-self*, which consequently is *implicit* in this consciousness. This moment of pure being-for-self is also *explicit* for the bondsman, for in the lord it exists for him as his *object*. Furthermore, his consciousness is not this dissolution of everything stable merely in principle; in his service he *actually* brings this about. Through his service he rids himself of his attachment to natural existence in every single detail; and gets rid of it by working on it.

195. However, the feeling of absolute power both in general, and in the particular form of service, is only implicitly this dissolution, and although the fear of the lord is indeed the beginning of wisdom, consciousness is not therein aware that it is a being-for-self. Through work, however, the bondsman becomes conscious of what he truly is. In the moment which corresponds to desire in the lord's consciousness, it did seem that the aspect of unessential relation to the thing fell to the lot of the bondsman, since in that relation the thing retained its independence. Desire has reserved to itself the pure negating of the object and thereby its unalloyed feeling of self. But that is the reason why this satisfaction is itself only a fleeting one, for it lacks the side of objectivity and permanence. Work, on the other hand, is desire held in check, fleetingness staved off; in other words, work forms and shapes the thing. The negative relation to the object becomes its *form* and something *permanent*, because it is precisely for the worker that the object has independence. This *negative* middle term or the formative *activity* is at the same time the individuality or pure being-for-self of consciousness which now, in the work outside of it, acquires an element of permanence. It is in this way, therefore, that consciousness, *qua* worker, comes to see in the independent being [of the object] its *own* independence.

196. But the formative activity has not only this positive significance that in it the pure being-for-self of the servile consciousness acquires an existence;

it also has negative significance with respect to its first moment, *fear*.[7] For, in fashioning the thing, the bondsman's own negativity, his being-for-self, becomes an object for him only through his setting at nought the existing *shape* confronting him. But this objective *negative* moment is none other than the alien being before which it has trembled. Now, however, he destroys this alien negative moment, posits *himself* as a negative in the permanent order of things, and thereby becomes *for himself*, someone existing on his own account. In the lord, the being-for-self is an 'other' for the bondsman, or is only *for* him [i.e. is not his own]; in fear, the being-for-self is present in the bondsman himself; in fashioning the thing, he becomes aware that being-for-self belongs to *him*, that he himself exists essentially and actually in his own right. The shape does not become something other than himself through being made external to him; for it is precisely this shape that is his pure being-for-self, which in this externality is seen by him to be the truth. Through this rediscovery of himself by himself, the bondsman realizes that it is precisely in his work wherein he seemed to have only an alienated existence that he acquires a mind of his own. For this reflection, the two moments of fear and service as such, as also that of formative activity, are necessary, both being at the same time in a universal mode. Without the discipline of service and obedience, fear remains at the formal stage, and does not extend to the known real world of existence. Without the formative activity, fear remains inward and mute, and consciousness does not become explicitly *for itself*. If consciousness fashions the thing without that initial absolute fear, it is only an empty self-centred attitude; for its form or negativity is not negativity *per se*, and therefore its formative activity cannot give it a consciousness of itself as essential being. If it has not experienced absolute fear but only some lesser dread, the negative being has remained for it something external, its substance has not been infected by it through and through. Since the entire contents of its natural consciousness have not been jeopardized, determinate being still *in principle* attaches to it; having a 'mind of one's own' is self-will, a freedom which is still enmeshed in servitude. Just as little as the pure form can become essential being for it, just as little is that form, regarded as extended to the particular, a universal formative activity, an absolute Notion; rather it is a skill which is master over some things, but not over the universal power and the whole of objective being.

B. Freedom of Self-consciousness

Stoicism, scepticism and the unhappy consciousness

197. For the independent self-consciousness, it is only the pure abstraction of the 'I' that is its essential nature, and, when it does develop its own differences, this differentiation does not become a nature that is objective and intrinsic to it. Thus this self-consciousness does not become an 'I' that in its

simplicity is genuinely self-differentiating, or that in this absolute differentiation remains identical with itself. On the other hand, the consciousness that is forced back into itself becomes, in its formative activity, its own object in the form of the thing it has fashioned, and at the same time sees in the lord a consciousness that exists as a being-for-self. But for the subservient consciousness as such, these two moments – *itself* as an independent object, and this object as a mode of consciousness, and hence its own essential nature – fall apart. Since, however, the form and the being-for-self are *for us*, or *in themselves*, the same, and since in the Notion of independent consciousness the *intrinsic* being is consciousness, the moment of intrinsic being or thinghood which received its form in being fashioned is no other substance than consciousness. We are in the presence of self-consciousness in a new shape, a consciousness which, as the infinitude of consciousness or as its own pure movement, is aware of itself as essential being, a being which *thinks* or is a free self-consciousness. For *to think* does not mean to be an *abstract* 'I', but an 'I' which has at the same time the significance of *intrinsic* being, of having itself for object, or of relating itself to objective being in such a way that its significance is the *being-for-self* of the consciousness for which it is [an object]. For in *thinking*, the object does not present itself in picture-thoughts but in *Notions*, i.e. in a distinct *being-in-itself* or intrinsic being, consciousness being immediately aware that this is not anything distinct from itself. What is pictured or figuratively conceived, what *immediately is*, has, as such, the form of being something other than consciousness; but a Notion is also something that *immediately is*, and this distinction, in so far as it is present in consciousness itself, is its determinate content; but since this content is at the same time a content grasped *in thought*, consciousness remains *immediately* aware of its unity with this determinate and distinct being, not, as in the case of a picture-thought, where consciousness still has specially to bear in mind that this is *its* picture-thought; on the contrary, the Notion is for me straightaway *my* Notion. In thinking, I *am free*, because I am not in an *other*, but remain simply and solely in communion with myself, and the object, which is for me the *essential* being, is in undivided unity my being-for-myself; and my activity in conceptual thinking is a movement within myself. It is essential, however, in thus characterizing this shape of self-consciousness to bear firmly in mind that it is *thinking* consciousness *in general*, that its object is an *immediate* unity of *being-in-itself* and *being-for-itself*. The selfsame consciousness that repels itself from itself becomes aware of itself as the element of *being-in-itself*; but at first it knows itself to be this element only as a universal mode of being in general, not as it exists objectively in the development and process of its manifold being.

198. This freedom of self-consciousness when it appeared as a conscious manifestation in the history of Spirit has, as we know, been called Stoicism. Its principle is that consciousness is a being that *thinks*, and that consciousness holds something to be essentially important, or true and good only in so far as it *thinks* it to be such.

199. The manifold self-differentiating expanse of life, with all its detail and complexity, is the object on which desire and work operate. This manifold activity has now contracted into the simple positing of differences in the pure movement of thinking. Essential importance no longer attaches to the difference as a specific *thing*, or as consciousness of a specific *natural existence*, as a feeling, or as desire and its object, whether this is posited by myself or by an alien consciousness. What alone has importance is the difference posited by *thought*, or the difference which from the very first is not distinct from myself. This consciousness accordingly has a negative attitude towards the lord and bondsman relationship. As lord, it does not have its truth in the bondsman, nor as bondsman is its truth in the lord's will and in his service; on the contrary, whether on the throne or in chains, in the utter dependence of its individual existence, its aim is to be free, and to maintain that lifeless indifference which steadfastly withdraws from the bustle of existence, alike from being active as passive, into the simple essentiality of thought. Self-will is the freedom which entrenches itself in some particularity and is still in bondage, while Stoicism is the freedom which always comes directly out of bondage and returns into the pure universality of thought. As a universal form of the World-Spirit, Stoicism could only appear on the scene in a time of universal fear and bondage, but also a time of universal culture which had raised itself to the level of thought.

200. Now, it is true that for this self-consciousness the essence is neither an other than itself, nor the pure abstraction of the 'I', but an 'I' which has the otherness within itself, though in the form of *thought*, so that in its otherness it has directly returned into itself. Yet at the same time this its essence is only an *abstract* essence. The freedom of self-consciousness is *indifferent* to natural existence and has therefore *let this equally go free*: the *reflection* is a *twofold* one. Freedom in thought has only *pure thought* as its truth, a truth lacking the fullness of life. Hence freedom in thought, too, is only the Notion of freedom, not the living reality of freedom itself. For the essence of that freedom is at first only thinking in general, the form as such [of thought], which has turned away from the independence of things and returned into itself. But since individuality in its activity should show itself to be alive, or in its thinking should grasp the living world as a system of thought, there would have to be present in *thought itself* a *content* for that individuality, in the one case a content of what is good, and in the other of what is true, in order that what is an object for consciousness should contain no other ingredient whatever except the Notion which is the essence. But here the Notion as an abstraction cuts itself off from the multiplicity of things, and thus has no content *in its own self* but one that is *given* to it. Consciousness does indeed destroy the content as an alien *immediacy* [*Sein*] when it *thinks* it; but the Notion is a *determinate* Notion, and this determinateness of the Notion is the alien element which it has within it. Stoicism, therefore, was perplexed when it was asked for what was called a 'criterion of truth as such', i.e. strictly speaking, for a *content* of thought itself. To the

question, *What* is good and true, it again gave for answer the *contentless* thought: The True and the Good shall consist in reasonableness. But this self-identity of thought is again only the pure form in which nothing is determined. The True and the Good, wisdom and virtue, the general terms beyond which Stoicism cannot get, are therefore in a general way no doubt uplifting, but since they cannot in fact produce any expansion of the content, they soon become tedious.

201. This thinking consciousness as determined in the form of abstract freedom is thus only the incomplete negation of otherness. *Withdrawn* from existence only into itself, it has not there achieved its consummation as absolute negation of that existence. The content, it is true, only counts as thought, but also as thought that is determinate and at the same time determinateness as such.

202. *Scepticism* is the realization of that of which Stoicism was only the Notion, and is the actual experience of what the freedom of thought is. This is *in itself* the negative and must exhibit itself as such. With the reflection of self-consciousness into the simple thought of itself, the independent existence or permanent determinateness that stood over against that reflection has, as a matter of fact, fallen outside of the infinitude of thought. In Scepticism, now, the wholly unessential and non-independent character of this 'other' becomes explicit *for consciousness*; the [abstract] thought becomes the concrete thinking which annihilates the being of the world in all its manifold determinateness, and the negativity of free self-consciousness comes to know itself in the many and varied forms of life as a real negativity.

It is clear that just as Stoicism corresponds to the *Notion* of the *independent* consciousness which appeared as the lord and bondsman relationship, so Scepticism corresponds to its *realization* as a negative attitude towards otherness, to desire and work. But although desire and work were unable to effect the negation for self-consciousness, this polemical bearing towards the manifold independence of things will, on the other hand, be successful, because it turns against them as a free self-consciousness that is already complete in its own self; more specifically, because it is *thinking*, or is in its own self infinite, and in this infinitude the independent things in their differences from one another are for it only vanishing magnitudes. The differences, which in the pure thinking of self-consciousness are only the abstraction of differences, here become the *entirety* of the differences, and the whole of differentiated being becomes a difference of self-consciousness.

203. Thus the foregoing has defined the nature of the activity of scepticism as such, and the way in which it operates. It exhibits the *dialectical movement* which Sense-certainty, Perception, and the Understanding each is; as also the unessential character of what, in the relationship of lord and bondsman, and for abstract thinking itself, is held to be a *determinate* element. That relationship at the same time embraces a *specific mode* in which ethical laws, too, are present as sovereign commands. The determinations in abstract thinking, however, are scientific Notions in which [formal] contentless thinking

spreads itself, attaching the Notion in fact in a merely external way to the being constituting its content, and which for it is independent, and holding as valid only *determinate* Notions, even though these are only pure abstractions.

204. Dialectic as a negative movement, just as it immediately *is*, at first appears to consciousness as something which has it at its mercy, and which does not have its source in consciousness itself. As Scepticism, on the other hand, it is a moment of self-consciousness, to which it does not *happen* that its truth and reality vanish without its knowing how, but which, in the certainty of its freedom, *makes* this 'other' which claims to be real, vanish. What Scepticism causes to vanish is not only objective reality as such, but its own relationship to it, in which the 'other' is held to be objective and is established as such, and hence, too, its *perceiving*, along with firmly securing what it is in danger of losing, viz. *sophistry*, and the truth it has itself determined and established. Through this self-conscious negation it procures for its own self the certainty of its freedom, generates the experience of that freedom, and thereby raises it to truth. What vanishes is the determinate element, or the moment of difference, which, whatever its mode of being and whatever its source, sets itself up as something fixed and immutable. It contains no permanent element, and must vanish before thought, because the 'different' is just this, not to be in possession of itself, but to have its essential being only in an other. Thinking, however, is the insight into this nature of the 'different', it is the negative essence, as simple.

205. The sceptical self-consciousness thus experiences in the flux of all that would stand secure before it its own freedom as given and preserved by itself. It is aware of this stoical indifference of a thinking which thinks itself, the unchanging and genuine certainty of itself. This self-certainty does not issue from something alien, whose complex development was deposited within it, a result which would leave behind it the process of its coming to be. On the contrary, consciousness itself is the *absolute dialectical unrest*, this medley of sensuous and intellectual representations whose differences coincide, and whose identity is equally again dissolved, for it is itself determinateness as contrasted with the non-identical. But it is just in this process that this consciousness, instead of being self-identical, is in fact nothing but a purely casual, confused medley, the dizziness of a perpetually self-engendered disorder. It is itself aware of this; for it itself maintains and creates this restless confusion. Hence it also admits to it, it owns to being a wholly contingent, single, and separate consciousness – a consciousness which is *empirical*, which takes its guidance from what has no reality for it, which obeys what is for it not an *essential* being, which does those things and brings to realization what it knows has no truth for it. But equally, while it takes itself in this way to be a single and separate, contingent and, in fact, animal life, and a *lost* self-consciousness, it also, on the contrary, converts itself again into a consciousness that is universal and self-identical; for it is the negativity of all singularity and all difference. From this self-identity, or within its own self, it falls back again into the former contingency and

confusion, for this same spontaneous negativity has to do solely with what is single and separate, and occupies itself with what is contingent. This consciousness is therefore the unconscious, thoughtless rambling which passes back and forth from the one extreme of self-identical self-consciousness to the other extreme of the contingent consciousness that is both bewildered and bewildering. It does not itself bring these two thoughts of itself together. At one time it recognizes that its freedom lies in rising above all the confusion and contingency of existence, and at another time equally admits to a relapse into occupying itself with what is unessential. It lets the unessential content in its thinking vanish; but just in doing so it is the consciousness of something unessential. It pronounces an absolute vanishing, but the pronouncement *is*, and this consciousness is the vanishing that is pronounced. It affirms the nullity of seeing, hearing, etc., yet it is itself seeing, hearing, etc. It affirms the nullity of ethical principles, and lets its conduct be governed by these very principles. Its deeds and its words always belie one another and equally it has itself the doubly contradictory consciousness of unchangeableness and sameness, and of utter contingency and non-identity with itself. But it keeps the poles of this its self-contradiction apart, and adopts the same attitude to it as it does in its purely negative activity in general. Point out likeness or identity to it, and it will point out unlikeness or non-identity; and when it is now confronted with what it has just asserted, it turns round and points out likeness or identity. Its talk is in fact like the squabbling of self-willed children, one of whom says *A* if the other says *B*, and in turn says *B* if the other says *A*, and who by contradicting *themselves* buy for themselves the pleasure of continually contradicting *one another*.

206. In Scepticism, consciousness truly experiences itself as internally contradictory. From this experience emerges a *new form* of consciousness which brings together the two thoughts which Scepticism holds apart. Scepticism's lack of thought about itself must vanish, because it is in fact *one* consciousness which contains within itself these two modes. This new form is, therefore, one which *knows* that it is the dual consciousness of itself, as self-liberating, unchangeable, and self-identical, and as self-bewildering and self-perverting, and it is the awareness of this self-contradictory nature of itself.

In Stoicism, self-consciousness is the simple freedom of itself. In Scepticism, this freedom becomes a reality, negates the other side of determinate existence, but really duplicates *itself*, and now knows itself to be a duality. Consequently, the duplication which formerly was divided between two individuals, the lord and the bondsman, is now lodged in one. The duplication of self-consciousness within itself, which is essential in the Notion of Spirit, is thus here before us, but not yet in its unity: the *Unhappy Consciousness* is the consciousness of self as a dual-natured, merely contradictory being.

207. This *unhappy, inwardly disrupted* consciousness, since its essentially contradictory nature is for it a *single* consciousness, must for ever have present in the one consciousness the other also; and thus it is driven out

of each in turn in the very moment when it imagines it has successfully attained to a peaceful unity with the other. Its true return into itself, or its reconciliation with itself will, however, display the Notion of Spirit that has become a living Spirit, and has achieved an actual existence, because it already possesses as a single undivided consciousness a dual nature. The Unhappy Consciousness itself *is* the gazing of one self-consciousness into another, and itself *is* both, and the unity of both is also its essential nature. But it is not as yet explicitly aware that this is its essential nature, or that it is the unity of both.

208. Since it is, to begin with, only the *immediate unity* of the two and so takes them to be, not the same, but opposites, one of them, viz. the simple Unchangeable, it takes to be the *essential* Being; but the other, the protean Changeable, it takes to be the unessential. The two are, for the Unhappy Consciousness, alien to one another; and because it is itself the consciousness of this contradiction, it identifies itself with the changeable consciousness, and takes itself to be the unessential Being. But as consciousness of unchangeableness, or of simple essential Being, it must at the same time set about freeing itself from the unessential, i.e. from itself. For though it indeed takes *itself* to be merely the Changeable, and the Unchangeable is, for it, an alien Being, yet it is *itself* a simple, hence unchangeable, consciousness, and hence is aware that this consciousness is its own essence, although in such a way that again it does not *itself* take the essence to be its own. The attitude it assigns to both cannot therefore be one of mutual indifference, i.e. it cannot itself be indifferent towards the Unchangeable; rather, it is itself directly both of them, and the relation of the two is for it a relation of essential being to the unessential, so that this latter has to be set aside; but since for it both are equally essential and contradictory, it is merely the contradictory movement in which one opposite does not come to rest in *its* opposite, but in it only produces itself afresh as an opposite.

209. Here, then, we have a struggle against an enemy, to vanquish whom is really to suffer defeat, where victory in one consciousness is really lost in its opposite. Consciousness of life, of its existence and activity, is only an agonizing over this existence and activity, for therein it is conscious that its essence is only its opposite, is conscious only of its own nothingness. Raising itself out of this consciousness it goes over into the Unchangeable; but this elevation is itself this same consciousness. It is, therefore, directly consciousness of the opposite, viz. of itself as a particular individual. The Unchangeable that enters into consciousness is through this very fact at the same time affected by individuality, and is only present with the latter; individuality, instead of having been extinguished in the consciousness of the Unchangeable, only continues to arise therefrom.

210. In this movement, however, consciousness experiences just this emergence of individuality in the Unchangeable, and of the Unchangeable in individuality. Consciousness becomes aware of individuality in general in the Unchangeable, and at the same time of its *own* individuality in the latter.

For the truth of this movement is just the *oneness* of this dual consciousness. This unity, however, in the first instance, becomes for it one in which the *difference* of both is still the dominant feature. Thus there exist for consciousness three different ways in which individuality is linked with the Unchangeable. Firstly, it again appears to itself as opposed to the Unchangeable, and is thrown back to the beginning of the struggle which is throughout the element in which the whole relationship subsists. Secondly, consciousness learns that individuality belongs to the Unchangeable itself, so that it assumes the form of individuality into which the entire mode of existence passes. Thirdly, it finds its own self as this particular individual in the Unchangeable. The first Unchangeable it knows only as the alien Being who passes judgement on the particular individual; since, secondly, the Unchangeable is a form of individuality like itself, consciousness becomes, thirdly, Spirit, and experiences the joy of finding itself therein, and becomes aware of the reconciliation of its individuality with the universal.

211. What is set forth here as the mode and relationship of the Unchangeable arose[8] as the *experience* through which the divided self-consciousness passes in its wretchedness. Now, this experience, it is true, is not *its own one-sided* movement, for it is itself the unchangeable consciousness, and this, consequently, is at the same time a particular individual consciousness too; and the movement is just as much a movement of the unchangeable consciousness, which makes its appearance in that movement as much as the other. For the movement runs through these moments: first, the Unchangeable is opposed to individuality in general; then, being itself an individual, it is opposed to another individual; and finally, it is one with it. But this reflection, so far as it is made by us, is here premature, for what has come before for us so far is only unchangeableness as unchangeableness of *consciousness*, which for that reason is not genuine unchangeableness, but one still burdened with an antithesis, not the Unchangeable in and for itself; we do not know, therefore, how the latter will behave. Here, we know only that for consciousness, which is our object here, the determinations indicated above appear in the Unchangeable.

212. For this reason, therefore, the unchangeable *consciousness* also retains in its very form the basic character of dividedness and being-for-self in contrast to the individual consciousness. Consequently, for the latter, the fact that the Unchangeable receives the form of individuality is only a *contingent* happening; just as it also merely *finds itself* opposed to it, so that the relation seems to result from nature.[9] That, finally, it does *find itself* in the Unchangeable, appears to it to be brought about partly, no doubt, by itself, or to take place because it is itself an individual; but this unity, both as regards its origin and the fact that it *is*, appears partly due to the Unchangeable; and the antithesis persists within this unity itself. In fact, through the Unchangeable's assuming a definite form, the moment of the beyond not only persists, but really is more firmly established; for if the beyond seems to have been brought closer to the individual consciousness through

the form of an actuality that is individual, it henceforth on the other hand confronts him as an opaque sensuous *unit* with all the obstinacy of what is *actual*. The hope of becoming one with it must remain a hope, i.e. without fulfilment and present fruition, for between the hope and its fulfilment there stands precisely the absolute contingency or inflexible indifference which lies in the very assumption of definite form, which was the ground of hope. By the nature of this *immediately present unit*, through the actual existence in which it has clothed itself, it necessarily follows that in the world of time it has vanished, and that in space it had a remote existence and remains utterly remote.

213. If at first the mere Notion of the divided consciousness was characterized by the effort to set aside its particular individuality and to become the unchangeable consciousness, its efforts from now on are directed rather to setting aside its relation with the pure *formless* Unchangeable, and to coming into relation only with the Unchangeable in its embodied or incarnate form. For the *oneness* of the particular individual with the Unchangeable is henceforth the essence and the object for this consciousness, just as in the mere Notion of it the formless abstract Unchangeable was the essential object; and the relation of this absolute dividedness of the Notion is now what it has to turn away from. The initially external relation to the incarnate Unchangeable as an alien reality has to be transformed into a relation in which it becomes absolutely one with it.

214. The movement in which the unessential consciousness strives to attain this oneness is itself threefold in accordance with the threefold relation this consciousness will have with its incarnate beyond: first, as pure consciousness; second, as a particular individual who approaches the actual world in the forms of desire and work; and third, as consciousness that is aware of its own being-for-self. We have now to see how these three modes of its being are present and determined in that general relationship.

215. At first, then, this consciousness being taken as *pure consciousness*, the incarnate Unchangeable when it is an object for pure consciousness seems to be present in its own proper nature. But this, its own proper nature, has not yet come into existence, as we have already remarked. In order that it should appear in consciousness in its own proper nature, this would certainly have to come about from *its* side, rather than from the side of consciousness. Thus its presence here is, at first, only one-sidedly due to consciousness, and just for that reason is not perfect and genuine, but remains burdened with imperfection or an antithesis.

216. But although the Unhappy Consciousness does not have the enjoyment of this presence, it has at the same time advanced beyond pure thinking in so far as this is the abstract thinking of Stoicism which turns its back on individuality altogether, and beyond the merely unsettled thinking of Scepticism – which is in fact only individuality in the form of an unconscious contradiction and ceaseless movement. It has advanced beyond both of these; it brings and holds together pure thinking and particular individuality,

but has not yet risen to that thinking where consciousness as a particular individuality is reconciled with pure thought itself. It occupies rather this intermediate position where abstract thinking is in contact with the individuality of consciousness *qua* individuality. The Unhappy Consciousness *is* this contact; it is the unity of pure thinking and individuality; also it *knows* itself to be this thinking individuality or pure thinking, and knows the Unchangeable itself essentially as an individuality. But what it does *not* know is that this its object, the Unchangeable, which it knows essentially in the form of individuality, is *its own self*, is itself the individuality of consciousness.

217. In this first mode, therefore, where we consider it as pure consciousness, it does not *relate* itself as a *thinking* consciousness to its object, but, though it is indeed *in itself*, or implicitly, a pure thinking individuality, and its object is just this pure thinking (although the *relation of one to the other is not itself pure thinking*), it is only a movement *towards* thinking, and so is devotion. Its thinking as such is no more than the chaotic jingling of bells, or a mist of warm incense, a musical thinking that does not get as far as the Notion, which would be the sole, immanent objective mode of thought. This infinite, pure inner feeling does indeed come into possession of its object; but this does not make its appearance in conceptual form, not as something [speculatively] comprehended, and appears therefore as something alien. What we have here, then, is the inward movement of the pure heart which *feels* itself, but itself as agonizingly self-divided, the movement of an infinite yearning which is certain that its essence is such a pure heart, a pure *thinking* which *thinks* of itself as a *particular individuality*, certain of being known and recognized by this object, precisely because the latter thinks of itself as an individuality. At the same time, however, this essence is the unattainable *beyond* which, in being laid hold of, flees, or rather has already flown. It has already flown; for it is in part the Unchangeable which thinks of itself as an individuality, and consciousness therefore directly attains in it its own self – *its own self*, but as the antithesis of the Unchangeable; instead of laying hold of the essence, it only *feels* it and has fallen back into itself. Since, in attaining itself, consciousness is unable to get away from itself as this antithesis to the Unchangeable, it has, instead of laying hold of the essence, only laid hold of what is unessential. Just as, on the one hand, when striving to find itself in the essence it takes hold only of its own separate existence, so on the other hand it cannot lay hold of the 'other' as an *individual* or as an *actual* Being. Where that 'other' is sought, it cannot be found, for it is supposed to be just a *beyond*, something that can *not* be found. When sought as a particular individual, it is not a *universal* individuality in the form of thought, not a *Notion*, but an individual in the form of an object, or an *actual* individual; an object of immediate sense-certainty, and for that very reason only something that has already vanished. Consciousness, therefore, can only find as a present reality the *grave* of its life. But because this grave is itself an *actual existence* and it is contrary to the nature of what actually exists to afford a lasting possession, the presence of

that grave, too, is merely the struggle of an enterprise doomed to failure. But having learned from experience that *the grave* of its *actual* unchangeable Being has *no actuality*, that the *vanished individuality*, because it has vanished, is not the true individuality, consciousness will abandon its quest for the unchangeable individuality as an *actual* existence, or will stop trying to hold on to what has vanished. Only then is it capable of finding individuality in its genuine or universal form.

218. But, in the first instance, *the return of the feeling heart into itself* is to be taken to mean that it has an *actual* existence as an *individual*. It is the *pure heart* which *for us* or *in itself* has found itself and is inwardly satiated, for although for itself in its feeling the essential Being is separated from it, yet this feeling is, in itself, a feeling of *self*; it has felt the object of its pure feeling and this object is itself. Thus it comes forward here as self-feeling, or as an actual consciousness existing on its own account. In this return into self there comes to view its second relationship, that of desire and work in which consciousness finds confirmation of that inner certainty of itself which we know it has attained, by overcoming and enjoying the existence alien to it, viz. existence in the form of independent things. But the Unhappy Consciousness merely *finds* itself *desiring* and *working*; it is not aware that to find itself active in this way implies that it is in fact certain of itself, and that its feeling of the alien existence is this self-feeling. Since it is not explicitly aware of this certainty, its inner life really remains a still incomplete self-certainty; that confirmation which it would receive through work and enjoyment is therefore equally incomplete; in other words, it must itself set at nought this confirmation so that it may indeed find in it confirmation, but only confirmation of what it is *for itself*, viz. of its dividedness.

219. The world of actuality to which desire and work are directed is no longer for this consciousness something *intrinsically null*, something merely to be set aside and consumed, but something like that consciousness itself, an *actuality broken in two*, which is only from one aspect intrinsically null, but from another aspect is also a sanctified *world*; it is the form of the Unchangeable, for this has retained individuality, and because, as the Unchangeable, it is a Universal, its individuality has in general the significance of all actuality.

220. If consciousness were aware of being an independent consciousness, and the world of actuality were for it an absolute nullity, then in work and enjoyment it would attain to a feeling of its independence, since the world of actuality would be nullified by itself. But since this actuality is for consciousness the form of the Unchangeable, it is unable of itself to nullify it. On the contrary, since it does succeed in setting it at nought and enjoying it, this comes about through the Unchangeable's itself having *surrendered* its embodied form, and having *relinquished* it for the enjoyment of consciousness. Consciousness, on its part, *likewise* makes its appearance as an actuality, but also as divided within itself, and in its work and enjoyment this dividedness displays itself as breaking up into a *relation* to the world of

actuality or a being which is *for itself*, and into a being that is *in itself*. That relation to actuality is the *changing* of it or *working on it*, the being-for-self which belongs to the *individual* consciousness as such. But, in this relation, it is also *in itself* or has intrinsic being; this aspect belongs to the Unchangeable beyond and consists of faculties and powers, a gift from an alien source, which the Unchangeable makes over to consciousness to make use of.

221. Accordingly, consciousness in its activity is, in the first instance, a relationship of two extremes. On one side it stands as actively present, while confronting it is a passive actuality: the two sides are in relation with one another, but both have also withdrawn into the Unchangeable and stand fast in themselves. It is, therefore, only a superficial element from each side that is involved in the moving interplay of their mutual opposition. The [passive] extreme of actuality is set aside by the active extreme; but the actuality, on its side, can only be set aside because its own unchangeable essence sets it aside, repels itself from itself, and hands over what is repelled to the active extreme. The active force appears as the *power* in which actuality is dissolved; for this very reason, however, the consciousness to which the *intrinsic* or essential Being is an 'other', regards this power which it displays in its activity to be the beyond of itself. Instead, therefore, of returning from its activity back into itself, and having obtained confirmation of its self-certainty, consciousness really reflects this activity back into the other extreme, which is thus exhibited as a pure universal, as the absolute power from which the activity started in all directions, and which is the essence both of the self-dividing extremes as they at first appeared, and of their interchanging relationship itself.

222. The fact that the unchangeable consciousness *renounces* and *surrenders* its embodied form, while, on the other hand, the particular individual consciousness *gives thanks* [for the gift], i.e. *denies* itself the satisfaction of being conscious of its *independence*, and assigns the essence of its action not to itself but to the beyond, through these two moments of *reciprocal self-surrender* of both parts, consciousness does, of course, gain a sense of its *unity* with the Unchangeable. But this unity is at the same time affected with division, is again broken within itself, and from it there emerges once more the antithesis of the universal and the individual. For though consciousness renounces the *show* of satisfying its feeling of self, it obtains the *actual* satisfaction of it; for it *has been* desire, work, and enjoyment; as consciousness it has *willed, acted*, and *enjoyed*. Similarly, even its *giving of thanks*, in which it acknowledges the other extreme as the essential Being and counts itself nothing, is its *own* act which counterbalances the action of the other extreme, and meets the self-sacrificing beneficence with a *like* action. If the other extreme delivers over to consciousness only the *surface* of its being, yet consciousness *also* gives thanks; and in surrendering its own action, i.e. its *essential* being, it really does more than the other which only sheds a superficial element of itself. Thus the entire movement is reflected not only in the actual desiring, working, and enjoyment, but even in the very giving of thanks where the reverse

seems to take place, in the *extreme of individuality*. Consciousness feels itself therein as this particular individual, and does not let itself be deceived by its own seeming renunciation, for the truth of the matter is that it has *not* renounced itself. What has been brought about is only the double reflection into the two extremes; and the result is the renewed division into the opposed consciousness of the *Unchangeable*, and the consciousness of willing, performing, and enjoying, and self-renunciation itself which *confronts* it; in other words, the consciousness of *independent individuality* in general.

223. With this appears the third relationship of the process of this consciousness, which proceeds from the second as a consciousness that has truly proved itself to be independent, by its will and its deed. In the first relationship it was merely the notion of an actual consciousness, or the inner feeling or heart which is not yet actual in action and enjoyment; the second is this actualization as an external action and enjoyment. Returned from this external activity, however, consciousness has *experienced* itself as actual and effective, or knows that it is in truth in and for itself. But here, now, is where the enemy is met with in his most characteristic form. In the struggle of the heart and emotions the individual consciousness is only a musical abstract moment. In work and enjoyment which make this unsubstantial existence a reality, it can directly forget *itself*, and the consciousness of its *own particular role* in this realization is cancelled out by the act of thankful acknowledgement. But this cancelling-out is in truth a return of consciousness into itself, and, moreover, into itself as the actuality which it knows to be true.

224. This third relationship in which this true actuality is one of the terms is the *relation* of that actuality, as a nothingness, to the universal Being. The process of this relation we have yet to consider.

225. To begin with, as regards the contradictory relation in which consciousness takes its own *reality* to be *immediately a nothingness*, its actual doing thus becomes a doing of nothing, its enjoyment a feeling of its wretchedness. Work and enjoyment thus lose all *universal content* and *significance*, for if they had any, they would have an absolute being of their own. Both withdraw into their mere particularity, which consciousness is set upon reducing to nothingness. Consciousness is aware of itself as *this actual individual* in the animal functions. These are no longer performed naturally and without embarrassment, as matters trifling in themselves which cannot possess any importance or essential significance for Spirit; instead, since it is in them that the enemy reveals himself in his characteristic shape, they are rather the object of serious endeavour, and become precisely matters of the utmost importance. This enemy, however, renews himself in his defeat, and consciousness, in fixing its attention on him, far from freeing itself from him, really remains for ever in contact with him, and for ever sees itself as defiled; and, since at the same time this object of its efforts, instead of being something essential, is of the meanest character, instead of being a universal, is the merest particular, we have here only a personality confined to its own

self and its own petty actions, a personality brooding over itself, as wretched as it is impoverished.

226. But to both of these moments, the feeling of its wretchedness and the poverty of its actions, is linked the consciousness of its unity with the Unchangeable. For the attempted direct destruction of what it actually is is *mediated* by the thought of the Unchangeable, and takes place in this *relation* to it. The *mediated* relation constitutes the essence of the negative movement in which consciousness turns against its particular individuality, but which, *qua relation*, is *in itself positive*, and will bring consciousness itself to an awareness of its *unity* with the Unchangeable.

227. This mediated relation is thus a syllogism in which the individuality, initially fixed in its antithesis to the *in-itself*, is united with this other extreme only through a third term. Through this middle term the one extreme, the Unchangeable, is brought into relation with the unessential consciousness, which equally is brought into relation with the Unchangeable only through this middle term; thus this middle term is one which presents the two extremes to one another, and ministers to each in its dealings with the other. This middle term is itself a conscious Being [the mediator], for it is an action which mediates consciousness as such; the content of this action is the extinction of its particular individuality which consciousness is undertaking.

228. In the mediator, then, this consciousness frees itself from action and enjoyment so far as they are regarded as its own. As a separate, independent extreme, it rejects the essence of its will, and casts upon the mediator or minister [priest] its own freedom of decision, and herewith the responsibility for its own action. This mediator, having a direct relationship with the unchangeable Being, ministers by giving advice on what is right. The action, since it follows upon the decision of someone else, ceases, as regards the doing or the *willing* of it, to be its own. But there is still left to the unessential consciousness the *objective* aspect, viz. the fruit of its labour, and its enjoyment. These, therefore, it rejects as well, and just as it renounces its *will*, so it renounces the *actuality* it received in work and enjoyment. It renounces them, partly as identified with the truth it has attained regarding its own self-conscious *independence* – inasmuch as what it does is foreign to it, a thinking and speaking of what is meaningless to it; partly, as identified with *external possessions* – when it gives away part of what it has acquired through work; and partly, also, as identified with the enjoyment it has had – when, in its fastings and mortifications, it once more completely denies itself that enjoyment.

229. Through these moments of surrender, first of its right to decide for itself, then of its property and enjoyment, and finally through the positive moment of practising what it does not understand, it truly and completely deprives itself of the consciousness of inner and outer freedom, of the actuality in which consciousness exists *for itself*. It has the certainty of having truly divested itself of its '*I*', and of having turned its immediate self-consciousness into a *Thing*, into an *objective* existence. Only through this *actual* sacrifice

could it demonstrate this self-renunciation. For only therein does the *deception* vanish which lies in the inner acknowledgement of gratitude through heart, sentiment, and tongue, an acknowledgement which indeed disclaims all power pertaining to its own independent existence, ascribing it all to a gift from above, but which in this very disclaimer, holds on to its own particular existence, does so outwardly in the possessions it does not surrender, inwardly in the consciousness of the decision it has itself made, and in the consciousness of its content which it has itself determined, which it has not exchanged for one coming from outside, which last would fill it up with what is meaningless for it.

230. But in the sacrifice actually carried out, consciousness, having nullified the *action* as its own doing, has also *in principle* obtained relief from its *misery*. That this relief has been obtained *in principle* is, however, the action of the other extreme of the syllogism, which is the essence possessed of *intrinsic being*. But that sacrifice made by the unessential extreme was at the same time not a one-sided action, but contained within itself the action of the other. For the surrender of one's own will is only from one aspect negative; in principle, however, or in itself, it is at the same time positive, viz. the positing of will as the will of an 'other', and specifically of will, not as a particular, but as a universal will. This positive meaning of the negatively posited particular will is taken by this consciousness to be the will of the other extreme, the will which, precisely because it is an 'other' for consciousness, becomes actual for it, not through the Unhappy Consciousness itself, but through a Third, the mediator as counsellor. Hence, for consciousness, its will does indeed become universal and essential will, but consciousness itself does not take itself to be this essential will. The surrender of its own will, as a *particular* will, is not taken by it to be in principle the positive aspect of universal will. Similarly, its giving up of possessions and enjoyment has only the same negative meaning, and the universal which thereby comes to be for it, is not regarded as its *own doing*. This *unity* of objectivity and being-for-self, which lies in the Notion of action, and which therefore becomes for consciousness essence and *object* – this unity is not the principle of its action, and so too it does not become an object *for consciousness*, directly and through itself. Rather, it lets the mediating minister express this certainty, a certainty which is itself still incomplete, that its misery is only *in principle* the reverse, i.e. that its action brings it only *in principle* self-satisfaction or blessed enjoyment; that its pitiable action too is only *in principle* the reverse, viz. an absolute action; that in principle, action is only really action when it is the action of a particular individual. But *for itself*, action and its own actual doing remain pitiable, its enjoyment remains pain, and the overcoming of these in a positive sense remains a *beyond*. But in this object, in which it finds that its own action and being, as being that of this *particular* consciousness, are being and action *in themselves*, there has arisen for consciousness the idea of *Reason*, of the certainty that, in its particular individuality, it has being absolutely *in itself*, or is all reality.

Notes

1 Miller's translation has 'since', instead of 'in so far as' in this sentence. The German word is 'indem' (in that . . .). I have rendered 'indem' as 'in so far as' here to make it clear that what is being considered is merely what self-consciousness *would* be without a relation to being, i.e. '*not* self-consciousness'. The fact that self-consciousness would fall short of genuine self-consciousness to the extent that it lacked a relation to being, explains why Hegel goes on in the following sentences to state that in self-consciousness properly understood, 'otherness is for it in the form of *a being*' and that self-consciousness thus incorporates consciousness. [s.h.]

2 Miller's translation has 'on its own account'. The German is 'für sich'. [s.h.]

3 Miller's translation has 'for self-consciousness'. The German word is 'sich'. [s.h.]

4 Miller's translation has 'the other self-consciousness equally gives it back again to itself'. The German text is '*zweitens* aber gibt es das andere Selbstbewußtsein ihm wieder ebenso zurück'. [s.h.]

5 See Hegel, *Phenomenology of Spirit*, p. 84 (not included in this collection). [s.h.]

6 Miller's translation just has 'the simple "I" is absolute mediation'. The German text is 'das einfache Ich [ist] der absolute Gegenstand, welcher aber für uns oder an sich die absolute Vermittlung ist'. [s.h.]

7 Miller's translation has 'it also has, in contrast with its first moment, the negative significance of *fear*'. The German text is 'sondern auch die negative [Bedeutung] gegen sein erstes Moment, die Furcht'. [s.h.]

8 Miller's translation has 'has appeared'. The German phrase is 'ergab sich'. [s.h.]

9 Miller's translation has 'from its own nature'. The German phrase is 'durch die Natur'. [s.h.]

9

Phenomenology of Spirit: Spirit. Absolute Freedom and Terror

584. Spirit thus comes before us as *absolute freedom*. It is self-consciousness which grasps the fact that its certainty of itself is the essence of all the spiritual 'masses', or spheres, of the real as well as of the supersensible world, or conversely, that essence and actuality are consciousness's knowledge of *itself*. It is conscious of its pure personality and therein of all spiritual reality, and all reality is solely spiritual; the world is for it simply its own will, and this is a general will. And what is more, this will is not the empty thought of will which consists in silent assent, or assent by a representative, but a real general will, the will of all *individuals* as such. For will is in itself the consciousness of personality, or of each, and it is as this genuine actual will that it ought to be, as the *self*-conscious essence of each and every personality, so that each, undivided from the whole, always does everything, and what appears as done by the whole is the direct and conscious deed of each.

585. This undivided Substance of absolute freedom ascends the throne of the world without any power being able to resist it. For since, in truth, consciousness alone is the element in which the spiritual beings or powers have their substance, their entire system which is organized and maintained by division into 'masses' or spheres has collapsed, now that the individual consciousness conceives the object as having no other essence than self-consciousness itself, or as being absolutely Notion. What made the Notion into an existent *object* was its diremption into separate *subsistent* spheres, but when the object becomes a Notion, there is no longer anything in it with a continuing existence; negativity has permeated all its moments. It comes into existence in such a way that each individual consciousness raises itself out of its allotted sphere, no longer finds its essence and its work in this particular sphere, but grasps itself as the *Notion* of will, grasps all spheres as the essence of this will, and therefore can only realize itself in a work which is a work of the whole. In this absolute freedom, therefore, all social groups or classes which are the spiritual spheres into which the whole is articulated

are abolished; the individual consciousness that belonged to any such sphere, and willed and fulfilled itself in it, has put aside its limitation; its purpose is the general purpose, its language universal law, its work the universal work.

586. The object and the [moment of] *difference* have here lost the meaning of *utility*, which was the predicate of all real being; consciousness does not begin its movement in the object as if this were something *alien* from which it first had to return into itself; on the contrary, the object is for it consciousness itself. The antithesis consists, therefore, solely in the difference between the *individual* and the *universal* consciousness; but the individual consciousness itself is directly in its own eyes that which had only the *semblance* of an antithesis; it is universal consciousness and will. The *beyond* of this its actual existence hovers over the corpse of the vanished independence of real being, or the being of faith, merely as the exhalation of a stale gas, of the vacuous *Être suprême*.

587. After the various spiritual spheres and the restricted life of the individual have been done away with, as well as his two worlds, all that remains, therefore, is the immanent movement of universal self-consciousness as a reciprocity of self-consciousness in the form of *universality* and of *personal* consciousness: the universal will goes *into itself* and is a *single, individual* will to which universal law and work stand opposed. But this *individual* consciousness is no less directly conscious of itself as universal will; it is aware that its object is a law given by that will and a work accomplished by it; therefore, in passing over into action and in creating objectivity, it is doing nothing individual, but carrying out the laws and functions of the state.

588. This movement is thus the interaction of consciousness with itself in which it lets nothing break loose to become a *free object* standing over against it. It follows from this that it cannot achieve anything positive, either universal works of language or of reality, either laws and general institutions of *conscious* freedom, or deeds and works of a freedom that *wills* them. The work which *conscious* freedom might accomplish would consist in that freedom, *qua universal* substance, making itself into an *object* and into an *enduring being*. This otherness would be the moment of difference in it whereby it divided itself into stable spiritual 'masses' or spheres and into the members of various powers. These spheres would be partly the 'thought-things' of a *power* that is separated into legislative, judicial, and executive powers; but partly, they would be the *real essences* we found in the real world of culture, and, looking more closely at the content of universal action, they would be the particular spheres of labour which would be further distinguished as more specific 'estates' or classes.[1] Universal freedom, which would have separated itself in this way into its constituent parts and by the very fact of doing so would have made itself into an *existent* Substance, would thereby be free from *particular* individuality, and would apportion the *plurality* of individuals to its various constituent parts. This, however, would restrict the activity and the being of the personality to a branch of the whole, to one kind of activity and being; when placed in the element of *being*, personality would have the

significance of a specific personality; it would cease to be in truth universal self-consciousness. Neither by the mere idea of obedience to *self-given* laws which would assign to it only a part of the whole, nor by its being *represented* in law-making and universal action, does self-consciousness let itself be cheated out of *reality*, the reality of *itself* making the law and accomplishing, not a particular work, but the universal work itself. For where the self is merely *represented* and is present only as an idea, there it is not *actual*; where it is represented by proxy, it *is not*.

589. Just as the individual self-consciousness does not find itself in this *universal work* of absolute freedom *qua* existent Substance, so little does it find itself in the *deeds* proper and *individual* actions of the will of this freedom. Before the universal can perform a deed it must concentrate itself into the One of individuality and put at the head an individual self-consciousness; for the universal will is only an *actual* will in a self, which is a One. But thereby all other individuals are excluded from the entirety of this deed and have only a limited share in it, so that the deed would not be a deed of the *actual universal* self-consciousness. Universal freedom, therefore, can produce neither a positive work nor a deed; there is left for it only *negative* action; it is merely the *fury* of destruction.

590. But the supreme reality and the reality which stands in the greatest antithesis to universal freedom, or rather the sole object that will still exist for that freedom, is the freedom and individuality of actual self-consciousness itself. For that universality which does not let itself advance to the reality of an organic articulation, and whose aim is to maintain itself in an unbroken continuity, at the same time creates a distinction within itself, because it is movement or consciousness in general. And, moreover, by virtue of its own abstraction, it divides itself into extremes equally abstract, into a simple, inflexible cold universality, and into the discrete, absolute hard rigidity and self-willed atomism of actual self-consciousness. Now that it has completed the destruction of the actual organization of the world, and exists now just for itself, this is its sole object, an object that no longer has any content, possession, existence or outer extension, but is merely this knowledge of itself as an absolutely pure and free individual self. All that remains of the object by which it can be laid hold of is solely its *abstract* existence as such. The relation, then, of these two, since each exists indivisibly and absolutely for itself, and thus cannot dispose of a middle term which would link them together, is one of wholly *unmediated* pure negation, a negation, moreover, of the individual as a being *existing* in the universal. The sole work and deed of universal freedom is therefore *death*, a death too which has no inner significance or filling, for what is negated is the empty point of the absolutely free self. It is thus the coldest and meanest of all deaths, with no more significance than cutting off a head of cabbage or swallowing a mouthful of water.

591. In this flat, commonplace monosyllable is contained the wisdom of the government, the abstract intelligence of the universal will, in the fulfilling of itself. The government is itself nothing else but the self-established

focus, or the individuality, of the universal will. The government, which wills and executes its will from a single point, at the same time wills and executes a specific order and action. On the one hand, it excludes all other individuals from its act, and on the other hand, it thereby constitutes itself a government that is a specific will, and so stands opposed to the universal will; consequently, it is absolutely impossible for it to exhibit itself as anything else but a *faction*. What is called government is merely the *victorious* faction, and in the very fact of its being a faction lies the direct necessity of its overthrow; and its being government makes it, conversely, into a faction, and [so] guilty. When the universal will maintains that what the government has actually done is a crime committed against it, the government, for its part, has nothing specific and outwardly apparent by which the guilt of the will opposed to it could be demonstrated; for what stands opposed to it as the *actual* universal will is only an unreal pure will, *intention*. *Being suspected*, therefore, takes the place, or has the significance and effect, of *being guilty*; and the external reaction against this reality that lies in the simple inwardness of intention, consists in the cold, matter-of-fact annihilation of this existent self, from which nothing else can be taken away but its mere being.

592. In this its characteristic *work*, absolute freedom becomes explicitly objective to itself, and self-consciousness learns what absolute freedom in effect is. *In itself*, it is just this *abstract self-consciousness*, which effaces all distinction and all continuance of distinction within it. It is as such that it is objective to itself; the *terror* of death is the vision of this negative nature of itself. But absolutely free self-consciousness finds this its reality quite different from what its own Notion of itself was, viz. that the universal will is merely the *positive* essence of personality, and that this latter knows itself in it only positively, or as preserved therein. Here, however, this self-consciousness which, as pure insight, completely separates its positive and its negative nature – completely separates the predicateless Absolute as pure *Thought* and as pure *Matter* – is confronted with the absolute *transition* of the one into the other as a present reality. The universal will, *qua* absolutely *positive*, actual self-consciousness, because it is this self-conscious reality heightened to the level of *pure* thought or of *abstract* matter, changes round into its negative nature and shows itself to be equally that which *puts an end to the thinking of oneself*, or to self-consciousness.

593. Absolute freedom as *pure* self-identity of the universal will thus has within it *negation*; but this means that it contains *difference* in general, and this again it develops as an *actual* difference. For pure *negativity* has in the self-identical universal will the element of subsistence, or the *Substance* in which its moments are realized; it has the matter which it can utilize in accordance with its own determinateness; and in so far as this Substance has shown itself to be the negative element for the individual consciousness, the organization of spiritual 'masses' or spheres to which the plurality of individual consciousnesses are assigned thus takes shape once more. These individuals who have felt the fear of death, of their absolute master, again

submit to negation and distinctions, arrange themselves in the various spheres, and return to an apportioned and limited task, but thereby to their substantial reality.

594. Out of this tumult, Spirit would be thrown back to its starting-point, to the ethical and real world of culture, which would have been merely refreshed and rejuvenated by the fear of the lord and master which has again entered men's hearts. Spirit would have to traverse anew and continually repeat this cycle of necessity if the result were only the complete interpenetration of self-consciousness and Substance – an interpenetration in which self-consciousness, which has experienced the negative power of its universal essence acting on it, would desire to know and find itself, not as this particular individual, but only as a universal, and therefore, too, would be able to endure the objective reality of universal Spirit, a reality excluding self-consciousness *qua* particular. But in absolute freedom there was no reciprocal action between a consciousness that is immersed in the complexities of existence, or that sets itself specific aims and thoughts, and a valid *external* world, whether of reality or thought; instead, the world was absolutely in the form of consciousness as a universal will, and equally self-consciousness was drawn together out of the whole expanse of existence or manifested aims and judgements, and concentrated into the simple self. The culture to which it attains in interaction with that essence is, therefore, the grandest and the last, is that of seeing its pure, simple reality immediately vanish and pass away into empty nothingness. In the world of culture itself[2] it does not get as far as to behold its negation or alienation in this form of pure abstraction; on the contrary, its negation is filled with a content, either honour or wealth, which it gains in place of the self that it has alienated from itself; or the language of Spirit and insight which the disrupted consciousness acquires; or it is the heaven of faith, or the Utility of the Enlightenment. All these determinations have vanished in the loss suffered by the self in absolute freedom; its negation is the death that is without meaning, the sheer terror of the negative that contains nothing positive, nothing that fills it with a content. At the same time, however, this negation in its real existence is not something alien; it is neither the universal inaccessible *necessity* in which the ethical world perishes, nor the particular accident of private possession, nor the whim of the owner on which the disrupted consciousness sees itself dependent; on the contrary, it is the *universal will* which in this its ultimate abstraction has nothing positive and therefore can give nothing in return for the sacrifice. But for that very reason it is immediately one with self-consciousness, or it is the pure positive, because it is the pure negative; and the meaningless death, the unfilled negativity of the self, changes round in its inner Notion into absolute positivity. For consciousness, the immediate unity of itself with the universal will, its demand to know itself as this specific point in the universal will, is changed round into the absolutely opposite experience. What vanishes for it in that experience is abstract *being* or the immediacy of that insubstantial point, and this

vanished immediacy is the universal will itself which it now knows itself to be in so far as it is a pure knowing or pure will. Consequently, it knows that will to be itself, and knows itself to be essential being; but not essential being as an *immediate existence*, not will as revolutionary government or anarchy striving to establish anarchy, nor itself as the centre of this faction or the opposite faction; on the contrary, the *universal will* is its *pure knowing and willing* and *it* is the universal will *qua* this pure knowing and willing. It does not lose *itself* in that will, for pure knowing and willing is much more *it* than is that atomic point of consciousness. It is thus the interaction of pure knowing with itself; pure *knowing qua essential being* is the universal will; but this essential being is abolutely nothing else but pure knowing. Self-consciousness is, therefore, the pure knowing of essential being *qua* pure knowing. Further, as an *individual self*, it is only the form of the subject or of real action, a form which is known by it as *form*. Similarly, *objective* reality, *being*, is for it simply a selfless form; for that reality would be something that is not known. This knowing, however, knows knowing to be essential being.

595. Absolute freedom has thus removed the antithesis between the universal and the individual will. The self-alienated Spirit, driven to the extreme of its antithesis in which pure willing and the agent of that pure willing are still distinct, reduces the antithesis to a transparent form and therein finds itself. Just as the realm of the real world passes over into the realm of faith and insight, so does absolute freedom leave its self-destroying reality and pass over into another land of self-conscious Spirit where, in this unreal world, freedom has the value of truth. In the thought of this truth Spirit refreshes itself, in so far as *it is* and remains *thought*, and knows this being which is enclosed within self-consciousness to be essential being in its perfection and completeness. There has arisen the new shape of Spirit, that of the *moral* Spirit.

Notes

1 Hegel's analysis of the 'real world of culture' forms the first part of his account of culture or 'self-alienated spirit' as a whole. The other parts of that account examine 'faith and pure insight', the Enlightenment and 'absolute freedom and terror'. For the analyses of the 'real world of culture', 'faith and pure insight' and the Enlightenment, see Hegel, *Phenomenology of Spirit*, pp. 297–355 (not included in this collection). [S.H.]

2 i.e. in the world of culture *before* the 'absolute freedom and terror' of the French Revolution. [S.H.]

10

Phenomenology of Spirit: Spirit. Absolute Knowing

804. Spirit [. . .] has shown itself to us to be neither merely the withdrawal of self-consciousness into its pure inwardness, nor the mere submergence of self-consciousness into substance, and the non-being of its [moment of] difference; but Spirit is *this movement* of the Self which empties itself of itself and sinks itself into its substance, and also, as Subject, has gone out of that substance into itself, making the substance into an object and a content at the same time as it cancels this difference between objectivity and content. That first reflection out of immediacy is the Subject's differentiation of itself from its substance, or the Notion's separation of itself from itself, the withdrawal into itself and the becoming of the pure 'I'. Since this difference is the pure act of 'I' = 'I', the Notion is the necessity and the uprising of *existence*, which has substance for its essence and subsists on its own account. But this subsistence of existence on its own account is the Notion posited in determinateness and is thus also its *immanent* movement, that of going down into the simple substance, which is Subject only as this negativity and movement. The 'I' has neither to cling to itself in the *form* of *self-consciousness* as against the form of substantiality and objectivity, as if it were afraid of the externalization of itself: the power of Spirit lies rather in remaining the selfsame Spirit in its externalization and, as that which is both *in itself* and *for itself*, in making its *being-for-self* no less merely a moment than its in-itself; nor is Spirit a *tertium quid* that casts the differences back into the abyss of the Absolute and declares that therein they are all the same; on the contrary, knowing is this seeming inactivity which merely contemplates how what is differentiated spontaneously moves in its own self and returns into its unity.

805. In this knowing, then, Spirit has concluded the movement in which it has shaped itself, in so far as this shaping was burdened with the difference of consciousness [i.e. of the latter from its object], a difference now overcome. Spirit has won the pure element of its existence, the Notion. The content, in accordance with the *freedom* of its *being*, is the self-alienating Self, or the immediate unity of self-knowledge. The pure movement of this

alienation, considered in connection with the content, constitutes the *necessity* of the content. The distinct content, as *determinate*, is in relation, is not 'in itself'; it is its own restless process of superseding itself, or *negativity*; therefore, negativity or diversity, like free being, is also the Self; and in this selflike *form* in which existence is immediately thought, the content is the *Notion*. Spirit, therefore, having won the Notion, displays its existence and movement in this ether of its life and is *Science*.[1] In this, the moments of its movement no longer exhibit themselves as specific *shapes of consciousness*, but – since consciousness's difference has returned into the Self – as *specific Notions* and as their organic self-grounded movement. Whereas in the phenomenology of Spirit each moment is the difference of knowledge and Truth, and is the movement in which the difference is cancelled, Science on the other hand does not contain this difference and the cancelling of it. On the contrary, since the moment has the form of the Notion, it unites the objective form of Truth and of the knowing Self in an immediate unity. The moment does not appear as this movement of passing back and forth, from consciousness or picture-thinking into self-consciousness, and conversely: on the contrary, its pure shape, freed from its appearance in consciousness, the pure Notion and its onward movement, depends solely on its pure *determinateness*. Conversely, to each abstract moment of Science corresponds a shape of manifest Spirit as such. Just as Spirit in its existence is not richer than Science, so too it is not poorer either in content. To know the pure Notions of Science in this form of shapes of consciousness constitutes the side of their reality, in accordance with which their essence, the Notion, which is posited in them in its *simple* mediation as *thinking*, breaks asunder the moments of this mediation and exhibits itself in accordance with the inner antithesis.

806. Science contains within itself this necessity of externalizing the form of the Notion, and it contains the passage of the Notion into *consciousness*. For the self-knowing Spirit, just because it grasps its Notion, is the immediate identity with itself which, in its difference, is the *certainty of immediacy*, or *sense-consciousness* – the beginning from which we started. This release of itself from the form of its Self is the supreme freedom and assurance of its self-knowledge.

807. Yet this externalization is still incomplete; it expresses the connection of its self-certainty with the object which, just because it is thus connected, has not yet won its complete freedom. The self-knowing Spirit knows not only itself but also the negative of itself, or its limit: to know one's limit is to know how to sacrifice oneself. This sacrifice is the externalization in which Spirit displays the process of its becoming Spirit in the form of *free contingent happening*, intuiting its pure Self as Time outside of it, and equally its Being as Space. This latter[2] becoming of Spirit, *Nature*, is its living immediate Becoming; Nature, the externalized Spirit, is in its existence nothing but this eternal externalization of its *continuing existence* and the movement which reinstates the *Subject*.

808. But the other side of its Becoming, *History*, is a *conscious*, self-*mediating* process – Spirit emptied out into Time; but this externalization, this kenosis,[3] is equally an externalization of itself; the negative is the negative of itself. This Becoming presents a slow-moving succession of Spirits, a gallery of images, each of which, endowed with all the riches of Spirit, moves thus slowly just because the Self has to penetrate and digest this entire wealth of its substance. As its fulfilment consists in perfectly *knowing* what *it is*, in knowing its substance, this knowing is its *withdrawal into itself* in which it abandons its outer existence and gives its existential shape over to recollection. Thus absorbed in itself, it is sunk in the night of its self-consciousness; but in that night its vanished outer existence is preserved, and this transformed existence – the former one, but now reborn of the Spirit's knowledge – is the new existence, a new world and a new shape of Spirit. In the immediacy of this new existence the Spirit has to start afresh to bring itself to maturity as if, for it, all that preceded were lost and it had learned nothing from the experience of the earlier Spirits. But recollection, the *inwardizing*, of that experience, has preserved it and is the inner being, and in fact the higher form of the substance. So although this Spirit starts afresh and apparently from its own resources to bring itself to maturity, it is none the less on a higher level that it starts. The realm of Spirits which is formed in this way in the outer world constitutes a succession in Time in which one Spirit relieved another of its charge and each took over the empire of the world from its predecessor. Their goal is the revelation of the depth of Spirit, and this is *the absolute Notion*. This revelation is, therefore, the raising-up [*Aufheben*] of its depth, or its *extension*, the negativity of this withdrawn 'I', a negativity which is its externalization or its substance; and this revelation is also the Notion's Time, in that this externalization is in its own self externalized, and just as it is in its extension, so it is equally in its depth, in the Self. The *goal*, Absolute Knowing, or Spirit that knows itself as Spirit, has for its path the recollection of the Spirits as they are in themselves and as they accomplish the organization of their realm. Their preservation, regarded from the side of their free existence appearing in the form of contingency, is History; but regarded from the side of their comprehended organization,[4] it is the Science of Knowing in the sphere of appearance:[5] the two together, comprehended History, form alike the inwardizing and the Calvary of absolute Spirit, the actuality, truth, and certainty of his throne, without which he would be lifeless and alone. Only

> from the chalice of this realm of spirits
> foams forth for Him his own infinitude.[6]

Notes

1   i.e. the *Science of Logic*. [S.H.]
2   Miller's translation has 'this last becoming'. The German phrase is 'dieses sein letzteres Werden'. [S.H.]

3 The phrase 'this kenosis' has been inserted by Miller. [S.H.]
4 Miller's translation has 'their [philosophically] comprehended organisation'. The German text is 'nach der Seite ihrer begriffenen Organisation'. [S.H.]
5 Phenomenology. [Translator's note.]
6 Adaptation of Schiller's *Die Freundschaft*. [Translator's note.]

Part III
Logic

Introduction

The *Science of Logic* was published in three parts between 1812 and 1816 while Hegel was rector of the Aegidiengymnasium in Nuremberg and engaged, besides his administrative duties, in teaching philosophy to school children. In October 1811, as he was working on the *Logic*, Hegel had written to his friend, Immanuel Niethammer, that 'I feel every year more inclined to make myself accessible, especially since my marriage'.[1] The text which eventually emerged, however, is one of the most difficult and daunting in the whole history of philosophy, exceeding in density and complexity both Plato's *Parmenides* and Kant's *Critique of Pure Reason*. Hegel revised the 'doctrine of being' in 1830–1, but the rest of the text remained untouched, and the book as a whole continues to present a formidable challenge to even its most sympathetic and assiduous readers.

The project of the *Logic* follows directly from that of the *Phenomenology*. The *Phenomenology* analyses a succession of forms of consciousness in which that which truly *is* – 'the True' (*das Wahre*) – is taken to stand over against consciousness in the form of an object or of another finite or infinite self. The conclusion reached by the *Phenomenology*, however, is that being cannot be regarded simply as confronting consciousness, but must be understood as disclosing itself *within* thought itself. This is not to say that the truth can be found within any mode of thought whatsoever, but that it will be found within the mode of thought which thinks *properly* – whatever that may turn out to mean. The first task facing absolute knowing or philosophy is thus to establish what it is to think properly, and in so doing to discover within thought (properly understood) the true character of being. This task is carried out by Hegel in the *Science of Logic*. The *Logic* thus represents Hegel's contribution both to logic and to ontology – to the clarification of what it is to *think* and of what it is to *be*.

If the *Logic* is rendered necessary systematically by the progression of the *Phenomenology* to absolute knowing, it is also rendered necessary historically by Kant's critical philosophy, as Hegel points out in the first part of his *Encyclopaedia* (1830). The great importance of Kant, Hegel tells us, is that he subjects to critical investigation the categories, such as substance and causality, that are used in metaphysics.[2] In Kant's own view, such a critical investigation shows that these categories only have objective validity in so far as they are used to determine the way things *appear* to us in sensuous intuition, and that, consequently, they cannot yield any knowledge of things in themselves. For reasons that were set out in the General Introduction above, however, Hegel does not accept this Kantian restriction of the categories to 'mere appearance' and does not wish to dismiss the pre-Kantian, metaphysical claim that we can know the true nature of being itself through thought. For Hegel, a *truly* critical investigation of the categories should not simply restrict their range of application, but should call into question the ways in which the categories themselves have traditionally been conceived. What makes a philosopher, such as Spinoza, an uncritical philosopher, in Hegel's view, is thus not that he believes knowledge of being itself can be gained through the concept of substance, but that he seeks such knowledge on the basis of a concept of substance whose meaning or definition he simply takes for granted. That is to say, Spinoza does not make thought and its categories the explicit object of his investigation and seek to establish without presuppositions how those categories are to be conceived.

Hegel's task in the *Science of Logic* is to carry out the true critique of the categories which, in his view, is prompted by Kant's philosophy, but which neither Spinoza, nor indeed Kant himself, undertook. Such a critique involves suspending the assumptions that have traditionally been made about the meaning of concepts such as 'substance' and 'causality' and working out *from scratch* how those concepts are to be conceived. This process of rigorous logical derivation will, Hegel believes, lead to the proper understanding of thought and its categories in and through which the true nature of being itself will be disclosed.

If the *Science of Logic* is to be a thoroughly critical science, and is not simply to take for granted what it is to think and what it is to be, it can begin with no determinate presuppositions about thought or being.[3] The *Logic* must thus begin with the most indeterminate thought that can be thought: the quite indeterminate thought of *being* as such – 'without any further determination'.[4] This is not the thought of existence or actuality, but the simple thought of *is* or *being*, whose meaning is as yet unspecified, but which is presupposed by everything else we think (including the thought that there *is* nothing at all). Hegel well recognizes that this thought of sheer being is an abstraction, but it is the least that can be thought. It is thus the most that *may* be thought, if we are not simply to take all further categories for granted but are to derive them from the very nature of thought itself.

Hegel's method in the *Science of Logic* is simply to render explicit the implications – and so to think the immanent development – of that initial indeterminate thought of being. Schelling claimed in the 1830s that Hegel moved the *Logic* along by contrasting the abstract concept of being with the more determinate concept of 'real being' and showing that pure being is '*not yet* real being', is merely being *in potentia*. 'With that interpolated *yet*,' Schelling writes, 'something to come which has yet to *be* is already promised, and with the help of this *yet* Hegel gets to *becoming*.'[5] In *Glas* Derrida continues this Schellingian reading of Hegel by pointing to the 'play of the *already* and the *not yet*' in Hegel's thought.[6] It is clear from Hegel's opening analysis of being–nothing–becoming, however, that this reading is inaccurate. In fact, the thought of pure being, as utterly indeterminate, disappears *immediately* into the thought of sheer nothing, and the thought of sheer and simple nothing disappears just as immediately into that of simple, indeterminate being. The thought of becoming thus arises because pure being proves to be not just pure and simple *being*, but the immediate *transition into*, and so *becoming of*, nothing, just as nothing proves to be not just nothing but the immediate becoming of being. The category of becoming arises, therefore, not, as Schelling claims, because pure being is thought to contain the promise of real being to come, but rather because pure being and pure nothing are unstable – and so pass dialectically into their opposites – in their very *immediacy*.

Pure being, in Hegel's account, proves to be becoming not by reference to some anticipated goal, but through its own immanent instability. Similarly, the thought of becoming settles into the thought of determinate being, not because of some craving for determinacy on Hegel's part, but because of the very nature of becoming itself. Becoming is the *vanishing* of being and nothing into one another; but it is thereby the vanishing of the very *difference* between pure being and pure nothing as such – their ceasing to be simply *other* than one another. In becoming, being and nothing thus do not just pass over into one *another*, but in fact pass over into their absolute *inseparability*. The thought of becoming thus leads immanently – through its very own structure – to the thought that being and nothing are utterly inseparable from, and one with, each other. This is the thought that being is inseparable from the not and that the not is inseparable from being: the thought of being as *determinate*, as being what it is solely in *not* being what it is not.

Hegel goes on to show that to be is not just to be determinate, but also to be 'something' in relation to 'other', to be 'limited', to be 'finite' and to be 'infinite'. In each case, the new concept which arises, arises immanently from the one that precedes it – without reference to an anticipated goal. The analysis is painstaking and abstract, but if Hegel is right, what is revealed here are not only the basic categories of thought but the (onto)logical structure of being itself.

In contemporary French philosophy much emphasis has been placed on the need to think difference non-dialectically. For example, in *Difference and Repetition* Deleuze talks of his concern to articulate 'a concept of difference without negation', that is, a difference without identity, opposition and contradiction.[7] Partly in order to enable those interested in the work of Deleuze and Derrida to see for themselves what Hegel has to say about difference – but also because of the intrinsic interest of Hegel's analysis – I have included the opening sections from the 'doctrine of essence' in this collection. As throughout the whole of the *Logic*, the structures analysed in the doctrine of essence are to be regarded both as concepts in terms of which we must think and as ontological structures to be encountered in the world. Hegel's claim in this section is therefore that illusion is in fact real – that seeming does occur – and that reflexivity (negativity) is actually at work in our world.

Although the analysis of essence proceeds immanently, like the analysis of being, the course of development in the doctrine of essence differs markedly from the development in the doctrine of being. This is due to the point of departure, which is no longer the sheer immediacy of being, but rather the thought of sheer *non-immediacy*, of '*sublated being*': the thought that *in essence* being is *not* simply immediate after all. The opening of the doctrine of essence explores the intrinsic ambiguity in this thought that the essence of being is sheer non-immediacy. Hegel shows first that, when the essence of being is thought as the simple and immediate negation of being's immediacy, it is turned into *something other* than that immediacy and being's immediacy in turn is left as *something other* than its essence. Hegel then shows, however, that being's immediacy cannot just be thought of as something other than its essence, because the concept of the essence of being as sheer non-immediacy actually dissolves the idea that there is any 'immediate being' at all. If the concept of the essence of being does away with the very idea of immediate being, immediate being must thus be thought of as not really being immediate after all, but as merely *seeming* to be. That is to say, the thought that in essence there is no immediate being necessarily reduces the immediacy with which we begin to mere illusion or *Schein*. But if the concept of essence reduces *all* immediacy to mere illusory being or seeming, then the thought of essence itself as immediately different from such seeming can in turn only be the thought of what essence *seems* to be. In fact, whatever immediacy essence is thought to have – whatever essence is taken to *be* – is necessarily negated by the very concept of essence itself into mere seeming and illusion. Indeed, in Hegel's view, this is all that essence ultimately proves to be: the movement of merely seeming to be, and so of not-really-being, what it 'is' – what Hegel calls 'the seeming of itself within itself' (*das Scheinen seiner in sich selbst*).[8] At this point, the very concept of essence appears to have been lost; but it is in fact the point at which a *productive* conception of essence first arises. For, once essence is thought of as mere seeming, as sheer not-being that is nevertheless *not* just nothing, essence is thought of as sheer negativity – sheer negativity *through which* there is, and must be, being. From the perspective of the doctrine of essence there is no simply *immediate* being; yet, from the very same point of view, there must be being because in essence there is *not* just *nothing*. Essence, understood properly, thus proves to be, not some transcendent realm beyond what what we see, but simply the not-just-nothing – 'the movement of nothing to nothing' – by virtue of which there is, and has to be, being.[9] Understood in this way, essence is *positing reflection.* Identity, for Hegel, is being, understood not just as immediate – not just as *being there* – but as *posited* or *constituted* by the movement of negativity, reflection and difference. From the point of view of the doctrine of essence, the ontological structures described in the doctrine of being – becoming, determinacy, finitude and infinity – are to be regarded as aspects of this *identity* of being and of all that such identity proves to be. They are thus not to be rejected out of hand, but are themselves to be understood as *constituted* by reflexivity.

The selections from the *Logic* end with short passages from the doctrine of the concept (or 'notion'). The concept is what being turns out to be *in truth*. Neither simple being, becoming and determinacy, nor essential seeming, reflexivity and identity, exhaust by themselves what it is to be, therefore, but they are in fact mere moments of being's true, *conceptual* structure. Whereas transition and relation to otherness are characteristic of sheer being, and positing, constituting and mediating are characteristic of essence and reflexivity, what is characteristic of being-as-concept is self-determination, self-differentiation and self-development. The concept, for Hegel, is thus 'free power', and can be called (as it is in the Christian religion) 'free love'[10] – the movement of differentiating and determining itself and of resolving its different moments into a complex, differentiated *unity*.

When the concept or notion is thought not just as such, but as determining itself to be a real, objective world, it is thought as fully self-determining and self-objectifying *reason* or absolute *Idea*: 'that which is objectively *true, or the true as such*'.[11] This Idea, according to Hegel, freely 'releases' or 'discloses' itself (*entschließt sich*) as nature. Nature, in other words, is simply that which being-as-Idea discloses itself actually *to be*. It is actually *existing* reason or Idea.[12] The lesson of the *Science of Logic* is thus that being is in truth not merely an indeterminate abstraction, but the concrete, rational realm of space and time.

The passages in Part III are taken from G. W. F. Hegel, *The Encyclopaedia Logic. Part 1 of the Encyclopaedia of the Philosophical Sciences with the Zusätze*, translated by T. F. Geraets, W. A. Suchting and H. S. Harris (Indianapolis: Hackett Publishing, 1991), and from G. W. F. Hegel, *Science of Logic*, translated by A. V. Miller, foreword by J. N. Findlay (Atlantic Highlands, NJ: Humanities Press International, 1989). For the German text of these passages, see G. W. F. Hegel, *Werke in zwanzig Bänden*, edited by E. Moldenhauer and K. M. Michel, 20 vols and Index (Frankfurt: Suhrkamp Verlag, 1969ff), vols 5, 6 and 8. The passages from the *Encyclopaedia Logic* marked 'Addition' are not by Hegel himself, but were compiled by Leopold von Henning, the editor of the 1840 edition, from transcripts of Hegel's lectures on logic made by his students. The numbered paragraphs and the remarks from the *Encyclopaedia*, as well as the text of the *Science of Logic*, were written by Hegel himself.

Logic

Notes

1 *Hegel: The Letters*, p. 258.
2 Hegel, *The Encyclopaedia Logic*, p. 81 (§ 41). See below, p. 153.
3 Hegel, *The Encyclopaedia Logic*, p. 124 (§ 78). See below, p. 168.
4 Hegel, *Science of Logic*, p. 82. See below, p. 187.
5 F. W. J. von Schelling, *On the History of Modern Philosophy*, translation, introduction and notes by Andrew Bowie (Cambridge: Cambridge University Press, 1994), p. 141.
6 J. Derrida, *Glas*, translated by J. P. Leavey, Jr. and R. Rand (Lincoln: University of Nebraska Press, 1986), p. 201.
7 G. Deleuze, *Difference and Repetition*, translated by P. Patton (London: Athlone Press, 1994), p. xx.
8 Hegel, *Science of Logic*, p. 398. See below, p. 218.
9 Hegel, *Science of Logic*, p. 400. See below, p. 219.
10 Hegel, *Science of Logic*, p. 603. See below, p. 246.
11 Hegel, *Science of Logic*, p. 755. See below, p. 246.
12 Hegel, *Science of Logic*, p. 843. See below, pp. 249–50.

11

Encyclopaedia Logic: Introduction

§ 1

Philosophy lacks the advantage, which the other sciences enjoy, of being able to *presuppose* its *ob-jects* as given immediately by representation.[1] And, with regard to its beginning and advance, it cannot *presuppose* the *method* of cognition as one that is already accepted. It is true that it does, initially, have its ob-jects in common with religion. Both of them have the *truth* in the highest sense of the word as their ob-ject, for both hold that *God* and God *alone* is the truth. Both of them also go on to deal with the realm of the finite, with *nature* and the *human spirit*, and with their relation to each other and to God as to their truth. Hence, philosophy can, of course, presuppose some *familiarity* with its ob-jects; in fact it *must* presuppose this, as well as an interest in these ob-jects. The reason is that in the order of time consciousness produces *representations* [*Vorstellungen*] of ob-jects before it produces *concepts* [*Begriffe*] of them; and that the *thinking* spirit only advances to thinking cognition and comprehension by going *through* representation and by converting itself *to* it.

But when we consider something in thought, we soon become aware that thoughtful consideration implies the requirement that the *necessity* of its content should be shown, and the very being, as well as the determinations, of its ob-jects should be proved. As a result, the familiarity with these ob-jects that was mentioned above is seen to be insufficient, and making – or granting the validity of – *presuppositions* and *assurances*, is seen to be inadmissible. The difficulty of making a beginning arises immediately, because a beginning (being something *immediate*) does make a presupposition or, rather, it is itself just that.

§ 2

To begin with, philosophy can be determined in general terms as a *thinking consideration* of ob-jects. But if it is correct (as indeed it is), that the *human being* distinguishes itself from the lower animals by thinking, then everything human is human because it is brought about through thinking, and for that reason alone. Now, since philosophy is a peculiar mode of thinking – a mode by which thinking becomes cognition, and conceptually comprehensive cognition at that – philosophical thinking will also be *diverse* from the thinking that is active in everything human and brings about the very humanity of what is human, even though it is also identical with this thinking, and *in-itself* there is only *One* thinking. This distinction is connected with the fact that the human import of consciousness, which is based on thinking, does not *appear in the form of thought* straightaway, but as feeling, intuition, representation – which are *forms* that have to be distinguished from thinking *itself as form*. [R]²

§ 3

Whatever kind it may be, the *content* that fills our consciousness is what makes up the *determinacy* of our feelings, intuitions, images and representations, of our purposes, duties, etc., and of our thoughts and concepts. Hence feeling, intuition, image, etc., are *the forms* of this content, a content that remains *one and the same*, whether it be felt, intuited, represented or willed, and whether it be *only* felt, or felt, intuited, etc., with an admixture of thought, or whether it is thought quite *without any admixture*. In any one of these forms or in a mixture of several of them, the content is *ob-ject* of our consciousness. But in this ob-jectivity the *determinacies of these forms join themselves onto the content*; with the result that each of these forms seems to give rise to a particular ob-ject, and that what is in-itself the same can look like a diverse content.

Remark: Since the determinacies of feeling, of intuition, of desire, of willing, etc., are generally called *representations*, inasmuch as we have *knowledge* of them, it can be said in general that philosophy puts *thoughts* and *categories*, but more precisely *concepts*, in the place of representations. Representations in general [or 'notions']³ can be regarded as *metaphors* of thoughts and concepts. But that we have these notions does not mean that we are aware of their significance for thinking, i.e., that we have the thoughts and concepts of them. Conversely, it is one thing to have thoughts and concepts, and another to know what the representations, intuitions and feelings are that correspond to them. – One side of what is called *the unintelligibility* of philosophy is related to this. The difficulty lies partly in the inability (which in-itself is just a *lack of practice*) to think abstractly, i.e., to hold on to pure thoughts and to move about in them. In our ordinary consciousness thoughts are affected by and united with the sensible and spiritual material with which we are familiar; and in thinking about something, in reflecting and arguing about it, we *mix* feelings, intuitions and representations with thoughts. (Categories, like *being*, or *singularity*, are already mingled into every proposition, even when it has a completely sensible content: 'This leaf *is* green.') But it is a very different thing to make the thoughts themselves, unmixed with anything else, into ob-jects. – The other aspect of the unintelligibility of philosophy is an impatient wish to have before us, in the mode of representation, what is in our consciousness as thought and concept. There is a saying that, when we have grasped a concept, we still do not know what to *think* with it. But there is nothing to be thought with a concept save the concept itself. What this saying means, however, is that we long for an *ordinary notion*, one that we are already *familiar* with; consciousness feels as if, together with the mode of representation, the very ground, where it stands solidly and is at home, has been pulled from under it. Finding itself displaced into the pure realm of the concept, it does not know *where* in the world it is. – Hence the writers, preachers, orators, etc., who tell their readers or listeners things that they already knew by heart, things that are familiar to them and even *self-explanatory*, are the ones that are most readily 'understood'.

§ 4

In its relation to our ordinary consciousness, philosophy would first have to show *the need* for its *peculiar mode of cognition*, or even to awaken this need. But in relation to the ob-jects of religion, i.e., to *truth* altogether, it would have to prove that we have the *ability* to reach their cognition on our own; and in relation to any *diversity* that comes to light between *religious* notions and its own diverging determinations, it would have to *justify* the latter.

§ 5

In order to reach a provisional agreement about the distinction that has been mentioned and the insight connected with it, namely, that the genuine *content* of our consciousness is *preserved* when it is translated into the form of thought and the concept, and even that it is not placed in its proper light until then, we can conveniently call to mind another *old prejudice*. This prejudgement holds that, when we want to experience what is *true* in ob-jects and occurrences, as well as in feelings, intuitions, opinions, notions, etc., then we must *think them over* [*nachdenken*]. And the very least that this thinking-over does in any case is to change our feelings, and notions, etc. into *thoughts*. [R]

§ 6

It is equally important, on the other hand, that philosophy should be quite clear about the fact that its content is nothing other than the basic import that is originally produced and produces itself in the domain of the living spirit, the content that is made into the *world*, the outer and inner world of consciousness; in other words, the content of philosophy is *actuality*. The first consciousness of this content is called *experience*. Within the broad realm of outer and inner thereness, a judicious consideration of the world already distinguishes that which is only *appearance*, transient and insignificant, from that which truly and in itself merits the name of *actuality*. Since philosophy is distinguished only in form from other ways of becoming conscious of this same identical import, its accord with actuality and experience is necessary. Indeed, this accord can be viewed as an outward touchstone, at least, for the truth of a philosophy; just as it has to be seen as the supreme and ultimate purpose of science to bring about the reconciliation of the reason that is conscious of itself with the reason that *is*, or actuality, through the cognition of this accord.

> *Remark*:   In the *Preface* to my *Philosophy of Right* [. . .] the following propositions will be found:
>
> > *What is rational, is actual,*
> > *and what is actual, is rational.*[4]

These simple propositions have seemed shocking to many and they have been attacked, even by those who are not ready to renounce the possession of philosophy, and certainly not that of religion. In the present context, we do not need to discuss religion, since the doctrines of the divine governance of the world express these propositions quite definitely. But as far as their philosophical meaning is concerned, we have to presuppose that the reader has enough education to know, not just that God is actual – that he is what is most actual, that he alone is genuinely actual – but also (with regard to the formal aspect) that quite generally, what is there is partly *appearance* and only partly actuality. In common life people may happen to call every brain wave, error, evil and suchlike 'actual', as well as every existence, however wilted and transient it may be. But even for our ordinary feeling, a contingent existence does not deserve to be called something-actual in the emphatic sense of the word; what contingently exists has no greater value than that which something-*possible* has; it is an existence which (although it is) can just as well *not be*. But when I speak of actuality, one should, of course, think about the sense in which I use this expression, given the fact that I dealt with actuality too in a quite elaborate *Logic*, and I distinguished it quite clearly and directly, not just from what is contingent, even though it has existence too, but also, more precisely, from being-there, from existence, and from other determinations.[5]

The notion that ideas and ideals are nothing but chimeras, and that philosophy is a system of pure phantasms, sets itself at once against the *actuality of what is rational*; but, conversely, the notion that ideas and ideals are something far too excellent to have actuality, or equally something too impotent to achieve actuality, is opposed to it as well. However, the severing of actuality from the Idea is particularly dear to the understanding, which regards its dreams (i.e., its abstractions) as something genuine, and is puffed up about the 'ought' that it likes to prescribe, especially in the political field – as if the world had had to wait for it, in order to learn how it ought to be, but is not. If the world were the way it ought to be, what then would become of the pedantic wisdom of the understanding's 'ought to be'? When the understanding turns against trivial, external and perishable ob-jects, institutions, situations, etc., with its 'ought' – ob-jects that may have a great relative importance for a certain time, and for particular circles – it may very well be in the right; and in such cases it may find much that does not correspond to correct universal determinations. Who is not smart enough to be able to see around him quite a lot that is not, in fact, how it ought to be? But this smartness is wrong when it has the illusion that, in its dealings with ob-jects of this kind and with their 'ought', it is operating within the [true] concerns of philosophical science. This science deals only with the Idea – which is not so impotent that it merely ought to be, and is not actual – and further with an actuality of which those ob-jects, institutions and situations are only the superficial outer rind.

§ 14

The same development of thinking that is presented in the history of philosophy is presented in philosophy itself, but freed from that historical outwardness, i.e., purely in the element of thinking. Free and genuine thought is inwardly *concrete*; hence it is *Idea*, and in all its universality it is *the* Idea or *the Absolute*. The science of it is essentially a *system*, since what is *concretely* true is so only in its inward self-unfolding and in taking and holding itself together in unity, i.e., as *totality*. Only through the distinguishing and determination of its distinctions, can what is concretely true be the necessity of these distinctions and the freedom of the whole.

> *Remark*: A philosophizing *without system* cannot be scientific at all; apart from the fact that philosophizing of this kind expresses on its own account a more subjective disposition, it is contingent with regard to its content. A content has its justification only as a moment of the whole, outside of which it is only an unfounded presupposition or a subjective certainty. Many philosophical writings restrict themselves like this – to the mere utterance of *dispositions* and *opinions*. – It is erroneous to understand by 'system' a philosophy whose principle is restricted and [kept] distinct from other principles; on the contrary, it is the principle of genuine philosophy to contain all particular principles within itself.

§ 15

Each of the parts of philosophy is a philosophical whole, a circle that closes upon itself; but in each of them the philosophical Idea is in a particular determinacy or element. Every single circle also breaks through the restriction of its element as well, precisely because it is inwardly [the] totality, and it grounds a further sphere. The whole presents itself therefore as a circle of circles, each of which is a necessary moment, so that the system of its peculiar elements constitutes the whole Idea – which equally appears in each single one of them.

§ 16

As an *Encyclopaedia*, science is not presented in the detailed development of its particularization; instead, it has to be restricted to the beginnings and the fundamental concepts of the particular sciences. [R]

Notes

1 The translators of *The Encyclopaedia Logic* use the hyphenated word 'ob-ject' to render the German word 'Gegenstand'. They translate 'Objekt' with 'object'. See *The Encyclopaedia Logic*, p. xxii. Material in square brackets in the passages from both *The Encyclopaedia Logic* and the *Science of Logic*, with one or two exceptions, has been added by the respective translators. [s.h.]

2 [R] indicates that the remark to a paragraph has been omitted. The remarks were written by Hegel himself. [s.h.]

3 The translators of *The Encyclopaedia Logic* use the word 'notion' (together with 'representation') to render the German word 'Vorstellung'. They do not follow Miller and use 'notion' to translate the word 'Begriff', but render that with 'concept'. [s.h.]

4 See Hegel, *Elements of the Philosophy of Right*, p. 20. See below, p. 325. [s.h.]

5 See Hegel, *Science of Logic*, pp. 541–53 (not included in this collection). [s.h.]

12

Encyclopaedia Logic: Preliminary Conception

§ 19

The Logic is the science of *the pure Idea*, that is, of the Idea in the abstract element of *thinking*.

> *Remark*: [. . .] The Logic is the *most difficult* science, inasmuch as it has to do, not with [sensible] intuitions nor even, like geometry, with abstract sense-representations, but with pure abstractions, and inasmuch as it requires a trained ability at withdrawing into pure thought, holding onto it and moving within it. It could, on the other hand, be viewed as the *easiest* science, because its content is nothing but our own thinking and its ordinary determinations, and because these are both the *simplest* and *what is elementary*. They are also what we are *most familiar* with: being, nothing, etc.; determinacy, magnitude, etc.; being-in-itself, being-for-itself, one, many and so on. But this familiarity only tends to make the study of the Logic more difficult. For one thing, we are prone to believe that it is not worthwhile to occupy oneself any further with what is so familiar. On the other hand, what we have to do is to become familiar with it in a way that is quite other than, and even opposed to, the one in which we are already used to it. [. . .] [A1–3][1]

§ 20

If we take thinking according to the most obvious notion of it, then it appears (α) first in its ordinary subjective significance, as one spiritual activity or faculty *side by side* with others such as sensation, intuition, imagination, etc., desire, volition, etc. What it *produces*, the determinacy or form of thought, is the *universal*, the abstract in general. Thus, *thinking* as an *activity* is the *active* universal, and indeed the *self*-actuating universal, since the act, or what is brought forth, is precisely the universal. Thinking represented as a *subject* is *that which thinks*, and the simple expression for the existing subject as thinker is '*I*'.

Remark: [. . .] Already in this preliminary exposition, we are speaking
of the distinction between the sensible, representation, and thought;
this distinction is altogether decisive for our grasp of the nature and the
kinds of cognition; so it will clarify matters if we call attention to this
distinction already at this point. – To elucidate the *sensible* we refer first
to its external origin, to the senses of sense organs. But simply naming
the organ does not give us the determination of what we apprehend
with it. The distinction of the *sensible* from thought is to be located in
the fact that the determination of the sensible is *singularity*, and since
the singular (in quite abstract terms, the atom) stands also within a
context, the sensible is a [realm of] mutual *externality* whose proximate
abstract forms are *juxtaposition* and *succession*. – *Representation* has sensible material of this kind as its content; but it is posited in the determination of its being *mine* – that the represented content is in *me* – and
of its *universality*, of its self-relation, or of its *simplicity*. – Apart from the
sensible, however, representation also has material that has sprung
from self-conscious thinking as its content, such as the notion of what
is right, of what is ethical or religious, and also of thinking itself; and
it is not very easy to see where the distinction between these *representations* and the *thoughts* of those contents is to be located. Here the
content is a thought, and the form of universality is present too, for
that form already belongs to a content as being in *me*, or, quite generally, as being a representation. The peculiarity of representation, however, is in general to be located in this fact also – that the content in it
stands at the same time in isolation. 'Right' and juridical and other
similar determinations certainly do not stand in the sensible mutual
externality of *space*. They do appear somehow in time, one after the
other; but their content is not itself represented as affected by time, as
passing away and changing in it. Nevertheless, these determinations,
which are in themselves spiritual, stand at the same time *in isolation*
upon the broad field of the inner, abstract universality of representation in general. In this isolation they are *simple*: right, duty, God.
Representation either sticks to the claim that right is right, God is God,
or, (at a more cultivated level) it points out determinations, such as that
God is the Creator of the world, that he is all-wise, almighty, etc. Here,
too, several isolated and simple determinations are strung together; but
they remain external to each other, in spite of the link that is allotted
to them in their subject. In this respect, representation agrees with the
understanding [*Verstand*], which is only distinct from it because it posits
relationships of universal and particular, or of cause and effect, etc.,
and therefore necessary relations between the isolated determinations
of representation – whereas representation leaves them *side by side*, in
its undetermined space, linked only by the simple 'and'. – The distinction between representation and thought is all the more important
because we can say in general that philosophy does nothing but transform

representations into thoughts – although, of course, it does go on to transform the mere thought into the Concept. [. . .] [A]

§ 21

(β) When thinking is taken as active with regard to ob-jects, as the *thinking-over* of something, then the universal – as the product of this activity – contains the value of the *matter*, what is *essential, inner, true*. [R] [A]

§ 22

(γ) Thinking it over *changes* something in the way in which the content is at first [given] in sensation, intuition or representation; thus, it is only *through the mediation* of an alteration that the *true* nature of the *ob-ject* comes into consciousness. [A]

§ 23

Because it is equally the case that in this thinking-over the genuine nature [of the ob-ject] comes to light, and that this thinking is *my* activity, this true nature is also the *product of my* spirit, [of me] as thinking subject. It is mine according to my simple universality as [universality] of the 'I' *being* simply *at home with itself*, or it is the product of my *freedom*.

> *Remark:* We often hear the expression 'thinking for oneself', as if it meant something important. But in fact one cannot think for someone else, any more than one can eat or drink for him; this expression is therefore a pleonasm. – Thinking immediately involves *freedom*, because it is the activity of the universal, a self-relating that is therefore abstract, a being-with-itself that is undetermined in respect of subjectivity, and which in respect of its *content* is, at the same time, only in the *matter* [itself] and in its determinations. So when one speaks of humility or modesty, and of arrogance, with reference to the doing of philosophy, and when this humility or modesty consists in not attributing any *particularity* of feature or agency to one's subjectivity, then philosophizing has to be absolved from arrogance at least, since thinking is only genuine with respect to its content in so far as it is immersed in the *matter* [*Sache*], and with respect to its form in so far as it is not a *particular* being or doing of the subject, but consists precisely in this, that consciousness conducts itself as an abstract 'I', as *freed* from *all particularity* of features, states, etc., and does only what is universal, in which it is identical with all individuals. – When Aristotle summons us to consider ourselves as *worthy* of conduct of this sort, then the worthiness that consciousness ascribes to itself consists precisely in the giving up of our *particular* opinions and beliefs and in allowing the *matter* [itself] to hold sway over us.[2]

§ 24

In accordance with these determinations, thoughts can be called *objective* thoughts; and among them the forms which are considered initially in ordinary logic and which are usually taken to be only forms of *conscious* thinking have to be counted too. Thus *logic* coincides with *metaphysics*, with the science of *things* grasped in *thoughts* that used to be taken to express the *essentialities* of the *things*. [R] [A1–3]

§ 25

The expression *objective thoughts* signifies the *truth* which ought to be the absolute *ob-ject*, not just the *goal* of philosophy. But at the same time this expression indicates in any case an antithesis – indeed, the very one whose determination and validity is the focus of our philosophical interest at the present time, and around which the quest for *truth* and for the cognition of it revolves. If the thought-determinations are afflicted with a fixed antithesis, i.e., if they are only of a *finite* nature, then they are inadequate to the truth which is absolutely in and for itself, and the truth cannot enter into thinking. The thinking that brings forth only *finite* determinations and moves within these alone is called *understanding* (in the more precise sense of the word). The *finitude* of the thought-determinations has further to be taken in two ways: first, they are *only subjective* and are permanently in antithesis to the objective; secondly, being quite generally of *limited content*, they persist both in their antithesis to each other, and (even more) in their antithesis to the Absolute. As a further introduction, we now ought to consider the *positions available to thinking with respect to objectivity*, in order to clarify the meaning of the Logic and to lead into the standpoint that is here given to it.

> *Remark*: In my *Phenomenology of Spirit,* which was for this reason described, when it was published, as the first part of the system of science, the procedure adopted was to begin from the first and simplest appearance of the spirit, from *immediate consciousness*, and to develop its dialectic right up to the standpoint of philosophical science, the necessity of which is shown by the progression. But for this purpose it was not possible to stick to the formal aspect of mere consciousness; for the standpoint of philosophical knowing is at the same time inwardly the richest in basic import and the most concrete one; so when it emerged as the result [of the development], it presupposed also the concrete shapes of consciousness, such as morality, ethical life, art and religion. Hence, the development of the *content*, or of the subject-matters of special parts of philosophical science, falls directly within that development of consciousness which seems at first to be restricted just to what is formal; that development has to take place behind the back of

consciousness so to speak, inasmuch as the content is related to consciousness as what is *in-itself*. This makes the presentation more complicated, and what belongs to the concrete parts [of the System] already falls partly within that introduction. – The examination that will be undertaken here has the even greater inconvenience that it can only be conducted descriptively [*historisch*] and argumentatively; but its principal aim is to contribute to the insight that the questions about the nature of *cognition*, about *faith* and so on, that confront us in the [realm of] representation, and which we take to be fully *concrete*, are in point of fact reducible to *simple* determinations of thought, which only get their genuine treatment in the Logic.

A) The First Position of Thought with Respect to Objectivity

Metaphysics

§ 26

The first position is the *naïve* way of proceeding, which, being still unconscious of the antithesis of thinking within and against itself, contains the *belief* that *truth* is [re]cognized, and what the objects genuinely are is brought before consciousness, through *thinking about* them. In this belief, thinking goes straight to the ob-jects; it reproduces the content of sense-experience and intuition out of itself, as a content of thought, and is satisfied with this as the truth. All philosophy in its beginnings, all of the sciences, even the daily doing and dealing of consciousness, lives in this belief.

§ 27

Because it is unconscious of its antithesis, this thinking *can*, in respect of its basic import, equally well be authentic *speculative* philosophizing; but it can also dwell within *finite* thought-determinations, i.e., within the *still unresolved* antithesis. Here, in the introduction, our concern can only be to consider this position of thinking with regard to its limit; so we shall begin by taking up this [finite] way of *philosophizing*. – In its most determinate development, which is also the one closest to us, this way of thinking was the *metaphysics of the recent past*, the way it was constituted among us before the Kantian philosophy. It is only in relation to the history of philosophy, however, that this metaphysics *belongs to the past*; for, on its own account, it is always present as the way in which the *mere understanding views* the ob-jects of reason. Hence, a closer examination of its procedure and its principal content has this more directly present interest for us too.

§ 28

This science regarded the thought-determinations as the *fundamental determinations of things*; and, in virtue of this presupposition, that the cognition of things as they are *in-themselves* results from the *thinking* of what *is*, it stood at a higher level than the later critical philosophizing. But two points should be noted. First, these determinations, in their abstraction, were taken to be valid on their own account, and capable of being *predicates of what is true*. In any case, this metaphysics presupposed that cognition of the Absolute could come about through the *attaching of predicates to it*; and it investigated neither the peculiar content and validity of the determinations of the understanding, nor yet this form of determining the Absolute by attaching predicates to it.

> *Remark*: *Being there* [*Dasein*] for instance, is a predicate of this kind like in the proposition, 'God is there'; or *finitude* and *infinity*, in the question whether the world is finite or infinite; or *simple* and *composite*, in the proposition, 'The soul is *simple*'; – or, again, 'The thing is *one*, a *whole*', etc. – There was no investigation of whether predicates of this kind are something true in and for themselves, nor of whether the form of the judgement could be the form of truth.

Addition: The presupposition of the older metaphysics was that of naïve belief generally, namely, that thinking grasps what things are *in-themselves*, that things only are what they genuinely are when they are [captured] in thought. Nature and the mind and heart of man are protean, constantly in a process of transformation, and the reflection that things as they immediately present themselves are not the things in themselves is an obvious one. – The standpoint of the older metaphysics referred to here is the opposite of the one that resulted from the Critical Philosophy. We can fairly say that this latter standpoint sends man to feed upon husks and chaff.

But, to be more precise about the procedure of the older metaphysics, we should note that it did not go beyond the thinking of mere *understanding*. It took up the abstract determinations of thought immediately, and let them count in their immediacy as predicates of what is true. When we are discussing thinking we must distinguish *finite* thinking, the thinking of the mere *understanding*, from the *infinite* thinking of *reason*. Taken in isolation, just as they are immediately given, the thought-determinations are *finite* determinations. But what is true is what is infinite within itself; it cannot be expressed and brought to consciousness through what is finite.

If we adhere to the modern notion that thinking is always restricted, then the expression 'infinite thinking' may appear quite astonishing. But, in fact, thinking is inwardly and essentially infinite. To put the point formally, 'finite' means whatever comes to an end, what *is*, but ceases to be where it connects with its other, and is thus restricted by it. Hence, the finite subsists in its relation to its other, which is its negation and presents itself as its limit. But thinking is at home with itself, it relates itself to itself, and is its own ob-ject. In so far as my ob-ject is a thought, I am at home with myself. Thus the I, or thinking, is infinite because it is related in thinking to an ob-ject that is itself. An ob-ject as such is an other, something negative that confronts me. But if thinking thinks itself, then it has an ob-ject that is at the same time not an ob-ject, i.e., an ob-ject that is sublated, ideal. Thus thinking as such, thinking in its purity, does not have any restriction within itself.

Thinking is only finite in so far as it stays within restricted determinations, which it holds to be ultimate. Infinite or speculative thinking, on the contrary, makes determinations likewise, but, in determining, in limiting, it sublates this defect again. Infinity must not be interpreted as an abstract, ever-receding beyond (the way it is in our ordinary notion of it), but in the simple manner specified above.

The thinking of the older metaphysics was *finite*, because that metaphysics moved in thought-determinations whose restrictions counted for it as something fixed, that would not be negated again. Thus, the question was asked, 'Does *thereness* belong to God?' and 'being-there' was thus treated as something purely positive, something ultimate and excellent. But we shall see later that *being-there* is in no way a merely positive determination, but one that is too lowly for the Idea, and unworthy of God. – Or again, the question of the finitude or infinity of the world was raised. Here infinity is sharply contrasted with finitude, yet it is easy to see that if the two are set against one another, then infinity, which is nevertheless supposed to be the whole, appears as *one* side only, and is limited by the finite.

But a limited infinity is itself only something finite. In the same sense the question was raised whether the soul is simple or composite. Thus simplicity, too, was counted as an ultimate determination, capable of grasping what is true. But 'simple' is a determination just as poor, abstract and one-sided as 'being-there', a determination which, as we shall see later, is incapable of grasping what is true because it is itself untrue. If the soul is considered only as simple, then it is determined as one-sided and finite by an abstraction of that kind.

Thus, the older metaphysics was concerned with the cognition of whether predicates of the kind here mentioned could be attached to its ob-jects. However, these predicates are restricted determinations of the understanding which express only a restriction, and not what is true. – We must notice particularly, at this point, that the metaphysical method was to 'attach' predicates to the ob-ject of cognition, e.g., to God. This then is an external reflection about the ob-ject, since the determinations (the predicates) are found ready-made in my representation, and are attached to the ob-ject in a merely external way. Genuine cognition of an ob-ject, on the other hand, has to be *such* that the ob-ject determines itself from within itself, and does not acquire its predicates in this external way. If we proceed by way of predication, the spirit gets the feeling that the predicates cannot exhaust what they are attached to.

From this point of view, therefore, the Orientals are quite right to call God the being who is Many-Named or Infinitely Named. Our mind and heart find no satisfaction in any of those finite determinations, so that the Oriental cognition consists in a restless seeking out of such predicates. In the case of finite things it is certainly true that they must be determined by means of finite predicates, and here the understanding with its activity has its proper place. Being itself finite, the understanding is cognizant only of the nature of the finite. Thus, if I call an action a 'theft', for instance, the action is thereby determined with regard to its essential content, and to [re]cognize this is sufficient for the judge. In the same way, finite things behave as 'cause' and 'effect', as 'force' and 'utterance', and when they are grasped according to these determinations, they are known in their finitude. But the ob-jects of reason cannot be determined through such finite predicates, and the attempt to do this was the defect of the older metaphysics.

§ 29

Predicates of this kind are, on their own account, a *restricted* content, and they show themselves to be inappropriate to the *fullness* of the *representation* (of God, nature, spirit, etc.) which they do not at all exhaust. Moreover, although they are connected with each other because they are predicates of One subject, they are nevertheless diverse through their content, so that they are taken up from *outside* and *in opposition to one another*. [R]

§ 30

Secondly, the ob-jects of this metaphysics were, it is true, totalities that belong in and for themselves to *reason*, to the thinking of the inwardly *concrete* universal: the *soul*, the *world, God*. But this metaphysics took them from *representation*, and when it applied the determinations-of-the-understanding to them, it grounded itself upon them, as *ready-made or given subjects*, and its only *criterion* of whether the predicates fitted, and were satisfactory or not, was that representation.

§ 31

The representations of the soul, of the world, of God, seem at first to provide thinking with a *firm hold*. But apart from the fact that the character of a particular subjectivity is mingled with them, and that therefore they can have a most diverse significance, what they need all the more is to receive their firm determination only through thinking. Every proposition expresses this need, because in it *what* the subject, i.e., the initial representation, is ought only to be indicated by the *predicate* (that is to say, in philosophy, by the thought-determination).

> *Remark*: In the proposition 'God *is* eternal, etc', we begin with the representation 'God'; but what he *is*, is not yet *known*; only the predicate states expressly what he *is*. In logical thinking, therefore, where the content is only and exclusively determined in the form of thought, it is first of all superfluous to make these determinations into predicates of propositions whose *subject* is God, or more vaguely the Absolute, and in addition there is the disadvantage that doing this sends us back to a criterion other than the nature of thought itself. – In any case, the form of the proposition, or more precisely that of the judgement, is incapable of expressing what is concrete (and what is true is concrete) and speculative; because of its form, the judgement is one-sided and to that extent false.

Addition: This metaphysics was not a free and objective thinking, for it did not allow the ob-ject to determine itself freely from within, but presupposed it as ready-made.

– As for free thinking, Greek philosophy thought freely, but Scholasticism did not, since, like this metaphysics, it adopted its content as something given, and indeed given by the Church. [...]

§ 32

Thirdly, this metaphysics became *dogmatism* because, given the nature of finite determinations, it had to assume that of *two opposed assertions* (of the kind that those propositions were) one must be *true*, and the other *false*.

Addition: *Dogmatism* has its first antithesis in *scepticism*. The ancient Sceptics gave the general name of 'dogmatism' to any philosophy that sets up definite theses. In this wider sense scepticism also counted properly speculative philosophy as dogmatic. But in the narrower sense dogmatism consists in adhering to one-sided determinations of the understanding while excluding their opposites. This is just the strict 'either-or', according to which (for instance) the world is *either* finite *or* infinite, but *not both*. On the contrary, what is genuine and speculative is precisely what does not have any such one-sided determination in it, and is therefore not exhausted by it; on the contrary, being a totality, it contains the determinations that dogmatism holds to be fixed and true in a state of separation from one another united within itself.

It often happens in philosophy that a one-sided view sets itself up beside the totality, claiming to be something particular and fixed *vis-à-vis* the latter. But, in fact, what is one-sided is not fixed and does not subsist on its own account; instead, it is contained within the whole as sublated. The dogmatism of the metaphysics of the understanding consists in its adherence to one-sided thought-determinations in their isolation, whereas the idealism of speculative philosophy involves the principle of totality and shows itself able to overgrasp the one-sidedness of the abstract determinations of the understanding. Thus, idealism will say, 'The soul is neither *just* finite nor *just* infinite, but is essentially *both* the one *and* the other, and hence *neither* the one *nor* the other'. In other words, these determinations are not valid when they are isolated from one another but only when sublated.

This idealism occurs even in our ordinary consciousness too. Accordingly, we say of sensible things that they are alterable, i.e., that they are and that they are not. – Regarding the determinations of the understanding we are more stubborn. As thought-determinations they count as more fixed, and indeed as fixed absolutely. We regard them as separated from one another by an infinite abyss, so that determinations that stand opposed to one another are never able to reach each other. The struggle of reason consists precisely in overcoming what the understanding has made rigid.

§ 33

In its orderly shape this metaphysics had, as its *first part*, Ontology, the doctrine of the *abstract determinations of essence*. In their manifoldness and finite validity, these determinations lack a principle; they must therefore be enumerated *empirically* and *contingently*, and their more precise *content* can only be based upon *representation*, [i.e.,] based upon the *assurance* that by one word one thinks precisely this, or perhaps also upon the word's etymology. What can be at issue in this context is merely the *correctness* of the analysis as it corresponds with the usage of language, and the empirical *exhaustiveness*, not the *truth* and *necessity* of these determinations in and for themselves.

> *Remark*:   The question whether being, being-there, or finitude, simplicity, compositeness, etc., are *concepts that are in and for themselves true*, must be surprising, if one is of the opinion that one can speak only of the truth *of a proposition*, and that the only question that can be raised with regard to a *concept* is whether (as people say) it can be truthfully '*attached*' to a subject or not. Untruth would depend on the contradiction to be found between the subject of the representation and the concept to be predicated of it. But since the Concept is something-concrete, and since it is itself every determinacy without exception, it is essentially, and within itself, a unity of distinct determinations. So, if truth were nothing more than lack of contradiction, one would have to examine first of all, with regard to each concept, whether it does not, on its own account, contain an inner contradiction of this kind.

§ 34

The *second part* was *Rational Psychology* or *Pneumatology*. This is concerned with the metaphysical nature of the *soul*, that is to say, of the spirit [taken] as a *thing*. [R]

Addition: [. . .] The older metaphysics considered the soul as a thing. But 'thing' is a very ambiguous expression. By a thing we understand first of all something that exists immediately, so that we have a sensible representation of it, and people have spoken of the soul in this way. The question has been raised therefore of where the soul has its seat. But if the soul has a seat, then it is in space, and is represented in a sensible way. And when we ask whether the soul is simple or composite, the same way of interpreting it as a thing is involved. This was a specially important question in connection with the immortality of the soul, which was considered to be conditional upon the simplicity of the soul. But, in fact, abstract simplicity is a determination that no more corresponds to the essence of the soul than compositeness.

As for the relationship between rational and empirical psychology, the first stands higher than the second in virtue of the fact that it sets itself the task of achieving the cognition of spirit through thought and of proving what it thinks as well; whereas empirical psychology starts from perception, and simply enumerates and describes what lies to hand there. If we want to grasp the spirit in thought, however, we must not be so coy about its particular characteristics. Spirit is activity in the sense in which the Schoolmen already said of God that he is absolute actuosity. The spirit's being active implies, however, that it manifests itself outwardly. Accordingly, it is not to be considered as an *ens* lacking all process, the way it was regarded in the older metaphysics, which separated a spirit's inwardness that lacked process from its outwardness. It is essential that the spirit be considered in its concrete actuality, in its energy, and more precisely in such a way that its utterances are recognized as being determined through its inwardness.

§ 35

The *third part, Cosmology*, dealt with the *world*, with its contingency, necessity and eternity, with its being limited in space and time, with the formal laws and their modifications, and further with the freedom of man and the origin of evil. [R]

Addition: [...] With regard to the way spirit appears in the world, the main questions raised in this cosmology were those concerning the freedom of man and the origin of evil. These are certainly questions of the highest interest; but to answer them in a satisfactory way, it is above all necessary not to cling to the abstract determinations of the understanding as if they were ultimate – as if each of the two terms of an antithesis could stand on its own, and were to be considered as something substantial and genuine in its isolation. This, however, was the standpoint of the older metaphysics, and also the general framework of these cosmological discussions. Because of this, they could not attain their purpose, namely, a comprehension of the phenomena of the world. The distinction between freedom and necessity was subjected to inquiry, for example, and these determinations were applied to nature and spirit in such a way that the operations of nature were considered to be subject to necessity, while those of spirit were free. This distinction is certainly essential, and it is grounded in the very core of spirit; but considered as abstractly confronting one another, freedom and necessity pertain to finitude only and are valid only on its soil. A freedom that had no necessity within it, and a mere necessity without freedom, are determinations that are abstract and hence untrue. Freedom is essentially concrete, eternally determinate within itself, and thus necessary at the same time. When people speak of necessity, it is usually initially understood as just determination from without; for instance, in finite mechanics, a body moves only when another body collides with it, and precisely in the direction imparted to it by this collision. This is a merely external necessity, however, not a genuinely inner necessity, for that is freedom.

The situation is the same with the antithesis between *good* and *evil* – one that is typical of the modern world, self-absorbed as it is. It is quite correct to consider evil as something that has a fixed character of its own, as something that is not the good – giving the antithesis its due – but only because its merely apparent and relative character should not be taken to mean that evil and good are all one in the Absolute, or, as it has lately been said, that evil is only something in the eye of the beholder. What is wrong here is that evil is looked on a something fixed and positive, whereas it is the negative that does not subsist on its own account, but only *wants* to be on its own account, and is in fact only the absolute semblance of inward negativity.

§ 36

The *fourth part, Natural* or *Rational Theology*, considered the concept of God or its possibility, the proof of his being-there and his attributes. [R]

Addition: The concern of this part of the older metaphysics was to establish how far reason could take us on its own account in the cognition of God. To have cognition of God through reason is certainly the highest task of science. Religion initially contains representations of God; these representations are communicated to us from our youth up as the doctrines of our religion, compiled in the Creed; and, in so far as the individual has faith in these teachings, and they are the truth for him, he has what he needs as a Christian. Theology, however, is the science of this faith. If theology provides a merely external enumeration and compilation of religious teachings, then it is not yet science. Even the merely historical treatment of its subject-matter that is in favour nowadays (for instance, the reporting of what this or that Church Father said) does not give theology a scientific character. Science comes only when we advance to the business of philosophy, i.e., the mode of thinking that involves comprehension. Thus, genuine theology is essentially, at the same time, Philosophy of Religion, and that is what it was in the Middle Ages too.

When we look more closely at the *Rational Theology* of the older metaphysics, we can see that it was a science of God that rested not upon *reason* but on the *understanding*, and its thinking moved only in abstract thought-determinations. While what was treated was the *concept* of God, it was the *representation* of God that formed the criterion for cognition. Thinking, however, must move freely within itself; all the same, it must be remarked at once that the result of this free thinking agrees with the content of the Christian religion, for the Christian religion is a revelation of reason. The rational theology of the older metaphysics, however, did not achieve any such agreement. Since it set out to determine the notion of God by means of thinking, what emerged as the concept of God was only the abstraction of positivity or reality in general, to the exclusion of negation, and God was accordingly defined as the *Supremely Real Essence*. But it is easy to see that, since negation was excluded from it, this Supremely Real Essence is precisely the opposite of what it should be and of what the understanding intended it to be. Instead of being what is richest, and utter fullness, it is instead rather the poorest, and utter emptiness – all on account of this abstract apprehension of it. The mind and heart rightly long for a concrete content, but concreteness is only present if the content contains within it determinacy, i.e., negation. When the concept of God is apprehended merely as that of the abstract or Supremely Real Essence, then God becomes for us a mere Beyond, and there can be no further talk of a cognition of God; for where there is no determinacy, no cognition is possible either. Pure light is pure darkness. [. . .]

If we cast another glance at the general procedure of this metaphysics in the light of our explanation, we find that it consisted in grasping the ob-jects of reason in abstract, finite determinations of the understanding, and making abstract identity into the [main] principle. But this infinity of the understanding, this pure Essence, is itself only something finite, for particularity is excluded from it, and this exclusion restricts and negates it. Instead of achieving concrete identity, this metaphysics held onto abstract identity; but what was good about it was the consciousness that thought alone constitutes the essentiality of what is. The material of this metaphysics was furnished by the earlier philosophers, and especially by the Scholastics. The understanding is, of course, one moment of speculative philosophy, but it is a moment at which we should not stop. Plato is not a metaphysician of this sort, and Aristotle still less so, although people usually believe the contrary.

B) The Second Position of Thought with Respect to Objectivity

I. Empiricism

§ 37

Empiricism was the initial result of a double need: there was the need first for a *concrete* content, as opposed to the abstract theories of the understanding that cannot advance from its universal generalizations to particularization and determination on its own, and secondly for a *firm hold* against the possibility of proving any claim at all in the field, and with the method, of the finite determinations. Instead of seeking what is true in thought itself, Empiricism proceeds to draw it from *experience*, from what is outwardly or inwardly present. [A]

§ 38

[. . .] On its *subjective* side, empirical cognition gets a firm hold from the fact that in perception consciousness has its *own immediate presence* and *certainty*.

> *Remark*:   In Empiricism there lies this great principle, that what is true must be in actuality and must be there for our perception. This principle is opposed to the 'ought' through which reflection inflates itself, and looks down upon what is actual and present in the name of a *Beyond* that can only have its place and thereness in the subjective understanding. Philosophy, like Empiricism, is cognizant [. . .] only of what *is*; it does not know that which only *ought* to be, and for that reason *is not there*. – On the subjective side we must recognize also the important principle of *freedom* that lies in Empiricism; namely, that what ought to count in our human knowing, we ought to see *for ourselves*, and to know *ourselves* as *present* in it. – But inasmuch as, so far as content is concerned, Empiricism restricts itself to what is finite, the *consistent* carrying through of its programme denies the supersensible altogether or at least its cognition and determinacy, and it leaves thinking with abstraction only, [i.e.,] with formal universality and identity. – The fundamental illusion in scientific empiricism is always that it uses the metaphysical categories of matter, force, as well as those of one, many, universality, and the infinite, etc., and it goes on to draw *conclusions*, guided by categories of this sort, presupposing and applying the forms of syllogizing in the process. It does all this without knowing that it thereby itself contains a metaphysics and is engaged in it, and that it is using those categories and their connections in a totally uncritical and unconscious manner. [A]

§39

In reflecting upon this principle it has been observed, to begin with, that in what is called 'experience' and what has to be distinguished from merely singular perceptions of single facts, there are *two* elements; one of them is the infinitely *manifold material* that isolates itself into single [bits] that stand on their own, the other is the *form*, the determinations of *universality* and *necessity*. It is true that empirical observation does show many perceptions of the same kind, even more than we can count; but universality is altogether something other than a great number. It is true that empirical observation also provides perceptions of alterations *that follow one after the other*, and of ob-jects that *lie side by side*; but it does not provide any *necessary* connection. Since, however, perception is to remain the foundation of what counts as truth, universality and necessity appear to be something *unjustified*, a subject-ive contingency, a mere habit, the content of which may be constituted the way it is or in some other way.

> *Remark*: An important consequence of this is that in this empirical approach juridical and ethical determinations and laws, as well as the content of religion, appear to be something contingent, and that their objectivity and inner truth have been given up.
>
> *Hume*'s scepticism, from which this reflective observation mainly starts, should be very carefully distinguished from *Greek scepticism*. In Humean scepticism, the *truth* of the empirical, the truth of feeling and intuition is taken as basic; and, on that basis, he attacks all universal determina-tions and laws, precisely because they have no justification by way of sense-perception. The old scepticism was so far removed from making feeling, or intuition, into the principle of truth that it turned itself against the sensible in the very first place instead. (Concerning modern scepticism as compared with ancient, see *Kritisches Journal der Philosophie*. Schelling and Hegel, eds., 1802, vol. 1, no. 2.)[3]

II. Critical philosophy

§ 40

Critical Philosophy has in common with Empiricism that it accepts experi-ence as the *only* basis for our cognitions; but it will not let them count as truths, but only as cognitions of appearances.

The distinction between the elements found in the analysis of experience – the *sensible material* and its *universal relations* – serves as the first starting-point. Combined with this we have the reflection (mentioned in the preced-ing paragraph [§ 39]) that only *what is singular* and only *what happens* are contained in perception [taken] on its own account. But at the same time, Critical Philosophy *holds on to the factum* that *universality* and *necessity*, being also essential determinations, are found to be present in what is called experience. And, because this element does not stem from the empirical as such, it belongs to the spontaneity of *thinking*, or is a priori. – The thought-determinations or *concepts of the understanding* make up *the objectivity* of the cognitions of experience. In general they contain *relations*, and hence *synthetic* a priori judgements (i.e., original relations of opposed terms) are formed by means of them. [R]

§ 41

First of all, the Critical Philosophy subjects to investigation the validity of the *concepts of the understanding* that are used in metaphysics, but also in the other sciences and in ordinary representation. This critique does not involve itself with the *content*, however, or with the determinate mutual relationship of these thought-determinations to each other; instead, it considers them according to the antithesis of *subjectivity* and *objectivity* in general. In the way that it is taken here, this antithesis relates to the distinction of the elements *within* experience (see the preceding paragraph [§ 40]). In this context 'objectivity' means the element of *universality* and *necessity*, i.e., of the thought-determinations themselves – the so-called a priori. But the Critical Philosophy extends the antithesis in such a way that experience *in its entirety* falls within *subjectivity*; i.e., both of these elements together are subjective, and nothing remains in contrast with subjectivity except the *thing-in-itself*.

The more detailed *forms* of the a priori, i.e., of thinking which, in spite of its objectivity, is interpreted as a merely subjective activity, are presented as follows – in a systematic order which, it may be remarked, rests only upon psychological-historical foundations.

Addition 1: Subjecting the determinations of the older metaphysics to investigation was without doubt a very important step. Naïve thinking went about unsuspectingly in the thought-determinations that were formed directly and spontaneously. No one asked, at that stage, to what extent these determinations would have value and validity [if taken] on their own account. We have already remarked earlier that thinking that is free is without presuppositions. By this standard, the thinking of the older metaphysics was not free, because, without further ado, it let its determinations count as something given in advance, or as an a priori, although reflection had not put them to the test.

By contrast, the Critical Philosophy set itself the task of investigating just how far the forms of thinking are in general capable of helping us reach the cognition of truth. More precisely, the faculty of cognition was to be investigated before cognition began. This certainly involves the correct insight that the forms of thinking themselves must be made the ob-ject of cognition; but there soon creeps in, too, the mistaken project of wanting to have cognition before we have any cognition, or of not wanting to go into the water before we have learned to swim. Certainly, the forms of thinking should not be used without investigation; but this process of investigation is itself a process of cognition. So the activity of the forms of thinking, and the critique of them, must be united within the process of cognition. The forms of thinking must be considered in and for themselves; they are the ob-ject and the activity of the ob-ject itself; they investigate themselves, [and] they must determine their own limits and point out their own defects. This is the same activity of thinking that will soon be taken into particular consideration under the name 'dialectic'; and we can only remark here, in a preliminary way, that it is not brought to bear on the thought-determinations from outside; on the contrary, it must be considered as dwelling within them.

The very first [task] in the Kantian philosophy, therefore, is for thinking to investigate how far it is capable of cognition. Nowadays we have gone beyond the Kantian philosophy, and everyone wants to go further. There are two ways of going further, however: one can go forward or backward. Looked at in the clear light of day, many of our philosophical endeavours are nothing but the (mistaken) procedure of the older metaphysics, an uncritical thinking on and on, of the kind that anyone can do.

Addition 2:   Kant's investigation of the thought-determinations suffers essentially from the defect that he did not consider them in and for themselves, but only to see whether they were *subjective* or *objective*. In ordinary language, to be 'objective' is to be present outside us and to come to us from outside through perception. Kant denied that the thought-determinations (cause and effect, for instance) were 'object-ive' in this sense, i.e., that they were given in perception; instead he regarded them as pertaining to our thinking itself or to the spontaneity of thinking, and so in *this* sense as subjective.

But all the same Kant calls the thought-product – and, to be precise, the universal and the necessary – 'objective', and what is only sensed, he calls 'subjective'. As a result, the linguistic usage mentioned above appears to have been stood on its head, and for that reason Kant has been charged with linguistic confusion. This, however, is a great injustice. More precisely, the situation is as follows: What ordinary consciousness is confronted with, what can be perceived by the senses (e.g., this animal, this star, etc.), appears to it as what subsists on its own account, or as what is independent. Thoughts, on the other hand, count for it as what is not self-standing, but rather dependent upon an other. In fact, however, what can be perceived by the senses is really secondary and not self-standing, while thoughts, on the contrary, are what is genuinely independent and primitive. It is in this sense that Kant called what measures up to thought (the universal and the necessary) 'objective'; and he was certainly quite right to do this. On the other hand, what is sensibly perceptible is certainly 'subjective', in that it does not have its footing within itself, and is as fleeting and transient as thought is enduring and inwardly stable. Nowadays we find this same determination of the distinction between the 'objective' and 'subjective', which Kant validated in the linguistic usage of the more highly educated consciousness. For example, people demand that the judgement of a work of art should be 'objective' and not 'subjective', and this is understood to mean that it should not be based on a contingent, particular feeling or mood of the moment, but should keep in mind the points of view that are universal and grounded in the essence of art. When dealing with something scientifically, we can distinguish between an 'objective' and a 'subjective' concern in the same sense.

Moreover, even the objectivity of thinking in Kant's sense is itself again only subjective in its form, because, according to Kant, thoughts, although they are universal and necessary determinations, are still *only our* thoughts, and are cut off from what the thing is *in-itself* by an impassable gulf. On the contrary, the true objectivity of thinking consists in this: that thoughts are not merely our thoughts, but at the same time the *In-itself* of things and of whatever else is ob-jective.

'Objective' and 'subjective' are convenient expressions which we employ currently; but their use can very easily give rise to confusion too. So far our explanation has shown that 'objectivity' has a threefold significance. *To start with*, it has the significance of what is externally present, as distinct from what is *only* subjective, meant, dreamed, etc.; *secondly*, it has the significance, established by Kant, of what is universal and necessary as distinct from the contingent, particular and subjective that we find in our sensation; and *thirdly*, it has the last-mentioned significance of the *In-itself* as thought-product, the significance of what is there, as distinct from what is only thought by us, and hence still distinct from the matter itself, or from the matter *in-itself*.

§ 42

(a) *The theoretical faculty*, cognition as such.

This philosophy points to the *original identity* of the 'I' within thinking (the transcendental unity of self-consciousness) as the determinate *ground* of the concepts of the understanding. The representations that are given through feeling and intuition are a *manifold* with regard to their *content*. They are equally manifold through their form, [i.e.,] through the *mutual externality* of sensibility in its two forms, space and time, which as forms of intuiting (as what is universal in it) are themselves a priori. Since the 'I' relates this manifold of sense-experience and intuiting to itself and unites it inwardly as within One consciousness (pure apperception), this manifold is brought into an identity, into an original combination. The determinate modes of this relating are the pure concepts of the understanding, the *categories*.

> *Remark*: We are all well aware that Kant's philosophy took the easy way in its *finding* of the categories. 'I', the unity of self-consciousness, is totally abstract and completely undetermined. So how are we to arrive at the *determinations* of the I, or at the categories? Fortunately, we can find the *various kinds of judgement* already specified empirically in the traditional logic. To judge, however, is to *think* a determinate ob-ject. So, the various modes of judgement that have already been enumerated give us the various *determinations of thinking*. – It remains the profound and enduring merit of *Fichte*'s philosophy to have reminded us that the *thought-determinations* must be exhibited in their *necessity*, and that it is essential for them to be *deduced*. – Fichte's philosophy ought to have had at least this effect upon the method of presenting a treatise on logic: that the thought-determinations in general, or the usual logical

material, the species of concepts, judgements and syllogisms, are no longer just taken from observation and thus apprehended only empirically, but are deduced from thinking itself. If thinking has to be able to prove anything at all, if logic must require that *proofs* are given, and if it wants to teach us how to prove [something], then it must above all be capable of proving its very own peculiar content, and able to gain insight into the necessity of this content. [A1–3]

§ 43

On the one hand, it is the categories that elevate mere perception into objectivity, into *experience*; but, on the other hand, these concepts, which are unities merely of subjective consciousness, are conditioned by the given material. They are empty on their own account and have their application and use only in experience, whose other component, the determinations of feeling and intuition, is equally something merely subjective. [A]

§ 44

The categories, therefore, are unfit to be determinations of the Absolute, which is not given in perception; hence the understanding, or cognition through the categories, cannot become cognizant of *things-in-themselves*.

> *Remark*: The *thing-in-itself* (and here 'thing' embraces God, or the spirit, as well) expresses the ob-ject, inasmuch as *abstraction* is made of all that it is for consciousness, of all determinations of feeling, as well as of all determinate thoughts about it. It is easy to see what is left, namely, what is *completely abstract*, or totally *empty*, and determined only as what is 'beyond'; the *negative* of representation, of feeling, of determinate thinking, etc. But it is just as simple to reflect that this *caput mortuum*[4] is itself only *the product* of thinking, and precisely of the thinking that has gone to the extreme of pure abstraction, the product of the empty 'I' that makes its own empty self-*identity* into its *ob-ject*. The *negative* determination that contains this abstract identity as [its] *ob-ject* is likewise entered among the Kantian categories, and, like that empty identity, it is something quite familiar. – We must be quite surprised, therefore, to read so often that one does not know what the *thing-in-itself* is; for nothing is easier to know than this.

§ 45

Now, it is *reason*, the faculty of the *unconditioned*, that sees what is conditioned in all this empiricial awareness of things. What is here called object of reason, the *unconditioned* or *infinite*, is nothing but the self-equivalent; in other words, it is that *original identity* of the *I* in thinking which was mentioned in § 42. This *abstract* 'I', or the thinking that makes this pure *identity* into its ob-ject or purpose, is called 'reason'. (See the remark to the preceding paragraph.) Our empirical cognitions are not appropriate for this identity that *lacks determinations* altogether, because they are always *determinate* in content. When an unconditioned of this sort is accepted as the Absolute and the Truth of reason (or as the *Idea*), then, of course, our empirical awareness is declared to be untrue, to be [only] *appearances*.

Addition: Kant was the first to emphasize the distinction between understanding and reason in a definite way, establishing the finite and conditioned as the subject-matter of the former, and the infinite and unconditioned as that of the latter. It must be recognized that to have established the finitude of the cognition that is based merely on experience and belongs to the understanding, and to have termed its content 'appearance', was a very important result of the Kantian philosophy. But we ought not to stop at this negative result, or to reduce the unconditioned character of reason to the merely abstract identity that excludes distinction. Since, upon this view, reason is regarded as simply going beyond the finite and conditioned character of the understanding, it is thereby itself degraded into something finite and conditioned, for the genuine infinite is not merely a realm beyond the finite: on the contrary, it contains the finite sublated within itself. The same holds for the *Idea* too, which Kant did indeed restore to honour, in that he vindicated it for reason, distinguishing it from the abstract determinations of the understanding and from merely sensible representations (all of which, even the latter, being habitually called 'ideas' in ordinary life). But, with regard to the Idea too, he halted at the negative aspect and at a mere 'ought'.

As for the interpretation of the ob-jects of our immediate consciousness, which form the content of empirical cognition, as mere *appearances*, this anyway must be regarded as a very important result of the Kantian philosophy. For our ordinary consciousness (i.e., the consciousness at the level of sense-perception and understanding) the ob-jects that it knows count as self-standing and self-founded in their isolation from one another; and when they prove to be related to each other, and conditioned by one another, their mutual dependence upon one another is regarded as something external to the ob-ject, and not as belonging to their nature. It must certainly be maintained against this that the ob-jects of which we have immediate knowledge are mere appearances, i.e., they do not have the ground of their being within themselves, but within something else. The further question, then, is how this other is determined. According to the Kantian philosophy, the things that we know about are only appearances for *us*, and what they are *in-themselves* remains for us an inaccessible beyond.

The naïve consciousness has rightly taken exception to this subjective idealism, according to which the content of our consciousness is something that is *only* ours, something posited only through *us*. In fact, the true situation is that the things of which we have immediate knowledge are mere appearances, not only *for us*, but also *in-themselves*, and that the proper determination of these things, which are in this sense 'finite', consists in having the ground of their being not within themselves but in the universal divine Idea. This interpretation must also be called idealism, but, as distinct from the subjective idealism of the Critical Philosophy, it is *absolute idealism*.

Although it transcends the ordinary realistic consciousness, still, this absolute ideal-ism can hardly be regarded as the private property of philosophy in actual fact, because, on the contrary, it forms the basis of all religious consciousness. This is because religion, too, regards the sum total of everything that is there, in short, the world before us, as created and governed by God.

§ 46

But the need arises to be cognizant of this identity or of the empty *thing-in-itself*. *To be cognizant*, however, means nothing else but the knowing of an ob-ject according to its *determinate* content. A determinate content, how-ever, contains a manifold *connection* within itself and is the basis for con-nections with many other ob-jects. So, this [Kantian] reason has nothing but the *categories* for its determination of the *thing-in-itself*, or of that infinite; and when it wants to use them for this purpose, it *flies off* (and becomes 'transcendent'). [R]

§ 47

(1) The *first unconditioned* that he considers is the *soul* (see § 34). – In my consciousness I always find myself (α) as the *determining subject*, (β) as a *singular* or as something abstractly simple, (γ) as what is *One* and *the same* in everything manifold of which I am conscious – as *something-identical*, (δ) as something *that distinguishes me* as thinking from *everything outside me*.

The procedure of the traditional metaphysics is correctly specified [by saying] that it sets the corresponding *categories*, or *thought-determinations*, in the place of these *empirical* determinations. This gives rise to four propositions: (α) the *soul is a substance*; (β) it is a *simple* substance; (γ) it is *numerically identical* with respect to the various times of its being-there; (δ) it stands in *relationship* to *what is spatial*.

Kant draws attention to the flaw involved in this transition: that two types of determination are confounded (*paralogism*), namely, empirical determina-tions with categories; *concluding* from the former to the latter, or in general replacing the first with the second, is quite unjustified.

It is obvious that this criticism expresses nothing other than the comment of Hume that we referred to above (§ 39): that thought-determinations in general – universality and necessity – are not found in perception, and that, both in its content and in its form, the empirical is diverse from the deter-mination of thought. [R]

Addition: 'Paralogisms' are basically defective syllogisms, whose defect consists, more precisely, in the fact that one and the same word is used in the two premises in diverse senses. According to Kant, the procedure of the older metaphysics in Rational Psychology is supposed to rest upon paralogisms of this kind; to be precise, merely empirical determinations of the soul are regarded by this psychology as pertaining to the soul in and for itself.

For that matter, it is quite correct to say that predicates like 'simplicity', 'unalterableness', etc., cannot be applied to the soul. This is not for the reason that Kant gives, however (viz., that reason would thereby overstep the limit assigned to it), but because the abstract determinations of the understanding are not good enough for the soul, which is something quite other than the merely simple, unalterable, etc. For instance, the soul is certainly simple self-identity; but at the same time, because it is active, it distinguishes itself inwardly, whereas what is *only* simple, i.e., simple in an abstract way, is (for that very reason) also dead at the same time. – The fact that, through his polemic against the older metaphysics, Kant removed those predicates from the soul and the spirit must be regarded a great result, but the reason that he gives for doing this is quite wrong.

§ 48

(2) In reason's attempt to be cognizant of the unconditioned [aspect] of the *second ob-ject* (§ 35), i.e., of *the world*, it gets involved in *antinomies*, i.e., in the assertion of two *opposed* propositions about *the same* ob-ject; and it finds, moreover, that each of the propositions must be affirmed with equal necessity. What follows from this is that the content of this 'world', whose determinations give rise to contradictions of this sort, cannot be *in-itself*, but can only be appearance. The *solution* is that the contradiction does not fall in the ob-ject in and for itself, but is only attributable to reason and to its cognition of the ob-ject.

> *Remark*: What is made explicit here is that it is the content itself, namely, the categories on their own account, that bring about the contradiction. This thought, that the contradiction which is posited by the determinations of the understanding in what is rational is *essential* and *necessary*, has to be considered one of the most important and profound advances of the philosophy of modern times. But the solution is as trivial as the viewpoint is profound; it consists merely in a tenderness for the things of this world. The stain of contradiction ought not to be in the essence of what is in the world; it has to belong *only* to thinking reason, to the *essence* of the *spirit*. It is not considered at all objectionable that the world *as it appears* shows contradictions to the spirit that observes it; the way the world is for subjective spirit, for *sensibility*, and for the *understanding*, is the world as it appears. But when the *essence* of what is in the world is compared with the *essence* of spirit, it may surprise us to see how naïvely the humble affirmation has been advanced, and repeated, that what is inwardly contradictory is not the essence of the world, but belongs to reason, the thinking essence. It does not help at all to express this by saying that reason *only* falls into contradiction through *the application of the categories*. For it is also asserted that this application is *necessary*, and that, for the purpose of

cognition, reason has no determinations other than the categories. Cognition really is *determining* and *determinate* thinking; if reason is only empty, indeterminate thinking, then it thinks *nothing*. But if reason is ultimately reduced to that *empty identity* (see the following paragraph), then it is, in the end, lucky to be freed from contradiction after all – through the easy sacrifice of all import and content.

It may also be remarked that, as a result of his failure to study the antinomy in more depth, Kant brings forward only *four* antinomies. He arrived at them by presupposing the table of categories just as he did in the case of the so-called paralogisms. While doing this he followed the procedure, which became so popular afterwards, of simply subsuming the determinations of an ob-ject under a ready-made *schema*, instead of deducing them from the Concept. I have pointed out further deficiencies in the treatment of the antinomies at appropriate points in my *Science of Logic*.[5] – The main point that has to be made is that antinomy is found not only in the four particular ob-jects taken from cosmology, but rather in *all* objects of all kinds, in *all* representations, concepts, and ideas. To know this, and to be cognizant of this property of ob-jects, belongs to what is essential in philosophical study; this is the property that constitutes what will determine itself in due course as the *dialectical* moment of logical thinking.

Addition: In the perspective of the older metaphysics it was assumed that, where cognition falls into contradictions, this is just an accidental aberration and rests on a subjective error in inferring and arguing. For Kant, on the contrary, it lies in the very nature of thinking to lapse into contradictions ('antinomies') when it aims at cognition of the infinite. In the remark to the above paragraph we have mentioned that the pointing out of the antinomies should be regarded as a very important advance for philosophical cognition, because in that way the rigid dogmatism of the metaphysics of the understanding is set aside and attention is directed to the dialect-ical movement of thinking. But, at the same time, it must be noted that here again Kant stopped at the merely negative result (that how things are in-themselves is unknowable), and did not penetrate to the cognition of the true and positive signific-ance of the antinomies. This true and positive significance (expressed generally) is that everything actual contains opposed determinations within it, and in consequence the cognition and, more exactly, the comprehension of an ob-ject amounts precisely to our becoming conscious of it as a concrete unity of opposed determinations. [. . .]

§ 49

(3) The *third* object of reason is *God* (§ 36); he has to be cognized, i.e., *determined by thinking*. But as opposed to simple *identity*, all determination is for the understanding only a *restriction*, i.e., a negation as such. Hence, all reality is to be taken only without restriction, i.e., as *indeterminate*, and

God, as the essential sum of all realities or as the supremely real Essence, becomes the *simple abstraction*; while the only determination that remains available for him is the just as strictly abstract determinacy of *being*. Abstract *identity* (which is what is here also is called 'concept') and *being* are the two moments that reason seeks to unify; this unification is the *Ideal* of reason.

§ 50

Two ways or forms are admissible for this unification: we can begin with *being* and pass on from there to the *abstraction of thinking*; or, conversely, we can effect the passage from the *abstraction* to *being*.

As far as beginning with being is concerned, this being, as what is immediate, presents itself as determined as an infinite manifold, as a world in all its fullness. This world can be determined more precisely as a collection of whatever infinitely many contingencies [there are] (in the *cosmological* proof); or as a collection of infinitely many *purposes* and *purposive* relationships (in the *physico-theological* proof). – *Thinking* of this fullness of being means stripping it of the form of the singularities and contingencies, and grasping it as a universal being, necessary in and for itself, one that is self-determining and active in accordance with universal purposes, one that is diverse from that contingent and singular collection: [i.e.,] grasping it as *God*. – The critique of this procedure is directed mainly against its being a syllogizing, a passage [from one being to another]. As such and in themselves, our *perceptions*, and their aggregate 'the world', do not show the universality that results from the purification of that content by thinking; so this universality is not justified by that empirical notion of the world. This elevation of thought from the empirical notion of the world to God is countered with the *Humean* standpoint (as was the case with the paralogisms; see § 47), the standpoint that proclaims the *thinking* of our perceptions to be inadmissible; i.e., the eliciting of the universal and necessary out of these perceptions. [R]

§ 51

The *other way of unification*, through which the *Ideal* is to be established, starts from the *abstraction of thinking* and goes *on to* the determination for which *being* alone remains; this is the *ontological proof* that *God is there*. The antithesis that occurs here is the one between *thinking* and *being*, whereas in the first way *being* is common to both sides, and the antithesis concerns only the distinction between what is singularized and what is universal. What the understanding sets against this second way is in-itself the same as was alleged before, namely that, just as the universal is not found to be present in the empirical, so, conversely, the determinate is not contained in the universal – and the determinate here is 'being'. In other words, 'being' cannot be deduced from the concept or analysed out of it.

Remark: One reason why Kant's critique of the ontological proof has been taken up, and accepted with so much unconditional acclaim, is undoubtedly that, in order to make quite clear what sort of distinction there is between thinking and being, Kant used the example of the *hundred dollars*.[6] With respect to their *concept*, these are equally one hundred, whether they are merely possible or actual; whereas, for the state of my fortune, this distinction is an essential one. – Nothing can be more obvious than that what I think or represent to myself is not yet *actual* because of that: nothing is more obvious than the thought that representing, or even the concept, falls short of being. – Calling such things as one hundred dollars a 'concept' can rightly be called a barbarism; but quite apart from that, those who repeat over and over again in their objections to the philosophical Idea, that *thinking and being* are *diverse*, surely ought to presuppose from the first that philosophers are familiar with this fact too. Can there in fact be a more trivial point of information than this? But then, too, we have to bear in mind that when we speak of 'God', we are referring to an ob-ject of quite another kind than one hundred dollars, or *any* other particular concept, notion, or whatever other name you want to give it. In fact what makes everything *finite* is this and *only* this: that *its being-there is diverse from its concept*. But God has to be expressly that which can only be '*thought as existing*', where the Concept includes being within itself. It is this unity of the Concept and of being that constitutes the concept of God. – It is true that this is still a formal determination of God, and one which, for that reason, only in fact contains the nature of the *Concept* itself. But it is easy to see that, even if it is taken in its totally abstract sense, the Concept includes *being* within itself. For however the Concept may be further determined, it is itself minimally the *immediate relation* to itself that emerges through the sublation of its mediation, and being is nothing else but that. – We might well say that it would be very odd if spirit's innermost core, the Concept, or even if I, or above all the concrete totality that God is, were not rich enough to contain within itself even so poor a determination as *being* is – for being is the poorest and the most abstract one of all. For thought, nothing can have less import than *being*. Only the notion that we have when we hear the word 'being', namely an *external, sensible* existence (like that of the paper which I have here in front of me), may be even poorer; but [at this point] we do not want to speak of the sensible existence of a restricted, perishable thing at all. – Besides, the trivial remark that thought and being are diverse may, at the most, hinder, but not abolish, the movement of man's spirit from the *thought* of God to the certainty that God *is*. Moreover, it is this passage, the absolute inseparability of the thought of God from his being, that has been restored to its rightful position by the theory of 'immediate knowing' or 'faith', which will be considered later.

C) The Third Position of Thought with Respect to Objectivity

Immediate knowing

§ 61

In the Critical Philosophy, thinking is interpreted as being *subjective*, and its *ultimate*, unsurpassable determination is *abstract universality*, or formal identity; thus, thinking is set in opposition to the truth, which is inwardly concrete universality. In this highest determination of thinking, which is reason, the categories are left out of account. – From the opposed standpoint thinking is interpreted as an activity *of the particular*, and in that way, too, it is declared to be incapable of grasping truth.

§ 62

As an activity of the particular, thinking has the *categories* as its only product and content. The way the understanding fixes them, these categories are *restricted* determinations, forms of what is *conditioned, dependent* and *mediated*. The Infinite, or the true, is not [present] for a thinking that is restricted in this way. Unlike the proofs that God is there, Critical Philosophy cannot make the passage to the Infinite. These thought-determinations are also called 'concepts'; and hence to 'comprehend' an ob-ject means nothing more than to grasp it in the form of something conditioned and mediated; so that inasmuch as it is what is true, infinite or unconditioned, it is transformed into something conditioned and mediated, and, instead of what is true being grasped in thinking, it is perverted into untruth.

> *Remark:*   This is the simple, one and only polemic that is advanced by the standpoint which asserts that God and the true can only be known immediately. In earlier times, every type of so-called anthropomorphic representation was banished from God as finite, and hence unworthy of the Infinite; and as a result he had already grown into something remarkably empty. But the thought-determinations were not generally considered anthropomorphic; on the contrary, thinking counted as what stripped the representations of the Absolute of their finitude – in accordance with the prejudice of all times, mentioned above, that it is only through [reflective] thinking that we arrive at the truth. But now, finally, even the thought-determinations in general are declared to be anthropomorphic, and thinking is explained as the activity of *just making* [the ob-ject] *finite*. – In Appendix VII of his *Letters on Spinoza*, Jacobi has expounded this polemic in the most determinate way, deriving it indeed from Spinoza's philosophy itself, and then using it to

attack cognition in general.[7] In this polemic, cognition is interpreted only as cognition of the finite, as the thinking progression through *sequences*, from one *conditioned* item to another *conditioned* one, where each condition is itself just something-conditioned once more. In other words, cognition is a progression through *conditioned conditions*. To explain and to comprehend, therefore, means to show that something is *mediated* through something *else*. Hence, every content is only a *particular*, *dependent* and *finite* one. God, or what is infinite and true, lies outside the mechanism of a connection of this kind to which cognition is supposed to be restricted. – Since Kant's philosophy posited the finitude of the categories most notably in the formal determination of their *subjectivity* alone, it is important that, in this polemic, the categories are dealt with in their determinacy, and the category as such is [re]cognized as being finite. – Jacobi had in view particularly the splendid successes of the natural sciences (the *sciences exactes*) in the cognition of the forces and laws of nature. But, of course, the Infinite does not allow itself to be found immanent in this domain of the finite; *Lalande* could say that he had searched all through the heavens, but he had not found God.[8] [. . .] The final result arising from investigations conducted in this domain was the *universal* as the *indeterminate* aggregate of finite outwardness – *matter*; and Jacobi saw, quite rightly, that this path of a mere progression by way of mediations can have no other issue.

§ 63

At the same time, it is asserted that the *truth is for the spirit* – so much so that it is through reason alone that man subsists, and this reason is *the knowledge of God*. But since mediated knowledge is supposed to be restricted simply to a finite content, it follows that reason is *immediate knowing, faith*.

> *Remark*:   [. . .] The expression 'believing' [. . .] carries with it the particular advantage that it calls *Christian religious* faith to mind, and seems to include it; it may quite easily even seem to be the same. Hence, this fideistic philosophizing looks essentially pious and Christian; and on the ground of this piety it claims for itself the freedom to make its assurances with even more pretension and authority. But we must not let ourselves be deceived by a semblance that can only sneak in because the same words are used. We must maintain the distinction firmly. The Christian faith implies an authority that belongs to the church, while, on the contrary, the faith of this philosophizing standpoint is just the authority of one's own subjective revelation. Moreover, the Christian faith is an objective content that is inwardly rich, a system of doctrine and cognition; whereas the content of this [philosophical] faith is inwardly so indeterminate that it may perhaps admit that content too – but equally it may embrace within it the belief that the

Dalaï-Lama, the bull, the ape, etc., is God, or it may, for its own part, restrict itself to *God in general*, to the 'highest essence'. Faith itself, in that would-be philosophical sense, is nothing but the dry abstraction of immediate knowing – a totally formal determination, which should not be mistaken for, or confounded with, the spiritual fullness of the Christian faith, either on the side of the faithful heart and the Holy Spirit that inhabits it, or on the side of the doctrine that is so rich in content.

Besides, what is called believing and immediate knowing here is just the same as what others have called inspiration, revelation of the heart, a content implanted in man by nature, and in particular sane human understanding (or 'common sense')[9] as well. All of these forms similarly make immediacy – i.e., the way that a content is found within consciousness, and is a fact in it – into their principle.

§ 64

What this immediate knowing knows is that the Infinite, the Eternal or God, that is [present] in our *representation* also *is* – that within our consciousness the certainty of its *being* is immediately and inseparably combined with our *representation* of it.

Remark: The last thing philosophy would want to do is to contradict these propositions of immediate knowing; on the contrary, it can congratulate itself upon the fact that *its own* old propositions, which even express its entire universal content, have somehow become also the general prejudices of the times – though in a quite unphilosophical way, to be sure. All there is to be surprised about, rather, is the fact that anyone could be of the opinion that these propositions are opposed to philosophy: namely, the propositions that what is held to be true is immanent in the spirit (§ 63), and that truth is [present] for the spirit (ibid). [. . .] The distinction between the assertions of immediate knowing and philosophy simply comes down in the end to this: that immediate knowing adopts an *excluding* posture or, in other words, it sets itself against the doing of philosophy. – But the proposition 'Cogito, ergo sum', which stands at the very centre, so to speak, of the entire concern of modern philosophy, was also uttered by its author in the mode of immediacy. [. . .] What Descartes says about the proposition that my being is inseparable from my thinking is that this connection is contained and indicated in the *simple intuition* of consciousness, that this connection is what is absolutely first; i.e., it is the principle, or what is most certain and evident, so that we cannot imagine any scepticism so extravagant as not to admit it. These statements are so eloquent and precise that the modern theses of Jacobi and others about this immediate connection can only count as useless repetitions.

§ 65

This standpoint is not content when it has shown that *mediate* knowing, taken *in isolation*, is inadequate for the [cognition of] truth; its peculiarity is that *immediate* knowing can only have the truth as its content when it is taken *in isolation*, to the *exclusion* of mediation. – Exclusions of this kind betray that this standpoint is a relapse into the metaphysical understanding, with its *Either-Or*; and hence it is really a relapse into the relationship of external mediation based upon clinging to the finite; i.e., to one-sided determinations beyond which this view mistakenly thinks that it has risen. But let us not push this point; exclusively immediate knowing is only asserted as *a fact*, and here, in the introduction, it only has to be taken up under the aspect of this external reflection. The important issue in-itself is the logical thinking of the antithesis of immediacy and mediation. But the standpoint of immediate knowing rejects the study of the nature of the matter, i.e., of the Concept, as one that leads to mediation and even to cognition. The genuine treatment of this topic, that of logical thinking, must find its own place within the Science itself.

> *Remark*: The entire second part of the *Logic*, the doctrine of *Essence*, deals with the essential self-positing unity of immediacy and mediation.

§ 66

So we stand by the position that immediate knowing has to be taken *as a fact*. But this means that our study is directed at the field of *experience*, and toward a *psychological* phenomenon. – In this connection we should point out, as one of the most common experiences, that truths, which we know very well to be the result of the most complicated, highly mediated studies, can present themselves immediately in the consciousness of those who are well versed in that kind of cognition. Like anyone who has been instructed in a science, a mathematician has solutions at his fingertips that were arrived at by a very complicated analysis; every educated human being has a host of general points of view and principles immediately present in his knowing, which have only emerged from his meditation on many things, and from the life experience of many years. The facility that we achieve in any kind of knowing, and also in art and technical skill, consists precisely in the fact that, when the occasion arises, we have this know-how, these ways of handling things, *immediately* in our consciousness, and even in our outwardly directed activity and in the limbs of our body. – Not only does the immediacy of knowing not exclude its mediation in all of these cases, but they are so far connected that the immediate knowing is even the product and result of the mediated knowing.

Remark: The connection of immediate *existence* with its mediation is just as trivial an insight; the seed and the parents are an immediate, originating existence with regard to the children, etc., which are the offspring. But, for all that the seed and the parents (in virtue of their just existing) are *immediate*, they are offspring as well; and, in spite of the mediation of their existence, the children, etc., are now immediate, for they *are* too. That I *am* in Berlin, which is my *immediate* present, is *mediated* by the journey I made to come here, etc.

§ 73

[. . .] The immediate knowing of God is only supposed to extend to [the affirmation] *that* God is, not *what* God is; for the latter would be a cognition and would lead to mediated knowing. Hence God, as the ob-ject of religion, is expressly restricted to *God in general*, to the indeterminate supersensible, and the content of religion is reduced to a minimum. [R]

§ 74

The general nature of the *form of immediacy* has still to be indicated briefly. For it is this form itself which, because it is *one-sided*, makes its very content one-sided and hence *finite*. It gives the *universal* the one-sidedness of an *abstraction*, so that God becomes an essence lacking all determination; but God can only be called spirit inasmuch as he is known as inwardly *mediating himself with himself*. Only in this way is he *concrete*, living and spirit; and that is just why the *knowing* of God as spirit contains mediation within it. – The form of immediacy gives to the *particular* the determination of *being*, or of relating *itself to itself*. But the particular is precisely the relating of itself to *another* outside it; through that form the *finite* is posited as absolute. Being totally abstract, this form is *indifferent* to *every content* and, just for that reason, it is receptive to any content; so it can sanction an idolatrous and immoral content just as easily as the reverse. Only the insight that the content is not independent, but is *mediated through an other*, reduces it to its finitude and untruth. And since the content brings mediation with it, this insight [too] is a knowing that contains mediation. But a content can only be [re]cognized as what is true, inasmuch as it is not mediated with an other, i.e., is not finite, so that it mediates itself with itself, and is in this way both mediation and immediate self-relation all in one. – That same understanding, which thinks that it has emancipated itself from finite knowing, and from the *the understanding's identity* [which is the principle] of metaphysics and of the Enlightenment, immediately makes this *immediacy, i.e., the abstract self-relation*, or the abstract identity, into the principle and criterion of truth once more. *Abstract thinking* (the form of reflective metaphysics) and *abstract intuiting* (the form of immediate knowing) are one and the same.

Addition: When the form of immediacy is held onto as firmly opposed to the form of mediation, then it becomes one-sided, and this one-sidedness is imparted to any content that is traced back to this form alone. In general, immediacy is abstract self-relation, and hence it is abstract identity or abstract universality at the same time. So if the universal in and for itself is taken only in the form of immediacy, it becomes just abstractly universal, and God acquires from this standpoint the significance of an Essence that is utterly indeterminate. To go on speaking of God as 'spirit' is simply to use an empty word, for, being both consciousness and self-consciousness, spirit is in any case a distinguishing of itself from itself and from an other, so that it is at once mediation.

§ 78

The *antithesis* between an independent immediacy of the content or of knowing, and, on the other side, an equally independent mediation that is irreconcilable with it, must be put aside, first of all, because it is a mere *presupposition* and an arbitrary *assurance*. All other presuppositions or assumptions must equally be given up when we enter into the Science, whether they are taken from representation or from thinking; for it is this Science, in which all determinations of this sort must first be investigated, and in which their meaning and validity like that of their antitheses must be [re]cognized.

> *Remark*:   Being a negative science that has gone through all forms of cognition, *scepticism* might offer itself as an introduction in which the nullity of such presuppositions would be exposed. But it would not only be a sad way, but also a redundant one, because, as we shall soon see, the dialectical moment itself is an essential one in the affirmative Science. Besides, scepticism would only have to find the finite forms empirically and unscientifically, and to take them up as given. To require a consummate scepticism of this kind, is the same as the demand that the Science should be preceded by *universal doubt*, i.e., by total *presuppositionlessness*. Strictly speaking, this requirement is fulfilled by the freedom that abstracts from everything, and grasps its own pure abstraction, the simplicity of thinking – in the resolve of *the will to think purely*.

More Precise Conception and Division of the *Logic*

§ 79

With regard to its form, the *logical* has three sides: (α) *the side of abstraction* or *of the understanding*, (β) *the dialectical* or *negatively rational side*, [and] (γ) *the speculative* or *positively rational* one.

Remark: These three sides do not constitute three *parts* of the Logic, but are *moments of everything logically real*; i.e., of every concept or of everything true in general. All of them together can be put under the first moment, that *of the understanding*; and in this way they can be kept separate from each other, but then they are not considered in their truth. – Like the division itself, the remarks made here concerning the determinations of the logical are only descriptive anticipations at this point.

§ 80

(α) Thinking as *understanding* stops short at the fixed determinacy and its distinctness *vis-à-vis* other determinacies; such a restricted abstraction counts for the understanding as one that subsists on its own account, and [simply] is.

Addition: When we talk about 'thinking' in general or, more precisely, about 'comprehension', we often have merely the activity of the understanding in mind. Of course, thinking is certainly an activity of the understanding to begin with, but it must not stop there and the Concept is not just a determination of the understanding. – The activity of the understanding consists generally in the bestowing of the form of universality on its content; and the universal posited by the understanding is, of course, an abstract one, which is held onto in firm opposition to the particular. But as a result, it is itself determined also as a particular again. Since the understanding behaves toward its ob-jects in a way that separates and abstracts them, it is thereby the opposite of immediate intuition and feeling, which, as such, deal entirely with the concrete and stick to that.

The oft-repeated complaints that are regularly made against thinking in general are connected with this antithesis between understanding and sense-experience. The burden of the complaints is that thinking is hard and one-sided and, if pursued consistently, leads to ruinous and destructive results. The first answer to these charges, in so far as they are justified in content, is that they do not apply to all thinking, and specifically not to rational thinking, but only to the thinking of the understanding.

But it should be added that even the thinking of the understanding must unquestionably be conceded its right and merit, which generally consists in the fact that without the understanding there is no fixity or determinacy in the domains either of theory or of practice. First, with regard to cognition, it begins by apprehending given ob-jects in their determinate distinctions. Thus, in the consideration of nature, for example, distinctions are drawn between matters, forces, kinds, etc., and they are marked off, each on its own account, in isolation one from another. In doing all this, thinking functions as understanding, and its principle here is identity, simple self-relation. So it is first of all this identity by which the advance from one determination to another is conditioned in cognition. Thus, for instance, in mathematics, magnitude is *the* one determination with respect to which a progression happens, all others being left out. In the same way we compare figures with one another in geometry, bringing out what is identical in them. In other areas of cognition, too, for instance, in jurisprudence, it is identity that is the primary means of progress. For, since we here infer one determination from another, our inferring is nothing but an advance in accordance with the principle of identity.

Understanding is just as indispensable in the practical sphere as it is in that of theory. Character is an essential factor in conduct, and a man of character is a man of understanding who (for that reason) has definite purposes in mind and pursues them with firm intent. As Goethe says,[10] someone who wants to do great things must know how to restrict himself. In contrast, someone who wants to do everything really wants to do nothing, and brings nothing off. There is a host of interesting things in the world; Spanish poetry, chemistry, politics, music are all very interesting, and we cannot blame a person who is interested in them. But if an individual in a definite situation is to bring something about, he must stick to something determinate and not dissipate his powers in a great many directions. Similarly, in the case of any profession, the main thing is to pursue it with understanding. For instance, the judge must stick to the law and give his verdict in accordance with it; he must not let himself be sidetracked by this or that; he must admit no excuse, and look neither to right nor left. – Furthermore, the understanding is an essential moment in culture generally. A cultivated person is not satisfied with what is cloudy and indeterminate; indeed, he grasps subject-matters in their fixed determinacy, while someone who is uncultivated sways uncertainly hither and thither, and it often takes much effort to come to an understanding with such a person as to what is under discussion, and get him to keep the precise point at issue steadily in view. [. . .] And finally, after what has been said already, it scarcely requires special mention that philosophy cannot do without the understanding either. Philosophizing requires, above all, that each thought should be grasped in its full precision and that nothing should remain vague and indeterminate.

But again, it is usually said also that the understanding must not go too far. This contains the valid point that the understanding cannot have the last word. On the contrary, it is finite, and, more precisely, it is such that when it is pushed to an extreme it overturns into its opposite. It is the way of youth to toss about in abstractions, whereas the man of experience does not get caught up in the abstract *either-or*, but holds onto the concrete.

§ 81

(β) The *dialectical* moment is the self-sublation of these finite determinations on their own part, and their passing into their opposites.

> *Remark*:   (1) The dialectical, taken separately on its own by the understanding, constitutes *scepticism*, especially when it is exhibited in scientific concepts. Scepticism contains the mere negation that results from the dialectic. (2) Dialectic is usually considered as an external art, which arbitrarily produces a confusion and a mere *semblance of contradictions* in determinate concepts, in such a way that it is this semblance, and not these determinations, that is supposed to be null and void, whereas on the contrary what is understandable would be true. Dialectic is

often no more than a subjective seesaw of arguments that sway back and forth, where basic import is lacking and the [resulting] nakedness is covered by the astuteness that gives birth to such argumentations. – According to its proper determinacy, however, the dialectic is the genuine nature that properly belongs to the determinations of the understanding, to things, and to the finite in general. Reflection is initially the transcending of the isolated determinacy and a relating of it, whereby it is posited in relationship but is nevertheless maintained in its isolated validity. The dialectic, on the contrary, is the *immanent* transcending, in which the one-sidedness and restrictedness of the determinations of the understanding displays itself as what it is, i.e., as their negation. That is what everything finite is: its own sublation. Hence, the dialectical constitutes the moving soul of scientific progression, and it is the principle through which alone *immanent coherence and necessity* enter into the content of science, just as all genuine, nonexternal elevation above the finite is to be found in this principle.

Addition 1: It is of the highest importance to interpret the dialectical [moment] properly, and to [re]cognize it. It is in general the principle of all motion, of all life, and of all activation in the actual world. Equally, the dialectical is also the soul of all genuinely scientific cognition. In our ordinary consciousness, not stopping at the abstract determinations of the understanding appears as simple fairness, in accordance with the proverb 'live and let live', so that one thing holds and the other does *also*. But a closer look shows that the finite is not restricted merely from the outside; rather, it sublates itself by virtue of its own nature, and passes over, of itself, into its opposite. Thus we say, for instance, that man is mortal; and we regard dying as having its ground only in external circumstances. In this way of looking at things, a man has two specific properties, namely, he is alive and *also* mortal. But the proper interpretation is that life as such bears the germ of death within itself, and that the finite sublates itself because it contradicts itself inwardly.

[. . .] Besides, the dialectic is not a new thing in philosophy. Among the Ancients, Plato is called the inventor of the dialectic, and that is quite correct in that it is in the Platonic philosophy that dialectic first occurs in a form which is freely scientific, and hence also objective. With Socrates, dialectical thinking still has a predominantly subjective shape, consistent with the general character of his philosophizing, namely, that of *irony*. Socrates directed his dialectic first against ordinary consciousness in general, and then, more particularly, against the Sophists. He was accustomed to pretend in his conversations that he wanted to be instructed more precisely about the matter under discussion; and in this connection he raised all manner of questions, so that the people with whom he conversed were led on to say the opposite of what had appeared to them at the beginning to be correct. When the Sophists called themselves teachers, for instance, Socrates, by a series of questions, brought the Sophist Protagoras to the point where he had to admit that all learning is merely recollection.

And by means of a dialectical treatment, Plato shows in his strictly scientific dialogues the general finitude of all fixed determinations of the understanding. Thus, for example, in the *Parmenides*, he deduces the Many from the One, and, notwithstanding that, he shows that the nature of the Many is simply to determine itself as the One. This was the grand manner in which Plato handled the dialectic. – In modern times it has mainly been Kant who reminded people of the dialectic again and reinstated it in its place of honour; as we have already seen (§ 48), he did this by working out the so-called antinomies of reason, which in no way involve a simple seesawing between [opposite] grounds as a merely subjective activity, but rather exhibit how each abstract determination of the understanding, taken simply on its own terms, overturns immediately into its opposite.

And, however much the understanding may, as a matter of habit, bristle at the dialectic, still the latter must in no way be regarded as present only for philosophical consciousness; on the contrary, what is in question here is found already in all other forms of consciousness, too, and in everyone's experience. Everything around us can be regarded an example of dialectic. For we know that, instead of being fixed and ultimate, everything finite is alterable and perishable, and this is nothing but the dialectic of the finite, through which the latter, being implicitly the other of itself, is driven beyond what it immediately is and overturns into its opposite.

[. . .] This dialectic is therefore recognized in many proverbs. The legal proverb, for instance, says, 'Summum ius summa iniuria', which means that if abstract justice is driven to the extreme, it overturns into injustice. Similarly, in politics, it is well known how prone the extremes of anarchy and despotism are to lead to one another. In the domain of individual ethics, we find the consciousness of dialectic in those universally familiar proverbs: 'Pride goes before a fall', 'Too much wit outwits itself', etc. – Feeling, too, both bodily and spiritual, has its dialectic. It is well known how the extremes of pain and joy pass into one another; the heart filled with joy relieves itself in tears, and the deepest melancholy tends in certain circumstances to make itself known by a smile. [A2]

§ 82

(γ) The *speculative* or *positively rational* apprehends the unity of the determinations in their opposition, the *affirmative* that is contained in their dissolution and in their transition. [R]

Addition: [. . .] What must be said is that, with respect to its true significance, the speculative is, neither provisionally nor in the end either, something merely subjective; instead, it expressly contains the very antitheses at which the understanding stops short (including therefore that of the subjective and objective, too), sublated within itself; and precisely for this reason it proves to be concrete and a totality. For this reason, too, a speculative content cannot be expressed in a one-sided proposition. If, for example, we say that 'the Absolute is the unity of the subjective and the objective', that is certainly correct; but it is still one-sided, in that it expresses only the aspect of *unity* and puts the emphasis on that, whereas in fact, of course, the subjective and the objective are not only identical but also distinct.

It should also be mentioned here that the meaning of the speculative is to be understood as being the same as what used in earlier times to be called 'mystical', especially with regard to the religious consciousness and its content. When we speak of the 'mystical' nowadays, it is taken as a rule to be synonymous with what is mysterious and incomprehensible; and, depending on the ways their culture and mentality vary in other respects, some people treat the mysterious and incomprehensible as what is authentic and genuine, while others regard it as belonging to the domain of superstition and deception. About this we must remark first that 'the mystical' is certainly something mysterious, but only for the understanding, and then only because abstract identity is the principle of the understanding. But when it is regarded as synonymous with the speculative, the mystical is the concrete unity of just those determinations that count as true for the understanding only in their separation and opposition. So if those who recognize the mystical as what is genuine say that it is something utterly mysterious, and just leave it at that, they are only declaring that for them, too, thinking has only the significance of an abstract positing of identity, and that in order to attain the truth we must renounce thinking, or, as they frequently put it, that we must 'take reason captive'. As we have seen, however, the abstract thinking of the understanding is so far from being something firm and ultimate that it proves itself, on the contrary, to be a constant sublating of itself and an overturning into its opposite, whereas the rational as such is rational precisely because it contains both of the opposites as ideal moments within itself. Thus, everything rational can equally be called 'mystical'; but this only amounts to saying that it transcends the understanding. It does not at all imply that what is so spoken of must be considered inaccessible to thinking and incomprehensible.

Notes

1 [A] indicates that an addition (or, as in this case, more than one addition) has been omitted. The additions were not written by Hegel himself, but were compiled by Leopold von Henning, the editor of the 1840 edition, from transcripts of Hegel's lectures on logic made by his students. [s.h.]

2 For a similar view, see Hegel, *The Encyclopaedia Logic*, p. 305 (§ 238 Addition): 'Philosophical thinking proceeds analytically in that it simply takes up its ob-ject, the Idea, and lets it go its own way, while it simply watches the movement and development of it, so to speak. To this extent philosophizing is wholly passive. But philosophical thinking is equally synthetic as well, and it proves to be the activity of the Concept [*Begriff*] itself. But this requires the effort to beware of our own inventions and particular opinions which are forever wanting to push themselves forward'. [s.h.]

3 See G. W. F. Hegel, 'Relationship of Skepticism to Philosophy, Exposition of its Different Modifications and Comparison of the Latest Form with the Ancient One', translated by H. S. Harris, in *Between Kant and Hegel: Texts in the Development of German Idealism*, translated and annotated by G. di Giovanni and H. S. Harris (Albany: SUNY Press, 1985), pp. 311–62. [s.h.]

4 This was the alchemist's term for the 'dead' precipitate that remained when all the 'living spirit' had been extracted or given off. [Translators' note.]

5 See Hegel, *Science of Logic*, pp. 190–9, 234–8. [s.h.]

6 I. Kant, *Critique of Pure Reason*, translated by N. Kemp Smith (London: Macmillan, 1929), p. 505 (B 627). [s.h.]

7 F. H. Jacobi, *The Main Philosophical Writings and the Novel Allwill*, translated from the German, with an introductory study, notes and bibliography by G. di Giovanni (Montreal and Kingston: McGill-Queen's University Press, 1994), pp. 370–8. [s.h.]

8 J.-J. Lalande (1732–1807), French astronomer whose tables of the planetary positions were considered the best available until the end of the eighteenth century. Hegel is said to have got this story from Jacobi or from J. F. Fries. [S.H.]

9 English in Hegel's own text. [S.H.]

10 In the poem *Natur und Kunst*: 'Wer Grosses will, muß sich zusammenraffen; / In der Beschränkung zeigt sich erst der Meister, / Und das Gesetz nur kann uns Freiheit geben' (*Werke*, Berlin edition, Aufbau Verlag, 1973, 2: 121). (The same moral is preached often in *Wilhelm Meister's Apprenticeship*.) [Translators' note.]

13

Science of Logic: Introduction

[. . .] In the *Phenomenology of Spirit* I have exhibited consciousness in its movement onwards from the first immediate opposition of itself and the object to absolute knowing. The path of this movement goes through every form of the *relation of consciousness to the object* and has the Notion [*Begriff*] of science for its result. This Notion therefore (apart from the fact that it emerges within logic itself) needs no justification here because it has received it in that work; and it cannot be justified in any other way than by this emergence in consciousness, all the forms of which are resolved into this Notion as into their truth.

[. . .] The Notion of pure science and its deduction is therefore presupposed in the present work in so far as the *Phenomenology of Spirit* is nothing other than the deduction of it. Absolute knowing is the *truth* of every mode of consciousness because, as the course of the *Phenomenology* showed, it is only in absolute knowing that the separation of the *object* from the *certainty of itself* is completely eliminated: truth is now equated with certainty and this certainty with truth.

Thus pure science presupposes liberation from the opposition of consciousness. It contains *thought in so far as this is just as much the object [Sache] in its own self, or the object in its own self in so far as it is equally pure thought.* As science, truth is pure self-consciousness in its self-development and has the shape of the self, so that the absolute truth of being is the known Notion and the Notion as such is the absolute truth of being.

This objective thinking, then, is the content of pure science. Consequently, far from it being formal, far from it standing in need of a matter to constitute an actual and true cognition, it is its content alone which has absolute truth, or, if one still wanted to employ the word matter, it is the veritable matter – but a matter which is not external to the form, since this matter is rather pure thought and hence the absolute form itself. Accordingly, logic is to be understood as the system of pure reason, as the realm of pure thought. This realm is truth as it is without veil and in its own absolute nature. It can therefore be said that this content is the exposition of God as he is in his eternal essence before the creation of nature and a finite mind.

Anaxagoras is praised as the man who first declared that *Nous*, thought, is the principle of the world, that the essence of the world is to be defined as thought. In so doing he laid the foundation for an intellectual view of the universe, the pure form of which must be logic. What we are dealing with in logic is not a thinking *about* something which exists independently as a base for our thinking and apart from it, nor forms which are supposed to provide mere signs or distinguishing marks of truth; on the contrary, the necessary forms and self-determinations of thought are the content and the ultimate truth itself. [. . .]

The exposition of what alone can be the true method of philosophical science falls within the treatment of logic itself; for the method is the consciousness of the form of the inner self-movement of the content of logic. In the *Phenomenology of Spirit* I have expounded an example of this method in application to a more concrete object, namely to consciousness. Here, we are dealing with forms of consciousness each of which in realizing itself at the same time resolves itself, has for its result its own negation – and so passes into a higher form. All that is necessary to achieve scientific progress – and it is essential to strive to gain this quite *simple* insight – is the recognition of the logical principle that the negative is just as much positive, or that what is self-contradictory does not resolve itself into a nullity, into abstract nothingness, but essentially only into the negation of its *particular* content, in other words, that such a negation is not all and every negation but the negation of a specific subject-matter which resolves itself, and consequently is a specific negation, and therefore the result essentially contains that from which it results; which strictly speaking is a tautology, for otherwise it would be an immediacy, not a result. Because the result, the negation, is a *specific* negation it has a *content*. It is a fresh Notion but higher and richer than its predecessor; for it is richer by the negation or opposite of the latter, therefore contains it, but also something more, and is the unity of itself and its opposite. It is in this way that the system of Notions as such has to be formed – and has to complete itself in a purely continuous course in which nothing extraneous is introduced.

I could not pretend that the method which I follow in this system of logic – or rather which this system in its own self follows – is not capable of greater completeness, of much elaboration in detail; but at the same time I know that it is the only true method. This is self-evident simply from the fact that it is not something distinct from its object and content; for it is the inwardness of the content, the dialectic which it possesses within itself, which is the mainspring of its advance. It is clear that no expositions can be accepted as scientifically valid which do not pursue the course of this method and do not conform to its simple rhythm, for this is the course of the subject-matter itself. [. . .]

14

Science of Logic: With What Must the Science Begin?

It is only in recent times that thinkers have become aware of the difficulty of finding a beginning in philosophy, and the reason for this difficulty and also the possibility of resolving it has been much discussed. What philosophy begins with must be either *mediated* or *immediate*, and it is easy to show that it can be neither the one nor the other; thus either way of beginning is refuted.

The *principle* of a philosophy does, of course, also express a beginning, but not so much a subjective as an *objective* one, the beginning of *everything*. The principle is a particular determinate *content* – water, the one, *nous*, idea, substance, monad, etc. Or, if it refers to the nature of cognition and consequently is supposed to be only a criterion rather than an objective determination – thought, intuition, sensation, ego, subjectivity itself. Then here too it is the nature of the content which is the point of interest. The beginning as such, on the other hand, as something subjective in the sense of being a particular, inessential way of introducing the discourse, remains unconsidered, a matter of indifference, and so too the need to find an answer to the question, With what should the beginning be made? remains of no importance in face of the need for a principle in which alone the interest of the matter in hand seems to lie, the interest as to what is the *truth*, the *absolute ground*.

But the modern perplexity about a beginning proceeds from a further requirement of which those who are concerned with the dogmatic demonstration of a principle or who are sceptical about finding a subjective criterion against dogmatic philosophizing, are not yet aware, and which is completely denied by those who begin, like a shot from a pistol, from their inner revelation, from faith, intellectual intuition, etc., and who would be exempt from *method* and logic. If earlier abstract thought was interested in the principle only as content, but in the course of philosophical development has been impelled to pay attention to the other side, to the behaviour of the cognitive process, this implies that the *subjective* act has also been grasped as an *essential* moment of objective truth, and this brings with it the need to unite the method with the content, the form with the principle.

Thus the principle ought also to be the beginning, and what is the first for thought ought also to be the first in the *process* of thinking.

Here we have only to consider how the *logical* beginning appears; the two sides from which it can be taken have already been named, to wit, either as a mediated result or as a beginning proper, as an immediacy. This is not the place to deal with the question apparently so important in present-day thought, whether the knowledge of truth is an immediate knowledge having a pure beginning, a faith, or whether it is a mediated knowledge. In so far as this can be dealt with *preliminarily* it has been done elsewhere.[1] Here we need only quote from it this, that there is nothing, nothing in heaven or in nature or mind or anywhere else which does not equally contain both immediacy and mediation, so that these two determinations reveal themselves to be *unseparated* and inseparable and the opposition between them to be a nullity. But as regards the philosophical discussion of this, it is to be found in every logical proposition in which occur the determinations of immediacy and mediation and consequently also the discussion of their opposition and their truth. Inasmuch as this opposition, as related to thinking, to knowing, to cognition, acquires the more concrete form of immediate or mediated *knowledge*, it is the nature of cognition simply as such which is considered within the science of logic, while the more concrete form of cognition falls to be considered in the philosophy of spirit and in the phenomenology of spirit. But to want the nature of cognition clarified *prior* to the science is to demand that it be considered *outside* the science; *outside* the science this cannot be accomplished, at least not in a scientific manner and such a manner is alone here in place.

The beginning is *logical* in that it is to be made in the element of thought that is free and for itself, in *pure knowing*. It is *mediated* because pure knowing is the ultimate, absolute truth of *consciousness*. In the Introduction it was remarked that the phenomenology of spirit is the science of consciousness, the exposition of it, and that consciousness has for result the *Notion* of science, i.e. pure knowing.[2] Logic, then, has for its presupposition the science of manifested spirit, which contains and demonstrates the necessity, and so the truth, of the standpoint occupied by pure knowing and of its mediation. In this science of manifested spirit the beginning is made from empirical, *sensuous* consciousness and this is *immediate* knowledge in the strict sense of the word; in that work there is discussed the significance of this immediate knowledge. Other forms of consciousness such as belief in divine truths, inner experience, knowledge through inner revelation, etc., are very ill-fitted to be quoted as examples of immediate knowledge as a little reflection will show. In the work just mentioned immediate consciousness is also the first and that which is immediate in the science itself, and therefore the presupposition; but in logic, the presupposition is that which has proved itself to be the result of that phenomenological consideration – the Idea as pure knowledge. *Logic is pure science*, that is, pure knowledge in the entire range of its development. But in the said result, this Idea has determined itself to be the certainty which has become truth, the certainty which, on the one hand, no longer has the object over against it but has internalized it, knows it as its own self – and, on the other hand, has given up the knowledge of itself as of something confronting the object of which it is only the annihilation, has divested itself of this subjectivity and is at one with its self-alienation.

Now starting from this determination of pure knowledge, all that is needed to ensure that the beginning remains immanent in its scientific development is to consider, or rather, ridding oneself of all other reflections and opinions whatever, simply to take up, *what is there before us*.

Pure knowing as concentrated into this unity has sublated all reference to an other and to mediation; it is without any distinction and as thus distinctionless, ceases itself to be knowledge; what is present is only *simple immediacy*.

Simple immediacy is itself an expression of reflection and contains a reference to its distinction from what is mediated. This simple immediacy, therefore, in its true expression is *pure being*. Just as *pure* knowing is to mean knowing as such, quite abstractly, so too pure being is to mean nothing but *being* in general: being, and nothing else, without any further specification and filling.

Here the beginning is made with being which is represented as having come to be through mediation, a mediation which is also a sublating of itself; and there is presupposed pure knowing as the outcome of finite knowing, of consciousness. But if no presupposition is to be made and the beginning itself is taken *immediately*, then its only determination is that it is to be the beginning of logic, of thought as such. All that is present is simply the resolve, which can also be regarded as arbitrary, that we propose to consider thought as such. Thus the beginning must be an *absolute*, or what is synonymous here, an *abstract* beginning; and so it *may not presuppose anything*, must not be mediated by anything nor have a ground; rather it is to be itself the ground of the entire science. Consequently, it must be purely and simply *an immediacy, or rather merely immediacy* itself. Just as it cannot possess any determination relatively to anything else, so too it cannot contain within itself any determination, any content; for any such would be a distinguishing and an interrelationship of distinct moments, and consequently a mediation. The beginning therefore is *pure being*.

To this simple exposition of what is only directly involved in the simplest of all things, the logical beginning, we may add the following further reflections; yet these cannot be meant to serve as elucidations and confirmations of that exposition – this is complete in itself – since they are occasioned by preconceived ideas and reflections and these, like all other preliminary prejudices, must be disposed of within the science itself where their treatment should be awaited with patience.

The insight that absolute truth must be a result, and conversely, that a result presupposes a prior truth which, however, because it is a first, objectively considered is unnecessary and from the subjective side is not known – this insight has recently given rise to the thought that philosophy can only begin with a *hypothetical* and *problematical* truth and therefore philosophizing can at first be only a quest. This view was much stressed by Reinhold in his later philosophical work and one must give it credit for the genuine interest on which it is based, an interest which concerns the speculative nature of the philosophical *beginning*. The detailed discussion of this view is at the same time an occasion for introducing a preliminary understanding of the meaning of progress in logic generally; for that view has a direct bearing on the advance; this it conceives to be such that progress in philosophy is rather a retrogression and a grounding or establishing by means of which we first obtain the result that what we began with is not something merely arbitrarily assumed but is in fact the *truth*, and also the *primary truth*.

It must be admitted that it is an important consideration – one which will be found in more detail in the logic itself – that the advance is a *retreat into the ground*, to what is *primary* and *true*, on which depends and, in fact, from which originates, that with which the beginning is made. Thus consciousness on its onward path from the immediacy with which it began is led back to absolute knowledge as its innermost *truth*. This last, the ground, is then also that from which the first proceeds, that which at first appeared as an immediacy. This is true in still greater measure of absolute spirit which reveals itself as the concrete and final supreme truth of all being, and which at the *end* of the development is known as freely externalizing itself, abandoning itself to the shape of an *immediate being*, opening or unfolding itself [*sich entschliessend*] into the creation of a world which contains all that fell into the development which preceded that result and which through this reversal of its position relatively to its beginning is transformed into something dependent on the result as principle. The essential requirement for the science of logic is not so much that the beginning be a pure immediacy, but rather that the whole of the science be within itself a circle in which the first is also the last and the last is also the first.

We see therefore that, on the other hand, it is equally necessary to consider as *result* that into which the movement returns as into its *ground*. In this respect the first is equally the ground, and the last a derivative; since the movement starts from the first and by correct inferences arrives at the last as the ground, this latter is a result. Further, the *progress* from that which forms the beginning is to be regarded as only a further determination of it, hence that which forms the starting-point of the development remains at the base of all that follows and does not vanish from it. The progress does not consist merely in the derivation of an other, or in the effected transition into a genuine other; and in so far as this transition does occur it is equally sublated again. Thus the beginning of philosophy is the foundation which is present and preserved throughout the entire subsequent development, remaining completely immanent in its further determinations.

Through this progress, then, the beginning loses the one-sidedness which attaches to it as something simply immediate and abstract; it becomes something mediated, and hence the line of the scientific advance becomes a *circle*. It also follows that because that which forms the beginning is still undeveloped, devoid of content, it is not truly known in the beginning; it is the science of logic in its whole compass which first constitutes the completed knowledge of it with its developed content and first truly grounds that knowledge.

But because it is the *result* which appears as the absolute ground, this progress in knowing is not something provisional, or problematical and hypothetical; it must be determined by the nature of the subject-matter itself and its content. The said beginning is neither an arbitrary and merely provisional assumption, nor is it something which appears to be arbitrarily and tentatively presupposed, but which is subsequently shown to have been properly made the beginning; not as is the case with the constructions one is directed to make in connection with the proof of a theorem in geometry, where it becomes apparent only afterwards in the proof that one took the right course in drawing just those lines and then, in the proof itself, in beginning with the comparison of those lines or angles; drawing such lines and comparing them are not an essential part of the proof itself.

Thus the *ground*, the *reason*, why the beginning is made with pure being in the pure science [of logic] is directly given in the science itself. This pure being is the unity into which pure knowing withdraws, or, if this itself is still to be distinguished as form from its unity, then being is also the content of pure knowing. It is when taken in this way that this *pure being*, this absolute immediacy has equally the character of something absolutely mediated. But it is equally essential that it be taken only in the one-sided character in which it is pure immediacy, *precisely because* here it is the beginning. If it were not this pure indeterminateness, if it were determinate, it would have been taken as something mediated, something already carried a stage further: what is determinate implies an other to a first. Therefore, it lies in the *very nature of a beginning* that it must be being and nothing else. To enter into philosophy, therefore, calls for no other preparations, no further reflections or points of connection.

We cannot really extract any further determination or *positive* content for the beginning from the fact that it is the beginning of philosophy. For here at the start, where the subject-matter itself is not yet to hand, philosophy is an empty word or some assumed, unjustified conception. Pure knowing yields only this negative determination, that the beginning is to be *abstract*. If pure being is taken as the *content* of pure knowing, then the latter must stand back from its content, allowing it to have free play and not determining it further. Or again, if pure being is to be considered as the unity into which knowing has collapsed at the extreme point of its union with the object, then knowing itself has vanished in that unity, leaving behind no difference from the unity and hence nothing by which the latter could be determined.

Nor is there anything else present, any content which could be used to make the beginning more determinate.

But the determination of *being* so far adopted for the beginning could also be omitted, so that the only demand would be that a pure beginning be made. In that case, we have nothing but the *beginning* itself, and it remains to be seen what this is. This position could also be suggested for the benefit of those who, on the one hand, are dissatisfied for one reason or another with the beginning with being and still more so with the resulting transition of being into nothing, and, on the other hand, simply know no other way of beginning a science than by *presupposing some general idea*, which is then *analysed*, the result of such analysis yielding the first specific concept in the science. If we too were to observe this method, then we should be without a particular object, because the beginning, as the beginning of *thought*, is supposed to be quite abstract, quite general, wholly form without any content; thus we should have nothing at all beyond the general idea of a mere beginning as such. We have therefore only to see what is contained in such an idea.

As yet there is nothing and there is to become something. The beginning is not pure nothing, but a nothing from which something is to proceed; therefore being, too, is already contained in the beginning. The beginning, therefore, contains both, being and nothing, is the unity of being and nothing; or is non-being which is at the same time being, and being which is at the same time non-being.

Further, in the beginning, being and nothing are present as *distinguished* from each other; for the beginning points to something else – it is a non-being which carries a reference to being as to an other; that which begins, as yet *is* not, it is only on the way to being. The being contained in the beginning is, therefore, a being which removes itself from non-being or sublates it as something opposed to it.

But again, that which begins already *is*, but equally, too, *is not* as yet. The opposites, being and non-being are therefore directly united in it, or, otherwise expressed, it is their *undifferentiated unity*.

The analysis of the beginning would thus yield the notion of the unity of being and nothing – or, in a more reflected form, the unity of differentiatedness and non-differentiatedness, or the identity of identity and non-identity. This concept could be regarded as the first, purest, that is, most abstract definition of the absolute – as it would in fact be if we were at all concerned with the form of definitions and with the name of the absolute. In this sense, that abstract concept would be the first definition of this absolute and all further determinations and developments only more specific and richer definitions of it. But let those who are dissatisfied with *being* as a beginning because it passes over into nothing and so gives rise to the unity of being and nothing, let them see whether they find this beginning which begins with the general idea of a *beginning* and with its analysis (which, though of course correct, likewise leads to the unity of being and nothing), more satisfactory than the beginning with being.

But there is a still further observation to be made about this procedure. The said analysis presupposes as familiar the idea of a beginning, thus following the example of other sciences. These presuppose their subject-matter and take it for granted that everyone has roughly the same general idea of it and can find in it the same determinations as those indicated by the sciences which have obtained them in one way or another through analysis, comparison and other kinds of reasoning. But that which forms the absolute beginning must likewise be something otherwise known; now if it is something concrete and hence is variously determined within itself, then this *internal relation* is presupposed as something known; it is thus put forward as an *immediacy* which, however, it is not; for it is a relation only as a relation of distinct moments, and it therefore contains *mediation* within itself. Further, with a concrete object, the analysis and the ways in which it is determined are affected by contingency and arbitrariness. Which determinations are brought out depends on what each person just *finds* in his own immediate, contingent idea. The relation contained in something concrete, in a synthetic unity, is *necessary* only in so far as it is not just given but is produced by the spontaneous return of the moments back into this unity – a movement which is the opposite of the analytical procedure, which is an activity belonging to the subject-thinker and external to the subject-matter itself.

The foregoing shows quite clearly the reason why the beginning cannot be made with anything concrete, anything containing a relation *within itself*. For such presupposes an internal process of mediation and transition of which the concrete, now become simple, would be the result. But the beginning ought not itself to be already a first *and* an other; for anything which is in its own self a first *and* an other implies that an advance has already been made. Consequently, that which constitutes the beginning, the beginning itself, is to be taken as something unanalysable, taken in its simple, unfilled immediacy, and therefore *as being*, as the completely empty being.

If impatience with the consideration of the abstract beginning should provoke anyone to say that the beginning should be made not with the beginning, but straightway with the subject-matter itself, well then, this subject-matter is nothing else but the said empty being; for what this subject-matter is, that will be explicated only in the development of the science and cannot be presupposed by it as known beforehand.

Whatever other form the beginning takes in the attempt to begin with something other than empty being, it will suffer from the defects already specified. Let those who are still dissatisfied with this beginning tackle the problem of avoiding these defects by beginning in some other way.

But we cannot leave entirely unmentioned an original beginning of philosophy which has recently become famous, the beginning with the *ego* [*Ich*].[3] It came partly from the reflection that from the first truth the entire sequel must be derived, and partly from the requirement that the *first* truth must be something with which we are acquainted, and still more, something of which we are *immediately certain*. This beginning is, in general, not a contingent idea which can be differently constituted in different subjects. For the ego, this immediate consciousness of self, at first appears to be itself both an immediacy and also something much more familiar to us than any other idea; anything else known belongs to the ego, it is true, but is still a content distinguished from it and therefore contingent; the ego, on the contrary, is the simple certainty of its own self. But the ego as such is *at the same time* also concrete, or rather, the ego is the most concrete of all things – the consciousness of itself as an infinitely manifold world. Before the ego, this concrete Being, can be made the beginning and ground of philosophy, it must be disrupted – this is the absolute act through which the ego purges itself of its content and becomes aware of itself as an abstract ego. Only this pure ego now is *not* immediate, is not the familiar, ordinary ego of our consciousness to which the science of logic could be directly linked for everyone. That act, strictly speaking, would be nothing else but the elevation to the standpoint of pure knowing where the distinction of subject and object has vanished. But as thus *immediately* demanded, this elevation is a subjective postulate; to prove itself a genuine demand, the progression of the concrete ego from immediate consciousness to pure knowing must have been indicated and exhibited through the necessity of the ego itself. Without this objective movement pure knowing, even in the shape of intellectual intuition, appears as an arbitrary standpoint, or even as one of the empirical *states* of consciousness with respect to which everything turns on whether or not it is found or can be produced in each and every individual. But inasmuch as this pure ego must be essential, pure knowing, and pure knowing is not *immediately* present in the individual consciousness but only as posited through the absolute act of the ego in raising itself to that standpoint, we lose the very advantage which is supposed to come from this beginning of philosophy, namely that it is something thoroughly familiar, something everyone finds in himself which can form the starting-point for further reflection; that pure ego, on the contrary, in its abstract, essential nature, is something unknown to the ordinary consciousness, something it does not find therein. Instead, such a beginning brings with it the disadvantage of the illusion that whereas the thing under discussion is supposed to be something familiar, the ego of empirical self-consciousness, it is in fact something far removed from it. When pure knowing is characterized as ego, it acts as a perpetual reminder of the subjective ego whose limitations should be forgotten, and it fosters the idea that the propositions and relations resulting from the further development of the ego are present and can already be found in the ordinary consciousness – for in fact it is this of which they are asserted. This confusion, far from clarifying the problem of a beginning, only adds to the difficulties involved and tends completely to mislead; among the uninitiated it has given rise to the crudest misunderstandings.

Further, as regards the *subjective* determinateness of the ego in general, it is true that pure knowing frees the ego from the restricted meaning imposed on it by the insuperable opposition of its object; but for this reason it would be *superfluous* at least to retain this subjective attitude and the determination of pure knowing as ego. This determination, however, not only introduces the disturbing ambiguity mentioned, but closely examined it also remains a subjective *ego*. The actual development of the science which starts from the ego shows that in that development the object has and retains the perennial character of an other for the ego, and that the ego which formed the starting-point is, therefore, still entangled in the world of appearance and is not the pure knowing which has in truth overcome the opposition of consciousness.

In this connection a further essential observation must be made, namely that although the ego could *in itself* or *in principle* [*an sich*] be characterized as pure knowing or as intellectual intuition and asserted as the beginning, we are not concerned in the science of logic with what is present only in *principle* or as something *inner*, but rather with the determinate reality *in thought* of what is inner and with the *determinateness* possessed by such an inner in this reality. But what, at the *beginning* of the science, is *actually present* of intellectual intuition – or of the eternal, the divine, the absolute, if its object be so named – cannot be anything else than a first, immediate, simple determination. Whatever richer name be given to it than is expressed by mere *being*, the consideration of such absolute must be restricted solely to the way in which it enters into our knowing as *thought* and is enunicated as such. True, intellectual intuition is the forcible rejection of mediation and the ratiocinative, external reflection; but what it enunciates above and beyond simple immediacy is something concrete, something which contains within itself diverse determinations. However, as we have remarked, the enunciation and exposition of such concrete beginning is a process of mediation which starts from *one* of the determinations and advances to the other, even though the latter returns to the first; it is a movement which at the same time may not be arbitrary or assertoric. Consequently, it is not the concrete something itself with which that exposition begins but only the simple immediacy from which the movement starts. And further, if something concrete is taken as the beginning, the conjunction of the determinations contained in it demand proof, and this is lacking.

If, therefore, in the expression of the absolute, or eternal, or God (and *God* has the absolutely undisputed right that the beginning be made with him) – if in the intuition or thought of these there is *implied more* than pure being – then this *more* must make its *appearance* in our knowing only as something *thought*, not as something imagined or figurately conceived; let what is present in intuition or figurate conception be as rich as it may, the determination which *first* emerges in knowing is simple, for only in what is simple is there nothing more than the pure beginning; only the immediate is simple, for only in the immediate has no advance yet been made from a *one* to an *other*. Consequently, whatever is intended to be expressed or implied beyond *being*, in the richer forms of representing the absolute or God, this is in the beginning only an empty word and only being; this simple determination which has no other meaning of any kind, this emptiness, is therefore simply as such the beginning of philosophy.

This insight is itself so simple that this beginning as such requires no preparation or further introduction; and, indeed, these preliminary, external reflections about it were not so much intended to lead up to it as rather to eliminate all preliminaries.

Notes

1　See Hegel, *The Encyclopaedia Logic*, pp. 108ff (§§ 61ff). See above pp. 163 ff. [S.H.]
2　See Hegel, *Science of Logic*, p. 48. See above p. 175. [S.H.]
3　This is a reference to Fichte. [S.H.]

15

Science of Logic: Doctrine of Being

Section One: Determinateness (Quality)

Being is the indeterminate *immediate*; it is free from determinateness in relation to *essence* and also from any which it can possess within itself. This reflectionless *being* is *being* as it is immediately in its own self alone.

Because it is indeterminate being, it lacks all quality; but *in itself*, the character of indeterminateness attaches to it only in contrast to what is *determinate* or qualitative. But *determinate* being stands in contrast to being in general, so that the very indeterminateness of the latter constitutes its quality. It will therefore be shown that the *first* being is in itself determinate, and therefore, *secondly*, that it passes over into *determinate being* [*Dasein*] – is *determinate being* – but that this latter as finite being sublates itself and passes over into the infinite relation of being to its own self, that is, *thirdly*, into *being-for-self*.

Chapter 1: Being

A. Being

Being, pure being, without any further determination. In its indeterminate immediacy it is equal only to itself. It is also not unequal relatively to an other; it has no diversity within itself nor any with a reference outwards. It would not be held fast in its purity if it contained any determination or content which could be distinguished in it or by which it could be distinguished from an other. It is pure indeterminateness and emptiness. There is *nothing* to be intuited in it, if one can speak here of intuiting; or, it is only this pure intuiting itself. Just as little is anything to be thought in it, or it is equally only this empty thinking. Being, the indeterminate immediate, is in fact *nothing*, and neither more nor less than *nothing*.

B. Nothing

Nothing, pure nothing: it is simply equality with itself, complete emptiness, absence of all determination and content – undifferentiatedness in itself. In so far as intuiting or thinking can be mentioned here, it counts as a distinction whether something or *nothing* is intuited or thought. To intuit or think nothing has, therefore, a meaning; both are distinguished and thus nothing *is* (exists) in our intuiting or thinking; or rather it is empty intuition and thought itself, and the same empty intuition or thought as pure being. Nothing is, therefore, the same determination, or rather absence of determination, and thus altogether the same as, pure *being*.

C. Becoming

1. Unity of being and nothing

Pure being and *pure nothing* are, therefore, the same. What is the truth is neither being nor nothing, but that being – does not pass over but has passed over – into nothing, and nothing into being. But it is equally true that they are not undistinguished from each other, that, on the contrary, they are not the same, that they are absolutely distinct, and yet that they are unseparated and inseparable and that each immediately *vanishes in its opposite*. Their truth is, therefore, this movement of the immediate vanishing of the one in the other: *becoming*, a movement in which both are distinguished, but by a difference which has equally immediately resolved itself.

> *Remark 1*: *The Opposition of Being and Nothing in Ordinary Thinking*: *Nothing* is usually opposed to *something*; but the being of *something* is already determinate and is distinguished from another *something*; and so therefore the nothing which is opposed to the something is also the nothing of a particular something, a determinate nothing. Here, however, nothing is to be taken in its indeterminate simplicity. Should it be held more correct to oppose to being, *non-being* instead of nothing, there would be no objection to this so far as the result is concerned, for in *non-being* the relation to *being* is contained: both being and its negation are enunciated in a *single* term, nothing, as it is in becoming. But we are concerned first of all not with the form of opposition (with the form, that is, also of *relation*) but with the abstract, immediate negation: nothing, purely on its own account, negation devoid of any relations – what could also be expressed if one so wished merely by 'not'.
>
> It was the *Eleatics*, above all Parmenides, who first enunciated the simple thought of *pure being* as the absolute and sole truth: *only being is, and nothing absolutely is not*, and in the surviving fragments of Parmenides this is enunciated with the pure enthusiasm of thought which has for

the first time apprehended itself in its absolute abstraction. As we know, in the oriental systems, principally in Buddhism, *nothing*, the void, is the absolute principle. Against that simple and one-sided abstraction the deep-thinking Heraclitus brought forward the higher, total concept of *becoming* and said: *being* as little *is*, as nothing *is*, or, all *flows*, which means, all is a *becoming*. The popular, especially oriental proverbs, that all that exists has the germ of death in its very birth, that death, on the other hand, is the entrance into new life, express at bottom the same union of being and nothing. But these expressions have a substratum in which the transition takes place; being and nothing are held apart in time, are conceived as alternating in it, but are not thought in their abstraction and consequently, too, not so that they are in themselves absolutely the same.

Ex nihilo nihil fit – is one of those propositions to which great importance was ascribed in metaphysics. In it is to be seen either only the empty tautology: nothing is nothing; or, if *becoming* is supposed to possess an actual meaning in it, then, since from *nothing* only *nothing becomes*, the proposition does not in fact contain *becoming*, for in it nothing remains nothing. Becoming implies that nothing does not remain nothing but passes into its other, into being. Later, especially Christian, metaphysics while rejecting the proposition that out of nothing comes nothing, asserted a transition from nothing into being; although it understood this proposition synthetically or merely imaginatively, yet even in the most imperfect union there is contained a point in which being and nothing coincide and their distinguishedness vanishes. The proposition: out of nothing comes nothing, nothing is just nothing, owes its peculiar importance to its opposition to *becoming* generally, and consequently also to its opposition to the creation of the world from nothing. Those who maintain the proposition: nothing is just nothing, and even grow heated in its defence, are unaware that in so doing they are subscribing to the abstract pantheism of the *Eleatics*, and also in principle to that of Spinoza. The philosophical view for which 'being is only being, nothing is only nothing', is a valid principle, merits the name of 'system of identity'; this abstract identity is the essence of pantheism. [. . .]

Remark 2: Defectiveness of the Expression 'Unity, Identity of Being and Nothing': Another contributory reason for the repugnance to the proposition about being and nothing must be mentioned; this is that the result of considering being and nothing, as expressed in the statement: being and nothing are one and the same, is incomplete. The emphasis is laid chiefly on their being one and the same, as in judgements generally, where it is the predicate that first states what the subject is. Consequently, the sense seems to be that the difference is denied, although at the same time it appears directly in the proposition; for this enunciates *both* determinations, being and nothing, and contains them as distinguished. At the same time, the intention cannot be that abstraction should be made from them and only the unity retained. Such a meaning would self-evidently be one-sided, because that from which abstraction is to be made is equally present and named in the proposition. Now in so far as the proposition: being and nothing are the same, asserts the identity of these determinations, but, in fact, equally contains them both as distinguished, the proposition is self-contradictory and cancels itself out. Bearing this in mind and looking at the proposition more closely, we find that it has a movement which involves the spontaneous vanishing of the proposition itself. But in thus vanishing, there takes place in it that which is to constitute its own peculiar content, namely, *becoming*.

The proposition thus *contains* the result, it is this *in its own self*. But the fact to which we must pay attention here is the defect that the result is not itself *expressed* in the proposition; it is an external reflection which discerns it therein. In this connection we must, at the outset, make this general observation, namely, that the proposition in the *form of a judgement* is not suited to express speculative truths; a familiarity with this fact is likely to remove many misunderstandings of speculative truths. Judgement is an *identical* relation between subject and predicate; in it we abstract from the fact that the subject has a number of determinatenesses other than that of the predicate, and also that the predicate is more extensive than the subject. Now if the content is speculative, the *non-identical* aspect of subject and predicate is also an essential moment, but in the judgement this is not expressed. It is the form of simple judgement, when it is used to express speculative results, which is very often responsible for the paradoxical and bizarre light in which much of recent philosophy appears to those who are not familiar with speculative thought.

To help express the speculative truth, the deficiency is made good in the first place by adding the contrary proposition: being and nothing are not the same, which is also enunciated as above. But thus there arises the further defect that these propositions are not connected, and therefore exhibit their content only in the form of an antinomy whereas their content refers to one and the same thing, and the determinations which are expressed in the two propositions are supposed to be in complete union – a union which can only be stated as an *unrest* of *incompatibles*, as a *movement*. The commonest injustice done to a speculative content is to make it one-sided, that is, to give prominence only to one of the propositions into which it can be resolved. It cannot then be denied that this proposition is asserted; *but the statement is just as false as it is true*, for once one of the propositions is taken out of the speculative content, the other must at least be equally considered and stated. Particular mention must be made here of that, so to speak, unfortunate word, 'unity'. Unity, even more than identity, expresses a subjective reflection; it is taken especially as the relation which arises from *comparison*, from external reflection. When this reflection finds the same thing in two *different objects*, the resultant unity is such that there is presupposed the complete *indifference* to it of the objects themselves which are compared, so that this comparing and unity does not concern the objects themselves and is a procedure and a determining external to them. Unity, therefore, expresses wholly *abstract* sameness and sounds all the more blatantly paradoxical the more the terms of which it is asserted show themselves to be sheer opposites. So far then, it would be better to say only *unseparatedness* and *inseparability*, but then the affirmative aspect of the relation of the whole would not find expression.

Thus the whole true result which we have here before us is *becoming*, which is not merely the one-sided or abstract unity of being and nothing. It consists rather in this movement, that pure being is immediate and simple, and for that very reason is equally pure nothing, that there *is* a difference between them, but a difference which no less sublates itself and is *not*. The result, therefore, equally asserts the difference of being and nothing, but as a merely fancied or imagined [*nur gemeinten*] difference.

It is the common opinion that being is rather the sheer other of nothing and that nothing is clearer than their absolute difference, and nothing seems easier than to be able to state it. But it is equally easy to convince oneself that this is impossible, that it is *unsayable. Let those who insist that being and nothing are different tackle the problem of stating in what the difference consists.* If being and nothing had any determinateness by which they were distinguished from each other then, as has been observed, they would be determinate being and determinate nothing, not the pure being and pure nothing that here they still are. Their difference is therefore completely empty, each of them is in the same way indeterminate; the difference, then, exists not in themselves but in a third, in subjective *opinion* [*Meinen*]. Opinion, however, is a form of subjectivity which is not proper to an exposition of this kind. But the third in which being and nothing subsist must also present itself here, and it has done so; it is *becoming*. In this, being and nothing are distinct moments; becoming only *is*, in so far as they are distinguished. This third is an other than they; they subsist only in an other, which is equivalent to saying that they are not self-subsistent. Becoming is as much the subsistence of being as it is of non-being; or, their subsistence is only their being in a *one*. It is just this their subsistence that equally sublates their difference.

The challenge to distinguish between being and nothing also includes the challenge to say what, then, is being and what is nothing. Those who are reluctant to recognize either one or the other as only a *transition* of the one into the other, and who assert this or that about being and nothing, let them state *what* it is they are speaking of, that is, put forward a *definition* of being and nothing and demonstrate its correctness. Without having satisfied this first requirement of the ancient science whose logical rules they accept as valid and apply in other cases, all that they maintain about being and nothing amounts only to assertions which are scientifically worthless. If elsewhere it has been said that existence, in so far as this at first is held to be synonymous with being, is the *complement* to *possibility*, then this presupposes another determination, possibility, and so being is not enunciated in its immediacy, but in fact as not self-subsistent, as conditioned. For being which is the outcome of *mediation* we shall reserve the term: *Existence*. But one *pictures* being to oneself, perhaps in the image of pure light as the clarity of undimmed seeing, and then nothing as pure night – and their distinction is linked with this very familiar sensuous difference. But, as a matter of fact, if this very seeing is more exactly imagined, one can readily perceive that in absolute clearness there is seen just as much, and as little, as in absolute darkness, that the one seeing is as good as the other, that pure seeing is a seeing of nothing. Pure light and pure darkness are two voids which are the same thing. Something can be distinguished only in determinate light or darkness (light is determined by darkness and so is darkened light, and darkness is determined by light, is illuminated darkness), and for this reason, that it is only darkened light and illuminated darkness which have within themselves the moment of difference and are, therefore, *determinate* being.

Remark 3:   *The Isolating of These Abstractions*: [. . .] In the pure reflection of the beginning as it is made in this logic with being as such, the transition is still concealed; because *being* is posited only as immediate, therefore *nothing* emerges in it only immediately. But all the subsequent determinations, like determinate being which immediately follows, are more concrete; in determinate being there is already *posited* that which contains and produces the contradiction of those abstractions and therefore their transition. When being is taken in this simplicity and immediacy, the recollection that it is the result of complete abstraction, and so for that reason alone is abstract negativity, nothing, is left behind, outside the science, which, within its own self, from *essence* onwards will expressly exhibit the said one-sided *immediacy* as a mediated immediacy where being is *posited* as *existence* and the mediating agent of this being is *posited* as *ground*.

In the light of such recollection, the transition from being into nothing can be represented, or, as it is said, *explained* and *made intelligible*, as something even easy and trivial; of course the being which is made the beginning of the science is *nothing*, for abstraction can be made from everything, and if abstraction is made from everything then *nothing* is left over. But, it may be continued, the beginning is thus not an affirmative, not being, but just nothing, and nothing is then also the *end*, at least as much as immediate being, and even more so. The shortest way is to let such reasoning take its course and then wait and see what is the nature of its boasted results. That *nothing* would be the result of such reasoning and that now the beginning should be made with nothing (as in Chinese philosophy), need not cause us to lift a finger, for before we could do so this nothing would no less have converted itself into being (see Section B above). [. . .] [R4]

2. Moments of becoming: Coming-to-be and ceasing-to-be

Becoming is the unseparatedness of being and nothing, not the unity which abstracts from being and nothing; but as the unity of *being* and *nothing* it is this *determinate* unity in which there *is* both being and nothing. But in so far as being and nothing, each unseparated from its other, *is*, each *is not*. They *are* therefore in this unity but only as vanishing, sublated moments. They sink from their initially imagined *self-subsistence* to the status of *moments*, which are still *distinct* but at the same time are sublated.

Grasped as thus distinguished, each moment is in this *distinguishedness* as a unity with the *other*. Becoming therefore contains being and nothing as *two* such unities, *each* of which is itself a unity of being and nothing; the one is being as immediate and as relation to nothing, and the other is nothing as immediate and as relation to being; the determinations are of unequal values in these unities.

Becoming is in this way in a double determination. In one of them, *nothing* is immediate, that is, the determination starts from nothing which relates itself to being, or in other words changes into it; in the other, *being* is immediate, that is, the determination starts from being which changes into nothing: the former is coming-to-be and the latter is ceasing-to-be.

Both are the same, *becoming*, and although they differ so in direction they interpenetrate and paralyse each other. The one is *ceasing-to-be*: being passes over into nothing, but nothing is equally the opposite of itself, transition into being, coming-to-be. This coming-to-be is the other direction: nothing passes over into being, but being equally sublates itself and is rather transition into nothing, is ceasing-to-be. They are not reciprocally sublated – the one does not sublate the other externally – but each sublates itself in itself and is in its own self the opposite of itself.

3. Sublation of becoming

The resultant equilibrium of coming-to-be and ceasing-to-be is in the first place *becoming* itself. But this equally settles into a stable unity. Being and nothing are in this unity only as vanishing moments; yet becoming as such *is* only through their distinguishedness. Their vanishing, therefore, is the vanishing of becoming or the vanishing of the vanishing itself. Becoming is an unstable unrest which settles into a stable result.

This could also be expressed thus: becoming is the vanishing of being in nothing and of nothing in being and the vanishing of being and nothing generally; but at the same time it rests on the distinction between them. It is therefore inherently self-contradictory, because the determinations it unites within itself are opposed to each other; but such a union destroys itself.

This result is the vanishedness of becoming, but it is not *nothing*; as such it would only be a relapse into one of the already sublated determinations, not the resultant of *nothing and being*. It is the unity of being and nothing which has settled into a stable oneness. But this stable oneness is being, yet no longer as a determination on its own but as a determination of the whole.

Becoming, as this transition into the unity of being and nothing, a unity which is in the form of being or has the form of the one-sided *immediate* unity of these moments, is *determinate being*.

> *Remark:*   *The Expression 'To Sublate'* [Aufheben]: *To sublate*, and the *sublated* (that which exists ideally as a moment), constitute one of the most important notions in philosophy. It is a fundamental determination which repeatedly occurs throughout the whole of philosophy, the meaning of which is to be clearly grasped and especially distinguished from *nothing*. What is sublated is not thereby reduced to nothing. Nothing is *immediate*; what is sublated, on the other hand, is the result of *mediation*; it is a non-being but as a *result* which had its origin in a being. It still has, therefore, *in itself* the *determinateness from which it originates*.
>
> *'To sublate'* has a twofold meaning in the language: on the one hand it means to preserve, to maintain, and equally it also means to cause to cease, to put an end to. Even 'to preserve' includes a negative element, namely, that something is removed from its immediacy and so from an existence which is open to external influences, in order to preserve it. Thus what is sublated is at the same time preserved; it has only lost its immediacy but is not on that account annihilated. The two definitions of 'to sublate' which we have given can be quoted as two dictionary *meanings* of this word. But it is certainly remarkable to find that a language has come to use one and the same word for two opposite meanings. It is a delight to speculative thought to find in the language words which have in themselves a speculative meaning; the German language has a number of such. The double meaning of the Latin *tollere* (which has become famous through the Ciceronian pun: *tollendum esse Octavium*) does not go so far; its affirmative determination signifies only a lifting-up. Something is sublated only in so far as it has entered into unity with its opposite; in this more particular signification as something reflected, it may fittingly be called a *moment*. In the case of the lever, weight and distance from a point are called its mechanical moments on account of the sameness of their effect, in spite of the contrast otherwise

between something real, such as a weight, and something ideal, such as a mere spatial determination, a line. We shall often have occasion to notice that the technical language of philosophy employs Latin terms for reflected determinations, either because the mother tongue has no words for them or if it has, as here, because its expression calls to mind more what is immediate, whereas the foreign language suggests more what is reflected.

The more precise meaning and expression which being and nothing receive, now that they are *moments*, is to be ascertained from the consideration of determinate being as the unity in which they are preserved. Being is being, and nothing is nothing, only in their contradistinction from each other; but in their truth, in their unity, they have vanished as these determinations and are now something else. Being and nothing are the same; *but just because they are the same they are no longer being and nothing*, but now have a different significance. In becoming they were coming-to-be and ceasing-to-be; in determinate being, a differently determined unity, they are again differently determined moments. This unity now remains their base from which they do not again emerge in the abstract significance of being and nothing.

Chapter 2: Determinate Being

In considering determinate being the emphasis falls on its determinate character; the determinateness is in the form of *being*, and as such it is *quality*. Through its quality, something is determined as opposed to an other, as *alterable* and *finite*; and as negatively determined not only against an other but also in its own self. This its negation as at first opposed to the finite something is the *infinite*; the abstract opposition in which these determinations appear resolves itself into the *infinity* which is free from the opposition, into *being-for-self*.

The treatment of determinate being falls therefore into three parts:

A.   Determinate being as such
B.   Something and other, finitude
C.   Qualitative infinity.

A. Determinate Being as Such

In determinate being (*a*) *as such*, its determinateness is first of all (*b*) to be distinguished as *quality*. This, however, is to be taken as well in the one determination of determinate being as in the other – as *reality* and *negation*. But in these determinatenesses determinate being is equally reflected into itself; and posited as such it is (*c*) *something*, a determinate being.

(a) Determinate being in general

From becoming there issues determinate being, which is the simple oneness of being and nothing. Because of this oneness it has the form of *immediacy*. Its mediation, becoming, lies behind it; it has sublated itself and determinate being appears, therefore, as a first, as a starting-point for the ensuing development. It is first of all in the one-sided determination of *being*; the other determination, *nothing*, will likewise display itself and in contrast to it.

It is not mere being, but determinate being [*Dasein*], etymologically taken, being in a certain *place*; but the idea of space is irrelevant here. Determinate being as the result of its becoming is, in general, being with a non-being such that this non-being is taken up into simple unity with being. *Non-being* thus taken up into being in such a way that the concrete whole is in the form of being, of immediacy, constitutes *determinateness* as such. [...]

Determinate being corresponds to *being* in the previous sphere, but being is indeterminate and therefore no determinations issue from it. *Determinate* being, however, is *concrete*; consequently a number of determinations, distinct relations of its moments, make their appearance in it.

(b) Quality

Because of the immediacy of the oneness of being and nothing in determinate being, they do not extend beyond each other; so far as determinate being is in the form of being, so far is it non-being, so far is it determinate. Being is not the *universal*, determinateness not the *particular*. Determinateness has not yet severed itself from being; and indeed it will no more sever itself from being, for the truth which from now on underlies them as ground is the unity of non-being with being; on this as ground all further determinations are developed. But the relation in which determinateness here stands to being is the immediate unity of both, so that as yet no differentiation of this unity is posited.

Determinateness thus isolated by itself in the form of *being* is *quality* – which is wholly simple and immediate. *Determinateness* as such is the more universal term which can equally be further determined as quantity and so on. Because of this simple character of quality as such, there is nothing further to be said about it.

Determinate being, however, in which nothing no less than being is contained, is itself the criterion for the one-sidedness of quality as a determinateness which is only *immediate* or only in the form of *being*. It is equally to be posited in the determination of nothing, whereby then the immediate or *affirmative* [*seiend*] determinateness is posited as a differentiated, reflected determinateness.[1] Nothing, as thus the determinate element of a determinateness, is equally something reflected, a *negative*.[2] Quality, taken in the distinct character of *being*, is *reality*; as burdened with a negative it is *negation* in general, likewise a quality but one which counts as a deficiency, and which further on is determined as limit, limitation.

Both are determinate being, but in *reality* as quality with the accent on *being*, the fact is concealed that it contains determinateness and therefore also negation. Consequently, reality is given the value only of something positive from which negation, limitation and deficiency are excluded. Negation taken as mere deficiency would be equivalent to nothing; but it is a *determinate* being, a quality, only determined with a non-being. [R]

(c) *Something*

In determinate being its determinateness has been distinguished as quality; in quality as determinately present [*als daseiender*], there *is* distinction – of reality and negation. Now although these distinctions are present in determinate being, they are no less equally void and sublated. Reality itself contains negation, is determinate being, not indeterminate, abstract being. Similarly, negation is determinate being, not the supposedly abstract nothing but posited here as it is in itself, as affirmatively present [*als seiend*], belonging to the sphere of determinate being. Thus quality is completely unseparated from determinate being, which is simply determinate, qualitative being.

This sublating of the distinction is more than a mere taking back and external omission of it again, or than a simple return to the simple beginning, to determinate being as such. The distinction cannot be omitted, for it *is*. What is, therefore, in fact present is determinate being in general, distinction in it, and sublation of this distinction; determinate being, not as devoid of distinction as at first, but as *again* equal to itself through sublation of the distinction, the simple oneness of determinate being *resulting* from this sublation. This sublatedness of the distinction is determinate being's *own* determinateness; it is thus *being-within-self* [*Insichsein*]: determinate being is *a determinate being, a something*.

Something is the *first negation of negation*, as simple self-relation in the form of being. Determinate being, life, thought, and so on, essentially determine themselves to become a determinate being, a living creature, a thinker (ego) and so on. This determination is of supreme importance if we are not to remain at the stage of determinate being, life, thought, and so on – also the Godhead (instead of God) – as generalities. In our ordinary way of thinking, *something* is rightly credited with reality. However, something is still a very superficial determination; just as reality and negation, determinate being and its determinateness, although no longer blank being and nothing, are still quite abstract determinations. It is for this reason that they are the most current expressions and the intellect which is philosophically untrained uses them most, casts its distinctions in their mould and fancies that in them it has something really well and truly determined. The negative of the negative is, as *something*, only the beginning of the subject [*Subjekt*] – being-within-self, only as yet quite indeterminate. It determines itself further on, first, as *a being-for-self* and so on, until in the Notion it first attains the concrete intensity of the subject. At the base of all these determinations lies the negative unity with itself. But in all this, care must be taken to distinguish between the *first* negation as negation *in general*, and the second negation, the negation of the negation: the latter is concrete, *absolute* negativity, just as the former on the contrary is only *abstract* negativity.

Something is the negation of the negation in the form of *being*; for this second negation is the restoring of the simple relation to self; but with this, something is equally *the mediation of itself with itself*. Even in the simple form of *something*, then still more specifically in *being-for-self*, *subject*, and so on, self-mediation is present; it is present even in *becoming*, only the mediation is quite abstract. In *something*, mediation with self is *posited*, in so far as something is determined as a simple identity. Attention can be drawn to the presence of mediation in general, as against the principle of the alleged mere immediacy of knowledge, from which mediation is supposed to be excluded; but there is no further need to draw particular attention to the moment of mediation, for it is to be found everywhere, in every Notion.

This mediation with itself which something is *in itself*, taken only as negation of the negation, has no concrete determinations for its sides; it thus collapses into the simple oneness which is *being*. Something *is*, and *is*, then, also a determinate being; further, it is *in itself* also *becoming*, which, however, no longer has only being and nothing for its moments. One of these, being, is now determinate being, and, further, a determinate being. The second is equally a *determinate* being, but determined as a negative of the something – an *other*. Something as a *becoming* is a transition, the moments of which are themselves somethings, so that the transition is *alteration* [*Veränderung*] – a becoming which has already become *concrete*. But to begin with, something alters only in its Notion; it is not yet *posited* as mediating and mediated, but at first only as simply maintaining itself in its self-relation, and its negative is posited as equally qualitative, as only an *other* in general.

B. Finitude

[. . .]

(a) *Something and an other*

1. Something and other are, in the first place, both determinate beings or somethings.

Secondly, each is equally an other. It is immaterial which is first named and solely for that reason called *something*; (in Latin, when they both occur in a sentence, both are called *aliud*, or 'the one, the other', *alius alium*; when there is reciprocity the expression *alter alterum* is analogous). If of two things we call one A, and the other B, then in the first instance B is determined as the other. But A is just as much the other of B. Both are, in the same way, *others*. The word 'this' serves to fix the distinction and the something which is to be taken affirmatively. But 'this' clearly expresses that this distinguishing and signalizing of the one something is a subjective designating falling outside the something itself. The entire determinateness falls into this external pointing out; even the expression 'this' contains no distinction; each and every something is just as well a 'this' as it is also an other. By 'this' we *mean* to express something completely determined; it is overlooked that speech, as a work of the understanding, gives expression only to universals, except in the *name* of a single object; but the individual name is meaningless, in the sense that it does not express a universal, and for the same reason appears as something merely posited and arbitrary; just as proper names, too, can be arbitrarily assumed, given or also altered.

Otherness thus appears as a determination alien to the determinate being thus characterized, or as the other *outside* the one determinate being; partly because a determinate being is determined as other only through being *compared* by a Third, and partly because it is only determined as other on account of the other which is outside it, but is not an other on its own account. At the same time, as has been remarked, every determinate being, even for ordinary thinking, determines itself as an other, so that there is no determinate being which is determined only as such, which is not outside a determinate being and therefore is not itself an other.

Both are determined equally as something and as other, and are thus the same, and there is so far no distinction between them. But this self-sameness of the determinations likewise arises only from external reflection, from the *comparing* of them; but the other as at first posited, although an other in relation to the something, is nevertheless also an other on its own account, apart from the something.

Thirdly, therefore, the other is to be taken as isolated, as in relation to itself, *abstractly* as the *other*; the τὸ ἕτερον of Plato, who opposes it as one of the moments of totality to the One, and in this way ascribes to the other a *nature* of its own. Thus the other, taken solely as such, is not the other of something but the other in its own self, that is, the other of itself. Such an other, determined as other, is physical nature; it is the other of spirit. This its determination is thus at first a mere relativity by which is expressed, not a quality of nature itself, but only a relation external to it. However, since spirit is the true something and nature, consequently, in its own self is only what it is as contrasted with spirit, the quality of nature taken as such is just this, to be the *other* in its own self, that which is *external to itself* (in the determinations of space, time and matter).

The other simply by itself is the other in its own self, hence the other of itself and so the other of the other – it is, therefore, that which is absolutely dissimilar within itself, that which negates itself, *alters* itself.[3] But in so doing it remains identical with itself, for that into which it alters is the other, and this is its sole determination; but what is altered is not determined in any different way but in the same way, namely, to be an other; in this latter, therefore, it only unites with its own self. It is thus posited as reflected into itself with sublation of the otherness, as a self-identical something from which, consequently, the otherness, which is at the same time a moment of it, is distinct[4] and does not appertain to the something itself.

2. Something *preserves* itself in its negative determinate being [*Nichtdasein*];[5] it is essentially *one* with it and essentially *not one* with it. It stands, therefore, in a *relation* to its otherness and is not simply its otherness. The otherness is at once contained in it and also still *separate* from it; it[6] is a *being-for-other* [*Sein für Anderes*].

Determinate being as such is immediate, without relation to an other; or, it is in the determination of *being*; but as including within itself non-being, it is *determinate* being, being negated within itself, and then in the first instance an other – but since at the same time it also preserves itself in its negation, it is only a *being-for-other*.

It preserves itself in its negative determinate being[7] and is being, but not being in general, but as self-related in *opposition* to its relation to other, as self-equal in opposition to its inequality. Such a being is *being-in-itself* [*Ansichsein*].

Being-for-other and being-in-itself constitute the two moments of the something. There are here present *two pairs* of determinations: 1. Something and other, 2. Being-for-other and being-in-itself. The former contain the unrelatedness of their determinateness; something and other fall apart. But their truth is their relation; being-for-other and being-in-itself are, therefore, the above determinations posited as *moments* of one and the same something, as determinations which are relations and which remain in their unity, in the unity of determinate being. Each, therefore, at the same time, also contains within itself its other moment which is distinguished from it.

Being and nothing in their unity, which is determinate being, are no longer being and nothing – these they are only outside their unity – thus in their unstable unity, in becoming, they are coming-to-be and ceasing-to-be. The being in something is *being-in-itself*. Being, which is self-relation, equality with self, is now no longer immediate, but is only as the non-being of otherness (as determinate being reflected into itself). Similarly, non-being as a moment of something is, in this unity of being and non-being, not negative determinate being in general, but an other, and more specifically – seeing that being is differentiated from it – at the same time a *relation* to its negative determinate being, a being-for-other.

Hence being-in-itself is, first, a negative relation to the negative determinate being, it has the otherness outside it and is opposed to it; in so far as something is *in itself* it is withdrawn from otherness and being-for-other. But secondly it has also present in it non-being itself, for it is itself the *non-being* of being-for-other.

But being-for-other is, first, a negation of the simple relation of being to itself which, in the first instance, is supposed to be determinate being and something; in so far as something is in an other or is for an other, it lacks a being of its own. But secondly it is not negative determinate being as pure nothing; it is negative determinate being which points to being-in-itself as to its own being which is reflected into itself, just as, conversely, being-in-itself points to being-for-other.

3. Both moments are determinations of what is one and the same, namely, the something. Something is *in itself* in so far as it has returned into itself out of the being-for-other. But something also has *in itself* (here the accent falls on *in*) or in *it* [*an ihm*], a determination or circumstance in so far as this circumstance is outwardly *in it*, is a being-for-other.[8]

This leads to a further determination. Being-in-itself and being-for-other are, in the first instance, distinct; but that something also has [outwardly] in *it*[9] the same character that it is *in itself*, and, conversely, that what it is as being-for-other it also is in itself – this is the identity of being-in-itself and being-for-other, in accordance with the determination that the something itself is one and the same something of both moments, which, therefore, are undividedly present in it. This identity is already formally given in the sphere of determinate being, but more expressly in the consideration of *essence* and of the relation of *inner* and *outer*, and most precisely in the consideration of the Idea as the unity of the Notion and *actuality*. People fancy that they are saying something lofty with the expression 'in itself', as they do in saying 'the inner'; but what something is *only in itself*, is also *only in it*; 'in itself' is only an abstract, and so even external determination. The expressions: there is nothing *in it*, or, there is something *in it*, imply, though somewhat obscurely, that what is *in* a thing also belongs to the thing's *being-in-itself*, to its inner, true worth.

It may be observed that the meaning of the *thing-in-itself* is here revealed; it is a very simple abstraction but for some while it counted as a very important determination, something superior, as it were, just as the proposition that we do not know what things are in themselves ranked as a profound piece of wisdom. Things are called 'in themselves' in so far as abstraction is made from all being-for-other, which means simply, in so far as they are thought devoid of all determination, as nothings. In this sense, it is of course impossible to know *what* the *thing-in-itself* is. For the question: *what*? demands that *determinations* be assigned; but since the things of which they are to be assigned are at the same time supposed to be *things in themselves*, which means, in effect, to be without any determination, the question is thoughtlessly made impossible to answer, or else only an absurd answer is given. The thing-in-itself is the same as that *absolute* of which we know nothing except that in it all is one. What is *in* these things-in-themselves, therefore, we know quite well; they are as such nothing but truthless, empty abstractions. What, however, the thing-in-itself is in truth, what truly is in itself, of this logic is the exposition, in which however something better than an abstraction is understood by 'in-itself', namely, what something is in its Notion; but the Notion is concrete within itself, is comprehensible simply as

Notion, and as determined within itself and the connected whole of its determinations, is cognizable. [. . .]

(b) *Determination, Constitution and Limit*[10]

[. . .]

Thus something *through its own nature* relates itself to the other, because otherness is posited in it as its own moment; its being-within-self includes the negation within it, by means of which alone it now has its affirmative determinate being. But the other is also qualitatively distinguished from this and is thus posited outside the something. The negation of its other is now the quality of the something, for it is as this sublating of its other that it is something. It is only in this sublation that the other is really opposed to another determinate being; the other is only externally opposed to the *first* something, or rather, since in fact they are *directly* connected, that is in their Notion, their connection is this, that determinate being has *passed over* into otherness, something into other, and something is just as much an other as the other itself is.[11] Now in so far as the being-within-self is the non-being of the otherness which is contained in it but which at the same time has a distinct being of its own, the something is itself the negation, *the ceasing of an other in it*; it is posited as relating itself negatively to the other and in so doing preserving itself; this other, the being-within-self of the something as negation of the negation, is its *in-itself*, and at the same time this sublation is *present in it* as a simple negation, namely, as its negation of the other something external to it. There is a *single* determinateness of both, which on the one hand is identical with the being-within-self of the somethings as negation of the negation, and on the other hand, since these negations are opposed to one another as other somethings, conjoins and equally disjoins them through their own nature, each negating the other: this determinateness is *limit*.

3. Being-for-other is the indeterminate, affirmative community of something with its other; in the limit the *non-being*-for-other becomes prominent, the qualitative negation of the other, which is thereby kept apart from the something which is reflected into itself. We must observe the development of this Notion, which manifests itself, however, rather as an entanglement and a contradiction. This contradiction is at once to be found in the circumstance that the limit, as something's negation reflected into itself, contains *ideally* in it the moments of something and other, and these, as distinguished moments, are at the same time posited in the sphere of determinate being as *really, qualitatively distinct*.

(a) Something, therefore, is immediate, self-related determinate being, and has a limit, in the first place, relatively to an other; the limit is the non-being of the other, not of the something itself: in the limit, something limits its other. But the other is itself a something in general, therefore the limit which something has relatively to the other is also the limit of the other as a something, its limit whereby it keeps the first something as *its* other apart from it, or is a *non-being of that something*; it is thus not only non-being of the other, but non-being equally of the one and of the other something, consequently of the something as such.

But the limit is essentially equally the non-being of the other, and so something at the same time *is* through its limit. It is true that something, in limiting the other, is subjected to being limited itself; but at the same time its limit is, as the ceasing of the other in it, itself only the being of the something; *through the limit something is what it is, and in the limit it has its quality.* This relationship is the outward manifestation of the fact that the limit is simple negation or the *first* negation, whereas the other is, at the same time, the negation of the negation, the being-within-self of the something.

Something, as an immediate determinate being, is, therefore, the limit relatively to another something, but the limit is present in the something itself, which is a something through the mediation of the limit which is just as much the non-being of the something. Limit is the mediation through which something and other each as well *is*, as *is not*.

(β) Now in so far as something in its limit both *is* and *is not*, and these moments are an immediate, qualitative difference, the negative determinate being and the determinate being of the something fall outside each other. Something has its determinate being *outside* (or, as it is also put, on the *inside*) of its limit; similarly, the other, too, because it is a something, is outside it. Limit is the *middle between* the two of them in which they cease. They have their determinate being *beyond* each other and *beyond* their limit; the limit as the non-being of each is the other of both.

It is in accordance with this difference of something from its limit that the line appears as line only outside its limit, the point; the plane as plane outside the line; the solid as solid only outside its limiting surface. It is primarily this aspect of limit which is seized by pictorial thought – the self-externality of the Notion – and especially, too, in reference to spatial objects.

(γ) But further, something as it is outside the limit, the unlimited something, is only a determinate being in general. As such, it is not distinguished from its other; it is only determinate being and therefore has the same determination as its other; each is only a something in general, or each is an other; thus both are the *same*. But this their primarily immediate determinate being is now posited with the determinateness as limit, in which both are what they are, distinguished from each other. Limit is, however, equally their *common* distinguishedness, their unity and distinguishedness, like determinate being. This double identity of both, determinate being and limit, contains this: that something has its determinate being only in the limit, and that since the limit and the determinate being are each at the same time the negative of each other, the something, which *is* only in its limit, just as much separates itself from itself and points beyond itself to its non-being, declaring this is to be its being and thus passing over into it.[12]

[. . .] Something with its immanent limit, posited as the contradiction of itself, through which it is directed and forced out of and beyond itself, is the *finite*.

(c) Finitude

[. . .] When we say of things that *they are finite*, we understand thereby that they not only have a determinateness, that their quality is not only a reality and an intrinsic determination, that finite things are not merely limited – as such they still have determinate being outside their limit – but that, on the contrary, non-being constitutes their nature and being. Finite things *are*, but their relation to themselves is that they are *negatively* self-related and in this very self-relation send themselves away beyond themselves, beyond their being. They *are*, but the truth of this being is their *end*. The finite not only alters, like something in general, but it *ceases to be*; and its ceasing to be is not merely a possibility, so that it could be without ceasing to be, but the being as such of finite things is to have the germ of decease as their being-within-self: the hour of their birth is the hour of their death.

[. . .] The finite is thus inwardly self-contradictory; it sublates itself, ceases to be. But this its result, the negative as such, is (α) its very *determination*;[13] for it [the finite] is the negative of the negative. Thus, in ceasing to be, the finite has not ceased to be;[14] it has become in the first instance only *another* finite which, however, is equally a ceasing-to-be as transition into another finite, and so on to *infinity*. But (β) closer consideration of this result shows that the finite in its ceasing-to-be, in this negation of itself has attained its being-in-itself, is *united with itself.* [. . .] In going beyond itself, therefore, it equally only unites with itself. This *identity with itself*, the negation of negation, is affirmative being and thus the other of the finite, of the finite which is supposed to have the first negation for its determinateness; this other is the *infinite*.

C. Infinity

The infinite in its simple Notion can, in the first place, be regarded as a fresh definition of the absolute; as indeterminate self-relation it is posited as *being* and *becoming*. The forms of *determinate being* find no place in the series of those determinations which can be regarded as definitions of the absolute, for the individual forms of that sphere are immediately posited only as determinatenesses, as finite in general. The infinite, however, is held to be absolute without qualification for it is determined expressly as negation of the finite, and reference is thus expressly made to limitedness in the infinite – limitedness of which being and becoming could perhaps be capable, even if not possessing or showing it – and the presence in the infinite of such limitedness is denied.

But even so, the infinite is not yet really free from limitation and finitude; the main point is to distinguish the genuine Notion of infinity from spurious infinity, the infinite of reason from the infinite of the understanding; yet the latter is the *finitized* infinite, and it will be found that in the very act of keeping the infinite pure and aloof from the finite, the infinite is only made finite.

[. . .] The infinite as thus posited over against the finite, in a relation wherein they are as qualitatively distinct others, is to be called the *spurious infinite*,[15] the infinite of the understanding, for which it has the value of the highest, the absolute Truth. The understanding is satisfied that it has truly reconciled these two, but the truth is that it is entangled in unreconciled, unresolved, absolute contradiction; it can only be brought to a consciousness of this fact by the contradictions into which it falls on every side when it ventures to apply and to explicate these its categories.

This contradiction occurs as a direct result of the circumstance that the finite remains as a determinate being opposed to the infinite, so that there are *two* determinatenesses; *there are* two worlds, one infinite and one finite, and in their relationship the infinite is only the *limit* of the finite and is thus only a determinate infinite, an *infinite which is itself finite*.

This contradiction develops its content into more explicit forms. The finite is real determinate being which persists as such even when transition is made to its non-being, to the infinite; this, as has been shown, has only the first, immediate negation for its determinateness relatively to the finite, just as the finite as opposed to that negation has, as negated, only the significance of an other and is, therefore, still [only] *something*. When, therefore, the understanding, raising itself above this finite world, ascends to its highest, to the infinite, this finite world remains for it on *this* side, so that the infinite is only set *above* or *beyond* the finite, is *separated* from it, with the consequence that the finite is separated from the infinite; each is *assigned* a *distinct* place – the finite as determinate being here, on *this* side, and the infinite, although the *in-itself* of the finite, nevertheless as a beyond in the dim, inaccessible distance, *outside* of which the finite is and remains.

As thus separated they are just as much essentially *connected* by the very negation which separates them. This negation which connects them – the *somethings* reflected into themselves – is the limit of the one relatively to the other, and that, too, in such a manner that each of them does not have the limit *in it* merely relatively to the other, but the negation is their *being-in-itself*; the limit is thus present in each on its own account, in separation from the other. But the limit is in the form of the first negation and thus both are limited, finite in themselves. However, each as affirmatively self-related is also the negation of its limit; each thus immediately repels the limit, as its non-being, from itself and, as qualitatively separated from it, posits it as *another being* outside it, the finite positing its non-being as this infinite and the infinite, similarly, the finite. It is readily conceded that there is a necessary transition from the finite to the infinite – necessary through the determination of the finite – and that the finite is raised to the form of being-in-itself, since the finite, although persisting as a determinate being, is at the same time *also* determined as *in itself* nothing and therefore as destined to bring about its own dissolution; whereas the infinite, although determined as burdened with negation and limit, is at the same time also determined as possessing *being-in-itself*, so that this abstraction of self-related affirmation constitutes its determination, and hence finite determinate being is not present in it. But it has been shown that the infinite itself attains affirmative being only *by means of* negation, as the negation of negation, and that when this its affirmation is taken as merely simple, qualitative being, the negation contained in it is reduced to a simple immediate negation and thus to a determinateness and limit, which then, as in contradiction with the being-in-itself of the infinite is posited as excluded from it, as not belonging to it, as, on the contrary, opposed to its being-in-itself, as the finite. As therefore each is in its own self and through its own determination the positing of its other, they are *inseparable*. But this their unity is *concealed* in their *qualitative* otherness, it is the *inner* unity which only lies at their base.

This determines the manner in which this unity is manifested: posited in *determinate being*, the unity is a changing or transition of the finite into the infinite, and vice versa; so that the infinite only *emerges* in the finite and the finite in the infinite, the other in the other; that is to say, each arises *immediately* and independently in the other, their connection being only an external one.

The process of their transition has the following detailed shape. We pass from the finite to the infinite. This transcending of the finite appears as an external act. In this void beyond the finite, what arises? What is the positive element in it? Owing to the inseparability of the infinite and the finite – or because this infinite remaining aloof on its own side is itself limited – there arises a limit; the infinite has vanished and its other, the finite, has entered. But this entrance of the finite appears as a happening external to the infinite, and the new limit as something that does not arise from the infinite itself but is likewise found as given. And so we are faced with a relapse into the previous determination which has been sublated in vain. But this new limit is itself only something which has to be sublated or transcended. And so again there arises the void, the nothing, in which similarly the said determinateness, a new limit, is encountered – *and so on to infinity*.

We have before us the alternating determination of the *finite* and the *infinite*; the finite is finite only in its relation to the ought or to the infinite, and the latter is only infinite in its relation to the finite. They are inseparable and at the same time mutually related as sheer others; each has in its own self the other of itself. Each is thus the unity of itself and its other and is in its determinateness *not* that which it itself is, and which its other is.

It is this alternating determination negating both its own self and its negation, which appears as the *progress to infinity*, a progress which in so many forms and applications is accepted as something ultimate beyond which thought does not go but, having got as far as this 'and so on to infinity', has usually reached its goal. This progress makes its appearance wherever *relative* determinations are pressed to the point of opposition, with the result that although they are in an inseparable unity, each is credited with a self-subsistent determinate being over against the other. The progress is, consequently, a *contradiction* which is not resolved but is always only enunciated as *present*.

What we have here is an abstract transcending of a limit, a transcending which remains incomplete because *it is not itself transcended*. Before us is the infinite; it is of course transcended, for a new limit is posited, but the result is rather only a return to the finite. This spurious infinity is in itself the same thing as the perennial ought; it is the negation of the finite it is true, but it cannot in truth free itself therefrom. The finite reappears *in the infinite itself* as its other, because it is only in its *connection* with its other, the finite, that the infinite is. The progress to infinity is, consequently, only the perpetual repetition of one and the same content, one and the same tedious *alternation* of this finite and infinite.

The infinity of the infinite progress remains burdened with the finite as such, is thereby limited and is itself *finite*. But this being so, the infinite progress would in fact be posited as the unity of the finite and the infinite; but this unity is not reflected on. Yet it is this unity alone which evokes the infinite in the finite and the finite in the infinite; it is, so to speak, the mainspring of the infinite progress. This progress is the *external* aspect of this unity at which ordinary thinking halts, at this perpetual repetition of one and the same alternation, of the vain unrest of advancing beyond the limit to infinity, only to *find* in this infinite a new limit in which, however, it is as little able to rest as in the infinite. This infinite has the fixed determination of a *beyond*, which cannot be reached, for the very reason that *it is not meant* to be reached, because the determinateness of the beyond, of the *affirmative* negation, is not let go. In accordance with this determination the infinite has the finite opposed to it as a being *on this side*, which is equally unable to raise itself into the infinite just because it has this determination of an *other*, of a *determinate being* which perpetually generates itself in its beyond, a beyond from which it is again distinct.

In this alternating determination of the finite and the infinite from one to the other and back again, their truth is already implicitly *present*, and all that is required is to take up what is before us.

[. . .] In the first place, the negation of the finite and infinite which is posited in the infinite progress can be taken as simple, hence as separate and merely successive. Starting from the finite, the limit is transcended, the finite negated. We now have its beyond, the infinite, but in this the limit *arises* again; and so we have the transcending of the infinite. This double sublation, however, is partly only an external affair, an alternation of the moments, and partly it is not yet posited as a *single unity*; the transcending of each moment starts independently, is a fresh act, so that the two processes fall apart. But in addition there is also present in the infinite progress their *connection*. First there is the finite, then this is transcended and this negative or beyond of the finite is the infinite, and then this negation is again transcended, so that there arises a new limit, a *finite* again. This is the complete, self-closing movement which has arrived at that which constituted the beginning; what arises is the *same* as that from which the movement *began*, that is, the finite is restored; it has therefore united *with itself*, has in its beyond only found *itself* again.

The same is the case with the infinite. In the infinite, the beyond of the limit, there arises only another limit which has the same fate, namely, that as finite it must be negated. Thus what is present again is the *same* infinite which had previously disappeared in the new limit; the infinite, therefore, through its sublating, through its transcending of the new limit, is not removed any further either from the finite – for the finite is only this, to pass over into the infinite – or from itself, for it has arrived *at its own self*.

Thus, both finite and infinite are this *movement* in which each returns to itself through its negation; they *are* only as *mediation* within themselves, and the affirmative of each contains the negative of each and is the negation of the negation. They are thus a *result*, and consequently not what they are in the determination of their *beginning*; the finite is not a *determinate being* on *its* side, and the infinite a *determinate being* or *being-in-itself* beyond the determinate being, that is, beyond the being determined as finite. The reason why understanding is so antagonistic to the unity of the finite and infinite is simply that it presupposes the limitation and the finite, as well as the in-itself, as *perpetuated*; in doing so it *overlooks* the negation of both which is actually present in the infinite progress, as also the fact that they occur therein only as moments of a whole and that they come on the scene only by means of their opposite, but essentially also by means of the sublation of their opposite.

If, at first, the return into self was considered to be just as much a return of the finite to itself as return of the infinite to itself, this very result reveals an error which is connected with the one-sidedness just criticized: first the finite and then the infinite is taken as the *starting-point* and it is only this that gives rise to *two* results. It is, however, a matter of complete indifference which is taken as the beginning; and thus the difference which occasioned the *double* result disappears of itself. This is likewise explicit in the line – unending in both directions – of the infinite progress in which each of the moments presents itself in equal alternation, and it is quite immaterial what point is fixed on or which of the two is taken as the beginning. They are distinguished in it but each is equally only the moment of the other. Since both the finite and the infinite itself are moments of the progress they are *jointly or in common the finite*, and since they are equally together negated in it and in the result, this result as negation of the finitude of both is called with truth the infinite. Their difference is thus the *double* meaning which both have. The finite has the double meaning of being first, only the finite *over against* the infinite which stands opposed to it, and secondly, of being the finite and *at the same time* the infinite opposed to it. The infinite, too, has the double meaning of being *one* of these two moments – as such it is the spurious infinite – and also the infinite in which both, the infinite and its other, are only moments. The infinite, therefore, as now before us is, in fact, the process in which it is deposed to being only *one* of its determinations, the opposite of the finite, and so to being itself only one of the finites, and then raising this its difference from itself into the affirmation of itself and through this mediation becoming the *true* infinite.

This determination of the true infinite cannot be expressed in the *formula* [. . .] of a *unity* of the finite and infinite; *unity* is abstract, inert self-sameness, and the moments are similarly only in the form of inert, simply affirmative being. The infinite, however, like its two moments, is essentially only as a *becoming*, but a becoming now *further determined* in its moments. Becoming, in the first instance, has abstract being and nothing for its determinations; as alteration, its moments possess determinate being, something and other; now, as the infinite, they are the finite and the infinite, which are themselves in process of becoming.

This infinite, as the consummated return into self, the relation of itself to itself, is *being* – but not indeterminate, abstract being, for it is posited as negating the negation; it is, therefore, also *determinate* being for it contains negation in general and hence determinateness. It *is* and *is there*, present before us. It is only the spurious infinite which is the *beyond*, because it is *only* the negation of the finite posited as *real* – as such it is the abstract, first negation; determined *only* as negative, the affirmation of *determinate* being is lacking in it; the spurious infinite, held fast as only negative, is even *supposed to be not there*, is supposed to be unattainable. However, to be thus unattainable is not its grandeur but its defect, which is at bottom the result of holding fast to the *finite* as such as a *merely affirmative being*. It is what is untrue that is unattainable, and such an infinite must be seen as a falsity. The image of the progress to infinity is the *straight line*, at the two limits of which alone the infinite is, and always only is where the line – which is determinate being – is not, and which goes *out beyond* to this negation of its determinate being, that is, to the indeterminate; the image of true infinity, bent back into itself, becomes the *circle*, the line which has reached itself, which is closed and wholly present, without *beginning* and *end*.

True infinity taken thus generally as *determinate* being which is posited as *affirmative* in contrast to the abstract negation, is *reality* in a higher sense than the former reality which was *simply* determinate; for here it has acquired a concrete content. It is not the finite which is the real, but the infinite. Thus reality is further determined as essence, Notion, Idea, and so on. It is, however, superfluous to repeat an earlier, more abstract category such as reality, in connection with the more concrete categories and to employ it for determinations which are more concrete than it is in its own self. Such repetition as to say that essence, or the Idea, is the real, has its origin in the fact that for untrained thinking, the most abstract categories such as being, determinate being, reality, finitude, are the most familiar.

The more precise reason for recalling the category of reality here is that the negation to which it is opposed as the affirmative is here negation of the negation; as such it is itself opposed to that reality which finite determinate being is. The negation is thus determined as ideality; ideal being [*das Ideelle*] is the finite as it is in the true infinite – as a determination, a content, which is distinct but is not an *independent, self-subsistent* being, but only a *moment*. Ideality has this more concrete signification which is not fully expressed by the negation of finite determinate being. [. . .]

Notes

1   Miller's translation has 'when it will be posited as a differentiated, reflected determinateness, no longer as immediate or in the form of being'. The German text is 'womit dann die unmittelbare oder die *seiende* Bestimmtheit als eine unterschiedene, reflektierte gesetzt wird'. Hegel's point here is that, when quality is thought or posited 'in the determination of nothing', a difference is introduced between negative and affirmative determinateness or quality. Immediate, affirmative determinateness thus comes to be thought, not simply as immediate, but as a *differentiated*, reflected determinateness (i.e., as reality *in relation to* negation). [s.h.]

2   Miller's translation has 'negation'. The German word is 'Verneinung'. In the following sentence Miller translates 'Verneinung' as 'negative', and reserves the word 'negation' for the German word 'Negation'. [s.h.]

3   The German word for 'other' is 'das Andere', and the German word for 'alteration' (or change) is 'Veränderung'. Hegel thus understands alteration as the process whereby what is other 'others' itself (*sich verändert*) into something else or comes to be other than what it is. Note that, unlike Aristotle and Kant, Hegel does not think that change (or the process of becoming other than what one is) presupposes an underlying *substratum*. See *The Complete Works of Aristotle*, edited by J. Barnes, 2 vols (Princeton: Princeton University Press, 1984), 1: 324–5 (*Physics*, 190a13–190b4), and Kant, *Critique of Pure Reason*, translated by N. Kemp Smith (London: Macmillan, 1929), pp. 216–17 (B230–2). [s.h.]

4   Miller's translation has (redundantly) 'from which . . . the otherness . . . is distinct from it'. [s.h.]

5   Miller's translation has 'in the negative of its determinate being'. The German text is 'in seinem Nichtdasein'. [s.h.]

6   i.e., something. [s.h.]

7   Miller's translation again has 'in the negative of its determinate being'. The German text is 'in seinem Nichtdasein'. [s.h.]

8   Miller's translation has 'within it' in line four of this paragraph, where the German text has 'an ihm'. This is inappropriate, since that which something has *an ihm* does not specifically lie *within* the thing (as opposed to on the surface), but simply belongs to *it* rather than something else. That which lies *within* the thing is what something is *in itself* or *an sich*. Hegel's point in this paragraph and the next is twofold. First, he is claiming that what belongs to something, belongs to it *outwardly* and so is evident from an external point of view (or for another). Second, he is claiming that the idea that there is a complete separation between what something

is in itself and what it is outwardly is in fact an abstraction. In truth, there is nothing within something that is not in some way outwardly evident, and there is nothing that is outwardly evident in a thing that does not in some way belong to what that thing is within itself. In translating 'an ihm' as 'in *it*', I am following the translation of Johnston and Struthers. See G. W. F. Hegel, *Science of Logic*, translated by W. H. Johnston and L. G. Struthers, 2 vols (London: George Allen and Unwin, 1929), 1: 133. [S.H.]

9   Miller's translation again has 'within it' for 'an ihm'. [S.H.]

10 The analyses of determination and constitution (subsections 1 and 2) have been omitted from this collection. [S.H.]

11 See Hegel, *Science of Logic*, pp. 117–18. See above, pp. 198–9. [S.H.]

12 Miller's translation has 'this double identity of both, of determinate being and limit' in line 9 of this paragraph. The German text is 'diese doppelte Identität beider, das Dasein und die Grenze'. Hegel's point here is that something and its other are identical with one another in so far as they are both *determinate* and both *limited*. To be determinate and to be limited are thus themselves one and the same thing – even though the limit is the *negation* of determinate being, the point at which determinate being ends. When the determinate being of something is itself understood to 'pass over' into the *non-being* of the thing in this way, then the thing is understood to be *finite*. [S.H.]

13 That is to say, the negative as such is what the finite itself intrinsically *is*. [S.H.]

14 It has continued to *be* finite, though *not* as it was before, and so has become a *different* finite. [S.H.]

15 'das *Schlecht-Unendliche*', also known as the 'Bad Infinite'. [S.H.]

16

Science of Logic:
Doctrine of Essence

The truth of *being* is *essence.*

Being is the immediate. Since knowing has for its goal knowledge of the true, knowledge of what being is *in and for itself,* it does not stop at the immediate and its determinations, but penetrates it on the supposition that at the back of this being there is something else, something other than being itself, that this background constitutes the truth of being. This knowledge is a mediated knowing for it is not found immediately with and in essence, but starts from an other, from being, and has a preliminary path to tread, that of going beyond being or rather of penetrating into it. Not until knowing *inwardizes, recollects* [*erinnert*] itself out of immediate being, does it through this mediation find essence. The German language has preserved essence in the past participle [*gewesen*] of the verb *to be;* for essence is past – but timelessly past – being.

When this movement is pictured as the path of knowing, then this beginning with being, and the development that sublates it, reaching essence as a mediated result, appears to be an activity of knowing external to being and irrelevant to being's own nature.

But this path is the movement of being itself. It was seen that being inwardizes itself through its own nature, and through this movement into itself becomes essence.

If, therefore, the absolute was at first defined as *being,* now it is defined as *essence.* Cognition certainly cannot stop short at manifold *determinate being,* nor yet at *being, pure being;* the reflection that immediately forces itself on one is that this *pure being,* the *negation* of everything finite, presupposes an *internalization,* a *recollection* [*Erinnerung*] and movement which has purified immediate, determinate being to pure being. Being is accordingly determined as essence, as a being in which everything determinate and finite is negated. It is thus the *indeterminate,* simple unity from which what is determinate has been eliminated in an *external manner;* the determinate element itself was external to this unity and, after this elimination, still remains confronting it; for it has not been sublated in itself but only relatively, only in relation to this unity. We have already mentioned that if essence is defined as the *sum total of all realities*, then these realities likewise are subordinate to the nature of the determinateness and to the abstractive reflection and this sum total reduces to empty oneness. Essence is in this way only a product, an artefact. *External* negation – and this is what abstraction is – only shifts the determinatenesses of being *away* from what is left over as Essence; it only puts them, so to speak, elsewhere, leaving them the affirmative character they possessed before. But in this way, essence is neither *in itself* nor *for itself*; what it is, it is through an other, the external, abstractive reflection; and it is for an other, namely for abstraction and, in general, for the simply affirmative being [*das Seiende*] that remains confronting it. Its character, therefore, is to lack all determinate character, to be inherently lifeless and empty.

But essence as it has here come to be, is what it is through a negativity which is not alien to it but is its very own, the infinite movement of being. It is being that is *in itself and for itself*; it is absolute *being-in-itself* in that it is indifferent to every determinateness of being, and otherness and relation-to-other have been completely sublated. But it is not only this being-in-itself; as mere being-in-itself it would be only the abstraction of pure essence; but it is equally essentially *being-for-self*; it is itself this negativity, the self-sublating of otherness and determinateness.

Essence as the completed return of being into itself is thus at first indeterminate essence. The determinatenesses of being are sublated in it; they are contained in essence *in principle* [*an sich*] but are not *posited in it*. Absolute essence in this simple equality with itself has *no determinate being*; but it must develop determinate being, for it is both *in itself* and *for itself*, i.e. it *differentiates* the determinations which are *implicit* [*an sich*] in it. Because it is self-repelling or indifferent to itself, *negative* self-relation, it sets itself over against itself and is infinite being-for-self only in so far as it is at one with itself in this its own difference from itself. This determining then is of a different nature from the determining in the sphere of being, and the determinations of essence have a different character from the determinatenesses of being. Essence is absolute unity of being-in-itself and being-for-itself; consequently its determining remains within this unity and is neither a becoming nor a transition, nor are the determinations themselves an *other* as other, or relations *to other*; they are self-subsistent, but at the same time only in their association with each other in this unity. Since essence is at first simple negativity, it now has to posit in its *own* sphere the determinateness that is only *implicit* in it, in order to give itself determinate being and then being-for-self.

In the *whole* of logic, essence occupies the same place as quantity does in the sphere of being; absolute indifference to limit. But quantity is this indifference in an *immediate* determination, and the limit is present in it as an immediately external determinateness, quantity passes over into quantum; the external limit is necessary to quantity and is *affirmatively present* in it [*ist an ihr seiend*]. In essence, on the other hand, the determinateness is not a simple immediacy but is present only as *posited* by essence itself; it is not free, but is present only as *connected* with its unity. The negativity of essence is *reflection*; and the determinations are *reflected*, posited by essence itself and remaining in essence as sublated.

Essence stands between *being* and *Notion*; it constitutes their mean, and its movement is the *transition* from being into the Notion. Essence is being-in-and-for-itself, but in the determination of being-in-itself; for the general determination of essence is to have proceeded from being, or to be the *first negation of being*. Its movement consists in positing within itself the negation or determination, thereby giving itself *determinate being* and becoming as infinite being-for-self what it is in itself. It thus gives itself its *determinate being* that is *equal* to its being-in-itself and becomes *Notion*. For the Notion is the absolute that in its determinate being is absolute, or is in and for itself. But the determinate being which essence gives itself is not yet determinate being as in and for itself, but as *given* by essence to itself, or as *posited*, and is consequently still distinct from the determinate being of the Notion.

At first, essence *shines* or *shows within itself*, or is reflection; secondly, it *appears*; thirdly, it *manifests* itself. In its movement, essence posits itself in the following determinations:

I.   As *simple* essence, essence in itself, which in its determinations remains within itself
II. As emerging into determinate being, or in accordance with its Existence and *Appearance*
III. As essence that is one with its Appearance, as *actuality*.[1]

Section One: Essence as Reflection Within Itself

Chapter 1: Illusory Being [*Schein*]

Essence that issues from being seems to confront it as an opposite; this immediate being is, in the first instance, the *unessential*.

But secondly, it is more than merely unessential being, it is essenceless being, it is *illusory being*.

Thirdly, this illusory being is not something external to or other than essence; on the contrary, it is essence's own illusory being. The showing of this illusory being within essence itself is *reflection*.

A. The Essential and the Unessential

Essence is *sublated being*. It is simple equality with itself, but only in so far as it is the *negation* of the sphere of being in general. Essence thus has immediacy confronting it as an immediacy from which it has become and which in this sublating has preserved and maintained itself. In this determination, essence itself is *simply affirmative [seiendes]*, immediate essence, and being is only a negative *in relation to* essence, not in and for itself; therefore essence is a *determinate* negation. In this way, being and essence are again related to each other as *others*; for *each has a being, an immediacy*, and these are indifferent to each other, and with respect to this being, being and essence are equal in value.

But at the same time, being, as contrasted with essence, is the unessential; in relation to essence, it has the determination of sublated being. Yet in so far as it is only related to essence simply as an other, essence is not strictly essence but only a differently determined being, the *essential*.

The distinction of essential and unessential has caused essence to relapse into the sphere of *determinate being*, since essence in its initial phase is determined as immediate, simply affirmative [*seiendes*] essence and hence only as *other* over against being. The sphere of determinate being is thereby made the base, and the fact that the being in this determinate being is being-in-and-for-itself, is a further determination external to determinate being itself; and conversely, while essence is indeed being-in-and-for-itself, it is so only in relation to an other, in a *specific* reference. Accordingly, in so far as the distinction is made of an essential and an unessential side in something [*Dasein*], this distinction is *externally* posited, a separation of one part of it from another that does not affect the something itself, a division which has its origin in a *third*. Such a division does not settle what is essential and what is unessential. It originates in some external standpoint and consideration and the same content can therefore be regarded now as essential and again as unessential.

Closer consideration shows that when essence is characterized as essential only relatively to what is unessential, it is because it is taken only as sublated being or determinate being. In this way, essence is only the *first* negation, or the negation which is a *determinateness* through which being becomes only determinate being, or the latter becomes only an other. But essence is the absolute negativity of being; it is being itself, but not determined only as an other, but being that has sublated itself both as immediate being and also as immediate negation, as negation that is infected with otherness. Thus being, or determinate being, has not preserved itself as an other – for we are in the sphere of essence – and the immediate that is still distinguished from essence is not merely an unessential determinate being but the immediate that is *in and for itself* a nullity; it is only a *non-essence, illusory* being.

B. Illusory Being

1. *Being is illusory being.*[2] The being of illusory being consists solely in the sublatedness of being, in its nothingness; this nothingness it has in essence

and apart from its nothingness, apart from essence, illusory being is *not*. It is the negative posited as negative.

Illusory being is all that still remains from the sphere of being. But it seems still to have an immediate side that is independent of essence and to be simply an other of essence. The other contains in general the two moments of determinate being and negated determinate being [*Nichtdasein*].[3] Since the unessential no longer has a being, all that remains to it of otherness is the pure moment of negated determinate being; illusory being is this *immediate*, negated determinate being in the determinateness of being, in such wise that it has determinate being only in relation to an other, only in its negated determinate being; the non-self-subsistent which *is* only in its negation. All that is left to it, therefore, is the pure determinateness of *immediacy*; it is *reflected* immediacy, that is, immediacy which *is* only by means of its negation and which, when contrasted with its *mediation*, is nothing but the empty determination of the immediacy of negated determinate being.

Thus *illusory being* is the phenomenon of scepticism, and the Appearance of idealism, too, is such an *immediacy*, which is not a something or a thing, in general, not an indifferent being that would still be, apart from its determinateness and connection with the subject. Scepticism did not permit itself to say 'It is'; modern idealism did not permit itself to regard knowledge as a knowing of the thing-in-itself; the illusory being of scepticism was supposed to lack any foundation of being, and in idealism the thing-in-itself was not supposed to enter into knowledge. But at the same time scepticism admitted a multitude of determinations of its illusory being, or rather its illusory being had for content the entire manifold wealth of the world. In idealism, too, Appearance embraces within itself the range of these manifold determinatenesses. This illusory being and this Appearance are *immediately* thus manifoldly determined. This content, therefore, may well have no being, no thing or thing-in-itself at its base; it remains on its own account as it is; the content has only been transferred from being into an illusory being, so that the latter has within itself those manifold determinatenesses, which are immediate, simply affirmative [*seiende*], and mutually related as others. Illusory being is, therefore, itself *immediately* determinate. It can have this or that content; whatever content it has, illusory being does not posit this itself but has it immediately. The various forms of idealism, Leibnizian, Kantian, Fichtean and others, have not advanced beyond being as determinateness, have not advanced beyond this immediacy, any more than scepticism did. Scepticism permits the content of its illusory being to be *given* to it; whatever content it is supposed to have, for scepticism it is *immediate*. The *monad* of Leibniz evolves its ideas and representations out of itself; but it is not the power that generates and binds them together, rather do they arise in the monad like bubbles; they are indifferent and immediate over against one another and the same in relation to the monad itself. Similarly, the Kantian Appearance is a *given* content of perception; it presupposes affections, determinations of the subject, which are immediate relatively to themselves and to the subject. It may well be that the infinite obstacle [*Anstoss*] of Fichte's idealism has no underlying thing-in-itself, so that it becomes purely a determinateness in the ego; but for the ego, this determinateness which it appropriates and whose externality it sublates is at the same time *immediate*, a *limitation* of the ego, which it can transcend but which has in it an element of indifference, so that although the limitation is in the ego, it contains an *immediate* non-being of the ego.

2. Illusory being, therefore, contains an immediate presupposition, a side that is independent of essence. But it does not have to be shown that illusory being, in so far as it is distinct from essence, sublates itself and withdraws into essence; for being in its totality has withdrawn into essence; illusory being is in itself a nullity; all that has to be shown is that the determinations which distinguish it from essence are determinations of essence itself, and further, that this *determinateness of essence* which illusory being is, is sublated in essence itself.

It is the immediacy of *non-being* that constitutes illusory being; but this non-being is nothing else but the negativity of essence present within it. In essence, being is non-being. Its intrinsic *nothingness* is the *negative nature of essence itself*. But the immediacy or indifference which this non-being contains is essence's own absolute being-in-itself. The negativity of essence is its equality with itself or its simple immediacy and indifference. Being has preserved itself in essence in so far as the latter in its infinite negativity has this equality with itself; it is through this that essence itself is being. The immediacy of the determinateness in illusory being over against essence is consequently nothing other than essence's own immediacy; but the immediacy is not simply affirmative [*seiend*], but is the purely mediated or reflected immediacy that is illusory being – being, not *as* being, but only as the determinateness of being as opposed to mediation; being as a moment.

These two moments, namely the nothingness which yet is and the being which is only a moment, or the implicit negativity and the reflected immediacy that constitute *the moments of illusory being*, are thus *the moments of essence itself*. What we have here is not an illusory show of being *in* essence, or an illusory show of essence *in* being; the illusory being in essence is not the illusory being of an other, but is illusory being *per se*, *the illusory being of essence itself*.

Illusory being is essence itself in the determinateness of being. Essence has an illusory being because it is *determinate* within itself and thereby distinguished from its absolute unity. But equally this determinateness is absolutely sublated in its own self. For essence is the self-subsistent, which *is* as self-mediated through its negation, which negation essence itself is; it is therefore the identical unity of absolute negativity and immediacy. – The negativity is negativity *per se*; it is its relation to itself and is thus in itself immediacy; but it is negative self-relation, a negating that is a repelling of itself, and the intrinsic immediacy is thus negative or *determinate* in regard to it. But this determinateness is itself absolute negativity, and this determining which is, as determining, immediately the sublating of itself, is a return-into-self.

Illusory being is the negative that has a being, but in an *other*, in its negation; it is a non-self-subsistent being which is in its own self sublated and null. As such, it is the negative returned into itself, non-self-subsistent being as in its own self not self-subsistent. This *self-relation* of the negative or of non-self-subsistent being is its *immediacy*; it is an *other* than the negative itself; it is its determinateness over against itself; or it is the negation directed against the negative. But negation directed against the negative is purely *self*-related negativity, the absolute sublating of the determinateness itself.

The *determinateness*, therefore, which illusory being is in essence is infinite determinateness; it is the purely *self*-coincident negative; it is thus the determinateness which as such is self-subsistent and indeterminate. Conversely, the self-subsistent, as self-related *immediacy*, is equally sheer determinateness and moment and *is* only as self-related negativity. This negativity that is identical with immediacy and immediacy that is thus identical with negativity, is *essence*. Illusory being, therefore, is essence itself, but essence in a determinateness, in such wise, however, that this is only a moment of essence and *essence* is the seeming of itself within itself.[4]

In the sphere of being, there *arises* over against being as an *immediacy*, non-being, which is likewise an *immediacy*, and their truth is *becoming*. In the sphere of essence, we have first essence opposed to the unessential, then essence opposed to illusory being, that is, to the unessential and to illusory being as the remainder of being. But both the unessential and illusory being,[5] and also the difference of essence from them, derive solely from the fact that essence is at first taken as an *immediate*, not as it is in itself, *namely*, not as an immediacy that *is* as pure mediation or absolute negativity. The first immediacy is thus only the *determinateness* of immediacy. The sublating of this determinateness of essence, therefore, consists simply and solely in showing that the unessential is only illusory being and that the truth is rather that essence contains the illusory being within itself as the infinite immanent movement that determines its immediacy as negativity and its negativity as immediacy, and is thus the seeming of itself within itself.[6] Essence in this its self-movement is *reflection*.

C. Reflection

Illusory being is the same thing as *reflection*; but it is reflection as *immediate*. For illusory being that has withdrawn into itself and so is estranged from its immediacy, we have the foreign word *reflection*.

Essence is reflection, the movement of becoming and transition that remains internal to it, in which the differentiated moment is determined simply as that which in itself is only negative, as illusory being. At the base of becoming in the sphere of being, there lies the determinateness of being, and this is relation to *other*. The movement of reflection, on the other hand, is the other as the *negation in itself*, which has a being only as self-related negation. Or, since the self-relation is precisely this negating of negation, the *negation as negation* is present in such wise that it has its being in its negatedness, as illusory being. Here, therefore, the other is not *being with a negation*, or limit, but *negation with the negation*. But the *first*, over against this other, the immediate or being, is only this very equality of the negation with itself, the negated negation, absolute negativity. This equality with itself, or *immediacy*, is consequently not a *first* from which the beginning was made and which passed over into its negation; nor is it an affirmatively present substrate that moves through reflection; on the contrary, immediacy is only this movement itself.

Consequently, becoming is essence, its reflective movement, is the *movement of nothing to nothing, and so back to itself*. The transition, or becoming, sublates itself in its passage; the *other* that in this transition comes to be, is not the non-being of a being, but the nothingness of a nothing, and this, to be the negation of a nothing, constitutes being. Being only *is* as the movement of nothing to nothing, and as such it is essence; and the latter does not *have* this movement *within it*, but is this movement as a being that is itself absolutely illusory, pure negativity, outside of which there is nothing for it to negate but which negates only its own negative, which latter *is* only in this negating.

This pure absolute reflection that is the movement from nothing to nothing determines itself further.

It is first, *positing reflection*.

Secondly, it forms the starting-point of the presupposed immediate and is thus *external reflection*.

But thirdly, it sublates this presupposition; and since reflection in sublating the presupposition *at the same time* presupposes it, it is *determining reflection*.

(a) Positing reflection

Illusory being is nothingness or the essenceless; but this nothingness or the essenceless does not have its being in an *other* in which its illusory being is reflected: on the contrary, its being is its own equality with itself. This interchange of the negative with itself has determined itself as the absolute reflection of essence.

This self-related negativity of essence is therefore the negating of its own self. Hence it is just as much *sublated* negativity as it is negativity; or it is itself both the negative, and simple equality with itself or immediacy. It consists, therefore, in *being itself* and *not itself* and that, too, in a single unity.

In the first place, reflection is the movement of nothing to nothing and is the negation that coincides with itself. This coincidence with itself is, in general, simple equality-with-self, immediacy. But this coincidence is not a transition of the negation into equality-with-self as into its otherness: on the contrary, reflection is transition as sublating of the transition; for reflection is immediate coincidence of the negative *with itself*. This coincidence is thus first, equality-with-self or immediacy; but secondly, this immediacy is the equality of *the negative* with itself, hence self-negating equality, the immediacy that is in itself the negative, the negative of itself, that consists in being that which it is not.

The self-relation of the negative is, therefore, its return [*Rückkehr*] into itself; it is immediacy as the sublating of the negative; but immediacy simply and solely *as* this relation or as *return from a negative*, and hence a self-sublating immediacy. This is *posited being or positedness* [*Gesetztsein*], immediacy purely and simply as *determinateness* or as self-reflecting. This immediacy which *is* only as return of the negative into itself, is that immediacy which constitutes the determinateness of illusory being and which previously seemed to be the starting-point of the reflective moment. But this immediacy, instead of being able to form the starting-point is, on the contrary, immediacy only as the return or as reflection itself. Reflection therefore is the movement which is return and is only therein that which begins or returns.[7]

It is a *positing* [*Setzen*] in so far as it is immediacy as a returning movement [*Rückkehren*]; for there is no other on hand, either an other *from* which or *into* which immediacy returns; it is, therefore, only as a returning movement, or as the negative of itself. Furthermore, this immediacy is the sublated negation and the sublated return-into-self. Reflection, as sublating the negative, is a sublating of *its other*, of immediacy. Since, therefore, it is immediacy as a returning movement, as a coincidence of the negative with itself, it is equally a negative of the negative as negative. Thus it is a *presupposing* [*Voraussetzen*]. – Or immediacy, as a returning movement, is only the negative of itself, only this, to be *not* immediacy; but reflection is the sublating of the negative of itself, it is a coincidence with itself; it therefore sublates its positing, and since in its positing it sublates its positing, it is a presupposing. – Reflection, in its presupposing, determines the return-into-self as the negative of itself, as that, the sublating of which is essence. The presupposing is the manner in which it relates itself to itself, but to itself as the negative of itself; only thus is it the self-relating negativity that remains internal to itself. Immediacy presents itself simply and solely as a return and is that negative which is the illusory being of the beginning, the illusory being which is negated by the return. Accordingly, the return of essence is its self-repulsion. In other words, reflection-into-self is essentially the presupposing of that from which it is the return.

It is only when essence has sublated its equality-with-self that it is equality-with-self. It presupposes itself and the sublating of this presupposition is essence itself; conversely, this sublating of its presupposition is the presupposition itself. Reflection therefore *finds before it* an immediate which it transcends and from which it is the return. But this return is only the presupposing of what reflection finds before it. What is thus found only *comes to be* through being *left behind*; its immediacy is sublated immediacy. Conversely, the sublated immediacy is the return-into-self, the *coming-to-itself* of essence, simple, self-equal being. Hence this coming-to-itself is the sublating of itself and is the self-repelling, presupposing reflection, and its self-repelling is the coming-to-itself of reflection.

It follows, therefore, from the foregoing consideration that the reflective movement is to be taken as an *absolute counterthrust* within itself.[8] For the presupposition of the return-into-self – that from which essence *comes* and *is* only as this return – is only in the return itself. The transcending of the immediate from which reflection starts is rather the outcome of this transcending; and the transcending of the immediate is the arrival at it. The movement, as an advance, immediately turns round upon itself and only so is self-movement – a movement which comes from itself in so far as *positing* reflection is *presupposing*, but, as *presupposing* reflection, is simply *positing* reflection.

Thus reflection is itself and its non-being, and is only itself, in that it is the negative of itself, for only thus is the sublating of the negative at the same time a coincidence with itself.

The immediacy that reflection, as a process of sublating, presupposes for itself is purely and simply a *positedness*, an immediacy that is *in itself* sublated, that is not distinct from the return-into-self and is itself only this movement of return. But at the same time it is determined as *negative*, as immediately *opposed* to something, therefore to an other. Thus reflection is *determinate*; and since, in accordance with this determinateness, it *has* a presupposition and starts from the immediate as its other, it is *external reflection*.

(b) External reflection

Reflection, as absolute reflection,[9] is essence that reflects its illusory being within itself and presupposes for itself only an illusory being, only positedness; as presupposing reflection, it is immediately only positing reflection. But external or real reflection presupposes itself as sublated, as the negative of itself. In this determination it is doubled: it is what is presupposed, or reflection-into-self, which is the immediate; and also it is reflection that is negatively self-related; it is related to itself as to its non-being.

External reflection therefore *presupposes* a being, *first*, not in the sense that its immediacy is only positedness or a moment, but, on the contrary, that this immediacy is self-relation and the determinateness is only a moment. Its relationship to its presupposition is such that the latter is the negative of reflection, but so that this negative *as* negative is sublated. Reflection in its positing, immediately sublates its positing and thus has an *immediate presupposition*. It therefore *finds* this before it as something from which it starts, and from which it is first the return-into-self, the negating of this its negative. But the fact that what is thus presupposed is a negative or is posited does not concern it; this determinateness belongs only to the positing reflection, but in the presupposing the positedness is present only as sublated. The determinations posited by the external reflection in the immediate are to that extent external to the latter. This external reflection in the sphere of being was the infinite; the finite ranked as the first, as the real; as the foundation, the abiding foundation, it forms the starting-point and the infinite is the reflection-into-self over against it.

This external reflection is the syllogism in which are the two extremes, the immediate and reflection-into-self; the middle term of the syllogism is the connection of the two, the determinate immediate, so that one part of the middle term, immediacy, belongs only to one of the extremes, the other, determinateness or negation, belongs only to the other extreme.

But a closer consideration of the action of external reflection shows it to be *secondly*, a positing of the immediate, which consequently becomes the negative or the determinate; but external reflection is immediately also the sublating of this its positing; for it *pre*supposes the immediate; in negating, it is the negating of this its negating. But in doing so it is immediately equally a *positing*, a sublating of the immediate negatively related to it, and this immediate from which it seemed to start as from something alien, *is* only in this its beginning. In this way, the immediate is not only *in itself* – that means, for us, or in external reflection – *identical* with reflection, but this identicalness is *posited*. For the immediate is determined by reflection as its negative or its other, but it is reflection itself that negates this determining. Hence the externality of reflection over against the immediate is sublated; its positing in which it negates itself, is the union of itself with its negative, with the immediate, and this union is the immediacy of essence itself. The fact is, therefore, that external reflection is not external, but is no less the immanent reflection of immediacy itself; in other words, the outcome of positing reflection is essence in and for itself. Reflection is thus *determining reflection*.

> *Remark*:   Reflection is usually taken in a subjective sense as the movement of the faculty of judgement that goes beyond a given immediate conception and seeks universal determinations for it or compares such determinations with it. Kant opposes *reflective judgement* to *determining judgement*.[10] He defines the faculty of judgement in general as the ability *to think the particular as subsumed under the universal. If the universal is given* (the rule, principle, law), then the faculty of judgement that subsumes the particular under it is *determinative*. But if only the particular is given *for which the universal is to be found*, then judgement is merely *reflective*. Here, then, to reflect is likewise to go beyond an immediate to the universal. On the one hand, it is only through this reference of the immediate to its universal that it is determined as a particular; by itself, it is only an individual or an immediate, simply affirmative being [*unmittelbares Seiendes*]. On the other hand, that to which it is referred is its universal, its rule, principle, law, in general, that which is reflected into itself, is self-related, essence or the essential.

But what is under discussion here is neither reflection at the level of consciousness, nor the more specific reflection of the understanding, which has the particular and the universal for its determinations, but of reflection generally. That reflection to which Kant ascribes the search for the universal of a given particular is clearly also only *external* reflection, which is related to the immediate as to something given. But in external reflection there is also implicit the notion of absolute reflection;[11] for the universal, the principle or rule and law to which it advances in its determining, counts as the essence of that immediate which forms the starting-point; and this immediate therefore counts as a nullity, and it is only the return from it, its determining by reflection, that is the positing of the immediate in accordance with its true being. Therefore, what reflection does to the immediate, and the determinations which issue from reflection, are not anything external to the immediate but are its own proper being.

It was external reflection, too, that recent philosophy had in mind when, as was the fashion for a while, it ascribed everything bad to reflection generally, regarding it and all its works as the polar opposite and hereditary foe of the absolute method of philosophizing. And intellectual reflection, in so far as it operates as external reflection, does in fact start from something immediately given which is alien to it, regarding itself as a merely formal activity which receives its content and material from outside and which, by itself, is only the movement conditioned by that content and material. Further, as will become more evident as soon as we come to consider determining reflection, the *reflected determinations* are of a different kind from the merely immediate determinations of being. The latter are more readily granted to be transient, merely relative and standing in relation to other; but the reflected determinations have the form of being-in-and-for-self. This makes them count as *essential*, and instead of passing over into their opposites they appear rather as absolute, free, and indifferent towards each other. Consequently, they are stubbornly opposed to their movement, their *being* is their self-identity in their determinateness, in accordance with which, even though they presuppose each other, they maintain themselves completely separate in this relation.

(c) Determining reflection

Determining reflection is in general the unity of *positing* and *external* reflection. This is to be considered in more detail.

1. External reflection starts from immediate being, *positing* reflection from nothing. External reflection, when it determines, posits an other – but this is essence – in the place of the sublated being; but positing reflection does not set its determination in place of another; positing *has* no presupposition.[12]

But that is why it is not the completed, determining reflection; the determination that it posits is consequently *only* something posited; it is an immediate, but not as equal to itself but as negating itself; it has an absolute relation to the return-into-self; it *is* only in reflection-into-self, but it is not this reflection itself.

What is *posited* is consequently an other, but in such a manner that the equality of reflection with itself is completely preserved; for what is posited *is* only as sublated, as a relation to the return-into-self. In the *sphere of being*, *determinate being* was the being in which negation was present, and being was the immediate base and element of this negation, which consequently was itself immediate. In the *sphere of essence, positedness* corresponds to determinate being. It is likewise a determinate being but its base is being as essence or as pure negativity; it is a determinateness or negation, not as affirmatively present [*seiend*] but immediately as sublated. *Determinate being is merely posited being or positedness*; this is the proposition of essence about determinate being. Positedness stands opposed, on the one hand, to determinate being, and on the other, to essence, and is to be considered as the middle term which unites determinate being with essence, and conversely, essence with determinate being. Accordingly, when it is said that a determination is *only* a positedness, this can have a twofold meaning; it is a positedness as opposed to determinate being or as opposed to essence. In the former meaning, determinate being is taken to be superior to positedness and the latter is ascribed to external reflection, to the subjective side. But in fact positedness is the superior; for as positedness, determinate being is that which it is in itself, a negative, something that is simply and solely related to the return-into-self. It is for this reason that positedness is *only* a positedness with respect to essence, as the negation of the accomplished return-into-self.

2. Positedness is not yet a determination of reflection; it is only determinateness as negation in general. But the positing is now in unity with external reflection; the latter is, in this unity, an absolute presupposing, that is, the repelling of reflection from itself, or the positing of the determinateness *as determinateness of itself*. Consequently, positedness is, as such, negation; but, as presupposed, it is also reflected into itself. Positedness is thus a *determination of reflection*.

The determination of reflection is distinct from the determinateness of being, from quality. The latter is immediate relation to other in general; positedness, too, is a relation to other, but to reflectedness-into-self. Negation as quality, is negation simply as *affirmative* [*seiend*]; being constitutes its ground and element. The determination of reflection, on the other hand, has for this ground reflectedness-into-self. Positedness fixes itself into a determination precisely because reflection is equality-with-self in its negatedness; its negatedness is consequently itself a reflection-into-self. Here the determination persists not through *being* but through its equality with itself. Because being, which supports quality, is not equal to the negation, quality is unequal within itself and hence a transitory moment vanishing in the other. The determination of reflection, on the other hand, is positedness *as* negation, negation which has negatedness as its ground; it is therefore not unequal within itself, and hence is *essential,* not transitory determinateness. It is *the equality with itself of reflection* that the negative possesses only as negative, as sublated or posited being, that enables the negative to persist.[13]

By virtue of this reflection-into-self the determinations of reflection appear as free essentialities floating in the void without attracting or repelling one another. In them the determinateness has established and infinitely fixed itself through the relation-to-self. It is the determinate that has brought into subjection its transitoriness and its mere positedness, or has bent back its reflection-into-other into reflection-into-self. These determinations hereby constitute determinate illusory being as it is in essence, essential illusory being. Because of this, *determining reflection* is reflection that has come forth from itself; the equality of essence with itself has perished in the negation, which is the dominant factor.

In the determination of reflection, therefore, there are two sides which at first are distinguished from one another. First, the determination is positedness, negation as such; secondly, it is reflection-into-self. As positedness, it is negation as negation; this accordingly is already its unity with itself. But at first, it is this only *in itself* or *in principle* [*an sich*], or, it is the immediate as sublating itself in its own self, as the other of itself. To this extent, reflection is an immanent determining. In the process, essence does not go outside itself; the differences are simply *posited*, taken back into essence. But according to the other side, they are not posited but reflected into themselves; the negation *as* negation is in an equality with itself, is not reflected into its other, into its non-being.

3. Now since the determination of reflection is as much a reflected relation within itself as it is positedness, this fact immediately throws more light on its nature. For as positedness, it is negation as such, a non-being over against an other, namely, *over against* absolute reflection-into-self, or over against essence. But as self-relation it is reflected into itself. This its reflection and the above positedness are distinct; its positedness is rather its sublatedness; but its reflectedness-into-self is its subsistence. In so far, therefore, as it is the positedness that is at the same time reflection-into-self, the determinateness of reflection is *the relation to its otherness within itself*. It is not an affirmative [*seiende*], quiescent determinateness, which would be related to an other in such a way that the related term and its relation are distinct from each other, the former a being-within-self, a something that excludes its other and its relation to this other from itself; on the contrary, the determination of reflection is in its own self the *determinate side* and the *relation* of this determinate side as determinate, that is, to its negation. Quality, through its relation, passes over into an other; in its relation its alteration begins. The determination of reflection, on the other hand, has taken its otherness back into itself. It is *positedness*, negation, which however bends back into itself the relation to other, and negation which is equal to

itself, the unity of itself and its other, and only through this is an *essentiality*. It is, therefore, positedness, negation; but as reflection-into-self it is at the same time the sublatedness of this positedness, infinite self-relation.

Chapter 2: The Essentialities or Determinations of Reflection

Reflection is determinate reflection; hence essence is determinate essence, or it is *an essentiality*.

Reflection is *the seeming of essence within itself* [*das Scheinen des Wesens in sich selbst*].[14] Essence, as infinite return-into-self, is not immediate but negative simplicity; it is a movement through distinct moments, absolute self-mediation. But it reflects itself into these its moments which consequently are themselves determinations reflected into themselves.

Essence is at first, simple self-relation, pure *identity*. This is its determination, but as such it is rather the absence of any determination.

Secondly, the proper determination is *difference*, a difference that is, on the one hand, external or indifferent, *diversity* in general, and on the other, is opposed diversity or *opposition*.

Thirdly, as *contradiction*, the opposition is reflected into itself and withdraws into its *ground*. [R]

A. Identity [*Identität*]

1. Essence is simple immediacy as sublated immediacy. Its negativity is its being; it is self-equal in its absolute negativity, through which otherness and relation-to-other has vanished in its own self into pure equality-with-self. Essence is therefore simple identity-with-self.

This identity-with-self is the *immediacy* of reflection. It is not that equality-with-self that *being* or even *nothing* is, but the equality-with-self that has brought itself to unity, not a restoration of itself from an other, but this pure origination from and within itself, *essential* identity. Consequently, it is not *abstract* identity or has not arisen through a relative negating which had taken place outside it, merely separating off the distinguished moment but otherwise leaving it afterwards as *simple affirmative* [*seiend*] as it was before. On the contrary, being and every determinateness of being has sublated itself not relatively, but in its own self: and this simple negativity of being in its own self is identity itself. So far, then, identity is still in general the same as essence.

Remark 1: *Abstract Identity*: Thinking that keeps to external reflection and knows of no other thinking but external reflection, fails to attain to a grasp of identity in the form just expounded, or of essence, which is the same thing. Such thinking always has before it only abstract identity, and apart from and alongside it, difference. In its opinion, reason is nothing more than a loom on which it externally combines and interweaves the warp, of say, identity, and then the woof of difference; or, also, again proceeding analytically, it now extracts especially identity and *then also again* obtains difference alongside it, is now a positing of likeness and *then also again* a positing of unlikeness – likeness when *abstraction* is made from difference, and unlikeness when abstraction is made from the positing of likeness. These assertions and opinions about what reason does must be completely set aside, since they are in a certain measure merely *historical*; the truth is rather that a consideration of everything that is, shows that *in its own self* everything is in its self-sameness different from itself and self-contradictory, and that in its differences, in its contradiction, it is self-identical, and is in its own self this movement of transition of one of these categories into the other, and for this reason, that each is in its own self the opposite of itself. The Notion of identity, that it is simple self-related negativity, is not a product of external reflection but has come from being itself. Whereas, on the contrary, that identity that is aloof from difference, and difference that is aloof from identity, are products of external reflection and abstraction, which arbitrarily clings to this point of indifferent difference.

2. This identity is, in the first instance, essence itself, not yet a determination of it, reflection in its entirety, not a distinct moment of it. As absolute negation it is the negation that immediately negates itself, a non-being and difference that vanishes in its arising, or a distinguishing by which nothing is distinguished, but which immediately collapses within itself. The distinguishing is the positing of non-being as non-being of the other. But the non-being of the other is sublation of the other and therewith of the distinguishing itself. Here, then, distinguishing is present as self-related negativity, as a non-being which is the non-being of itself, a non-being which has its non-being not in another but in its own self. What is present, therefore, is self-related, reflected difference, or pure, *absolute difference*.

In other words, identity is the reflection-into-self that is identity only as internal repulsion, and is this repulsion as reflection-into-self, repulsion which immediately takes itself back into itself. Thus it is identity as difference that is identical with itself. But difference is only identical with itself in so far as it is not identity but absolute non-identity. But non-identity is absolute in so far as it contains nothing of its other but only itself, that is, in so far as it is absolute identity with itself.

Identity, therefore, is *in its own self* absolute non-identity. But it is also the *determination* of identity as against non-identity. For as reflection-into-self it posits itself as its own non-being; it is the whole, but, as reflection, it posits itself as its own moment, as positedness, from which it is the return into itself. It is only as such moment of itself that it is identity as such, as *determination* of simple equality with itself in contrast to absolute difference. [R2]

B. Difference [*Unterschied*]

(*a*) *Absolute difference*

Difference is the negativity which reflection has within it, the nothing which is said in enunciating identity, the essential moment of identity itself which, as negativity of itself, determines itself and is distinguished from difference.

1. This difference is difference *in and for itself*, *absolute difference*, the *difference of essence*. It is difference in and for itself, not difference resulting from anything external, but *self-related*, therefore *simple* difference. It is essential to grasp absolute difference as *simple*. In the absolute difference of *A* and *not-A* from each other, it is the *simple not* which, as such, constitutes it. Difference itself is the simple Notion. Two things are *different*, it is said, *in that* they, etc. '*In that*', that is, in one and the same respect, in the same ground of determination.[15] It is the *difference of reflection*, not the *otherness of determinate being*. One determinate being and another determinate being are posited as falling apart, each of them, as determined against the other, has an *immediate being* for itself. The *other of essence*, on the contrary, is the other in and for itself, not the other as other of an other, existing outside it but simple determinateness in itself. In the sphere of determinate being, too, otherness and determinateness proved to be of this nature, to be simple determinateness, identical opposition; but this identity revealed itself only as the *transition* of one determinateness into the other. Here, in the sphere of reflection, difference appears as reflected difference, which is thus posited as it is in itself.

2. Difference in itself is self-related difference; as such, it is the negativity of itself, the difference not of an other, but *of itself from itself*; it is not itself but its other. But that which is different from difference is identity. Difference is therefore itself and identity. Both together constitute difference; it is the whole, and its moment. It can equally be said that difference, as simple, is no difference; it is this only when it is in relation with identity; but the truth is rather that, as difference, it contains equally identity and this relation itself. Difference is the whole and its own *moment*, just as identity equally is its whole and its moment. This is to be considered as the essential nature of reflection and as the *specific, original ground of all activity and self-movement*. Difference and also identity, make themselves into a moment or a positedness because, as reflection, they are negative relation-to-self.

Difference as thus unity of itself and identity, is *in its own self determinate difference*. It is not transition into an other, not relation to an other outside it: it has its other, identity, within itself, just as identity, having entered into the determination of difference, has not lost itself in it as its other, but preserves itself in it, is its reflection-into-self and its moment.

3. Difference possesses both moments, identity and difference; both are thus a *positedness*, a determinateness. But in this positedness each is *self-relation*. One of them, identity, is itself immediately the moment of reflection-into-self; but equally, the other is difference, difference in itself, reflected difference. Difference, in that it has two moments that are themselves reflections-into-self, is *diversity*.

(b) Diversity [Verschiedenheit]

1. Identity *falls apart* within itself into diversity because, as absolute difference, it posits itself as its own negative within itself, and these its moments, namely, itself and the negative of itself, are reflections-into-self, are self-identical; or, in other words, precisely because identity itself immediately sublates its negating and in its *determination is reflected into itself*. The distinguished terms *subsist* as indifferently different towards one another because each is self-identical, because identity constitutes its ground and element; in other words, the difference is what it is, only in its very opposite, in identity.

Diversity constitutes the otherness as such of reflection. The other of determinate being has for its ground immediate *being* in which the negative subsists. But in reflection it is self-identity, reflected immediacy, that constitutes the subsistence of the negative and its indifference.

The moments of difference are identity and difference itself. They are [merely] diverse when they are reflected into themselves, that is, when they are *self-related*; as such, they are *in the determination of identity*, they are only relation-to-self; the identity is not related to the difference, nor is the difference related to the identity; as each moment is thus only *self*-related, they are *not determined* against one another. Now because in this manner they are not different in themselves, the *difference* is *external* to them. The *diverse* moments are, therefore, mutually related, not as identity and difference, but merely as simply *diverse* moments, that are indifferent to one another and to their determinateness.

2. In diversity, as the indifference of difference, reflection has become, in general, *external* to itself; difference is merely a *posited* or sublated being, but it is itself the total reflection. When considered more closely, both identity and difference, as has just been demonstrated, are reflections, each of which is unity of itself and its other; each is the whole. Consequently, the determinateness in which they are *only* identity or *only* difference, is sublated. Therefore they are not qualities, because through the reflection-into-self, their determinateness is at the same time only a negation. What is present, therefore, is this duality, *reflection-into-self* as such, and determinateness as negation or *positedness*. Positedness is the reflection that is external to itself;

it is the negation as negation – and so therefore *in itself* or *implicity*, the self-related negation and reflection-into-self, but only implicitly; it is relation to the negation as something external to it.

Thus the reflection that is implicit, and external reflection, are the two determinations into which the moments of difference, namely, identity and difference, posited themselves. They are these moments themselves in so far as they have now determined themselves. *Reflection in itself* is identity, but determined as being indifferent to difference, not as simply not possessing difference, but as being self-identical in its relation with it; it is *diversity*. It is identity that has so reflected itself into itself that it is really the *one* reflection of the two moments into themselves; both are reflections-into-self. Identity is this one reflection of both, which contains difference only as an indifferent difference and is simply diversity. *External reflection*, on the other hand, is their *determinate* difference, not as an absolute reflection-into-self, but as a determination to which the [merely] implicit reflection is indifferent; difference's two moments, identity and difference itself, are thus externally posited determinations, not determinations in and for themselves.

Now this external identity is *likeness*, and external difference, *unlikeness*. *Likeness*, it is true, is identity, but only as a positedness, an identity that is not in and for itself. Similarly, *unlikeness* is difference, but as an external difference that is not in and for itself the difference of the unlike itself. Whether or not something is like something else does not concern either the one or the other; each of them is only self-referred, is in and for itself what it is; identity or non-identity, as likeness or unlikeness, is the verdict of a third party distinct from the two things.

3. External reflection relates what is diverse to likeness and unlikeness. This relation, which is a *comparing*, passes to and fro between likeness and unlikeness. But this relating to likeness and unlikeness, back and forth, is external to these determinations themselves; also, they are related not to one another but each, by itself, to a third. In this alternation, each stands forth immediately on its own. External reflection is, as such, external to itself; the *determinate* difference is the negated absolute difference. Therefore it is not simple, not reflection-into-self; on the contrary, it has this outside it. Its moments, therefore, fall asunder and are related also as mutually external to the reflection-into-self confronting them.

In the self-alienated reflection, therefore, likeness and unlikeness appear as mutually unrelated, and in relating them to *one and the same* thing, it separates them by the introduction of '*in so far*', of *sides* and *respects*. The diverse, which are one and the same, to which both likeness and unlikeness are related, are therefore, *from one side* like one another, but *from another side* are unlike, and *in so far* as they are like, they are not unlike. *Likeness* is related only to itself, and similarly *unlikeness* is only unlikeness.

But by this separation of one from the other they merely sublate themselves. The very thing that was supposed to hold off contradiction and dissolution from them, namely, that something is *like* something else *in one respect, but is unlike it in another* – this holding apart of likeness and unlikeness is their destruction. For both are determinations of difference; they are relations to one another, the one being what the other is not; like is not unlike and unlike is not like; and both essentially have this relation and have no meaning apart from it; as determinations of difference, each is what it is as *distinct* from its other. But through this mutual indifference, likeness is only self-referred, and unlikeness similarly is self-referred and a reflective determination on its own; each, therefore, is like itself; the difference has vanished, since they cannot have any determinateness over against one another; in other words, each therefore is only likeness.

This indifferent point of view or external difference thus sublates itself and is in its own self the negativity of itself. It is the negativity that belongs to the comparer in the act of comparing. The comparer goes from likeness to unlikeness and from this back to likeness, and therefore lets the one vanish in the other and is, in fact, *the negative unity of both*. This unity, in the first instance, lies beyond the compared and also beyond the moments of the comparison as a subjective act falling outside them. But, as we have seen, this negative unity is, in fact, the very nature of likeness and unlikeness. The independent self-reference which each of them is, is in fact the self-reference that sublates their distinctiveness and so, too, themselves.

From this side, likeness and unlikeness, as moments of external reflection and as external to themselves, vanish together in their likeness. But further, this their *negative* unity is also *posited* in them; they have, namely the [merely] *implicit* reflection outside them, or are the likeness and unlikeness of a *third party*, of an other than they.[16] And so likeness is not like itself; and unlikeness, as unlike not itself but something else unlike it, is itself likeness. The like and the unlike are therefore *unlike themselves*. Consequently each is this reflection: likeness, that it is itself and unlikeness, and unlikeness, that it is itself and likeness.

Likeness and unlikeness formed the side of *positedness* as against the compared or the diverse which had determined itself as the [merely] *implicit* reflection contrasted with them. But this diverse[17] as thus determined has equally lost its determinateness as against them. Likeness and unlikeness,[18] the determinations of external reflection, are just this merely implicit reflection which the diverse as such is supposed to be, the merely indeterminate difference of the diverse. The *implicit* reflection is self-relation without the negation, abstract self-identity, and so simply positedness itself. The merely diverse, therefore, passes over through positedness into negative reflection. The diverse is the merely posited difference, therefore the difference that is no difference, and therefore in its own self the negation of itself. Thus likeness and unlikeness themselves, that is, positedness, returns through indifference or the implicit reflection back into the negative unity with itself, into the reflection which the difference of likeness and unlikeness in its own self is. Diversity, whose *indifferent* sides are just as much simply and solely *moments* of one negative unity, is *opposition*. [R]

(*c*) *Opposition* [Gegensatz]

In opposition, the *determinate reflection*, difference, finds its completion. It is the unity of identity and diversity; its moments are diverse in one identity and thus are *opposites*.[19]

Identity and *difference* are the moments of difference held within itself; they are *reflected* moments of its unity. But *likeness* and *unlikeness* are the self-alienated reflection; their self-identity is not merely the indifference of each towards the other distinguished from it, but towards being-in-and-for-self as such, an identity-with-self over against the identity that is reflected into itself; it is therefore the *immediacy* that is not reflected into itself. The positedness of the sides of the external reflection is accordingly a *being*, just as their non-positedness is a *non-being*.

Closer consideration shows the moments of opposition to be positedness reflected into itself or determination in general. Positedness is likeness and unlikeness; these two reflected into themselves constitute the determinations of opposition. Their reflection-into-self consists in this, that each is in its own self the unity of likeness and unlikeness. Likeness is only in the reflection that compares on the basis of unlikeness, and therefore is mediated by its other, indifferent moment; similarly, unlikeness is only in the same reflective relationship in which likeness is. Therefore each of these moments is, in its determinateness, the whole. It is the whole in so far as it also contains its other moment; but this its other is an indifferent, *simple affirmative* moment; thus each contains reference to its non-being, and is only reflection-into-self or the whole, as essentially connected with its non-being.

This self-*likeness* reflected into itself that contains within itself the reference to unlikeness, is the positive; and the unlikeness that contains within itself the reference to its non-being, to likeness, is the negative. Or, both are a positedness; now in so far as the differentiated determinateness is taken as a differentiated *determinate self-reference* of positedness, the opposition is, on the one hand, *positedness* reflected into its likeness to itself and on the other hand, *positedness* reflected into its unlikeness to itself – the positive and the negative. The positive is positedness as reflected into self-likeness; but what is reflected is positedness, that is, the negation as negation, and so this reflection-into-self has reference-to-other for its determination. The negative is positedness as reflected into unlikeness; but the positedness is unlikeness itself, and this reflection is therefore the identity of unlikeness with itself and absolute self-reference. Each is the whole; the positedness reflected into likeness-to-self contains unlikeness, and the positedness reflected into unlikeness-to-self also contains likeness.

The positive and the negative are thus the sides of the opposition that have become self-subsistent. They are self-subsistent in that they are the reflection of the *whole* into themselves, and they belong to the opposition in so far as this is the *determinateness* which, as a whole, is reflected into itself. On account of their self-subsistence, they constitute the *implicitly* determined opposition. Each is itself and its other; consequently, each has *its determinate-ness* not in an other, but *in its own self*. Each is self-referred, and the reference to its other is only a self-reference. This has a twofold aspect: each is a reference to its non-being as a sublating of this otherness within it; thus its non-being is only a moment in it. But on the other hand positedness here has become a being, an indifferent subsistence; consequently, the other of itself which each contains is also the non-being of that in which it is supposed to be contained only as a moment. Each therefore *is*, only in so far as its *non-being is*, and is in an identical relationship with it.

The determinations which constitute the positive and negative consist, therefore, in the fact that the positive and negative are, in the first place, absolute *moments* of the opposition; their subsistence is inseparably *one* reflection; it is a single mediation in which each *is* through the non-being of its other, and so *is* through its other or its own non-being. Thus they are simply *opposites*; in other words, *each* is only the opposite of the other, the one is not as yet positive, and the other is not as yet negative, but both are negative to one another. In the first place, then, each *is*, *only in so far as the other is*; it is what it is, through the other, through its own non-being; it is only a *positedness*; secondly, it is, *in so far as the other is not*; it is what it is, through the non-being of the other; it is *reflection-into-self*. But these two are the *one* mediation of the opposition as such, in which they are simply only *posited moments*.

Further, however, this mere positedness is simply reflected into itself; in accordance with this moment of *external reflection* the positive and negative are *indifferent* to that first identity in which they are only moments; in other words, since that first reflection is the positive's and negative's own reflection into themselves, each is in its own self its positedness, so each is indifferent to this its reflection into its non-being, to its own positedness. The two sides are thus merely diverse[20] and in so far as their being determined as positive and negative constitutes their positedness in relation to one another, each is not in its own self so determined but is only determinateness in general. Therefore, although one of the determinatenesses of positive and negative belongs to each side, they can be changed round, and each side is of such a kind that it can be taken equally well as positive as negative.

But thirdly, the positive and negative are not only something posited, not merely an indifferent something, but their *positedness*, or the *reference-to-other in a unity which they are not themselves, is taken back* into each. Each is in its own self positive and negative: the positive and negative are the determination of reflection in and for itself; it is only in this reflection of opposites into themselves that they are positive and negative. The positive has within itself the reference-to-other in which the determinateness of the positive is; similarly, the negative is not a negative as contrasted with an other, but likewise possesses within itself the determinateness whereby it is negative.

Thus each [the positive as well as the negative] is a self-subsistent, independent unity-with-self. The positive is, indeed, a positedness, but in such wise that for it the positedness is only positedness as sublated. It is the *not-opposite*, the sublated opposition, but as a side of the opposition itself. As positive, something is, of course, determined with reference to an otherness, but in such a manner that its nature is to be *not* something posited; it is the reflection-into-self that negates the otherness. But the other of itself, the negative, is itself no longer a positedness or moment, but a self-subsistent *being*; thus the negating reflection of the positive is immanently determined as *excluding* from itself this its *non-being*.

The negative, as such absolute reflection, is not the immediate negative but the negative as a sublated positedness, the negative in and for itself, which is based positively on itself. As reflection-into-self it negates its relationship to other; its other is the positive, a self-subsistent being; consequently, its negative relation to it is to exclude it. The negative is the independently existing opposite contrasted with the positive, which is the determination of the sublated opposition – the self-based *whole opposition* opposed to the self-identical positedness.

The positive and negative are therefore not merely *implicitly* [*an sich*] positive and negative, but explicitly and actually so [*an und für sich*]. They are *implicitly* positive and negative in so far as one makes abstraction from their exclusive relation to other and only takes them in accordance with their determination. Something is *in itself* positive or negative when it is supposed to be so determined not merely *relatively to an other*. But when the positive and negative are taken, not as positedness, and therefore not as opposites, then each is the immediate, *being* and *non-being*. But the positive and negative are moments of opposition; their in-itself constitutes merely the form of their reflectedness-into-self. Something is *in itself* positive, apart from the relation to the negative; and something is *in itself* negative, apart from the relation to the positive;[21] in this determination, one clings merely to the abstract moment of this reflectedness. But the positive or negative *in itself* essentially implies that to be an opposite is not merely a moment, does not stem from comparison, but is a determination belonging to the sides of the opposition themselves. They are therefore not positive or negative *in themselves* apart from the relation to other; on the contrary, *this relation* – an exclusive relation – constitutes their determination or in-itself; in it, therefore, they are at the same time explicitly and actually [*an und für sich*] positive or negative. [R]

C. Contradiction [*Widerspruch*]

1. Difference as such contains its two sides as *moments*; in diversity they fall *indifferently* apart; in opposition as such, they are sides of the difference, one being determined only by the other, and therefore only moments; but they are no less determined within themselves, mutually indifferent and mutually exclusive: the *self-subsistent determinations of reflection*.

One is the positive, the other the negative, but the former as the intrinsically positive, the latter as the intrinsically negative. Each has an indifferent self-subsistence of its own through the fact that it has within itself the relation to its other moment; it is thus the whole, self-contained opposition. As this whole, each is mediated with itself *by its other* and *contains* it. But further, it is mediated with itself by the *non-being of its other*; thus it is a unity existing on its own and it *excludes* the other from itself.

The self-subsistent determination of reflection that contains the opposite determination, and is self-subsistent in virtue of this inclusion, at the same time also excludes it; in its self-subsistence, therefore, it excludes from itself its own self-subsistence. For this consists in containing within itself its opposite determination – through which alone it is not a relation to something external – but no less immediately in the fact that it is itself, and also excludes from itself the determination that is negative to it. It is thus *contradiction*.

Difference as such is already *implicitly* contradiction; for it is the *unity* of sides which are, only in so far as they are *not one* – and it is the *separation* of sides which are, only as separated *in the same relation*. But the positive and negative are the *posited* contradiction because, as negative unities, they are themselves the positing of themselves, and in this positing each is the sublating of itself and the positing of its opposite. They constitute the determining reflection as *exclusive*; and because the excluding of the sides is a single act of distinguishing and each of the distinguished sides in excluding the other is itself the whole act of exclusion, each side in its own self excludes itself.

If we consider the two determinations of reflection on their own, then the positive is *positedness* as reflected *into likeness to itself*, positedness that is not a relation to an other, a subsistence, therefore, in so far as positedness is *sublated* and *excluded*. But with this, the positive makes itself into the *relation of a non-being* – into a *positedness*. It is thus the contradiction that, in positing identity with itself by *excluding* the negative, it makes itself into the *negative* of what it excludes from itself, that is, makes itself into its opposite. This, as excluded, is posited as free from that which excludes it, and therefore as reflected into itself and as itself exclusive. The exclusive reflection is thus a positing of the positive as excluding its opposite, so that this positing is immediately the positing of its opposite which it excludes.

This is the absolute contradiction of the positive, but it is immediately the absolute contradiction of the negative; the positing of each is a *single* reflection. The negative, considered on its own over against the positive, is positedness as reflected *into unlikeness to itself*, the negative as negative. But the negative is itself the unlike, the non-being of an opposite; therefore its reflection into its unlikeness is rather its relation to itself. Negation *in general* is the negative as quality, or *immediate* determinateness; but the negative *as negative*, is related to the negative of itself, to its opposite. If this negative is only taken as identical with the first, then it, too, like the first, is merely immediate; and so they are not taken as mutual opposites and therefore not as negatives; the negative is not an immediate at all. But now, since it is also just as much a fact that each is the same as its opposite, this relation of the unlike is just as much their identical relation.

This is therefore the same contradiction that the positive is, namely, positedness or negation as self-relation. But the positive is only *implicitly* this contradiction, whereas the negative is the contradiction *posited*; for the latter, in virtue of its reflection-into-self which makes it a negative in and for itself or a negative that is identical with itself, is accordingly determined as a non-identical, as excluding identity. The negative is this, to be *identical with itself in opposition to identity*, and consequently, through its excluding reflection to exclude itself from itself.

The negative is, therefore, the whole opposition based, as opposition, on itself, absolute difference that *is not related to an other*; as opposition, it excludes identity from itself – but in doing so excludes itself; for as *self-relation* it is determined as the very identity that it excludes.

2. Contradiction resolves itself. In the self-excluding reflection we have just considered, positive and negative, each in its self-subsistence, sublates itself; each is simply the transition or rather the self-transposition of itself into its opposite. This ceaseless vanishing of the opposites into themselves is the *first unity* resulting from contradiction; it is the null.

But contradiction contains not merely the negative, but also the positive; or, the self-excluding reflection is at the same time *positing* reflection; the result of contradiction is not merely a nullity. The positive and negative constitute the *positedness* of the self-subsistence. Their own negation of themselves sublates the *positedness* of the self-subsistence. It is this which in truth perishes in contradiction.

The reflection-into-self whereby the sides of opposition are converted into self-subsistent self-relations is, in the first instance, their self-subsistence as *distinct* moments; as such they are only *implicitly* this self-subsistence, for they are still opposites, and the fact that they are *implicitly* self-subsistent constitutes their positedness. But their excluding reflection sublates this positedness, converts them into explicitly self-subsistent sides, into sides which are self-subsistent not merely *implicitly* or *in themselves* but through their negative relation to their opposite; in this way, their self-subsistence is also posited. But further, through this their positing, they make themselves into a positedness. *They destroy themselves* in that they determine themselves as self-identical, yet in this determination are rather the negative, an identity-with-self that is a relation-to-other.

However, this excluding reflection, looked at more closely, is not merely this formal determination. It is an *implicit* self-subsistence and is the sublating of this positedness, and it is only through this sublating that it becomes explicitly and in fact a self-subsistent unity. True, through the sublating of otherness or positedness, we are again presented with positedness, the negative of an other. But in point of fact, this negation is not merely the first, immediate relation-to-other again, not positedness as a sublated immediacy, but as a sublated positedness. The excluding reflection of self-subsistence, being exclusive, converts itself into a positedness, but is just as much a sublating of its positedness. It is a sublating self-relation; in this, it first sublates the negative, and secondly, posits itself as a negative, and it is only this negative that it sublates; in sublating the negative, it posits and sublates itself at the same time. In this way, the *exclusive determination itself* is that *other* of itself whose negation it is; consequently, the sublating of this positedness is not again a positedness as the negative of an other, but is a uniting with itself, the positive unity with itself. Self-subsistence is thus through *its own* negation a unity returned into itself, since it returns into itself through the negation of *its own* positedness. It is the unity of essence, being identical with itself through the negation, not of an other, but of itself.[22]

3. According to this positive side, in which the self-subsistence in opposition, as the excluding reflection, converts itself into a positedness which it no less sublates, opposition is not only *destroyed* [*zugrunde gegangen*] but has withdrawn *into its ground*. The excluding reflection of the self-subsistent opposition converts this into a negative, into something posited; it thereby reduces its primarily self-subsistent *determinations*, the positive and negative, to the status of *mere* determinations; and the positedness, being thus made into a positedness, has simply returned into its unity with itself; it is *simple essence*, but essence as *ground*. Through the sublating of its inherently self-contradictory determinations, essence has been restored, but with this determination, that it is the excluding unity of reflection – a simple unity that determines itself as a negative, but in this positedness is immediately like itself and united with itself.

In the first place, therefore, the self-subsistent opposition through its contradiction *withdraws* into ground; this opposition is the *prius*, the immediate, that forms the starting-point, and the sublated opposition or the sublated positedness is itself a positedness. Thus *essence as ground is a positedness*, something that has become. But conversely, what has been posited is only this, that opposition or positedness is a sublated positedness, only is *as* positedness. Therefore essence as ground is the excluding reflection in such wise that it makes its own self into a positedness, that the opposition from which we started and which was the immediate, is the merely posited, determinate self-subsistence of essence, and that opposition is merely that which sublates itself within itself, whereas essence is that which, in its determinateness, is reflected into itself. Essence as ground excludes *itself* from itself, it posits *itself*; its positedness – which is what is excluded – is only *as* positedness, as identity of the negative with itself. This self-subsistent is the negative *posited* as negative; it is self-contradictory and therefore remains immediately in essence as in its ground.

The resolved contradiction is therefore ground, essence as unity of the positive and negative. In opposition, the determination has attained to self-subsistence; but ground is this completed self-subsistence; in it, the negative is self-subsistent essence, but as a negative; as self-identical in this negativity, ground is just as much the positive. Opposition and its contradiction is, therefore, in ground as much abolished as preserved. Ground is essence as positive identity-with-self, which, however, at the same time relates itself to itself as negativity, and therefore determines itself and converts itself into an excluded positedness; but this positedness is the whole self-subsistent essence, and essence is ground, as self-identical and positive in this its negation. The self-contradictory, self-subsistent opposition was therefore already itself ground; all that was added to it was the determination of unity-with-self, which results from the fact that each of the self-subsistent opposites sublates itself and makes itself into its opposite, thus falling to the ground [*zugrunde geht*]; but in this process it at the same time only unites with itself; therefore, it is only in falling to the ground [*in seinem Untergange*], that is, in its positedness or negation, that the opposite is really the essence that is reflected into and identical with itself. [R1,2]

> *Remark 3*:   *The Law of Contradiction*: If, now, the first determinations of reflection, namely, identity, difference and opposition, have been put in the form of a law, still more should the determination into which they pass as their truth, namely, contradiction, be grasped and enunciated as a law: *everything is inherently contradictory*, and in the sense that this law in contrast to the others expresses rather the truth and the essential nature of things. The contradiction which makes its appearance in opposition, is only the developed nothing that is contained in identity and that appears in the expression that the law of identity says *nothing*. This negation further determines itself into difference and opposition, which now is the posited contradiction.
>
> But it is one of the fundamental prejudices of logic as hitherto understood and of ordinary thinking, that contradiction is not so characteristically essential and immanent a determination as identity; but in fact, if it were a question of grading the two determinations and they had to be kept separate, then contradiction would have to be taken as the profounder determination and more characteristic of essence. For as against contradiction, identity is merely the determination of the simple immediate, of dead being; but contradiction is the root of all movement and vitality; it is only in so far as something has a contradiction within it that it moves, has an urge and activity.
>
> In the first place, contradiction is usually kept aloof from things, from the sphere of being and of truth generally; it is asserted that *there is nothing that is contradictory*. Secondly, it is shifted into subjective reflection by which it is first posited in the process of relating and comparing. But even in this reflection, it does not really exist, for it is said that the *contradictory* cannot be *imagined* or *thought*. Whether it occurs in actual things or in reflective thinking, it ranks in general as a contingency, a kind of abnormality and a passing paroxysm of sickness.
>
> Now as regards the assertion that *there is* no contradiction, that it does not exist, this statement need not cause us any concern; an absolute

determination of essence must be present in every experience, in every-thing actual, as in every notion. We made the same remark above in connection with the *infinite*, which is the contradiction as displayed in the sphere of being. But common experience itself enunciates it when it says that at least *there is* a *host* of contradictory things, contradictory arrangements, whose contradiction exists not merely in an external reflection but in themselves. Further, it is not to be taken merely as an abnormality which only occurs here and there, but is rather the neg-ative as determined in the sphere of essence, the principle of all self-movement, which consists solely in an exhibition of it. External, sensuous motion itself is contradiction's immediate existence. Something moves, not because at one moment it is here and at another there, but because at one and the same moment it is here and not here, because in this 'here', it at once is and is not. The ancient dialecticians must be granted the contradictions that they pointed out in motion; but it does not follow that therefore there is no motion, but on the contrary, that motion is *existent* contradiction itself.

Similarly, internal self-movement proper, *instinctive urge* in general, (the appetite or *nisus* of the monad, the entelechy of absolutely simple essence), is nothing else but the fact that something is, in one and the same respect, *self-contained and* deficient, *the negative of itself.* Abstract self-identity is not as yet a livingness, but the positive, being in its own self a negativity, goes outside itself and undergoes alteration. Some-thing is therefore alive only in so far as it contains contradiction within it, and moreover is this power to hold and endure the contradiction within it. But if an existent in its positive determination is at the same time incapable of reaching beyond its negative determination and hold-ing the one firmly in the other, is incapable of containing contradiction within it, then it is not the living unity itself, not ground, but in the contradiction falls to the ground [*zugrunde geht*]. *Speculative thinking* consists solely in the fact that thought holds fast contradiction, and in it, its own self, but does not allow itself to be dominated by it as in ordinary thinking, where its determinations are resolved by contradic-tion only into other determinations or into nothing.

If the contradiction in motion, instinctive urge, and the like, is masked for ordinary thinking, in the simplicity of these determinations, contra-diction is, on the other hand, immediately represented in the *determina-tions of relationship.* The most trivial examples of above and below, right and left, father and son, and so on *ad infinitum*, all contain opposition in each term. That *is* above, which is *not* below; 'above' is specifically just this, not to be 'below', and only *is, in so far as* there is a 'below'; and conversely, each determination implies its opposite. Father is the other of son, and son the other of father, and each only *is* as this other of the other; and at the same time, the one determination only is, in relation to the other; their being is a *single* subsistence. The father also has an existence of his own apart from the son-relationship; but then he is not father but simply man; just as above and below, right and left, are each also a reflection-into-self and are something apart from their relationship, but then only places in general. Opposites, therefore, contain contradiction in so far as they are, in the same respect, negatively related to one another or *sublate each other* and are *indifferent* to one another. Ordinary thinking when it passes over to the moment of the *indifference* of the determinations, forgets their negative unity and so retains them merely as 'differents' in general, in which determination right is no longer right, nor left left, etc. But since it has, in fact, right and left before it, these determinations are before it as self-negating, the one being in the other, and each in this unity being [at the same time] not self-negating but indifferently for itself.

Therefore though ordinary thinking everywhere has contradiction for its content, it does not become aware of it, but remains an external reflection which passes from likeness to unlikeness, or from the negative relation to the reflection-into-self, of the distinct sides. It holds these two determinations over against one another and has in mind *only them*, but not their *transition*, which is the essential point and which contains the contradiction. *Intelligent* reflection, to mention this here, consists, on the contrary, in grasping and asserting contradiction. Even though it does not express the Notion of things and their relationships and has for its material and content only the determinations of ordinary thinking, it does bring these into a relation that contains their contradiction and allows *their Notion to show or shine through* the contradiction. Thinking reason, however, sharpens, so to say, the blunt difference of diverse terms, the mere manifoldness of pictorial thinking, into *essential* difference, into *opposition*. Only when the manifold terms have been driven to the point of contradiction do they become active and lively towards one another, receiving in contradiction the negativity which is the indwelling pulsation of self-movement and spontaneous activity [*Lebendigkeit*].

We have already remarked that the basic determination in the ontological proof of the existence of God is *the sum total of all realities*.[23] It is usually shown, first of all, that this determination is *possible* because it is free from *contradiction*, reality being taken only as reality without any limitation. We remarked that this sum total thus becomes simple indeterminate being, or if the realities are, in fact, taken as a plurality of determinate beings, [turns] into the sum-total of all negations. More precisely, when the difference of reality is taken into account, it develops from difference into opposition, and from this into contradiction, so that in the end the sum total of all realities simply becomes absolute contradiction within itself. Ordinary – but not speculative – thinking, which abhors contradiction, as nature abhors a vacuum, rejects this conclusion; for in considering contradiction, it stops short at the one-sided *resolution* of it into *nothing*, and fails to recognize the positive side of contradiction where it becomes *absolute activity* and absolute ground.

In general, our consideration of the nature of contradiction has shown that it is not, so to speak, a blemish, an imperfection or a defect in something if a contradiction can be pointed out in it. On the contrary, every determination, every concrete thing, every Notion, is essentially a unity of distinguished and distinguishable moments, which, by virtue of the *determinate, essential difference*, pass over into contradictory moments. This contradictory side of course resolves itself into nothing, it withdraws into its negative unity. Now the thing, the subject, the Notion, is just this negative unity itself; it is inherently self-contradictory, but it is no less the *contradiction resolved*: it is the *ground* that contains and supports its determinations. The thing, subject, or Notion, as reflected into itself in its sphere, is its resolved contradiction, but its entire sphere is again also *determinate, different*; it is thus a finite sphere and this means a *contradictory* one. It is not itself the resolution of this higher contradiction but has a higher sphere for its negative unity, for its ground. Finite things, therefore, in their indifferent multiplicity are simply this, to be contradictory and *disrupted within themselves and to return into their ground*. As will be demonstrated later, the true inference from a finite and contingent being to an absolutely necessary being does not consist in inferring the latter from the former as from a being that *is and remains the ground*; on the contrary, the inference is from a being that, as is also directly implied in *contingency*, is only in a state of collapse and is *inherently self-contradictory*; or rather, the true inference consists in showing that contingent being in its own self withdraws into its ground in which it is sublated, and further, that by this withdrawal it posits the ground only in such a manner that it rather makes itself into a positedness. In ordinary inference, the *being* of the finite appears as ground of the absolute; because the finite is, therefore the absolute is. But the truth is that the absolute is, because the finite is the inherently self-contradictory opposition, because it is *not*. In the former meaning, the inference runs thus: the being of the finite is the being of the absolute; but in the latter, thus: the non-being of the finite is the being of the absolute.

Notes

1 Hegel's analyses of existence, appearance and actuality are not included in this collection. [s.h.]

2 'Das Sein ist Schein'. 'Schein' can also be translated as 'seeming' (the term I have used in my introduction to Part III on Logic). [s.h.]

3 See Hegel, *Science of Logic*, p. 116: 'The second is equally a *determinate* being, but determined as a negative of the something – an *other*', and p. 119: 'Something *preserves* itself in its negative determinate being [*Nichtdasein*]'. See above, pp. 198, 200. [s.h.]

4 Miller's translation has 'the reflection of itself within itself'. The German text is 'das Scheinen seiner in sich selbst'. [s.h.]

5   Miller's translation has 'both essence and illusory being'. The German text is '[. . .] das Unwesentliche und der Schein als Reste des Seins. Aber sie beide, sowie der Unterschied des Wesens von ihnen'. [S.H.]

6   Miller's translation again has 'the reflection of itself within itself'. The German text is 'das Scheinen seiner in sich selbst'. [S.H.]

7   Miller's translation has 'Reflection therefore is the movement that starts or returns only in so far as the negative has already returned into itself'. The German text is 'Die Reflexion ist also die Bewegung, die, indem sie die Rückkehr ist, erst darin das ist, das anfängt oder das zurückkehrt'. [S.H.]

8   Miller's translation has '*absolute recoil* upon itself'. The German phrase is '*absoluter Gegenstoß* in sich'. [S.H.]

9   i.e. positing reflection. [S.H.]

10   I. Kant, *Critique of Judgement*, translated, with an introduction, by W. Pluhar (Indianapolis: Hackett Publishing, 1987), pp. 18–19 (Second Introduction, section IV). [S.H.]

11   i.e. positing reflection. [S.H.]

12   Miller's translation has 'the determination thus posited is not put in the place of an other; the positing *has* no presupposition'. The German text is 'das Setzen setzt seine Bestimmung nicht an die Stelle eines Anderen; es *hat* keine Voraussetzung'. [S.H.]

13   Miller's translation has 'It is *the equality of reflection with itself* that possesses the negative only as negative, as sublated or posited being'. The German text is 'Die *Sichselbstgleichheit der Reflexion*, welche das Negative nur als Negatives, als Aufgehobenes oder Gesetztes hat'. [S.H.]

14   Miller's translation has 'the showing of the illusory being of essence within essence itself'. The German text is 'das Scheinen des Wesens in sich selbst'. [S.H.]

15   Miller's translation has '"*In that*" is, in one and the same respect'. The German text is '*Darin*, d.h. in einer und derselben Rücksicht'. [S.H.]

16   i.e. of the diverse. [S.H.]

17   Miller's translation has 'this positedness as thus determined'. The German text is 'Aber dieses hat damit seine Bestimmtheit'. I read 'dieses' as referring back to 'das Verglichene oder das Verschiedene' ('the compared or the diverse') in the previous sentence. [S.H.]

18   Miller's translation has 'But likeness and unlikeness'. The German text is 'Eben die Gleichheit und die Ungleichheit'. [S.H.]

19   Miller's translation has 'It is the unity of identity and difference; its moments are different in one identity'. The German text is 'Er ist die Einheit der Identität und der Verschiedenheit; seine Momente sind in *einer* Identität verschiedene'. [S.H.]

20   Miller's translation has 'merely different'. The German text is 'bloß verschiedene'. [S.H.]

21   Reading 'positive' for 'negative'. [Translator's note.]

22   Hegel's point here is that the positive and the negative are both *self-excluding* determinations. That which holds sway and 'subsists' in the self-destruction of the positive and the negative is thus this very activity of self-exclusion itself. In the following paragraphs Hegel conceives of this activity of self-exclusion – of 'excluding reflection' – as the *ground* of the positive and the negative. The activity of grounding, for Hegel, is thus itself simply the activity of excluding oneself from oneself and setting this excluded self over against oneself as the 'grounded'. [S.H.]

23   See Hegel, *Science of Logic*, p. 112 (not included in this collection). For related passages, see Hegel, *The Encyclopaedia Logic*, p. 75 (§ 36 Addition) and p. 94 (§ 49) (above pp. 150, 160–1). [S.H.]

17

Science of Logic: Doctrine of the Notion [Concept]

The Notion in General

What the *nature of the Notion* is, can no more be stated offhand than can the Notion of any other object. It might perhaps seem that, in order to state the Notion of an object, the logical element were presupposed and that therefore this could not in turn have something else for its presupposition, nor be deduced; just as in geometry logical propositions as applied to magnitude and employed in that science, are premised in the form of *axioms*, determinations of cognition that *have not been and cannot be deduced*. Now although it is true that the Notion is to be regarded, not merely as a subjective presupposition but as the *absolute foundation*, yet it can be so only in so far as it has *made* itself the foundation. Abstract immediacy is no doubt a *first*; yet in so far as it is abstract it is, on the contrary mediated, and therefore if it is to be grasped in its truth its foundation must first be sought. Hence this foundation, though indeed an immediate, must have made itself immediate through the sublation of mediation.

From this aspect the *Notion* is to be regarded in the first instance simply as the third to *being* and *essence*, to the *immediate* and to *reflection*. Being and essence are so far the moments of its *becoming*; but it is their *foundation* and *truth* as the identity in which they are submerged and contained. They are contained in it because it is their *result*, but no longer as *being* and *essence*. That determination they possess only in so far as they have not withdrawn into this their unity.

Objective logic therefore, which treats of *being* and *essence* constitutes properly the *genetic exposition of the Notion.* [. . .]

Section One: Subjectivity

Chapter 1: The Notion

[. . .] This universal Notion, which we have now to consider here, contains the three moments: *universality, particularity* and *individuality*. The difference and the determinations which the Notion gives itself in its distinguishing, constitute the side which was previously called *positedness*. As this is identical in the Notion with being-in-and-for-self, each of these moments is no less the *whole* Notion than it is a *determinate* Notion and *a determination* of the Notion.

In the first instance, it is the *pure Notion* or the determination of *universality*. But the pure or universal Notion is also only a *determinate* or *particular* Notion, which takes its place alongside other Notions. Because the Notion is a totality, and therefore in its universality or pure identical self-relation is essentially a determining and a distinguishing, it therefore contains within itself the standard by which this form of its self-identity, in pervading and embracing all the moments, no less immediately determines itself to be only the *universal* over against the distinguishedness of the moments.

Secondly, the Notion is thereby posited as this *particular* or *determinate* Notion, distinct from others.

Thirdly, individuality is the Notion reflecting itself out of the difference into absolute negativity. This is, at the same time, the moment in which it has passed out of its identity into its *otherness*, and becomes the *judgement*.[1]

A. The Universal Notion

The pure Notion is the absolutely infinite, unconditioned and free. It is here, at the outset of the discussion which has the Notion for its *content*, that we must look back once more at its genesis. *Essence* is the *outcome* of *being*, and the Notion the *outcome* of essence, therefore also of being. But this becoming has the significance of a self-*repulsion*, so that it is rather the *outcome* which is the *unconditioned* and *original*. *Being*, in its transition into essence, has become an *illusory being* or a *positedness*, and *becoming* or transition into an *other* has become a positing; and conversely, the *positing* or reflection of essence has sublated itself and has restored itself as a being that is *not posited*, that is *original*. The Notion is the interfusion of these moments, namely, qualitative and original being is such only as a positing, only as a return-into-self, and this pure reflection-into-self is a sheer *becoming-other* or *determinateness* which, consequently, is no less an infinite, self-relating *determinateness*.

Thus the Notion is, in the first instance, the *absolute self-identity* that is such only as the negation of negation or as the infinite unity of the negativity with itself. This *pure relation* of the Notion to itself, which is this relation by positing itself through the negativity, is the *universality* of the Notion.

As *universality* is the utterly *simple* determination, it does not seem capable of any explanation; for an explanation must concern itself with definitions and distinctions and must apply predicates to its object, and to do this to what is simple, would alter rather than explain it. But the simplicity which constitutes the very nature of the universal is such that, through absolute negativity, it contains *within itself* difference and determinateness in the highest degree. *Being* is simple as *immediate* being; for that reason it is only something *meant* or *intended* and we cannot say of it what it is; therefore, it is one with its other, with *non-being*. Its Notion is just this, to be a simplicity that immediately vanishes in its opposite; it is *becoming*. The *universal*, on the contrary, is that *simplicity* which, because it is the Notion, no less possesses *within itself* the *richest content*.

First, therefore, it is the simple relation to itself; it is only *within itself*. *Secondly*, however, this identity is *within itself* absolute *mediation*, but it is not something *mediated*. The universal that is *mediated*, namely, the *abstract* universal that is opposed to the particular and the individual, this will be discussed later when we are dealing with the determinate notion.[2] Yet even the *abstract* universal involves this, that in order to obtain it we are required to *leave out* other determinations of the concrete. These determinations, simply as such, are *negations*; equally, too, the *omitting* of them is a *negating*. So that even with the abstraction, we have the negation of the negation. But this double negation is conceived of as though it were *external* to the abstraction, as though not only were the other omitted properties of the concrete distinct from the one retained, which is the content of the abstract universal, but also as though this operation of omitting the other properties and retaining the one were a process outside the properties themselves. To such an *externality* in face of that movement, the universal has not yet determined itself; it is still within itself that absolute mediation which is, precisely, the negation of the negation or absolute negativity.

By virtue of this original unity it follows, in the first place, that the first negative, or the *determination*, is not a limitation for the universal which, on the contrary, *maintains itself therein* and is positively identical with itself. The categories of being were, as Notions, essentially these identities of the determinations with themselves in their limitation or otherness; but this identity was only *in itself* the Notion; it was not yet manifested. Consequently, the qualitative determination as such was lost in its other and had for its truth a determination *distinct* from itself. The universal, on the contrary, even when it posits itself in a determination, *remains* therein what it is. It is the soul [*Seele*] of the concrete which it indwells, unimpeded and equal to itself in the manifoldness and diversity of the concrete. It is not dragged into the process of becoming, but *continues* itself through that process undisturbed and possesses the power of unalterable, undying self-preservation.

But even so, it does not merely *show*, or have an *illusory being*, in its other, like the determination of reflection; this, as a *correlate*, is not merely self-related but is a *positive relating* of itself to its other in which it *manifests itself*; but, in the first instance, it only *shows* in it, and this illusory being of each in the other, or their reciprocal determining, along with their self-dependence, has the form of an external act. The *universal*, on the contrary, is posited as the *essential being* of its determination, as the latter's *own positive nature*. For the determination that constitutes its negative is, in the Notion, simply and solely a *positedness*; in other words, it is, at the same time, essentially only the negative of the negative, and is only as this identity of the negative with itself, which is the universal. Thus the universal is also the *substance* of its determinations; but in such wise that what was a *contingency* for substance, is the Notion's own self-*mediation*, its own *immanent reflection*. But this mediation which, in the first instance, raises contingency to *necessity*, is the *manifested* relation; the Notion is not the abyss of formless substance, or necessity as the *inner* identity of things or states distinct from, and limiting, one another; on the contrary, as absolute negativity, it is the shaper and creator, and because the determination is not a limitation but is just as much utterly sublated, or posited, the illusory being is now manifestation, the manifestation *of the identical*.

The universal is therefore *free* power; it is itself and takes its other within its embrace, but without *doing violence* to it; on the contrary, the universal is, in its other, in peaceful communion with itself. We have called it free power, but it could also be called *free love* and *boundless blessedness*, for it bears itself towards its other as towards *its own self*; in it, it has returned to itself.

We have just mentioned *determinateness*, although the Notion, being as yet only the universal and only self-*identical*, has not yet advanced to that stage. However, we cannot speak of the universal apart from determinateness which to be more precise is particularity and individuality, for the universal, in its absolute negativity, contains determinateness in and for itself. The determinateness, therefore, is not introduced from outside when we speak of it in connection with the universal. As negativity in general or in accordance with the *first*, *immediate* negation, the universal contains determinateness generally as *particularity*; as the *second* negation, that is, as negation of the negation, it is *absolute determinateness* or *individuality* and *concreteness*. The universal is thus the totality of the Notion; it is a concrete, and far from being empty, it has through its Notion a *content*, and a content in which it not only maintains itself but one which is its own and immanent in it. We can, indeed, abstract from the content: but in that case we do not obtain the universal of the Notion but only the *abstract* universal, which is an isolated, imperfect moment of the Notion and has no truth. [. . .]

Section Three: The Idea

The Idea is the *adequate Notion*, that which is objectively *true*, or the *true as such*. When anything whatever possesses truth, it possesses it through its Idea, or, *something possesses truth only in so far as it is Idea*. [. . .]

Having reached the result that the Idea is the unity of the Notion and objectivity, is the true, it must not be regarded merely as a *goal* to which we have to approximate but which itself always remains a kind of *beyond*; on the contrary, we must recognize that everything actual *is* only in so far as it possesses the Idea and expresses it. It is not merely that the object, the objective and subjective world in general, *ought to be congruous* with the Idea, but they are themselves the congruence of Notion and reality; the reality that does not correspond to the Notion is mere *Appearance*, the subjective, contingent, capricious element that is not the truth. When it is said that no object is to be found in experience that is perfectly congruous with the *Idea*, one is opposing the Idea as a subjective standard to the actual; but what anything actual is supposed in truth *to be*, if its Notion is not in it and if its objectivity does not correspond to its Notion at all, it is impossible to say; for it would be nothing. It is true that the mechanical and chemical object, like the non-spiritual subject and the spirit that is conscious only of the finite, not of its essence, do not, according to their various natures, have their Notion existent in them *in its own free form*. But they can only be true at all in so far as they are the union of their Notion and reality, of their soul and their body. Wholes like the state and the church cease to exist when the unity of their Notion and their reality is dissolved; man, the living being, is dead when soul and body are parted in him; dead nature, the mechanical and chemical world – taking, that is, the dead world to mean the inorganic world, otherwise it would have no positive meaning at all – dead nature, then, if it is separated into its Notion and its reality, is nothing but the subjective abstraction of a thought form and a formless matter. *Spirit* that was not Idea, was not the unity of the Notion with its own self, or the Notion that did not have the Notion itself for its reality would be dead, spiritless spirit, a material object.

The Idea being the unity of Notion and reality, *being* has attained the significance of *truth*; therefore what now *is* is only what is Idea. Finite things are finite because they do not possess the complete reality of their Notion within themselves, but require other things to complete it – or, conversely, because they are presupposed as objects, hence possess the Notion as an external determination. The highest to which they attain on the side of this finitude is external purposiveness. That actual things are not congruous with the Idea is the side of their *finitude* and *untruth*, and in accordance with this side they are *objects*, determined in accordance with their various spheres and in the relationships of objectivity, either mechanically, chemically or by an external end. That the Idea has not completely leavened its reality, has imperfectly subdued it to the Notion, this is a possibility arising from the fact that the Idea itself has a *restricted content*, that though it is essentially the unity of Notion and reality, it is no less essentially their difference; for only the object is their immediate, that is, merely *implicit* unity. But if an object, for example the state, *did not correspond at all* to its Idea, that is, if in fact it was not the Idea of the state at all, if its reality, which is the self-conscious individuals, did not correspond at all to the Notion, its soul and its body would have parted; the former would escape into the solitary regions of thought, the latter would have broken up into the single individualities. But because the Notion of the state so essentially constitutes the nature of these individualities, it is present in them as an urge so powerful that they are impelled to translate it into reality, be it only in the form of external purposiveness, or to put up with it as it is, or else they must needs perish. The worst state, one whose reality least corresponds to the Notion, in so far as it still exists, is still Idea; the individuals still obey a dominant Notion. [...]

Chapter 3: The Absolute Idea

[...] It is in this manner that each step of the *advance* in the process of further determination, while getting further away from the indeterminate beginning is also *getting back nearer* to it, and that therefore, what at first sight may appear to be different, the retrogressive grounding of the beginning, and the *progressive further determining* of it, coincide and are the same. The method, which thus winds itself into a circle, cannot anticipate in a development in time that the beginning is, as such, already something derived; it is sufficient for the beginning in its immediacy that it is simple universality. In being that, it has its complete condition; and there is no need to claim apologetically that it may only be accepted *provisionally* and *hypothetically*.[3] Whatever objections to it might be raised – say, the limitations of human knowledge, the need to examine critically the instrument of cognition before starting to deal with the subject-matter – are themselves *presuppositions*, which as *concrete determinations* involve the demand for their mediation and proof. Since therefore they possess no formal advantage over the *beginning* with the subject-matter against which they protest, but on the contrary themselves require deduction on account of their more concrete content, their claim to prior consideration must be treated as an empty presumption. They have an untrue content, for they convert what we know to be finite and untrue into something incontestable and absolute, namely, a *limited* cognition determined as *form* and *instrument relatively to its content*; this untrue cognition is itself also the form, the process of seeking grounds, that is retrogressive. The method of truth, too, knows the beginning to be incomplete, because it is a beginning; but at the same time it knows this incompleteness to be a necessity, because truth only comes to be itself through the negativity of immediacy. The impatience that insists *merely* on getting beyond the *determinate* – whether called beginning, object, the finite, or in whatever other form it be taken – and finding itself immediately in the absolute, has before it as cognition nothing but the empty negative, the abstract infinite; in other words, a *presumed* absolute, that is presumed because it is not *posited*, not *grasped*; grasped it can only be through the *mediation* of cognition, of which the universal and immediate is a moment, but the truth itself resides only in the extended course of the process and in the conclusion. To meet the subjective needs of unfamiliarity and its impatience, a survey of the *whole* may of course be given *in advance* – by a division for reflection which, after the manner of finite cognition, specifies the particular of the universal as something *already there* and to be awaited in the course of the science. Yet this affords us nothing more than a picture for *ordinary thinking*; for the genuine transition from the universal to the particular and to the whole that is determined in and for itself, in which whole that first universal itself according to its true determination is again a moment, is alien to the above manner of division, and is alone the mediation of the science itself.

By virtue of the nature of the method just indicated, the science exhibits itself as a *circle* returning upon itself, the end being wound back into the beginning, the simple ground, by the mediation; this circle is moreover a *circle of circles*, for each individual member as ensouled by the method is reflected into itself, so that in returning into the beginning it is at the same time the beginning of a new member. Links of this chain are the individual sciences [of logic, nature and spirit], each of which has an *antecedent* and a *successor* – or, expressed more accurately, *has* only the *antecedent* and *indicates* its *successor* in its conclusion.

Thus then logic, too, in the absolute Idea, has withdrawn into that same simple unity which its beginning is; the pure immediacy of being in which at first every determination appears to be extinguished or removed by abstraction, is the Idea that has reached through mediation, that is, through the sublation of mediation, a likeness correspondent to itself. The method is the pure Notion that relates itself only to itself; it is therefore the *simple self-relation* that is *being*. But now it is also *fulfilled being*, the *Notion that comprehends* itself, being as the *concrete* and also absolutely *intensive* totality. In conclusion, there remains only this to be said about this Idea, that in it, first, the *science of logic* has grasped its own Notion. In the sphere of *being*, the beginning of its *content*, its Notion appears as a knowing in a subjective reflection external to that content. But in the Idea of absolute cognition the Notion has become the Idea's own content. The Idea is itself the pure Notion that has itself for subject-matter and which, in running itself as subject-matter through the totality of its determinations, develops itself into the whole of its reality, into the system of the science [of logic], and concludes by apprehending this process of comprehending itself, thereby superseding its standing as content and subject-matter and cognizing the Notion of the science. Secondly, this Idea is still logical, it is enclosed within pure thought, and is the science only of the divine *Notion*. True, the systematic exposition is itself a realization of the Idea but confined within the same sphere. Because the pure Idea of cognition is so far confined within subjectivity, it is the *urge* to sublate this, and pure truth as the last result becomes also the *beginning of another sphere and science*. It only remains here to indicate this transition.

The Idea, namely, in positing itself as absolute *unity* of the pure Notion and its reality and thus contracting itself into the immediacy of *being*, is the *totality* in this form – nature. But this determination has not *issued from a process* of becoming, nor is it a *transition*, as when above, the subjective Notion in its totality *becomes objectivity*, and the *subjective end becomes life*. On the contrary, the pure Idea in which the determinateness or reality of the Notion is itself raised into Notion, is an absolute *liberation* for which there is no longer any immediate determination that is not equally *posited* and itself Notion; in this freedom, therefore, no transition takes place; the simple being to which the Idea determines itself remains perfectly transparent to it and is the Notion that, in its determination, abides with itself. The passage is therefore to be understood here rather in this manner, that the Idea *freely releases* itself in its absolute self-assurance and inner poise. By reason of this freedom, the form of its determinateness is also utterly free – the *externality of space and time* existing absolutely on its own account without the moment of subjectivity. In so far as this externality presents itself only in the abstract immediacy of being and is apprehended from the standpoint of conscious ness, it exists as mere objectivity and external life; but in the Idea it remains essentially and actually [*an und für sich*] the totality of the Notion, and science in the relationship to nature of divine cognition. But in this next resolve of the pure Idea to determine itself as external Idea, it thereby only posits for itself the mediation out of which the Notion ascends as a free Existence that has withdrawn into itself from externality, that completes its self-liberation in the *science of spirit*, and that finds the supreme Notion of itself in the science of logic as the self-comprehending pure Notion.

Notes

1 Hegel's separate analyses of the particular or determinate Notion, individuality and judgement are not included in this collection, though the analysis of the universal Notion which follows does touch on the nature of particularity and individuality. [s.h.]
2 Not included in this collection. Miller's translation has 'specific Notion', instead of 'determinate Notion'. The German text is 'bei dem bestimmten Begriffe'. [s.h.]
3 Miller's translation has 'there is no need to deprecate the fact that it may only be accepted *provisionally* and *hypothetically*'. The German text is 'es braucht nicht depreziert zu werden, daß man ihn nur *provisorisch* und *hypothetisch* gelten lassen möge'. 'Deprezieren' means to 'apologise'. [s.h.]

Part IV

Philosophy of Nature and Philosophy of Subjective Spirit

Introduction

Hegel's *Philosophy of Nature* forms the second part of his *Encyclopaedia* (1830), where it is presented in a series of numbered paragraphs, with supplementary remarks and additions, rather than in a continuous text. It has drawn (profoundly ignorant) ridicule from Karl Popper, who dismissed Hegel's account of sound and heat as 'gibberish',[1] but many other, much more discerning philosophers have acknowledged the considerable importance of Hegel's work. J. N. Findlay rightly sees in the *Philosophy of Nature* 'an integral part of Hegel's system' that is based on an 'informed and accurate' grasp of the science of his day;[2] and Heidegger, though critical of Hegel, regarded the latter's conception of time as 'the most radical way in which the ordinary understanding of time has been given form conceptually, and one which has received too little attention'.[3] The paragraphs selected here include those devoted to space and time, those concerned with the general conception of the philosophy of nature as such, as well as those which deal with the organism, disease, death and the transition to spirit (which particularly interest Derrida in *Glas*).

Hegel's project in the *Philosophy of Nature* is a continuation of the ontological project of the *Science of Logic*. Having reached the conclusion at the end of the *Logic* that being is to be understood not just as immediacy, reflexivity or conceptual development, but as *nature*, Hegel now has to determine fully what nature is. His aim is not to ground any particular scientific conception of nature, but to provide a philosophical account of the very structure of nature itself. His aim, in other words, is to produce an account of nature to compare with, indeed to surpass, those offered by Aristotle in the *Physics*, Kant in the *Metaphysical Foundations of Natural Science*, or Schelling in the *Ideas for a Philosophy of Nature*. Following the method of the *Logic*, Hegel starts with the least that nature can be understood to be – sheer externality, or space – and proceeds to show that the basic features of nature can be derived directly and immanently from space itself. Time is thus understood by Hegel, not as a separate 'form of intuition', as it is by Kant, but as the self-negating or 'self-sublation' of space itself.[4] Place is understood as a spatial point enduring through time.[5] Motion is understood as the process whereby place *changes* – the process whereby place ceases to be *this* place and becomes *another* place. And matter is understood to be the exclusive, self-relating space that is preserved in motion across space.[6] In his account of the organism, which concludes the *Philosophy of Nature*, Hegel then shows how disease and death are immanent to life itself, and how, as the universality of their genus comes to be *for* living beings themselves, *spirit* eventually emerges from nature.[7]

Spirit, for Hegel, is nothing other than self-determining freedom, and his account of the most immediate form of such freedom – the freedom of individual subjectivity – is to be found in the *Philosophy of Subjective Spirit*, the first section of the *Philosophy of Spirit* which forms the third part of the *Encyclopaedia* (1830). Though far less influential historically than the *Phenomenology of Spirit*, Hegel's study of subjective spirit has nevertheless engaged the interest of many subsequent philosophers, most notably that of Derrida who analysed Hegel's theory of signs in the essay 'The Pit and the Pyramid' in *Margins of Philosophy*.[8] The *Philosophy of Subjective Spirit* itself contains a sub-section entitled 'Phenomenology'. There is, however, an important difference between the project of the *Philosophy of Subjective Spirit* and that of the *Phenomenology of Spirit*. The *Phenomenology* does not set out to determine the ontological structure of consciousness – what consciousness ultimately *is* – but only to examine the dialectical consequences of the various ways in which consciousness *takes* itself and its objects, that is, the consequences of the various ways in which consciousness and its objects *appear* to consciousness itself. The main conclusion reached by the *Phenomenology*, as we know, is that consciousness cannot sustain its favoured idea that the 'True' confronts it as an object, and that, consequently, the true nature of being must be understood as disclosing itself *within* consciousness and thought itself. Once it has been established in this way that thought can indeed find the truth within itself, thought can begin to do philosophy, rather than mere phenomenology. In the *Logic* and the *Philosophy of Nature*, as we have seen, philosophical thought determines being as quality, essential reflexivity, conceptual development, reason (or Idea), space, time and matter, culminating in organic life and the emergence of spirit. The task of determining what it is to be spirit then falls – initially – to the *Philosophy of Subjective Spirit*. In contrast to that of the *Phenomenology*, therefore, the purpose of the *Philosophy of Subjective Spirit* is an avowedly ontological one: to continue the work of philosophy and to determine, not just what consciousness takes itself to be, but what spirit (or the mind) in truth *is*.

Hegel's intention in this section of the *Encyclopaedia* thus differs strikingly from that of Kant in the *Critique of Pure Reason*, even though the two philosophers provide comparable analyses of intuition, imagination and understanding. Kant's claim is a purely transcendental one: to show how intuition, imagination and understanding function as conditions of the possibility of experience. The first *Critique* is thus not to be understood as providing an account of those faculties *in themselves*; indeed, Kant denies that any ontological account of the mind itself can be given. Hegel, by contrast, is seeking to offer precisely such an account.

Similarly, Hegel's project differs from those of Descartes and Locke, even though his remarks on memory and attention can be usefully compared with what they have to say on these topics. Unlike Descartes and Locke, Hegel is not doing epistemology in the *Philosophy of Subjective Spirit* and is not primarily concerned with determining how we can know objects in the world. He is doing ontology and seeking to understand what the basic activities of the mind *are*.

Each activity of the mind discussed by Hegel is to be understood specifically as a form of subjective freedom. Those activities that are discussed later by Hegel presuppose those that come earlier, and render explicit what is only implicit in those earlier activities. Consequently, those treated later exhibit greater freedom than those treated earlier, and Hegel's account as a whole thus shows how human subjectivity progressively emancipates itself from nature. The passages selected here do not cover all the activities of the mind that Hegel analyses, but concentrate on the following: sensation, in which we are still primarily determined by things in nature; consciousness, in which we freely conceive of what we sense as an object; intuition, in which (through attention) we freely conceive of what we sense as an encompassing realm of space and time; recollection and associative imagination in which we freely retain images of things and associate them with one another; productive imagination in which we freely produce symbols and signs in which to give expression to subjective images and meanings; mechanical memory in which we freely abstract from meaning, hold a series of purely meaningless signs in our mind and thereby become conscious of ourselves as 'abstract subjectivity'; thought in which we freely render our abstract subjectivity determinate in acts of conceiving, judging and reasoning; and, finally, will in which we freely determine ourselves through thought to be practical. The objective world that the free human will builds for itself – the world of society, the state, and history – is analysed by Hegel in the *Philosophy of Right* and the *Lectures on the Philosophy of World History*.

The passages in Part IV are taken from G. W. F. Hegel, *Philosophy of Nature. Being Part Two of the Encyclopaedia of the Philosophical Sciences (1830)*, translated by A. V. Miller, with foreword by J. N. Findlay (Oxford: Clarendon Press, 1970) and G. W. F. Hegel, *Philosophy of Mind. Being Part Three of the Encyclopaedia of the Philosophical Sciences (1830)*, translated by W. Wallace, together with the *Zusätze* in Boumann's text (1845), translated by A. V. Miller, with foreword by J. N. Findlay (Oxford: Clarendon Press, 1971). For the German text of these passages, see G. W. F. Hegel, *Werke in zwanzig Bänden*, edited by E. Moldenhauer and K. M. Michel, 20 vols and Index

(Frankfurt: Suhrkamp Verlag, 1969ff), vols 9 and 10. The passages marked 'Addition' are not by Hegel himself, but were compiled by Karl Michelet (the editor of the 1842 edition of the *Encyclopaedia Philosophy of Nature*) and Ludwig Boumann (the editor of the 1845 edition of the *Encyclopaedia Philosophy of Spirit* [or *Mind*]) from transcripts of Hegel's lectures made by his students. The numbered paragraphs and the remarks were written by Hegel himself.

Notes

1 K. R. Popper, *The Open Society and its Enemies* (1945), 2 vols (London: Routledge, 1966), 2: 28.
2 J. N. Findlay, *Hegel: A Re-examination* (New York: Oxford University Press, 1958), p. 267.
3 M. Heidegger, *Being and Time*, translated by J. Macquarrie and E. Robinson (Oxford: Blackwell, 1962), p. 480.
4 G. W. F. Hegel, *Philosophy of Nature. Being Part Two of the Encyclopaedia of the Philosophical Sciences (1830)*, translated by A. V. Miller, with foreword by J. N. Findlay (Oxford: Clarendon Press, 1970), p. 34 (§ 257 Addition). See below, p. 265.
5 Hegel, *Philosophy of Nature*, p. 40 (§ 260 Addition). See below, p. 268.
6 Hegel, *Philosophy of Nature*, p. 41 (§ 261). See below, p. 269.
7 Hegel, *Philosophy of Nature*, p. 443 (§ 376). See below, p. 281.
8 J. Derrida, *Margins of Philosophy*, translated, with additional notes, by A. Bass (Brighton: The Harvester Press, 1982), pp. 69–108.

18

Philosophy of Nature: Introduction

§ 245

In man's *practical* approach to Nature, the latter is, for him, something immediate and external; and he himself is an external and therefore sensuous individual, although in relation to natural objects, he correctly regards himself as *end*. A consideration of Nature according to this relationship yields the standpoint of *finite* teleology (§ 205). In this, we find the correct presupposition that Nature does not itself contain the absolute, final end (§§ 207–11).[1] But if this way of considering the matter starts from particular, *finite* ends, on the one hand it makes them into presuppositions whose contingent content may in itself be even insignificant and trivial. On the other hand, the end-relationship demands for itself a deeper mode of treatment than that appropriate to external and finite relationships, namely, the mode of treatment of the Notion, which in its own general nature is immanent and therefore is immanent in Nature as such. [A]

§ 246

What is now called *physics* was formerly called *natural philosophy*, and it is also a *theoretical*, and indeed a *thinking* consideration of Nature; but, on the one hand, it does not start from determinations which are external to Nature, like those ends already mentioned; and secondly, it is directed to a knowledge of the *universal* aspect of Nature, a universal which is also *determined* within itself – directed to a knowledge of forces, laws and genera, whose content must not be a simple aggregate, but arranged in orders and classes, must present itself as an organism. As the Philosophy of Nature is a *comprehending* [*begreifend*] treatment, it has as its object the same *universal*, but *explicitly*, and it considers this universal in its *own immanent necessity* in accordance with the self-determination of the Notion.

> *Remark*: The relation of philosophy to the empirical sciences was discussed in the general introduction [to the *Encyclopaedia*].[2] Not only

must philosophy be in agreement with our empirical knowledge of Nature, but the *origin* and *formation* of the Philosophy of Nature pre-supposes and is conditioned by empirical physics. However, the course of a science's origin and the preliminaries of its construction are one thing, while the science itself is another. In the latter, the former can no longer appear as the foundation of the science; here, the foundation must be the necessity of the Notion.

It has already been mentioned that, in the progress of philosophical knowledge, we must not only give an account of the object *as determined by its Notion*, but we must also name the *empirical* appearance corre-sponding to it, and we must show that the appearance does, in fact, correspond to its Notion. However, this is not an appeal to experience in regard to the necessity of the content. Even less admissible is an appeal to what is called *intuition* [*Anschauung*], which is usually noth-ing but a fanciful and sometimes fantastic exercise of the imagination on the lines of *analogies*, which may be more or less significant, and which impress determinations and schemata on objects only *externally* (§ 231, Remark).[3]

Addition: [. . .] The Philosophy of Nature takes up the material which physics has prepared for it empirically, at the point to which physics has brought it, and recon-stitutes it, so that experience is not its final warrant and base. Physics must therefore work into the hands of philosophy, in order that the latter may translate into the Notion the abstract universal transmitted to it, by showing how this universal, as an intrinsically necessary whole, proceeds from the Notion. The philosophical way of putting the facts is no mere whim, once in a way to walk on one's head for a change, after having walked for a long while on one's legs, or once in a way to see our everyday face bedaubed with paint: no, it is because the method of physics does not satisfy the Notion, that we have to go further.

What distinguishes the Philosophy of Nature from physics is, more precisely, the kind of metaphysics used by them both; for metaphysics is nothing else but the entire range of the universal determinations of thought, as it were, the diamond net into which everything is brought and thereby first made intelligible. Every educated consciousness has its metaphysics, an instinctive way of thinking, the absolute power within us of which we become master only when we make it in turn the object of our knowledge. Philosophy in general has, as philosophy, other categories than those of the ordinary consciousness: all education [*Bildung*] reduces to the distinc-tion of categories. All revolutions, in the sciences no less than in world history, originate solely from the fact that Spirit, in order to understand and comprehend itself with a view to possessing itself, has changed its categories, comprehending itself more truly, more deeply, more intimately, and more in unity with itself. Now the inadequacy of the thought-determinations used in physics can be traced to two points which are closely bound up with each other. (α) The universal of physics is abstract or only formal; its determination is not immanent in it and it does not pass over into particularity. (β) The determinate content falls for that very reason outside the universal; and so is split into fragments, into parts which are isolated and detached from each other, devoid of any necessary connection, and it is just this which stamps it as only finite. If we examine a flower, for example, our understanding notes its particular qualities; chemistry dismembers and analyses it. In this way, we separate colour, shape of the leaves, citric acid, etheric oil, carbon, hydrogen, etc.; and now we say that the plant consists of all these parts.

> If you want to describe life and gather its meaning,
> To drive out its spirit must be your beginning,
> Then though fast in your hand lie the parts one by one
> The spirit that linked them, alas is gone
> And 'Nature's Laboratory' is only a name
> That the chemist bestows on't to hide his own shame.

as Goethe says.[4] Spirit cannot remain at this stage of thinking in terms of detached, unrelated concepts [*Verstandesreflexion*] and there are two ways in which it can advance beyond it. (α) The naïve mind [*der unbefangene Geist*], when it vividly contemplates Nature, as in the suggestive examples we often come across in Goethe, feels the life and the universal relationship in Nature; it divines that the universe is an organic whole and a totality pervaded by Reason, and it also feels in single forms of life an intimate oneness with itself; but even if we put together all those ingredients of the flower the result is still not a flower. And so, in the Philosophy of Nature, people have fallen back on intuition [*Anschauung*] and set it above reflective thought; but this is a mistake, for one cannot philosophize out of intuition. (β) What is intuited must also be thought, the isolated parts must be brought back by thought to simple universality; this thought unity is the Notion, which contains the specific differences, but as an immanent self-moving unity. The determinations of philosophical universality are not indifferent; it is the universality which fulfils itself, and which, in its diamantine identity, also contains difference.

The true infinite is the unity of itself and the finite; and this, now, is the category of philosophy and so, too, of the Philosophy of Nature. If genera and forces are the inner side of Nature, the universal, in face of which the outer and individual is only transient, then still a third stage is demanded, namely, the inner side of the inner side, and this, according to what has been said, would be the unity of the universal and the particular.

> To Nature's heart there penetrates no mere created mind:
> Too happy if she but display the outside of her rind.
> ★   ★   ★   ★
> I swear – of course but to myself – as rings within my ears
> That same old warning o'er and o'er again for sixty years,
> And thus a thousand times I answer in my mind: –
> With gladsome and ungrudging hand metes Nature from her store:
> She keeps not back the core,
> Nor separates the rind,
> But all in each both rind and core has evermore combined.[5]

In grasping this inner side, the one-sidedness of the theoretical and practical approaches is transcended, and at the same time each side receives its due. The former contains a universal without determinateness, the latter an individuality without a universal; the cognition which comprehends [*begreifendes Erkennen*] is the middle term in which universality does not remain on *this* side, in *me*, over against the individuality of the objects: on the contrary, while it stands in a negative relation to things and assimilates them to itself, it equally finds individuality in them and does not encroach upon their independence, or interfere with their free self-determination. The cognition which comprehends is thus the unity of the theoretical and practical approaches: the negation of individuality is, as negation of the negative, the affirmative universality which gives permanence to its determinations; for the true individuality is at the same time within itself a universality. [. . .]

§ 247

Nature has presented itself as the Idea in the form of *otherness*. Since therefore the Idea is the negative of itself, or is *external to itself*, Nature is not merely external in relation to this Idea (and to its subjective existence, Spirit); the truth is rather that *Externality* constitutes the specific character in which Nature, as Nature, exists. [A]

§ 248

In this externality, the determinations of the Notion have the show of an *indifferent subsistence* and *isolation* [*Vereinzelung*] in regard to each other, and the Notion, therefore, is present only as something inward. Consequently, Nature exhibits no freedom in its existence, but only *necessity* and *contingency*. [R] [A]

§ 249

Nature is to be regarded as a *system of stages*, one arising necessarily from the other and being the proximate truth of the stage from which it results: but it is not generated *naturally* out of the other but only in the inner Idea which constitutes the ground of Nature. *Metamorphosis* pertains only to the Notion as such, since only *its* alteration is development. But in Nature, the Notion is partly only something inward, partly existent only as a living individual: *existent* metamorphosis, therefore, is limited to this individual alone.

> *Remark*: It has been an inept conception of ancient and also recent Philosophy of Nature to regard the progression and transition of one natural form and sphere into a higher as an outwardly-actual production which, however, to be made *clearer*, is relegated to the *obscurity* of the past. It is precisely externality which is characteristic of Nature, that is, differences are allowed to fall apart and to appear as indifferent to each other: the dialectical Notion which leads forward the *stages*, is the inner side of them. A thinking consideration must reject such nebulous, at bottom, sensuous ideas, as in particular the so-called *origination*, for example, of plants and animals from water, and then the *origination* of the more highly developed animal organisms from the lower, and so on. [A]

§ 250

The *contradiction* of the Idea, arising from the fact that, as Nature, it is external to itself, is more precisely this: that on the one hand there is the *necessity* of its forms which is generated by the Notion, and their rational determination in the organic totality; while on the other hand, there is their indifferent *contingency* and indeterminable irregularity. In the sphere of Nature contingency and determination from without has its right, and this contingency is at its greatest in the realm of concrete individual forms, which however, as products of Nature, are concrete only in an *immediate* manner. The *immediately* concrete thing is a group of properties, external to one another and more or less indifferently related to each other; and for that very reason, the simple subjectivity which exists for itself is also indifferent and abandons them to contingent and external determination. This is the *impotence* of Nature, that it preserves the determinations of the Notion only *abstractly*, and leaves their detailed specification to external determination.

> *Remark*:   The infinite wealth and variety of forms and, what is most irrational, the contingency which enters into the external arrangement of natural things, have been extolled as the sublime freedom of Nature, even as the divinity *of* Nature, or at least the divinity present *in* it. This confusion of contingency, caprice, and disorder, with freedom and rationality is characteristic of sensuous and unphilosophical thinking. This impotence of Nature sets limits to philosophy and it is quite improper to expect the Notion to comprehend – or as it is said, construe or deduce – these contingent products of Nature. It is even imagined that the more trivial and isolated the object, the easier is the task of deducing it.[6] Undoubtedly, traces of determination by the Notion are to be found even in the most particularized object, although these traces do not exhaust its nature. Traces of this influence of the Notion and of this inner coherence of natural objects will often surprise the investigator, but especially will they seem startling, or rather incredible, to those who are accustomed to see only contingency in natural, as in human, history. One must, however, be careful to avoid taking such trace of the Notion for the total determination of the object, for that is the route to the analogies previously mentioned.
>
> In the impotence of Nature to adhere strictly to the Notion in its realization, lies the difficulty and, in many cases, the impossibility of finding fixed distinctions for classes and orders from an empirical consideration of Nature. Nature everywhere blurs the essential limits of species and genera by intermediate and defective forms, which continually furnish counter examples to every fixed distinction; this even occurs within a specific genus, that of man, for example, where monstrous births, on the one hand, must be considered as belonging to the genus, while on the other hand, they lack certain essential determinations

characteristic of the genus. In order to be able to consider such forms as defective, imperfect and deformed, one must presuppose a fixed, invariable type. This type, however, cannot be furnished by experience, for it is experience which also presents these so-called monstrosities, deformities, intermediate products, etc. The fixed type rather presupposes the self-subsistence and dignity of the determination stemming from the Notion.

§ 251

Nature is, in itself, a living Whole. The movement through its stages is more precisely this: that the Idea *posits* itself as that which it is *in itself*; or what is the same thing, that it returns *into itself* out of its immediacy and externality which is *death*, in order to be, first a *living creature*, but further, to sublate this determinateness also in which it is only Life, and to give itself an existence as Spirit, which is the truth and the final goal of Nature and the genuine actuality of the Idea. [A]

Notes

1 Paragraphs in *The Encyclopaedia Logic* not included in this collection. Material in square brackets in the passages from both the *Philosophy of Nature* and the *Philosophy of Subjective Spirit* has been added by the respective translators and also by me. [S.H.]

2 See, for example, Hegel, *The Encyclopaedia Logic*, pp. 28–9 (§ 6). See above, pp. 135–7. [S.H.]

3 Paragraph in *The Encyclopaedia Logic* not included in this collection. [S.H.]

4 J. W. von Goethe, *Faust*, Part One, Studierzimmer, ll. 1936–41. English version by William Wallace, taken from: G. W. F. Hegel, *Logic. Being Part One of the Encyclopaedia of the Philosophical Sciences (1830)*, translated by W. Wallace, with foreword by J. N. Findlay (Oxford: Clarendon Press, 1975), p. 309. Hegel himself only quotes the last four lines, and puts them in a different order. Wallace's translation is inserted here by Miller. [S.H.]

5 J. W. von Goethe, *Zur Morphologie*, vol. 1, part 3. English version by Wallace, taken from: Hegel, *Logic. Being Part One of the Encyclopaedia of the Philosophical Sciences (1830)*, p. 327. Wallace's translation is inserted here by Miller. [S.H.]

6 It was in this – and other respects too – quite naïve sense that Herr Krug once challenged the Philosophy of Nature to perform the feat of deducing *only* his pen. One could perhaps give him hope that *his* pen would have the glory of being deduced, if ever philosophy should advance so far and have such a clear insight into every great theme in heaven and earth, past and present, that there was nothing more important to comprehend. [Hegel's note.] [See G. W. F. Hegel, 'How the Ordinary Human Understanding Takes Philosophy (as Displayed in the Works of Mr Krug)', in *Between Kant and Hegel: Texts in the Development of German Idealism*, translated and annotated by G. di Giovanni and H. S. Harris (Albany: SUNY Press, 1985), pp. 292–310. S.H.]

19

Philosophy of Nature: Mechanics. Space and Time

(1) Space

§ 254

The first or immediate determination of Nature is *Space*: the abstract *universality of Nature's self-externality*, self-externality's mediationless indifference. It is a wholly ideal *side-by-sideness* [*Nebeneinander*] because it is self-externality; and it is absolutely *continuous*, because this asunderness is still quite *abstract*, and contains no specific difference within itself.

> *Remark*: A number of different theories have been put forward about the nature of space. I will mention only the Kantian definition that space, like time, is a form of *sensuous intuition*. It has also become usual elsewhere to lay down as a principle that space must be regarded only as something subjective in our ideas. Disregarding what belongs in the Kantian conception to subjective idealism and its determinations, there remains the correct definition that space is a mere form, i.e. an *abstraction*, that of immediate *externality*. It is not permissible to speak of *points of space*, as if they constituted the positive element of space, since space, on account of its lack of difference, is only the possibility and not the actual *positedness* of being-outside-of-one-another and of the negative, and is therefore absolutely continuous; the point, the being-for-self, is consequently rather the *negation* of space, a negation which is posited in space. This also settles the question of the infinitude of space (§ 100, Remark).[1] Space is simply pure Quantity, only no longer as a logical determination, but as existing immediately and externally. Nature, consequently, does not begin with the qualitative but with the quantitative, because its determination is not, like Being in Logic, the abstractly First and immediate, but a Being already essentially *mediated* within itself, an external- and other-being.

Addition:　Our procedure consists in first fixing the thought demanded by the necessity of the Notion and then in asking how this thought appears in our ordinary ideas. The further requirement is that in intuition, space shall correspond to the thought of pure self-externality. Even if we were mistaken in this, it would not affect the truth of our thought. In the empirical sciences the reverse method is followed; there the first thing is the empirical intuition of space, and only thereafter do we come to the thought of space. In order to prove that space accords with our thought, we must compare the idea of space with the determination of our notion. The filling of space does not affect space itself; the Heres are side by side and do not interfere with each other. The Here is not yet place, but only the possibility of Place; the Heres are completely the same, and this abstract plurality without real interruption or limit is, precisely, externality. The Heres are also different; but the difference is equally no difference, i.e. it is an abstract difference. Space is therefore punctiformity, but a negative [*nichtig*] punctiformity, and so perfect continuity. To fix a point is to interrupt space: but space is absolutely uninterrupted thereby. The point has meaning only in so far as it is spatial, and so external both to itself and to others; Here contains within itself an Above, Below, Right and Left. Something which was not external in its own self but only to an Other, would be a point; but there is no such point, because no Here is ultimate. However remotely I place a star, I can go beyond it, for the universe is nowhere nailed up with boards. This is the complete externality of space. But the Other of the point is just as much a self-externality as the point is, and therefore the two are undistinguished and unseparated. Beyond its limit, as its *otherness*, space is still in community with itself, and this unity in asunderness is continuity. The unity of these two moments, discreteness and continuity, is the objectively determined Notion of space. This Notion, however, is only the abstraction of space, which is often regarded as absolute space. This is thought to be the truth of space; but relative space is something much higher, for it is the determinate space of some material body. It is rather the truth of abstract space to exist as a material body. [...]

§ 255

Space, as in itself the Notion as such, contains within itself the *differences* of the Notion. (*a*) In the indifference of space, these are immediately the three *dimensions*, which are merely *diverse* and possess no determination whatever. [R]

§ 256

(*β*) The difference of space is, however, essentially a determinate, qualitative difference. As such, it is (*a*), first, the *negation* of space itself, because this is immediate *differenceless* self-externality, the *point*. (*β*) But the negation is the negation *of space*, i.e. it is itself spatial. The point, as essentially this relation, i.e. as sublating itself, is the *line*, the first other-being, i.e. spatial being, of the point. (*γ*) The truth of other-being is, however, negation of the negation. The line consequently passes over into the plane, which, on the one hand, is a determinateness opposed to line and point, and so surface, simply as such, but, on the other hand, is the sublated negation of space. It is thus the restoration of the spatial totality which now contains the negative moment within itself, an *enclosing surface* which separates off a *single* whole space.

> *Remark*:   That the line does not consist of points, nor the plane of lines, follows from their Notion; for the line is rather the point existing *outside* of itself, i.e. *relating* itself to space and sublating itself, and the plane, similarly, is the sublated line existing outside of itself. [. . .] [A]

(2) Time

§ 257

Negativity, as point, relates itself to space, in which it develops its determinations as line and plane; but in the sphere of self-externality, negativity is equally *for itself* and so are its determinations; but, at the same time, these are posited in the sphere of self-externality, and negativity, in so doing, appears as indifferent to the inert side-by-sideness of space. Negativity, thus posited for itself, is Time.

Addition: Space is the immediate existence of Quantity in which everything subsists, even the limit having the form of subsistence; this is the defect of space. Space is this contradiction, to be infected with negation, but in such wise that this negation falls apart into indifferent subsistence. Since space, therefore, is only this inner negation of itself, the self-sublating of its moments is its truth. Now time is precisely the existence of this perpetual self-sublation; in time, therefore, the point has actuality. Difference has stepped out of space; this means that it has ceased to be this indifference, it is for itself in all its unrest, is no longer paralysed. This pure Quantity, as self-existent difference, is what is negative in itself, Time; it is the negation of the negation, the self-relating negation. Negation in space is negation attached to an Other; the negative in space does not therefore yet receive its due. In space the plane is indeed a negation of the negation, but in its truth it is distinct from space. The truth of space is time, and thus space becomes time; the transition to time is not made subjectively by us, but made by space itself. In pictorial thought, space and time are taken to be quite separate: we have space and *also* time; philosophy fights against this 'also'.

§ 258

Time, as the negative unity of self-externality, is similarly an out-and-out abstract, ideal being. It is that being which, inasmuch as it *is*, is *not*, and inasmuch as it is *not*, *is*: it is Becoming directly *intuited*; this means that differences, which admittedly are purely *momentary*, i.e. directly self-sublating, are determined as *external*, i.e. as external to *themselves*.

Remark: Time, like space, is a *pure form* of *sense* or *intuition*, the non-sensuous sensuous; but, as in the case of space, the distinction of object-ivity and a subjective consciousness confronting it, does not apply to time. If these determinations were applied to space and time, the former would then be abstract objectivity, the latter abstract subjectivity. Time is the same principle as the I = I of pure self-consciousness, but this principle, or the simple Notion, still in its uttermost externality and abstraction – as intuited mere *Becoming*, pure being-within-self as sheer coming-out-of-self.

Time is *continuous*, too, like space, for it is the negativity abstractly relating self to self, and in this abstraction there is as yet no real difference.

Everything, it is said, *comes to be* and *passes away* in time. If abstrac-tion is made from *everything*, namely from what fills time, and also from what fills space, then what we have left over is empty time and empty space: in other words, these abstractions of externality are pos-ited and represented as if they were for themselves. But it is not *in* time that everything comes to be and passes away, rather time itself is the *becoming*, this coming-to-be and passing away, the *actually existent ab-straction, Chronos*, from whom everything is born and by whom its offspring is destroyed. The real is certainly distinct from time, but is also essentially identical with it. What is real is limited, and the Other to this negation is *outside* it; therefore the determinateness in it is self-external and is consequently the contradiction of its being; the abstrac-tion of this externality and unrest of its contradiction is time itself. The finite is perishable and *temporal* because, unlike the Notion, it is not in its own self total negativity; true, this negativity is immanent in it as its universal essence, but the finite is not adequate to this essence: it is *one-sided*, and consequently it is related to negativity as to the power that dominates it. The Notion, however, in its freely self-existent iden-tity as I = I, is in and for itself absolute negativity and freedom. Time, therefore, has no power over the Notion, nor is the Notion in time or temporal; on the contrary, *it* is the power over time, which is this negat-ivity only *qua* externality. Only the natural, therefore, is subject to time in so far as it is finite; the True, on the other hand, the Idea, Spirit, is *eternal*. But the notion of eternity must not be grasped negatively as abstraction from time, as existing, as it were, outside of time; nor in a sense which makes eternity come *after* time, for this would turn eternity into futurity, one of the moments of time.

Addition: Time is not, as it were, a receptacle in which everything is placed as in a flowing stream, which sweeps it away and engulfs it. Time is only this abstraction of destruction. It is because things are finite that they are in time; it is not because they are in time that they perish; on the contrary, things themselves are the temporal, and to be so is their objective determination. It is therefore the process of actual things themselves which makes time; and though time is called omnipotent, it is also completely impotent. The Now has a tremendous right; it *is* nothing as the individual Now, for as I pronounce it, this proudly exclusive Now dissolves, flows away and falls into dust. *Duration* is the universal of all these Nows, it is the sublatedness of this process of things which do not endure. And though things endure, time still passes away and does not rest; in this way, time appears to be independent of, and distinct from, things. But if we say that time passes away even though things endure, this merely means that although some things endure, change is nevertheless apparent in others, as for example in the course of the sun; and so, after all, things are in time. A final shallow attempt to attribute rest and duration to things is made by representing change as gradual. If everything stood still, even our imagination, then we should endure, there would be no time. But all finite things are temporal, because sooner or later they are subject to change; their duration is thus only relative.

Absolute timelessness is distinct from duration; the former is eternity, from which natural time is absent. But in its Notion, time itself is eternal; for time as such – not any particular time, nor Now – is its Notion, and this, like every Notion generally, is eternal, and therefore also absolute Presence. Eternity will not come to be, nor was it, but it *is*. The difference therefore between eternity and duration is that the latter is only a relative sublating of time, whereas eternity is infinite, i.e. not relative, duration but duration reflected into self. [...]

§ 259

The dimensions of time, *present, future* and *past,* are the *becoming* of externality as such, and the resolution of it into the differences of being as passing over into nothing, and of nothing as passing over into being. The immediate vanishing of these differences into *singularity* is the present as *Now* which, as singularity, is *exclusive* of the other moments, and at the same time completely *continuous* in them, and is only this vanishing of its being into nothing and of nothing into its being.

> *Remark*: The *finite* present is the *Now* fixed as *being* and distinguished as the concrete unity, and hence as the affirmative, from what is *negative*, from the abstract moments of past and future; but this being is itself only abstract, vanishing into nothing. Furthermore, in Nature where time is a *Now*, being does not reach the *existence* of the difference of these dimensions; they are, of necessity, only in subjective imagination, in *remembrance* and *fear* or *hope*. But the past and future of time as *being* in Nature, are space, for space is negated time; just as sublated space is immediately the point, which developed for itself is time. [...]

Addition: The dimensions of time complete the determinate content of intuition in that they posit for intuition the Notion of time, which is *becoming*, in its totality or reality; this consists in positing each of the abstract moments of the unity which becoming is, as the whole, but under opposite determinations. Each of these two determinations is thus itself a unity of being and nothing; but they are also distinguished. This difference can only be that of coming-to-be and passing away. In the one case, in the Past (in Hades), being is the foundation, the starting-point; the Past has been actual as history of the world, as natural events, but posited under the category of non-being which is added to it. In the other case, the position is reversed; in the Future, non-being is the first determination, while being is later, though of course not in time. The middle term is the indifferent unity of both, so that neither the one nor the other is the determinant. The Present *is*, only because the Past is not; conversely, the being of the Now is determined as not-being, and the non-being of its being is the Future; the Present is this negative unity. The non-being of the being which is replaced by the Now, is the Past; the being of the non-being which is contained in the Present, is the Future. In the positive meaning of time, it can be said that only the Present *is*, that Before and After are not. But the concrete Present is the result of the Past and is pregnant with the Future. The true Present, therefore, is eternity. [. . .]

(3) **Place and Motion**

§ 260

Space is within itself the contradiction of indifferent asunderness and differenceless continuity, the pure negativity of itself, and the *transition, first of all, into time*. Similarly, time is the immediate *collapse* into indifference, into undifferentiated asunderness or *space*, because its opposed moments which are held together in unity, immediately sublate themselves. In this way, the *negative* determination in space, the *exclusive* point, no longer only implicitly [or in itself] conforms to the Notion, but is *posited* and *concrete* within itself, through the total negativity which is time; the point, as thus concrete, is *Place* (§§ 255, 256).

Addition: If we refer back to the exposition of the notion of duration, we see that this immediate unity of space and time is already the ground of their being; for the negative of space is time, and the positive, i.e. the being of the differences of time, is space. But space and time are posited unequally therein, in other words, their unity is manifested only as a movement of transition of the one into the other, so that the beginning and the realization, the result, fall asunder. But it is precisely the result which enunciates their ground and truth. What persists is the equality-with-self into which time has retreated; this is space, for the characteristic of space is to be indifferent existence in general. The point exists here in its truth, namely as a universal, and for this reason it is a whole space as a totality of dimensions. This Here is now equally time, a Present which immediately sublates itself, a Now which has been. The Here is at the same time a Now, for it is the point of duration. This unity of Here and Now is Place.

§ 261

Place, as this *posited* identity of space and time is equally, at first, the posited *contradiction* which space and time are each in themselves. Place is spatial, and therefore indifferent, *singularity*; and it is this only as a *spatial Now*, as time, so that place is immediately indifferent towards itself as *this* place, is external to itself, the negation of itself, and is *another place*. This *vanishing* and *self-regeneration* of space in time and of time in space, a process in which time posits itself spatially as *place*, but in which place, too, as indifferent spatiality, is immediately posited as *temporal*: this is *Motion*. This becoming, however, is itself just as much the collapse within itself of its contradiction, the *immediately identical* and *existent* unity of both, namely, *Matter*. [R]

Addition: One place only points to another place, and so sublates itself and becomes another; but the difference is likewise sublated. Each place, taken by itself, is only *this* place, that is, they are all the same as each other; in other words, Place is simply the universal Here. Something occupies its place, then changes it; another place arises, but, both before and after, something occupies its place and does not leave it. This dialectic which is inherent in Place was enunciated by Zeno when he showed that nothing moves: for motion would be a change of place, but the arrow does not leave its place. This dialectic is precisely the infinite Notion which the Here is; for time is posited in its own self. There are three different places: the present place, the place about to be occupied, and the place which has just been vacated; the vanishing of the dimensions of time is paralysed. But at the same time there is only *one* place, a universal of these places, which remains unchanged through all the changes; it is duration, existing immediately in accordance with its Notion, and as such it is Motion. That Motion is what we have expounded, is self-evident; this Notion of it conforms to our intuition of it. Its essence is to be the immediate unity of Space and Time; it is Time which has a real existence through Space, or Space which is first truly differentiated by Time. Thus we know that Space and Time pertain to Motion; the velocity, the quantum of Motion, is Space in relation to a specific Time elapsed. It is also said that Motion is a relation of Space and Time; but the specific nature of this relation has to be comprehended. It is in Motion that Space and Time first acquire actuality.

Just as Time is the purely formal soul of Nature, and Space, according to Newton, is the sensorium of God, so Motion is the Notion of the veritable soul of the world. We are accustomed to regard it as a predicate or a state; but Motion is, in fact, the Self, the Subject as Subject, the abiding of vanishing. The fact that Motion appears as a predicate is the immediate necessity of its self-extinction. Rectilinear motion is not Motion in and for itself, but Motion in subjection to an Other in which it has become a predicate or a sublated moment. The restoration of the duration of the Point, as opposed to its motion, is the restoration of Place as unmoved. But this restored Place is not immediate Place, but Place which has returned out of alteration, and is the result and ground of Motion. As forming a dimension, i.e. as opposed to the other moments, it is the centre. This return of the line is the circle; it is the Now, Before and After which have closed together in a unity in which these dimensions are indifferent, so that Before is equally After, and vice versa. It is in circular motion that the necessary paralysis of these dimensions is first posited in space. Circular motion is the spatial or subsistent unity of the dimensions of time. The point proceeds towards a place which is its future, and leaves one which is the past; but what it has left behind is at the same time what it has still to reach: it has been already at the place which it is reaching. Its goal is the point which is its past; and this is the truth of time, that the goal is not the future but the past. The motion which relates itself to the centre is itself the *plane*, motion as the synthetic whole in which exist its moments, the extinction of the motion in the centre, the motion itself and its relation to its extinction, namely the radii of the circle. But this plane itself moves and becomes the other of itself, a complete space; or the reversion-into-self, the immobile centre, becomes a universal point in which the whole is peacefully absorbed. In other words, it is motion in its essence, motion which has sublated the distinctions of Now, Before and After, its dimensions or its Notion. In the circle, these are in a unity; the circle is the restored Notion of duration, Motion extinguished within itself. There is posited *Mass*, the persistent, the self-consolidated, which exhibits motion as its possibility.

   Now this is how we conceive the matter: since there is motion, something moves; but this something which persists is matter. Space and Time are filled with Matter. Space does not conform to its Notion; it is therefore the Notion of Space itself which gives itself existence in Matter. Matter has often been made the starting-point, and Space and Time have then been regarded as forms of it. What is right in this standpoint is that Matter is what is real in Space and Time. But these, being abstract, must present themselves here as the First, and then it must appear that Matter is their truth. Just as there is no Motion without Matter, so too, there is no Matter without Motion. Motion is the process, the transition of Time into Space and of Space into Time: Matter, on the other hand, is the relation of Space and Time as a peaceful identity. Matter is the first reality, existent being-for-self; it is not merely the abstract being, but the positive existence of Space, which, however, excludes other spaces. The point *should* also be exclusive: but because it is only an abstract negation, it does not yet exclude. Matter is exclusive relation-to-self, and is thus the first real limit in Space. What is called the filling of Space and Time, the palpable and tangible, what offers resistance and what, in its being-for-other, is also for itself, all this is attained simply in the unity of Space and Time.

§ 262

Through the moment of its negativity, of its abstract *separation into parts*, matter holds itself asunder in opposition to its self-identity; this is the *repulsion* of matter. But since these different parts are one and the same, matter is no less essentially the negative unity of this sundered being-for-self and is therefore continuous; this is its *attraction*. Matter is inseparably both and is the negative unity of these two moments, singularity. But this singularity as still *distinguished* from the *immediate* asunderness of matter and consequently *not yet posited* as *material*, is an *ideal* singularity, a *centre: gravity*.

   Remark: By his attempt at a so-called *construction* of matter in his *Metaphysical Elements of Natural Science*, Kant has, among other things, the merit of having started towards a *notion* of matter, and of having revived with this attempt, the concept of a *philosophy of Nature*. But in so doing he postulated the forces of attraction and repulsion, determinations of the reflective Understanding, as fixed mutual opposites, and whereas he should have made matter result from them he presupposed it as something ready-made, so that what is to be attracted and repelled is already matter. I have demonstrated in detail the confusion which prevails in this Kantian exposition, in my system of Logic [. . .].[2] Besides, only *heavy* matter is that totality and real existence in which attraction and repulsion can occur; it possesses the ideal moments of the Notion, of singularity or subjectivity. For this reason, attraction and repulsion are not to be taken as independent of each other or as forces on their own account; matter results from them only as moments of the Notion; but it is the presupposition of their manifestation.

It is essential to distinguish *gravity* from mere *attraction*. The latter is only the sublating of discreteness and yields only continuity. Gravity, on the other hand, is the reduction of both discrete and continuous particularity to unity as a negative relation to self, to *singularity*, to a *subjectivity* which, however, is still quite abstract. Now in the sphere of the first *immediacy* of Nature, this self-external continuity is still posited as the *existent*; it is first in the sphere of Physics that material reflection-into-self begins.[3] Consequently, *singularity*, although present as a determination of the Idea, is here *outside* the material element. In the first place, therefore, matter itself is essentially *heavy*; this is not an external property, nor can it be separated from matter. Gravity constitutes the substantiality of matter; this itself is the *nisus* [*Streben*], the striving to reach the *centre*; but − and this is the other essential determination of matter − this centre falls *outside it*. It can be said that matter is attracted by the centre, i.e. its existence as a self-external continuum is negated; but if the centre itself is conceived as material, then the attraction is merely reciprocal, is at the same time a being-attracted, so that the centre again exists in distinction from them both. The centre, however, is not to be taken as material; for the characteristic of the material object is, precisely, to posit its centre *outside itself*. It is not the centre, but the striving to reach it, which is immanent in matter. Gravity is, so to speak, the confession of the nullity of the self-externality of matter in its being-for-self, of its lack of self-subsistence, of its contradiction.

It can also be said that gravity is the being-within-self of matter, in this sense, that just because it is not yet in its own self a centre or subjectivity, it is still indeterminate, undeveloped, and undisclosed, the form is not yet material.

Where the centre lies, is determined by the heavy matter of which it is the centre; matter, as mass, is determinate, and so also, therefore, is its *nisus*, which is the positing − and so a determinate positing − of the centre.

Addition: Matter is spatial separation; it offers resistance and in doing so repels itself from itself: this is repulsion, by which matter posits its reality and fills space. But the separated parts which mutually repel each other are only a One, many Ones; each is what the other is. The One repels itself only from itself; this is the sublating of the separation of what is for itself: attraction. These two together, as gravity, constitute the Notion of matter; gravity is the predicate of matter and constitutes the substance of this Subject. The unity of gravity is only an Ought, a longing, the most unhappy *nisus* to which matter is eternally condemned; for this unity does not come to itself or reach itself. If matter attained what it seeks in gravity, it would melt into a single point. The reason why this unity is not realized here, is because repulsion, no less than attraction, is an essential moment of matter. The dull, obscure unity does not become free; but since, all the same, matter has as its specific character the positing of the Many in the One, it is not so foolish as those would-be philosophers who keep the One and the Many apart, and in this respect they are refuted by matter itself. The two unities of attraction and repulsion, although forming the inseparable moments of gravity, do not unite to form a single, ideal unity; this unity first attains its explicit existence in Light, as we shall see later.[4] Matter seeks a place outside the Many; and since there is not yet any difference between the parts which are seeking this place, there is no reason why one should be nearer than another. They are at equal distances on the periphery; the point they seek is the centre, and this extends in every dimension so that the next determination we have is the *sphere*. Although gravity is a mode of the inwardness of matter and not its lifeless externality, nevertheless this inwardness does not yet have its place here; matter is still that which is without inwardness, is the Notion of the Notionless. [. . .]

Notes

1   Paragraph in *The Encyclopaedia Logic* not included in this collection. [S.H.]
2   See Hegel, *Science of Logic*, pp. 178–84 (not included in this collection). [S.H.]
3   This refers not to physics as a natural science, but to a later section of the *Philosophy of Nature* which is not included in this collection. [S.H.]
4   See Hegel, *Philosophy of Nature*, p. 87ff (§ 275ff) (not included in this collection). [S.H.]

20

Philosophy of Nature: Organics. The Animal Organism

§ 350

The organic individuality exists as *subjectivity* in so far as the externality proper to shape is *idealized* into members, and the organism in its process outwards preserves inwardly the unity of the self. This is the *animal* nature which, in the actuality and externality of immediate singularity, is equally, on the other hand, the *inwardly reflected* self of *singularity*, *inwardly* present *subjective* universality.

Addition: In the animal, light has found itself, for the animal arrests its relationship to an other; it is the self which is for the self – the existing unity of distinct moments which are pervaded by it. The goal of the plant's development is to become for-itself, but it does not transcend the stage of two independently existing individuals, viz. the plant itself and the bud, which are not in the form of ideal moments: these two posited in a unity are the animal nature. The animal organism is therefore this duplication of subjectivity, which no longer, as in the plant, exists as duplicated, but only as the unity of this duplication. There thus exists in the animal the veritable subjective unity, a unitary soul [*Seele*], the immanent infinitude of form which is set forth in the externality of the body; and this soul in turn stands in relationship with an inorganic Nature, with an outer world. But the subjectivity of the animal consists in preserving itself in its bodily nature and in its contact with an outer world and, as the universal, remaining at home with itself. The life of the animal as this highest point of Nature is thus the absolute idealism of possessing within itself the determinateness of its bodily nature in a perfectly fluid form – the incorporation of the immediate into the subject and its possession as incorporated.

Here, therefore, heaviness is first truly overcome; the centre has become a filled centre, which has itself for fulcrum and first, as such, is a truly self-subsistent centre. In the solar system we have the sun and other members which have an independent existence, and are related to each other, not according to their physical nature, but only according to the nature of space and time. Now if the animal organism, too, is a sun, then in it the stars are related to each other according to their physical nature, and are taken back into the sun, which holds them within itself in one individuality. The animal is the existent Idea in so far as its members are purely and simply moments of the form, perpetually negating their independence and bringing themselves back into their unity, which is the reality of the Notion and is for the Notion. If a finger is cut off, it is no longer a finger, but a process of chemical decomposition sets in. In the animal, the fully achieved unity is for the implicit unity, and this latter is the soul [*Seele*], the Notion, which is present in the body in so far as this is the process of idealization. The asunderness of spatial exist-ence has no truth for the soul, which is unitary, finer than a point. People have been at pains to find the soul; but this is a contradiction. There are millions of points in which the soul is everywhere present; and yet it is not at any one point, simply because the asunderness of space has no truth for it. This point of subjectivity is to be adhered to, the others are only predicates of life. But this subjectivity is not yet for-itself as pure, universal subjectivity; it is not aware of itself in thought, but only in feeling and intuition. That is to say, it is only reflected into itself in the individual which, reduced to a simple determinateness, is posited as ideal; it is objective to itself only in a specific, particular state and is the negation of any such determin-ateness, but does not transcend it – in the same way that sensual man can indulge every appetite, but not get beyond it in order to grasp himself in thought as universal.

§ 351

The animal has freedom of *self-movement* because its subjectivity is, like light, ideality freed from gravity, a free time which, as removed from real externality, *spontaneously determines its place*. Bound up with this is the animal's possession of a *voice*, for its *subjectivity* as *real* ideality (soul), dominates the abstract ideality of time and space and displays its self-movement as a free vibration *within itself*; it has animal *heat* as a permanent *process of the dissolution* of cohesion and of the enduring self-subsistence of the parts in the permanent preservation of shape: further, [it nourishes itself by] an *interrupted intus-susception* as a self-individualizing relationship to an individual, non-organic nature. But above all, as the individuality which in determinateness is for itself immediately *universal*, simply abiding with itself and preserving itself, it has *feeling* – the *existent* ideality of being determined.

Addition: [. . .] (*a*) The animal as sensuous is heavy, remains tied to the Centre; but the particular place it occupies is not determined by gravity. Gravity is the universal determination of matter, but it also determines the *particular* place; the mechanical relationship of gravity consists precisely in this, that something, in being determined in space, has its determination therein only in something outside it. But the animal, as self-related singularity, does not occupy this particular place as the result of an external determination, because, as a singularity which is turned back into self, it is indifferent to non-organic Nature, and in free movement is merely related to it by space and time generally. The particularization of place lies therefore in the animal's own power, and is not posited by an other; it is the animal itself which gives itself this place. In any other thing, this particularization is fixed, be-cause the thing is not a self which is for itself. True, the animal does not escape from the general determination of being in a particular place; but *this* place is posited by the animal itself. And it is for this very reason that the subjectivity of the animal is not simply distinguished from external Nature, but the animal distinguishes itself from it; and this is an extremely important distinction, this positing of itself as the pure negativity of *this* place, and *this* place, and so on. The whole of Physics is the form which develops in contradistinction to gravity; but in Physics the form does not yet attain to this freedom in face of the torpor [*Dumpfheit*] of gravity, and it is in the subjectivity of the animal that this being-for-self over against gravity is first posited. The physical individuality, too, does not escape from gravity since even its process contains determinations of place and gravity.

(β) Voice is a high privilege of the animal which can appear wonderful; it is the utterance of sensation, of self-feeling. The animal makes manifest that it is inwardly for-itself, and this manifestation is voice. But it is only the sentient creature that can show outwardly that it is sentient. Birds of the air and other creatures emit cries when they feel pain, need, hunger, repletion, pleasure, joyfulness, or are in heat: the horse neighs when it goes to battle; insects hum; cats purr when pleased. But the voice of the bird when it launches forth in song is of a higher kind; and this must be reckoned as a special manifestation in birds over and above that of voice generally in animals. For while fish are dumb in their element of water, birds soar freely in theirs, the air; separated from the objective heaviness of the earth, they fill the air with themselves, and utter their self-feeling in their own particular element. Metals have sound, but this still is not voice; voice is the spiritualized mechanism which thus utters itself. The inorganic does not show its specific quality until it is stimulated from outside, gets struck; but the animal sounds of its own accord. What is subjective announces its psychic nature [*als dies Seelenhafte*] in vibrating inwardly and in merely causing the air to vibrate. This independent subjectivity is, quite abstractly, the pure process of time, which in the concrete body, is self-realizing time, vibration, and sound. Sound belongs to the animal in such a manner that it is the animal's own activity that makes the bodily organism vibrate. But nothing is outwardly altered thereby; there is only movement, and the movement produced is only abstract, pure vibration, and this produces only an alteration of place but an alteration which is equally cancelled again – a negation of specific gravity and cohesion which, however, are equally reinstated. The voice is the closest to Thought; for here pure subjectivity becomes objective, not as a particular actuality, as a state or a sensation, but in the abstract element of space and time.

(γ) With voice there is linked animal heat. The chemical process also yields heat which can rise to the intensity of fire, but it is transitory. The animal, on the other hand, as the lasting process of self-movement, of consuming and producing itself, perpetually negates and reproduces what is material and must therefore perpetually generate heat. [. . .]

§ 352

The animal organism as living universality is the Notion which passes through its three determinations as syllogisms, each of which is *in itself* the same *totality* of the substantial unity, and, at the same time, in keeping with the determination of the form, *transition* into the others, so that the totality as existent *results* from this process. It is only as this self-reproductive being, not as a mere being (*nicht als Seiendes*), that the living creature *is* and *preserves itself*; it only is, in making itself what it is, and is the antecedent End which is itself only result. The organism is therefore, like the plant, to be considered (a) as individual Idea which in its process is only *self*-related, and inwardly coalesces with self – Shape; (b) as Idea which enters into relationship with its other, its non-organic nature, and posits this inwardly as ideal – Assimilation; (c) Idea as entering into relationship with an other which is itself a living individual, so that in the other it is in relationship with itself – the Genus-process.[1] [A]

1. The Process of the Genus

§ 368[2]

Genus and species

The genus, in its implicit universality, *particularizes* itself at first simply into *species*. At the base of the *different forms* and *classes* of animals is the universal *type of the Animal*, determined by the Notion; Nature exhibits this type, partly in the various *stages of its development* from the simplest organization to the most perfect, in which it is the instrument of spirit, and partly in the various *circumstances* and *conditions* of *elemental Nature*. An animal species, developed to the point of singularity, distinguishes itself from others in and through its own self, and through the negation of them is *for itself*. The natural fate of the individuals in this hostile relationship, in which others are reduced to an inorganic nature, is a *violent* death. [R] [A]

2. The Sex-relation

§ 369

This first diremption of the genus into species and the further determination of these to the point of immediate, exclusive being-for-self of *singularity*, is only a negative and hostile attitude towards others. But the genus is also an essentially affirmative relation of the singularity to itself in it; so that while the latter, as an individual, excludes another individual, it continues itself in this *other* and in this *other* feels its own self. This relationship is a *process* which begins with a *need*; for the individual as a *singular* does not accord with the genus immanent in it, and yet at the same time is the identical self-relation of the genus in *one* unity; it thus has the *feeling* of this defect. The genus is therefore present in the individual as a straining against the inadequacy of its single actuality, as the urge to obtain its self-feeling in the other of its genus, to integrate itself through union with it and through this mediation to close the genus with itself and bring it into existence – *copulation*.

Addition: The process of the animal with its non-organic nature has made the ideality of the latter explicit, and the animal has thereby demonstrated in its own self its self-feeling and its objectivity. It is not merely an implicit self-feeling, but a self-feeling which exists and is alive. The division of the sexes is such that the extremes are totalities of self-feeling; the animal's instinct is to produce itself as a self-feeling, as totality. Now in the constructive instinct, the organic became a dead product, freely released, it is true, from the organism, but only a superficial form imposed on an external material, and this did not therefore confront itself as a free, indifferent subject: here, on the contrary, both sides are independent individuals as in the process of assimilation, but with this difference, that they are not related to each other as organic and non-organic beings; on the contrary, both are organisms and belong to the genus, so that they exist only as one species. Their union is the disappearance of the sexes into which the simple genus has developed. The animal has an object with which it feels itself immediately identical; this identity is the moment of the first process (of formation) which is added to the determination of the second (of assimilation). This attitude [*Verhalten*] of an individual to another of its kind is the substantial relation of the genus. The nature of each permeates both; and both exist within the sphere of this universality. The process consists in this, that they become in reality what they are in themselves, namely, one genus, the same subjective vitality. Here, the Idea of Nature is actual in the male and female couple; their identity, and their being-for-self, which up till now were only for us in our reflection, are now, in the infinite reflection into self of the two sexes, felt by themselves. This feeling of universality is the highest to which the animal can attain; but its concrete universality never becomes for it a theoretical object of intuition: else it would be Thought, Consciousness, in which alone the genus attains a free existence. The contradiction is, therefore, that the universality of the genus, the identity of individuals, is distinct from their particular individuality; the individual is only one of two, and does not exist as unity but only as a singular. The activity of the animal is to sublate this difference. The genus, as the foundation, is one extreme of the syllogism, for every process has the form of the syllogism. The genus is the impelling subjectivity into which is placed the vitality which wants to produce itself. The mediation, the middle term of the syllogism, is the tension between this essential nature of the individuals and the incongruity of their single actuality; and it is this which impels them to have their self-feeling only in the other. The genus, in giving itself actuality, which, because it has the form of immediate existence is, of course, only a single actuality, closes itself with the other extreme, that of singularity.

The *formation of the differentiated sexes* must be different, their determinateness against each other must exist as posited by the Notion, because, as differentiated moments [*Differente*], they are an urge [*Trieb*]. But the two sides are not merely, as in the chemical sphere, implicitly neutral; on the contrary, on account of the original identity of formation, the same type underlies both the *male and female genitals*, only that in one or the other, one or the other part predominates: in the female, it is necessarily the passive moment [*das Indifferente*], in the male, the moment of duality [*das Entzweite*], of opposition. This identity is most striking in the lower animals: 'In some grasshoppers (e.g. *Gryllus verruccivorus*) the large testicles, composed of vessels rolled together in bundles, resemble the ovaries which are equally large and composed of bundles of similarly rolled-up oviducts. Also in the male horse-fly, not only does the outline of the testicles present the same shape as the thicker [*gröbere*] larger ovaries, but they, too, consist of almost oval, elliptical, delicate vesicles which, with their base, stand up on the substance of the testicles like ova on an ovary.'[3] The greatest difficulty has been experienced in discovering the female uterus in the male genitals. The scrotum has ineptly been mistaken for it,[4] simply because the testicles present a definite correspondence to the female ovary. But it is rather the prostate in the male which corresponds to the female uterus; in the male, the uterus is reduced to a gland, to an indifferent generality. This has been very well demonstrated by Ackermann in his hermaphrodite,[5] which has a uterus as well as other, male, organs [*Formationen*]; but this uterus not only occupies the place of the prostate, but the ejaculatory ducts also pass through its substance and open into the *crista galli* in the urethra. Also, the female *labia pudendi* are shrunken scrota: consequently, in Ackermann's hermaphrodite, the *labia pudendi* were filled with a kind of testicular secretion. Lastly, the medial line of the scrotum is split in the female and forms the vagina. In this way, a complete understanding is obtained of the conversion of one sex into the other. Just as in the male, the uterus is reduced to a mere gland, so, on the other hand, the male testicle remains enclosed in the ovary in the female, does not emerge into opposition, does not develop on its own account into active brain [*Gehirn*]; and the clitoris is inactive feeling in general. In the male, on the other hand, we have instead active feeling, the swelling heart, the effusion of blood into the *corpora cavernosa* and the meshes of the spongy tissue of the urethra; to this male effusion of blood correspond the female menses. In this way, the reception [*Empfangen*] by the uterus, as a simple retention, is, in the male, split into the productive brain and the external heart. Through this difference, therefore, the male is the active principle, and the female is the receptive, because she remains in her undeveloped unity.

Procreation must not be reduced to the ovary and the male semen, as if the new product were merely a composition of the forms or parts of both sides; the truth is that the female contains the material element, but the male contains the subjectivity. *Conception* is the contraction of the whole individual into the simple, self-surrendering unity, into its representation [*Vorstellung*]; the seed is this simple representation itself – simply a single point, like the name and the entire self. Conception, therefore, is nothing else but this, that the opposite moments, these abstract representations, become one.

§ 370

The *product* is the *negative identity* of the differentiated individuals and is, as *realized* [*gewordene*] *genus*, an asexual life. But on its *natural* side, this product is only *in principle* [*an sich*] this genus, distinct from the individuals whose difference [from one another] has perished in it, and is itself an immediate *singular*, destined to develop into the same natural individuality, into the same difference and perishable existence. This process of propagation spends itself in the spurious infinite progress. The genus preserves itself only through the destruction of the individuals who, in the process of generation, fulfil their destiny and, in so far as they have no higher destiny, in this process meet their death.

Addition: Thus the animal organism has run through its cycle and is now the asexual and fecund universal; it has become the absolute genus which, however, is the death of this individual. The lower animal organisms, e.g. butterflies, die, therefore, immediately after copulation; for they have sublated their singularity in the genus and their singularity is their life. Higher organisms survive the generative act since they possess a higher kind of independence; and their death is the culmination of the process in their structure, which we shall come across later as disease. The genus, which produces itself through negation of its differences, does not, however, exist in and for itself but only in a series of single living beings: and thus the sublation of the contradiction is always the beginning of a fresh one. In the genus-process the separate individual creatures perish; for they are distinct only outside of this unity of the process, which is the true actuality. Love, on the other hand, is the feeling in which the self-seeking of the individual and its separated existence is negated, and the individual form [*Gestalt*] therefore perishes and cannot preserve itself. For only that preserves itself which, as absolute, is self-identical; and that is the universal which is for the universal. But in the animal, the genus does not exist as such but only in principle [*an sich*]; it is only in spirit that it exists in and for itself in its eternity. The transition to the existent genus takes place in principle [*an sich*], in the Idea, in the Notion, that is to say, in the eternal creation; but there the sphere of Nature is closed.

3. The Genus and the Individual

§ 371

a. *The disease of the individual*

In the two preceding relationships, the self-mediation of the genus with itself is the process of its diremption into individuals and the sublation of its difference. But since the genus also (§ 357)[6] assumes the shape of external universality, of an inorganic nature against the individual, it attains to existence in the latter in an abstract, negative manner. In this relationship of an external existence, the individual organism can just as well not conform to its genus as preserve itself in it through its return into self (§ 366).[7] It finds itself in a state of disease when one of its systems or organs, *stimulated* into conflict with the inorganic power [*Potenz*], establishes itself in isolation and persists in its particular activity against the activity of the whole, the fluidity and all-pervading process of which is thus obstructed. [A]

§ 372

The characteristic *manifestation* of disease is, therefore, that the identity of the entire organic process displays itself as the *successive* course of the vital movement through its distinct moments: sensibility, irritability, and reproduction, i.e. as *fever*, which, however, as process of the *totality* in opposition to the *isolated* [*vereinzelte*] activity, is just as much the effort towards, and the beginning of, *cure*. [A]

§ 373

b. Therapy

The medicine provokes the organism to put an end to the *particular* irritation in which the formal activity of the *whole* is fixed and to restore the fluidity of the particular organ or system within the whole. This is brought about by the medicine as an irritant, but one which is difficult to assimilate and overcome, so that the organism is confronted by something alien to it against which it is compelled to exert its strength. In acting against something external to it, the organism breaks out from the limitation with which it had become identified and in which it was entangled and against which it cannot react so long as the limitation is not an object for it. [R] [A]

§ 374

In disease, the animal is entangled with a non-organic power [*Potenz*] and is held fast in one of its particular systems or organs in opposition to the unity of its vitality. Its organism, as a determinate existence, has a certain quantitative strength and is, indeed, capable of overcoming its dividedness; but the organism can just as well succumb to it and find in it the manner of its death. The animal, in overcoming and ridding itself of particular inadequacies, does not put an end to the general inadequacy which is inherent in it, namely, that its Idea is only the *immediate* Idea, that, as animal, it stands *within Nature*, and its subjectivity is only *implicitly* the Notion but is not *for its own self* the Notion. The inner universality therefore remains opposed to the natural singularity of the living being as the *negative* power from which the animal suffers violence and perishes, because natural existence [*Dasein*] as such does not itself contain this universality and is not therefore the reality which corresponds to it. [A]

§ 375

c. The self-induced destruction of the individual

The universality which makes the animal, as a singular, a *finite* existence, reveals itself in it as the abstract power which terminates the internal process active within the animal, a process which is itself abstract (§ 356).[8] The disparity between its finitude and universality is its *original disease* and the inborn *germ of death*, and the removal of this disparity is itself the accomplishment of this destiny. The individual removes this disparity in giving its singularity the form of universality; but in so far as this universality is abstract and immediate, the individual achieves only an *abstract objectivity* in which its activity has become deadened and ossified and the process of life has become the inertia of *habit*; it is in this way that the animal brings about its own destruction.

Addition: [. . .] In Nature [. . .] universality is manifested only negatively, in that subjectivity is sublated in it. The form in which this separation is accomplished is, precisely, the consummation of the singular, which converts itself into the universal but cannot endure this universality. In life, the animal maintains itself, it is true, against its non-organic nature and its genus; but its genus, as the universal, in the end retains the upper hand. The living being, as a singular, dies from the habit of life, in that it lives itself into its body, into its reality. Vitality makes itself, for itself, into the universal, in that the activities become universal; and it is in this universality that the vitality itself dies; for since vitality is a process, opposition is necessary to it, and now the other which it should have had to overcome is for it no longer an other. Just as in the spiritual sphere, old people dwell more and more within themselves and their kind, and their general ideas and conceptions tend to occupy their interest to the exclusion of what is particular, with the result that tension, *interest* *[inter esse]* falls away and they are contented in this processless habit: so, too, it is in the physical sphere. The absence of opposition to which the organism progresses is the repose of the dead; and this repose of death overcomes the inadequacy of disease, this inadequacy being therefore the primary cause of death.

§ 376

But this achieved identity with the universal is the sublation of the *formal* *opposition* between the *immediate* singularity of the individuality and its *universality*; and this is only one side, and that the abstract side, namely, the *death of the natural being*. But in the Idea of life, subjectivity is the Notion, and it is thus *in itself* the absolute *being-within-self* of *actuality* and concrete universality. Through the sublation of the *immediacy* of its reality just demonstrated, subjectivity has coalesced with itself; the last *self-externality* of Nature has been sublated and the Notion, which in Nature is present only *in principle* [*an sich seiende Begriff*], has become *for itself*. With this, Nature has passed over into its truth, into the subjectivity of the Notion whose *objectivity* is itself the sublated immediacy of singularity, is *concrete universality*; so that the Notion is posited as having for its *determinate being* the reality which corresponds to it, namely, the Notion – and this is *spirit* [*Geist*].

Addition: Above this death of Nature, from this dead husk, proceeds a more beautiful Nature, *spirit*. The living being ends with this division and this abstract coalescence within itself. But the one moment contradicts the other: that which has coalesced is for that reason identical – Notion or genus and reality, or subject and object, are no longer divided; and that which has repelled and divided itself is for that very reason not abstractly identical. The truth is their unity as distinct moments; therefore in this coalescence and in this division, what is sublated is only *formal* opposition because of the intrinsic identity of the moments, and similarly, what is negated is only *formal* identity, because of their division. That is to say, in more concrete terms, the Notion of life, the genus, life in its universality, repels from itself its reality which has become a totality within it, but it is in itself identical with this reality, is Idea, is absolutely preserved, is the Divine, the Eternal, and therefore abides in this reality; and what has been sublated is only the form, the inadequacy of natural existence, the still only abstract externality of time and space. The living being is, it is true, the supreme mode of the Notion's existence in Nature; but here, too, the Notion is present only in principle [*an sich*], because the Idea exists in Nature only as a singular. Certainly, in locomotion the animal is completely liberated from gravity, in sensation it feels itself, in voice it hears itself; in the genus-process the genus exists, but still only as a singular. Now since this existence is still inadequate to the universality of the Idea, the Idea must break out of this circle and by shattering this inadequate form make room for itself. Therefore, instead of the third moment in the genus-process sinking back again into singularity, the other side, death, is the sublating of the singular and therewith the emergence of the genus, the procession of spirit; for the negation of natural being, i.e. of immediate singularity, is this, that the universal, the genus, is posited and that, too, in the form of genus. *In the individuality*, this movement of the two sides is the process which sublates itself and whose *result is consciousness*, unity, the unity in and for itself of both, as self, not merely as genus in the inner Notion of the singular. Herewith, the Idea exists *in* the self-subsistent subject, for which, as organ of the Notion, everything is ideal and fluid; that is, the subject *thinks*, makes everything in space and time its own and in this way has universality, i.e. its own self, present within it. Since in this way the universal is now *for* the universal, therefore the Notion is *for itself*; this is first manifested in spirit in which the Notion makes itself objective to itself, but in doing so, the existence of the Notion, as Notion, is *posited*. Thought, as this universal which exists for itself, is *immortal being*; mortal being is that in which the Idea, the universal, exists in an inadequate form.

This is the transition from Nature to spirit; in the living being Nature finds its consummation and has made its peace, in that it is transformed into a higher existence. Spirit has thus proceeded from Nature. The goal of Nature is to destroy itself and to break through its husk of immediate, sensuous existence, to consume itself like the phoenix in order to come forth from this externality rejuvenated as spirit. Nature has become an other to itself in order to recognize itself again as Idea and to reconcile itself with itself. But it is one-sided to regard spirit in this way as having only *become* an actual existence after being merely a potentiality. True, Nature is the immediate – but even so, as the other of spirit, its existence is a relativity: and so, as the negative, its being is only posited, derivative. It is the power of free spirit which sublates this negativity; spirit is no less *before* than *after* Nature, it is not merely the metaphysical Idea of it. Spirit, just because it is the goal of Nature, is *prior* to it, Nature has proceeded from spirit: not empirically, however, but in such a manner that spirit is already from the very first implicitly present in Nature which is spirit's own presupposition. But spirit in its infinite freedom gives Nature a free existence and the Idea is active in Nature as an inner necessity; just as a free man of the world is sure that his action is the world's activity. Spirit, therefore, itself proceeding, *in the first instance*, from the immediate, but *then* abstractly apprehending itself, wills to achieve its own liberation by fashioning Nature out of itself; this action of spirit is philosophy.

With this, we have brought our treatment of Nature to its boundary. Spirit, which has apprehended itself, also wills to know itself in Nature, to make good again the loss of itself. This reconciliation of spirit with Nature and with actuality is alone its genuine liberation, in which it sheds its merely personal habits of thought and ways of looking at things. This liberation from Nature and Nature's necessity is the

Notion of the Philosophy of Nature. The forms which Nature wears are only forms of the Notion, although in the element of externality; it is true that these forms, as grades of Nature, are grounded in the Notion, but even where the Notion gathers itself together in sensation, it is still not yet present to itself as Notion. The difficulty of the Philosophy of Nature lies just in this: first, because the material element is so refractory towards the unity of the Notion, and, secondly, because spirit has to deal with an ever-increasing wealth of detail. None the less, Reason must have confidence in itself, confidence that in Nature the Notion speaks to the Notion and that the veritable form of the Notion which lies concealed beneath Nature's scattered and infinitely many shapes, will reveal itself to Reason.

Let us briefly survey the field we have covered. At first, the Idea was, in gravity, freely disbanded into a body whose members are the free heavenly bodies; then this externality fashioned itself inwardly into properties and qualities which, belonging to an individual unity, had in the chemical process an immanent and physical movement. Finally, in the living being, gravity is disbanded into members in which the subjective unity abides. The aim of these lectures has been to give a picture of Nature in order to subdue this Proteus: to find in this externality only the mirror of ourselves, to see in Nature a free reflex of spirit: to know God, not in the contemplation of him as spirit, but in this his immediate existence.

Notes

1 Hegel's analyses of shape and assimilation have not been included in this collection. [s.h.]

2 In his edition of 1842, Karl Ludwig Michelet renumbered § 368 as § 370, § 369 as § 368, and § 370 as § 369. Miller's translation preserves Michelet's numbering, but I have restored the numbering adopted by Hegel himself in the 1830 edition of the *Encyclopaedia*. [s.h.]

3 G. H. von Schubert, *Ahnungen einer allgemeinen Geschichte des Lebens* (Leipzig, 1806/1821), part 1, p. 185. [Hegel's note.]

4 Schubert, *Ahnungen einer allgemeinen Geschichte des Lebens*, part 1, pp. 205–6. [Hegel's note.]

5 Hegel is referring here to J. F. Ackermann, *Infantis androgyni historia et ichnographia* (Jena, 1805). See G. W. F. Hegel, *Philosophy of Nature*, edited and translated with an introduction and explanatory notes by M. J. Petry, 3 vols. (London: George Allen and Unwin, 1970), 3: 353–4. [s.h.]

6 Paragraph of the *Philosophy of Nature* not included in this collection. [s.h.]

7 Paragraph of the *Philosophy of Nature* not included in this collection. [s.h.]

8 Paragraph of the *Philosophy of Nature* not included in this collection. [s.h.]

21

Philosophy of Spirit: Introduction

§ 377

The knowledge of Mind [*Geist*] is the highest and hardest, just because it is the most 'concrete' of sciences.[1] The significance of that 'absolute' command-ment, *Know thyself* – whether we look at it in itself or under the historical circumstances of its first utterance – is not to promote mere self-knowledge in respect of the *particular* capacities, character, propensities, and foibles of the single self. The knowledge it commands means that of man's genuine reality – of what is essentially and ultimately true and real – of mind as the true and essential being. Equally little is it the purport of mental philo-sophy[2] to teach what is called *knowledge of men* – the knowledge whose aim is to detect the *peculiarities*, passions, and foibles of other men, and lay bare what are called the recesses of the human heart. Information of this kind is, for one thing, meaningless, unless on the assumption that we know the *universal* – man as man, and, that always must be, as mind. And for another, being only engaged with casual, insignificant, and *untrue* aspects of mental life, it fails to reach the underlying essence of them all – the mind itself.

Addition: The difficulty of the philosophical cognition of mind consists in the fact that in this we are no longer dealing with the comparatively abstract, simple logical Idea, but with the most concrete, most developed form achieved by the Idea in its self-actualization. Even finite or subjective mind, not only absolute mind, must be grasped as an actualization of the Idea. The treatment of mind is only truly philo-sophical when it cognizes the Notion of mind in its living development and actual-ization, which simply means, when it comprehends mind as a type of the absolute Idea. But it belongs to the nature of mind to cognize its Notion. Consequently, the summons to the Greeks of the Delphic Apollo, *Know thyself*, does not have the mean-ing of a law externally imposed on the human mind by an alien power; on the contrary, the god who impels to self-knowledge is none other than the absolute law of mind itself. Mind is, therefore, in its every act only apprehending itself, and the aim of all genuine science is just this, that mind shall recognize itself in everything in heaven and on earth. An out-and-out Other simply does not exist for mind. Even the oriental does not wholly lose himself in the object of his worship; but the Greeks were the first to grasp expressly as mind what they opposed to themselves as the Divine, although even they did not attain, either in philosophy or in religion, to a knowledge of the absolute infinitude of mind; therefore with the Greeks the relation of the human mind to the Divine is still not one of absolute freedom. It was Christianity, by its doctrine of the Incarnation and of the presence of the Holy Spirit in the community of believers, that first gave to human consciousness a perfectly free relationship to the infinite and thereby made possible the comprehensive know-ledge of mind in its absolute infinitude.

Henceforth, such a knowledge alone merits the name of a philosophical treat-ment. Self-knowledge in the usual trivial meaning of an inquiry into the foibles and faults of the single self has interest and importance only for the individual, not for philosophy; but even in relation to the individual, the more the focus of interest is shifted from the general intellectual and moral nature of man, and the more the inquiry, disregarding duties and the genuine content of the will, degenerates into a self-complacent absorption of the individual in the idiosyncrasies so dear to him, the less is the value of that self-knowledge. The same is true of the so-called knowledge of *human nature* which likewise is directed to the peculiarities of individual minds. This knowledge is, of course, useful and necessary in the conduct of life, especially in bad political conditions where right and morality have given place to the self-will, whims and caprice of individuals, in the field of intrigues where characters do not rely on the nature of the matter in hand but hold their own by cunningly exploiting the peculiarities of others and seeking by this means to attain their arbitrary ends. For philosophy, however, this knowledge of human nature is devoid of interest in so far as it is incapable of rising above the consideration of contingent particularities to the understanding of the characters of great men, by which alone the true nature of man in its serene purity is brought to view. But this knowledge of human nature can even be harmful for philosophy if, as happens in the so-called pragmatic treatment of history, through failure to appreciate the substantial character of world-historical individuals and to see that great deeds can only be carried out by great characters, the supposedly clever attempt is made to trace back the greatest events in history to the accidental idiosyncrasies of those heroes, to their presumed petty aims, propensit-ies, and passions. In such a procedure history, which is ruled by divine Providence, is reduced to a play of meaningless activity and contingent happenings.

§ 378

Pneumatology, or, as it was also called, Rational Psychology, has been already alluded to in the Introduction to the Logic as an *abstract* and generalizing metaphysic of the subject.[3] *Empirical* (or inductive) psychology, on the other hand, deals with the 'concrete' mind: and, after the revival of the sciences, when observation and experience had been made the distinctive methods for the study of concrete reality, such psychology was worked on the same lines as other sciences. In this way it came about that the metaphysical the-ory was kept outside the inductive science, and so prevented from getting any concrete embodiment or detail: while at the same time the inductive science clung to the conventional commonsense metaphysic, with its analysis into forces, various activities, etc., and rejected any attempt at a 'speculative' treatment.

The books of Aristotle on the Soul,[4] along with his discussions on its special aspects and states, are for this reason still by far the most admirable, perhaps even the sole, work of philosophical value on this topic. The main aim of a philosophy of mind can only be to reintroduce unity of idea and principle into the theory of mind, and so reinterpret the lesson of those Aristotelian books.

Addition: Genuinely speculative philosophy, which excludes the mode of treatment discussed in the previous Paragraph which is directed to the unessential, isolated, empirical phenomena of mind, also excludes the precisely opposite mode of so-called Rational Psychology or Pneumatology, which is concerned only with abstractly universal determinations, with the supposedly unmanifested essence, the 'in-itself' of mind. For speculative philosophy may not take its subject-matter from picture-thinking [*Vorstellung*] as a *datum*, nor may it determine such given material merely by categories of the abstractive intellect [*Verstand*] as the said psychology did when it posed the question whether mind or soul is simple and immaterial, whether it is substance. In these questions mind was treated as a thing; for these categories were regarded, in the general manner of the abstractive intellect, as inert, fixed; as such, they are incapable of expressing the nature of mind. Mind is not an inert being but, on the contrary, absolutely restless being, pure activity, the negating or ideality of every fixed category of the abstractive intellect; not abstractly simple but, in its simplicity, at the same time a distinguishing of itself from itself; not an essence that is already finished and complete before its manifestation, keeping itself aloof behind its host of appearances, but an essence which is truly actual only through the specific forms of its necessary self-manifestation; and it is not, as that psychology supposed, a soul-thing only externally connected with the body, but is inwardly bound to the latter by the unity of the Notion. [. . .]

Notes

1   Wallace translates '*Geist*' as 'mind', but this word can also be translated as 'spirit'. [S.H.]
2   'Philosophie des Geistes'. [S.H.]
3   See Hegel, *The Encyclopaedia Logic*, p. 71 (§ 34). See above, p. 148. [S.H.]
4   See, especially, *The Complete Works of Aristotle*, edited by J. Barnes, 2 vols (Princeton: Princeton University Press, 1984), 1: 641–92 [*On the Soul*]. [S.H.]

22

Philosophy of Subjective Spirit: Anthropology and Phenomenology of Spirit

Anthropology. Sensation [*Empfindung*]

§ 400

Sensibility (feeling) is the form of the dull stirring, the inarticulate breathing, of the spirit through its unconscious and unintelligent individuality, where every definite feature is still 'immediate' – neither specially developed in its content nor set in distinction as objective to subject, but treated as belonging to its most special, its natural peculiarity. The content of sensation is thus limited and transient, belonging as it does to natural, immediate being – to what is therefore qualitative and finite. [R] [A]

§ 401

What the sentient soul finds within it is, on one hand, the naturally immediate, as 'ideally' in it and made its own. On the other hand and conversely, what originally belongs to the central individuality [*Fürsichsein*] (which as further deepened and enlarged is the conscious ego and free mind) gets the features of the natural corporeity, and is so felt. In this way we have two spheres of feeling. One, where what at first is a corporeal affection (e.g. of the eye or of any bodily part whatever) is made feeling (sensation) by being driven inward, memorized in the soul's self-centred part. Another, where affections originating in the mind and belonging to it, are in order to be felt, and to be as if found, invested with corporeity. [. . .] [R]

Addition: The content of sensation either originates in the outer world or belongs to the soul's interior; a sensation is therefore either external or internal. Here we have to consider the latter class of sensations only in so far as they are corporealized; on the side of their inwardness they are proper to the sphere of psychology. The external sensations, on the other hand, are exclusively the subject-matter of Anthropology.

The first thing to be said about the last-named class of sensations is that we receive them through the various senses. The sentient subject is thus determined from outside, that is to say, his corporeity is determined by something external. The various modes of this determining constitute the different external sensations. Each such different mode is a general possibility of being determined, a circle of single sensations. Seeing, for example, contains the indefinite possibility of a multiplicity of visual sensations. The universal nature of the ensouled individual is also displayed in the fact that the individual is not tied to one single thing in the specific modes of sensation but embraces a whole circle of particulars. If, on the contrary, I could see only what was blue, this limitation would be a quality of me. But since, in contrast to natural things, I am the universal that is at home with itself in the determinateness, I can see any colour, or rather the whole range of different colours.

The general modes of sensation are related to the physical and chemical qualities of natural objects, the necessity of which has to be demonstrated in the Philosophy of Nature, and are mediated by the various sense-organs.[1] The fact that in general the sensation of the external world falls asunder into such diverse, mutually indifferent modes of sensation, lies in the nature of its content, since this is sensuous; but the sensuous is synonymous with the self-external in such a manner that even the internal sensations by their mutual externality acquire a sensuous character.

Now why we have just the familiar *five* senses, no more and no less, with their distinctive forms, the rational necessity of this must, in a philosophical treatment, be demonstrated. This is done when we grasp the senses as representations of the Notion's moments. These moments are, as we know, only *three*. But the five senses reduce quite naturally to three groups of senses. The first is formed by the senses of physical *ideality*, the second by those of *real difference*, and the third comprises the sense of *earthly totality*.

As representing the Notion's moments, each of these three groups must form a totality in itself. But now the first group contains the sense of what is abstractly universal, abstractly ideal, and therefore of what is not truly a totality. Here, therefore, the totality cannot exist as a concrete, but only as a sundered totality, as one which is split up into *two abstract* moments. This is why the first group embraces two senses – *sight* and *hearing*. For sight, the ideal element is in the form of a simple self-relation, and for hearing it exists as a product of the negation of the material element. The second group as the group of difference, represents the sphere of *process*, of decomposition and dissolution of concrete corporeity. But from the determination of difference, a doubling of the senses of this group at once follows. The second group contains, therefore, the senses of *smell* and *taste*. The former is the sense of the abstract, the latter the sense of the concrete, process. Lastly the third group embraces only one sense, that of *feeling* or *touch*, because touch is the sense of the *concrete* totality.

Let us now consider more closely the individual senses.

Sight is the sense of that physical ideality which we call light. We can say of light that it is, as it were, physicalized space. For light, like space, is indivisible, a serene ideality, extension absolutely devoid of determination, without any reflection-into-self, and therefore without internality. Light manifests something else and this manifesting constitutes its essential nature; but within itself it is abstract self-identity, the opposite of Nature's asunderness appearing within Nature itself, and therefore immaterial matter. For this reason light does not offer resistance, contains no limitation, expands illimitably in all directions, is absolutely weightless, imponderable. It is only with this ideal element and with its obscuration by the element of darkness, in other words, with colour, that sight has to do. Colour is what is seen, light is the medium of seeing. The really material aspect of corporeity, on the other hand, does not as yet concern us in seeing. Therefore the objects we see can be remote from us. In seeing things we form, as it were, a merely theoretical, not as yet a practical, relationship; for in seeing things we let them continue to exist in peace and relate ourselves only to their ideal side. On account of this independence of sight of corporeity proper, it can be called the noblest sense. On the other hand, sight is a very imperfect sense because by it the object does not present itself to us immediately as a spatial totality, not as *body*, but always only as surface, only according to the two dimensions of width and height, and we only get to see the body in its total shape by looking at it from various points of view and seeing it successively in all its dimensions. The most distant objects originally appear to sight, as we can observe in children, on one and the same surface as those nearest to us, just because sight does not directly see *depth*. Only in noticing that to the depth we have perceived by touch there corresponds something dark, a shadow, do we come to believe that where a shadow becomes visible we see a depth. Connected with this is the fact that we do not directly perceive by sight the measure of the distance of the body but can only infer it from the smaller or greater appearance of objects.

In contrast to sight which is the sense of ideality devoid of any inwardness, hearing is the sense of the pure inwardness of the corporeal. Just as sight is connected with physicalized space, with light, so hearing is connected with physicalized time, with sound. For in sound, corporeity has become posited as time, as the movement, the vibration of the body internally, a trembling, a mechanical shock in which the body, without having to alter its relative position as a whole body, moves only its parts, posits its inner spatiality as temporal, and therefore overcomes its indifferent asunderness, thereby letting its pure inwardness [become] manifest, but immediately restoring itself from the superficial alteration it suffered from the mechanical shock. But the medium through which sound reaches our hearing is not alone the element of air but in still greater measure the concrete corporeity stretching between us and the sonorous object: the earth, for example, for when the ear is held to the ground cannonades can sometimes be heard which could not be heard through the medium of air alone.

The senses of the second group are related to *real* corporeity; but not as yet to real corporeity as a being-for-self and as offering resistance, but only in so far as it is in a state of dissolution, has entered into its *process*. This process is a necessary one. Bodies are, of course, destroyed partly by external, contingent causes; but apart from this contingent destruction bodies perish by their own nature, destroy themselves, but in such a manner that their destruction seems to approach them from outside. This is the action of air which gives rise to the silent, imperceptible process of the spontaneous dissipation of all bodies, the volatilization of all vegetable and animal forms. Now although both smell and taste are connected with spontaneously dissolving corporeity, yet these two senses are distinguished from each other by the fact that smell receives body in the *abstract*, simple, indeterminate process of volatilization or evaporation; taste, on the other hand, is connected with the *real* concrete process of body and with the chemical qualities issuing from that process, namely, sweetness, bitterness, alkalinity, acidity, and saltiness. For taste, a direct contact with the object is indispensable, whereas for smell this is not so. In hearing, such contact is still less necessary and in sight is completely absent.

As already remarked, the third group contains only the one sense of feeling. Since this is located chiefly in the fingers it is also called touch. Touch is the most concrete of all the senses; for its distinctive nature is the connection – not with the abstractly universal or ideal physical element, nor with the self-separating qualities of the corporeal – but with the solid reality of the latter. It is, therefore, really only for touch that there is a self-existent Other, a self-existent individual, over against the sentient subject as another self-existent individual. This is why touch is the sense affected by gravity, that is, by the unity sought by bodies which hold on to their being-for-self and do not enter into the process of dissolution but offer resistance. In general, it is material being-for-self which is for touch. But to the different modes of this being-for-self there belongs not only weight but also the kind of *cohesion* – hardness, softness, rigidity, brittleness, roughness, smoothness. But it is not only perdurable, solid corporeity which is for touch, but also the negativity of this material being-for-self, namely, *heat*. By this, the specific gravity and cohesion of bodies are altered. Hence, this alteration affects what is essential in the nature of body; it can therefore be said that also in being affected by heat, *solid* corporeity is for touch. Lastly, shape with its three dimensions comes within the province of touch; for determinateness in the sphere of mechanics appertains entirely to touch. [. . .]

Phenomenology of Spirit [Mind]. Consciousness

§ 413

Consciousness constitutes the reflected or correlational grade of mind: the grade of mind as *appearance*. Ego [*Ich*] is infinite self-relation of mind, but as subjective or as self-certainty. The immediate identity of the natural soul has been raised to this pure 'ideal' self-identity; and what the former *contained* is for this self-subsistent reflection set forth as an *object*. The pure abstract freedom of mind lets go from it its specific qualities – the soul's natural life – to an equal freedom as an independent *object*. It is of this latter, as external to it, that the *ego* is in the first instance aware (conscious), and as such it is Consciousness. Ego, as this absolute negativity, is implicitly the identity in the otherness: the *ego* is itself that other and stretches over the object (as if that object were implicitly cancelled) – it is one side of the relationship and the whole relationship – the light, which manifests itself and something else too. [A]

(α) *Sensuous consciousness*

§ 418

Consciousness is, first, *immediate* consciousness, and its reference to the object accordingly the simple and underived certainty of it. The object similarly, being immediate, an existent, reflected in itself, is further characterized as immediately singular. This is sense-consciousness.

Remark: Consciousness – as a case of correlation – comprises only the categories belonging to the abstract ego or formal thinking; and these it treats as features of the object (§ 415).[2] Sense-consciousness therefore is aware of the object as an existent, a something, an existing thing, a singular, and so on. It appears as wealthiest in matter, but as poorest in thought. That wealth of matter is made out of sensations: they are the *material* of consciousness (§ 414),[3] the substantial and qualitative, what the soul in its anthropological sphere *is* and finds *in itself*. This material the ego (the reflection of the soul in itself) separates from itself, and puts it first under the category of being. Spatial and temporal Singularness, *here* and *now* (the terms by which in the *Phenomenology of the Mind* [...] I described the object of sense-consciousness)[4] strictly belongs to *intuition*. At present the object is at first to be viewed only in its correlation to *consciousness*, i.e. a something *external* to it, and not yet as external on its own part, or as being beside and out of itself.[5] [A]

§ 419

The *sensible* as something [*Etwas*] becomes an *other*:[6] the reflection in itself of this *something*, the *thing*, has *many* properties; and as a single (thing) [*als Einzelnes*] in its immediacy has several *predicates*. The muchness of the sense-singular thus becomes a breadth – a variety of relations, reflectional attributes, and universalities. These are logical terms introduced by the thinking principle, i.e. in this case by the Ego, to describe the sensible. But the Ego as itself apparent sees in all this characterization a change in the object; and sensuous consciousness, so construing the object, is sense-perception.

Addition: The content of sensuous consciousness is in itself dialectical. It is supposed to be *the* single, isolated individual; but it is just this that makes it not *a* single individual but all individuals, and just by excluding from itself the individual content of another it relates itself to another, proves that it goes out of and beyond itself, that it is dependent on another, is mediated by it and has the other within itself. The proximate truth of what is *immediately* individual is therefore its relatedness to another. The determinations of this relation are those which are called determinations of reflection, and the consciousness which apprehends these determinations is *perception*.

(β) *Sense-perception* [Wahrnehmen]

§ 420

Consciousness, having passed beyond the sensible, wants to take the object in its truth, not as merely immediate, but as mediated, reflected in itself, and universal. Such an object is a combination of sense qualities with attributes of wider range by which thought defines concrete relations and connections.

Hence the identity of consciousness with the object passes from the abstract identity of 'I am sure' to the definite identity of 'I know, and am aware'.[7]

> *Remark*: The particular grade of consciousness on which Kantism conceives the mind is perception: which is also the general point of view taken by ordinary consciousness, and more or less by the sciences. The sensuous certitudes of single apperceptions or observations form the starting-point: these are supposed to be elevated to truth, by being regarded in their bearings, reflected upon, and on the lines of definite categories turned at the same time into something necessary and universal, viz. *experiences*.

Addition: Although perception starts from observation of sensuous materials it does not stop short at these, does not confine itself simply to smelling, tasting, seeing, hearing and feeling [touching], but necessarily goes on to relate the sensuous to a universal which is not observable in an immediate manner, to cognize each individual thing as an internally coherent whole: in force, for example, to comprehend all its manifestations; and to seek out the connections and mediations that exist between separate individual things. While therefore the merely sensuous consciousness merely *shows* things, that is to say, exhibits them in their immediacy, perception, on the other hand, apprehends the connectedness of things, demonstrates that when such and such circumstances are present such and such a thing follows, and thus begins to demonstrate the truth of things. This demonstration is, however, still defective, not final. For that by which something is hereby supposed to be demonstrated is itself *presupposed*, and consequently in need of demonstration; with the result that in this field one goes from one presupposition to another and lapses into the progress to infinity. This is the standpoint occupied by empiricism. Everything must be experienced. But if it is philosophy we are supposed to be discussing, then we must rise above this empirical demonstration which remains tied to presuppositions, to a proof of the absolute necessity of things. [. . .]

Notes

1 See Hegel, *Philosophy of Nature*, Physics, pp. 85–272 (§§ 272–336) (not included in this collection). [S.H.]
2 Paragraph of the *Philosophy of Subjective Spirit* not included in this collection. [S.H.]
3 Paragraph of the *Philosophy of Subjective Spirit* not included in this collection. [S.H.]
4 See Hegel, *Phenomenology of Spirit*, pp. 58–66. See above, pp. 79–86. [S.H.]
5 'noch nicht als an ihm selbst Äußerliches oder als Außersichsein'. [S.H.]
6 On the dialectic of something and other, see Hegel, *Science of Logic*, pp. 116–20. See above, pp. 198–201. Wallace's translation has 'somewhat', instead of 'something'. [S.H.]
7 'Damit ist die Identität des Bewußtseins mit dem Gegenstand nicht mehr die abstrakte der *Gewißheit*, sondern die *bestimmte*, ein *Wissen*'. [S.H.]

23

Philosophy of Subjective
Spirit: Psychology

(α) Intuition [*Anschauung*]

§ 446

The mind which as soul is naturally determined – which as consciousness
relates to this determinacy as to an outward object[1] – but which as intelligence *finds itself* so characterized – is (1) an inarticulate embryonic life, in
which it is to itself as it were palpable and has the whole *material* of its
knowledge. In consequence of the immediacy in which it is thus originally,
it is in this stage only as an individual and possesses a vulgar subjectivity. It
thus appears as mind in the guise of *feeling*. [R]

Addition: We have already had on two occasions to speak of *feeling*, but on each
occasion in a different connection. First, we had to consider it in connection with
soul, and more precisely at the point where soul, awaking from its self-confined
natural life, finds within itself the determinations of the content of its sleeping
nature: it is just this that makes it a feeling soul. But by overcoming the restrictedness
of sensation it attains to the feeling of its Self, of its totality, and lastly, apprehending
itself as 'I', awakes to consciousness.[2] At the stage of consciousness, we again spoke
of feeling. But there, the determinations of feeling were the manifested material of
consciousness separated from soul in the shape of an independent object.[3] Now,
thirdly and lastly, feeling signifies the form which mind as such, which is the unity
and truth of soul and consciousness, gives itself in the first instance. In this form
of mind, the content of feeling is liberated from the double one-sidedness which
attached to it, on the one hand, at the stage of soul, and, on the other hand, at the
stage of consciousness. For that content is now characterized as being in itself both
objective and subjective; and mind's activity is now directed only towards making
itself *explicitly* the unity of subjectivity and objectivity.

§ 447

The characteristic form of feeling is that though it is a mode of some
'affection', this mode is simple. Hence feeling, even should its import be

most sterling and true, has the form of casual particularity – not to mention that its import may also be the most scanty and most untrue. [R] [A]

§ 448

(2) As this immediate finding is broken up into elements, we have the one factor in *Attention* – the abstract *identical* direction of mind (in feeling, as also in all other more advanced developments of it) – an active self-collection – the factor of fixing it as our own, but with an as yet only formal autonomy of intelligence.[4] Apart from such attention there is nothing for the mind. The other factor is to invest the special quality of feeling, as contrasted with this inwardness of mind, with the character of something existent, but as a *negative* or as the abstract otherness of itself. Intelligence thus defines the content of sensation as something that is out of itself, projects it into time and space, which are the forms in which it is intuitive. To the view of consciousness the material is only an object of consciousness, a relative other: from mind it receives the rational characteristic of being *the other of itself* (§§ 247, 254).[5]

Addition: [. . .] Accordingly, the activity of intuition produces to begin with simply a shifting of sensation away from us, a transformation of what is sensed into an object existing outside of us. The content of sensation is not altered by this attention; on the contrary, it is here still one and the same thing in mind and in the external object, so that mind here has not as yet a content peculiar to itself which it could compare with the content of intuition. Consequently, what intuition brings about is merely the transformation of the form of internality into that of externality. This forms the first manner, one which is still formal, in which intelligence becomes a determining activity. About the significance of this externality two remarks must be made: first, that the sensed object in becoming external to the inwardness of mind, receives the form of self-externality, since the mental or the rational constitutes the object's own nature. Secondly, we must remark that since this transformation of the sensed object originates in mind as such, the former thereby acquires a *mental* [*geistig*], i.e. an *abstract* externality and by this acquires that universality which can *immediately* belong to an external thing, namely, a universality that is still quite formal, without content. But the form of the Notion itself falls apart in this abstract externality. Accordingly, the latter has the dual form of space and of time (cf. §§ 254–9).[6] Sensations are therefore made spatial and temporal by intuition. The spatial aspect presents itself as the form of indifferent juxtaposition [*Nebeneinandersein*] and quiescent subsistence; the temporal aspect, on the other hand, presents itself as the form of unrest, of the immanently negative, of successiveness, of arising and vanishing, so that the temporal *is*, in that it *is not*, and *is not*, in that it *is*. But both forms of abstract externality are identical with one another in the sense that each is in its own self utterly discrete and at the same time utterly continuous. Their continuity, which includes within itself absolute discreteness, consists precisely in the abstract *universality* of the externality, a universality which derives from mind and has not yet developed any *actual* separation into parts.

But when we said that what is sensed receives from the intuiting mind the form of the spatial and temporal, this statement must not be understood to mean that space and time are only subjective forms. This is what Kant wanted to make them. But things are in truth themselves spatial and temporal; this double form of asunderness is not one-sidedly given to them by our intuition, but has been originally imparted to them by the implicit, infinite spirit, by the creative eternal Idea.[7] Since, therefore, our intuitive mind honours the determinations of sensation by giving them the abstract form of space and time, thereby making them into real objects as well as assimilating them to itself, the supposition of subjective idealism that we receive only the *subjective* results of our determining activity and not the object's own determinations is completely refuted. However, the answer to those who stupidly attach quite extraordinary importance to the question as to the *reality* of space and time, is that space and time are extremely meagre and superficial determinations, consequently, that things obtain very little from these forms and the loss of them, were this in some way possible, would therefore amount to very little. Cognitive thinking does not halt at these forms; it apprehends things in their Notion in which space and time are contained as ideal moments. Just as in external Nature space and time, by the dialectic of the Notion immanent in them, raise themselves into matter (§ 261)[8] as their truth, so free intelligence is the self-existent dialectic of these forms of immediate asunderness.

§ 449

(3) When intelligence reaches a concrete unity of the two factors, that is to say, when it is at once self-collected in this externally existing material, and yet in this self-collectedness [*Erinnerung in-sich*] sunk in the out-of-selfness, it is *Intuition*.[9]

Addition: [. . .] First of all, as regards the relation of intuition to representation [*Vorstellung*], the former has only this in common with the latter, that in both forms of mind the object is separate from me and at the same time also my own. But the object's character of being mine is only implicitly present in intuition and first becomes explicit in representation. In intuition, the objectivity of the content predominates. Not until I reflect that it is I who have the intuition, not until then do I occupy the standpoint of representation.

But with reference to the relation of intuition to consciousness, the following remark must be made. In the broadest sense of the word, one could of course give the name of intuition to the immediate or sensuous consciousness considered in § 418.[10] But if this name is to be taken in its proper significance, as rationally it must, then between that consciousness and intuition the essential distinction must be made that the former, in the *unmediated*, quite abstract certainty of itself, relates itself to the *immediate* individuality of the object, an individuality sundered into a multiplicity of aspects; whereas intuition is consciousness *filled* with the certainty of Reason, whose object is *rationally* determined and consequently not an individual torn asunder into its various aspects but a totality, a unified fullness of determinations. [. . .]

But the necessity for going beyond mere intuition, lies in the fact that intelligence, according to its Notion, is *cognition*, whereas intuition is not as yet a *cognitive* awareness of the subject-matter since as such it does not attain to the *immanent development* of the substance of the subject-matter but confines itself rather to seizing the *unexplicated* substance still wrapped up in the inessentials of the external and contingent. Intuition is, therefore, only the *beginning* of cognition and it is to this its status that Aristotle's saying refers, that all knowledge starts from wonder.[11] For since subjective Reason, as intuition, has the certainty, though only the indeterminate certainty, of finding itself again in the object, which to begin with is burdened with an irrational form, the object inspires it with wonder and awe. But philosophical thinking must rise above the standpoint of wonder. It is quite erroneous to imagine that one truly knows the object when one has an immediate intuition of it. Perfect cognition belongs only to the pure thinking of Reason which comprehends its object, and only he who has risen to this thinking possesses a perfectly determinate, true intuition. With him intuition forms only the substantial form into which his completely developed cognition concentrates itself again. In immediate intuition, it is true that I have the entire object before me; but not until my cognition of the object developed in all its aspects has returned into the form of simple intuition does it confront my intelligence as an articulated, systematic totality. In general, it is the educated man who has an intuition free from a mass of contingent detail and equipped with a wealth of rational insights. An intelligent, educated man, even though he does not philosophize, can grasp the essentials, the core, of the subject-matter in its simple qualitative nature. Reflection is, however, always necessary to achieve this. People often imagine that the poet, like the artist in general, must go to work purely intuitively. This is absolutely not the case. On the contrary, a genuine poet, before and during the execution of his work, must meditate and reflect; only in this way can he hope to bring out the heart, or the soul, of the subject-matter, freeing it from all the externalities in which it is shrouded and by so doing, *organically* develop his intuition.

§ 450

At and towards this its own out-of-selfness [*Außersichsein*], intelligence no less essentially directs its attention. In this its immediacy it is an awaking to itself, a recollection of itself. Thus intuition becomes a concretion of the material with the intelligence, which makes it its own, so that it no longer needs this immediacy, no longer needs to find the content.

Addition: At the standpoint of mere intuition we are outside of ourselves, in the elements of space and time, these two forms of asunderness. Here intelligence is immersed in the external material, is one with it, and has no other content than that of the intuited object. Therefore, in intuition we can become unfree in the highest degree. But, as we already remarked in the Addition to § 448, intelligence is the *self-existent dialectic* of this immediate asunderness.[12] Accordingly, mind posits intuition as its own, pervades it, makes it into something inward, recollects (inwardizes) itself in it, becomes present to itself in it, and hence free. By this withdrawal into itself, intelligence raises itself to the stage of mental representation. In representation, mind *has* intuition; the latter is *ideally present* in mind, it has not *vanished* or merely *passed away*. Therefore, when speaking of an intuition that has been raised to a representation, language is quite correct in saying: I *have* seen this. By this is expressed no mere past, but also in fact *presence*; here the past is purely *relative* and exists only in the *comparison* of *immediate* intuition with what we now have in representation. But the word 'have', employed in the perfect tense, has quite peculiarly the meaning of presence; what I have seen is something not merely that I *had*, but still *have*, something, therefore, that is present in me. In this use of the word 'have' can be seen a general sign of the inwardness of the modern mind, which makes the reflection, not merely that the past in its immediacy has passed away, but also that in mind the past is still preserved.

(β) Representation (or Mental Idea) [*Vorstellung*]

§ 451

Representation is this recollected or inwardized intuition, and as such is the middle between that stage of intelligence where it finds itself immediately subject to modification and that where intelligence is in its freedom, or, as thought. The representation is the property of intelligence; with a preponderating subjectivity, however, as its right of property is still conditioned by immediacy,[13] and the representation cannot as it stands be said to *be*. The path of intelligence in representations is to render the immediacy inward, to invest itself with intuitive action in itself, and at the same time to get rid of the subjectivity of the inwardness, and inwardly divest itself of it; so as to be in itself in an *externality* of its own. But as representation begins from intuition and the ready-found material of intuition, the intuitional contrast still continues to affect its activity, and makes its concrete products still 'syntheses', which do not grow to the concrete immanence of the notion till they reach the stage of thought. [A]

(αα) Recollection [*Erinnerung*]

§ 452

Intelligence, as it at first recollects the intuition, places the content of feeling in its own inwardness – in a space and a time of its own. In this way that content is (1) an *image* or picture, liberated from its original immediacy and abstract singleness amongst other things, and received into the universality of the ego. The image loses the full complement of features proper to intuition, and is arbitrary or contingent, isolated, we may say, from the external place, time and immediate context in which the intuition stood. [A]

§ 453

(2) The image is of itself transient, and intelligence itself is as attention its time and also its place, its when and where. But intelligence is not only

consciousness and actual existence, but *qua* intelligence is the subject and
the potentiality of its own specializations. The image when thus kept in
mind is no longer existent, but stored up out of consciousness.[14]

> *Remark*:   To grasp intelligence as this night-like mine or pit [*Schacht*] in
> which is stored a world of infinitely many images and representations,
> yet without being in consciousness, is from the one point of view the
> universal postulate which bids us treat the notion as concrete, in the
> way we treat, for example, the germ as affirmatively containing, in
> virtual possibility, all the qualities that come into existence in the sub-
> sequent development of the tree. Inability to grasp a universal like this,
> which, though intrinsically concrete, still continues *simple*, is what has
> led people to talk about special fibres and areas as receptacles of par-
> ticular ideas. It was felt that what was diverse should in the nature of
> things have a local habitation peculiar to itself. But whereas the reversion
> of the germ from its existing specializations to its simplicity in a purely
> potential existence takes place only in another germ – the germ of the
> fruit; intelligence *qua* intelligence shows the potential coming to free
> existence in its development, and yet at the same time collecting itself
> in its inwardness. Hence from the other point of view intelligence is to
> be conceived as this subconscious mine, i.e. as the *existent* universal in
> which the different has not yet been realized in its separations. And it is
> indeed this potentiality which is the first form of universality offered in
> mental representation. [A]

§ 454

(3) An image thus abstractly treasured up needs, if it is to exist, an actual
intuition: and what is strictly called Remembrance [*Erinnerung*] is the reference of the image to an intuition – and that as a subsumption of the
immediate single intuition (impression) under what is in point of form
universal, under the representation (idea) with the same content.[15] Thus
intelligence recognizes the specific sensation and the intuition of it as what
is already its own – in them it is still within itself: at the same time it is
aware that what is only its (primarily) internal image is also an immediate
object of intuition, by which it is authenticated. The image, which in the
mine of intelligence was only its *property*, now that it has been endued with
externality, comes actually into its *possession*. And so the image is at once
rendered distinguishable from the intuition and separable from the blank
night in which it was originally submerged. Intelligence is thus the force
which can give forth its property, and dispense with external intuition for its
existence in it. This 'synthesis' of the internal image with the recollected
[*erinnerten*] existence is *representation* proper: by this synthesis the internal
now has the qualification of being able to be presented before intelligence
and to have its existence in it.

Addition: The manner in which the images of the past lying hidden in the dark depths of our inner being become our actual possession, is that they present themselves to our intelligence in the luminous, plastic shape of an *existent* intuition of *similar* content, and that with the help of this *present* intuition we recognize them as intuitions we have already had. Thus it happens, for example, that we recognize out of hundreds of thousands a man whose image was already quite dim in our mind, as soon as we catch sight of him again. If, therefore, I am to *retain* something in my memory, I must have repeated intuitions of it. At first, the image will, of course, be recalled not so much by myself as by the corresponding immediate intuition; but the image, by being frequently recalled in this way, acquires such intense vividness and is so present to me that I no longer need the external intuition to remind me of it. It is in this way that children pass from intuition to recollection. The more educated a man is, the less he lives in immediate intuition, but, in all his intuitions, at the same time lives in recollections; so that for him there is little that is altogether new but, on the contrary, the substantial import of most new things is something already familiar to him. Similarly, an educated man contents himself for the most part with his images and seldom feels the need of immediate intuition. The curious multitude, on the other hand, are always hurrying to where there is something to gape at.

(ββ) Imagination [*Einbildungskraft*]

§ 455

(1) The intelligence which is active in this possession is the *reproductive imagination*, where the images issue from the inward world belonging to the ego, which is now the power over them. The images are in the first instance referred to this external, immediate time and space which is treasured up along with them. But it is solely in the conscious subject, where it is treasured up, that the image has the individuality in which the features composing it are conjoined: whereas their original concretion, i.e. at first only in space and time, as a *unit* of intuition, has been broken up. The content reproduced, belonging as it does to the self-identical unity of intelligence, and an out-put from its universal mine, has a general idea (representation) to supply the link of association for the images which according to circumstances are more abstract or more concrete ideas.

> *Remark*: The so-called *laws of the association of ideas* were objects of great interest, especially during that outburst of empirical psychology which was contemporaneous with the decline of philosophy. In the first place, it is not *Ideas [Ideen]* (properly so called) which are associated. Secondly, these modes of relation are not *laws*, just for the reason that there are so many laws about the same thing, as to suggest a caprice and a contingency opposed to the very nature of law. It is a matter of chance whether the link of association is something pictorial, or an intellectual category, such as likeness and contrast, reason and consequence.

The train of images and representations suggested by association is the sport of vacant-minded ideation, where, though intelligence shows itself by a certain formal universality, the matter is entirely pictorial. – Image and Representation,[16] if we leave out of account the more precise definition of those forms given above, present also a distinction in content. The former is the more sensuously concrete idea, whereas the idea (representation), whatever be its content (from image, notion, or idea [*Idee*]), has always the peculiarity, though belonging to intelligence, of being in respect of its content given and immediate. It is still true of this idea or representation, as of all intelligence, that it finds its material, as a matter of fact, to *be* so and so; and the universality which the aforesaid material receives by ideation is still abstract. Mental representation is the mean in the syllogism of the elevation of intelligence, the link between the two significations of self-relatedness – viz. *being* and *universality*, which in consciousness receive the title of object and subject. Intelligence complements what is merely found by the attribution of universality, and the internal and its own by the attribution of being, but a being of its own institution. (On the distinction of representations and thoughts, see Introduction to the Logic, § 20 note.)[17]

Abstraction, which occurs in the ideational activity by which general ideas are produced (and ideas *qua* ideas virtually have the form of generality), is frequently explained as the incidence of many similar images one upon another and is supposed to be thus made intelligible. If this superimposing is not to be mere accident and without principle, a force of attraction in like images must be assumed, or something of the sort, which at the same time would have the negative power of rubbing off the dissimilar elements against each other. This force is really intelligence itself – the self-identical ego which by its internalizing recollection gives the images *ipso facto* generality, and subsumes the single intuition under the already internalized image (§ 453).[18]

Addition: The second stage of development of representation is, as we have already indicated in the Addition to § 451, imagination.[19] The manner in which the first form of mental representation, recollection, has raised itself to this stage is that intelligence, emerging from its abstract inward being into determinateness, disperses the night-like darkness enveloping the wealth of its images and banishes it by the luminous clarity of a present image.

But imagination, in its turn, contains three forms into which it unfolds itself. It is, in general, the determinant of the images.

At first, however, it does no more than determine the images as entering into existence. As such, it is merely reproductive imagination. This has the character of a merely formal activity.

But, secondly, imagination not merely recalls the images existent in it but connects them with one another and in this way raises them to *general* ideas or representations. Accordingly, at this stage, imagination appears as the activity of *associating* images.

The third stage in this sphere is that in which intelligence posits its *general* ideas or representations as identical with the *particular* aspect of the image and so gives the former a pictorial existence. This sensuous existence has the double form of symbol and sign, so that this third stage comprises creative imagination [*Phantasie*], which produces symbols and signs, the latter forming the transition to memory.

Reproductive Imagination

The first activity is the formal one of reproducing images. It is true that pure thoughts can also be reproduced, but imagination has to do not with them but only with images. But the production of images by imagination occurs *voluntarily* and without the help of an immediate intuition. It is this that distinguishes this form of ideating intelligence from mere recollection, which does not operate spontaneously but requires a present intuition and *involuntarily* causes the images to appear.

Associative Imagination

A higher activity than the simple reproduction of images is the connecting of them with one another. The content of the images has, on account of its immediacy or sensuousness, the form of finitude, of relation to an Other. Now since here it is I in general who determine or posit, I, too, posit this connection. By this, intelligence gives the images a subjective bond in place of their objective one. But the former still has in part the shape of externality relatively to what is thereby connected. I have, for example, the image of an object before me; to this image is linked quite externally the image of persons with whom I have talked about this object, or who own it, etc. Often the images are linked together only by space and time. Ordinary social conversation mostly rambles on from one idea to another in a very external and contingent manner. It is only when the conversation has a definite aim that it acquires a firmer coherence. The various moods of feeling impart a characteristic touch to every representation – a gay mood, a touch of gaiety, a sad mood, a touch of sadness. Even more is this true of the passions. The degree of intelligence also produces a difference in the way images are connected; clever, witty persons are therefore distinguished from ordinary folk in this respect, too; a clever person seeks out images that contain something substantial and profound. Wittiness connects ideas which, although remote from one another, none the less have in fact an inner connection. Punning, too, must be included in this sphere; the deepest passion can give itself up to this pastime; for a great mind, even in the most unfortunate circumstances, knows how to bring everything it encounters into relation with its passion.

§ 456

Thus even the association of ideas is to be treated as a subsumption of the individual under the universal, which forms their connecting link. But here intelligence is more than merely a general form: its inwardness is an internally definite, concrete subjectivity with a substance and value of its own, derived from some interest, some latent concept or Ideal principle [*Idee*], so far as we may by anticipation speak of such. Intelligence is the power which wields the stores of images and ideas belonging to it, and which thus (2) freely combines and subsumes these stores in obedience to its peculiar tenor. Such is creative imagination [*Phantasie*] – symbolic, allegoric, or poetical imagination – where the intelligence gets a definite embodiment in this store of ideas and informs them with its general tone. These more or less concrete, individualized creations are still 'syntheses': for the material, in which the subjective principles and ideas get a mentally pictorial existence, is derived from the data of intuition.

Addition: Images are already more universal than intuitions; they still have, however, a sensuously concrete content whose connection with another such content is myself. Now it is in turning my attention to this connection that I arrive at *general* ideas, or to ideas (representations) in the strict sense of this word. For that which connects the single images to one another consists precisely in what is common to them. This common element is either any one *particular* side of the object raised to the form of *universality*, such as, for example, in the rose, the red colour; or the *concrete universal*, the genus, for example, in the rose, the plant; but in each case it is an idea (representation) which comes into being through the dissolution by intelligence of the empirical connection of the manifold determinations of the object. In generating general ideas, intelligence is spontaneously active; it is, therefore, a stupid mistake to assume that general ideas arise, without any help from the mind, by a number of similar images coming into contact with one another, that, for example, the red colour of the rose seeks the red of other images in my head, and thus conveys to me, a mere spectator, the general idea of red. Of course, the *particular* element belonging to the image is something given; but the analysis of the concrete individuality of the image and the resultant form of universality come, as remarked, from myself. [. . .]

In the subjective sphere where we now find ourselves, the *general* idea is the inward side; the image, on the other hand, is the external side. These two mutually opposed determinations, to begin with, still fall apart, but in their dividedness are one-sided. The former lacks externality, figuration, and the latter, elevation to the expression of a determinate universal. The truth of these two sides is, therefore, their unity. More exactly, this unity, the imaging of the universal and the generalization of the image, comes about not by the general idea uniting with the image to form a *neutral*, so to speak, *chemical* product, but by the idea actively proving itself to be the *substantial* power over the image, subjugating it as an *accident*, making itself into the image's soul, and becoming in the image *for itself*, inwardizing itself, manifesting its own self. Intelligence, having brought about this unity of the universal and the particular, of the inward and the outward, of idea (representation) and intuition, and in this way restoring the totality present in intuition as now authenticated, the ideating activity is completed within itself in so far as it is productive imagination. This forms the formal aspect of art; for art represents the true universal, or the Idea [*Idee*] in the form of sensuous existence, of the image.

§ 457

In creative imagination intelligence has been so far perfected as to need no aids for intuition. Its self-sprung ideas have pictorial existence. This pictorial creation of its intuitive spontaneity is subjective – still lacks the side of existence. But as the creation unites the internal idea with the vehicle of materialization, intelligence has therein *implicitly* returned both to identical self-relation and to immediacy. As reason, its first start was to appropriate the immediate datum in itself (§§ 445, 455 Remark), i.e. to universalize it; and now its action as reason (§ 438) is from the present point directed towards giving the character of an existent to what in it has been perfected to concrete auto-intuition.[20] In other words, it aims at making itself *be* and be a fact. Acting on this view, it is self-uttering, intuition-producing: the imagination which creates signs.

> *Remark*: Productive imagination [*Phantasie*] is the centre in which the universal and being, one's own and what is picked up, internal and external, are completely welded into one. The preceding 'syntheses' of intuition, recollection, etc., are unifications of the same factors, but they are 'syntheses'; it is not till creative imagination that intelligence ceases to be the vague mine and the universal, and becomes an individuality, a concrete subjectivity, in which the self-reference is defined both to being and to universality. The creations of imagination are on all hands recognized as such combinations of the mind's own and inward with the matter of intuition; what further and more definite aspects they have is a matter for other departments. For the present this internal studio of intelligence is only to be looked at in these abstract aspects. – Imagination, when regarded as the agency of this unification, is reason, but only a formal reason,[21] because the matter or theme it embodies is to imagination *qua* imagination a matter of indifference; while reason *qua* reason also insists upon the *truth* of its content.
>
> Another point calling for special notice is that, when imagination elevates the internal meaning to an image and intuition, and this is expressed by saying that it gives the former the character of an *existent*, the phrase must not seem surprising that intelligence makes itself *be* as a *thing*; for its ideal import is itself, and so is the aspect which it imposes upon it. The image produced by imagination of an object is a bare mental or subjective intuition: in the sign or symbol it adds intuitability proper; and in mechanical memory it completes, so far as it is concerned, this form of *being*.

Addition: As we have seen in the Addition to the previous Paragraph, in creative imagination the general idea or representation constitutes the subjective element which gives itself objectivity in the image and thereby authenticates itself. This authentication is, however, itself immediately still a subjective one, since intelligence in the first instance still has regard to the given content of the images, is guided by it in symbolizing its general ideas. This conditioned, only relatively free, activity of intelligence we call *symbolic* imagination. This selects for the expression of its general ideas only that sensuous material whose independent signification corresponds to the specific content of the universal to be symbolized. Thus, for example, the strength of Jupiter is represented by the eagle because this is looked upon as strong. *Allegory* expresses the subjective element more by an *ensemble* of separate details. Lastly, *poetic* imagination, though it is freer than the plastic arts in its use of materials, may only select such sensuous material as is adequate to the content of the idea to be represented.

But intelligence necessarily progresses from subjective authentication of the general idea mediated by the image, to its objective, absolute authentication. For since the content of the general idea to be authenticated unites only with itself in the content of the image serving as symbol, this mediated form of the authentication, of this unity of subjectivity and objectivity, straightway changes into the form of immediacy. By this dialectical movement, the general idea reaches the point where it no longer needs the image's content for its authentication, but is authenticated in and for itself alone, is, therefore, immediately valid. Now the general idea, liberated from the image's content, in making its freely selected external material into something that can be intuitively perceived, produces what has to be called a sign – in specific distinction from symbol. The sign must be regarded as a great advance on the symbol. Intelligence, in indicating something by a sign, has finished with the content of intuition, and the sensuous material receives for its soul a signification foreign to it. Thus, for example, a cockade, or a flag, or a tomb-stone, signifies something totally different from what it immediately indicates. The arbitrary nature of the connection between the sensuous material and a general idea occurring here, has the necessary consequence that the significance of the sign must first be learned. This is especially true of language signs.

§ 458

In this unity (initiated by intelligence) of an independent representation with an intuition, the matter of the latter is, in the first instance, something accepted, something immediate or given (for example, the colour of the cockade, etc.). But in the fusion of the two elements, the intuition does not count positively or as representing itself, but as representative of something else. It is an image, which has received as its soul and meaning an independent mental representation. This intuition is the *Sign*.

> *Remark*: The sign is some immediate intuition, representing a totally different import from what naturally belongs to it; it is the pyramid into which a foreign soul has been conveyed, and where it is conserved. The *sign* is different from the *symbol*: for in the symbol the original characters (in essence and conception) of the visible object are more or less identical with the import which it bears as symbol; whereas in the sign, strictly so-called, the natural attributes of the intuition, and the connotation of which it is a sign, have nothing to do with each other. Intelligence therefore gives proof of wider choice and ampler authority in the use of intuitions when it treats them as designatory (significative) rather than as symbolical.

In logic and psychology, signs and language are usually foisted in somewhere as an appendix, without any trouble being taken to display their necessity and systematic place in the economy of intelligence.[22] The right place for the sign is that just given: where intelligence – which as intuiting generates the form of time and space, but appears as recipient of sensible matter, out of which it forms ideas – now gives its own original ideas a definite existence from itself, treating the intuition (or time and space as filled full) as its own property, deleting the connotation which properly and naturally belongs to it, and conferring on it an other connotation as its soul and import. This sign-creating activity may be distinctively named 'productive' Memory (the primarily abstract 'Mnemosyne'); since memory [*Gedächtnis*], which in ordinary life is often used as interchangeable and synonymous with remembrance (recollection), and even with conception and imagination, has always to do with signs only.

§ 459

The intuition – in its natural phase a something given and given in space – acquires, when employed as a sign, the peculiar characteristic of existing only as superseded and sublimated [*aufgehoben*]. Such is the negativity of intelligence; and thus the truer phase of the intuition used as a sign is existence in *time* (but its existence vanishes in the moment of being), and if we consider the rest of its external psychical quality, its *institution* by intelligence, but an institution growing out of its (anthropological) own naturalness. This institution of the natural is the vocal note, where the inward idea manifests itself in adequate utterance. The vocal note [*Ton*] which receives further articulation to express specific ideas – speech and, its system, language – gives to sensations, intuitions, conceptions, a second and higher existence than they naturally possess – invests them with the right of existence in the ideational realm.

Remark: Language here comes under discussion only in the special aspect of a product of intelligence for manifesting its ideas in an external medium. If language had to be treated in its concrete nature, it would be necessary for its vocabulary or material part to recall the anthropological or psychophysiological point of view (§ 401),[23] and for the grammar or formal portion to anticipate the standpoint of analytic understanding. With regard to the elementary *material* of language, while on one hand the theory of mere accident has disappeared, on the other the principle of imitation has been restricted to the slight range it actually covers – that of vocal objects. Yet one may still hear the German language praised for its wealth – that wealth consisting in its special expression for special sounds – *Rauschen, Sausen, Knarren*, etc.; – there have been collected more than a hundred such words, perhaps: the humour of the moment creates fresh ones when it pleases. Such superabundance in the realm of sense and of triviality contributes nothing to form the real wealth of a cultivated language. The strictly raw material of language itself depends more upon an inward symbolism than a symbolism referring to external objects; it depends, i.e. on anthropological articulation, as it were the posture in the corporeal act of oral utterance. For each vowel and consonant accordingly, as well as for their more abstract elements (the posture of lips, palate, tongue in each) and for their combinations, people have tried to find the appropriate signification. But these dull subconscious beginnings are deprived of their original importance and prominence by new influences, it may be by external agencies or by the needs of civilization. Having been originally sensuous intuitions, they are reduced to signs, and thus have only traces left of their original meaning, if it be not altogether extinguished. As to the *formal* element, again, it is the work of analytic intellect [*Verstand*] which informs language with its categories: it is this logical instinct which gives rise to grammar. The study of languages still in their original state, which we have first really begun to make acquaintance with in modern times, has shown on this point that they contain a very elaborate grammar and express distinctions which are lost or have been largely obliterated in the languages of more civilized nations. It seems as if the language of the most civilized nations has the most imperfect grammar, and that the same language has a more perfect grammar when the nation is in a more uncivilized state than when it reaches a higher civilization. (Cf. W. von Humboldt's *Essay on the Dual*.)

In speaking of vocal (which is the original) language, we may touch, only in passing, upon written language – a further development in the particular sphere of language which borrows the help of an externally practical activity. It is from the province of immediate spatial intuition to which written language proceeds that it takes and produces the signs (§ 454).[24] In particular, hieroglyphics uses spatial figures to designate *ideas*; alphabetical writing, on the other hand, uses them to designate vocal notes which are already signs. Alphabetical writing thus consists of signs of signs – the words or concrete signs of vocal language being analysed into their simple elements, which severally receive designation. – Leibniz's practical mind misled him to exaggerate the advantages which a complete written language, formed on the hieroglyphic method (and hieroglyphics are used even where there is alphabetic writing, as in our signs for the numbers, the planets, the chemical elements, etc.), would have as a universal language for the intercourse of nations and especially of scholars. But we may be sure that it was rather the intercourse of nations (as was probably the case in Phoenicia, and still takes place in Canton – see *Macartney's Travels* by Staunton) which occasioned the need of alphabetical writing and led to its formation. At any rate a comprehensive hieroglyphic language for ever completed is impracticable. Sensible objects no doubt admit of permanent signs; but, as regards signs for mental objects, the progress of thought and the continual development of logic lead to changes in the views of their internal relations and thus also of their nature; and this would involve the rise of a new hieroglyphical denotation. Even in the case of sense-objects it happens that their names, i.e. their signs in vocal language, are frequently changed, as, for example, in chemistry and mineralogy. Now that it has been forgotten what names properly are, viz. externalities which of themselves have no sense, and only get signification as signs, and now that, instead of names proper, people ask for terms expressing a sort of definition, which is frequently changed capriciously and fortuitously, the denomination, i.e. the composite name formed of signs of their generic characters or other supposed characteristic properties, is altered in accordance with the differences of view with regard to the genus or other supposed specific property. It is only a stationary civilization, like the Chinese, which admits of the hieroglyphic language of that nation; and its method of writing moreover can only be the lot of that small part of a nation which is in exclusive possession of mental culture. – The progress of the vocal language depends most closely on the habit of alphabetical writing; by means of which only does vocal language acquire the precision and purity of its articulation. The imperfection of the Chinese vocal language is notorious: numbers of its words possess several utterly different meanings, as many as ten and twenty, so that, in speaking, the distinction is made perceptible merely by accent and intensity, by speaking low and soft or crying out. The European, learning to speak Chinese, falls into the most ridiculous blunders before he has mastered these absurd refinements of accentuation. Perfection here consists in the opposite of that *parler sans accent* which in Europe is justly required of an educated speaker. The hieroglyphic mode of writing keeps the Chinese vocal language from reaching that objective precision which is gained in articulation by alphabetic writing.

Alphabetic writing is on all accounts the more intelligent: in it the *word* – the mode, peculiar to the intellect, of uttering its ideas most worthily – is brought to consciousness and made an object of reflection. Engaging the attention of intelligence, as it does, it is analysed; the work of sign-making is reduced to its few simple elements (the primary postures of articulation) in which the sensuous factor [*das Sinnliche*] in speech is brought to the form of universality, at the same time that in this elementary phase it acquires complete precision and purity. Thus alphabetic writing retains at the same time the advantage of vocal language, that the ideas have names strictly so called: the name is the simple sign for the exact idea, i.e. the simple plain idea, not decomposed into its features and compounded out of them. Hieroglyphics, instead of springing from the direct analysis of sensible signs, like alphabetic writing, arise from an antecedent analysis of ideas. Thus a theory readily arises that all ideas may be reduced to their elements, or simple logical terms, so that from the elementary signs chosen to express these (as, in the case of the Chinese *Koua*, the simple straight stroke, and the stroke broken into two parts) a hieroglyphic system would be generated by their composition. This feature of hieroglyphic – the analytical designations of ideas – which misled Leibniz to regard it as preferable to alphabetic writing is rather in antagonism with the fundamental desideratum of language – the name. To want a name means that for the immediate idea (which, however ample a connotation it may include, is still for the mind simple in the name), we require a simple immediate sign which for its own sake does not suggest anything, and has for its sole function to signify and represent sensibly the simple idea as such. It is not merely the image-loving and image-limited intelligence that lingers over the simplicity of ideas and reintegrates them from the more abstract factors into which they have been analysed: thought too reduces to the form of a simple thought the concrete connotation which it 'resumes' and reunites from the mere aggregate of attributes to which analysis has reduced it. Both alike require such signs, simple in respect of their meaning: signs, which though consisting of several letters or syllables and even decomposed into such, yet do not exhibit a combination of several ideas. – What has been stated is the principle for settling the value of these written languages. It also follows that in hieroglyphics the relations of concrete mental ideas to one another must necessarily be tangled and perplexed, and that the analysis of these (and the proximate results of such analysis must again be analysed) appears to be possible in the most various and divergent ways. Every divergence in analysis would give rise to another formation of the written name; just as in modern times (as already noted, even in the region of sense) muriatic acid has undergone several changes of name. A hieroglyphic written language would require a philosophy as stationary as is the civilization of the Chinese.

What has been said shows the inestimable and not sufficiently appreciated educational value of learning to read and write an alphabetic character. It leads the mind from the sensibly concrete image to attend to the more formal structure of the vocal word and its abstract elements, and contributes much to give stability and independence to the inward realm of mental life. Acquired habit subsequently effaces the peculiarity by which alphabetic writing appears, in the interest of vision, as a roundabout way to ideas by means of audibility; it makes them a sort of hieroglyphic to us, so that in using them we need not consciously realize them by means of tones, whereas people unpractised in reading utter aloud what they read in order to catch its meaning in the sound. Thus, while (with the faculty which transformed alphabetic writing

into hieroglyphics) the capacity of abstraction gained by the first practice remains, hieroglyphic reading is of itself a deaf reading and a dumb
writing. It is true that the audible (which is in time) and the visible
(which is in space), each have their own basis, one no less authoritative
than the other. But in the case of alphabetic writing there is only a
single basis: the two aspects occupy their rightful relation to each other:
the visible language is related to the vocal only as a sign, and intelligence expresses itself immediately and unconditionally by speaking. –
The instrumental function of the comparatively non-sensuous element
of tone for all ideational work shows itself further as peculiarly important in memory which forms the passage from representation to thought.

§ 460

The name, combining the intuition (an intellectual production) with its
signification [*Bedeutung*], is primarily a single transient product; and conjunction of the idea (which is inward) with the intuition (which is outward)
is itself outward. The reduction of this outwardness to inwardness is (verbal)
Memory.

(γγ) Memory [*Gedächtnis*]

§ 461

Under the shape of memory the course of intelligence passes through the
same inwardizing (recollecting) functions, as regards the intuition of the
word, as representation in general does in dealing with the first immediate
intuition (§ 451).[25] (1) Making its own the synthesis achieved in the sign,
intelligence, by this inwardizing (memorizing) elevates the *single* synthesis to
a universal, i.e. permanent, synthesis, in which name and meaning are for it
objectively united, and renders the intuition (which the name originally is) a
representation. Thus the import (connotation) and sign, being identified,
form one representation: the representation in its inwardness is rendered
concrete and gets existence for its import: all this being the work of memory
which retains names (retentive Memory).

Addition: We shall consider memory under the three forms of:

1   the memory which retains names (retentive memory);
2   reproductive memory;
3   mechanical memory.

   Of primary importance here, therefore, is the retention of the meaning of names,
of our ability to remember the ideas objectively linked to language-signs. Thus when
we hear or see a word from a foreign language, its meaning becomes present to our

mind; but it does not follow that the converse is true, that we can produce for our ideas the corresponding word-signs in that language. We learn to speak and write a language later than we understand it.

§ 462

The name is thus the thing [*Sache*] so far as it exists and counts in the ideational realm. (2) In the name, *Reproductive* memory has and recognizes the thing, and with the thing it has the name, apart from intuition and image. The name, as giving an *existence* to the content in intelligence, is the externality of intelligence to itself; and the inwardizing or recollection of the name, i.e. of an intuition of intellectual origin, is at the same time a self-externalization to which intelligence reduces itself on its own ground. The association of the particular names lies in the meaning of the features sensitive, representative, or cogitant – series of which the intelligence traverses as it feels, represents, or thinks.

> *Remark*: Given the name lion, we need neither the actual vision of the animal, nor its image even: the name alone, if we *understand* it, is the unimaged simple representation. We *think* in names.
>
> The recent attempts – already, as they deserved, forgotten – to rehabilitate the Mnemonic of the ancients, consist in transforming names into images, and thus again deposing memory to the level of imagination. The place of the power of memory is taken by a permanent tableau of a series of images, fixed in the imagination, to which is then attached the series of ideas forming the composition to be learned by rote. Considering the heterogeneity between the import of these ideas and those permanent images, and the speed with which the attachment has to be made, the attachment cannot be made otherwise than by shallow, silly, and utterly accidental links. Not merely is the mind put to the torture of being worried by idiotic stuff, but what is thus learnt by rote is just as quickly forgotten, seeing that the same tableau is used for getting by rote every other series of ideas, and so those previously attached to it are effaced. What is mnemonically impressed is not like what is retained in memory really got by heart, i.e. strictly produced from within outwards, from the deep pit of the ego, and thus recited, but is, so to speak, read off the tableau of fancy. – Mnemonic is connected with the common prepossession about memory, in comparison with fancy and imagination; as if the latter were a higher and more intellectual activity than memory. On the contrary, memory has ceased to deal with an image derived from intuition – the immediate and incomplete mode of intelligence; it has rather to do with an object which is the product of intelligence itself – such a *without-book* as remains locked up in the *within-book* of intelligence,[26] and is, within intelligence, only its outward and existing side.

Addition: The word as *sounded* vanishes in *time*; the latter thus demonstrates itself in the former to be an *abstract*, that is to say, merely *destructive*, negativity. The true, concrete negativity of the language-sign is *intelligence*, since by this the sign is changed from something outward to something inward and as thus transformed is preserved. Words thus attain an existence animated by thought. This existence is absolutely necessary to our thoughts. We only know our thoughts, only have definite, actual thoughts, when we give them the form of objectivity, of a being distinct from our inwardness, and therefore the shape of externality, and of an externality, too, that at the same time bears the stamp of the highest inwardness. The articulated sound, the *word*, is alone such an inward externality. To want to think without words as Mesmer once attempted is, therefore, a manifestly irrational procedure which, as Mesmer himself admitted, almost drove him insane. But it is also ridiculous to regard as a defect of thought and a misfortune, the fact that it is tied to a word; for although the common opinion is that it is just the *ineffable* that is the most excellent, yet this opinion, cherished by conceit, is unfounded, since what is ineffable is, in truth, only something obscure, fermenting, something which gains clarity only when it is able to put itself into words. Accordingly, the word gives to thoughts their highest and truest existence. Of course, one can also indulge in a mass of verbiage, yet fail to grasp the matter in hand. But then what is at fault is not the word, but a defective, vague, superficial thinking. Just as the true *thought* is the very thing itself, so too is the *word* when it is employed by genuine thinking. Intelligence, therefore, in filling itself with the word, receives into itself the nature of the thing. But this reception has, at the same time, the meaning that intelligence thereby takes on the nature of a *thing* and to such a degree that subjectivity, in its distinction from the thing, becomes quite empty, a mindless container of words, that is, a mechanical memory. In this way the profusion of remembered words can, so to speak, switch round to become the extreme alienation of intelligence. The more familiar I become with the meaning of the word, the more, therefore, that this becomes united with my inwardness, the more can the objectivity, and hence the definiteness, of meaning, vanish and consequently the more can memory itself, and with it also the words, become something bereft of mind.

§ 463

(3) As the interconnection of the names lies in the meaning, the conjunction of their meaning with the reality as names is still an (external) synthesis; and intelligence in this its externality has not made a complete and simple return into self. But intelligence is the universal – the single plain truth of its particular self-divestments [*Entäußerungen*]; and its consummated appropriation of them abolishes that distinction between meaning and name. This supreme inwardizing of representation is the supreme self-divestment of intelligence, in which it renders itself the mere *being*, the universal space of names as such, i.e. of meaningless words. The ego, which is this abstract being, is, because subjectivity, at the same time the power over the different names – the link which, having nothing in itself, fixes in itself series of them and keeps them in stable order. So far as they merely *are*, and intelligence is here itself this *being* of theirs, its power is a merely abstract subjectivity – memory;

which, on account of the complete externality in which the members of such series stand to one another, and because it is itself this externality (subjective though that be), is called mechanical (§ 195).[27]

> *Remark*:   A composition is, as we know, not thoroughly conned by rote, until one attaches no meaning to the words. The recitation of what has been thus got by heart is therefore of course accentless. The correct accent, if it is introduced, suggests the meaning: but this introduction of the signification of an idea disturbs the mechanical nexus and therefore easily throws out the reciter. The faculty of conning by rote series of words, with no principle governing their succession, or which are separately meaningless, for example, a series of proper names, is so supremely marvellous, because it is the very essence of mind to be at home with itself [*bei sich selbst zu sein*];[28] whereas in this case the mind is estranged in itself, and its action is like machinery. But it is only as uniting subjectivity with objectivity that the mind is at home with itself;[29] and in the case before us – after it has in intuition been at first so external as to pick up its facts ready made, and in representation inwardizes or recollects this datum and makes it its own – it proceeds as memory to make itself external in itself, so that what is its own assumes the guise of something found. Thus one of the two dynamic factors of thought, viz. objectivity, is here put in intelligence itself as a quality of it. – It is only a step further to treat memory as mechanical – the act implying no intelligence – and as thereby only justified by its uses, its indispensability perhaps for other purposes and functions of mind. But by so doing we overlook the proper signification it has in the mind.[30]

§ 464

If it is to be the fact [*Sache*] and true objectivity, the mere name as an existent requires something else – to be interpreted by the representing intellect. Now in the shape of mechanical memory, intelligence is at once that external objectivity and the meaning. In this way intelligence is explicitly made an *existence* of this identity, i.e. it is explicitly active as such an identity which as reason it is implicitly. Memory is in this manner the passage into the function of *thought*, which no longer has a *meaning*, i.e. its objectivity is no longer severed from the subjective, and its inwardness does not need to go outside for its existence.

> *Remark*:   The German language has etymologically assigned memory [*Gedächtnis*], of which it has become a foregone conclusion to speak contemptuously, the high position of direct kindred with thought [*Gedanke*]. – It is not matter of chance that the young have a better memory than the old, nor is their memory solely exercised for the sake of utility. The young have a good memory because they have not yet reached the

stage of reflection; their memory is exercised with or without design so as to level the ground of their inner life to pure being or to pure space in which the fact, the implicit content, may reign and unfold itself with no antithesis to a subjective inwardness. Genuine ability is in youth generally combined with a good memory. But empirical statements of this sort help little towards a knowledge of what memory intrinsically is. To comprehend the position and meaning of memory and to understand its organic interconnection with thought is one of the hardest points, and hitherto one quite unregarded in the theory of mind. Memory *qua* memory is itself the merely *external* mode, or merely *existential* aspect of thought, and thus needs a complementary element. The passage from it to thought is to our view or implicitly the identity of reason with this existential mode: an identity from which it follows that reason only exists in a subject, and as the function of that subject. Thus active reason is *Thinking*.

(γ) Thinking [*Denken*]

§ 465

Intelligence is recognitive: it cognizes an intuition, but only because that intuition is already its own (§ 454); and in the name it rediscovers the fact [*Sache*] (§ 462):[31] but now it finds *its* universal in the double signification of the universal as such, and of the universal as immediate or as being – finds that is the genuine universal which is its own unity overlapping and including its other, viz. being. Thus intelligence is explicitly, and on its own part cognitive: *virtually* it is the universal – its product (the thought) is the thing: it is a plain identity of subjective and objective. It knows that what is *thought, is*, and that what *is*, only *is* in so far as it is a thought (§§ 5, 21);[32] the thinking of intelligence is to *have thoughts*: these are as its content and object.

Addition: Thinking is the third and last main stage in the development of intelligence; for in it the *immediate, implicit* unity of subjectivity and objectivity present in intuition is restored out of the opposition of these two sides in representation as a unity enriched by this opposition, hence as a unity both in essence and in actuality. The end is accordingly bent back into the beginning. Whereas, then, at the stage of representation the unity of subjectivity and objectivity effected partly by imagination and partly by mechanical memory – though in the latter I do violence to my subjectivity – still retains a subjective character, in thinking, on the other hand, this unity receives the form of a unity that is both subjective and objective, since it knows itself to be the *nature of the thing*. Those who have no comprehension of philosophy become speechless, it is true, when they hear the proposition that *Thought* is *Being*. None the less, underlying all our actions is the presupposition of the unity of Thought and Being. It is as rational, thinking beings that we make this presupposition. But it is well to distinguish between only *being* thinkers, and *knowing* ourselves as thinkers. The former we always are in all circumstances; but the latter, on the contrary, is perfectly true only when we have risen to *pure* thinking. Pure thinking knows that it alone, and not feeling or representation, is capable of grasping the truth of things, and that the assertion of Epicurus that the true is what is sensed, must be pronounced a complete perversion of the nature of mind. Of course, thinking must not stop at abstract, formal thinking, for this breaks up the content of truth, but must always develop into concrete thinking, to a cognition that *comprehends* its object.

§ 466

But cognition by thought is still in the first instance formal: the universality and its being is the plain subjectivity of intelligence. The thoughts therefore are not yet fully and freely determinate, and the representations which have been inwardized to thoughts are so far still the given content. [A]

§ 467

As dealing with this given content, thought is (α) *understanding* [*Verstand*] with its formal identity, working up the representations, that have been memorized, into species, genera, laws, forces, etc., in short into categories – thus indicating that the raw material does not get the truth of its being save in these thought-forms. As intrinsically infinite negativity, thought is (β) essentially an act of partition – *judgement*, which, however, does not break up the concept again into the old antithesis of universality and being, but distinguishes on the lines supplied by the interconnections peculiar to the concept. Thirdly (γ), thought supersedes the formal distinction and institutes at the same time an identity of the differences – thus being formal *reason*[33] or inferential understanding. Intelligence, as the act of thought, cognizes. And (α) understanding out of its generalities (the categories) *explains* the individual, and is then said to comprehend or understand itself: (β) in the judgement it explains the individual to be a universal (species, genus). In these forms the *content* appears as given: (γ) but in inference (syllogism) it characterizes a content from itself, by superseding that form-difference. With the perception of the necessity, the last immediacy still attaching to formal thought has vanished. [R]

Addition: Prior to Kant, no distinction had been made between Understanding and Reason. But unless one wants to sink to the level of the vulgar consciousness which crudely obliterates the distinct forms of pure thought, the following distinction must be firmly established between Understanding and Reason: that for the latter, the object is determined in and for itself, is the identity of content and form, of universal and particular, whereas for the former it falls apart into form and content, into universal and particular, and into an empty 'in-itself' to which the determinateness is added from outside; that, therefore, in the thinking of the Understanding, the content is indifferent to its form, while in the comprehensive thinking of Reason the content produces its form from itself.

But though Understanding has this inherent defect just indicated, it is none the less a necessary moment of rational thinking. Its activity consists, in general, in making abstraction. When it separates the contingent from the essential it is quite in its right and appears as what in truth it ought to be. Therefore, one who pursues a substantial aim is called a man of understanding. Without Understanding, no firm character is possible, for this requires a man to hold firmly to his individual, essential nature. But also, conversely, Understanding can give to a one-sided determination the form of universality and thereby become the opposite of sound common sense, which is endowed with a sense for what is essential.

The second moment of pure thinking is judging. Intelligence which, as Understanding, forcibly separates from one another and from the object the various *abstract determinations* immediately united in the concrete individuality of the object, necessarily proceeds, in the first place, to *connect* the object with these *general determinations* of thought, hence to consider the object as *relation*, as an objective togetherness, as a totality. This activity of intelligence is often, but incorrectly, called comprehension; for from this standpoint the object is still grasped as something given, as dependent on something else by which it is conditioned. The circumstances which condition an object still have the value here of self-subsistent existences. Hence the identity of the interrelated phenomena is still only internal, and just for that reason merely external. Here, therefore, the Notion does not as yet reveal itself in its own shape, but in the form of an irrational necessity.

Only on the third stage of pure thinking is the Notion as such known. Therefore, this stage represents comprehension in the strict sense of the word. Here the universal is known as self-particularizing, and from the particularization gathering itself together into individuality; or, what is the same thing, the particular loses its self-subsistence to become a moment of the Notion. Accordingly, the universal is here no longer a form external to the content, but the true form which produces the content from itself, the self-developing Notion of the thing. Consequently, on this stage, thinking has no other content than itself, than its own determinations which constitute the immanent content of the form; in the object, it seeks and finds only itself. Here, therefore, the object is distinguished from thought only by having the form of being, or subsisting on its own account. Thus thinking stands here in a completely free relation to the object.

In this thinking, which is identical with its object, intelligence reaches its consummation, its goal; for now it is *in fact* that which in its immediacy it was only *supposed* to be, self-knowing truth, self-cognizing Reason. *Knowing* now constitutes the *subjectivity* of Reason, and *objective* Reason is posited as a *Knowing*. This reciprocal interpenetration of thinking subjectivity and objective Reason is the final result of the development of theoretical mind through the stages, antecedent to pure thinking, of intuition and mental representation.

§ 468

Intelligence which, as theoretical, appropriates an immediate mode of being, is, now that it has completed *taking possession,* in its own *property*: the last negation of immediacy has implicitly required that the intelligence shall itself determine its content. Thus thought, as free notion, is now also free in point of *content*. But when intelligence is aware that it is determinative of the content, which is *its* mode no less than it is a mode of being, it is Will.

Addition: Pure thinking is, to begin with, a disinterested [*unbefangenes*] activity in which it is absorbed in the object. But this action necessarily also becomes *objective to itself*. Since objective cognition is absolutely at home with itself in the object, it must recognize that *its* determinations are determinations of the *object*, and that, conversely, the *objectively* valid determinations *immediately present* in the object are *its* determinations. By this recollection [*Erinnerung*], this *withdrawal into itself* of intelligence, the latter becomes *will*. For the ordinary consciousness this transition does not, of course, exist; on the contrary, for ordinary thinking, thought and will fall outside of each other. But in truth, as we have just seen, thought determines itself into will and remains the substance of the latter; so that without thought there can be no will, and even the uneducated person wills only in so far as he has thought; the animal, on the other hand, because it does not think is also incapable of possessing a will.

§ 469

As will, the mind is aware that it is the author of its own conclusions, the origin of its self-fulfilment. Thus fulfilled, this independency or individuality forms the side of existence or of *reality* for the Idea of mind. As will, the mind steps into actuality; whereas as cognition it is on the soil of notional generality. Supplying its own content, the will is self-possessed, and in the widest sense free: this is its characteristic trait. Its finitude lies in the formalism that the spontaneity of its self-fulfilment means no more than a general and abstract ownness, not yet identified with matured reason. It is the function of the essential will to bring liberty to exist in the formal will, and it is therefore the aim of that formal will to fill itself with its essential nature, i.e. to make liberty [*Freiheit*] its pervading character, content, and aim, as well as its sphere of existence. The essential freedom of will is, and must always be, a thought: hence the way by which will can make itself objective mind is to rise to be a thinking will – to give itself the content which it can only have as it thinks itself.

> *Remark*:   True liberty, in the shape of ethical life,[34] consists in the will finding its purpose in a universal content, not in subjective or selfish interests. But such a content is only possible in thought and through thought: it is nothing short of absurd to seek to banish thought from the ethical, religious and law-abiding life.

Addition: Intelligence has demonstrated itself to be mind that withdraws into itself from the object, that recollects itself in it and recognizes its *inwardness* as *objectivity*. Conversely, will at the start of its self-objectification is still burdened with the form of subjectivity. But here, in the sphere of *subjective* mind, we have only to pursue this externalization to the point where volitional intelligence becomes objective mind, that is, to the point where the product of will ceases to be merely enjoyment and starts to become deed and action.

Now, in general, the course of development of practical mind is as follows.

At first, will appears in the form of immediacy; it has not yet *posited* itself as intelligence freely and objectively determining itself, but only *finds* itself as such objective determining. As such, it is (1) *practical feeling*, has a *single* content and is itself an *immediately individual, subjective* will which, as we have just said, feels itself as objectively determining, but still lacks a content that is liberated from the form of subjectivity, a content that is truly objective and universal in and for itself. For this reason, will is, to begin with, only *implicitly* or *notionally*, free. But it belongs to the Idea of freedom that the will should make its Notion, which is *freedom itself*, its content or aim. When it does this it becomes *objective* mind, constructs for itself a world of its freedom, and thus gives to its true content a self-subsistent existence. But will achieves this aim only by ridding itself of its [abstract] individuality, by developing its initially only implicit universality into a content that is universal in and for itself.

The next step on this path is made by will when (2), as impulse, it goes on to make the agreement of its inward determinateness with objectivity, which in feeling is only *given*, into an agreement that *ought* first to be *posited* by will.

The further step consists (3) in the subordination of *particular* impulses to a *universal* one – happiness. But since this universal is only a universality of reflection, it remains external to the particular aspect of the impulses, and is connected with this particular aspect only by the wholly abstract individual will, that is, by *caprice*.

Both the indeterminate universal of happiness as well as the immediate particularity of impulses and the abstract individuality of caprice are, in their mutual externality, untrue, and that is why they come together in the will that wills the *concrete* universal, the Notion of freedom which, as already remarked, forms the goal of practical mind.

Notes

1 Wallace's translation has 'The mind which as soul is physically conditioned – which as consciousness stands to this condition on the same terms as to an outward object.' The German text is 'Der Geist, der als *Seele natürlich* bestimmt, als *Bewußtsein* im Verhältnis zu dieser Bestimmtheit als zu einem *äußeren* Objekte ist.' [S.H.]

2 See G. W. F. Hegel, *Philosophy of Mind. Being Part Three of the Encyclopaedia of the Philosophical Sciences (1830)*, translated by W. Wallace, together with the *Zusätze* in Boumann's text (1845), translated by A. V. Miller, with foreword by J. N. Findlay (Oxford: Clarendon Press, 1971), pp. 71–122 (§§ 399–407). For §§ 400–1, see above, pp. 287–90. [S.H.]

3 See Hegel, *Philosophy of Mind*, pp. 158–9 (§ 418 Remark). See above, p. 291. [S.H.]

4 'formell'. Wallace's translation has 'nominal'. [S.H.]

5 'das Andere seiner selbst'. Wallace's translation has 'its very other'. See Hegel, *Philosophy of Nature*, pp. 13–14, 28–9. See above, pp. 260, 263. [S.H.]

6 See Hegel, *Philosophy of Nature*, pp. 28–37. See above, pp. 263–7. [S.H.]

7 Miller (following Wallace) has 'by the intrinsically infinite mind'. The German phrase is 'von dem an sich seienden unendlichen Geiste, von der schöpferischen

ewigen Idee'. Miller's translation is misleading because it suggests that the eternal Idea or *logos* through which there is space and time is some kind of absolute mind or consciousness. In fact Hegel is suggesting that the eternal Idea as such is merely spirit that is *implicit* and so *not yet* conscious or for itself. (Note that the phrase 'an sich seiend' is an adjectival phrase qualifying 'Geist', not an adverbial phrase qualifying 'unendlich'.) The argument of the *Philosophy of Nature* and the *Philosophy of Spirit* shows that there is no consciousness or mind at all until nature – the Idea in the form of otherness – comes to consciousness of itself in and through certain finite living beings (such as human beings). [S.H.]

8   See Hegel, *Philosophy of Nature*, p. 41. See above, pp. 268–9. [S.H.]
9   'Anschauung'. Wallace's translation has 'Intuition or Mental Vision'. [S.H.]
10 See Hegel, *Philosophy of Mind*, pp. 158–60. See above, pp. 290–1. [S.H.]
11 See *The Complete Works of Aristotle*, edited by J. Barnes, 2 vols (Princeton: Princeton University Press, 1984), 2: 1554 (*Metaphysics* I, 2, 982b11–14).
12 See Hegel, *Philosophy of Mind*, p. 198. See above, p. 295. [S.H.]
13 'noch bedingt durch die Unmittelbarkeit'. Wallace's translation has 'still conditioned by contrast with the immediacy'. [S.H.]
14 'bewußtlos aufbewahrt'. [S.H.]
15 The Humean terms 'impression' and 'idea' are introduced here by Wallace, not Hegel. [S.H.]
16 'Vorstellung'. Wallace's translation has 'Idea'. [S.H.]
17 Hegel, *The Encyclopaedia Logic*, pp. 49–50. See above, p. 140. [S.H.]
18 See Hegel, *Philosophy of Mind*, p. 204. See above, pp. 297–8. [S.H.]
19 Not included in this collection. [S.H.]
20 §§ 438, 445 from the *Philosophy of Subjective Spirit* are not included in this collection. For § 455 Remark, see above, pp. 299–300. Wallace refers mistakenly to § 435. [S.H.]
21 'formell'. Wallace's translation has 'nominal'. [S.H.]
22 'in dem Systeme der Tätigkeit der Intelligenz'. [S.H.]
23 See Hegel, *Philosophy of Mind*, pp. 75–88. Parts of § 401 and its Addition are printed above, pp. 287–90. [S.H.]
24 See Hegel, *Philosophy of Mind*, pp. 205–6. See above, pp. 298–9. [S.H.]
25 See Hegel, *Philosophy of Mind*, pp. 201–2. See above, p. 297. [S.H.]
26 'einem solchen *Auswendigen*, welches in das Inwendige der Intelligenz eingeschlossen bleibt'. [S.H.]
27 Paragraph from the *Encyclopaedia Logic* not included in this collection. [S.H.]
28 Wallace's translation has 'to have its wits about it'. [S.H.]
29 'bei sich'. Wallace's translation has 'has its wits about it'. [S.H.]
30 The mistake here lies not in regarding memory as mechanical, but in thinking that mechanical memory is justified only in so far as it serves 'other purposes of mind'. In Hegel's view, mechanical memory has its own intrinsic value as the expression of 'abstract subjectivity' (see § 463). To make this clear, I have replaced Wallace's phrase 'in which case it is only' with the phrase 'and as thereby only'. The relevant German text is: 'Es liegt nahe, das Gedächtnis als eine mechanische, als eine Tätigkeit des Sinnlosen zu fassen, wobei es etwa nur durch seinen Nutzen, vielleicht seine Unentbehrlichkeit für andere Zwecke und Tätigkeiten des Geistes gerechtfertigt wird'. [S.H.]
31 See Hegel, *Philosophy of Mind*, pp. 205–6, 219–21. See above, pp. 298–9, 310–11. [S.H.]
32 See Hegel, *The Encyclopaedia Logic*, pp. 28, 52–4. See above, pp. 135, 141. [S.H.]
33 'formell'. Wallace's translation has 'nominal'. [S.H.]
34 'Sittlichkeit'. Wallace's translation has 'moral life'. [S.H.]

Part V

Philosophy of Objective Spirit: Philosophy of Right and Philosophy of History

Introduction

A condensed version of Hegel's *Philosophy of Objective Spirit* is to be found in the second section of the *Philosophy of Spirit* (the third part of the *Encyclopaedia* [1830]), but it is developed in much more detail in the *Elements of the Philosophy of Right*, a handbook for use in lectures published in 1820, and in the *Lectures on the Philosophy of World History*, delivered by Hegel in Berlin between 1822 and 1831. It is from these latter works that the passages selected here have been chosen. The *Philosophy of Right* was regarded by some in the past as nothing more than the expression of 'the spirit of the Prussian Restoration'.[1] It is now recognized, however, to be one of the greatest works of social and political philosophy ever written. Its specific purpose is to continue Hegel's philosophical project by examining what it is for human freedom to be *objective*.

Hegel actually begins with the still subjective freedom of choice. He proceeds to show, however, that freedom comes to be something objective when it is understood not only as that which *can* be exercised, but as that which *must* be recognized by all – that is, as *right*. Right is initially conceived by Hegel as the right freely to appropriate for oneself things which do not themselves have rights: the right to property. It is then further determined as the right to engage in deliberate action in pursuit of one's welfare in the light of principles that have been freely established by reason (such as the Kantian principle that truly moral action is action carried out 'for the sake of duty'). Human freedom becomes fully objective, according to Hegel, when it takes the form, not only of individual property ownership and action, but also of a living *community* of free beings – an objective society or world of human freedom. The three main elements of such free or 'ethical' community (*Sittlichkeit*) are (*a*) marriage, in which two people freely commit themselves to a life lived together in love, (*b*) civil society, in which people freely labour in order to produce goods to meet their needs and organize themselves into estates and corporations (by which Hegel understands trade associations or guilds, not individual companies), and (*c*) the state, in which citizens freely submit themselves to laws and institutions which are recognized to secure justice and individual welfare.

In the course of the *Philosophy of Right* Hegel offers several analyses which have since become well-known and are worthy of particular consideration. He argues, for example, that choice – often regarded as the epitome of freedom – is not actually as free as one might think, because it is dependent on what we are *given* to choose by society or nature.[2] He also claims – famously and not uncontroversially – that Kant's categorical imperative is insufficient as a guide to moral action because 'it is possible to justify any wrong or immoral action by this means'. One can, for example, quite well will that theft and murder 'should become a universal law', if one is happy to countenance the total disappearance of property or 'the complete *absence of human life*'.[3] In his account of civil society, Hegel anticipates Marx by arguing that the smooth and proper functioning of a economy geared towards ever increasing productivity actually leads to overproduction and poverty.[4] Unlike Marx, however, Hegel does not believe that the very system of production and exchange *as such* leads to poverty. Consequently, he does not think that the removal of poverty and its attendant alienation requires the abolition of such an economic system. This is because Hegel holds that corporations within an exchange economy can effectively guard against overproduction (and therefore, by implication, guard against poverty) by limiting the number of producers in a given industry and by encouraging those who do produce to work together for a common end rather than seek 'external manifestations of success in [their] trade' by *outproducing* one another.[5] In spite of clear similarities between himself and Marx, therefore, Hegel differs from Marx by advocating, not communism, but a reformed – indeed, socialized – exchange economy in which freedom of trade is promoted but in which this freedom 'should not be such as to prejudice the general good'.[6]

The highest freedom is enjoyed, according to Hegel, when freedom of choice, moral action and economic activity are situated within the rational state. Such a state, it should be noted, is not the totalitarian 'Hegelian' Moloch of myth. It is an organized community of citizens who live under laws and institutions that guarantee their rights and promote their individual welfare, and who, as a result, feel free to trust those laws and institutions.[7] The defining feature of a free state for Hegel is thus not, as is commonly held today, that the legislature and the executive are legitimated by the *decision* or *vote* of the people as a whole (though Hegel does insist that deputies to the lower house be elected by members of corporations).[8] It is that the citizens see that their rights and individual welfare are actually secured by the state and its laws and so recognize that 'the community is the substantial basis and end'.[9]

If the *Philosophy of Right* demonstrates that true, objective freedom is freedom within the rational state, the *Lectures on the Philosophy of World History* demonstrate that such freedom emerges in the modern world as the result of the complex *historical* development of the human spirit. Indeed, in the passages selected here from his introduction to the lectures, Hegel argues that spirit is historical by its very nature and that history in turn is nothing but the development of spirit to true freedom. This does not mean that Hegel believes everything that has happened in the past has led inexorably to human emancipation. It means that he applies the word 'history' specifically to those activities and events, amongst the vicissitudes and reversals of human fortune, that *have actually* led to, and sustained, human emancipation. History, for Hegel, thus does not encompass all that human beings have done. It encompasses the specific series of political, social, economic, aesthetic, religious and philosophical transformations that have been brought about by – and that have themselves promoted – the move from what Hegel takes to be the ancient oriental conception that 'one [i.e. the emperor or despot] is free', through the Greek and Roman conception that 'some are free', to the Christian (and modern, secular) conception that 'all men as such are free, and that man is by nature free'.[10]

Hegel's introduction to the *Lectures on the Philosophy of World History* includes well-known remarks on the role of 'great individuals' in history, as well as on the 'cunning of reason' whereby self-interested human passion has, in spite of itself, often furthered the cause of human liberation.[11] In the main text of the lectures (not represented in this collection), Hegel then gives a detailed account of the political and cultural histories of China, India, Persia, Greece, Rome and Christian Europe. At the end of Hegel's account, it becomes clear that the idea of the free and rational state is not realized in the modern world in its pure form, but that the most advanced modern nations, such as France, England and Germany, distort to some degree the very freedom and rationality they incarnate. Thus, if the *Philosophy of Right* shows us what true, objective freedom in the state is, the sobering lesson of history, as Hegel already notes in the *Philosophy of Right* itself, is that 'the state is not a work of art; it exists in the world, and hence in the sphere of arbitrariness, contingency, and error, and bad behaviour may disfigure it in many respects'.[12]

The passages in Part V are taken from G. W. F. Hegel, *Elements of the Philosophy of Right*, edited by A. W. Wood, translated by H. B. Nisbet (Cambridge: Cambridge University Press, 1991), and G. W. F. Hegel, *Lectures on the Philosophy of World History. Introduction: Reason in History*, translated by H. B. Nisbet, with an introduction by D. Forbes (Cambridge: Cambridge University Press, 1975). The German text of the *Philosophy of Right* can be found in Hegel, *Werke in zwanzig Bänden*, vol. 7, and the German text of Hegel's introduction to his *Lectures on the Philosophy of World History* can be found in G. W. F. Hegel, *Vorlesungen über die Philosophie der Weltgeschichte. Erste Hälfte: Die Vernunft in der Geschichte*, edited by J. Hoffmeister (Hamburg: Felix Meiner, 1955). The passages from the *Philosophy of Right* marked 'Addition' are not by Hegel himself but were compiled by Eduard Gans (the editor of the 1833 edition) from transcripts of Hegel's lectures made by his students. The passages from the introduction to the *Lectures on the Philosophy of World History* which are in Roman type (i.e. *not* in italic) are not by Hegel either, but were compiled by Georg Lasson (the editor of the 1917, 1920 and 1930 editions), again from student transcripts of Hegel's lectures. The numbered paragraphs and the remarks from the *Philosophy of Right* and the passages from the *Lectures on the Philosophy of World History* which are italicized were written by Hegel himself.

Notes

1 R. Haym, 'Preußen und die Rechtsphilosophie' (*Hegel und seine Zeit*), in *Materialien zu Hegels Rechtsphilosophie*, edited by M. Riedel, 2 vols (Frankfurt: Suhrkamp Verlag, 1975), 1: 366.
2 Hegel, *Elements of the Philosophy of Right*, p. 49 (§ 15 Addition). See below. p. 334.
3 Hegel, *Elements of the Philosophy of Right*, p. 162 (§ 135). See below, p. 350.
4 Hegel, *Elements of the Philosophy of Right*, p. 266 (§ 243). See below, p. 374.
5 Hegel, *Elements of the Philosophy of Right*, pp. 270–2 (§§ 251–3). See below, pp. 377–8.
6 Hegel, *Elements of the Philosophy of Right*, p. 263 (§ 236 Addition). See below, p. 372.
7 Hegel, *Elements of the Philosophy of Right*, pp. 276, 288 (§§ 258, 268). See below, pp. 380, 384.
8 Hegel, *Elements of the Philosophy of Right*, p. 348 (§ 309 and Addition). See below, pp. 391–2.
9 Hegel, *Elements of the Philosophy of Right*, pp. 287–8 (§§ 265 Addition; 268). See below, pp. 383–4.
10 G. W. F. Hegel, *Lectures on the Philosophy of World History. Introduction: Reason in History*, translated by H. B. Nisbet, with an introduction by D. Forbes (Cambridge: Cambridge University Press, 1975), p. 54. See below, p. 402.
11 Hegel, *Lectures on the Philosophy of World History*, pp. 83, 89. See below, pp. 410, 413.
12 Hegel, *Elements of the Philosophy of Right*, pp. 279, 282–3 (§§ 258 Addition; 260 Addition). See below, pp. 381–2.

24

Philosophy of Right: Preface and Introduction

Preface

[...]

> What is rational is actual;
> and what is actual is rational.

Alienation/
Reconciliation

This conviction is shared by every ingenuous consciousness as well as by philosophy, and the latter takes it as its point of departure in considering both the *spiritual* and the *natural* universe. If reflection, feeling, or whatever form the subjective consciousness may assume regards the *present* as *vain* and looks beyond it in a spirit of superior knowledge, it finds itself in a vain position; and since it has actuality only in the present, it is itself mere vanity. Conversely, if the *Idea* is seen as 'only an idea', a representation [*Vorstellung*] in the realm of opinion, philosophy affords the opposite insight that nothing is actual except the Idea. For what matters is to recognize in the semblance of the temporal and transient the substance which is immanent and the eternal which is present. For since the rational, which is synonymous with the Idea, becomes actual by entering into external existence [*Existenz*], it emerges in an infinite wealth of forms, appearances and shapes and surrounds its core with a brightly coloured covering in which consciousness at first resides, but which only the concept can penetrate in order to find the inner pulse, and detect its continued beat even within the external shapes. But the infinitely varied circumstances which take shape within this externality as the essence manifests itself within it, this infinite material and its organization, are not the subject-matter of philosophy. To deal with them would be to interfere in things [*Dinge*] with which philosophy has no concern, and it can save itself the trouble of giving good advice on the subject. Plato could well have refrained from recommending nurses never to stand still with children but to keep rocking them in their arms; and Fichte likewise need not have perfected his *passport regulations* to the point of 'constructing', as the expression ran, the requirement that the passports of suspect persons should carry not only their personal description but also their painted likeness.[1] In deliberations of this kind, no trace of philosophy remains, and it can the more readily abstain from such ultra-wisdom because it is precisely in relation to this infinite multitude of subjects that it should appear at its most liberal. In this way, philosophical science will also show itself furthest removed from the hatred which the vanity of superior wisdom displays towards a multitude of circumstances and institutions – a hatred in which pettiness takes the greatest of pleasure, because this is the only way in which it can attain self-esteem [*Selbstgefühl*].

This treatise, therefore, in so far as it deals with political science, shall be nothing other than an attempt *to comprehend and portray the state as an inherently rational entity*. As a philosophical composition, it must distance itself as far as possible from the obligation to construct a *state as it ought to be*; such instruction as it may contain cannot be aimed at instructing the state on how it ought to be, but rather at showing how the state, as the ethical universe, should be recognized.

Ἰδοὺ Ῥόδος, ἰδοὺ καὶ τὸ πήδημα.
Hic Rhodus, *hic* saltus.[2]

To comprehend *what is* is the task of philosophy, for *what is* is reason. As far as the individual is concerned, each individual is in any case a *child of his time*; thus philosophy, too, is *its own time comprehended in thoughts*. It is just as foolish to imagine that any philosophy can transcend its contemporary world as that an individual can overleap his own time or leap over Rhodes. If his theory does indeed transcend his own time, if it builds itself a world *as it ought to be*, then it certainly has an existence, but only within his opinions – a pliant medium in which the imagination can construct anything it pleases.

With little alteration, the saying just quoted would read:

Here is the rose, dance *here*.[3]

What lies between reason as self-conscious spirit and reason as present actuality, what separates the former from the latter and prevents it from finding satisfaction in it, is the fetter of some abstraction or other which has not been liberated into [the form of] the concept. To recognize reason as the rose in the cross of the present and thereby to delight in the present – this rational insight is the *reconciliation* with actuality which philosophy grants to those who have received the inner call *to comprehend*, to preserve their subjective freedom in the realm of the substantial, and at the same time to stand with their subjective freedom not in a particular and contingent situation, but in what has being in and for itself.

This is also what constitutes the more concrete sense of what was described above in more abstract terms as the *unity of form and content*.[4] For *form* in its most concrete significance is reason as conceptual cognition, and *content* is reason as the substantial essence of both ethical and natural actuality; the conscious identity of the two is the philosophical Idea. – It is a great obstinacy, the kind of obstinacy which does honour to human beings, that they are unwilling to acknowledge in their attitudes [*Gesinnung*] anything which has not been justified by thought – and this obstinacy is the characteristic property of the modern age, as well as being the distinctive principle of Protestantism. What Luther inaugurated as faith in feeling and in the testimony of the spirit is the same thing that the spirit, at a more mature stage of its development, endeavours to grasp in the *concept* so as to free itself in the present and thus find itself therein. It has become a famous saying that 'a half-philosophy leads away from God' – and it is the same half-measure which defines cognition as an *approximation* to the truth – 'whereas true philosophy leads to God';[5] the same applies to philosophy and the state. Reason is not content with an approximation which, as something 'neither cold nor hot', it 'spews out of its mouth';[6] and it is as little content with that cold despair which confesses that, in this temporal world, things are bad or at best indifferent, but that nothing better can be expected here, so that for this reason alone we should live at peace with actuality. The peace which cognition establishes with the actual world has more warmth in it than this.

A further word on the subject of *issuing instructions* on how the world ought to be: philosophy, at any rate, always comes too late to perform this function. As the *thought* of the world, it appears only at a time when actuality has gone through its formative process and attained its completed state. This lesson of the concept is necessarily also apparent from history, namely that it is only when actuality has reached maturity that the ideal appears opposite the real and reconstructs this real world, which it has grasped in its substance, in the shape of an intellectual realm. When philosophy paints its grey in grey, a shape of life has grown old, and it cannot be rejuvenated, but only recognized, by the grey in grey of philosophy; the owl of Minerva begins its flight only with the onset of dusk.

But it is time to conclude this foreword; as a foreword, its function was in any case merely to make external and subjective comments on the point of view of the work to which it is prefaced. If a content is to be discussed philosophically, it will bear only scientific and objective treatment; in the same way, the author will regard any criticism expressed in a form other than that of scientific discussion of the matter [*Sache*] itself merely as a subjective postscript and random assertion, and will treat it with indifference.

Introduction

§ 1

The subject-matter of *the philosophical science of right* is the *Idea of right* – the concept of right and its actualization. [R] [A]

§ 2

The science of right is *a part of philosophy*. It has therefore to develop the *Idea*, which is the reason within an object [*Gegenstand*], out of the concept; or what comes to the same thing, it must observe the proper immanent development of the thing [*Sache*] itself. As a part [of philosophy], it has a determinate *starting-point*, which is the *result* and truth of what *preceded* it, and what preceded it is the so-called *proof* of that result. Hence the concept of right, so far as its *coming into being* is concerned, falls outside the science of right; its deduction is presupposed here and is to be taken as *given*. [A] [R]

§ 4

The basis [*Boden*] of right is the *realm of spirit* in general and its precise location and point of departure is the *will*; the will is *free*, so that freedom constitutes its substance and destiny [*Bestimmung*] and the system of right is the realm of actualized freedom, the world of spirit produced from within itself as a second nature.

Addition: (H,G).[7] The freedom of the will can best be explained by reference to physical nature. For freedom is just as much a basic determination of the will as weight is a basic determination of bodies. If matter is described as heavy, one might think that this predicate is merely contingent; but this is not so, for nothing in matter is weightless: on the contrary, matter is weight itself. Heaviness constitutes the body and is the body. It is just the same with freedom and the will, for that which is free is the will. Will without freedom is an empty word, just as freedom is actual only as will or as subject. But as for the connection between the will and thought, the following remarks are necessary. Spirit is thought in general, and the human being is distinguished from the animal by thought. But it must not be imagined [*sich vorstellen*] that a human being thinks on the one hand and wills on the other, and that he has thought in one pocket and volition in the other, for this would be an empty representation [*Vorstellung*]. The distinction between thought and will is simply that between theoretical and practical attitudes. But they are not two separate faculties; on the contrary, the will is a particular way of thinking – thinking translating itself into existence [*Dasein*], thinking as the drive to give itself existence. This distinction between thought and will can be expressed as follows. When I think of an object [*Gegenstand*], I make it into a thought and deprive it of its sensuous quality; I make it into something which is essentially and immediately mine. For it is only when I think that I am with myself [*bei mir*], and it is only by comprehending it that I can penetrate an object; it then no longer stands opposed to me, and I have deprived it of that quality of its own which it had for itself in opposition to me. Just as Adam says to Eve: 'You are flesh of my flesh and bone of my bone', so does spirit say: 'This is spirit of my spirit, and its alien character has disappeared.' Every representation [*Vorstellung*] is a generalization, and this is inherent in thought. To generalize something means to think it. 'I' is thought and likewise the universal. When I say 'I', I leave out of account every particularity such as my character, temperament, knowledge [*Kenntnisse*], and age. 'I' is totally empty; it is merely a point – simple, yet active in this simplicity. The colourful canvas of the world is before me; I stand opposed to it and in this [theoretical] attitude I overcome [*aufhebe*] its opposition and make its content my own. 'I' is at home in the world when it knows it, and even more so when it has comprehended it. So much for the theoretical attitude. The practical attitude, on the other hand, begins with thought, with the 'I' itself, and seems at first to be opposed [to the world] because it immediately sets up a separation. In so far as I am practical or active, i.e. in so far as I act, I determine myself, and to determine myself means precisely to posit a difference. But these differences which I posit are nevertheless also mine, the determinations apply to me, and the ends to which I am impelled belong to me. Now even if I let go of these determinations and differences, i.e. if I posit them in the so-called external world, they still remain mine: they are what I have done or made, and they bear the imprint of my mind [*Geist*]. This, then, is the distinction between theoretical and practical attitudes; the relationship between them must now be described. The theoretical is essentially contained within the practical; the idea [*Vorstellung*] that the two are separate must be rejected, for one cannot have a will without intelligence. On the contrary, the will contains the theoretical within itself. The will determines itself, and this determination is primarily of an inward nature, for what I will I represent to myself as my object [*Gegenstand*]. The animal acts by instinct, it is impelled by something inward and is therefore also practical; but it has no will, because it does not represent to itself what it desires. It is equally impossible to adopt a theoretical attitude or to think without a will, for in thinking we are necessarily active. The content of what is thought certainly takes on the form of being; but this being is something mediated, something posited by our activity. These distinct attitudes are therefore inseparable: they are one and the same thing, and both moments can be found in every activity, of thinking and willing alike. [R]

§ 5

The will contains (a) the element of *pure indeterminacy* or of the 'I''s pure reflection into itself, in which every limitation, every content, whether present immediately through nature, through needs, desires and drives, or given and determined in some other way, is dissolved; this is the limitless infinity of *absolute abstraction* or *universality*, the pure thinking of oneself.

> *Remark*:   Those who regard thinking as a particular and distinct *faculty*, divorced from the will as an equally distinct *faculty*, and who in addition even consider that thinking is prejudicial to the will – especially the good will – show from the very outset that they are totally ignorant of the nature of the will (a remark which we shall often have occasion to make on this same subject). – Only *one aspect* of the will is defined here – namely this *absolute possibility* of *abstracting* from every determination in which I find myself or which I have posited in myself, the flight from every content as a limitation. If the will determines itself in this way, or if representational thought [*die Vorstellung*] considers this aspect in itself

[*für sich*] as freedom and holds fast to it, this is *negative* freedom or the freedom of the understanding. – This is the freedom of the void, which is raised to the status of an actual shape and passion. If it remains purely theoretical, it becomes in the religious realm the Hindu fanaticism of pure contemplation; but if it turns to actuality, it becomes in the realm of both politics and religion the fanaticism of destruction, demolishing the whole existing social order, eliminating all individuals regarded as suspect by a given order, and annihilating any organization which attempts to rise up anew. Only in destroying something does this negative will have a feeling of its own existence [*Dasein*]. It may well believe that it wills some positive condition, for instance the condition of universal equality or of universal religious life, but it does not in fact will the positive actuality of this condition, for this at once gives rise to some kind of order, a particularization both of institutions and of individuals; but it is precisely through the annihilation of particularity and of objective determination that the self-consciousness of this negative freedom arises. Thus, whatever such freedom believes [*meint*] that it wills can in itself [*für sich*] be no more than an abstract representation [*Vorstellung*], and its actualization can only be the fury of destruction.

Addition: (H,G). It is inherent in this element of the will that I am able to free myself from everything, to renounce all ends, and to abstract from everything. The human being alone is able to abandon all things, even his own life: he can commit suicide. The animal cannot do this; it always remains only negative, in a determination which is alien to it and to which it merely grows accustomed. The human being is pure thinking of himself, and only in thinking is he this power to give himself universality, that is, to extinguish all particularity, all determinacy. This negative freedom or freedom of the understanding is one-sided, but this one-sidedness always contains within itself an essential determination and should therefore not be dismissed; but the defect of the understanding is that it treats a one-sided determination as unique and elevates it to supreme status. This form of freedom occurs frequently in history. The Hindus, for example, place the highest value on mere persistence in the knowledge of one's simple identity with oneself, on remaining within this empty space of one's inwardness like colourless light in pure intuition, and on renouncing every activity of life, every end, and every representation [*Vorstellung*]. In this way, the human being becomes *Brahman*. There is no longer any distinction between the finite human being and Brahman; instead, every difference [*Differenz*] has disappeared in this universality. This form [of freedom] appears more concretely in the active fanaticism of both political and religious life. An example of this was the Reign of Terror in the French Revolution, during which all differences of talents and authority were supposed to be cancelled out [*aufgehoben*]. This was a time of trembling and quaking and of intolerance towards everything particular. For fanaticism wills only what is abstract, not what is articulated, so that whenever differences emerge, it finds them incompatible with its own indeterminacy and cancels them [*hebt sie auf*]. This is why the people, during the French Revolution, destroyed once more the institutions they had themselves created, because all institutions are incompatible with the abstract self-consciousness of equality.

§ 6

(β) In the same way, 'I' is the transition from undifferentiated indeterminacy to *differentiation, determination,* and the *positing* of a determinacy as a content and object. – This content may further be given by nature, or generated by the concept of spirit. Through this positing of itself as something *determinate*, 'I' steps into existence [*Dasein*] in general – the absolute moment of the *finitude* or *particularization* of the 'I'.

> *Remark*:   This second moment of *determination* is just as much *negativity* and cancellation [*Aufheben*] as the first – for it is the cancellation of the first abstract negativity. – Just as the particular is in general contained within the universal, so in consequence is this second moment already contained within the first and is merely a *positing* of what the first already *is in itself*. The first moment – that is, the first as it is for itself – is not true infinity or the *concrete* universality of the concept, but only something *determinate* and one-sided. For since it is abstraction from all determinacy, it is itself not *without* determinacy; and the fact that it is abstract and one-sided constitutes its determinacy, deficiency and finitude. – The differentiation and determination of the two moments referred to is to be found in the philosophy of Fichte and likewise in that of Kant etc., except that in Fichte – to confine ourselves to his presentation – 'I', as the unbounded (in the first proposition of his *Theory of Knowledge* [*Wissenschaftslehre*]), is taken purely and simply as something *positive* (and thus as the universality and identity of the understanding). Consequently, this abstract 'I' *for itself* is supposed to be *the truth*; and *limitation* – i.e. the *negative* in general, whether as a given external limit or as an activity of the 'I' itself – is therefore something *added* to it (in the second proposition). – The further step which speculative philosophy had to take was to apprehend the *negativity* which is immanent within the universal or the identical, as in the 'I' – a step the need for which is not perceived by those who fail to apprehend the *dualism* of *infinity* and *finitude*, even in that immanent and abstract form in which Fichte understood it.

Addition: (H,G). This second moment appears as the opposing one. It is to be apprehended in its universal mode: it belongs to freedom, but does not constitute the whole of freedom. The 'I' here emerges from undifferentiated indeterminacy to become differentiated, to posit something determinate as its content and object [*Gegenstand*]. I do not merely will – I will something. A will which, as described in the previous paragraph, wills only the abstract universal, wills *nothing* and is therefore not a will at all. The particular [thing] which the will wills is a limitation, for the will, in order to be a will, must in some way limit itself. The fact that the will wills *something* is the limit or negation. Thus particularization is what as a rule is called finitude. Reflective thought usually regards the first moment, namely the indeterminate, as the absolute and higher moment, and conversely regards the limited as a mere negation of this indeterminacy. But this indeterminacy is itself merely a negation with regard to the determinate, to finitude: 'I' is this solitude and absolute negation. The indeterminate will is to this extent just as one-sided as that which exists in mere determinacy.

§ 7

(γ) The will is the unity of both these moments – *particularity* reflected *into itself* and thereby restored to *universality*. It is *individuality* [*Einzelheit*], the *self-determination* of the 'I', in that it posits itself as the negative of itself, that is, as *determinate* and *limited*, and at the same time remains with itself [*bei sich*], that is, in its *identity with itself* and universality; and in this determination, it joins together with itself alone. – 'I' determines itself in so far as it is the self-reference of negativity. As this *reference to itself*, it is likewise indifferent to this determinacy; it knows the latter as its own and as *ideal*, as a mere possibility by which it is not restricted but in which it finds itself merely because it posits itself in it. – This is the *freedom* of the will, which constitutes the concept or substantiality of the will, its gravity, just as gravity constitutes the substantiality of a body. [R]

Addition: (H). What is properly called the will contains both the preceding moments. 'I' as such is primarily pure activity, the universal which is with itself [*bei sich*]; but this universal determines itself, and to that extent is no longer with itself but posits itself as an other and ceases to be the universal. Then the third moment is that 'I' is with itself in its limitation, in this other; as it determines itself, it nevertheless still remains with itself and does not cease to hold fast to the universal. This, then, is the concrete concept of freedom, whereas the two previous moments have been found to be thoroughly abstract and one-sided. But we already possess this freedom in the form of feeling [*Empfindung*], for example in friendship and love. Here, we are not one-sidedly within ourselves, but willingly limit ourselves with reference to an other, even while knowing ourselves in this limitation as ourselves. In this determinacy, the human being should not feel determined; on the contrary, he attains his self-awareness only by regarding the other as other. Thus, freedom lies neither in indeterminacy nor in determinacy, but is both at once. The will which limits itself exclusively to a *this* is the will of the stubborn person who considers himself unfree unless he has *this* will. But the will is not tied to something limited; on the contrary, it must proceed further, for the nature of the will is not this one-sidedness and restriction. Freedom is to will something determinate, yet to be with oneself [*bei sich*] in this determinacy and to return once more to the universal.

§ 11

The will which is free as yet only *in itself* is the *immediate* or *natural* will. The determinations of the difference which is posited within the will by the self-determining concept appear within the immediate will as an *immediately* present content: these are the *drives, desires and inclinations* by which the will finds itself naturally determined. This content, along with the determinations developed within it, does indeed originate in the will's rationality and it is thus rational in itself; but expressed in so immediate a form, it does not yet have the form of rationality. *For me*, this content is admittedly entirely *mine*; but this form and that content are still different, so that the will is *a finite will within itself*. [R] [A]

§ 14

The finite will, purely with regard to its form, is the self-reflecting *infinite 'I'* which is with itself [*bei sich selbst*] (see § 5). As such, it *stands above* its content, i.e. its various drives, and also above the further individual ways in which these are actualized and satisfied. At the same time, since it is only formally infinite, it is *tied* to this content as to the determinations of its nature and of its external actuality (see §§ 6 and 11); but since it is indeterminate, it is not restricted to this or that content in particular. To this extent, this content is only a possible one for the reflection of the 'I' into itself; it may or may not be mine; and 'I' is the *possibility* of determining myself to this or to something else, of *choosing* between these determinations which the 'I' must in this respect regard as external.

§ 15

The freedom of the will, according to this determination, is *arbitrariness* [*Willkür*], in which the following two factors are contained: free reflection, which abstracts from everything, and dependence on an inwardly or externally given content and material. Since this content, which is necessary *in itself* as an end, is at the same time determined as a possible content in opposition to free reflection, it follows that arbitrariness is *contingency* in the shape of will.

> *Remark:*   The commonest idea [*Vorstellung*] we have of freedom is that of
> arbitrariness – the mean position of reflection between the will as deter-
> mined solely by natural drives and the will which is free in and for
> itself. When we hear it said that freedom in general consists in *being
> able to do as one pleases*, such an idea [*Vorstellung*] can only be taken to
> indicate a complete lack of intellectual culture [*Bildung des Gedankens*];
> for it shows not the least awareness of what constitutes the will which is
> free in and for itself, or right, or ethics, etc. Reflection, the *formal*
> universality and unity of self-consciousness, is the will's *abstract* cer-
> tainty of its freedom, but it is not yet the *truth* of this freedom, because
> it does not yet have itself as its content and end, so that the subjective
> side is still something other than the objective [*die gegenständliche*]; the
> content of this self-determination therefore also remains purely and
> simply finite. Instead of being the will in its truth, arbitrariness is rather
> the will as *contradiction*. – In the controversy which arose chiefly at the

time of Wolff's metaphysics as to whether the will is actually free or whether our knowledge of its freedom is merely a delusion, it was arbitrariness which people had in mind. To the certainty of this abstract self-determination, *determinism* rightly opposed the *content*, which, as something *encountered*, is not contained in that certainty and therefore *comes to it from outside* – although 'outside' here denotes drive or representation [*Vorstellung*], or simply the fact that the consciousness is filled in such a way that its content is not derived from its own self-determining activity as such. Accordingly, since only the formal element of free self-determination is immanent within arbitrariness, whereas the other element is something given to it, arbitrariness may indeed be called a delusion if it is supposed to be equivalent to freedom. In all reflective philosophy, as in that of Kant and subsequently in Fries's utterly superficial revision of it, freedom is nothing other than this formal self-activity.

Addition: (H). Since I have the possibility of determining myself in this or that direction – that is, since I am able to choose – I possess an arbitrary will, and this is what is usually called freedom. The choice which I have lies in the universality of the will, whereby I can make this or that [thing] mine. This [thing] which is mine is a particular content and is therefore incompatible with me; thus it is separate from me and is only potentially mine, just as I am only the potentiality of uniting with it. The choice therefore lies in the indeterminacy of the 'I' and the determinacy of the content. Because of this content, the will is consequently not free, although it has in itself the aspect of infinity in a formal sense. None of these contents is in keeping with it, and it does not truly have itself in any of them. It is inherent in arbitrariness that the content is not determined as mine by the nature of my will, but by *contingency*; thus I am also dependent on this content, and this is the contradiction which underlies arbitrariness. The common man thinks that he is free when he is allowed to act arbitrarily, but this very arbitrariness implies that he is not free. When I will what is rational, I act not as a particular [*partikulares*] individual, but in accordance with the concepts of ethics in general: in an ethical act, I vindicate not myself but the thing [*die Sache*]. But a person who does something perverse gives the greatest prominence to his particularity [*Partikularität*]. The rational is the high road which everyone follows and where no one stands out from the rest. When great artists complete a work, we can say that it *had* to be so; that is, the artist's particularity has completely disappeared and no *mannerism* is apparent in it. Phidias has no mannerisms; the shape itself lives and stands out. But the poorer the artist is, the more we see of himself, of his particularity and arbitrariness. If we stop our enquiry at arbitrariness, at the human being's ability to will this or that, this does indeed constitute his freedom; but if we bear firmly in mind that the content of what he wills is a given one, it follows that he is determined by it and is in this very respect no longer free.

§ 16

Whatever the will has decided to choose (see § 14), it can likewise relinquish (see § 5). But with this possibility of proceeding in turn beyond any other content which it may substitute for the previous one, and so on *ad infinitum*, it does not escape from finitude, because every such content is different from the form [of the will] and therefore finite; and the opposite of determinacy – namely indeterminacy, indecision, or abstraction – is only the other, equally one-sided moment.

§ 17

That contradiction which is the arbitrary will (see § 15) makes its *appearance* as a *dialectic* of drives and inclinations which conflict with each other in such a way that the satisfaction of one demands that the satisfaction of the other be subordinated or sacrificed, and so on; and since a drive is merely the simple direction of its own determinacy and therefore has no yardstick within itself, this determination that it should be subordinated or sacrificed is the contingent decision of arbitrariness – whether the latter is guided by calculations of the understanding as to which drive will afford the greater satisfaction, or by any other consideration one cares to name. [A]

§ 20

When reflection applies itself to the drives, representing them, estimating them, and comparing them with one another and then with the means they employ, their consequences etc., and with a sum total of satisfaction – i.e. with *happiness* – it confers *formal universality* upon this material and purifies it, in this external manner, of its crudity and barbarity. This cultivation of the universality of thought is the absolute value of *education* (cf. § 187) [below].

Addition: (H). In happiness, thought already has some power over the natural force of the drives, for it is not content with the instantaneous, but requires a whole of happiness. This is connected with education to the extent that education likewise implements a universal. But two moments are present in the ideal of happiness: the first is a universal which is superior to all particularities; but secondly, since the content of this universal is in turn merely universal pleasure, the individual and particular, i.e. a finite quantity, reappears at this point, and we are compelled to return to the drive. Since the content of happiness lies in the subjectivity and feeling [*Empfindung*] of everyone, this universal end is itself particular [*partikular*], so that no true unity of content and form is yet present within it.

§ 21

The truth, however, of this formal universality, which is indeterminate for itself and encounters its determinacy in the material already mentioned, is *self-determining universality, the will, or freedom.* When the will has universality, or itself as infinite form, as its content, object [*Gegenstand*], and end, it is free not only *in itself* but also *for itself* – it is the Idea in its truth. [R] [A]

§ 22

The will which has being in and for itself is *truly infinite*, because its object [*Gegenstand*] is itself, and therefore not something which it sees as *other* or as a *limitation*; on the contrary, it has merely returned into itself in its object. Furthermore, it is not just a possibility, predisposition, or *capacity* (*potentia*), but the *infinite in actuality* (*infinitum actu*), because the concept's existence [*Dasein*] or objective [*gegenständliche*] externality is inwardness itself.

> *Remark*: If one therefore speaks only of the free will as such, without specifying that it is the will which is free in and *for itself*, one is speaking only of the *predisposition* towards freedom or of the natural and finite will (see § 11), and therefore not – whatever one may say and believe – of the free will. – When the understanding regards the infinite merely as something negative and hence as *beyond its sphere*, it believes that it is doing the infinite all the more honour by pushing it ever further away and distancing it as something alien. In the free will, the truly infinite has actuality and presence – the will itself is the idea which is present within itself. [A]

§ 23

Only in this freedom is the will completely *with itself* [*bei sich*], because it has reference to nothing but itself, so that every relationship of *dependence* on something *other* than itself is thereby eliminated. – It is *true*, or rather it is *truth* itself, because its determination consists in being in its *existence* [*Dasein*] – i.e. as something opposed to itself – what it is in its concept; that is, the pure concept has the intuition of itself as its end and reality.

§ 27

The absolute determination or, if one prefers, the absolute drive, of the free spirit (see § 21) is to make its freedom into its object [*Gegenstand*] – to make it objective both in the sense that it becomes the rational system of the spirit itself, and in the sense that this system becomes immediate actuality. [. . .] This enables the spirit to be for itself, as Idea, what the will is in itself. The abstract concept of the Idea of the will is in general *the free will which wills the free will*.

§ 28

Action

The activity of the will consists in cancelling [*aufzuheben*] the contradiction between subjectivity and objectivity and in translating its ends from their subjective determination into an objective one, while at the same time remaining *with itself* in this objectivity. Apart from the formal mode of consciousness

[. . .] in which objectivity is present only as immediate actuality, this activity is the *essential development* of the substantial content of the Idea (see § 21), a development in which the concept determines the *Idea*, which is *itself* at first *abstract*, to [produce] the totality of its system. This totality, as the substantial element, is independent of the opposition between a merely subjective end and its realization, and is *the same* in both of these forms.

§ 29

Right is any existence [*Dasein*] in general which is the *existence* of the *free will*. Right is therefore in general freedom, as Idea. [R]

§ 30

Right is something *utterly sacred*, for the simple reason that it is the existence [*Dasein*] of the absolute concept, of self-conscious freedom. – But the *formalism* of right – and also of duty – arises out of the different stages in the development of the concept of freedom. In opposition to the more formal, i.e. *more abstract* and hence more limited kind of right, that sphere and stage of the spirit in which the spirit has determined and actualized within itself the further moments contained in its Idea possesses a higher right, for it is the *more concrete* sphere, richer within itself and more truly universal.

> *Remark*: Each stage in the development of the Idea of freedom has its distinctive right, because it is the existence of freedom in one of its own determinations. When we speak of the opposition between morality or ethics and *right*, the right in question is merely the initial and formal right of abstract personality. Morality, ethics and the interest of the state – each of these is a distinct variety of right, because each of them gives determinate shape and existence to *freedom*. They can come into *collision* only in so far as they are all in equal measure rights; if the moral point of view of the spirit were not also a right – i.e. freedom in one of its forms – it could not possibly come into collision with the right of personality or with any other right, because every right embodies the concept of freedom, the highest determination of spirit, in relation to which everything else is without substance. But a collision also contains this further moment: it imposes a limitation whereby one right is subordinated to another; only the right of the world spirit is absolute in an unlimited sense.

§ 31

The method whereby the concept, in science, develops out of itself and is merely an *immanent* progression and production of its own determinations is likewise assumed to be familiar from logic. Its progress does not depend on the assertion that various circumstances *are present* or on the subsequent *application* of the universal to such material of extraneous origin.

> *Remark*: The moving principle of the concept, which not only dissolves the particularizations of the universal but also produces them, is what I call *dialectic*. I consequently do not mean that kind of dialectic which takes an object [*Gegenstand*], proposition, etc. given to feeling or to the immediate consciousness in general, and dissolves it, confuses it, develops it this way and that, and is solely concerned with deducing its opposite – a negative mode which frequently appears even in Plato. Such dialectic may regard as its final result the opposite of a given idea [*Vorstellung*], or, as in the uncompromising manner of ancient scepticism, its contradiction, or, in a lame fashion, an *approximation* to the truth, which is a modern half-measure. The higher dialectic of the concept consists not merely in producing and apprehending the determination as an opposite and limiting factor, but in producing and apprehending the *positive* content and result which it contains; and it is this alone which makes it a *development* and immanent progression. This dialectic, then, is not an *external* activity of subjective thought, but the *very soul* of the content which puts forth its branches and fruit organically. This development of the Idea as the activity of its own rationality is something which thought, since it is subjective, merely observes, without for its part adding anything extra to it. To consider something rationally means not to bring reason to bear on the object from outside in order to work upon it, for the object is itself rational for itself; it is the spirit in its freedom, the highest apex of self-conscious reason, which here gives itself actuality and engenders itself as an existing world; and the sole business of science is to make conscious this work which is accomplished by the reason of the thing [*Sache*] itself.

§ 32

The *determinations* in the development of the concept are on the one hand themselves concepts, but on the other hand, since the concept is essentially Idea, they have the form of existence [*Dasein*], and the series of concepts which results is therefore at the same time a series of *shapes*; this is how science should regard them. [R]

Addition: (H). The Idea must continually determine itself further within itself, for it is initially no more than an abstract concept. But this initial abstract concept is never abandoned. On the contrary, it merely becomes continually richer in itself, so that the last determination is also the richest. Those determinations which previously existed only in themselves thereby attain their free self-sufficiency, but in such a way that the concept remains the soul which holds everything together and which arrives at its own differentiation only through an immanent process. One cannot therefore say that the concept arrives at anything new; on the contrary, the last determination coincides in unity with the first. Thus, even if the concept appears to have become fragmented in its existence, this is merely a semblance, as is subsequently confirmed when all its details finally return in the concept of the universal. In the empirical sciences, it is customary to analyse what is found in representational thought [*Vorstellung*], and when the individual instance has been reduced to the common quality, this common quality is then called the concept. This is not how we proceed, for we merely wish to observe how the concept determines itself, and we force ourselves not to add anything of our own thoughts and opinions. What we obtain in this way, however, is a series of thoughts and another series of existent shapes, in which it may happen that the temporal sequence of their actual appearance is to some extent different from the conceptual sequence. Thus, we cannot say, for example, that property existed before the family, although property is nevertheless dealt with first. One might accordingly ask at this point why we do not begin with the highest instance, that is, with the concretely true. The answer will be that we wish to see the truth precisely in the form of a result, and it is essential for this purpose that we should first comprehend the abstract concept itself. What is actual, the shape which the concept assumes, is therefore from our point of view only the subsequent and further stage, even if it should itself come first in actuality. The course we follow is that whereby the abstract forms reveal themselves not as existing for themselves, but as untrue.

Notes

1 See Plato, *Laws* 789b–790a; J. G. Fichte, *Grundlage des Naturrechts nach Prinzipien der Wissenschaftslehre* (Jena/Leipzig: C. E. Gabler, 1796–1797), § 21, 2. [S.H.]

2 'Here is Rhodes, jump here'. This saying is drawn from one of Aesop's fables, *The Braggart*. [Editor's (i.e. A. Wood's) note.]

3 In Greek, *Rhodos* means either 'Rhodes' or 'rose', and in Latin, *salta* means either 'jump' or 'dance'. The pun suggests to Hegel that to meet the challenge of comprehending the rationality of the actual is also to find a way of rejoicing in the present. [Editor's note.]

4 See Hegel, *Elements of the Philosophy of Right*, p. 10 (passage not included in this collection). [S.H.]

5 'A little taste of philosophy perhaps moves one to atheism, but more of it leads back to religion' (Francis Bacon, *The Advancement of Learning, Works*, 1, eds Spedding, Ellis and Heath (London: Longman, 1857–1874), p. 436). [Editor's note.]

6 'So then because thou art lukewarm, and neither hot nor cold, I will spue thee out of my mouth' (Revelation 3:16). [Editor's note.]

7 'H' indicates that the addition was derived by Eduard Gans from a transcript of Hegel's lectures made by H. G. Hotho in 1822–3, 'G' indicates that the addition was derived from a transcript made by K. G. von Griesheim in 1824–5, and 'H,G' indicates that the addition was derived from both of these transcripts. The complete original texts of Hotho's and Griesheim's transcripts are to be found in vols 3 and 4 respectively of G. W. F. Hegel, *Vorlesungen über Rechtsphilosophie. 1818–1831*, edited by K.-H. Ilting, 4 vols (Stuttgart: Frommann-Holzboog, 1973–4). With one or two exceptions, material in square brackets in the passages from both the *Philosophy of Right* and the *Lectures on the Philosophy of World History* has been included by the translator, H. B. Nisbet. [S.H.]

25

Philosophy of Right:
Abstract Right and Morality

Abstract Right

§ 34

The will which is free in and for itself, as it is in its *abstract* concept, is in the determinate condition of *immediacy*. Accordingly, in contrast with reality, it is its own negative actuality, whose reference to itself is purely abstract – the *inherently individual* [*in sich einzelner*] will of a *subject*. In accordance with the moment of *particularity* of the will, it has in addition a content consisting of determinate ends, and as *exclusive individuality* [*Einzelheit*], it simultaneously encounters this content as an external world immediately confronting it. [A]

§ 35

The *universality* of this will which is free for itself is formal universality, i.e. the will's self-conscious (but otherwise contentless) and *simple* reference to itself in its individuality [*Einzelheit*]; to this extent, the subject is a *person*. It is inherent in *personality* that, as *this* person, I am completely determined in all respects (in my inner arbitrary will, drive, and desire, as well as in relation to my immediate external existence [*Dasein*]), and that I am finite, yet totally pure self-reference, and thus know myself in my finitude as *infinite, universal,* and *free*. [R] [A]

§ 36

Personality contains in general the capacity for right and constitutes the concept and the (itself abstract) basis of abstract and hence *formal* right. The commandment of right is therefore: *be a person and respect others as persons*.

§ 41

The person must give himself an external sphere of freedom in order to have being as Idea. The person is the infinite will, the will which has being in and for itself, in this first and as yet wholly abstract determination. Consequently, this sphere distinct from the will, which may constitute the sphere of its freedom, is likewise determined as *immediately different* and ✓ *separable* from it.

Addition: (H). The rational aspect of property is to be found not in the satisfaction of needs but in the superseding of mere subjectivity of personality. Not until he has property does the person exist as reason. Even if this first reality of my freedom is in an external thing [*Sache*] and is thus a poor kind of reality, the abstract personality in its very immediacy can have no other existence [*Dasein*] than in the determination of immediacy.

§ 42

What is immediately different from the free spirit is, for the latter and in itself, the external in general – a *thing* [*Sache*], something unfree, impersonal, and without rights. [R] [A]

§ 44

A person has the right to place his will in any thing [*Sache*]. The thing thereby becomes *mine* and acquires my will as its substantial end (since it has no such end within itself), its determination and its soul – the absolute *right of appropriation* which human beings have over all things [*Sachen*]. [R]

Addition: (H). All things [*Dinge*] can become the property of human beings, because the human being is free will and, as such, exists in and for himself, whereas that which confronts him does not have this quality. Hence everyone has the right to make his will a thing [*Sache*] or to make the thing his will, or, in other words, to supersede the thing and transform it into his own; for the thing, as externality, has no end in itself, and is not infinite self-reference but something external to itself. A living creature (the animal) is also external in this way and is to that extent itself a thing [*Sache*]. The will alone is infinite, *absolute* in relation to everything else, whereas the other, for its part, is merely *relative*. Thus to appropriate something means basically only to manifest the supremacy of my will in relation to the thing [*Sache*] and to demonstrate that the latter does not have being in and for itself and is not an end in itself. This manifestation occurs through my conferring upon the thing an end other than that which it immediately possessed; I give the living creature, as my property, a soul other than that which it previously had; I give it my soul. The free will is consequently that idealism which does not consider things [*Dinge*], as they are, to be in and for themselves, whereas realism declares them to be absolute, even if they are found only in the form of finitude. Even the animal has gone beyond this realist philosophy, for it consumes things [*Dinge*] and thereby proves that they are not absolutely self-sufficient.

§ 45

To have even external power over something constitutes *possession*, just as the particular circumstance that I make something my own out of natural need, drive and arbitrary will is the particular interest of possession. But the circumstance that I, as free will, am an object [*gegenständlich*] to myself in what I possess and only become an actual will by this means constitutes the genuine and rightful element in possession, the determination of *property.*

> *Remark*: In relation to needs – if these are taken as primary – the possession of property appears as a means; but the true position is that, from the point of view of freedom, property, as the first *existence* [*Dasein*] of freedom, is an essential end for itself.

§ 46

Since my will, as personal and hence as the will of an individual [*des Einzelnen*], becomes objective in property, the latter takes on the character of *private property*; and common property, which may by its nature be owned by separate individuals, takes on the determination of an *inherently* [*an sich*] *dissolvable* community in which it is in itself [*für sich*] a matter [*Sache*] for the arbitrary will whether or not I retain my share in it. [R] [A]

§ 47

As a person, I am myself an *immediate individual* [*Einzelner*]; in its further determination, this means in the first place that I am *alive* in this *organic body*, which is my undivided external existence [*Dasein*], *universal* in content, the real potentiality of all further-determined existence. But as a person, I at the same time possess *my life and body*, like other things [*Sachen*], only *in so far as I so will it*.

> *Remark*: [. . .] I have these limbs and my life only *in so far as I so will it*; the animal cannot mutilate or destroy itself, but the human being can.

Addition: (G). Animals are indeed in possession of themselves: their soul is in possession of their body. But they have no right to their life, because they do not will it.

§ 48

In so far as the body is immediate existence [*Dasein*] it is not commensurate with the spirit; before it can be the spirit's willing organ and soul-inspired instrument, it must first be *taken possession of* by the spirit (see § 57).[1] – But *for others*, I am essentially a free entity within my body while I am in immediate possession of it.

> *Remark*: It is only because I am alive as a free entity within my body that this living existence [*Dasein*] may not be misused as a beast of burden. In so far as I am alive, my soul (the concept and, on a higher level, the free entity) and my body are not separated; my body is the existence [*Dasein*] of freedom, and I feel through it. It is therefore only a sophistical understanding, devoid of any Idea, which can make a distinction whereby the *thing-in-itself* [*Ding an sich*], the soul, is neither touched nor affected if the *body* is abused and the *existence* [*Existenz*] of the person is subjected to the power of another. *I* can withdraw into myself from my existence [*Existenz*] and make it external to me – I can keep particular feelings outside myself and be free even if I am in chains. But this is *my* will; *for others*, I am in my body. I am *free for the other* only in so far as I am free in my *existence* [*Dasein*]: this is an identical proposition (see my *Science of Logic*, vol. I [first edition, 1812], pp. 49ff.).[2] Violence done to *my body* by others is violence done to me.
>
> Because I feel, contact with or violence to my body touches me immediately as *actual* and *present*. This constitutes the difference between personal injury and infringement of my external property; for in the latter, my will does not have this immediate presence and actuality.

§ 49

In relation to external things, the *rational* aspect is that I possess property; the *particular* aspect, however, includes subjective ends, needs, arbitrariness talents, external circumstances, etc. (see § 45). It is on these that mere possession as such depends, but this particular aspect, in this sphere of abstract personality, is not yet posited as identical with freedom. *What* and *how much* I possess is therefore purely contingent as far as right is concerned. [R]

Addition: (H). The equality which one might wish to introduce, for example, with reference to the distribution of goods would in any case be destroyed again within a short time, because all resources are dependent on diligence. But if something is impracticable, it ought not to be put into practice either. For while human beings are certainly equal, they are equal only as persons, that is, in relation to the source of their possessions. Accordingly, everyone ought to have property. If we therefore wish to speak of equality, it is this equality which we should consider. But this equality is distinct from the determination of particularity, from the question of how much I possess. In this context, it is false to maintain that justice requires everyone's property to be equal; for it requires only that everyone should have property. Particularity, in fact, is the very condition to which inequality is appropriate and in which equality would be contrary to right. It is perfectly correct that human beings often covet the goods of others; but this is precisely what is contrary to right, for right is that which remains indifferent to particularity.

Morality [*Moralität*]

§ 105

The moral point of view is the point of view of the will in so far as the latter is *infinite* not only *in itself* but also *for itself* [. . .]. This reflection of the will into itself and its identity for itself, as opposed to its being-in-itself and immediacy and the determinacies which develop within the latter, determine the *person* as a *subject*.

§ 113

The expression of the will as *subjective* or *moral* is *action*. Action contains the following determinations: (α) it must be known by me in its externality as mine; (β) its essential relation [*Beziehung*] to the concept is one of obligation; and (γ) it has an *essential* relation [*Beziehung*] to the will of others.

> *Remark*: Only with the expression of the moral will do we come to
> *action*. The *existence* [*Dasein*] which the will gives to itself in formal
> right is located in an *immediate thing* [*Sache*] and is itself immediate.
> [. . .]

§ 117

The autonomously acting will, in the ends which it pursues in relation to the existence [*Dasein*] it has before it, has an *idea* [*Vorstellung*] *of the circumstances which that existence involves*. But since, on account of this presupposition, the will is *finite*, the objective phenomenon [*gegenständliche Erscheinung*] is *contingent* for it, and may contain something other than what was present in the will's idea [*Vorstellung*] of it. It is, however, the right of the will to recognize as its *action*, and to accept *responsibility* for, only those aspects of its *deed* which it knew to be presupposed within its end, and which were present in its *purpose*. – I can be made *accountable* for a deed only if *my will was responsible* for it – *the right of knowledge*. [A]

§ 118

Furthermore, action has multiple *consequences* in so far as it is translated into external existence [*Dasein*]; for the latter, by virtue of its context in external necessity, develops in all directions. These consequences, as the [outward] *shape* whose *soul* is the *end* to which the action is directed, belong to the action as an integral part of it. But the action, as the end translated into the *external world*, is at the same time exposed to external forces which attach to it things quite different from what it is for itself, and impel it on into remote and alien consequences. The will thus has the right *to accept responsibility* only for the first set of consequences, since they alone were part of its purpose. [R]

Addition: (H). The fact that I recognize only what I had an idea [*Vorstellung*] of constitutes the transition to intention. For I can be made responsible only for what I knew of the circumstances. But necessary consequences attach themselves to every action – even if what I initiate is purely individual and immediate – and they are to that extent the universal element contained within it. It is true that I cannot foresee those consequences which might be prevented, but I must be familiar with the universal nature of the individual deed. What is at issue here is not the individual aspect but the whole, which concerns not the determinate character of the particular action but its universal nature. The transition from purpose to intention consists, then, in the fact that I ought to be aware not only of my individual action, but also of the universal which is associated with it. When it emerges in this manner, the universal is what I have willed, i.e. my *intention*.

§ 119

The external existence [*Dasein*] of an action is a varied set of connections which may be regarded as infinitely divided into *individual units* [*Einzelheiten*], and the action itself can be thought of as having *touched only one of these units in the first instance*. But the truth of the *individual* [*des Einzelnen*] is the *universal*, and the determinate character of the action for itself is not an isolated content confined to one external unit, but a *universal* content containing within itself all its various connections. The purpose, as emanating from a *thinking* agent, contains not just the individual unit, but essentially that *universal aspect* already referred to – the *intention*. [R] [A]

§ 120

The *right of intention* is that the *universal* quality of the action shall have being not only *in itself*, but shall be *known* by the agent and thus have been present all along in his subjective will; and conversely, what we may call the right of the *objectivity* of the action is the right of the action to assert itself as known and willed by the subject as a *thinking agent*.[3] [R]

§ 121

The universal quality of an action is the varied *content* of the action in general, reduced to the *simple form* of universality. But the subject, as reflected into itself and hence as a *particular* entity in relation to the particularity of the objective realm, has its own particular content in its end, and this is the soul and determinant of the action. The fact that this moment of the *particularity* of the agent is contained and implemented in the action constitutes *subjective freedom* in its more concrete determination, i.e. the *right of the subject* to find its *satisfaction in the action*. [A]

§ 122

This particular aspect gives the action its subjective *value* and *interest* for me. In contrast with this end – i.e. *the intention from the point of view of its content* – the immediate character of the action in its further content is reduced to a means. In so far as such an end is a finite one, it may in turn be reduced to a means to some further intention, and so on in an infinite progression.

§ 123

For the content of these ends, all that presents itself here is (a) formal activity itself, inasmuch as the subject *actively* commits itself to whatever it is to regard and promote as its end – for human beings wish to act in support of whatever interests them, or should interest them, as their own. (β) But the as yet abstract and formal freedom of subjectivity has a more determinate content only in its *natural subjective existence* [*Dasein*] – its needs, inclinations, passions, opinions, fancies, etc. The satisfaction of this content is *welfare* or *happiness*, both in its particular determinations and in its universal aspect – the ends of finitude in general. [R]

Addition: (H). In so far as the determinations of happiness are present and given, they are not true determinations of freedom, which is not truly present for *itself* until it has adopted the good as an end in itself. We may ask at this point whether the human being has a right to set himself ends which are not based on freedom, but solely on the fact that the subject is a living being. The fact that he is a living being is not contingent, however, but in accordance with reason, and to that extent he has a right to make his needs his end. There is nothing degrading about being alive, and we do not have the alternative of existing in a higher spirituality. It is only by raising what is present and given to a self-creating process that the higher sphere of the good is attained (although this distinction does not imply that the two aspects are incompatible).

Against Kant

§ 124

[. . .]

> *Remark*:   The right of the subject's *particularity* to find satisfaction, or – to put it differently – the right of *subjective freedom*, is the pivotal and focal point in the difference between *antiquity* and the *modern* age. This right, in its infinity, is expressed in Christianity, and it has become the universal and actual principle of a new form of the world. Its more specific shapes include love, the romantic, the eternal salvation of the individual as an end, etc.; then there are morality and conscience, followed by the other forms, some of which will come into prominence below as the principle of civil society and as moments of the political

constitution, while others appear within history at large, particularly in the history of art, the sciences and philosophy. [. . .]

§ 125

Subjectivity, with its *particular* content of *welfare*, is reflected into itself and infinite, and consequently also has reference to the universal, to the will which has being in itself. This [universal] moment, initially posited within this particularity itself, includes *the welfare of others* – or in its complete, but wholly empty determination, the welfare of *all*. The welfare of *many other* particular beings in general is thus also an essential end and right of subjectivity. But since the *universal which has being in and for itself*, as distinct from such particular [kinds of] content, has not so far been determined beyond the stage of *right*, these ends of particularity, different as they are from the universal, may be in conformity with it – but alternatively, they may not.

§ 126

My particularity, however, like that of others, is only a right at all in so far as I am *free*. It cannot therefore assert itself in contradiction to this substantial basis on which it rests; and an intention to promote my welfare and that of others – and in the latter case in particular it is called a *moral intention* – cannot justify an *action which is wrong*. [R] [A]

§ 127

The *particularity* of the interests of the natural will, taken together as a simple *totality*, is personal existence [*Dasein*] as *life*. *In extreme danger* and in collision with the rightful property of someone else, this life may claim (not in equity, but as a right) a *right of necessity* [*Notrecht*] for the alternatives are an infinite injury [*Verletzung*] to existence with total loss of rights, and an injury only to an individual and limited existence of freedom, whereby right as such and the capacity for rights of the injured party, who has been injured only in *this* specific property, continue to be recognized.

> *Remark*: From the right of necessity arises the benefit of competence, whereby a debtor is permitted to retain his tools, agricultural implements, clothes, and in general as much of his resources – i.e. of the property of his creditors – as is deemed necessary to support him, even in his accustomed station in society.

Addition: (H). Life, as the totality of ends, has a right in opposition to abstract right. If, for example, it can be preserved by stealing a loaf, this certainly constitutes an infringement of someone's property, but it would be wrong to regard such an action as common theft. If someone whose life is in danger were not allowed to take measures to save himself, he would be destined to forfeit all his rights; and since he would be deprived of life, his entire freedom would be negated. There are certainly many prerequisites for the preservation of life, and if we look to the future, we must concern ourselves with such details. But the only thing that is necessary is to live *now*; the future is not absolute, and it remains exposed to contingency. Consequently, only the necessity [*Not*] of the immediate present can justify a wrong action, because its omission would in turn involve committing a wrong – indeed the ultimate wrong, namely the total negation of the existence of freedom. The *beneficium competentiae*[4] is of relevance here, because links of kinship and other close relationships entail the right to demand that no one should be sacrificed completely for the sake of right.

§ 129

The *good* is the *Idea, as the unity of the *concept* of the will and the *particular will*, in which abstract right, welfare, the subjectivity of knowing, and the contingency of external existence [*Dasein*], as *self-sufficient for themselves*, are superseded; but they are at the same time *essentially contained* and *preserved* within it. – [The good is] *realized freedom, the absolute and ultimate end of the world*. [A]

§ 130

Within this idea, welfare has no validity for itself as the existence [*Dasein*] of the individual and particular will, but only as *universal* welfare and essentially as *universal in itself*, i.e. in accordance with freedom; welfare is not a good without *right*. Similarly, right is not the good without welfare (*fiat iustitia* should not have *pereat mundus* as its consequence).[5] Thus, since the good must necessarily be actualized through the particular will, and since it is at the same time the latter's substance, it has an *absolute right* as distinct from the abstract right of property and the particular ends of welfare. In so far as either of the latter moments is distinguished from the good, it has validity only in so far as it is in conformity with it and subordinate to it.

§ 132

The *right of the subjective will* is that whatever it is to recognize as valid should be *perceived* by it *as good*, and that it should be held responsible for an action – as its aim translated into external objectivity – as right or wrong, good or evil, legal or illegal, according to its cognizance [*Kenntnis*] of the value which that action has in this objectivity.

> *Remark*:   The *good* is in general the essence of the will in its *substantiality* and *universality* – the will in its truth; the good therefore exists without exception only *in thought* and *through thought*. Consequently, the assertion that human beings cannot know [*erkennen*] the truth, but have to do only with appearances, or that thought is harmful to the good will,

and other similar notions [*Vorstellungen*], deprive the spirit both of intellectual and of all ethical worth and dignity. – The right to recognize
nothing that I do not perceive as rational is the highest right of the
subject, but by virtue of its subjective determination, it is at the same
time *formal*; on the other hand, *the right of the rational* – as the objective
– over the subject remains firmly established. – Because of its formal
determination, insight is equally capable of being *true* and of being
mere *opinion* and *error*. From the point of view of what is still the
sphere of morality, the individual's attainment of this right of insight
depends upon his particular subjective education. I may require of
myself and regard it as an inner subjective right that my insight into an
obligation should be based on *good* reasons and that I should be *convinced* by it, and in addition, that I should recognize it in terms of its
concept and nature. But whatever I may require in order to satisfy my
conviction that an action is good, permissible, or impermissible – and
hence that the agent is in this respect responsible for it – in no way
detracts from the *right of objectivity*. [. . .]

§ 133

The relation of the good to the particular subject is that the good is the
essential character of the subject's will, which thus has an unqualified *obligation* in this connection. Because *particularity* is distinct from the good and
falls within the subjective will, the good is initially determined only as
universal abstract essentiality – i.e. as *duty*. In view of this determination, *duty*
should be done *for the sake of duty*.

Addition: (H). The essential element of the will for me is duty. Now if I know
nothing apart from the fact that the good is my duty, I do not go beyond duty in the
abstract. I should do my duty for its own sake, and it is in the true sense my own
objectivity that I bring to fulfilment in doing so. In doing my duty, I am with myself
[*bei mir selbst*] and free. The merit and exalted viewpoint of Kant's moral philosophy
are that it has emphasized this significance of duty.

§ 134

Since action for itself requires a particular content and a determinate end,
whereas duty in the abstract contains nothing of the kind, the question
arises: *what is duty?* For this definition [*Bestimmung*], all that is available so
far is this: to do *right*, and to promote *welfare*, one's own welfare and welfare
in its universal determination, the welfare of others (see § 119). [A]

§ 135

These determinations, however, are not contained in the determination of
duty itself. But since both of them are conditional and limited, they give rise

to the transition to the higher sphere of the *unconditional*, the sphere of duty. Hence all that is left for duty itself, in so far as it is the essential or universal element in the moral self-consciousness as it is related within itself to itself alone, is abstract universality, whose determination is *identity without content* or the abstractly *positive*, i.e. the indeterminate.

> Remark: However essential it may be to emphasize the pure and uncon-
> ditional self-determination of the will as the root of duty – for know-
> ledge [*Erkenntnis*] of the will first gained a firm foundation and point of
> departure in the philosophy of Kant, through the thought of its infinite
> autonomy (see § 133) – to cling on to a merely moral point of view
> without making the transition to the concept of ethics reduces this gain
> to an *empty formalism,* and moral science to an empty rhetoric of *duty
> for duty's sake*. From this point of view, no immanent theory of duties is
> possible. One may indeed bring in material *from outside* and thereby
> arrive at *particular* duties, but it is impossible to make the transition to
> the determination of particular duties from the above determination of
> duty as *absence of contradiction*, as *formal correspondence with itself*, which
> is no different from the specification of *abstract indeterminacy*; and even
> if such a particular content for action is taken into consideration, there
> is no criterion within that principle for deciding whether or not this
> content is a duty. *On the contrary*, it is possible to justify any wrong or
> immoral mode of action by this means. – Kant's further form – the
> capacity of an action to be envisaged as a *universal* maxim – does yield
> a more *concrete* representation [*Vorstellung*] of the situation in question,
> but it does not in itself [*für sich*] contain any principle apart from
> formal identity and that absence of contradiction already referred to. –
> The fact that *no property* is present is in itself [*für sich*] no more contra-
> dictory than is the non-existence of this or that individual people,
> family, etc., or the complete *absence of human life*. But if it is already
> established and presupposed that property and human life should exist
> and be respected, then it is a contradiction to commit theft or murder;
> a contradiction must be a contradiction with something, that is, with
> a content which is already fundamentally present as an established
> principle. Only to a principle of this kind does an action stand in a
> relation [*Beziehung*] of agreement or contradiction. But if a duty is to
> be willed merely as a duty and not because of its content, it is a *formal
> identity* which necessarily excludes every content and determination.
> [. . .] [A]

§ 136

Because of the abstract character of the good, the other moment of the Idea, i.e. *particularity* in general, falls within subjectivity. Subjectivity, in its universality reflected into itself, is the absolute inward certainty of itself; it is that which posits particularity, and it is the determining and decisive factor – *the conscience.* [A]

§ 137

True conscience is the disposition to will what is good *in and for itself*; it therefore has fixed principles, and these have for it the character of determinacy and duties which are objective for themselves. In contrast to its content – i.e. truth – conscience is merely the *formal aspect* of the activity of the will, which, as *this* will, has no distinctive content of its own. But the objective system of these principles and duties and the union of subjective knowledge with this system are present only when the point of view of ethics has been reached. Here, within the formal point of view of morality, conscience lacks this objective content, and is thus for itself the infinite formal certainty of itself, which for this very reason is at the same time the certainty of *this* subject.

> *Remark*: [...] The point of view of morality, which is distinguished in this treatise from that of ethics, includes only the formal conscience; the true conscience has been mentioned only in order to indicate its different character, and to prevent the possible misunderstanding to the effect that we are here discussing the true conscience rather than the formal conscience, which is in fact our exclusive concern. The true conscience is contained in the ethical disposition, which will be considered only in the following section. The religious conscience, however, lies completely outside this sphere. [A]

§ 138

This subjectivity, as abstract self-determination and pure certainty of itself alone, *evaporates* into itself all *determinate* aspects of right, duty and existence [*Dasein*], inasmuch as it is the power of *judgement* which determines solely from within itself what is good in relation to a given content, and at the same time the power to which the good, which is at first only an idea [*vorgestellt*] and an *obligation*, owes its *actuality*. [R] [A]

§ 139

Where all previously valid determinations have vanished and the will is in a state of pure inwardness, the self-consciousness is capable of making into its principle either *the universal in and for itself*, or the *arbitrariness* of its *own particularity*, giving the latter precedence over the universal and realizing it through its actions – i.e. it is capable of being *evil*.

> *Remark*: Conscience, as formal subjectivity, consists simply in the possibility of turning at any moment to *evil*; for both morality and evil have

their common root in that self-certainty which has being for itself and knows and resolves for itself. [. . .]

Addition: (H). The abstract certainty which knows itself as the basis of everything has within it the possibility of willing the universal of the concept, but also that of making a particular content into its principle and realizing this content. It follows that the abstraction of self-certainty is always a part of *evil*, which is the second of these alternatives, and that *only* the human being is good – but only in so far as he can also be evil. Good and evil are inseparable, and their inseparability derives from the fact that the concept becomes its own object [*Gegenstand*] and, as object, immediately embodies the determination of difference. The evil will wills something opposed to the universality of the will, whereas the good acts in accordance with its true concept. [. . .]

§ 140

The self-consciousness knows how to discover a *positive* aspect in its own end (see § 135); for this end, as part of the purpose of an *actual concrete* action, necessarily has a positive aspect. By virtue of this positive aspect, [which it regards] as a *duty and admirable intention*, the self-consciousness is able to assert that its action is good both *for others* and *for itself*. But because of its self-reflection and consequent awareness of the universal character of the will, it is also in a position to compare with this universal character the essentially *negative* content of its action, which is simultaneously present *within it*. To assert that this action is good for *others* is *hypocrisy*; and to assert that it is good for the self-consciousness *itself* is to go to the even greater extreme at which *subjectivity declares itself absolute*.

Remark: This last and most abstruse form of evil, whereby evil is perverted into good and good into evil and the consciousness, knowing
that it has the power to accomplish this reversal, consequently knows
itself as absolute, is the greatest extreme of subjectivity from the point
of view of morality. It is the form to which evil has advanced in our
time – thanks to philosophy, i.e. to a shallowness of thought which has
twisted a profound concept into this shape and has presumed to call
itself philosophy, just as it has presumed to call evil good. [. . .] The
supreme form in which this subjectivity is completely comprehended
and expressed is that to which the term 'irony', borrowed from Plato,
has been applied. Only the name is taken from Plato, however, for
Plato used it of a method which Socrates employed in personal dialogue to defend the Idea of truth and justice against the complacency
of the uneducated consciousness and that of the Sophists; but it was
only this consciousness which he treated ironically, not the Idea itself.
Irony concerns only a manner of speaking in relation to *people*; without
this personal direction, the essential movement of thought is dialectic,

and Plato was so far from treating the dialectic in itself [*für sich*], let alone irony, as the ultimate factor and as the Idea itself that, on the contrary, he ended the to and fro of thought, and particularly of sub- jective opinion, by submerging it in the substantiality of the Idea. The only possible culmination – and this must now be discussed – of that subjectivity which regards itself as the ultimate instance is reached when it *knows* itself as that power of resolution and decision on [mat- ters of] truth, and duty which is already implicitly [*an sich*] present within the preceding forms. Thus, it does indeed consist in knowledge of the objective side of ethics, but without that self-forgetfulness and self-renunciation which seriously immerses itself in this objectivity and makes it the basis of its action. Although it has a relation [*Beziehung*] to this objectivity, it at the same time distances itself from it and knows *itself* as that which *wills* and *resolves in a particular way* but may *equally well* will and resolve otherwise. – 'You in fact honestly accept a law as existing in and for itself' [it says to others]; 'I do so, too, but I go further than you, for I am also beyond this law and can do *this or that* as I please. It is not the thing [*Sache*] which is excellent, it is I who am excellent and master of both law and thing; I *merely play* with them as with my own caprice, and in this ironic consciousness in which I let the highest of things perish, I *merely enjoy myself.*' – In this shape, subjectiv- ity is not only *empty* of all ethical *content* [*die Eitelkeit alles sittlichen Inhalts*] in the way of rights, duties, and laws, and is accordingly evil (evil, in fact, of an inherently wholly universal kind); in addition, its form is that of *subjective* emptiness [*Eitelkeit*], in that it knows itself as this emptiness of all content and, in this knowledge, knows *itself* as the absolute. [. . .]

Addition: (H). Representational thought [*Vorstellung*] can go further and transform the evil will into a semblance of goodness. Even if it cannot alter the nature of evil, it can nevertheless make it appear to be good. For every action has a positive aspect, and since the determination of good as opposed to evil can likewise be reduced to the positive, I can maintain that my action is good with reference to my intention. Thus, evil is connected with good not only within the consciousness, but also in its positive aspect. If the self-consciousness passes its action off as good only for the benefit of other people, it takes the form of *hypocrisy*; but if it is able to assert that the deed is good in its own estimation, too, we have reached that even higher level of subjectivity which knows itself as absolute. For subjectivity of this kind, good and evil in and for themselves have disappeared, and it can pass off as good or evil whatever its wishes and its ability dictate. This is the point of view of absolute sophistry which sets itself up as a legislator and refers the distinction between good and evil to its own arbitrary will. As for hypocrisy, this includes above all those religious hypocrites (or Tartuffes) who comply with all ceremonial requirements and may even be pious in themselves [*für sich*], while at the same time doing whatever they please. Nowadays, there is no longer much talk of hypocrites, partly because this accusation appears too harsh, and partly because hypocrisy in its immediate shape has more or less disappeared. This barefaced lie and cloak of goodness has now become too transparent not to be seen through, and the distinction between doing good on the one hand and evil on the other is no longer present to the same extent since increasing education has made such antithetical determinations seem less clear-cut. Instead, hypocrisy has now assumed the subtler guise [*Gestalt*] of *probabilism*, which consists in the attempt to represent a transgression as something good from the point of view of one's own conscience. This can only occur where morality and goodness are determined by an authority, so that there are as many reasons as there are authorities for maintaining that evil is good. Casuistic theologians, especially Jesuits, have worked on these cases of conscience and endlessly multiplied them.

As these cases are refined to the highest pitch of subtlety, numerous collisions arise, and the antithesis of good and evil becomes so blurred that, in individual instances, the opposite poles prove interchangeable. All that is asked for is *probability*, that is, an approximation to goodness which can be substantiated by some reason or by some authority. Thus, this point of view has the peculiar determination of possessing only an abstract content; the concrete content is presented as inessential – or rather, it is allowed to depend on mere opinion. In this way, someone may have committed a crime while willing the good. If, for example, an evil man is murdered, the assertion that the murderer wished to resist evil and to diminish it can be passed off as the positive aspect [of the deed]. The next step beyond probabilism is that it is no longer someone else's authority or assertion that counts, but the subject itself, i.e. its *own* conviction, which can *alone* make something good. The inadequacy of this is that everything is made to refer solely to conviction, and that there is no longer any right which has being in and for itself, a right for which this conviction would merely be the form. It is not, of course, a matter of indifference whether I do something from habit or custom or because I am thoroughly persuaded of its truth. But objective truth is also different from my conviction, for the latter makes no distinction whatsoever between good and evil; conviction always remains conviction, and the bad can only be that of which I am not convinced. While this point of view is that of a supreme instance which obliterates good and evil, it at the same time acknowledges that it is subject to error, and to this extent, it is brought down from its exalted position and again becomes contingent and appears to deserve no respect. Now this form is *irony*, the consciousness that such a principle of conviction is of little value and that, within this supreme criterion, only arbitrariness prevails. This point of view was in fact a product of Fichte's philosophy, which maintains that the 'I' is absolute, i.e. that it is absolute certainty, the universal selfhood [*Ichheit*] whose further development leads to objectivity. It cannot in fact be said of Fichte that he made the arbitrary will of the subject into a principle in the practical sphere, but this [principle of the] particular, in the sense of Friedrich von Schlegel's 'particular selfhood', was itself later elevated to divine status in relation to the good and the beautiful. This implies that objective goodness is merely something constructed by my conviction, sustained by me alone, and that I, as lord and master, can make it come and go [as I please]. As soon as I relate myself to something objective, it ceases to exist for me, and so I am poised above an immense void, conjuring up shapes and destroying them. This supremely subjective point of view can arise only in a highly cultivated age in which faith has lost its seriousness, which now exists essentially only in the vanity of all things.

§ 141

For the *good* as the substantial universal of freedom, but still as something *abstract*, determinations of some kind are therefore *required*, as is a determining principle (although this principle is *identical* with the good itself). For the *conscience* likewise, as the purely abstract principle of determination, it is required that its determinations should be universal and objective. Both of them [i.e. the good and the conscience], if raised in this way to independent totalities [*für sich zur Totalität*], become the indeterminate which *ought* to be determined. – But the integration of these two relative totalities into absolute identity has already been accomplished *in itself*, since this very subjectivity of *pure self-certainty*, melting away for itself in its emptiness, is *identical* with the *abstract universality* of the good: the identity – which is accordingly *concrete* – of the good and the subjective will, the truth of them both, is *ethical life*. [R] [A]

Notes

1 Paragraph not included in this collection. [S.H.]
2 See also Hegel, *Science of Logic*, pp. 117–22. See above pp. 198–201. [S.H.]
3 My purpose, for Hegel, is the immediate act I propose to carry out (e.g. building a house or driving a car). My intention is the *kind* of action (the 'universal') I take my proposed act to be (e.g. one with broadly beneficial or broadly deleterious consequences). The right of intention is thus the right only to be held responsible for the particular kind of action I take my act to be (for the *particular universal* that I will). The right of objectivity is the corresponding 'right of the action' to be understood properly as the kind of action it actually is. The right of objectivity thus requires that I be held responsible, not just for what I myself intend through my act, but for what I, as rational agent, *should* recognize to be my act's general consequences. In the following paragraphs Hegel seeks to reconcile the demands of subjective particularity and of rational understanding, by claiming (*a*) that we all have the right to fulfil our own particular intentions through our actions and gain satisfaction thereby (§ 121), but (*b*) that we must in turn recognize the right of others to gain satisfaction for themselves and that we must also respect the demands of right as such (§§ 125, 126). [S.H.]
4 'Beneficence of need'. Under certain provisions deriving from Roman law, a debtor or unsuccessful defendant in a civil action could not be required to pay more than his means permitted; for example, he could not be deprived of the tools necessary to ply his trade. [Editor's (i.e. A. Wood's) note.]
5 The Latin saying which Hegel splits into two parts means roughly: 'Let justice be done, even if the world should perish'. [Translator's note.]

26

Philosophy of Right: Ethical Life

§ 142

Ethical life [*Sittlichkeit*] is the *Idea of freedom* as the living good which has its knowledge and volition in self-consciousness, and its actuality through self-conscious action. Similarly, it is in ethical being that self-consciousness has its motivating end and a foundation which has being in and for itself. Ethical life is accordingly the *concept of freedom which has become the existing* [*vorhandenen*] *world and the nature of self-consciousness.*

§ 144

(a) The objective sphere of ethics, which takes the place of the abstract good, is substance made *concrete* by subjectivity *as infinite form*. It therefore posits *distinctions* within itself which are thus determined by the concept. These distinctions give the ethical a fixed *content* which is necessary for itself, and whose existence [*Bestehen*] is exalted above subjective opinions and preferences: they are *laws and institutions which have being in and for themselves*. [A]

§ 145

The fact that the ethical sphere is the *system* of these determinations of the Idea constitutes its *rationality*. In this way, the ethical sphere is freedom, or the will which has being in and for itself as objectivity, as a circle of necessity whose moments are the *ethical powers* which govern the lives of individuals. In these individuals – who are accidental to them – these powers have their representation [*Vorstellung*], phenomenal shape [*erscheinende Gestalt*], and actuality. [A]

§ 146

(β) In this *actual self-consciousness* [which it now possesses], the substance knows itself and is thus an object [*Objekt*] of knowledge. In relation to the subject, the ethical substance and its laws and powers are on the one hand an object [*Gegenstand*], inasmuch as *they are*, in the supreme sense of self-sufficiency. They are thus an absolute authority and power, infinitely more firmly based than the being of nature. [R]

§ 147

On the other hand, they are not something *alien* to the subject. On the contrary, the subject bears *spiritual witness* to them as to *its own essence*, in which it has its *self-awareness* [*Selbstgefühl*] and lives as in its element which is not distinct from itself – a relationship which is immediate and closer to identity than even [a relationship of] *faith* or *trust*. [R]

§ 148

All these substantial determinations are *duties* which are binding on the will of the individual; for the individual, as subjective and inherently undetermined – or determined in a particular way – is distinct from them and *consequently stands in a relationship to them* as to his own substantial being. [R]

§ 149

A binding duty can appear as a *limitation* only in relation to indeterminate subjectivity or abstract freedom, and to the drives of the natural will or of the moral will which arbitrarily determines its own indeterminate good. The individual, however, finds his *liberation* in duty. On the one hand, he is liberated from his dependence on mere natural drives, and from the burden he labours under as a particular subject in his moral reflections on obligation and desire; and on the other hand, he is liberated from that indeterminate subjectivity which does not attain existence [*Dasein*] or the objective determinacy of action, but remains *within itself* and has no actuality. In duty, the individual liberates himself so as to attain substantial freedom.

Addition: (H). Duty places limits only on the arbitrary will of subjectivity and clashes only with that abstract good to which subjectivity clings. When people say that they want to be free, this means primarily only that they want to be free in an abstract sense, and every determination and division [*Gliederung*] within the state is regarded as a limitation of that freedom. To this extent, duty is not a limitation of freedom, but only of freedom in the abstract, that is, of unfreedom: it is the attainment of essential being, the acquisition of affirmative freedom.

§ 150

The ethical, in so far as it is reflected in the naturally determined character of the individual as such, is *virtue*; and in so far as virtue represents nothing

more than the simple adequacy of the individual to the duties of the circumstances [*Verhältnisse*] to which he belongs, it is *rectitude*.

> *Remark*:   In an ethical community, it is easy to say *what* someone must
> do and *what* the duties are which he has to fulfil in order to be virtu-
> ous. He must simply do what is prescribed, expressly stated, and known
> to him within his situation. Rectitude is the universal quality which
> may be required of him, partly by right and partly by ethics. But from
> the point of view of morality, rectitude can easily appear as something
> of a lower order, beyond which one must impose further demands on
> oneself and others. For the craving to be something *special* [*Besonderes*]
> is not satisfied with the universal, with what has being in and for itself;
> only in the *exceptional* does it attain consciousness of its distinctiveness.
> [. . .] [A]

§ 151

But if it is simply *identical* with the actuality of individuals, the ethical [*das
Sittliche*], as their general mode of behaviour, appears as *custom* [*Sitte*]; and
the *habit* of the ethical appears as a *second nature* which takes the place of the
original and purely natural will and is the all-pervading soul, significance, and
actuality of individual existence [*Dasein*]. It is *spirit* living and present as a
world, and only thus does the substance of spirit begin to exist as spirit. [A]

§ 152

In this way, *ethical substantiality* has attained its *right*, and the latter has
attained *validity*. That is, the self-will of the individual [*des Einzelnen*], and
his own conscience in its attempt to exist for itself and in opposition to the
ethical substantiality, have disappeared; for the ethical character knows that
the end which moves it is the universal which, though itself unmoved, has
developed through its determinations into actual rationality, and it recognizes that its own dignity and the whole continued existence [*Bestehen*] of its
particular ends are based upon and actualized within this universal. Subjectivity is itself the absolute form and existent actuality of substance, and the
difference between the subject on the one hand and substance as its object
[*Gegenstand*], end, and power on the other is the same as their difference in
form, both of which differences have disappeared with equal immediacy. [R]

§ 153

The *right of individuals* to their *subjective determination to freedom* is fulfilled
in so far as they belong to ethical actuality; for their *certainty* of their own
freedom has its *truth* in such objectivity, and it is in the ethical realm that
they *actually* possess *their own* essence and their *inner* universality (see § 147).

Remark: When a father asked him for advice about the best way of educating his son in ethical matters, a Pythagorean replied: 'Make him the *citizen of a state with good laws*.' (This saying has also been attributed to others.)

Addition: (H). Those pedagogical experiments in removing people from the ordinary life of the present and bringing them up in the country (cf. Rousseau's *Emile*) have been futile, because one cannot successfully isolate people from the laws of the world. Even if young people have to be educated in solitude, no one should imagine that the breath of the spiritual world will not eventually find its way into this solitude and that the power of the world spirit is too weak for it to gain control of such remote regions. The individual attains his right only by becoming the citizen of a good state.

§ 154

The right of individuals to their *particularity* is likewise contained in ethical substantiality, for particularity is the mode of outward appearance in which the ethical exists.

§ 155

Hence *duty* and *right* coincide in this identity of the universal and the particular will, and in the ethical realm, a human being has rights in so far as he has duties, and duties in so far as he has rights. In abstract right, I have the right and someone else has the corresponding duty; and in morality, it is merely an *obligation* that the right of my own knowledge and volition, and of my welfare, should be united with my duties and exist objectively. [A]

§ 156

The ethical substance, as containing self-consciousness which has being for itself and is united with its concept, is the *actual spirit* of a family and a people. [A]

Section 1: The Family

§ 158

The family, as the *immediate substantiality* of spirit, has as its determination the spirit's *feeling* [*Empfindung*] of its own unity, which is *love*. Thus, the disposition [appropriate to the family] is to have self-consciousness of one's individuality *within this unity* as essentiality which has being in and for itself, so that one is present in it not as an independent person [*eine Person für sich*] but as a *member*.

Addition: (H,G). Love means in general the consciousness of my unity with another, so that I am not isolated on my own [*für mich*], but gain my self-consciousness only through the renunciation of my independent existence [*meines Fürsichseins*] and through knowing myself as the unity of myself with another and of the other with me. But love is a feeling [*Empfindung*], that is, ethical life in its natural form. In the state, it is no longer present. There, one is conscious of unity as law; there, the content must be rational, and I must know it. The first moment in love is that I do not wish to be an independent person in my own right [*für mich*] and that, if I were, I would feel deficient and incomplete. The second moment is that I find myself in another person, that I gain recognition in this person [*daß ich in ihr gelte*], who in turn gains recognition in me. Love is therefore the most immense contradiction; the understanding cannot resolve it, because there is nothing more intractable than this punctiliousness of the self-consciousness which is negated and which I ought nevertheless to possess as affirmative. Love is both the production and the resolution of this contradiction. As its resolution, it is ethical unity.

§ 161

Marriage, as the *immediate ethical relationship*, contains *first* the moment of *natural* vitality; and since it is a substantial relationship, this involves life in its totality, namely as the actuality of the *species* [*Gattung*] and its process. [. . .] But *secondly*, in self-consciousness, the *union* of the natural sexes, which was merely *inward* (or had being only *in itself*) and whose existence [*Existenz*] was for this very reason merely external, is transformed into a *spiritual* union, into self-conscious love.

Addition: (G). Marriage is essentially an ethical relationship. Formerly, especially under most systems of natural law, it was considered only in its physical aspect or natural character. It was accordingly regarded only as a sexual relationship, and its other determinations remained completely inaccessible. But it is equally crude to interpret marriage merely as a civil contract, a notion [*Vorstellung*] which is still to be found even in Kant.[1] On this interpretation, marriage gives contractual form to the arbitrary relations between individuals, and is thus debased to a contract entitling the parties concerned to use one another. A third and equally unacceptable notion is that which simply equates marriage with love; for love, as a feeling [*Empfindung*], is open in all respects to contingency, and this is a shape which the ethical may not assume. Marriage should therefore be defined more precisely as rightfully ethical [*rechtlich sittliche*] love, so that the transient, capricious and purely subjective aspects of love are excluded from it.

§ 181

The family disintegrates, in a natural manner and essentially through the principle of personality, into a *plurality* of families whose relation to one another is in general that of self-sufficient concrete persons and consequently of an external kind. In other words, the moments which are bound together in the unity of the family, as the ethical Idea which is still in its concept, must be released from the concept to [attain] self-sufficient reality. This is the stage of *difference* [*Differenz*]. To put it first in abstract terms, this gives the determination of *particularity* which is related to *universality*, but in such a way that the latter is its basis – though still only its *inner* basis; consequently, this universality is present only as a formal *appearance* in the particular [*auf formelle, in das Besondere nur scheinende Weise*]. This relation of reflection accordingly represents in the first instance the loss of ethical life; or, since the latter, as the essence, necessarily *appears* [. . .], this relation constitutes the *world of appearance* of the ethical, i.e. *civil society*. [R] [A]

Section 2: Civil Society

§ 182

The concrete person who, as a *particular* person, as a totality of needs and a mixture of natural necessity and arbitrariness, is his own end, is *one principle* of civil society. But this particular person stands essentially in *relation* [*Beziehung*] to other similar particulars, and their relation is such that each asserts itself and gains satisfaction through the others, and thus at the same time through the exclusive *mediation* of the form of *universality*, which is *the second principle*.

Addition: (H,G). Civil society is the [stage of] difference [*Differenz*] which intervenes between the family and the state, even if its full development [*Ausbildung*] occurs later than that of the state; for as difference, it presupposes the state, which it must have before it as a self-sufficient entity in order to subsist [*bestehen*] itself. Besides, the creation of civil society belongs to the modern world, which for the first time allows all determinations of the Idea to attain their rights. If the state is represented as a unity of different persons, as a unity which is merely a community [of interests], this applies only to the determination of civil society. Many modern exponents of constitutional law have been unable to offer any view of the state but this. In civil society, each individual is his own end, and all else means nothing to him. But he cannot accomplish the full extent of his ends without reference to others; these others are therefore means to the end of the particular [person]. But through its reference to others, the particular end takes on the form of universality, and gains satisfaction by simultaneously satisfying the welfare of others. Since particularity is tied to the condition of universality, the whole [of civil society] is the sphere [*Boden*] of mediation in which all individual characteristics [*Einzelheiten*], all aptitudes, and all accidents of birth and fortune are liberated, and where the waves of all passions surge forth, governed only by the reason which shines through them. Particularity, limited by universality, is the only standard by which each particular [person] promotes his welfare.

§ 183

The selfish end in its actualization, conditioned in this way by universality, establishes a system of all-round interdependence, so that the subsistence

[*Subsistenz*] and welfare of the individual [*des Einzelnen*] and his rightful existence [*Dasein*] are interwoven with, and grounded on, the subsistence, welfare and rights of all, and have actuality and security only in this context. – One may regard this system in the first instance as the *external state*, the *state of necessity* and *of the understanding*.[2]

§ 187

Individuals, as citizens of this state, are *private persons* who have their own interest as their end. Since this end is mediated through the universal, which thus *appears* to the individuals as a *means*, they can attain their end only in so far as they themselves determine their knowledge, volition and action in a universal way and make themselves *links* in the chain of this *continuum* [*Zusammenhang*]. In this situation, the interest of the Idea, which is not present in the consciousness of these members of civil society as such, is the *process* whereby their individuality [*Einzelheit*] and naturalness are raised, both by natural necessity and by their arbitrary needs, *to formal freedom* and formal *universality of knowledge and volition*, and subjectivity is *educated* in its particularity. [R] [A]

A. The System of Needs

§ 189

Particularity, in its primary determination as that which is opposed to the universal of the will in general (see § 6),[3] is *subjective need*, which attains its objectivity, i.e. its *satisfaction*, by means of (α) external things [*Dinge*], which are likewise the *property* and product of the needs and *wills* of others and of (β) activity and work, as the mediation between the two aspects. The end of subjective need is the satisfaction of subjective *particularity*, but in the relation [*Beziehung*] between this and the needs and free arbitrary will of others, *universality* asserts itself, and the resultant manifestation [*Scheinen*] of rationality in the sphere of finitude is *the understanding*. This is the chief aspect which must be considered here, and which itself constitutes the conciliatory element within this sphere. [R]

Addition: (H,G). There are certain universal needs, such as food, drink, clothing, etc., and how these are satisfied depends entirely on contingent circumstances. The soil is more or less fertile in different places, the years are more or less productive, one man is industrious and the other lazy. But this proliferation of arbitrariness generates universal determinations from within itself, and this apparently scattered and thoughtless activity is subject to a necessity which arises of its own accord. To discover the necessity at work here is the object [*Gegenstand*] of political economy, a science which does credit to thought because it finds the laws underlying a mass of contingent occurrences. It is an interesting spectacle to observe here how all the interconnections have repercussions on others, how the particular spheres fall into groups, influence others, and are helped or hindered by these. This interaction, which is at first sight incredible since everything seems to depend on the arbitrary will of the individual [*des Einzelnen*], is particularly worthy of note; it bears a resemblance to the planetary system, which presents only irregular movements to the eye, yet whose laws can nevertheless be recognized.

a. The nature of needs and their satisfaction

§ 190

The ways and means by which the *animal* can satisfy its needs are limited in scope, and its needs are likewise limited. Though sharing this dependence, the *human being* is at the same time able to transcend it and to show his universality, first by *multiplying* his needs and means [of satisfying them], and secondly by *dividing* and *differentiating* the concrete need into individual parts and aspects which then become different needs, *particularized* and hence *more abstract*.

> Remark: In right, the object [*Gegenstand*] is the *person*; at the level of morality, it is the *subject*, in the family, the *family-member*, and in civil society in general, the *citizen* (in the sense of *bourgeois*). Here, at the level of needs [. . .], it is that concretum *of representational thought* which we call *the human being*; this is the first, and in fact the only occasion on which we shall refer to *the human being* in this sense.

Addition: (H). The animal is a particular entity [*ein Partikulares*] which has its instinct and the means of satisfying it, means whose bounds cannot be exceeded. There are insects which are tied to a specific plant, and other animals whose sphere is wider and which can live in different climates; but there is always a limiting factor in comparison with the sphere which is open to the human being. The need for food and clothing, the necessity of renouncing raw food and of making it fit to eat and destroying its natural immediacy, means that the human being's life is less comfortable than that of the animal – as indeed it ought to be, since man is a spiritual being. The understanding, which can grasp distinctions, brings multiplicity into these needs; and since taste and utility become criteria of judgement, the needs themselves are also affected by them. In the end, it is no longer need but opinion which has to be satisfied, and it is a distinctive feature of education that it resolves the concrete into its particulars. The very multiplication of needs has a restraining influence on desire, for if people make use of many things, the pressure to obtain any one of these which they might need is less strong, and this is a sign that necessity [*die Not*] in general is less powerful.

§ 191

In the same way, the *means* employed by particularized needs, and in general the ways in which these are satisfied, are *divided* and *multiplied* so that they in turn become relative ends and abstract needs. It is an infinite process of multiplication which is in equal measure a *differentiation* of these determinations and a *judgement* on the suitability of the means to their ends – i.e. [a process of] *refinement*.

Addition: (H). What the English call 'comfortable' is something utterly inexhaustible; its ramifications are infinite, for every comfort in turn reveals its less comfortable side, and the resulting inventions are endless. A need is therefore created not so much by those who experience it directly as by those who seek to profit from its emergence.

§ 192

Needs and means, as existing in reality [*als reelles Dasein*], become a *being* [*Sein*] for *others* by whose needs and work their satisfaction is mutually conditioned. That abstraction which becomes a quality of both needs and means (see § 191) also becomes a determination of the mutual relations [*Beziehung*] between individuals. This universality, as the *quality of being recognized*, is the moment which makes isolated and abstract needs, means, and modes of satisfaction into *concrete*, i.e. *social* ones. [A]

§ 193

This moment thus becomes a particular end-determinant for the means themselves and their ownership, and also for the way in which needs are satisfied. In addition, it immediately involves the requirement of *equality* in this respect with others. On the one hand, the need for this equality, together with *imitation* as the process whereby people make themselves like others, and on the other hand the need of *particularity* (which is likewise present here) to assert itself through some distinctive quality, themselves become an actual source of the multiplication and expansion of needs.

§ 194

Within social needs, as a combination of immediate or natural needs and the spiritual needs of *representational thought* [*Vorstellung*], the spiritual needs, as the universal, predominate. This social moment accordingly contains the aspect of *liberation*, because the strict natural necessity of need is concealed and man's relation is to *his own opinion*, which is universal, and to a necessity imposed by himself alone, instead of simply to an external necessity, to inner contingency, and to *arbitrariness*. [R]

§ 195

This liberation is *formal*, because the particularity of the ends remains the basic content. The tendency of the social condition towards an indeterminate multiplication and specification of needs, means, and pleasures – i.e. *luxury* – a tendency which, like the distinction between natural and educated[4] needs, has no limits [*Grenzen*], involves an equally infinite increase in dependence and want. These are confronted with a material which offers infinite resistance, i.e. with external means whose particular character is that they are the property of the free will [of others] and are therefore absolutely unyielding. [A]

b. The nature of work

§ 196

The mediation whereby appropriate and *particularized* means are acquired and prepared for similarly *particularized* needs is *work*. By the most diverse processes, work specifically applies to these numerous ends the material which is immediately provided by nature. This process of formation gives the means their value and appropriateness, so that man, as a consumer, is chiefly concerned with *human* products, and it is human effort which he consumes. [A]

§ 197

The variety of determinations and objects [*Gegenstände*] which are worthy of interest is the basis from which *theoretical education* develops. This involves not only a variety of representations [*Vorstellungen*] and items of knowledge [*Kenntnissen*], but also an ability to form such representations [*des Vorstellens*] and pass from one to the other in a rapid and versatile manner, to grasp complex and general relations [*Beziehungen*], etc. – it is the education of the understanding in general, and therefore also includes language. – *Practical education* through work consists in the self-perpetuating need and *habit of being occupied* in one way or another, in the *limitation of one's activity* to suit both the nature of the material in question and, in particular, the arbitrary will of others, and in a habit, acquired through this discipline, of *objective* activity and *universally applicable* skills. [A]

§ 198

The universal and objective aspect of work consists, however, in that [process of] *abstraction* which confers a specific character on means and needs and hence also on production, so giving rise to the *division of labour*. Through this division, the work of the individual [*des Einzelnen*] becomes *simpler*, so that his skill at his abstract work becomes greater, as does the volume of his output. At the same time, this abstraction of skill and means makes the *dependence* and *reciprocity* of human beings in the satisfaction of their other needs complete and entirely necessary. Furthermore, the abstraction of production makes work increasingly *mechanical*, so that the human being is eventually able to step aside and let a *machine* take his place.

c. Resources [and estates]

§ 199

In this dependence and reciprocity of work and the satisfaction of needs, *subjective selfishness* turns into a *contribution towards the satisfaction of the needs of everyone else.* By a dialectical movement, the particular is mediated by the universal so that each individual, in earning, producing, and enjoying on his own account [*für sich*], thereby earns and produces for the enjoyment of others. This necessity which is inherent in the interlinked dependence of each on all now appears to each individual in the form of *universal and permanent resources* (see § 170)[5] in which, through his education and skill, he has an opportunity to share; he is thereby assured of his livelihood, just as the universal resources are maintained and augmented by the income which he earns through his work.

§ 200

The *possibility of sharing* in the universal resources – i.e. of holding *particular resources* – is, however, *conditional* upon one's own immediate basic assets (i.e. capital) on the one hand, and upon one's skill on the other; the latter in turn is itself conditioned by the former, but also by contingent circumstances whose variety gives rise to *differences* in the *development* of natural physical and mental [*geistigen*] aptitudes which are already unequal in themselves [*für sich*]. In this sphere of particularity, these differences manifest themselves in every direction and at every level, and, in conjunction with other contingent and arbitrary circumstances, necessarily result in *inequalities in the resources and skills* of individuals. [R]

§ 201

The infinitely varied means and their equally infinite and intertwined movements of reciprocal production and exchange *converge*, by virtue of the universality inherent in their content, and become *differentiated* into *universal masses.* In consequence, the whole complex [*Zusammenhang*] evolves into *particular systems* of needs, with their corresponding means, varieties of work, modes of satisfaction, and theoretical and practical education – into systems to which individuals are separately assigned, i.e. into different *estates* [*Stände*].

Addition: (H). The manner in which the universal resources are shared depends on every particular characteristic of the individuals concerned; but the universal differences into which civil society is particularized are necessary in character. While the family is the primary basis of the state, the estates are the second. The latter are of special importance, because private persons, despite their selfishness, find it necessary to have recourse to others. This is accordingly the root which links selfishness with the universal, i.e. with the state, which must take care to ensure that this connection is a firm and solid one.

§ 202

The estates are determined, in accordance with *the concept*, as the *substantial* or immediate estate, the reflecting or *formal* estate, and lastly, the *universal* estate.

§ 203

(a) The *substantial* estate has its resources in the natural products of the *soil* which it cultivates – soil which is capable of being exclusively private property, and which requires not just indeterminate exploitation, but formation of an objective kind. Given the association of work and acquisition with fixed *individual* seasons, and the dependence of the yield on the varying character of natural processes, the end to which need is directed in this case becomes that of *provision* for the future. But because of the conditions to which it is subject, this provision retains the character of a [mode of] subsistence [*Subsistenz*] in which reflection and the will of the individual play a lesser role, and thus its substantial disposition in general is that of an immediate ethical life based on the family relationship and on trust.

> *Remark*: The proper beginning and original foundation of states has rightly been equated with the introduction of *agriculture* and of *marriage*. For the former principle brings with it the cultivation of the soil, and in consequence exclusively private property (cf. Remark to § 170),[6] and it reduces the nomadic life of savages, who seek their livelihood in constant movement, to the tranquillity of civil law [*Privatrecht*] and the secure satisfaction of needs. This is accompanied by the restriction [*Beschränkung*] of sexual love to marriage, and the marriage bond is in turn extended to become a *lasting* and inherently [*in sich*] universal union, while need becomes *care for the family* and possession becomes *family property*. Security, consolidation, lasting satisfaction of needs, etc. – qualities by which these institutions primarily recommend themselves – are nothing but forms of universality and shapes assumed by rationality, the absolute and ultimate end, as it asserts itself in these objects [*Gegenständen*]. [...]

Addition: (H). In our times, the [agricultural] economy, too, is run in a reflective manner, like a factory, and it accordingly takes on a character like that of the second estate and opposed to its own character of naturalness. Nevertheless, this first estate will always retain the patriarchal way of life and the substantial disposition associated with it. The human being reacts here with immediate feeling [*Empfindung*] as he accepts what he receives; he thanks God for it and lives in faith and confidence that this goodness will continue. What he receives is enough for him; he uses it up, for it will be replenished. This is a simple disposition which is not concerned with the acquisition of wealth; it may also be described as that of the *old nobility*, which consumed whatever it had. In this estate, the main part is played by nature, and human industry is subordinate to it. In the second estate, however, it is the understanding itself which is essential, and the products of nature can be regarded only as raw materials.

§ 204

(b) The *estate of trade and industry* [*Stand des Gewerbes*] has the task of *giving form* to natural products, and it relies for its livelihood on its *work*, on *reflection* and the understanding, and essentially on its mediation of the needs and work of others. What it produces and enjoys, it owes chiefly to *itself* and to its own activity. – Its business is in turn subdivided into work performed in a relatively concrete manner in response to individual [*einzelne*] needs and at the request of individuals [*Einzelner*] (*the estate of craftsmanship*); more abstract work of mass production which supplies individual needs but is more universally in demand (*the estate of manufacturers*); and the business of exchanging separate commodities [*Mittel*] for one another, chiefly through the universal means of exchange, namely money, in which the abstract value of all goods is actualized (*the estate of commerce*).

Addition: (H). In the estate of trade and industry, the individual [*Individuum*] has to rely on himself, and this feeling of selfhood is intimately connected with the demand for a condition in which right is upheld. The sense of freedom and order has therefore arisen mainly in towns. The first estate, on the other hand, has little need to think for itself:[7] what it gains is an alien gift, a gift of nature. This feeling of dependence is fundamental to it, and may easily be coupled with a willingness to accept whatever may befall it at the hands of other people. The first estate is therefore more inclined to subservience, the second estate to freedom.

§ 205

(c) The *universal estate* has *the universal interests* of society as its business. It must therefore be exempted from work for the direct satisfaction of its needs, either by having private resources, or by receiving an indemnity from the state which calls upon its services, so that the private interest is satisfied through working for the universal.

§ 206

On the one hand, the *estates*, as particularity become objective to itself, are divided in this way into different general categories in accordance with the concept. But on the other hand, the question of which particular estate the *individual* will belong to is influenced by his natural disposition, birth and circumstances, although the ultimate and essential determinant is *subjective opinion* and the *particular arbitrary will*, which are accorded their right, their merit, and their honour in this sphere. Thus, *what* happens in this sphere through *inner necessity* is at the same time *mediated by the arbitrary will*, and for the subjective consciousness, it has the shape of being the product of its own will.

> *Remark*: In this respect, too, in relation to the principle of particularity and subjective arbitrariness, a difference emerges between the political life of east and west, and of the ancient and modern worlds. In the former, the division of the whole into estates came about *objectively and of its own accord*, because it is rational *in itself*; but the principle of subjective particularity was at the same time denied its rights, as when, for example, the allocation of individuals to specific estates was left to the rulers, as in Plato's *Republic* [. . .] (415 a–d), or to birth *alone*, as in the *Indian caste-system*. [. . .]

§ 207

The individual attains actuality only by entering into *existence* [*Dasein*] in general, and hence into *determinate particularity*; he must accordingly limit himself *exclusively* to one of the *particular* spheres of need. The ethical disposition within this system is therefore that of *rectitude* and the *honour of one's estate*, so that each individual, by a process of self-determination, makes himself a member of one of the moments of civil society through his activity, diligence and skill, and supports himself in this capacity; and only through this mediation with the universal does he simultaneously provide for himself and gain *recognition* in his own eyes [*Vorstellung*] and in the eyes of others. – *Morality* has its proper place in this sphere, where reflection on one's own actions and the ends of welfare and of particular needs are dominant, and where contingency in the satisfaction of the latter makes even contingent and individual help into a duty. [R]

Addition: (H). When we say that a human being must be *somebody* [*etwas*], we mean that he must belong to a particular estate; for being somebody means that he has substantial being. A human being with no estate is merely a private person and does not possess actual universality. On the other hand, the individual [*der Einzelne*] in his particularity may see himself as the universal and believe that he would be lowering himself if he became a member of an estate. This is the false notion [*Vorstellung*] that, if something attains an existence [*Dasein*] which is necessary to it, it is thereby limiting and surrendering itself.

C. The Police and the Corporation

§ 230

In the *system of needs*, the livelihood and welfare of each individual [*jedes Einzelnen*] are a *possibility* whose actualization is conditioned by the individual's own arbitrary will and particular nature, as well as by the objective system of needs. Through the administration of justice, *infringements* of property or personality are annulled. But the right *which is actually present in particularity* means not only that *contingencies* which interfere with this or that end should be *cancelled* [*aufgehoben*] and that the *undisturbed security* of *persons* and *property* should be guaranteed, but also that the livelihood and welfare of individuals should be *secured* – i.e. that *particular welfare* should be *treated as a right* and duly *actualized*.

a. The police [Polizei]

§ 231

In so far as the principle by which this or that end is governed is still that of the particular will, that authority [*Macht*] of the universal which guarantees security remains, on the one hand, primarily limited to the sphere of *contingencies*, and on the other, it remains an *external order*.

§ 232

Apart from crimes which the universal authority [*Macht*] must prevent or bring to justice – i.e. contingency in the shape of arbitrary evil – the permissible arbitrariness of inherently [*für sich*] rightful actions and of the private use of property also has external relations [*Beziehungen*] with other individuals [*Einzelne*], as well as with other public arrangements designed to further a common end. Through this universal aspect, private actions become a contingent matter which passes out of my control [*Gewalt*] and which can wrong or harm other people or actually does so.

§ 233

There is admittedly *only* a *possibility* that harm may be done. But the fact that no harm is done is, as a contingency, likewise no more than that. This is the aspect of *wrong* which is inherent in such actions, and which is consequently the ultimate reason [*Grund*] for penal justice as implemented by the police.

§ 234

The relations [*Beziehungen*] of external existence [*Dasein*] fall within the infinite of the understanding; consequently, no boundary is present *in itself* between what is harmful and what is harmless (even with regard to crime), between what is suspicious and what is not suspicious, or between what should be prohibited or kept under surveillance and what should be exempted from prohibitions, surveillance and suspicion, inquiry and accountability. The more precise determinations will depend on custom, the spirit of the rest of the constitution, prevailing conditions, current emergencies, etc.

Addition: (H). No fixed determinations are possible here, and no absolute boundaries can be drawn. Everything here is personal; subjective opinion comes into play, and the spirit of the constitution and current dangers will determine the more precise circumstances. In times of war, for example, various things which are otherwise harmless must be regarded as harmful. Because of these aspects of contingency and arbitrary personality, the police takes on a certain character of *maliciousness*. When reflection is highly developed, the police may tend to draw everything it can into its sphere of influence, for it is possible to discover some potentially harmful aspect in everything. On such occasions, the police may proceed very pedantically and disrupt the ordinary life of individuals. But however troublesome this may be, no objective boundary line can be drawn here.

§ 235

In the indeterminate multiplication and interdependence of daily needs, the *procurement* and *exchange of means* to satisfy these (a process on whose unimpeded continuance everyone relies) and the need to make the requisite inquiries and negotiations as short as possible give rise to aspects of common interest in which the business *of one* is at the same time carried out on behalf of *all*; they also give rise to means and arrangements which may be of use to the community. These *universal functions* and arrangements *of public utility* require oversight and advance provision on the part of the public authority [*Macht*].

§ 236

The differing interests of producers and consumers may come into collision with each other, and even if, *on the whole*, their correct relationship reestablishes itself automatically, its adjustment also needs to be consciously regulated by an agency which stands above both sides. The right to regulate individual matters in this way (e.g. by deciding the value of the commonest necessities of life) is based on the fact that, when commodities in completely universal everyday use are publicly marketed, they are offered not so much to a particular individual [*Individuum*] as such, as to the individual in a universal sense, i.e. to the public; and the task of upholding the public's right not to be cheated and of inspecting market commodities may, as a common concern, be entrusted to a public authority [*Macht*]. – But the main reason why some universal provision and direction are necessary is that large branches of industry are dependent on external circumstances and remote combinations whose full implications cannot be grasped by the individuals [*Individuen*] who are tied to these spheres by their occupation.

> *Remark*: At the opposite extreme to freedom of trade and commerce in civil society are public arrangements to provide for and determine the work of everyone. These included, for example, the building of the pyramids in ancient times, and other enormous works in Egypt and Asia which were undertaken for public ends, and in which the work of the individual [*des Einzelnen*] was not mediated by his particular arbitrary will and particular interest. This interest invokes the freedom of trade and commerce against regulation from above; but the more blindly it immerses itself in its selfish ends, the more it requires such regulation to bring it back to the universal, and to moderate and shorten the duration of those dangerous convulsions to which its collisions give rise, and which should return to equilibrium by a process of unconscious necessity.

Addition: (H). The aim of oversight and provisions on the part of the police is to mediate between the individual [*Individuum*] and the universal possibility which is available for the attainment of individual ends. The police should provide for street-lighting, bridge-building, the pricing of daily necessities and public health. Two main views are prevalent on this subject. One maintains that the police should have oversight over everything, and the other maintains that the police should have no say in such matters, since everyone will be guided in his actions by the needs of others. The individual [*der Einzelne*] must certainly have a right to earn his living in this way or that; but on the other hand, the public also has a right to expect that necessary tasks will be performed in the proper manner. Both viewpoints must be satisfied, and the freedom of trade should not be such as to prejudice the general good.

§ 237

Now even if the possibility exists for individuals to share in the universal resources, and even if this possibility is guaranteed by the public authority [*Macht*], it remains – apart from the fact that such a guarantee must always be incomplete – open to contingencies of a subjective kind. This is increasingly the case the more it takes such conditions as skill, health, capital, etc. for granted.

§ 238

Initially, the family is the substantial whole whose task it is to provide for this particular aspect of the individual, both by giving him the means and skills he requires in order to earn his living from the universal resources, and by supplying his livelihood and maintenance in the event of his incapacity to look after himself. But civil society tears the individual [*Individuum*] away from family ties, alienates the members of the family from one another, and recognizes them as self-sufficient persons. Furthermore, it substitutes its own soil for the external inorganic nature and paternal soil from which the individual [*der Einzelne*] gained his livelihood, and subjects the existence [*Bestehen*] of the whole family itself to dependence on civil society and to contingency. Thus, the individual [*Individuum*] becomes a *son of civil society*, which has as many claims upon him as he has rights in relation to it.

Addition: (H). Admittedly, the family must provide food for its individual members [*Einzelnen*], but in civil society, the family is subordinate and merely lays the foundations; its effectiveness is no longer so comprehensive. Civil society, on the other hand, is the immense power which draws people to itself and requires them to work for it, to owe everything to it, and to do everything by its means. Thus, if a human being is to be a member of civil society, he has rights and claims in relation to it, just as he had in relation to his family. Civil society must protect its members and defend their rights, just as the individual [*der Einzelne*] owes a duty to the rights of civil society.

§ 239

In this character as a *universal family*, civil society has the duty and right, in the face of *arbitrariness* and contingency on the part of *the parents*, to supervise and influence the *education* [*Erziehung*] of children in so far as this has a bearing on their capacity to become members of society, and particularly if this education is to be completed not by the parents themselves, but by others. In so far as communal arrangements can be made for this purpose, it is likewise incumbent upon civil society to make them. [A]

§ 240

In the same way, society has the duty and right to act as guardian on behalf of those who destroy the security of their own and their family's livelihood by their extravagance, and to implement their end and that of society in their place.

Addition: (G). In Athens, the law obliged every citizen to give an account of his means of support; the view nowadays is that this is a purely private matter. On the one hand, it is true that every individual has an independent existence [*ist jedes Individuum für sich*]; but on the other, the individual is also a member of the system of civil society, and just as every human being has a right to demand a livelihood from society, so also must society protect him against himself. It is not just starvation which is at stake here; the wider viewpoint is the need to prevent a rabble from emerging. Since civil society is obliged to feed its members, it also has the right to urge them to provide for their own livelihood.

§ 241

Not only arbitrariness, however, but also contingent physical factors and circumstances based on external conditions (see § 200) may reduce individuals to *poverty*. In this condition, they are left with the needs of civil society and yet – since society has at the same time taken from them the natural means of acquisition (see § 217),[8] and also dissolves [*aufhebt*] the bond of the family in its wider sense as a kinship group (see § 181) – they are more or less deprived of all the advantages of society, such as the ability to acquire skills and education in general, as well as of the administration of justice, health care and often even of the consolation of religion. For the *poor*, the universal authority [*Macht*] takes over the role of the family with regard not only to their immediate deficiencies, but also to the disposition of laziness, viciousness, and the other vices to which their predicament and sense of wrong give rise.

§ 242

The subjective aspect of poverty, and in general of every kind of want to which all individuals are exposed, even in their natural environment, also requires *subjective* help, both with regard to the *particular* circumstances and with regard to *emotion* and *love*. This is a situation in which, notwithstanding all universal arrangements, *morality* finds plenty to do. But since this help, both in itself [*für sich*] and in its effects, is dependent on contingency, society endeavours to make it less necessary by identifying the universal aspects of want and taking steps to remedy them. [R]

§ 243

When the activity of civil society is unrestricted, it is occupied internally with *expanding its population and industry*. – On the one hand, as the association [*Zusammenhang*] of human beings through their needs is *universalized*, and with it the ways in which means of satisfying these needs are devised and made available, the *accumulation of wealth* increases; for the greatest profit is derived from this twofold universality. But on the other hand, the *specialization* [*Vereinzelung*] and *limitation* of particular work also increase, as do likewise the *dependence* and *want* of the class [*Klasse*] which is tied to such work; this in turn leads to an inability to feel and enjoy the wider freedoms, and particularly the spiritual advantages, of civil society.

§ 244

When a large mass of people sinks below the level of a certain standard of living – which automatically regulates itself at the level necessary for a member of the society in question – that feeling of right, integrity [*Rechtlichkeit*] and honour which comes from supporting oneself by one's own activity and work is lost. This leads to the creation of a *rabble*, which in turn makes it much easier for disproportionate wealth to be concentrated in a few hands.

Addition: (G). The lowest level of subsistence [*Subsistenz*], that of the rabble, defines itself automatically, but this minimum varies greatly between different peoples. In England, even the poorest man believes he has his rights; this differs from what the poor are content with in other countries. Poverty in itself does not reduce people to a rabble; a rabble is created only by the disposition associated with poverty, by inward rebellion against the rich, against society, the government, etc. It also follows that those who are dependent on contingency become frivolous and lazy, like the *lazzaroni* of Naples, for example. This in turn gives rise to the evil that the rabble do not have sufficient honour to gain their livelihood through their own work, yet claim that they have a right to receive their livelihood. No one can assert a right against nature, but within the conditions of society hardship at once assumes the form of a wrong inflicted on this or that class. The important question of how poverty can be remedied is one which agitates and torments modern societies especially.

§ 245

If the direct burden [of support] were to fall on the wealthier class, or if direct means were available in other public institutions (such as wealthy hospitals, foundations or monasteries) to maintain the increasingly impoverished mass at its normal standard of living, the livelihood of the needy would be ensured without the mediation of work; this would be contrary to the principle of civil society and the feeling of self-sufficiency and honour among its individual members. Alternatively, their livelihood might be mediated by work (i.e. by the opportunity to work) which would increase the volume of production; but it is precisely in overproduction and the lack of a proportionate number of consumers who are themselves productive that the evil [*Übel*] consists [*besteht*], and this is merely exacerbated by the two expedients in question. This shows that, despite an *excess of wealth*, civil society in *not wealthy enough* – i.e. its own distinct resources are not sufficient – to prevent an excess of poverty and the formation of a rabble.

Remark: The example of *England* permits us to study these phenomena [*Erscheinungen*] on a large scale, especially the results achieved by poor-rates, boundless donations, and equally limitless private charity, and above all by the abolition [*Aufheben*] of the corporations. There (especially in Scotland), it has emerged that the most direct means of dealing with poverty, and particularly with the renunciation of shame and honour as the subjective bases of society and with the laziness and extravagance which give rise to a rabble, is to leave the poor to their fate and direct them to beg from the public.

§ 246

This inner dialectic of society drives it – or in the first instance *this specific society* – to go beyond its own confines and look for consumers, and hence the means it requires for subsistence [*Subsistenz*], in other nations [*Völkern*] which lack those means of which it has a surplus or which generally lag behind it in creativity, etc.

§ 247

Just as the earth, the firm and *solid ground*, is a precondition of the principle of family life, so is the *sea* the natural element for industry, whose relations with the external world it enlivens. By exposing the pursuit of gain to danger, industry simultaneously rises above it; and for the ties of the soil and the limited circles of civil life with its pleasures and desires, it substitutes the element of fluidity, danger and destruction. Through this supreme medium of communication, it also creates trading links between distant countries, a legal [*rechtlichen*] relationship which gives rise to contracts; and at the same time, such trade [*Verkehr*] is the greatest educational asset [*Bildungsmittel*] and the source from which commerce derives its world-historical significance. [R]

§ 248

This extended link also supplies the means necessary for *colonization* – whether sporadic or systematic – to which the fully developed civil society is driven, and by which it provides part of its population with a return to the family principle in a new country, and itself with a new market and sphere of industrial activity.

Addition: (G). Civil society is driven to establish colonies. The increase of population alone has this effect; but a particular factor is the emergence of a mass of people who cannot gain satisfaction for their needs by their work when production exceeds the needs of consumers. Sporadic colonization is found particularly in Germany. The colonists move to America or Russia and retain no links with their home country, to which they are consequently of no service. The second variety of colonization, quite different from the first, is systematic. It is initiated by the state, which is aware of the proper way of carrying it out and regulates it accordingly. [...] The liberation of colonies itself proves to be of the greatest advantage to the mother state, just as the emancipation of slaves is of the greatest advantage to the master.

§ 249

What the police provides for in the first instance is the actualization and preservation of the universal which is contained within the particularity of civil society, [and it does so] as *an external order and arrangement* for the protection and security of the masses of particular ends and interests which have their subsistence [*Bestehen*] in this universal; as the higher guiding authority, it also provides for those interests which extend beyond the society in question (see § 246). In accordance with the Idea, particularity itself makes this universal, which is present in its immanent interests, the end and object [*Gegenstand*] of its will and activity, with the result that *the ethical returns* to civil society as an immanent principle; this constitutes the determination of the *corporation*.

b. *The corporation*

§ 250

The *agricultural estate*, in view of the substantiality of its natural and family life, has within itself, in immediate form, the concrete universal in which it lives. The *universal estate*, by definition [*in seiner Bestimmung*], has the universal for itself as its basis and as the end of its activity. The intermediate estate, i.e. the estate of trade and industry, is essentially concerned with the *particular*, and the corporation is therefore specially characteristic of it.

§ 251

The work performed by civil society is divided into different branches according to its particular nature. Since the inherent likeness of such particulars, as the quality *common* to them all, comes into existence [*Existenz*] in the *association*, the *selfish* end which pursues its own particular interest comprehends [*faßt*] and expresses itself at the same time as a universal end; and the member of civil society, in accordance with his *particular skill*, is a member of a corporation whose universal end is therefore wholly *concrete*, and no wider in scope than the end inherent in the trade which is the corporation's proper business and interest.

§ 252

By this definition [*Bestimmung*], the corporation has the right, under the supervision of the public authority [*Macht*], to look after its own interests within its enclosed sphere, to admit members in accordance with their objective qualification of skill and rectitude and in numbers determined by the universal context, to protect its members against particular contingencies, and to educate others so as to make them eligible for membership. In short, it has the right to assume the role of a *second* family for its members, a role which must remain more indeterminate in the case of civil society in general, which is more remote from individuals and their particular requirements. [R]

§ 253

In the corporation, the family not only *has* its firm basis in that its livelihood is *guaranteed* – i.e. it has secure *resources* (see § 170)[9] – on condition of its [possessing a certain] *capability*, but the two [i.e. livelihood and capability] are also *recognized*, so that the member of a corporation has no need to demonstrate his competence and his regular income and means of support – i.e. the fact that he *is somebody* – by any further *external evidence*. In this way, it is also recognized that he belongs to a whole which is itself a member of society in general, and that he has an interest in, and endeavours to promote, the less selfish end of this whole. Thus, he has *his honour in his estate*.

> *Remark*: As a guarantor of resources, the institution of the corporation corresponds to the introduction of agriculture and private property in another sphere (see Remark to § 203). – When complaints are made about that luxury and love of extravagance of the professional [*gewerbetreibenden*] classes which is associated with the creation of a rabble (see § 244), we must not overlook, in addition to the other causes [of this phenomenon] (e.g. the increasingly mechanical nature of work), its *ethical* basis as implied in what has been said above. If the individual [*der Einzelne*] is not a member of a legally recognized [*berechtigten*] corporation (and it is only through legal recognition that a community becomes a corporation), he is without the *honour of belonging to an estate*, his isolation reduces him to the selfish aspect of his trade, and his livelihood and satisfaction lack *stability*. He will accordingly try to gain *recognition* through the external manifestations of success in his trade, and these are without limit [*unbegrenzt*], because it is impossible for him to live in a way appropriate to his estate if his estate does not exist; for a community can *exist* in civil society only if it is legally constituted and recognized. Hence no way of life of a more general kind appropriate to such an estate can be devised. – Within the corporation, the help which poverty receives loses its contingent and unjustly [*mit Unrecht*] humiliating character, and wealth, in fulfilling the duty it owes to its association, loses the ability to provoke arrogance in its possessor and envy in others; rectitude also receives the true recognition and honour which are due to it.

§ 254

In the corporation, the so-called *natural right* to practise one's skill and thereby earn what there is to earn is limited only to the extent that, in this context, the skill is rationally determined. That is, it is freed from personal opinion and contingency, from its danger to oneself and others, and is recognized, guaranteed, and at the same time raised to a conscious activity for a common end.

§ 255

The *family* is the first *ethical* root of the state; the *corporation* is the second, and it is based in civil society. The former contains the moments of subjective particularity and objective universality in *substantial* unity; but in the latter, these moments, which in civil society are at first divided into the *internally reflected* particularity of need and satisfaction and abstract legal [*rechtlichen*] universality, are inwardly united in such a way that particular welfare is present as a right and is actualized within this union.

> *Remark*:   The sanctity of marriage and the honour attaching to the cor-
> poration are the two moments round which the disorganization of civil
> society revolves.

Addition: (H). When the corporations were abolished [*aufgehoben*] in recent times, it was with the intention that the individual [*der Einzelne*] should look after himself. But even if we accept this, the corporation does not affect the individual's obligation to earn his living. In our modern states, the citizens have only a limited share in the universal business of the state; but it is necessary to provide ethical man with a universal activity in addition to his private end. This universal [activity], which the modern state does not always offer him, can be found in the corporation. We saw earlier that, in providing for himself, the individual [*das Individuum*] in civil society is also acting for others.[10] But this unconscious necessity is not enough; only in the corporation does it become a knowing and thinking [part of] ethical life. The corporation, of course, must come under the higher supervision of the state, for it would otherwise become ossified and set in its ways, and decline into a miserable guild system. But the corporation in and for itself is not an enclosed guild; it is rather a means of giving the isolated trade an ethical status, and of admitting it to a circle in which it gains strength and honour.

§ 256

The end of the corporation, which is limited and finite, has its truth in the *end which is universal* in and for itself and in the absolute actuality of this end. So likewise do the separation and relative identity which were present in the external organization of the police. The sphere of civil society thus passes over into the *state*. [R]

Section 3: The State

§ 257

The state is the actuality of the ethical Idea – the ethical spirit as substantial will, *manifest* and clear to itself, which thinks and knows itself and implements what it knows in so far as it knows it. It has its immediate existence [*Existenz*] in *custom* and its mediate existence in the *self-consciousness* of the individual [*des Einzelnen*], in the individual's knowledge and activity, just as self-consciousness, by virtue of its disposition, has its *substantial freedom* in the state as its essence, its end, and the product of its activity. [R]

§ 258

The state is the actuality of the substantial *will*, an actuality which it possesses in the particular *self-consciousness* when this has been raised to its universality; as such, it is the *rational* in and for itself. This substantial unity is an absolute and unmoved end in itself, and in it, freedom enters into its highest right, just as this ultimate end possesses the highest right in relation to individuals [*die Einzelnen*], whose *highest duty* is to be members of the state.

> *Remark*: If the state is confused with civil society and its determination is equated with the security and protection of property and personal freedom, *the interest of individuals* [*der Einzelnen*] *as such* becomes the ultimate end for which they are united; it also follows from this that membership of the state is an optional matter. – But the relationship of the state to the individual [*Individuum*] is of quite a different kind. Since the state is objective spirit, it is only through being a member of the state that the individual [*Individuum*] himself has objectivity, truth and ethical life. *Union* as such is itself the true content and end, and the destiny [*Bestimmung*] of individuals [*Individuen*] is to lead a universal life; their further particular satisfaction, activity, and mode of conduct have this substantial and universally valid basis as their point of departure and result. – Considered in the abstract, rationality consists in general in the unity and interpenetration of universality and individuality [*Einzelheit*]. Here, in a concrete sense and in terms of its content, it consists in the unity of objective freedom (i.e. of the universal substantial will) and subjective freedom (as the freedom of individual [*individuellen*] knowledge and of the will in its pursuit of particular ends). And in terms of its form, it therefore consists in self-determining action in accordance with laws and principles based on *thought* and hence *universal*. [. . .]

Addition: (G). The state in and for itself is the ethical whole, the actualization of freedom, and it is the absolute end of reason that freedom should be actual. The state is the spirit which is present in the world and which *consciously* realizes itself therein, whereas in nature, it actualizes itself only as the other of itself, as dormant spirit. Only when it is present in consciousness, knowing itself as an existent object [*Gegenstand*], is it the state. Any discussion of freedom must begin not with individuality [*Einzelheit*] or the individual self-consciousness, but only with the essence of self-consciousness; for whether human beings know it or not, this essence realizes itself as a self-sufficient power of which single individuals [*die einzelnen Individuen*] are only moments. The state consists in the march of God in the world,[11] and its basis is the power of reason actualizing itself as will. In considering the Idea of the state, we must not have any particular states or particular institutions in mind; instead, we should consider the Idea, this actual God, in its own right [*für sich*]. Any state, even if we pronounce it bad in the light of our own principles, and even if we discover this or that defect in it, invariably has the essential moments of its existence [*Existenz*] within itself (provided it is one of the more advanced states of our time). But since it is easier to discover deficiencies than to comprehend the affirmative, one may easily fall into the mistake of overlooking the inner organism of the state in favour of individual [*einzelne*] aspects. The state is not a work of art; it exists in the world, and hence in the sphere of arbitrariness, contingency and error, and bad behaviour may disfigure it in many respects. But the ugliest man, the criminal, the invalid, or the cripple is still a living human being; the affirmative aspect – life – survives [*besteht*] in spite of such deficiencies, and it is with this affirmative aspect that we are here concerned.

A. Constitutional Law

§ 260

The state is the actuality of concrete freedom. But *concrete freedom* requires that personal individuality [*Einzelheit*] and its particular interests should reach their full *development* and gain *recognition of their right* for itself (within the system of the family and of civil society), and also that they should, on the one hand, *pass over* of their own accord into the interest of the universal, and on the other, knowingly and willingly acknowledge this universal interest even as their own *substantial spirit*, and *actively pursue it* as their *ultimate end*. The effect of this is that the universal does not attain validity or fulfilment without the interest, knowledge and volition of the particular, and that individuals do not live as private persons merely for these particular interests without at the same time directing their will to a universal end [*in und für das Allgemeine wollen*] and acting in conscious awareness of this end. The principle of modern states has enormous strength and depth because it allows the principle of subjectivity to attain fulfilment in the *self-sufficient extreme* of personal particularity, while at the same time *bringing it back to substantial unity* and so preserving this unity in the principle of subjectivity itself.

Addition: (H, G). The Idea of the state in modern times has the distinctive characteristic that the state is the actualization of freedom not in accordance with subjective caprice, but in accordance with the concept of the will, i.e. in accordance with its universality and divinity. Imperfect states are those in which the Idea of the state is still invisible [*eingehüllt*] and where the particular determinations of this Idea have not yet reached free self-sufficiency. In the states of classical antiquity, universality was indeed already present, but particularity [*Partikularität*] had not yet been released and set at liberty and brought back to universality, i.e. to the universal end of the whole. The essence of the modern state is that the universal should be linked with the complete freedom of particularity [*Besonderheit*] and the well-being of individuals, and hence that the interest of the family and of civil society must become focused on the state; but the universality of the end cannot make further progress without the personal [*eigene*] knowledge and volition of the particular individuals [*der Besonderheit*], who must retain their rights. Thus, the universal must be activated, but subjectivity on the other hand must be developed as a living whole. Only when both moments are present [*bestehen*] in full measure can the state be regarded as articulated and truly organized.

§ 261

In relation to the spheres of civil law [*Privatrecht*] and private welfare, the spheres of the family and civil society, the state is on the one hand an *external* necessity and the higher power to whose nature their laws and interests are subordinate and on which they depend. But on the other hand, it is their *immanent* end, and its strength consists in the unity of its universal and ultimate end with the particular interest of individuals, in the fact that they have *duties* towards the state to the same extent as they also have rights (see § 155). [R] [A]

§ 262

The actual Idea is the spirit which divides itself up into the two ideal spheres of its concept – the family and civil society – as its finite mode, and thereby emerges from its ideality to become infinite and actual spirit for itself. In so doing, it allocates the material of its finite actuality, i.e. individuals as a *mass*, to these two spheres, and in such a way that, in each individual case [*am Einzelnen*], this allocation appears to be *mediated* by circumstances, by the individual's arbitrary will and personal [*eigene*] choice of vocation [*Bestimmung*] (see § 185 and the appended Remark).[12]

Addition: (H). In Plato's republic, subjective freedom is not yet recognized, because individuals still have their tasks assigned to them by the authorities [*Obrigkeit*]. In many oriental states, this assignment is governed by birth. But subjective freedom, which must be respected, requires freedom of choice on the part of individuals.

§ 263

In these spheres in which its moments, individuality [*Einzelheit*] and particularity, have their immediate and reflected reality, spirit is present as their objective universality which *manifests itself in them* [*als ihre in sie scheinende objektive Allgemeinheit*] as the power of the rational in necessity (see § 184),[13] i.e. as the *institutions* considered above.[14] [A]

§ 264

Individuals as a mass are themselves spiritual natures, and they therefore embody a dual moment, namely the extreme of *individuality* [*Einzelheit*] which knows and wills *for itself*, and the extreme of *universality* which knows and wills the substantial. They can therefore attain their right in both of these respects only in so far as they have actuality both as private and as substantial persons. In the spheres in question [i.e. family and civil society], they attain their right in the first respect directly; and in the second respect, they attain it by discovering their essential self-consciousness in [social] institutions as that *universal* aspect of their particular interests which has being in itself, and by obtaining through these institutions an occupation and activity directed towards a universal end within a corporation.

§ 265

These institutions together form the *constitution* – that is, developed and actualized rationality – in the realm of *particularity*, and they are therefore the firm foundation of the state and of the trust and disposition of individuals towards it. They are the pillars on which public freedom rests, for it is within them that particular freedom is realized and rational; hence the union of freedom and necessity is present *in itself* within these institutions.

Addition: (G). It has already been noted that the sanctity of marriage and the institutions in which civil society takes on an ethical appearance constitute the stability of the whole – that is, the universal is simultaneously the concern [*Sache*] of each [individual] as a particular [entity]. What matters most is that the law of reason should merge with the law of particular freedom, and that my particular end should become identical with the universal; otherwise, the state must hang in the air. It is the self-awareness of individuals which constitutes the actuality of the state, and its stability consists in the identity of the two aspects in question. It has often been said that the end of the state is the happiness of its citizens. This is certainly true, for if their welfare is deficient, if their subjective ends are not satisfied, and if they do not find that the state as such is the means to this satisfaction, the state itself stands on an insecure footing.

§ 266

But the spirit is objective and actual to itself not only as this necessity and as a realm of appearance, but also as the *ideality* and inner dimension of these. Thus, this substantial universality becomes *its own object* [*Gegenstand*] and end, with the result that the necessity in question similarly becomes its own object and end in the *shape* of freedom.

§ 267

The *necessity* in ideality is the *development* of the Idea within itself; as *subjective* substantiality, it is the [individual's] political *disposition*, and as *objective* substantiality – in contrast with the former – it is the *organism* of the state, the *political* state proper and *its constitution*. [A]

§ 268

The political *disposition*, i.e. *patriotism* in general, is certainty based on *truth* (whereas merely subjective certainty does not originate in *truth*, but is only opinion) and a volition which has become *habitual*. As such, it is merely a consequence of the institutions within the state, a consequence in which rationality is *actually* present, just as rationality receives its practical application through action in conformity with the state's institutions. – This disposition is in general one of *trust* (which may pass over into more or less educated insight), or the consciousness that my substantial and particular interest is preserved and contained in the interest and end of an other (in this case, the state), and in the latter's relation to me as an individual [*als Einzelnem*]. As a result, this other immediately ceases to be an other for me, and in my consciousness of this, I am free.

> *Remark*: Patriotism is frequently understood to mean only a willingness to perform *extraordinary* sacrifices and actions. But in essence, it is that disposition which, in the normal conditions and circumstances of life, habitually knows that the community is the substantial basis and end. [...]

Addition: (H). Uneducated people delight in argument [*Räsonieren*] and fault-finding, for it is easy to find fault, but difficult to recognize the good and its inner necessity. Education in its early stages always begins with fault-finding, but when it is complete, it sees the positive element in everything. In religion, it is equally easy to say that this or that is superstition, but it is infinitely more difficult to comprehend the truth which it contains. Thus people's apparent political disposition should be distinguished from what they genuinely will; for inwardly, they in fact will the thing [*Sache*], but they fasten on to details and delight in the vanity of claiming superior insight. They trust that the state will continue to exist [*bestehen*] and that particular interests can be fulfilled within it alone; but habit blinds us to the basis of our entire existence [*Existenz*]. It does not occur to someone who walks the streets in safety at night that this might be otherwise, for this habit of [living in] safety has become second nature, and we scarcely stop to think that it is solely the effect of particular institutions. Representational thought often imagines that the state is held together by force; but what holds it together is simply the basic sense of order which everyone possesses.

§ 269

The [*political*] disposition takes its particularly determined *content* from the various aspects of the organism of the state. This *organism* is the development of the Idea in its differences and their objective actuality. These different aspects are accordingly the *various powers* [within the state] with their corresponding tasks and functions, through which the universal continually *produces* itself. It does so in a *necessary* way, because these various powers are determined by the *nature of the concept*; and it *preserves* itself in so doing, because it is itself the presupposition of its own production. This organism is the *political constitution*. [A]

§ 270

The fact that the end of the state is both the universal interest as such and the conservation of particular interests within the universal interest as the substance of these constitutes (1) the *abstract actuality* or substantiality of the state. But this substantiality is (2) the *necessity* of the state, for it divides itself up into the conceptual *differences* within the state's functions; and these differences, by virtue of this substantiality, are likewise actual and *fixed* determinations or powers. (3) But this very substantiality is the spirit which knows and wills itself as having *passed through the form of education*. The state therefore *knows* what it wills, and knows it in its *universality* as something *thought*. Consequently, it acts and functions in accordance with known ends and recognized principles, and with laws which are laws not only *in themselves* but also for the consciousness; and it likewise acts in determinate knowledge [*Kenntnis*] of existing circumstances and relations in so far as its actions have relevance to these. [R] [A]

§ 273

The political state is therefore divided into three substantial elements:

(a) the power to determine and establish the universal – the *legislative* power;
(b) the subsumption of *particular* spheres and individual cases under the universal – the *executive power*;
(c) subjectivity as the ultimate decision of the will – *the power of the sovereign*, in which the different powers are united in an individual unity which is thus the apex and beginning of the whole, i.e. of *constitutional monarchy*.

> *Remark:* The development [*Ausbildung*] of the state to constitutional monarchy is the achievement of the modern world, in which the substantial Idea has attained infinite form. The *history* of this immersion of

the world spirit in itself or – and this amounts to the same thing – this free development in which the Idea releases its moments (and they are only its moments) from itself as totalities, and in so doing contains them in that ideal unity of the concept in which real rationality consists [*besteht*] – the history of this true formation [*Gestaltung*] of ethical life is the concern [*Sache*] of universal world history. [. . .] [A]

a. The power of the sovereign

§ 279

Sovereignty, which is initially only the *universal* thought of this ideality, can *exist* only as *subjectivity* which is certain of itself, and as the will's abstract – and to that extent ungrounded – *self-determination* in which the ultimate decision is vested. This is the individual aspect of the state as such, and it is in this respect alone that the state itself is *one*. But subjectivity attains its truth only as a *subject*, and personality only as a *person*, and in a constitution which has progressed to real rationality, each of the three moments of the concept has its distinctive [*ausgesonderte*] shape which is *actual for itself*. This absolutely decisive moment of the whole, therefore, is not individuality in general, but *one* individual, the *monarch*. [R]

Addition: (G). In the organization of the state (which in this case means constitutional monarchy), the one thing which we must bear in mind is the internal necessity of the Idea; all other considerations are irrelevant. The state must be regarded as a great architectonic edifice, a hieroglyph of reason which becomes manifest in actuality. All considerations of mere utility, externality, and the like must therefore be excluded from a philosophical treatment [of this subject]. Representational thought can easily comprehend that the state is the self-determining and completely sovereign will, the ultimate source of decisions. But it is more difficult to grasp this 'I will' as a person, for this [formula] does not imply that the monarch may act arbitrarily: on the contrary, he is bound by the concrete content of the advice he receives, and if the constitution is firmly established, he often has nothing more to do than to sign his name. But this *name* is important: it is the ultimate instance and *non plus ultra*. It could be said that an organic articulation was already present in the beautiful democracy of Athens, but we can see at once that the Greeks based the ultimate decision on completely external phenomena [*Erscheinungen*] such as oracles, the entrails of sacrificial animals and the flight of birds, and that they regarded nature as a power which proclaimed and expressed by these means what was good for human beings. At that time, self-consciousness had not yet arrived at the abstraction of subjectivity, nor had it yet realized that an 'I will' must be pronounced by man himself on the issue to be decided. This 'I will' constitutes the great difference between ancient and modern worlds, so that it must have its own distinct existence [*Existenz*] in the great edifice of the state. Unfortunately, however, this determination is regarded as merely external and discretionary.

b. *The executive power*

§ 287

The execution and application of the sovereign's decisions, and in general the continued implementation and upholding of earlier decisions, existing laws, institutions and arrangements to promote common ends, etc., are distinct from the decisions themselves. This task of *subsumption* in general belongs to the *executive power*, which also includes the powers of the *judiciary* and the *police*; these have more immediate reference to the particular affairs of civil society, and they assert the universal interest within these [particular] ends.

§ 288

The *particular* common interests which fall within civil society, and which lie outside the universal interest of the state as the interest which has being in and for itself (see § 256), are administered by the corporations (see § 251) which represent the communities and the various professions [*Gewerbe*] and estates, with their authorities [*Obrigkeit*], supervisors, administrators, etc. On the one hand, the business of these administrators is to look after the *private property* and *interests* of these *particular* spheres, and in this respect, their authority [*Autorität*] is based in part on the trust of their fellow-citizens and equals. On the other hand, these circles must be subordinated to the higher interests of the state. Thus, the filling of such offices will in general involve a mixture of popular election by the interested parties, and confirmation and determination by a higher authority.

§ 289

The task of *upholding*, within these particular rights, *legality* and the *universal interest of the state*, and that of bringing these rights back to the universal, need to be performed by delegates of the executive power, i.e. the executive *civil servants* and the higher consultative bodies. The latter necessarily work together in groups, and they converge in their supreme heads who are in touch with the monarch himself.

> *Remark*: Just as civil society is the field of conflict in which the private interest of each individual comes up against that of everyone else, so do we here encounter the conflict between private interests and particular concerns of the community, and between both of these together and the higher viewpoints and ordinances of the state. The spirit of the corporation, which arises when the particular spheres gain legal recognition [*Berechtigung*], is now at the same time inwardly transformed

into the spirit of the state, because it finds in the state the means of sustaining its particular ends. This is the secret of the patriotism of the citizens in the sense that they know the state as their substance, for it is the state which supports their particular spheres and the legal recognition, authority and welfare of these. In so far as the *rooting of the particular in the universal* is contained *immediately* in the spirit of the corporation, it is in this spirit that such depth and strength of *disposition* as the state possesses are to be found. [. . .]

§ 290

The *division* [*Teilung*] *of labour* (see § 198) likewise makes its appearance in the business of the executive. The *organization* of official bodies accordingly faces the formal but difficult task of ensuring that civil life shall be governed in a *concrete* manner from below, where it is concrete, but that the business in question shall be divided into its *abstract* branches and dealt with by distinct bodies; the latter should function as separate centres whose activities should again converge both at the lowest level and in a concrete overview on the part of the supreme executive.

Addition: (G). The most important issue for the executive power is the division of functions. The executive power is concerned with the transition from the universal to the particular and individual, and its functions must be divided in accordance with its different branches. The difficulty, however, is [that of ensuring] that they also come together again at upper and lower levels. For although the power of the police and that of the judiciary, for example, are divergent, they do converge in every particular case [*Geschäft*]. The expedient which is often employed in these circumstances is to appoint a State Chancellor, Prime Minister or Cabinet Council in order to simplify the highest level of government. But this may have the result that everything is again controlled from above by ministerial power, and that functions are, to use the common expression, centralized. This is associated with a high degree of facility, speed and effectiveness in measures adopted for the universal interest of the state. A regime of this kind was introduced by the French Revolution and further developed by Napoleon, and it still exists [*besteht*] in France today. On the other hand, France lacks corporations and communal associations [*Kommunen*] – that is, circles in which particular and universal interests come together. Admittedly, these circles gained too great a degree of self-sufficiency in the Middle Ages, when they became states within the state and behaved in an obdurate manner like independently established bodies. But although this ought not to happen, it can still be argued that the proper strength of states resides in their [internal] communities [*Gemeinden*]. In these, the executive encounters legitimate [*berechtigte*] interests which it must respect; and since the administration can only encourage such interests – although it must also supervise them – the individual finds protection for the exercise of his rights, so that his particular [*partikulares*] interest is bound up with the preservation of the whole. For some time now, organization has always been directed from above, and efforts have been devoted for the most part to this kind of organization, despite the fact that the lower level of the masses as a whole can easily be left in a more or less disorganized state. Yet it is extremely important that the masses should be organized, because only then do they constitute a power or force; otherwise, they are merely an aggregate, a collection of scattered atoms. Legitimate power is to be found only when the particular spheres are organized.

c. *The Legislative Power*

§ 298

The *legislative power* has to do with the laws as such, in so far as they are in need of new and further determination, and with those internal concerns of the state whose content is wholly universal. This power is itself a part of the constitution, which it presupposes and which to that extent lies in and for itself outside the sphere which the legislative power can determine directly; but the constitution does undergo further development through the further evolution of the laws and the progressive character of the universal concerns of government. [A]

§ 300

In the legislative power as a whole, the other two moments have a primary part to play, namely the *monarchy* as the power of ultimate decision, and the *executive power* as the advisory moment which has concrete knowledge [*Kenntnis*] and oversight of the whole with its numerous aspects and the actual principles which have become established within it, and knowledge of the needs of the power of the state in particular. The final element [in the legislature] is the *Estates*. [A]

§ 302

Viewed as a *mediating* organ, the Estates stand between the government at large on the one hand and the people in their division into particular spheres and individuals [*Individuen*] on the other. Their determination requires that they should embody in equal measure both the *sense* and *disposition* of the *state* and *government* and the *interests* of *particular* circles and *individuals* [*Einzelnen*]. At the same time, this position means that they share the mediating function of the organized power of the executive, ensuring on the one hand that the power of the sovereign does not appear as an isolated *extreme* – and hence simply as an arbitrary power of domination – and on the other, that the particular interests of communities, corporations and individuals [*Individuen*] do not become isolated either. Or more important still, they ensure that individuals do not present themselves as a *crowd* or *aggregate*, unorganized in their opinions and volition, and do not become a massive power in opposition to the organic state. [R]

Addition: (H). The constitution is essentially a system of mediation. In despotic states, where there are only rulers [*Fürsten*] and people, the people function – if they function at all – merely as a destructive mass opposed to all organization. But when it becomes part of the organism, the mass attains its interests in a legitimate and orderly manner. If, however, such means are not available, the masses will always express themselves in a barbarous manner. This is why, in despotic states, the despot always treats the people with indulgence and vents his wrath only on his immediate circle. In the same way, the people in such states pay only modest taxes, whereas in constitutional states, the taxes become higher as a result of the people's own consciousness. In fact, in no country are so many taxes paid as in England.

§ 305

One of the estates of civil society contains the principle which is in itself capable of being adapted to this political relation [*Beziehung*], namely the estate of natural ethical life; its basis is the life of the family and, as far as its livelihood is concerned, landed property. Thus, in its particular aspect, this estate shares that independent volition and natural determination which is also contained in the moment [*Element*] of sovereignty.

§ 306

This estate is better equipped for its political role and significance inasmuch as its resources are equally independent of the resources of the state and of the uncertainty of trade, the quest for profit, and all variations in property. It is likewise independent of the favour of the executive power and of the masses, and is even protected *against its own arbitrariness* by the fact that those members of this estate who are called to this vocation [*Bestimmung*] do not have the same right as other citizens either to dispose freely of their entire property or to know that it will pass on to their children in proportion to the equal degree of love that they feel for them. Thus, their resources become *inalienable inherited property*, burdened with primogeniture. [A]

§ 308

The second section of the Estates encompasses the *changing* element in *civil society*, which can play its part only by means of *deputies*; the external reason for this is the sheer number of its members, but the essential reason lies in the nature of its determination and activity. In so far as these deputies are elected by civil society, it is immediately evident that, in electing them, society acts *as what it is*. That is, it is not split up into individual atomic units which are merely assembled for a moment to perform a single temporary act and have no further cohesion; on the contrary, it is articulated into its associations, communities, and corporations which, although they are already in being, acquire in this way a political connotation. In the entitlement of this estate to elect deputies at the request of the sovereign power, and in the entitlement of the first estate to appear [in person] [. . .], the existence [*Existenz*] of the Estates and of their assembly acquires its own constitutional guarantee.

> *Remark*: The idea [*Vorstellung*] that *all* individuals ought to participate in deliberations and decisions on the universal concerns of the state – on the grounds that they are all members of the state and that the concerns of the state are the concerns of *everyone*, so that everyone has a *right* to share in them with his own knowledge and volition – seeks to implant in the organism of the state a *democratic* element *devoid of rational form*, although it is only by virtue of its rational form that the state is an organism. This idea [*Vorstellung*] appears plausible precisely because it stops short at the *abstract* determination of membership of the state and because superficial thinking sticks to abstractions. Rational deliberation or the consciousness of the Idea [*Idee*] is *concrete*, and it coincides to that extent with true *practical* sense, which is itself nothing other than rational sense or the sense of the Idea; it must not, however, be confused with the mere routine of business and the horizon of a limited sphere. The concrete state is *the whole, articulated into its particular circles*. Each member of the state is a *member* of an *estate* of this kind, and only in this objective determination can he be considered in relation to the state. His universal determination in general includes two moments, for he is a *private person* and at the same time a *thinking* being with consciousness and volition of the *universal*. But this consciousness and volition remain empty and lack *fulfilment* and actual *life* until they are filled with particularity, and this is [to be found in] a particular estate and determination. Otherwise, the individual remains a *generic category* [*Gattung*], but only within the *next* generic category does he attain his *immanent* universal *actuality*. – Consequently, it is within the sphere of his corporation, community, etc. (see § 251) that the individual first attains his actual and living determination as *universal*, and it remains open to him to enter any sphere, including the universal estate, for which his aptitude qualifies him. The idea [*Vorstellung*] that *everyone* should participate in the concerns of the state entails the further assumption that *everyone is an expert on such matters*; this is also absurd, notwithstanding the frequency with which we hear it asserted. In public opinion, however (see § 316),[15] the way is open for everyone to express and give effect to his subjective opinions on the universal.

§ 309

Since deputies are elected to deliberate and decide on matters of *universal* concern, the aim of such elections is to appoint individuals who are credited by those who elect them with a better understanding of such matters than they themselves possess. It is also the intention that these individuals will not subordinate the universal interest to the particular interest of a community or corporation, but will give it their essential support. Their position is accordingly not that of commissioned or mandated agents, especially since the purpose [*Bestimmung*] of their assembly is to provide a forum for live exchanges and collective deliberations in which the participants instruct and convince one another.

Addition: (G). The introduction of representation [*Repräsentation*] means that consent is not given directly by everyone but only by authorized deputies, for the individual [*der Einzelne*] is no longer involved as an infinite person. Representation is based on trust, but trust is not the same thing as giving my vote *in person*. Majority decisions are also at variance with the principle that I should be personally present in anything which imposes an obligation on me. I can trust a person if I believe that he has sufficient insight to treat my cause [*Sache*] as if it were his own, and to deal with it in the light of his own best knowledge and conscience. Thus, the principle of the individual subjective will is no longer applicable, for the trust is vested in a cause, in the principles of a human being and his conduct, actions and concrete sense in general. It is therefore desirable that anyone who becomes a member of the Estates should possess a character, insight, and will consistent with his task of participating in universal concerns. For it is not essential that the individual [*Individuum*] should have a say as an abstract individual entity; on the contrary, all that matters is that his interests should be upheld in an assembly which deals with universal issues. The electors require a guarantee that the elected deputy will promote and accomplish this end.

§ 311

In view of the fact that the deputies are elected by civil society, it is also desirable that they should be familiar with and party to its special needs, frustrations and particular interests. Given the nature of civil society, the deputies are elected by the various corporations (see § 308), and this simple mode of procedure is not impaired by abstractions and atomistic notions [*Vorstellungen*] [of society]. Consequently, it directly fulfils the requirement referred to above, and the election itself is either completely superfluous or can be reduced to an insignificant play of arbitrary opinion.

> *Remark*: It is clearly in the general interest that the deputies should include individuals who are thoroughly familiar with, and personally involved in, each particular major branch of society (e.g. commerce, manufacturing industries, etc.) – an important consideration which the idea [*Vorstellung*] of loose and indeterminate elections leaves entirely to chance. Each of these branches of society, however, has the same right as the others to be represented. If the deputies are regarded as *representatives*, this term cannot be applied to them in an organic and rational sense unless they are *representatives* not of *individuals* as a crowd, but of one of the essential *spheres* of society, i.e. of its major interests. Thus,

representation no longer means the *replacement* of one individual *by another*; on the contrary, the interest itself is *actually present* in its representative, and the latter is there to represent the objective element he himself embodies. – As for mass elections, it may also be noted that, in large states in particular, the electorate inevitably becomes *indifferent* in view of the fact that a single vote has little effect when numbers are so large; and however highly they are urged to value the right to vote, those who enjoy this right will simply fail to make use of it. As a result, an institution of this kind achieves the opposite of its intended purpose [*Bestimmung*], and the election comes under the control of a few people, of a faction, and hence of that particular and contingent interest which it was specifically designed to neutralize.

B. International Law [*Das äußere Staatsrecht*]

§ 330

International law [*das äußere Staatsrecht*] applies to the *relations* between independent states. What it contains *in and for itself* therefore assumes the form of an *obligation*, because its actuality depends on *distinct and sovereign wills*. [A]

§ 331

The nation state [*das Volk als Staat*] is the spirit in its substantial rationality and immediate actuality, and is therefore the absolute power on *earth*; each state is consequently a sovereign and independent entity in relation to others. The state has a primary and absolute entitlement to be a sovereign and independent power *in the eyes of others*, i.e. *to be recognized* by them. At the same time, however, this entitlement is purely formal, and the requirement that the state should be recognized simply because it is a state is abstract. Whether the state does in fact have being in and for itself depends on its content – on its constitution and [present] condition; and recognition, which implies that the two [i.e. form and content] are identical, also depends on the perception and will of the other state.

> *Remark*: Without relations [*Verhältnis*] with other states, the state can no more be an actual individual [*Individuum*] than an individual [*der Einzelne*] can be an actual person without a relationship [*Relation*] with other persons (see § 322).[16] On the other hand, the legitimacy of a state, and more precisely – in so far as it has external relations – of the power of its sovereign, is a purely *internal* matter (one state should not interfere in the internal affairs of another). On the other hand, it is equally essential that this legitimacy should be *supplemented* by recognition

on the part of other states. But this recognition requires a guarantee that the state will likewise recognize those other states which are supposed to recognize it, i.e. that it will respect their independence; accordingly, these other states cannot be indifferent to its internal affairs. – In the case of a nomadic people, for example, or any people at a low level of culture, the question even arises of how far this people can be regarded as a state. The religious viewpoint (as in former times with the Jewish and Mohammedan nations [*Völkern*]) may further entail a higher opposition which precludes that universal identity that recognition requires. [A]

§ 332

The immediate actuality in which states coexist is particularized into various relations which are determined by the independent arbitrary wills of both parties, and which accordingly possess the formal nature of *contracts* in general. The subject-matter [*Stoff*] of these contracts, however, is infinitely less varied than it is in civil society, in which individuals [*die Einzelnen*] are mutually interdependent in innumerable respects, whereas independent states are primarily wholes which can satisfy their own needs internally.

§ 333

The principle of *international law* [*Völkerrecht*], as that *universal* right which ought to have international validity in and for itself (as distinct from the particular content of positive treaties), is that *treaties*, on which the mutual obligations of states depend, *should be observed*. But since the sovereignty of states is the principle governing their mutual relations, they exist to that extent in a state of nature in relation to one another, and their rights are *actualized* not in a universal will with constitutional powers over them, but in their own particular wills. Consequently, the universal determination of international law remains only an *obligation*, and the [normal] condition will be for relations governed by treaties to alternate with the suspension [*Aufhebung*] of such relations.

> *Remark:* There is no praetor to adjudicate between states, but at most arbitrators and mediators, and even the presence of these will be contingent, i.e. determined by particular wills. Kant's idea [*Vorstellung*] of a *perpetual peace* guaranteed by a federation of states which would settle all disputes and which, as a power recognized by each individual state, would resolve all disagreements so as to make it impossible for these to be settled by war presupposes an *agreement* between states. But this agreement, whether based on moral, religious or other grounds and considerations, would always be dependent on particular sovereign wills, and would therefore continue to be tainted with contingency.

§ 334

Consequently, if no agreement can be reached between particular wills, conflicts between states can be settled only by *war*. Since the sphere of the state is extensive and its relations [*Beziehungen*] through its citizens are extremely varied, it may easily suffer injuries [*Verletzungen*] on many occasions. But which of these injuries should be regarded as a specific breach of treaties or as an injury to the recognition and honour of the state remains *inherently [an sich]* indeterminable; for a state may associate its infinity and honour with any one of its individual interests, and it will be all the more inclined to take offence if it possesses a strong individuality which is encouraged, as a result of a long period of internal peace, to seek and create an occasion [*Stoff*] for action abroad.

§ 335

Furthermore, the state, as a wholly spiritual entity, cannot confine itself simply to noting that an *injury* has actually taken place. On the contrary, a further cause of discord arises in the *idea* [*Vorstellung*] of such an injury as a *danger* threatening from another state, in changing estimates of greater and lesser degrees of probability, in conjectures as to the other state's intentions, etc.

§ 336

The relationship of states to one another is a relationship between independent entities and hence between *particular* wills, and it is on this that the very validity of treaties depends. But the *particular will* of the whole, *as far as its content is concerned*, is its own *welfare* in general. Consequently, this welfare is the supreme law for a state in its relations with others, especially since the Idea of the state is precisely that the opposition between right as abstract freedom and the particular content which fills it, i.e. the state's own welfare, should be superseded within it, and it is on this Idea as a *concrete* whole that the initial recognition of states is based (see § 331).

§ 337

The substantial welfare of the state is its welfare as a *particular* state in its specific interest and condition and in its equally distinctive external circumstances in conjunction with the particular treaties which govern them. Its government is accordingly a matter of *particular wisdom*, not of universal providence (cf. Remark to § 324),[17] just as its end in relation to other states and its principle for justifying wars and treaties is not a universal (philanthropic) thought, but its actually offended or threatened welfare in *its specific particularity*. [R]

§ 338

The fact that states reciprocally recognize each other as such remains, *even in war* – as the condition of rightlessness [*Rechtlosigkeit*], force and contingency – a *bond* whereby they retain their validity for each other in their being in and for themselves, so that even in wartime, the determination of war is that of something which ought to come to an end. War accordingly entails the determination of international law [*Völkerrecht*] that it should preserve the possibility of peace – so that, for example, ambassadors should be respected and war should on no account be waged either on internal institutions and the peace of private and family life, or on private individuals.

Addition: (G). Modern wars are accordingly waged in a humane manner, and persons do not confront each other in hatred. At most, personal enmities will arise at military outposts, but in the army as such, hostility is something indeterminate which takes second place to the duty which each respects in the other.

§ 339

Otherwise, the conduct of states towards one another in wartime (e.g. in the taking of prisoners), and concessions of rights in peacetime to the citizens of another state for the purpose of private contacts, etc. will depend primarily on national *customs*, for these are the universal aspect of behaviour which is preserved under all circumstances.

Addition: (G). The European nations [*Nationen*] form a family with respect to the universal principle of their legislation, customs and culture [*Bildung*], so that their conduct in terms of international law is modified accordingly in a situation which is otherwise dominated by the mutual infliction of evils [*Übeln*]. The relations between states are unstable, and there is no praetor to settle disputes; the higher praetor is simply the universal spirit which has being in and for itself, i.e. the world spirit.

§ 340

Since states function as *particular* entities in their mutual relations, the broadest view of these relations will encompass the ceaseless turmoil not just of external contingency, but also of passions, interests, ends, talents and virtues, violence [*Gewalt*], wrongdoing, and vices in their inner particularity. In this turmoil, the ethical whole itself – the independence of the state – is exposed to contingency. The principles of the *spirits of nations* [*Volksgeister*] are in general of a limited nature because of that particularity in which they have their objective actuality and self-consciousness as *existent* individuals, and their deeds and destinies in their mutual relations are the manifest [*erscheinende*] dialectic of the finitude of these spirits. It is through this dialectic that the *universal* spirit, *the spirit of the world*, produces itself in its freedom from all limits, and it is this spirit which exercises its right – which is the highest right of all – over finite spirits in *world history* as the *world's court of judgement* [*Weltgericht*].

C. World History

§ 341

The *element* of the *universal spirit's* existence [*Dasein*] is intuition and image in art, feeling and representational thought in religion, and pure and free thought in philosophy. In *world history*, it is spiritual actuality in its entire range of inwardness and externality. World history is a court of judgement [*Gericht*] because, in its *universality* which has being in and for itself, the *particular* – i.e. the Penates, civil society, and the spirits of nations [*Völkergeister*] in their multifarious actuality – is present only as *ideal*, and the movement of spirit within this element is the demonstration of this fact.

§ 342

Furthermore, it is not just the *power* of spirit which passes judgement in world history – i.e. it is not the abstract and irrational necessity of a blind fate. On the contrary, since spirit in and for itself is *reason*, and since the being-for-itself of reason in spirit is knowledge, world history is the necessary development, from the *concept* of the freedom of spirit alone, of the *moments* of reason and hence of spirit's self-consciousness and freedom. It is the exposition and the *actualization of the universal spirit.*

§ 343

The history of spirit is its own *deed*; for spirit is only what it does, and its deed is to make itself – in this case as spirit – the object of its own consciousness, and to comprehend itself in its interpretation of itself to itself. This comprehension is its being and principle, and the *completion* of an act of comprehension is at the same time its alienation [*Entäußerung*] and transition. To put it in formal terms, the spirit which comprehends this comprehension *anew* and which – and this amounts to the same thing – returns into itself from its alienation, is the spirit at a stage higher than that at which it stood in its earlier [phase of] comprehension. [R]

§ 346

Since history is the process whereby the spirit assumes the shape of events and of immediate natural actuality, the stages of its development are present as *immediate natural principles*; and since these are natural, they constitute a plurality of separate entities [*eine Vielheit außereinander*] such that *one of them is allotted to each nation* [*Volke*] in its *geographical* and *anthropological* existence [*Existenz*].

§ 347

The nation [*Volk*] to which such a moment is allotted as a *natural* principle is given the task of implementing this principle in the course of the self-development of the world spirit's self-consciousness. This nation is the *dominant* one in world history for this epoch, *and only once in history can it have this epoch-making role* (see § 346). In contrast with this absolute right which it possesses as bearer of the present stage of the world spirit's development, the spirits of other nations are without rights, and they, like those whose epoch has passed, no longer count in world history.

> *Remark*: The particular history of a world-historical nation contains, on the one hand, the development of its principle from its latent [*eingehüllten*] childhood phase until it blossoms out in free ethical self-consciousness and makes its mark in universal history, and on the other, the period of its decline and fall – for these denote the emergence within it of a higher principle which is simply the negative of its own. This signifies the spirit's transition to the higher principle and hence the transition of world history to *another* nation. From this period onwards, the previous nation has lost its absolute interest, and although it will also positively absorb the higher principle and incorporate it in its own development, it will react to it as to an extraneous element rather than with immanent vitality and vigour. It will perhaps lose its independence, or it may survive or eke out its existence as a particular state or group of states and struggle on in a contingent manner with all kinds of internal experiments and external conflicts.

Notes

1 See I. Kant, *The Metaphysics of Morals*, introduction, translation, and notes by M. Gregor (Cambridge: Cambridge University Press, 1991), p. 96 (*The Doctrine of Right*, § 24). [s.h.]

2 'Not- und Verstandesstaat'. See F. Schiller, *On the Aesthetic Education of Man. In a Series of Letters*, edited and translated with an introduction, commentary and glossary of terms by E. M. Wilkinson and L. A. Willoughby (Oxford: Clarendon Press, 1967), p. 22 (4th Letter). [s.h.]

3 The first edition, and the Suhrkamp edition, refer to § 60, but Ilting's edition refers to § 6, which makes much better sense. [Translator's note.] See above, p. 331. [s.h.]

4 The first edition, and the Suhrkamp edition, read *ungebildetem* ('uneducated'). I follow Ilting's edition, whose reading *gebildetem* ('educated') makes better sense. [Translator's note.]

5 Paragraph not included in this collection. [S.H.]
6 Not included in this collection. [S.H.]
7 'Hat . . . wenig selbst zu denken'; this seems to be a misreading by Gans of the equivalent phrase in Hotho's notes (Hegel, *Vorlesungen über Rechtsphilosophie* [Ilting edition], 3: 630), 'hat wenig sich selbst zu danken' ('owes little to its own efforts'). [Translator's note.]
8 Paragraph not included in this collection. [S.H.]
9 Paragraph not included in this collection. [S.H.]
10 See Hegel, *Elements of the Philosophy of Right*, p. 233 (§ 199). See above, p. 366. [S.H.]
11 'Es ist der Gang Gottes in der Welt, daß der Staat ist'. This might also be translated as: 'it is the way of God in the world, that the state exists'. [S.H.]
12 Not included in this collection. [S.H.]
13 Not included in this collection. [S.H.]
14 i.e. the family, estates and corporations. See Hegel, *Elements of the Philosophy of Right*, pp. 234, 272 (§§ 201 Addition, 255). See above, pp. 367, 379. [S.H.]
15 Not included in this collection. [S.H.]
16 Not included in this collection. [S.H.]
17 Not included in this collection. [S.H.]

27

Philosophy of History: Introduction

---

*[. . .] We must first of all note that the object we have before us, i.e. world history, belongs to the **realm of the spirit**. The world as a whole comprehends both physical and spiritual nature. Physical nature also plays a part in world history. [. . .] But the spirit and the course of its development are the true substance of history. [. . .]*

a. The determination [Bestimmung] of spirit

*The first thing we must do is to define **the abstract determination of spirit**. It must, however, be pointed out* that the spirit is not in itself abstract, for it is not an abstraction invented by man; on the contrary, it is entirely individual, active, and absolutely alive: it is consciousness, but it is also the object of consciousness – for it is in the nature of the spirit to have itself as its object. The spirit, then, is capable of thought, and its thought is that of a being which itself exists, and which thinks that it exists and how it exists. It possesses knowledge: but knowledge is consciousness of a rational object. Besides, the spirit only has consciousness in so far as it is conscious of itself; in other words, I only know an object in so far as I know myself and my own determination through it, for whatever I am is also an object of my consciousness, and I am not just this, that or the other, but only what I **know** myself to be. I know my object, and I know myself; the two are inseparable. Thus the spirit forms a definite conception of itself and of its essential nature. It can only have a spiritual content; and its sole content and interest are spiritual. This, then, is how the spirit acquires a content: it does not find its content outside itself, but makes itself its own object and its own content. Knowledge is its form and function, but its content is the spiritual itself. Thus the spirit is by nature self-sufficient or free.

The nature of spirit can best be understood if we contrast it with its direct opposite, which is matter. Just as gravity is the substance of matter, so also can it be said that freedom is the substance of spirit. It is immediately obvious to everyone that freedom is one of the various attributes of spirit; but philosophy teaches us that all the attributes of spirit exist only by virtue of freedom, that all are merely means of attaining freedom, and that the sole object which they all seek and to whose realization they all contribute is freedom. Speculative philosophy has shown that freedom is the one authentic property of spirit. Matter possesses gravity in so far as it is impelled to move towards a central point; it is essentially composite, and consists entirely of discrete parts which all tend towards a centre; thus matter has no unity. It is made up of separate elements and aspires to a condition of unity; it thus endeavours to overcome itself and seeks its own opposite. If it were to succeed, it would no longer be matter, but would have ceased to exist as such; it strives towards ideality, for unity is its ideal existence. Spirit, on the other hand, is such that its centre is within itself; it too strives towards its centre, but it has its centre within itself. Its unity is not something external; it always finds it within itself, and exists in itself and with itself. Matter has its substance outside itself; spirit, on the other hand, is self-sufficient being, which is the same thing as freedom. For if I am dependent, I am beholden to something other than myself, and cannot exist without this external point of reference. If, however, I am self-sufficient, I am also free.

When the spirit strives towards its centre, it strives to perfect its own freedom; and this striving is fundamental to its nature. To say that spirit exists would at first seem to imply that it is a completed entity. On the contrary, it is by nature active, and activity is its essence; it is its own product, and is therefore its own beginning and its own end. Its freedom does not consist in static being, but in a constant negation of all that threatens to destroy freedom. The business of spirit is to produce itself, to make itself its own object, and to gain knowledge of itself; in this way, it exists for itself. Natural objects do not exist for themselves; for this reason, they are not free. The spirit produces and realizes itself in the light of its knowledge of itself; it acts in such a way that all its knowledge of itself is also realized. Thus everything depends on the spirit's self-awareness; if the spirit knows that it is free, it is altogether different from what it would be without this knowledge. For if it does not know that it is free, it is in the position of a slave who is content with his slavery and does not know that his condition is an improper one. It is the sensation of freedom alone which makes the spirit free, although it is in fact always free in and for itself. [. . .]

Given this abstract definition, we can say that world history is the record of the spirit's efforts to attain **knowledge** *of what it is* **in itself***. The* **Orientals** *do not know that the spirit or man as such are free in themselves. And because they do not know this, they are not themselves free. They only know that One is free; but for this very reason, such freedom is mere arbitrariness, savagery and brutal passion, or a milder and tamer version of this which is itself only an accident of nature, and equally arbitrary. This One is therefore merely a despot, not a free man and a human being. The consciousness of freedom first awoke among the* **Greeks,** *and they were accordingly free; but, like the Romans, they only knew that* **Some,** *and not all men as such, are free. Plato and Aristotle did not know this either; thus the Greeks not only had slaves, on which their life and the* *continued existence of their estimable freedom depended, but their very freedom itself was on the one hand only a fortuitous, undeveloped, transient, and limited efflorescence, and, on the other, a harsh servitude of all that is humane and proper to man. The* **Germanic** *nations, with the rise of Christianity, were the first to realize that man is by nature free, and that freedom of the spirit is his very essence. This consciousness first dawned in religion, in the innermost region of the spirit; but to incorporate the same principle into secular existence was a further problem, whose solution and application require long and arduous cultural exertions. For example, slavery did not immediately [come to an end] with the adoption of Christianity; still less did freedom at once predominate in states, or governments and constitutions become rationally organized and founded upon the principle of freedom. This* **application** *of the principle to secular affairs, the penetration and transformation of secular life by the principle of freedom, is the long process of which history itself [is made up]. I have already drawn attention to this* **distinction** *between the* **principle** *as such and its application – i.e. its* **introduction** *and* **execution** *in the actual world of the spirit and of life [. . .].*[1] *It is one of the basic articles of philosophical science, and its vital importance must not be overlooked. The same distinction applies not only to the* **Christian** *principle of the self-consciousness of freedom which I have mentioned provisionally here, it applies just as essentially to the principle of* **freedom** *in general. World history is the progress of the consciousness of freedom – a progress whose necessity it is our business to comprehend.*

These general remarks on the different degrees of knowledge of freedom – firstly, that of the Orientals, who knew only that **One** *is free, then that of the Greek and Roman world, which knew that* **Some** *are free, and finally, our own knowledge that* **All** *men as such are free, and that* **man** *is* **by nature** *free – supply us with the divisions we shall observe in our survey of world history and which will help us to organise our discussion of it. But these are only provisional remarks thrown out in passing; several other concepts must first be explained.*

The spirit's consciousness of its freedom (which is the precondition of the reality of this **freedom***) has been defined as spiritual reason in its determinate form, hence as the destiny of the spiritual world, and – since the latter is the substantial world and the physical world [is] subordinated to it (or, in speculative terminology, has no truth in comparison with it) – as the ultimate end of the world in general. But that this freedom, as defined above, still remains an indefinite term which is capable of infinite interpretations, and that, since it is the highest concept of all, it is open to an infinite number of misunderstandings, confusions, and errors and covers every possible kind of extravagance – all this has never been known and experienced so fully as in the present age; but we must make do for the moment with this general definition. We have also stressed the importance of the infinite difference between the principle – i.e. that which exists only* **in itself** *– and its realization. For freedom in itself carries with it the infinite necessity of attaining consciousness – for freedom, by definition, is self-knowledge – and hence of realizing itself: it is itself the end of its own operations, and the sole end of the spirit.*

The substance of the spirit is freedom. From this, we can infer that its end in the historical process is the freedom of the subject to follow its own conscience and morality, and to pursue and implement its own universal ends; it also implies that the subject has infinite value and that it must become conscious of its supremacy. The end of the world spirit is realized in substance through the freedom of each individual.

The spirits of the nations are the links in the process whereby the spirit arrives at free recognition of itself. Nations, however, exist **for** themselves – for we are not concerned here with spirit **in** itself – and as such, they have a natural existence. In so far as they are nations, their principles are natural ones; and since their principles differ, the nations themselves are also naturally different. Each has its own principle which it seeks to realize as its end; if it has attained this end, it has no further task to perform in the world.

The spirit of a nation should thus be seen as the development of a principle; this principle is at first bound up with an indistinct impulse which gradually works its way out and seeks to attain objective reality. A natural spirit of this kind is a determinate spirit, a concrete whole; it **must** gain recognition in its determinate form. Since it is a spirit, it can only be understood in spiritual terms, by means of thought, and it is we who understand it in this way; the next step is for the national spirit to understand itself in turn by the same means. We must therefore examine the determinate concept or principle of the spirit in question. This principle is extremely rich in content, and it assumes many forms in the course of its development; for the spirit is living and active, and is concerned only with its own productions. The spirit, as it advances towards its realization, towards self-satisfaction and self-knowledge, is the sole motive force behind all the deeds and aspirations of the nation. Religion, knowledge, the arts, and the destinies and events of history are all aspects of its evolution. This, and not the natural influences at work upon it (as the derivation of the word *natio* from *nasci* might suggest), determines the nation's character. In its active operations, the national spirit at first knows only the ends of its determinate reality, but not its own nature. But it is nevertheless endowed with an impulse to formulate its thoughts. Its supreme activity is thought, so that when it reaches the height of its powers, its aim is to comprehend itself. The ultimate aim of the spirit is to know itself, and to comprehend itself not merely intuitively but also in terms of thought. It must and will succeed in its task; but this very success is also its downfall, and this in turn heralds the emergence of a new phase and a new spirit. The individual national spirit fulfils itself by merging with the principle of another nation, so that we can observe a progression, growth and succession from one national principle to another. The task of philosophical world history is to discover the continuity within this movement. [. . .]

The aim of world history, therefore, is that the spirit should attain knowledge of its own true nature, that it should objectivize this knowledge and transform it into a real world, and give itself an objective existence. The essential point to note is that this aim is itself a product of the spirit. The spirit is not a natural entity like an animal, for the animal is no more than its immediate existence. The spirit is such that it produces itself and makes itself what it is. Thus the first form it assumes in its real existence is the outcome of its own activity. Its essential being is actuosity, not static existence, for it has produced itself, it has come to exist for itself, and made itself what it is by its own agency. It can only be said to have a true existence if it has produced itself, and its essential being is process in the absolute sense. This process, in which it mediates itself with itself by its own unaided efforts, has various distinct moments; it is full of movement and change, and is determined in different ways at different times. It consists essentially of a series of separate stages, and world history is the expression of the divine process which is a graduated progression in which the spirit comes to know and realize itself and its own truth. Its various stages are stages in the self-recognition of the spirit; and the essence of the spirit, its supreme imperative, is that it should recognize, know and realize itself for what it is. It accomplishes this end in the history of the world; it produces itself in a series of determinate forms, and these forms are the nations of world history. Each of them represents a particular stage of development, so that they correspond to epochs in the history of the world. Or on a more fundamental level, they are the principles in which the spirit has discovered itself, and which it is impelled to realize. There is therefore an essential connection between them in which the nature of the spirit alone is expressed.

World history is the expression of the divine and absolute process of the spirit in its highest forms, of the progression whereby it discovers its true nature and becomes conscious of itself. The specific forms it assumes at each of these stages are the national spirits of world history, with all the determinate characteristics of their ethical life, their constitutions, their art, their religion and their knowledge. The world spirit has an infinite urge and an irresistible impulse to realize these stages of its development; for this sequence and its realization are its true concept. World history merely shows how the spirit gradually attains consciousness and the will to truth; it progresses from its early glimmerings to major discoveries and finally to a state of complete consciousness. We have already discussed the ultimate end of this process.[2] The principles of the national spirits in their necessary progression are themselves only moments of the one universal spirit, which ascends through them in the course of history to its consummation in an all-embracing **totality**. [. . .]

The immediate question which now presents itself is this: what means does the Idea employ to realize itself? This is the second point we have to consider here.

b. *The means of its realization*

*This question of the **means** whereby freedom creates a world for itself leads us to the phenomenon of history proper. Whereas freedom as such is primarily an* *internal concept, the means it employs belong to the external and phenomenal world which confronts us directly in history. An initial* **survey of history**, *however, would indicate that the actions of men are governed by their needs, passions and interests, by the attitudes and aims to which these give rise, and by their own character and abilities; we gain the impression that, in this scene of activity, these needs, passions, interests, etc., are the sole* **motive forces**. *Individuals do at times pursue more general ends such as* **goodness**, *but the good they pursue is invariably of a limited character. Worthy patriotic sentiments are of this kind, for they may well be directed towards a country whose importance in relation to the world as a whole and to its universal end is negligible; and the same is true of love of one's family or friends, and indeed of moral rectitude in general. In short, all* **virtues** *come under this category. We may well see the ends of reason realized in the virtues of individual subjects and in their sphere of inflence: but these are only isolated individuals who constitute but a small proportion of the mass of mankind when we compare them with all the others, and the extent to which their virtues are effective is relatively limited. But in many cases, passions, private interests and the satisfaction of selfish impulses are the most potent force. What makes them powerful is [that] they do not heed any of the restraints which justice and morality seek to impose upon them, and the elemental power of passion has a more immediate hold over man than that artificial and laboriously acquired discipline of order and moderation, justice and morality.*

When we contemplate this display of passions, and consider the historical consequences of their violence and of the irrationality which is associated with them (and even more so with good intentions and worthy aims); when we see the evil, the wickedness, and the downfall of the most flourishing empires the human spirit has created; and when we are moved to profound pity for the untold miseries of individual human beings — we can only end with a feeling of sadness at the transience of everything. And since all this destruction is not the work of mere nature but of the will of man, our sadness takes on a moral quality, for the good spirit in us (if we are at all susceptible to it) eventually revolts at such a spectacle. Without rhetorical exaggeration, we need only compile an accurate account of the misfortunes which have overtaken the finest manifestations of national and political life, and of personal virtues or innocence, to see a most terrifying picture take shape before our eyes. Its effect is to intensify our feelings to an extreme pitch of hopeless sorrow with no redeeming circumstances to counterbalance it. We can only harden ourselves against it or escape from it by telling ourselves that it was ordained by fate and could not have been otherwise. There is nothing we can do about it now, and we react against the lassitude into which such sorrowful reflections can plunge us and return to our customary attitudes, to the aims and interests of the present, which [call for] activity rather than laments over the past. Indeed, we retreat into that selfish complacency which stands on the calmer shore and, from a secure position, smugly looks on at the distant spectacle of confusion and wreckage. But even as we look upon history as an altar on which the happiness of nations, the wisdom of states, and the virtue of individuals are slaughtered, our thoughts inevitably impel us to ask: **to whom**, *or* **to what ultimate end** *have these* *monstrous sacrifices been made? This usually leads in turn to those general consid-erations from which our whole enquiry began. From this beginning, we proceeded to define those same events which afford so sad a spectacle for gloomy sentiments and brooding reflection as no more than the **means** whereby what we have specified as the substantial destiny, the absolute and final end, or in other words, the true **result** of world history, is realized. From the very outset, we rejected the path of reflection as a means of ascending from the spectacle of historical detail to the universal principle behind it. Besides, such sentimental reflections have no real interest in transcending the attitudes and emotions which go along with them, or in solving the enigmas of providence to which they give rise. They are content instead to derive a lugubrious satisfaction from the empty and futile sublimities which the negative results of history evoke. Let us therefore return to the point of view we originally adopted; and the moments we shall discover within it will furnish us with the essential definitions we require in order to answer the questions which such scenes from history present.*

*The first thing we have to notice is this: what we have hitherto called the principle, or ultimate end, or destiny, or the nature and concept of the spirit **in itself**, is purely **universal and abstract**. A principle, fundamental rule or law is something universal and implicit, and as such, it has not attained complete reality, however true it may be in itself. Aims, principles and the like are present at first in our thoughts and inner intentions, or even in books, but not yet in reality itself. In other words, that which exists only **in itself** is a possibility or potentiality which has not yet emerged into existence. A second moment is necessary before it can attain reality – that of actuation or realization; and its principle is the will, the activity of mankind in the world at large. It is only by means of this activity that the original concepts or implicit determinations are realized and actualized.*

*Laws and principles have no immediate life or validity in themselves. The activity which puts them into operation and endows them with real existence has its source in the needs, impulses, inclinations and passions of man. If I put something into practice and give it a real existence, I must have some personal interest in doing so; I must be personally involved in it, and hope to obtain satisfaction through its accomplishment – in other words, my own interest must be at stake. To have an interest in something means to be implicated and involved in it, and an end which I am actively to pursue must in some way or other be my own end. It is **my** end which must be satisfied, even if the end for which I am working has many other sides to it which have nothing to do with me. This infinite right of the subject is the second essential moment of freedom, in that the subject must itself be satisfied by whatever activity or task it performs. And if men are to be interested in anything, they must be actively engaged in it; that is, they look for their own interest in whatever end they work for, and they wish to identify themselves with it and find their own self-esteem confirmed by it. But there is a possible misunderstanding here which we must take care to avoid: a common and justified form of censure or criticism is to say of someone that he is an interested party – in other words, that he is merely seeking some personal advantage and this alone; he is solely concerned with furthering his own cause, regardless of the* *common weal, and the latter interests him only in so far as he can turn it to his personal advantage, even at the expense of actively detracting from the general cause, jeopardizing it, or sacrificing it altogether. But anyone who actively supports a cause is not just an interested party – he is interested **in the cause itself**. Language accurately reproduces this distinction. Thus nothing can happen, nothing can be accomplished unless the individuals concerned can also gain satisfaction for themselves as particular individuals. For they have their own special needs, impulses and interests which are peculiar to themselves – peculiar to themselves inasmuch as they are separate individuals, although the same needs, impulses and interests may be no different in content from those of others, and may in fact be shared by them. Such interests include not only those dictated by personal needs and volitions, but also those which arise out of personal beliefs and convictions (or at least out of personal conjectures and opinions) – provided, of course, that the desire to reflect, to analyse, and to think rationally is already awake. Under these conditions, people also expect that the cause for which they are supposed to act should appeal to them personally, and at all events, that they should be able to enter into it with the backing of their own opinions and convictions regarding its goodness, justice, utility, the reward they hope to reap from it, and so on. This moment is particularly applicable to our own age, in which people are much less inclined to accept things on trust or on the strength of external authority and wish to act in support only of those causes to which they can assent with their own understanding and their independent convictions and opinions. [. . .]*

*We may therefore conclude that nothing whatsoever has been accomplished without the active interest of those concerned in it; and since interest can be described as passion (in so far as the whole individuality, to the exclusion of all other actual or possible interests and aims, applies itself to an object with every fibre of the will, and concentrates all its needs and resources on attaining its end), we may say without qualification that **nothing great** has been accomplished in the world **without passion**. Passion is the subjective or formal aspect of the energy of active volition – irrespective of its actual content or end – and this distinction between form and content also applies to all personal convictions, opinions and conscience. For the content of my convictions and the end to which my passions are directed are of vital importance when it comes to deciding whether the one or the other is of a true and substantial nature. But conversely, if its nature is indeed such, it must inevitably attain real existence as that moment of the subjective will which includes all such factors as needs, impulses and passions, as well as personal attitudes, opinions and convictions.*

From this examination of the second essential moment in the realization of historical ends, it is evident – if we stop for a moment to consider the political implications – that a state will be well constituted and internally powerful if the private interest of its citizens coincides with the general end of the state, so that the one can be satisfied and realized through the other; this proposition is an extremely important one. But for the state to achieve this unity, numerous institutions must be set up and appropriate mechanisms invented, and the understanding must go through *prolonged struggles before it discovers what is in fact appropriate. Conflicts with individual interests and passions are also inevitable, and the latter must be subjected to a long and rigorous process of discipline before the ultimate unity is achieved. The moment at which the state attains this unity marks the most flourishing period in its history, when its virtue, strength and prosperity are at their height. But **world history** does not begin with **any conscious end**, as do all **particular associations** set up by men. Even man's social instinct entails the conscious purpose of securing his life and property, and as soon as a society has come into being, such purposes at once take on an even more definite shape. The aim is now to defend the city of Athens or Rome, for instance, and with every new evil or exigency which arises, the problem becomes more specific still. World history begins with its **universal end** – that the **concept** of the spirit should be realized – existing only **in itself**, i.e. as mere **nature**; it is as yet only an inward, basic, unconscious impulse, and the whole activity of world history, as already mentioned, is a constant endeavour to make this impulse conscious. Thus, what we have called the subjective element – i.e. needs, impulses, passions, particular interests, and opinions or subjective ideas – is immediately present to itself from the beginning in the shape of **natural being** or **natural will**. This vast conglomeration of volition, interests and activities is the sum total of **instruments** and means which the world spirit employs to accomplish its end, to make this end conscious and to give it reality; and its end is simply that of finding itself, of coming to terms with itself, and of contemplating its own actuality. All these expressions of individual and national life, in seeking and fulfilling their **own** ends, are at the same time the **means** and **instruments of a higher purpose** and wider enterprise of which they are themselves ignorant and which they nevertheless unconsciously carry out. This, however, may be open to question, and it has indeed been questioned and often denied altogether, or dismissed and condemned as pure fantasy or as a figment of mere philosophy. But I have made my position clear on this issue from the very beginning, and stated our initial assumption or belief (which I put forward only as anticipating the result of our enquiry, without any further pretensions for the moment) that **reason rules the world**, and consequently its history, and continues to do so. In relation to this universal substance which exists in and for itself, everything else is in a subordinate position and acts only as a means to serve its interests. This universal reason exists as an immanent principle within history, in which and through which it fulfils itself. That the union of the universal substance, which exists in and for itself, with the particular and the subjective, is the sole truth, is a **speculative** proposition which is dealt with in this general form by logic. But in the actual **process** of world history, seen as something as yet incomplete, we find that the subjective element or consciousness is [not] yet in a position to know the true nature of the ultimate end of history, the concept of the spirit. For the latter has not yet become the content of its needs and interests; and although the subjective consciousness is still unaware of it, the universal substance is nevertheless present in its particular ends and realizes itself through them. Since, as I have said, the speculative aspect of this relationship belongs to the province of logic, this is not the place for me to define and analyse* *its concept and to make it, so to speak,* **intelligible**. *But I can at least attempt, by means of examples, to give a clearer impression of its nature.*

This relationship between the subjective consciousness and the universal substance is such that the actions of human beings in the history of the world produce an effect altogether different from what they themselves intend and accomplish, from what they immediately recognize and desire. Their own interest is gratified; but at the same time, they accomplish a further purpose, a purpose which was indeed implicit in their own actions but was not part of their conscious intentions. By way of analogy, let us imagine a man who, from motives of revenge – perhaps of justified revenge, in that he may himself have suffered unjustly – set light to someone else's house; this at once means that a connection is established between the immediate deed and a train of circumstances, albeit external circumstances, which have nothing to do with the original deed regarded purely in isolation. The deed as such consisted, let us say, in applying a small flame to a small portion of a beam. What this deed itself does not accomplish takes place of its own accord; the ignited portion is connected with further sections of the beam, these in turn are connected with the timberwork of the entire house, which is itself connected with other houses, and a widespread conflagration [results]; this conflagration destroys the property of many other people apart from that of the individual against whom the revenge was directed, and it may even cost many of them their lives. All this was not part of the original deed itself, nor of its perpetrator's intention. But the same action contains yet another general implication: in the intention of its instigator, it was purely a means of gaining revenge on an individual by destroying his property; but it is also a crime, which carries its punishment with it. The perpetrator may not have been conscious of this, and it may not have been his remotest intention, but it is nevertheless the universal and substantial essence of the deed itself, and a necessary consequence of it.

The main purpose of this example is to show that an action may have implications which transcend the intention and consciousness of the agent. The above example has the further peculiarity [that] the substance of the act, and consequently the act itself in its entirety, reacts upon the individual who performed it; it recoils upon him and destroys him, thereby annulling the original act itself (inasmuch as it constitutes a crime) and restoring the authority of justice. But there is no need to stress this aspect here, as it applies only to a specific instance; and besides, I have already said that I wished only to establish an analogy.

But I should like to mention a further example, to which we shall have occasion to return later at the appropriate moment.[3] As an actual historical instance, it exemplifies that combination of the universal and the particular, of an apparently necessary determination and an apparently contingent purpose, in the peculiar form with which we are at present chiefly concerned. **Caesar**, *in danger [of losing] the position to which he had ascended – a position in which he was not yet superior to the others who stood at the head of the state, but at least on an equal footing with them – opposed his rivals with the intention of preserving himself, his position, his honour and his security. He was in danger [of succumbing] to those who [were] on the point of becoming his enemies, but who at the same time had the* *formal constitution of the state (and hence the authority of outward legality) on the side of their own personal ends. But since their power gave them sovereignty over the provinces of the Roman Empire, his victory over them simultaneously enabled him to conquer the whole empire itself. He thereby became the sole ruler of the state, although he left the form of the constitution intact. But the means by which he achieved his own (originally negative) end, i.e. the undivided sovereignty of Rome, was at the same time an inherently necessary determination in the history of Rome and of the world. Thus not just his own personal advantage was involved, for his work was the product of an impulse which accomplished the end for which his age was ready. Such are the great men of history: the substance of their own particular ends is the will of the world spirit. Their true power resides in this inner content, which is present in the universal unconscious instinct of mankind. All men are driven on by an inward compulsion, and they are incapable of resisting the individual who has taken it upon himself to execute one of the ends of history in the course of furthering his own personal interests. On the contrary, the nations flock to his standard, for he reveals to them and carries out what is already their own immanent impulse. [. . .]*

The great individuals of world history, therefore, are those who seize upon this higher universal and make it their own end. It is they who realize the end appropriate to the higher concept of the spirit. To this extent, they may be called **heroes**. They do not find their aims and vocation in the calm and regular system of the present, in the hallowed order of things as they are. Indeed, their justification does not lie in the prevailing situation, for they draw their inspiration from another source, from that hidden spirit whose hour is near but which still lies beneath the surface and seeks to break out without yet having attained an existence in the present. For this spirit, the present world is but a shell which contains the wrong kind of kernel. It might, however, be objected that everything which deviates from the established order – whether intentions, aims, opinions, or so-called ideals – is likewise different from what is already there. Adventures of all kinds have such ideals, and their activities are based on attitudes which conflict with the present circumstances. But the fact that all such attitudes, sound reasons, or general principles differ from existing ones does not mean to say that they are justified. The only true ends are those whose content has been produced by the absolute power of the inner spirit itself in the course of its development; and world-historical individuals are those who have willed and accomplished not just the ends of their own imagination or personal opinions, but only those which were appropriate and necessary. Such individuals know what is necessary and timely, and have an inner vision of what it is.

It is possible to distinguish between the insight of such individuals and the realization that even such manifestations of the spirit as this are no more than moments within the universal Idea. To understand this is the prerogative of philosophy. World-historical individuals have no need to do so, as they are men of practice. They do, however, know and will their own enterprise, because the time is ripe for it, and it is already inwardly present. Their business is to know this universal principle, which is the necessary and culminating stage in the development of their world, to make it their end, and to devote their energy to its realization. They derive the universal principle whose realization they accomplish from within themselves; it is not, however, their own invention, but is eternally present and is merely put into practice by them and honoured in their persons. But since they draw it from within themselves, from a source which was not previously available, they appear to derive it from themselves alone; and the new world order and the deeds they accomplish appear to be their own achievement, their personal interest and creation. But right is on their side, for they are the far-sighted ones: they have discerned what is true in their world and in their age, and have recognized the concept, the next universal to emerge. And the others, as already remarked, flock to their standard, for it is they who express what the age requires. They are the most far-sighted among their contemporaries; they know best what issues are involved, and whatever they do is right. The others feel that this is so, and therefore have to obey them. Their words and deeds are the best that could be said and done in their time. Thus, the great individuals of history can only be understood within their own context; and they are admirable simply because they have made themselves the instruments of the substantial spirit. This is the true relationship between the individual and his universal substance. For this substance is the source of everything, the sole aim, the sole power, and the sole end which is willed by such individuals; it seeks its satisfaction through them and is accomplished by them. It is this which gives them their power in the world, and only in so far as their ends are compatible with that of the spirit which has being in and for itself do they have absolute right on their side – although it is a right of a wholly peculiar kind.

The state of the world is not yet fully known, and the aim is to give it reality. This is the object of world-historical individuals, and it is through its attainment that they find satisfaction. They can discern the weakness of what still appears to exist in the present, although it possesses only a semblance of reality. The spirit's inward development has outgrown the world it inhabits, and it is about to progress beyond it. Its self-consciousness no longer finds satisfaction in the present, but its dissatisfaction has not yet enabled it to discover what it wants, for the latter is not yet positively present; its status is accordingly negative. The world-historical individuals are those who were the first to formulate the desires of their fellows explicitly. It is not easy for us to know what we want; indeed, we may well want something, yet still remain in a negative position, a position of dissatisfaction, for we may as yet be unconscious of the positive factor. But the individuals in question knew what they wanted, and what they wanted was of a positive nature. They do not at first create satisfaction, however, and the aim of their actions is not that of satisfying others in any case. If this were so, they would certainly have plenty to do, because their fellows do not know what the age requires or even what they themselves desire. But to try to resist these world-historical individuals is a futile undertaking, for they are irresistibly driven on to fulfil their task. Their course is the correct one, and even if the others do not believe that it corresponds to their own desires, they nevertheless adopt it or acquiesce in it. There is a power within them which is stronger than they are, even if it appears to them as something external and alien and runs counter to what they consciously believe they want. For the spirit in its further evolution is the inner soul of all individuals, although it remains in a state of unconsciousness until great men call it to life. It is the true object of all men's desires, and it is for this reason that it exerts a power over them to which they surrender even at the price of denying their conscious will; they follow these leaders of souls because they feel the irresistible power of their own inner spirit pulling them in the same direction.

If we go on to examine the fate of these world-historical individuals, we see that they had the good fortune [to be] the executors of an end which marked a stage in the advance of the universal spirit. But as individual subjects, they also have an existence distinct from that of the universal substance, an existence in which they cannot be said to have enjoyed what is commonly called happiness. They did not wish to be happy in any case, but only to attain their end, and they succeeded in doing so only by dint of arduous labours. They knew how to obtain satisfaction and to accomplish their end, which is the universal end. With so great an end before them, they boldly resolved to challenge all the beliefs of their fellows. Thus it was not happiness that they chose, but exertion, conflict and labour in the service of their end. And even when they reached their goal, peaceful enjoyment and happiness were not their lot. Their actions are their entire being, and their whole nature and character are determined by their ruling passion. When their end is attained, they fall aside like empty husks. They may have undergone great difficulties in order to accomplish their purpose, but as soon as they have done so, they die early like Alexander, are murdered like Caesar, or deported like Napoleon. One may well ask what they gained for themselves. What they gained was that concept or end which they succeeded in realizing. Other kinds of gain, such as peaceful enjoyment, were denied them. The fearful consolation that the great men of history did not enjoy what is called happiness – which is possible only in private life, albeit under all kinds of different external circumstances – this consolation can be found in history by those who are in need of it. It is needed by the envious, who resent all that is great and outstanding and who accordingly try to belittle it and to find fault with it. The existence of such outstanding figures only becomes bearable to them because they know that such men did not enjoy happiness. In this knowledge, envy sees a means of restoring the balance between itself and those whom it envies. Thus, it has often enough been demonstrated even in our own times that princes are never happy on their thrones; this enables men not to grudge them their thrones, and to accept the fact that it is the princes rather than they themselves who sit upon them. The free man, however, is not envious, for he readily acknowledges and rejoices in the greatness of others.

But such great men are fastened upon by a whole crowed of envious spirits who hold up their passions as weaknesses. It is indeed possible to interpret their lives in terms of passion, and to put the emphasis on moral judgements by declaring that it was their passions which motivated them. Of course, they were men of passion, for they were passionately dedicated to their ends, which they served with their whole character, genius and nature. In such individuals, then, that which is necessary in and for itself assumes the form of passion. Great men of this kind admittedly do seem to follow only the dictates of their passions and of their own free will, but the object of their will is universal, and it is this which constitutes their pathos. Passion is simply the energy of their ego, and without this, they could not have accomplished anything.

In this respect, the aim of passion and that of the Idea are one and the same; passion is the absolute unity of individual character and the universal. The way in which the spirit in its subjective individuality here coincides exactly with the Idea has an almost animal quality about it. [...]

The particular interests of passion cannot therefore be separated from the realization of the universal; for the universal arises out of the particular and determinate and its negation. The particular has its own interests in world history; it is of a finite nature, and as such, it must perish. Particular interests contend with one another, and some are destroyed in the process. But it is from this very conflict and destruction of particular things that the universal emerges, and it remains unscathed itself. For it is not the universal Idea which enters into opposition, conflict and danger; it keeps itself in the background, untouched and unharmed, and sends forth the particular interests of passion to fight and wear themselves out in its stead. It is what we may call the **cunning of reason** that it sets the passions to work in its service, so that the agents by which it gives itself existence must pay the penalty and suffer the loss. For the latter belong to the phenomenal world, of which part is worthless and part is of positive value. The particular is as a rule inadequate in relation to the universal, and individuals are sacrificed and abandoned as a result. The Idea pays the tribute which existence and the transient world exact, but it pays it through the passions of individuals rather than out of its own resources. Caesar had to do what was necessary to overthrow the decaying freedom of Rome; he himself met his end in the struggle, but necessity triumphed: in relation to the Idea, freedom was subordinate to the external events. [...]

c. *The material of its realization*

*The third point to be considered is the nature of the **end to be realized** by these means, in other words, the form it assumes in reality. We have spoken hitherto of **means**, but in the realization of a subjective and finite end we must also take*

*account of the **material** which is available or which has to be procured in order
that the end may be realized. The question we must answer is accordingly this:
what is the material in which the ultimate end of reason is realized?*

The changes in historical existence presuppose a medium within which
such changes occur. But as we have seen, it is the subjective will which
implements them. Thus, in this case too, the first part of our answer is once
again the subject itself, the needs of men, and the realm of subjectivity in
general. The rational attains existence within the medium of human knowledge and volition. We have seen how the subjective will has an end which
represents the truth of a reality (in so far as it embodies some great passion
of world-historical significance). When its passions are limited, however, the
subjective will is dependent, and it can only satisfy its particular ends within
this position of dependence. But as already pointed out, it too has a substantial life, a reality in which it moves as in its essential being and which
constitutes the aim of its existence. This essential being, the unity of the
subjective will and the universal, is the ethical whole, and its concrete
manifestation is the **state**. The state is the reality within which the individual has and enjoys his freedom, but only in so far as he knows, believes
in and wills the universal. This, then, is the focal point of all the other
concrete aspects of the spirit, such as justice, art, ethics, and the amenities
of existence. Within the state, freedom becomes its own object and achieves
its positive realization. But this does not mean that the subjective will of the
individual is implemented and satisfied through the universal will, and that
the latter is merely a means to the end of the former. Nor is the universal
will merely a community of human beings within which the freedom of all
individuals has to be limited. To imagine that freedom is such that the
individual subject, in its co-existence with other subjects, must limit its
freedom in such a way that this collective restriction, the mutual constraint
of all, leaves everyone a limited area in which to act as he pleases, is to interpret freedom in purely negative terms; on the contrary, justice, ethical life
and the state, and these alone, are the positive realization and satisfaction of
freedom. The random inclinations of individuals are not the same thing as
freedom. That kind of freedom on which restrictions are imposed is mere
arbitrariness, which exists solely in relation to particular needs.

Only in the state does man have a rational existence. The aim of all education is to ensure that the individual does not remain purely subjective but
attains an objective existence within the state. The individual can certainly
make the state into a means of attaining this or that end. But the truth is
realized only in so far as each individual wills the universal cause itself and
has discarded all that is inessential. Man owes his entire existence to the
state, and has his being within it alone. Whatever worth and spiritual reality
he possesses are his solely by virtue of the state. For as a knowing being, he
has spiritual reality only in so far as his being, i.e. the rational itself, is his
object and possesses objective and immediate existence for him; only as
such does he possess consciousness and exist in an ethical world, within the

legal and ethical life of the state. For the truth is the unity of the universal and the subjective will, and the universal is present within the state, in its laws and in its universal and rational properties.

The subjective will – or passion – is the activating and realizing principle; the Idea is the inner essence, and the state is the reality of ethical life in the present. For the state is the unity of the universal, essential will and the will of the subject, and it is this which constitutes ethical life. The individual who lives within this unity has an ethical existence, and his value consists solely in this substantiality. **Sophocles'** Antigone says: 'The divine commands are not of yesterday, nor of today; no, they live eternally, and no one could say whence they came.'[4] The laws of ethics are not contingent, for they are the rational itself. The aim of the state is that the substance which underlies the real activity and dispositions of men should be recognized and made manifest, and that it should ensure its own continuity. The absolute interest of reason requires that this ethical whole should be present; and it is from this interest of reason that the justification and merit of those heroes who have founded states – however primitive the latter may have been – are derived. The state does not exist for the sake of the citizens; it might rather be said that the state is the end, and the citizens are its instruments. But this relation of end and means is not at all appropriate in the present context. For the state is not an abstraction which stands in opposition to the citizens; on the contrary, they are distinct moments like those of organic life, in which no one member is either a means or an end. The divine principle in the state is the Idea made manifest on earth. [. . .]

Notes

1 See Hegel, *Lectures on the Philosophy of World History*, p. 35 (not included in this collection). [s.h.]
2 Hegel, *Lectures on the Philosophy of World History*, p. 55. See above, p. 402. [s.h.]
3 See, for example, Hegel, *Lectures on the Philosophy of World History*, p. 89. See above, p. 413. [s.h.]
4 *Greek Tragedies*, eds D. Grene and R. Lattimore, 3 vols (Chicago: University of Chicago Press, 1960), 1: 196 (Sophocles, *Antigone*, ll. 455–6). [s.h.]

Part VI

Philosophy of Absolute Spirit: Aesthetics, Philosophy of Religion and History of Philosophy

Introduction

The freedom that is afforded by life in the state and by historical action is concrete and objective. It is the freedom, not just to let one's inner imagination play, but to achieve actual satisfaction of one's needs through property ownership, labour and human companionship. Nevertheless, such freedom and satisfaction are regarded by Hegel as ultimately restricted and finite, because they are achieved through fulfilling particular aims – doing well in this particular job, building a family with this particular person – which of necessity are open to change and may be supplanted by others. *Absolute* freedom and satisfaction, according to Hegel, can only be found by bringing to mind that which is itself absolute: the absolute character or *truth* of being and of human spiritual freedom. Such absolute freedom is attained in the three forms of absolute self-knowledge or spirit: art, religion and philosophy.

Hegel gives a brief account of the forms of absolute spirit in the third section of the *Philosophy of Spirit* (which forms part three of the *Encyclopaedia* [1830]). But they are given much more extensive treatment in his voluminous *Lectures on Aesthetics*, *Lectures on the Philosophy of Religion* and *Lectures on the History of Philosophy*, which were delivered in Berlin throughout the 1820s and have since exercised enormous influence on aesthetic theorists such as A. C. Bradley and Benedetto Croce, theologians such as Karl Barth and Eberhard Jüngel, and philosophers such as Heidegger, Adorno and Derrida.

In art, Hegel maintains, stone, wood, coloured pigment and sound are worked into the visible and audible expression of human freedom and of the differentiated unity of being itself. When they are rendered sensuously intuitable in this way, freedom and unity appear as *beauty*. In the passages from the *Aesthetics* selected here Hegel discusses various examples of beautiful freedom and unity, including the 'serene peace and bliss' of the classical Greek sculpture, the 'well-being and delight in life' suffusing Murillo's pictures of beggar-boys, and the 'free self-reliance' of the characters in tragic drama.[1] Much of what Hegel says about beauty shows the influence of Winckelmann, Kant, Schiller and Schelling. Yet he also departs from them in many significant ways. In particular, he displays a much higher regard for Dutch painting than either Winckelmann or Schelling.

Hegel goes on to sketch the distinction between symbolic art (in which true freedom and beauty are actually lacking), classical art (in which spirit and body are united in the most harmonious beauty) and romantic art (which achieves the most inward beauty, but also makes space for the sheer externality of nature). He also describes the modern situation in which the artist is free to choose any style or content, provided 'it does not contradict the formal law of being simply beautiful and capable of artistic treatment'.[2] It should be noted, by the way, that Hegel does *not* maintain anywhere that art dies in the modern world. He concedes that 'art has ceased to be the supreme need of the spirit', but he clearly acknowledges a continuing role for modern art. Indeed, he expresses the hope that 'art will always rise higher and come to perfection'.[3]

The selections from the *Aesthetics* conclude with Hegel's famous account of tragedy and comedy, including his influential reading of Sophocles' *Antigone* and his less well-known, but also profoundly illuminating, interpretation of the comedy of Aristophanes. Tragedy, for Hegel, is generated by heroic characters who are unable to renounce their ambitions or their justified passions and so destroy themselves. Comedy, by contrast, shows characters who are 'not seriously tied to the finite world with which they are engaged' and who can thus give up their foolish concerns and still remain happily secure in themselves.[4]

Religion, according to Hegel – in particular, the Christian religion – reinforces the lesson of comedy by teaching that the deepest spiritual freedom comes through the willingness to let go of *all* that one holds dear, even to the point of death. For the Christian, this readiness to let go of what is one's own – which is the mark of *love* – is revealed to be the true way of humanity in the life and death of Jesus Christ. The Christian also believes that through Christ love is revealed to be the true nature of God or the Absolute as such.[5] This, Hegel tells us, is because 'religion has pictorial thinking [*Vorstellung*] as its form of consciousness'.[6] That is to say, whereas philosophy knows the Absolute to be reason or Idea unfolding as nature and human freedom, Christian faith *pictures* such absolute reason as – and *feels* it to be – divine love at work in the world and within ourselves.

Measured against the knowledge afforded by philosophy, Christianity – like art – fails to disclose fully the true nature of absolute reason. In Hegel's view, however, human beings are imaginative, feeling beings, and cannot live by pure concepts alone. It is thus essential not only that we know and understand the truth through thought, but also that we picture and feel it in the inwardness of faith (and, indeed, see and hear it given sensuous expression in art). Moreover, Hegel thinks that it is in fact wholly appropriate to picture absolute reason as *love* because, like love, reason 'is the resolution of the contradictions posited by it'.[7] The work of absolute reason in the world is thus just *like* the work of love in so far as both bring about profound unity in difference. Furthermore, not only is love the right image for reason, but when absolute reason determines itself to be not just nature, but human freedom and ethical life (in particular, marriage), it actually *becomes* love itself. According to Hegel, therefore, even though religion may not attain to the clarity of philosophy, 'when we say, "God is love", we are saying something very great and true'.[8]

Hegel's *Lectures on the Philosophy of Religion* offer a philosophical account of all the major world religions. The passages selected here (from the lectures of 1827) concentrate on Hegel's account of Christianity, however, because it is in Christianity that he believes the truth is pictured most concretely. Of particular importance, to my mind, are the passages setting out Hegel's conception of the triune God, his comparison of Christ and Socrates, his interpretation of Christ's death as manifesting infinite love and as thus taking away the sheer negativity of death (as putting death itself 'to death'), and his understanding of the religious community – the church – as itself Holy Spirit.

Religious experience of the truth, like aesthetic experience of it, is absolutely essential to true human freedom, in Hegel's view. Nevertheless, neither art nor religion provides the highest freedom, because neither presents the truth in the transparent and fully self-determining form of conceptual understanding. This task falls to philosophy – more specifically, to dialectical logic, philosophy of nature and philosophy of spirit. The project of Hegel's *Lectures on the History of Philosophy*, which crown his philosophical system, is to show how philosophy has developed from its beginning with Thales and the other Pre-Socratics to the point at which it recognizes – with Hegel himself – that it must proceed immanently and dialectically if it is to understand properly what it is to think and what it is to be.

In the passages from the introduction to the lectures selected here, Hegel points first to the parallel he sees between the development of philosophy in history and the conceptual development in the *Logic*. 'The succession of philosophical systems in history,' he maintains, 'is the same as their succession in the logical derivation of the categories of the Idea'.[9] The historical development of philosophy is not random, therefore, but is determined by the path that thought must take as it comes to understand the nature of being, freedom and thought itself more fully. The development of philosophy is not, however, utterly independent of the overall development of civilization as a whole – of social, political and cultural development. This is because a given philosophy articulates in conceptual form the understanding of being and freedom that informs the whole culture and society in which it arises. Philosophy develops, therefore, as culture and society develop, and the path trodden by philosophical thought proves to be one and the same as that trodden by civilization as a whole – the path laid down by our developing comprehension of ourselves and the world we inhabit.

Any modern interpretation of a philosophy – be it of Aristotle's, Kant's or Hegel's own – must thus place that philosophy in relation not only to other philosophies, but also to the total historical context in which it emerges. This, indeed, is one of the enduring legacies of Hegel's thought, inherited from Herder and passed on to Marx, Nietzsche, Heidegger and Gadamer: that philosophy is necessarily and irreducibly *historical*. What distinguishes Hegel from his historicist successors is his conviction that the historical development of philosophy – as, indeed, of society, art and religion – is itself the work of *reason*: the rational process wherein the absolute nature of reason itself is gradually revealed and brought to consciousness.

Hegel's account of absolute spirit completes his system of philosophy. Four things should be noted about this account. First of all, absolute spirit must be recognized to be thoroughly historical – an utter contradiction to some. Secondly, the different forms of absolute spirit – art, religion and philosophy – must be understood to develop together and so must each be conceived in relation to the others. Thirdly, within the process of their combined development, each form of absolute spirit must be recognized to achieve the highest comprehension of which it is capable at a different time in history. Religion comes to picture the Absolute as love long before philosophy comes to comprehend it fully as self-determining reason or Idea; and art presents the truth in the form of perfect beauty before religion pictures it as love. Fourthly, in spite of the fact that art, religion and philosophy reach maturity at different times in history and disclose the truth with differing degrees of clarity, all three continue to be necessary in the modern world, because the human spirit *by its very nature* needs to see and hear the truth given sensuous expression, to picture and feel the truth in faith, and to understand the truth in thought. If one bears these four things in mind, it becomes clear that absolute spirit is a highly complex phenomenon. Indeed, it exemplifies within itself the very unity-in-difference which it declares to be the truth.

The passages in Part VI are taken from G. W. F. Hegel, *Aesthetics. Lectures on Fine Art*, translated by T. M. Knox (Oxford: Clarendon Press, 1975), G. W. F. Hegel, *Lectures on the Philosophy of Religion* (One Volume Edition: The Lectures of 1827), edited by P. C. Hodgson, translated by R. F. Brown, P. C. Hodgson and J. M. Stewart, with the assistance of H. S. Harris (Berkeley: University of California Press, 1988), and G. W. F. Hegel, *Introduction to the Lectures on the History of Philosophy*, translated by T. M. Knox and A. V. Miller (Oxford: Clarendon Press, 1985). The German text of the *Aesthetics* can be found in Hegel, *Werke in zwanzig Bänden*, vols 13, 14 and 15, and the German text of the *Lectures on the Philosophy of Religion* can be found in G. W. F. Hegel, *Vorlesungen. Ausgewählte Nachschriften und Manuskripte*, vols 3–5: *Vorlesungen über die Philosophie der Religion*, edited by W. Jaeschke (Hamburg: Felix Meiner, 1983ff). Neither text was written by Hegel himself. The text of the *Aesthetics* was compiled by H. G. Hotho (the editor of the 1835 edition) from Hegel's own papers and from student transcripts of his lectures. The text of the *Lectures on the Philosophy of Religion* which is used here was compiled by Walter Jaeschke (the editor of the most recent edition), once more from student transcripts of Hegel's lectures. The German text of the first passage from the *Introduction to the Lectures on the*

History of Philosophy ('Concept and Aim') is to be found in Hegel, *Werke in zwanzig Bänden*, vol. 20. (pp. 475–80). This passage was written by Hegel himself in 1820. The German text of the other passages is to be found in G. W. F. Hegel, *Einleitung in die Geschichte der Philosophie*, edited by J. Hoffmeister (Hamburg: Felix Meiner, 1940). This work was not written by Hegel himself, but was compiled by Johannes Hoffmeister from student transcripts of Hegel's lectures.

Notes

1 G. W. F. Hegel, *Aesthetics: Lectures on Fine Art*, translated by T. M. Knox (Oxford: Clarendon Press, 1975), pp. 157, 170, 1195. See below, pp. 432, 436, 450.
2 Hegel, *Aesthetics*, p. 605. See below, p. 442.
3 Hegel, *Aesthetics*, p. 103. See below, p. 428.
4 Hegel, *Aesthetics*, pp. 1197, 1221. See below, pp. 451, 469.
5 Hegel, *Lectures on the Philosophy of Religion*, pp. 418, 466. See below, pp. 488–9, 499.
6 Hegel, *Aesthetics*, p. 103. See below, p. 428.
7 Hegel, *Lectures on the Philosophy of Religion*, p. 420. See below, p. 490. See also Hegel, *Elements of the Philosophy of Right*, p. 199 (§ 158 Addition). See above, p. 360.
8 Hegel, *Lectures on the Philosophy of Religion*, p. 418. See below, p. 489.
9 G. W. F. Hegel, *Introduction to the Lectures on the History of Philosophy*, translated by T. M. Knox and A. V. Miller (Oxford: Clarendon Press, 1985), p. 22. See below, p. 510.

28

Aesthetics: The Ideal

Introduction

[. . .] Now the highest content which the subject can comprise in himself is what we can point-blank call *freedom*. Freedom is the highest destiny of the spirit. In the first place, on its purely formal side, it consists in this, that in what confronts the subject there is nothing alien and it is not a limitation or a barrier; on the contrary, the subject finds himself in it. Even under this formal definition of freedom, all distress and every misfortune has vanished, the subject is reconciled with the world, satisfied in it, and every opposition and contradiction is resolved. But, looked at more closely, freedom has the rational in general as its content: for example, morality in action, truth in thinking. But since freedom at first is only subjective and not effectively achieved, the subject is confronted by the unfree, by the purely objective as the necessity of nature, and at once there arises the demand that this opposition be reconciled. [. . .]

Consequently, man strives further in the realm of spirit to obtain satisfaction and freedom in knowing and willing, in learning and actions. The ignorant man is not free, because what confronts him is an alien world, something outside him and in the offing, on which he depends, without his having made this foreign world for himself and therefore without being at home in it by himself as in something his own. The impulse of curiosity, the pressure for knowledge, from the lowest level up to the highest rung of philosophical insight arises only from the struggle to cancel this situation of unfreedom and to make the world one's own in one's ideas and thought. Freedom in action issues in the opposite way, from the fact that the rationality of the will wins actualization. This rationality the will actualizes in the life of the state. In a state which is really articulated rationally all the laws and organizations are nothing but a realization of freedom in its essential characteristics. When this is the case, the individual's reason finds in these institutions only the actuality of his own essence, and if he obeys these laws, he coincides, not with something alien to himself, but simply with what is his own. Caprice [*Willkür*], of course, is often equally called 'freedom'; but caprice is only non-rational freedom, choice and self-determination issuing not from the rationality of the will but from fortuitous impulses and their dependence on sense and the external world.

Now man's physical needs, as well as his knowing and willing, do indeed get a satisfaction in the world and do resolve in a free way the antithesis of subjective and objective, of inner freedom and externally existent necessity. But nevertheless the content of this freedom and satisfaction remains *restricted*, and thus this freedom and self-satisfaction retain too an aspect of *finitude*. But where there is finitude, opposition and contradiction always break out again afresh, and satisfaction does not get beyond being relative. In law and its actualization, for example, my rationality, my will and its freedom, are indeed recognized; I count as a person and am respected as such; I have property and it is meant to remain mine; if it is endangered, the court sees justice done to me. But this recognition and freedom are always solely confined to single relative matters and their single objects: this house, this sum of money, this specific right, this specific law, etc., this single action and reality. What confronts consciousness here is single circumstances which indeed bear on one another and make up a totality of relations, but only under purely relative categories and innumerable conditions, and, dominated by these, satisfaction may as easily be momentary as permanent.

Now, at a higher level, the life of the state, as a whole, does form a perfect totality in itself: monarch, government, law-courts, the military, organization of civil society, and associations, etc., rights and duties, aims and their satisfaction, the prescribed modes of action, duty-performance, whereby this political whole brings about and retains its stable reality – this entire organism is rounded off and completely perfected in a genuine state. But the *principle* itself, the actualization of which is the life of the state and wherein man seeks his satisfaction, is still once again *one-sided* and inherently abstract, no matter in how many ways it may be articulated without and within. It is only the rational freedom of the *will* which is explicit here; it is only in the *state* – and once again only this *individual* state – and therefore again in a *particular* sphere of existence and the isolated reality of this sphere, that freedom is actual. Thus man feels too that the rights and obligations in these regions and their mundane and, once more, *finite* mode of existence are insufficient; he feels that both in their objective character, and also in their relation to the subject, they need a still higher confirmation and sanction.

What man seeks in this situation, ensnared here as he is in finitude on every side, is the region of a higher, more substantial, truth, in which all oppositions and contradictions in the finite can find their final resolution, and freedom its full satisfaction. This is the region of absolute, not finite, truth. The highest truth, truth as such, is the resolution of the highest opposition and contradiction. In it validity and power are swept away from the opposition between freedom and necessity, between spirit and nature, between knowledge and its object, between law and impulse, from opposition and contradiction as such, whatever forms they may take. Their validity and power *as* opposition and contradiction is gone. Absolute truth proves that neither freedom by itself, as subjective, sundered from necessity, is absolutely a true thing nor, by parity of reasoning, is truthfulness to be ascribed to necessity isolated and taken by itself. The ordinary consciousness, on the other hand, cannot extricate itself from this opposition and either remains despairingly in contradiction or else casts it aside and helps itself in some other way. But philosophy enters into the heart of the self-contradictory characteristics, knows them in their essential nature, i.e. as in their one-sidedness not absolute but self-dissolving, and it sets them in the harmony and unity which is truth. To grasp this Concept [*Begriff*] of truth is the task of philosophy. [...]

Now, owing to its preoccupation with truth as the absolute object of consciousness, art too belongs to the absolute sphere of the spirit, and therefore, in its content, art stands on one and the same ground with religion (in the stricter sense of the word) and philosophy. For, after all, philosophy has no other object but God and so is essentially rational theology and, as the servant of truth, a continual divine service.

Owing to this sameness of content the three realms of absolute spirit differ only in the *forms* in which they bring home to consciousness their object, the Absolute.

The differences between these forms are implied in the nature of absolute spirit itself. The spirit in its truth is absolute. Therefore it is not an essence lying in abstraction beyond the objective world. On the contrary, it is present within objectivity in the finite spirit's recollection or inwardization of the essence of all things – i.e. the finite apprehends itself in its own essence and so itself becomes essential and absolute. Now the *first* form [art] of this apprehension is an immediate and therefore *sensuous* knowing, a knowing, in the form and shape of the sensuous and objective itself, in which the Absolute is presented to intuition [*Anschauung*][1] and feeling. Then the *second* form [religion] is *pictorial* thinking,[2] while the *third* and last [philosophy] is the *free* thinking of absolute spirit.

(*a*) Now the form of *sensuous intuition* is that of art, so that it is art which sets truth before our minds in the mode of sensuous configuration, a sensuous configuration which in this its appearance has itself a loftier, deeper sense and meaning, yet without having the aim of making the Concept as such in its universality comprehensible by way of the sensuous medium; for it is precisely the *unity* of the Concept with the individual appearance which is the essence of the beautiful and its production by art. Now of course this unity achieved in art is achieved not only in sensuous externality but also in the sphere of imagination [*Vorstellung*], especially in poetry; but still in this too, the most spiritual of the arts, the union of meaning with its individual configuration is present, even if for the imaginative consciousness, and every content is grasped in an immediate way and brought home to the imagination. In general, we must state at once that while art has truth, i.e. the spirit, as its proper subject-matter, it cannot provide a vision of the same by means of particular natural objects as such, i.e. by means of the sun, for example, the moon, the earth, stars, etc. Such things are visible existents, it is true, but they are isolated and, taken by themselves, cannot provide a vision of the spiritual.

Now in giving art this absolute position we are expressly rejecting the [. . .] idea which assumes that art is useful for some varied ulterior subject-matter or other interests foreign to itself. On the other hand, *religion* makes use of art often enough to bring religious truth home to people's feelings or to symbolize it for the imagination, and in that event of course art stands in the service of a sphere different from itself. Yet when art is present in its supreme perfection, then precisely in its figurative mode it contains the kind of exposition most essential to and most in correspondence with the content of truth. Thus, for example, in the case of the Greeks, art was the highest form in which the people represented the gods to themselves and gave themselves some awareness of truth. This is why the poets and artists became for the Greeks the creators of their gods, i.e. the artists gave the nation a definite idea of the behaviour, life, and effectiveness of the Divine, or, in other words, the definite content of religion. And it was not as if these ideas and doctrines were already there, *in advance* of poetry, in an abstract mode of consciousness as general religious propositions and categories of thought, and then later were only clothed in imagery by artists and given an external adornment in poetry; on the contrary, the mode of artistic production was such that what fermented in these poets they could work out *only* in this form of art and poetry. At other levels of the religious consciousness, where the religious content is less amenable to artistic representation, art has in this respect a more restricted field of play.

This is the original true standing of art as the first and immediate satisfaction of absolute spirit.

But just as art has its 'before' in nature and the finite spheres of life, so too it has an 'after', i.e. a region which in turn transcends art's way of apprehending and representing the Absolute. For art has still a limit in itself and therefore passes over into higher forms of consciousness. This limitation determines, after all, the position which we are accustomed to assign to art in our contemporary life. For us art counts no longer as the highest mode in which truth fashions an existence for itself. In general it was early in history that thought passed judgement against art as a mode of illustrating the idea of the Divine; this happened with the Jews and Mohammedans, for example, and indeed even with the Greeks, for Plato opposed the gods of Homer and Hesiod starkly enough. With the advance of civilization a time generally comes in the case of every people when art points beyond itself. For example, the historical elements in Christianity, the Incarnation of Christ, his life and death, have given to art, especially painting, all sorts of opportunities for development, and the Church itself has nursed art or let it alone; but when the urge for knowledge and research, and the need for inner spirituality, instigated the Reformation, religious ideas were drawn away from their wrapping in the element of sense and brought back to the inwardness of heart and thinking. Thus the '*after*' of art consists in the fact that there dwells in the spirit the need to satisfy itself solely in its own inner self as the true form for truth to take. Art in its beginnings still leaves over something mysterious, a secret foreboding and a longing, because its creations have not completely set forth their full content for imaginative vision. But if the perfect content has been perfectly revealed in artistic shapes, then the more far-seeing spirit rejects this objective manifestation and turns back into its inner self. This is the case in our own time. We may well hope that art will always rise higher and come to perfection, but the form of art has ceased to be the supreme need of the spirit. No matter how excellent we find the statues of the Greek gods, no matter how we see God the Father, Christ and Mary so estimably and perfectly portrayed: it is no help; we bow the knee no longer [before these artistic portrayals].

(*b*) Now the next sphere, which transcends the realm of art, is religion. *Religion* has pictorial thinking [*Vorstellung*] as its form of consciousness, for the Absolute has [been] removed[3] from the objectivity of art into the inwardness of the subject and is now given to pictorial thinking in a subjective way, so that mind and feeling, the inner subjective life in general, becomes the chief factor. This advance from art to religion may be described by saying that for the religious consciousness art is only *one* aspect. If, that is to say, the work of art presents truth, the spirit, as an object in a sensuous mode and adopts this form of the Absolute as the adequate one, then religion adds to this the worship [*Andacht*] given by the inner self in its relation to the absolute object. For worship does not belong to art as such. Worship only arises from the fact that now by the subject's agency the heart is permeated with what art makes objective as externally perceptible, and the subject so identifies himself with this content that it is its *inner* presence in ideas and depth of feeling which becomes the essential element for the existence of the Absolute. Worship is the community's cult in its purest, most inward, most subjective form – a cult in which objectivity is, as it were, consumed and digested, while the objective content, now stripped of its objectivity, has become a possession of mind and feeling.

(*c*) Finally, the *third* form of absolute spirit is *philosophy*. For in religion God, to begin with, is an external object for consciousness, since we must first be taught what God is and how he has revealed and still reveals himself; next, religion does work in the element of the inner life, and stirs and animates the community. But the inwardness of the heart's worship and our pictorial thinking is not the highest form of inwardness. As this purest form of knowledge we must recognize untrammelled *thinking* in which philosophy brings to our minds the same content [as in religion] and thereby attains that most spiritual worship in which thinking makes its own and knows conceptually what otherwise is only the content of subjective feeling or pictorial thinking. In this way the two sides, art and religion, are united in philosophy: the *objectivity* of art, which here has indeed lost its external sensuousness but therefore has exchanged it for the highest form of the objective, the form of thought, and the *subjectivity* of religion which has been purified into the subjectivity of *thinking*. For thinking on one side is the most inward, closest, subjectivity – while true thought, the Idea, is at the same time the most real and most objective universality which only in thinking can apprehend itself in the form of its own self.

With this indication of the difference between art, religion and philosophy we must here be content.

The sensuous mode of consciousness is the earlier one for man, and so, after all, the earlier stages of religion were a religion of art and its sensuous representation. Only in the religion of the spirit is God now known as spirit in a higher way, more correspondent with thought; this at the same time makes it plain that the manifestation of truth in a sensuous form is not truly. adequate to the spirit. [. . .]

The Ideal As Such

1. Beautiful individuality

The most general thing which can be said in a merely formal way about the ideal of art, on the lines of our previous considerations, comes to this, that, on the one hand, the true has existence and truth only as it unfolds into external reality; but, on the other hand, the externally separated parts, into which it unfolds, it can so combine and retain in unity that now every part of its unfolding makes this soul, this totality, appear in each part. If we take the human form as the nearest illustration of this, it is [. . .] a totality of organs into which the Concept is dispersed, and it manifests in each member only some particular activity and partial emotion. But if we ask in which particular organ the whole soul appears as soul, we will at once name the eye; for in the eye the soul is concentrated and the soul does not merely see through it but is also seen in it. Now as the pulsating heart shows itself all over the surface of the human, in contrast to the animal, body, so in the same sense it is to be asserted of art that it has to convert every shape in all points of its visible surface into an eye, which is the seat of the soul and brings the spirit into appearance. – Or, as Plato cries out to the star in his familiar distich: 'When thou lookest on the stars, my star, oh! would I were the heavens and could see thee with a thousand eyes',[4] so, conversely, art makes every one of its productions into a thousand-eyed Argus, whereby the inner soul and spirit is seen at every point. And it is not only the bodily form, the look of the eyes, the countenance and posture, but also actions and events, speech and tones of voice, and the series of their course through all conditions of appearance that art has everywhere to make into an eye, in which the free soul is revealed in its inner infinity.

(*a*) With this demand for thoroughgoing possession of soul there arises at once the further question *what* this soul is, the eyes of which all points in the phenomenal world are to become. More precisely still, the question is what sort of soul it is that by its nature shows itself qualified to gain its true manifestation through art. For people[5] speak even of a specific 'soul' of metals, minerals, stars, animals, numerously particularized human characters and their expressions, using the word 'soul' in an ordinary sense. But, for things in nature, such as stones, plants, etc., the word 'soul', in the meaning given to it above, can only be used metaphorically. The soul of merely natural things is explicitly finite and transitory, and should be called 'specific nature' rather than 'soul'. [. . .]

The animation and life of *spirit* alone is free infinity; as such, the spirit in real existence is self-aware as something inner, because in its manifestation it reverts into itself and remains at home with itself. To spirit alone, therefore, is it given to impress the stamp of its own infinity and free return into itself upon its external manifestation, even though through this manifestation it is involved in restriction. Now spirit is only free and infinite when it actually comprehends its universality and raises to universality the ends it sets before itself; but, for this reason, it is capable by its own nature, if it has *not* grasped this freedom, of existing as restricted content, stunted character and a mind crippled and superficial. In a content of such null worth the infinite manifestation of spirit again remains only formal, for in that case we have nothing but the abstract form of self-conscious spirit, and its content contradicts the infinity of spirit in its freedom. It is only by virtue of a genuine and inherently substantial content that restricted and mutable existence acquires independence and substantiality, so that then both determinacy and inherent solidity, content that is both substantial and restrictedly exclusive, are actual in one and the same thing; and hereby existence gains the possibility of being manifested in the restrictedness of its own content as at the same time universality and as the soul which is alone with itself. – In short, art has the function of grasping and displaying existence, in its appearance, as *true*, i.e. in its suitability to the content which is adequate to itself, the content which is both implicit and explicit. Thus the truth of art cannot be mere correctness, to which the so-called imitation of nature is restricted; on the contrary, the outer must harmonize with an inner which is harmonious in itself, and, just on that account, can reveal itself as itself in the outer.

(*b*) Now since art brings back into this harmony with its true Concept what is contaminated in other existents by chance and externality, it casts aside everything in appearance which does not correspond with the Concept and only by this purification does it produce the Ideal. This may be given out to be flattery by art, as, for example, it is said depreciatingly of portrait painters that they flatter. But even the portrait painter, who has least of all to do with the Ideal of art, *must* flatter, in the sense that all the externals in shape and expression, in form, colour, features, the purely natural side of imperfect existence, little hairs, pores, little scars, warts, all these he must let go, and grasp and reproduce the subject in his universal character and enduring personality. It is one thing for the artist simply to imitate the face of the sitter, its surface and external form, confronting him in repose, and quite another to be able to portray the true features which express the inmost soul of the subject. For it is throughout necessary for the Ideal that the outer form should explicitly correspond with the soul. So, for example, in our own time what has become the fashion, namely what are called *tableaux vivants*,[6] imitate famous masterpieces deliberately and agreeably, and the accessories, costume, etc., they reproduce accurately; but often enough we see ordinary faces substituted for the spiritual expression of the subjects and this produces an inappropriate effect. Raphael's Madonnas, on the other hand, show us forms of expression, cheeks, eyes, nose, mouth, which, as forms, are appropriate to the radiance, joy, piety, and also the humility of a mother's love. Of course someone might wish to maintain that all women are capable of this feeling, but not every cast of countenance affords a satisfactory and complete expression of this depth of soul.

(*c*) Now the nature of the artistic Ideal is to be sought in this reconveyance of external existence into the spiritual realm, so that the external appearance, by being adequate to the spirit, is the revelation thereof. Yet this is a reconveyance into the inner realm which at the same time does not proceed to the universal in its abstract form, i.e. to the *extreme* which *thinking* is, but remains in the *centre* where the purely external and the purely internal coincide. Accordingly, the Ideal is actuality, withdrawn from the profusion of details and accidents, in so far as the inner appears itself in this externality, lifted above and opposed to universality, as living individuality. For the individual subjective life which has a substantive content in itself and at the same time makes this content appear on itself externally, stands in this centre. In this centre the substantiality of the content cannot emerge explicitly in its universality in an abstract way; it remains still enclosed in individuality and therefore appears intertwined with a determinate existent, which now, for its part, freed from mere finitude and its conditions, comes together with the inwardness of the soul into a free harmony. Schiller in his poem *Das Ideal und das Leben*[7] [The Ideal and Life] contrasts actuality and its griefs and battles with the 'still shadow-land of beauty'. Such a realm of shadows is the Ideal; the *spirits* appearing in it are dead to immediate existence, cut off from the indigence of natural life, freed from the bonds of dependence on external influences and all the perversions and convulsions inseparable from the finitude of the phenomenal world. But all the same the Ideal treads into the sensuous and the natural form thereof, yet it still at the same time draws this, like the sphere of the external, back into itself, since art can bring back the apparatus, required by external appearance for its self-preservation, to the limits within which the external can be the manifestation of spiritual freedom. Only by this process does the Ideal exist in externality, self-enclosed, free, self-reliant, as sensuously blessed in itself, enjoying and delighting in its own self. The ring of this bliss resounds throughout the entire appearance of the Ideal, for however far the external form may extend, the soul of the Ideal never loses itself in it. And precisely as a result of this alone is the Ideal genuinely beautiful, since the beautiful exists only as a total though subjective unity; wherefore too the subject who manifests the Ideal must appear collected together in himself again into a higher totality and independence out of the divisions in the life of other individuals and their aims and efforts.

(α) In this respect, amongst the fundamental characteristics of the Ideal we may put at the top this serene peace and bliss, this self-enjoyment in its own achievedness and satisfaction. The ideal work of art confronts us like a blessed god. For the blessed gods [of Greek art], that is to say, there is no final seriousness in distress, in anger, in the interests involved in finite spheres and aims, and this positive withdrawal into themselves, along with the negation of everything particular, gives them the characteristic of serenity and tranquillity. In this sense Schiller's phrase holds good: 'Life is serious, art cheerful.'[8] Often enough, it is true, pedants have poked fun at this, on the ground that art in general, and especially Schiller's own poetry, is of a most serious kind; and after all in fact ideal art does not lack seriousness – but even in the seriousness cheerfulness or serenity remains its inherent and essential character. This force of individuality, this triumph of concrete freedom concentrated in itself, is what we recognize especially in the works of art of antiquity in the cheerful and serene peace of their shapes. And this results not at all from a mere satisfaction gained without struggle, but on the contrary, only when a deeper breach has rent the subject's inner life and his whole existence. For even if the heroes of tragedy, for example, are so portrayed that they succumb to fate, still the heart of the hero recoils into simple unity with itself, when it says: 'It is so.' The subject in this case still always remains true to himself; he surrenders what he has been robbed of, yet the ends he pursues are not just taken from him; he renounces them and thereby does not lose *himself*. Man, the slave of destiny, may lose his life, but not his freedom. It is this self-reliance which even in grief enables him to preserve and manifest the cheerfulness and serenity of tranquillity.

(β) It is true that in romantic art the distraction and dissonance of the heart goes further and, in general, the oppositions displayed in it are deepened and their disunion may be maintained. So, for example, in portraying the Passion, painting sometimes persists in expressing the derision in the expressions of the military tormentors with the horrible grimaces and grins on their faces; and with this retention of disunion, especially in sketches of vice, sin and evil, the serenity of the Ideal is then lost, for even if the distraction does not remain so fixedly as this, still something, if not ugly every time, at least not beautiful often comes into view. In another school of painting, the older Netherlandish one,[9] there is displayed an inner reconciliation of the heart in its honesty and truthfulness to itself as well as in its faith and unshakeable confidence, but this firmness does not achieve the serenity and satisfaction of the Ideal. Even in romantic art, however, although suffering and grief affect the heart and subjective inner feeling more deeply there than is the case with the ancients, there do come into view a spiritual inwardness, a joy in submission, a bliss in grief and rapture in suffering, even a delight in agony. Even in the solemnly religious music of Italy this pleasure and transfiguration of grief resounds through the expression of lament. This expression in romantic art generally is 'smiling through tears'. Tears belong to grief, smiles to cheerfulness, and so smiling in weeping denotes this inherent tranquillity amidst agony and suffering. Of course smiling here ought not to be a mere sentimental emotion, a frivolous and self-conceited attitude of the man to misfortunes and his minor personal feelings; on the contrary, it must appear as the calmness and freedom of beauty despite all grief – as it is said of Chimena in the *Romances of the Cid*: 'How beautiful she was in tears.'[10] On the other hand, a man's lack of self-control is either ugly and repugnant, or else ludicrous. Children, e.g., burst into tears on the most trifling occasions, and this makes us smile. On the other hand, tears in the eyes of an austere man who keeps a stiff upper lip[11] under the stress of deep feeling convey a totally different impression of emotion.

But laughter and tears may fall apart in abstraction from one another and in this abstraction they have been used inappropriately as a motif for art, as for instance in the laughter chorus of [C. M. F. E.] von Weber's *Der Freischütz* [1821]. Laughing as such is an outburst which yet ought not to remain unrestrained if the Ideal is not to be lost. The same abstraction occurs in the similar laughter in a duet from Weber's *Oberon* [1826] during which one may be anxious and distressed for the throat and lungs of the prima donna! How differently moving, on the other hand, is the inextinguishable laughter of the gods in Homer, which springs from the blessed tranquillity of the gods and is only cheerfulness and not abstract boisterousness. Neither, on the other side, should tears, as unrestrained grief, enter the ideal work of art, as when, for example, such abstract inconsolability is to be heard in Weber's *Der Freischütz*, to mention it again. In music in general, song is this joy and pleasure in self-awareness, like the lark's singing in the freedom of the air. Shrieking, whether of grief or mirth, is not music at all. Even in suffering, the sweet tone of lament must sound through the griefs and alleviate them, so that it seems to us worth while so to suffer as to understand this lament. This is the sweet melody, the song in all art.

(γ) In this fundamental principle the modern doctrine of irony too has its justification in a certain respect, except that irony, on the one hand, is often bare of any true seriousness and likes to delight especially in villains, and, on the other hand, ends in mere heartfelt longing instead of in acting and doing. Novalis, for example, one of the nobler spirits who took up this position, was driven into a void with no specific interests, into this dread of reality, and was wound down as it were into a spiritual decline. This is a longing which will not let itself go in actual action and production, because it is frightened of being polluted by contact with finitude, although all the same it has a sense of the deficiency of this abstraction. True, irony implies the absolute negativity in which the subject is related to himself in the annihilation of everything specific and one-sided; but since this annihilation, as was indicated above in our consideration of this doctrine, affects not only, as in comedy, what is inherently null which manifests itself in its hollowness, but equally everything inherently excellent and solid, it follows that irony as this art of annihilating everything everywhere, like that heart-felt longing, acquires, at the same time, in comparison with the true Ideal, the aspect of inner inartistic lack of restraint. For the Ideal requires an inherently substantive content which, it is true, by displaying itself in the form and shape of the outer as well, comes to particularity and therefore to restrictedness, though it so contains the restrictedness in itself that everything *purely* external in it is extinguished and annihilated. Only on account of this negation of pure externality is the specific form and shape of the Ideal a manifestation of that substantive content in an appearance according with artistic vision and imagination.

2. The relation of the Ideal to nature

[. . .] Some maintain that the natural forms with which spirit is clothed are already in their actual appearance – an appearance not recreated by art – so perfect, so beautiful, and so excellent in themselves that there cannot be still another beauty evincing itself as higher and, in distinction from what is there confronting us, as ideal, since art is not even capable of reaching altogether what is already met with in nature. On the other hand, there is a demand that there should be found for art independently, in contrast to reality, forms and representations of another and more ideal kind. [. . .] While others, with the 'Ideal' on their lips, look down on vulgarity and speak of it contemptuously, [some speak] of the Idea and the Ideal with similar superiority and contempt.

But in fact there is in the world of spirit something vulgarly natural both within and without. It is vulgar externally just because the inner side is vulgar, and in its action and all its external manifestations the latter brings into appearance only the aims of envy, jealousy, avarice in trifles and in the sensuous sphere. Even this vulgarity art can take as its material, and has done so. But in that case either there remains [. . .] the representation as such, the cleverness of production, as the sole essential interest, and in that case it would be useless to expect a cultivated man to show sympathy with the whole work of art, i.e. with a topic of this kind, or else the artist must make something further and deeper out of it through his treatment of the subject. It is especially the so-called *genre* painting which has not despised such topics and which has been carried by the Dutch [*Holländer*] to the pitch of perfection. Now what has led the Dutch to this *genre?* What is it that is expressed in these little pictures which prove to have the highest power of attraction? They cannot be called pictures of vulgarity and then be just set aside altogether and discarded. For, if we look at it more closely, the proper subject-matter of these paintings is not so vulgar as is usually supposed.

The Dutch have selected the content of their artistic representations out of their own experience, out of their own life in the present, and to have actualized this present once more through art too is not to be made a reproach to them. What the contemporary world has brought before our vision and our spirit must also belong to that world if it is to claim our whole interest. In order to ascertain what engrossed the interest of the Dutch at the time of these paintings, we must ask about Dutch history. The Dutch themselves have made the greatest part of the land on which they dwell and live; it has continually to be defended against the storms of the sea, and it has to be maintained. By resolution, endurance, and courage, townsmen and countrymen alike threw off the Spanish dominion of Philip II, son of Charles V (that mighty King of the World), and by fighting won for themselves freedom in political life and in religious life too in the religion of freedom. This citizenship, this love of enterprise, in small things as in great, in their own land as on the high seas, this painstaking as well as cleanly and neat well-being, this joy and exuberance in their own sense that for all this they have their own activity to thank, all this is what constitutes the general content of their pictures. This is no vulgar material and stuff which, it is true, is not to be approached by a man of high society who turns up his nose at it, convinced of the superiority of courts and their appendages. Fired by a sense of such vigorous nationality, Rembrandt painted his famous Night Watch, now in Amsterdam, Van Dyck so many of his portraits, Wouwerman his cavalry scenes, and even in this category are those rustic carousels, jovialities and convivial merriments.

To cite a contrast, we have, for example, good *genre* paintings in our exhibition this year too [1828], but in skill of representation they fall far below the Dutch pictures of the same kind, and even in content they cannot rise to freedom and joyfulness like that of the Dutch. For example, we see a woman going into an inn to scold her husband. Here we have nothing but a scene of snarling and vicious people.[12] On the other hand, with the Dutch in their taverns, at weddings and dances, at feasting and drinking, everything goes on merrily and jovially, even if matters come to quarrels and blows; wives and girls join in and a feeling of freedom and gaiety animates one and all. This spiritual cheerfulness in a justified pleasure, which enters even pictures of animals and which is revealed as satisfaction and delight – this freshly awakened spiritual freedom and vitality in conception and execution – constitutes the higher soul of pictures of this kind.

In the like sense the beggar boys of Murillo (in the Central Gallery at Munich) are excellent too. Abstractly considered, the subject-matter here too is drawn from 'vulgar nature': the mother picks lice out of the head of one of the boys while he quietly munches his bread; on a similar picture two other boys, ragged and poor, are eating melon and grapes.[13] But in this poverty and semi-nakedness what precisely shines forth within and without is nothing but complete absence of care and concern – a Dervish could not have less – in the full feeling of their well-being and delight in life. This freedom from care for external things and the inner freedom made visible outwardly is what the Concept of the Ideal requires. In Paris there is a portrait of a boy by Raphael:[14] his head lies at rest, leaning on an arm, and he gazes out into the wide and open distance with such bliss of carefree satisfaction that one can scarcely tear oneself away from gazing at this picture of spiritual and joyous well-being. The same satisfaction is afforded by those boys of Murillo. We see that they have no wider interests and aims, yet not at all because of stupidity; rather do they squat on the ground content and serene, almost like the gods of Olympus; they do nothing, they say nothing; but they are people all of one piece without any surliness or discontent; and since they possess this foundation of all excellence, we have the idea that anything may come of these youths. These are totally different modes of treatment from those we see in that quarrelsome choleric woman, or in the peasant who ties up his whip, or the postillion who sleeps on straw.[15]

But such *genre* pictures must be small and appear, even in the whole impression they give to our vision, as something insignificant which we have got beyond, so far as the external subject-matter and the content of the painting goes. It would be intolerable to see such things worked out life-size and therefore claiming that we should really be satisfied with them and their like in their entirety.

In this way what is generally called 'vulgarity' must be interpreted if it is to have the right of entry into art.

Now of course there are higher, more ideal, materials for art than the representation of such joy and bourgeois excellence in what are always inherently insignificant details. For men have more serious interests and aims which enter in through the unfolding and deepening of spirit and in which men must remain in harmony with themselves. The higher art will be that which has as its task the representation of this higher content. [. . .]

Notes

1 Knox's translation has 'contemplation'. [S.H.]
2 'das vorstellende Bewußtsein'. Material in square brackets in the passages collected here from the lectures on *Aesthetics*, the *Philosophy of Religion* and the *History of Philosophy* has been included by the respective translators. A very few such insertions are my own. [S.H.]
3 Knox's translation omits the word 'been'. [S.H.]
4 Diogenes Laertius, *Plato*, 23, § 29. [Translator's note.]
5 A hit at Schelling and other philosophers of nature. [Translator's note.]
6 i.e. beautiful women set in a frame, to imitate some artist's picture. [Translator's note.]
7 This poem of Schiller's third period appeared first in 1795 in *Die Horen*. [Translator's note.]

8   The last line of Schiller's prologue to *Wallenstein* (1798–1800). [S.H.]
9   Knox's translation has 'Flemish'. The German word is 'niederländisch'. Hegel has in mind paintings from the fifteenth century, before the distinction between Flemish and Dutch artists was made. [S.H.]
10 The quotation is from Herder's poetic version of the *Romances of the Cid*, I. 6. [Translator's note.]
11 'eines ernsten, gehaltenen Mannes'. [S.H.]
12 The painting concerned is probably *Sermon* by Constantin Schrötter. See *Hegel in Berlin. Preußische Kulturpolitik und idealistische Ästhetik. Zum 150. Todestag des Philosophen*, edited by O. Pöggeler et al. (Berlin: Staatsbibliothek Preußischer Kuturbesitz, 1981), p. 236. [S.H.]
13 See S. Houlgate, *Freedom, Truth and History: An Introduction to Hegel's Philosophy* (London: Routledge, 1991), pp. 133–4. Hegel visited Munich in 1815. [S.H.]
14 Raphael, *Portrait d'un jeune homme*. Hegel visited the Louvre in September 1827. [Translator's note.]
15 The picture of the peasant and his whip is by Schrötter, the one of the sleeping postilion by Heidecker. See *Hegel in Berlin*, p. 237. [S.H.]

29

Aesthetics: The Particular Forms of Art

Introduction

What up to this point we have dealt with [. . .] concerned the actuality of the Idea of the beautiful as the Ideal of art, but [no matter] under how many aspects we also developed the Concept of the ideal work of art, still all our distinctions bore only on the ideal work of art in *general*. But, like the Idea, the Idea of the beautiful is a totality of essential differences which must issue as such and be actualized. Their actualization we may call on the whole the *particular forms* of art, as the development of what is implicit in the Concept of the Ideal and comes into existence through art. Yet if we speak of these art forms as different species of the Ideal, we may not take 'species' in the ordinary sense of the word, as if here the particular forms came from without to the Idea as their universal genus and had become modifications of it: on the contrary, 'species' should mean nothing here but the distinctive and therefore more concrete determinations of the Idea of the beautiful and the Ideal of art itself. The general character of [artistic] representation, i.e., is here made determinate not from without but in itself through its own Concept, so that it is this Concept which is spread out into a totality of particular modes of artistic formation.

Now, in more detail, the forms of art, as the actualizing and unfolding of the beautiful, find their origin in the Idea itself, in the sense that through them the Idea presses on to representation and reality, and whenever it is explicit to itself either only in its abstract determinacy or else in its concrete totality, it also brings itself into appearance in another real formation. This is because the Idea as such is only truly Idea as developing itself explicitly by its own activity; and since as Ideal it is immediate appearance, and indeed with its appearance is the identical Idea of the beautiful, so also at every particular stage on which the Ideal treads the road of its unfolding there is immediately linked with every *inner* determinacy another *real* configuration. It is therefore all one whether we regard the advance in this development as an inner advance of the Idea in itself or of the shape in which it gives itself existence. Each of these two sides is immediately bound up with the other. The consummation of the Idea as content appears therefore simultaneously as also the consummation of form; and conversely the deficiencies of the artistic shape correspondingly prove to be a deficiency of the Idea which constitutes the inner meaning of the external appearance and in that appearance becomes real to itself. Thus if [...] we encounter art-forms at first which are still inadequate in comparison with the true Ideal, this is not the sort of case in which people ordinarily speak of unsuccessful works of art which either express nothing or lack the capacity to achieve what they are supposed to represent; on the contrary, the specific shape which every content of the Idea gives to itself in the particular forms of art is always adequate to that content, and the deficiency or consummation lies only in the relatively untrue or true determinateness in which and as which the Idea is explicit to itself. This is because the content must be true and concrete in itself before it can find its truly beautiful shape.

In this connection, as we saw already in the general division of the subject [...], we have three chief art-forms to consider:

(i) The *Symbolic*. In this the Idea still *seeks* its genuine expression in art, because in itself it is still abstract and indeterminate and therefore does not have its adequate manifestation on and in itself, but finds itself confronted by what is external to itself, external things in nature and human affairs. Now since it has only an immediate inkling of its own abstractions in this objective world or drives itself with its undetermined universals into a concrete existence, it corrupts and falsifies the shapes that it finds confronting it. This is because it can grasp them only arbitrarily, and therefore, instead of coming to a complete identification, it comes only to an accord, and even to a still abstract harmony, between meaning and shape; in this neither completed nor to be completed mutual formation, meaning and shape present, equally with their affinity, their mutual externality, foreignness and incompatibility.

(ii) But, secondly, the Idea, in accordance with its essential nature, does not stop at the abstraction and indeterminacy of universal thoughts but is in itself free infinite subjectivity and apprehends this in its actuality as spirit. Now spirit, as free subject, is determined through and by itself, and in this self-determination, and also in its own nature, has that external shape, adequate to itself, with which it can close as with its absolutely due reality. On this entirely harmonious unity of content and form, the second art-form, the *classical*, is based. Yet if the consummation of this unity is to become actual, spirit, in so far as it is made a topic for art, must not yet be the purely absolute spirit which finds its adequate existence only in spirituality and inwardness, but the spirit which is still particular and therefore burdened with an abstraction. That is to say, the free subject, which classical art configurates outwardly, appears indeed as essentially universal and therefore freed from all the accident and mere particularity of the inner life and the outer world, but at the same time as filled solely with a universality particularized within itself. This is because the external shape is, as such, an external determinate particular shape, and for complete fusion [with a content] it can only present again in itself a specific and therefore restricted content, while too it is only the inwardly particular spirit which can appear perfectly in an external manifestation and be bound up with that in an inseparable unity.

Here art has reached its own essential nature by bringing the Idea, as spiritual individuality, directly into harmony with its bodily reality in such a perfect way that external existence now for the first time no longer preserves any independence in contrast with the meaning which it is to express, while conversely the inner [meaning], in its shape worked out for our vision, shows there only itself and in it is related to itself affirmatively.

(iii) But, thirdly, when the Idea of the beautiful is comprehended as absolute spirit, and therefore as the spirit which is free in its own eyes, it is no longer completely realized in the external world, since its true determinate being it has only in itself as spirit. It therefore dissolves that classical unification of inwardness and external manifestation and takes flight out of externality back into itself. This provides the fundamental typification of the *romantic* art-form; the content of this form, on account of its free spirituality, demands more than what representation in the external world and the bodily can supply; in romantic art the shape is externally more or less indifferent, and thus that art reintroduces, in an opposite way from the symbolic, the separation of content and form.

In this way, symbolic art *seeks* that perfect unity of inner meaning and external shape which classical art *finds* in the presentation of substantial individuality to sensuous contemplation, and which romantic art *transcends* in its superior spirituality.

The End of the Romantic Form of Art

Art, as it has been under our consideration hitherto, had as its basis the unity of meaning and shape and so the unity of the artist's subjective activity with his topic and work. Looked at more closely, it was the specific kind of this unification [at each stage] which provided, for the content and its corresponding portrayal, the substantial norm penetrating all artistic productions.

In this matter we found at the beginning of art, in the East, that the spirit was not yet itself explicitly free; it still sought for its Absolute in nature and therefore interpreted nature as in itself divine. Later on, the vision of classical art represented the Greek gods as naïve and inspired, yet even so essentially as individuals burdened with the natural human form as with an *affirmative* feature. Romantic art for the first time deepened the spirit in its own inwardness, in contrast to which the flesh, external reality and the world in general was at first posited as *negative*, even though the spirit and the Absolute had to appear in this element alone; yet at last this element could be given validity for itself again in a more and more positive way.

(a) These ways of viewing the world constitute religion, the substantial spirit of peoples and ages, and are woven into, not art alone, but all the other spheres of the living present at all periods. Now just as every man is a child of his time in every activity, whether political, religious, or scientific, and just as he has the task of bringing out the essential content and the therefore necessary form of that time, so it is the vocation of art to find for the spirit of a people the artistic expression corresponding to it. Now so long as the artist is bound up with the specific character of such a world-view and religion, in immediate identity with it and with firm faith in it, so long is he genuinely in earnest with this material and its representation; i.e. this material remains for him the infinite and true element in his own consciousness – a material with which he lives in an original unity as part of his inmost self, while the form in which he exhibits it is for him as artist the final, necessary and supreme manner of bringing before our contemplation the Absolute and the soul of objects in general. By the substance of his material, a substance immanent in himself, he is tied down to the specific mode of its exposition. For in that case the material, and therefore the form belonging to it, the artist carries immediately in himself as the proper essence of his existence which he does not imagine for himself but which he *is*; and therefore he only has the task of making this truly essential element objective to himself, to present and develop it in a living way out of his own resources. Only in that event is the artist completely inspired by his material and its presentation; and his inventions are no product of caprice, they originate in him, out of him, out of this substantial ground, this stock, the content of which is not at rest until through the artist it acquires an individual shape adequate to its inner essence. If, on the other hand, we nowadays propose to make the subject of a statue or a painting a Greek god, or, Protestants as we are today, the Virgin Mary, we are not seriously in earnest with this material. It is the innermost faith which we lack here, even if the artist in days when faith was still unimpaired did not exactly need to be what is generally called a pious man, for after all in every age artists have not as a rule been the most pious of men! The requirement is only this, that for the artist the content [of his work] shall constitute the substance, the inmost truth, of his consciousness and make his chosen mode of presentation necessary. For the artist in his production is at the same time a creature of nature, his skill is a *natural* talent; his work is not the pure activity of comprehension which confronts its material entirely and unites itself with it in free thoughts, in pure thinking; on the contrary, the artist, not yet released from his *natural* side, is united *directly* with the subject-matter, believes in it, and is identical with it in accordance with his very own self. The result is then that the artist is entirely absorbed in the object; the work of art proceeds entirely out of the undivided inwardness and force of genius; the production is firm and unwavering, and in it the full intensity [of creation] is preserved. This is the fundamental condition of art's being present in its integrity.

(β) On the other hand, in the position we have been forced to assign to art in the course of its development, the whole situation has altogether altered. This, however, we must not regard as a mere accidental misfortune suffered by art from without owing to the distress of the times, the sense for the prosaic, lack of interest, etc.; on the contrary, it is the effect and the progress of art itself which, by bringing before our vision as an object its own indwelling material, at every step along this road makes its own contribution to freeing art from the content represented. What through art or thinking we have before our physical or spiritual eye as an object has lost all absolute interest for us if it has been put before us so completely that the content is exhausted, that everything is revealed, and nothing obscure or inward is left over any more. For interest is to be found only in the case of lively activity [of mind]. The spirit only occupies itself with objects so long as there is something secret, not revealed, in them. This is the case so long as the material is identical with the substance of our own being. But if the essential world-views implicit in the concept of art, and the range of the content belonging to these, are in every respect revealed by art, then art has got rid of this content which on every occasion was determinate for a particular people, a particular age, and the true need to resume it again is awakened only with the need to turn *against* the content that was alone valid hitherto; thus in Greece Aristophanes rose up against his present world, and Lucian against the whole of the Greek past, and in Italy and Spain, when the Middle Ages were closing, Ariosto and Cervantes began to turn against chivalry.

Now contrasted with the time in which the artist owing to his nationality and his period stands with the substance of his being within a specific world-view and its content and forms of portrayal, we find an altogether opposed view which in its complete development is of importance only in most recent times. In our day, in the case of almost all peoples, criticism, the cultivation of reflection, and, in our German case, freedom of thought have mastered the artists too, and have made them, so to say, a *tabula rasa* in respect of the material and the form of their productions, after the necessary particular stages of the romantic art-form have been traversed. Bondage to a particular subject-matter and a mode of portrayal suitable for this material alone are for artists today something past, and art therefore has become a free instrument which the artist can wield in proportion to his subjective skill in relation to any material of whatever kind. The artist thus stands above specific consecrated forms and configurations and moves freely on his own account, independent of the subject-matter and mode of conception in which the holy and eternal was previously made visible to human apprehension. No content, no form, is any longer immediately identical with the inwardness, the nature, the unconscious substantial essence of the artist; every material may be indifferent to him if only it does not contradict the formal law of being simply beautiful and capable of artistic treatment. Today there is no material which stands in and for itself above this relativity, and even if one matter be raised above it, still there is at least no absolute need for its representation by *art*. Therefore the artist's attitude to his topic is on the whole much the same as the dramatist's who brings on the scene and delineates different characters who are strangers to him. The artist does still put his genius into them, he weaves his web out of his own resources but only out of what is purely universal or quite accidental there, whereas its more detailed individualization is not his. For this purpose he needs his supply of pictures, modes of configuration, earlier forms of art which, taken in themselves, are indifferent to him and only become important if they seem to him to be those most suitable for precisely this or that material. Moreover, in most arts, especially the visual arts, the topic comes to the artist from the outside; he works to a commission, and in the case of sacred or profane stories, or scenes, portraits, ecclesiastical buildings, etc., he has only to see what he can make of his commission. For, however much he puts his heart into the given topic, that topic yet always remains to him a material which is not in itself directly the substance of his own consciousness. It is therefore no help to him to adopt again, as that substance, so to say, past world-views, i.e. to propose to root himself firmly in one of these ways of looking at things, e.g. to turn Roman Catholic as in recent times many have done for art's sake in order to give stability to their mind and to give the character of something absolute to the specifically limited character of their artistic product in itself.[1] The artist need not be forced first to settle his accounts with his mind or to worry about the salvation of his own soul. From the very beginning, before he embarks on production, his great and free soul must know and possess its own ground, must be sure of itself and confident in itself. The great artist today needs in particular the free development of the spirit; in that development all superstition, and all faith which remains restricted to determinate forms of vision and presentation, is degraded into mere aspects and features. These the free spirit has mastered because he sees in them no absolutely sacrosanct conditions for his exposition and mode of configuration, but ascribes value to them only on the strength of the higher content which in the course of his re-creation he puts into them as adequate to them.

In this way every form and every material is now at the service and command of the artist whose talent and genius is explicitly freed from the earlier limitation to one specific art-form.

(γ) But if in conclusion we ask about the content and the forms which can be considered as *peculiar* to this stage of our inquiry in virtue of its general standpoint, the answer is as follows.

The universal forms of art had a bearing above all on the absolute truth which art attains, and they had the origin of their particular differences in the specific interpretation of what counted for consciousness as absolute and carried in itself the principle for its mode of configuration. In this matter we have seen in symbolic art natural meanings appearing as the *content*, natural things and human personifications as the *form* of the representation; in classical art spiritual individuality, but as a corporeal, not inwardized, present over which there stood the abstract necessity of fate; in romantic art spirituality with the subjectivity immanent therein, for the inwardness of which the external shape remained accidental. In this final art-form too, as in the earlier ones, the Divine is the absolute subject-matter of art. But the Divine had to objectify itself, determine itself, and therefore proceed out of itself into the secular content of subjective personality. At first the infinity of personality lay in honour, love and fidelity, and then later in particular individuality, in the specific character which coalesced with the particular content of human existence. Finally this cohesion with such a specific limitation of subject-matter was cancelled by humour which could make every determinacy waver and dissolve and therefore made it possible for art to transcend itself. Yet in this self-transcendence art is nevertheless a withdrawal of man into himself, a descent into his own breast, whereby art strips away from itself all fixed restriction to a specific range of content and treatment, and makes *Humanus* its new holy of holies: i.e. the depths and heights of the human heart as such, mankind in its joys and sorrows, its strivings, deeds and fates.[2] Herewith the artist acquires his subject-matter in himself and is the human spirit actually self-determining and considering, meditating, and expressing the infinity of its feelings and situations: nothing that can be living in the human breast is alien to that spirit any more.[3] This is a subject-matter which does not remain determined artistically in itself and on its own account; on the contrary, the specific character of the topic and its outward formation is left to capricious invention, yet no interest is excluded – for art does not need any longer to represent only what is absolutely at home at one of its specific stages, but everything in which man as such is capable of being at home.

In face of this breadth and variety of material we must above all make the demand that the actual presence of the spirit today shall be displayed at the same time throughout the mode of treating this material. The modern artist, it is true, may associate himself with the classical age and with still more ancient times; to be a follower of Homer, even if the last one, is fine, and productions reflecting the medieval veering to romantic art will have their merits too; but the universal validity, depth, and special idiom of some material is one thing, its mode of treatment another. No Homer, Sophocles, etc., no Dante, Ariosto or Shakespeare can appear in our day; what was so magnificently sung, what so freely expressed, has been expressed; these are materials, ways of looking at them and treating them which have been sung once and for all. Only the present is fresh, the rest is paler and paler.

The French must be reproached on historical grounds, and criticized on the score of beauty, for presenting Greek and Roman heroes, Chinese, and Peruvians, as French princes and princesses and for ascribing to them the motives and views of the time of Louis XIV and XV; yet, if only these motives and views had been deeper and finer in themselves, drawing them into present-day works of art would not be exactly bad. On the contrary, all materials, whatever they be and from whatever period and nation they come, acquire their artistic truth only when imbued with living and contemporary interest. It is in this interest that artistic truth fills man's breast, provides his own mirror-image, and brings truth home to our feelings and imagination. It is the appearance and activity of imperishable humanity in its many-sided significance and endless all-round development which in this reservoir of human situations and feelings can now constitute the absolute content of our art.

If after thus determining in a general way the subject-matter peculiar to this stage, we now look back at what we have considered in conclusion as the forms of the dissolution of romantic art, we have stressed principally how art falls to pieces, on the one hand, into the imitation of external objectivity in all its contingent shapes; on the other hand, however, into the liberation of subjectivity, in accordance with its inner contingency, in humour. Now, finally, still within the material indicated above, we may draw attention to a coalescence of these extremes of romantic art. In other words, just as in the advance from symbolic to classical art we considered the transitional forms of image, simile, epigram, etc., so here in romantic art we have to make mention of a similar transitional form. In those earlier modes of treatment the chief thing was that inner meaning and external shape fell apart from one another, a cleavage partly superseded by the subjective activity of the artist and converted, particularly in epigram, so far as possible into an identification. Now romantic art was from the beginning the deeper disunion of the inwardness which was finding its satisfaction in itself and which, since objectivity does not completely correspond with the spirit's inward being, remained broken or indifferent to the objective world. In the course of romantic art this opposition developed up to the point at which we had to arrive at an exclusive interest, either in contingent externality or in equally contingent subjectivity. But if this satisfaction in externality or in the subjective portrayal is intensified, according to the principle of romantic art, into the heart's deeper immersion in the object, and if, on the other hand, what matters to humour is the object and its configuration within its subjective reflex, then we acquire thereby a growing intimacy with the object, a sort of *objective* humour. Yet such an intimacy can only be partial and can perhaps be expressed only within the compass of a song or only as part of a greater whole. For if it were extended and carried through within objectivity, it would necessarily become action and event and an objective presentation of these. But what we may regard as necessary here is rather a sensitive abandonment of the heart in the object, which is indeed unfolded but remains a *subjective* spirited movement of imagination and the heart – a fugitive notion, but one which is not purely accidental and capricious but an inner movement of the spirit devoted entirely to its object and retaining it as its content and interest.

In this connection we may contrast such final blossomings of art with the old Greek epigram in which this form appeared in its first and simplest shape. The form meant here displays itself only when to talk of the object is not just to name it, not an inscription or epigraph which merely says in general terms what the object is, but only when there are added a deep feeling, a felicitous witticism, an ingenious reflection, and an intelligent movement of imagination which vivify and expand the smallest detail through the way that poetry treats it. But such poems to or about something, a tree, a mill-lade, the spring, etc., about things animate or inanimate, may be of quite endless variety and arise in any nation, yet they remain of a subordinate kind and, in general, readily become lame. For especially when reflection and speech have been developed, anyone may be struck in connection with most objects and circumstances by some fancy or other which he now has skill enough to express, just as anyone is good at writing a letter. With such a general sing-song, often repeated even if with new nuances, we soon become bored. Therefore at this stage what is especially at stake is that the heart, with its depth of feeling, and the spirit and a rich consciousness shall be entirely absorbed in the circumstances, situation, etc., tarry there, and so make out of the object something new, beautiful and intrinsically valuable.

A brilliant example of this, even for the present and for the subjective spiritual depth of today, is afforded especially by the Persians and Arabs in the eastern splendour of their images, in the free bliss of their imagination which deals with its objects entirely contemplatively. The Spaniards and Italians too have done excellent work of this kind. Klopstock does say[4] of Petrarch: 'Petrarch sang songs of his Laura, beautiful to their admirer, but to the lover – nothing.' Yet Klopstock's love-poems are full only of moral reflections, pitiable longing and strained passion for the happiness of immortality – whereas in Petrarch we admire the freedom of the inherently ennobled feeling which, however much it expresses desire for the beloved, is still satisfied in itself. For the desire, the passion, cannot be missing in the sphere of these subjects, provided it be confined to wine and love, the tavern and the glass, just as, after all, the Persian pictures are of extreme voluptuousness. But in its subjective interest imagination here removes the object altogether from the scope of practical desire; it has an interest only in this imaginative occupation, which is satisfied in the freest way with its hundreds of changing turns of phrase and conceits, and plays in the most ingenious manner with joy and sorrow alike. Amongst modern poets those chiefly possessed of this equally ingenious freedom of imagination, but also of its subjectively more heartfelt depth, are Rückert, and Goethe in his *West-östlicher Divan*. Goethe's poems in the *Divan* are particularly and essentially different from his earlier ones. In *Willkommen und Abschied* [Welcome and Farewell], e.g., the language and the depiction are beautiful indeed, and the feeling is heartfelt, but otherwise the situation is quite ordinary, the conclusion trivial, and imagination and its freedom has added nothing further. Totally different is the poem called *Wiederfinden* [Meeting again] in the *Divan*. Here love is transferred wholly into the imagination, its movement, happiness and bliss. In general, in similar productions of this kind we have before us no subjective longing, no being in love, no desire, but a pure delight in the topics, an inexhaustible self-yielding of imagination, a harmless play, a freedom in toying alike with rhyme and ingenious metres – and, with all this, a depth of feeling and a cheerfulness of the inwardly self-moving heart which through the serenity of the outward shape lift the soul high above all painful entanglement in the restrictions of the real world.

With this we may close our consideration of the particular forms into which the ideal of art has been spread in the course of its development. I have made these forms the subject of a rather extensive investigation in order to exhibit the content out of which too their mode of portrayal has been derived. For it is the content which, as in all human work, so also in art is decisive. In accordance with its essential nature, art has nothing else for its function but to set forth in an adequate sensuous present what is itself inherently rich in content, and the philosophy of art must make it its chief task to comprehend in thought what this fullness of content and its beautiful mode of appearance are.

Notes

1 Friedrich Schlegel, for example, converted to Catholicism in 1808. [s.h.]
2 Hegel is alluding to Goethe's poem, *Die Geheimnisse*, written in 1784–5 (ll. 245–6). See M. Donougho, 'Remarks on "Humanus heißt der Heilige . . ."', in *Hegel-Studien* 17 (1982): 214–25. [s.h.]
3 Hegel is obviously alluding to the familiar line of Terence. [Translator's note.] See Terence, *The Comedies*, translated with an introduction by B. Radice (Harmondsworth: Penguin Classics, 1976), p. 104 (*Heauton Timorumenos*: 'I'm human, so any human interest is my concern'). Hegel quotes a version of this line earlier in the *Aesthetics* (p. 46, not included in this collection). [s.h.]
4 In *Die künftige Geliebte* (The Future Sweetheart), 1747. [Translator's note.]

30

Aesthetics: Tragedy, Comedy and Drama

The Genres of Dramatic Poetry and the Chief Features it has had in History

If we glance back briefly on the course we have followed in our consideration of dramatic art up to now, we first established what its principle is in its
general and particular characteristics as well as what it is in relation to the
public. Then, secondly, we saw that a drama presents to us live the whole
development of a complete and specific action, and therefore it imperatively
needs a fully visible presentation, and this can only be given artistically by
actual performance in the theatre. But if the action is thus to be made real
objectively, it must itself be altogether determined and finished in itself in
poetic conception and treatment. But this can only be done if, thirdly,
dramatic poetry is split into different *genres* which borrow their type, whether
it involves oppositions or their reconciliation, from the difference between
the ways in which the characters and their aims, their conflict and the outcome of the whole action are brought on the scene. The chief modes arising
from this difference and having a varied historical development are tragedy
and comedy, as well as the conciliation of these two modes of treatment,
which only in dramatic poetry become of such essential importance that
they may serve as the basis for the division of its different *genres*.

In explaining these points in more detail we have

(a) first to bring out the general principle of tragedy, comedy and the so-
called 'drama';
(b) secondly, to indicate the character of classical and modern dramatic
poetry, their difference having been produced in the course of the historical development of tragedy and comedy;
(c) thirdly, to consider the concrete forms which comedy and tragedy especially have been able to take within this difference.

(a) The Principle of Tragedy, Comedy and Drama

The essential principle for discriminating the kinds of epic poetry depended on whether the substantive material to be portrayed in an epic was expressed in its universality or related in the form of objective characters, deeds and events.

Lyric, conversely, is divided into a series of different modes of expression by the degree and manner in which the subject-matter is more loosely or more tightly interwoven with the person whose inner life that subject-matter reveals.

Dramatic poetry, finally, makes central the collisions between characters and between their aims, as well as the necessary resolution of this battle. Consequently the principle for distinguishing its *genres* can only be derived from the relation of individuals to their aim and what it involves. The specific character of this relation is also what decides the particular manner of the dramatic conflict and outcome and so provides the essential type of the whole course of events in its living and artistic presentation.

As the principal points for consideration in this matter we must, in general, emphasize those features which in their harmony constitute the essence of every true action: (i) what is in *substance* good and great, the Divine actualized in the world, as the foundation of everything genuine and absolutely eternal in the make-up of an individual's character and aim; (ii) the *subject*, the individual himself in his unfettered self-determination and freedom. In whatever form dramatic poetry brings the action on the stage, what is really effective in it is absolute truth, but the specific way in which this effectiveness comes on the scene takes a different, and indeed an opposed, form according to whether what is kept dominant in the individuals and their actions and conflicts is their substantive basis or alternatively their subjective caprice, folly and perversity.

In this connection we have to examine the principle for the following *genres*:

(α) for tragedy, taken in its substantive and original typical form;
(β) for comedy, in which the mastery of all relations and ends is given as much to the individual in his willing and action, as to external contingency;
(γ) for drama, i.e. for a play in the narrower sense of the word, as occupying a middle position between these first two kinds.

(α) At this point I will make brief mention of only the most general basic characteristics of tragedy; their concrete particularization can come into view only in the light of the stages in tragedy's historical development.

(αα) The true content of the tragic action is provided, so far as concerns the *aims* adopted by the tragic characters, by the range of the substantive and independently justified powers that influence the human will: family love between husband and wife, parents and children, brothers and sisters; political life also, the patriotism of the citizens, the will of the ruler; and religion existent, not as a piety that renounces action and not as a divine judgement in man's heart about the good or evil of his actions, but on the contrary, as an active grasp and furtherance of actual interests and circumstances. A similar excellence belongs to the genuinely tragic *characters*. Throughout they are what they can and must be in accordance with their essential nature, not an ensemble of qualities separately developed epically in various ways; on the contrary, even if they are living and individual themselves, they are simply the *one* power dominating their own specific character; for, in accordance with their own individuality, they have inseparably identified themselves with some single particular aspect of those solid interests we have enumerated above, and are prepared to answer for that identification. Standing on this height, where the mere accidents of the individual's purely personal life disappear, the tragic heroes of dramatic art have risen to become, as it were, works of sculpture, whether they be living representatives of the substantive spheres of life or individuals great and firm in other ways on the strength of their free self-reliance; and so in this respect the statues and images of the gods, rather abstract in themselves, explain the lofty tragic characters of the Greeks better than all other commentaries and notes.

In general terms, therefore, we may say that the proper theme of the original type of tragedy is the Divine; not, however, the Divine as the object of the religious consciousness as such, but as it enters the world and individual action. Yet in this actual appearance it does not lose its substantive character, nor does it see itself there as inverted into the opposite of itself. In this form the spiritual substance of will and accomplishment is the concrete ethical order [*das Sittliche*]. For if we take the ethical order in its direct genuineness and do not interpret it from the point of view of subjective reflection as abstract morality [*das formell Moralische*], then it is the Divine made real in the world and so the substantive basis which in all its aspects, whether particular or essential, provides the motive for truly human action, and it is in action itself that these aspects develop and actualize this their essence.

(ββ) Everything that forces its way into the objective and real world is subject to the principle of particularization; consequently the ethical powers, just like the agents, are differentiated in their domain and their individual appearance. Now if, as dramatic poetry requires, these thus differentiated powers are summoned into appearance as active and are actualized as the specific aim of a human 'pathos' which passes over into action, then their harmony is cancelled and they come on the scene in *opposition* to one another in reciprocal independence. In that event a single action will under certain circumstances realize an aim or a character which is one-sidedly isolated in its complete determinacy, and therefore, in the circumstances presupposed, will necessarily rouse against it the opposed 'pathos' and so lead to inevitable conflicts. The original essence of tragedy consists then in the fact that within such a conflict each of the opposed sides, if taken by itself, has *justification*; while each can establish the true and positive content of its own aim and character only by denying and infringing the equally justified power of the other. The consequence is that in its ethical life [*Sittlichkeit*],[1] and because of it, each is nevertheless involved in *guilt*.

The general reason for the necessity of these conflicts I have touched upon already. The substance of ethical life, as a concrete unity, is an ensemble of *different* relations and powers which only in a situation of inactivity, like that of the blessed gods, accomplish the work of the spirit in the enjoyment of an undisturbed life. But the very nature of this ensemble implies its transfer from its at first purely abstract *ideality* into its actualization in *reality* and its appearance in the mundane sphere. Owing to the nature of the real world, the mere *difference* of the constituents of this ensemble becomes perverted into *opposition* and collision, once individual characters seize upon them on the territory of specific circumstances. Only from this point of view can we be really serious about those gods who dwell in their peaceful tranquillity and unity solely on Olympus and in the heaven of imagination and religious ideas, but who, when they now come actually to life as a specific 'pathos' in a human individual, lead, despite all their justification, to guilt and wrong owing to their particular specification and the opposition to which this leads.

(γγ) In this way however, an unresolved contradiction is set up; it does appear in the real world but cannot maintain itself there as the substance of reality and what is genuinely true; its proper claim is satisfied only when it is annulled as a contradiction. However justified the tragic character and his aim, however necessary the tragic collision, the third thing required is the tragic resolution of this conflict. By this means eternal justice is exercised on individuals and their aims in the sense that it restores the substance and unity of ethical life with the downfall of the individual who has disturbed its peace. For although the characters have a purpose which is valid in itself, they can carry it out in tragedy only by pursuing it one-sidedly and so contradicting and infringing someone else's purpose. The truly substantial thing which has to be actualized, however, is not the battle between particular aims or characters, although this too has its essential ground in the nature of the real world and human action, but the reconciliation in which the specific individuals and their aims work together harmoniously without opposition and without infringing on one another. Therefore what is superseded in the tragic denouement is only the *one-sided* particular which had not been able to adapt itself to this harmony, and now (and this is the tragic thing in its action), unable to renounce itself and its intention, finds itself condemned to total destruction, or, at the very least, forced to abandon, if it can, the accomplishment of its aim.

In this connection Aristotle, as every one knows, laid it down [*Poetics*, 1449[b] 26] that the true effect of tragedy should be to arouse pity and fear and accomplish the catharsis of these emotions. By 'emotions' Aristotle did not mean mere feeling, my subjective sense of something corresponding with me or not, the agreeable or disagreeable, the attractive or the repulsive – this most superficial of all criteria which only recently has been proposed as the principle of dramatic success or failure. For the only important thing for a work of art is to present what corresponds with reason and spiritual truth, and if we are to discover the principle of this, we must direct our attention to totally different considerations. Even in the case of Aristotle's dictum we must therefore fix our eyes not on the mere feelings of pity and fear but on the nature of the subject-matter which by its artistic appearance is to purify these feelings. A man can be frightened in face of, on the one hand, something finite and external to him, or, on the other hand, the power of the Absolute. What a man has really to fear is not an external power and oppression by it, but the might of the ethical order which is one determinant of his own free reason and is at the same time that eternal and inviolable something which he summons up against himself if once he turns against it. Like fear, pity too has two kinds of object. The first is the object of ordinary emotion, i.e. sympathy with someone else's misfortune and suffering which is felt as something finite and negative. Provincial females are always ready with compassion of this sort. For if it is only the negative aspect, the negative aspect of misfortune, that is emphasized, then the victim of misfortune is degraded. True pity, on the contrary, is sympathy at the same time with the sufferer's ethical justification, with the affirmative aspect, the substantive thing that must be present in him. Beggars and rascals cannot inspire us with pity of this kind. Therefore if the tragic character has inspired in us a fear of the power of the ethical order that he has violated, then if in his misfortune he is to arouse a tragic sympathy he must be a man of worth and goodness himself. For it is only something of intrinsic worth which strikes the heart of a man of noble feelings and shakes it to its depths. After all, therefore, we should not confuse our interest in a tragic denouement with a naïve sense of satisfaction that our sympathy should be claimed by a sad story, by a misfortune as such. Such miseries may befall a man, without his contributing to them and without his fault, merely as a result of the conjuncture of external accidents and natural circumstances, as a result of illness, loss of property, death, etc., and the only interest in them by which we should properly be gripped is our eagerness to rush to the man's help. If we cannot help, then spectacles of wretchedness and distress are only harrowing. A truly tragic suffering, on the contrary, is only inflicted on the individual agents as a consequence of their own deed which is both legitimate and, owing to the resulting collision, blameworthy, and for which their whole self is answerable.

Above mere fear and tragic sympathy there therefore stands that sense of reconciliation which the tragedy affords by the glimpse of eternal justice. In its absolute sway this justice overrides the relative justification of one-sided aims and passions because it cannot suffer the conflict and contradiction of naturally harmonious ethical powers to be victorious and permanent in truth and actuality.

In virtue of this principle, tragedy rests primarily on the contemplation of such a conflict and its resolution. Consequently, owing to its whole manner of presentation, it is dramatic poetry alone which is capable of making the entire range and course of tragedy into the principle of a work of art and developing it completely. It is for this reason that I have only now taken the opportunity to speak of the tragic outlook, although it is at work extensively and variously, even if to a lesser extent, in the other arts also.

(β) In tragedy the eternal substance of things emerges victorious in a reconciling way, because it strips away from the conflicting individuals only their false one-sidedness, while the positive elements in what they willed it displays as what is to be retained, without discord but affirmatively harmonized. In comedy, conversely, it is subjectivity, or personality, which in its infinite assurance retains the upper hand. For, granted the cleavage of dramatic poetry into different *genres*, it is only these two fundamental features of action which can confront one another as the basis of such *genres*. In tragedy the individuals destroy themselves through the one-sidedness of their otherwise solid will and character, or they must resignedly accept what they had opposed even in a serious way. In comedy there comes before our contemplation, in the laughter in which the characters dissolve everything, including themselves, the victory of their own subjective personality which nevertheless persists self-assured.

(αα) The general ground for comedy is therefore a world in which man as subject or person has made himself completely master of everything that counts to him otherwise as the essence of what he wills and accomplishes, a world whose aims are therefore self-destructive because they are unsubstantial. Nothing can be done, for example, to help a democratic nation where the citizens are self-seeking, quarrelsome, frivolous, bumptious, without faith or knowledge, garrulous, boastful and ineffectual: such a nation destroys itself by its own folly. But it does not follow at all that every unsubstantial action is comical on account of this nullity. In this matter the laughable is often confused with the comical. Every contrast between something substantive and its appearance, between an end and the means may be laughable; this is a contradiction in which the appearance cancels itself and the realization of an end is at the same time the end's own destruction. But for the comical we must make a deeper demand. For example, there is nothing comical about the vices of mankind. A proof of this is given us by satire, all the more tediously, the cruder are the colours in which it paints the contradiction between what actually exists in the world and what virtuous men ought to be. Neither need follies, senselessness, silliness, be comical, taken in and by themselves, although we laugh at them. In general, nowhere can more contradiction be found than in the things that people laugh at. The flattest and most tasteless things can move people to laughter, and they often laugh all the same at the most important and profound matters if they see in them only some wholly insignificant aspect which contradicts their habits and day-to-day outlook. In such a case their laughter is only an expression of a self-complacent wit, a sign that they are clever enough to recognize such a contrast and are aware of the fact. There is also the laughter of derision, scorn, despair, etc. On the other hand, the comical as such implies an infinite light-heartedness and confidence felt by someone raised altogether above his own inner contradiction and not bitter or miserable in it at all: this is the bliss and ease of a man who, being sure of himself, can bear the frustration of his aims and achievements. A narrow and pedantic mind is least of all capable of this when for others his behaviour is laughable in the extreme.

(ββ) I will touch generally on only the following more detailed points in connection with the sort of thing that can serve as the situation of a comical action.

In the first place, the characters and their aims are entirely without substance and contradictory and therefore they cannot accomplish anything. Avarice, for example, both in its aim and in the petty means it uses appears from beginning to end as inherently null. For the avaricious man takes the dead abstraction of wealth, money as such, as the ultimate reality beyond which he will not go; and he tries to attain this cold pleasure by depriving himself of every other concrete satisfaction, while nevertheless he cannot gain his chosen end because his aim and his means are helpless in face of cunning, betrayal, etc. But if an individual is *serious* in identifying himself with such an inherently false aim and making it the one real thing in his life, then, the more he still clings to it after he has been deprived of its realization, the more miserable he becomes. In such a picture there is none of the real essence of the comical, just as there is none anywhere when on one side there is the painfulness of the man's situation, and on the other side mere ridicule and malicious joy. Therefore there is more of the comic in a situation where petty and futile aims are to be brought about with a show of great seriousness and elaborate preparations, but where, precisely because what the individual willed was something inherently trivial, he is not ruined in fact when his purpose fails but can surmount this disaster with cheerfulness undisturbed.

In the second place, the converse situation occurs where individuals plume themselves on the *substantial* quality of their characters and aims, but as instruments for accomplishing something substantial their characters are the precise opposite of what is required. In this case the substantial quality is purely imaginary and has become in itself and in the eyes of onlookers an appearance giving itself the look and the value of something important; but this involves between aim and character, action and personality a contradiction whereby an achievement of the imagined character and aim is frustrated. An example of this kind of thing is the *Ecclesiazusae* of Aristophanes. There the women wish to decide on and to found a new political constitution, but they still retain all the whims and passions of women.

A third type, in addition to the first two, is based on the use of external contingencies. Through their various and peculiar complications situations arise in which aims and their accomplishment, inner character and external circumstances, are put in contrast with one another comically and then they lead to an equally comic solution.

(γγ) But the comical rests as such throughout on contradictory contrasts both between aims in themselves and also between their objects and the accidents of character and external circumstances, and therefore the comic action requires a solution almost more stringently than a tragic one does. In a comic action the contradiction between what is absolutely true and its realization in individuals is posed more profoundly.

Yet what is destroyed in this solution cannot be either fundamental principle or individual character.[2]

For, as genuine art, comedy too has to submit to the obligation of using its presentation to bring the absolutely rational into appearance, not at all as what is broken up and perverted in itself but on the contrary as what assigns neither the victory nor, in the last resort, permanence, in the real world to folly and unreason, to false oppositions and contradictions. Aristophanes, for example, did not make fun of what was truly ethical in the life of the Athenians, or of their genuine philosophy, true religious faith and serious art. On the contrary what he does put before our eyes in its self-destructive folly is the downright opposite of the genuine actuality of the state, religion, and art,[3] i.e. what he exhibits is sophistry, the deplorable and lamentable character of tragedy, flighty gossip, litigiousness, etc., and the aberrations of the democracy out of which the old faith and morals had vanished. Only in our day could a Kotzebue succeed in giving the palm to a moral excellence which is a form of baseness and in palliating and countenancing what can only exist in order to be destroyed.

But neither should subjective personality as such come to grief in comedy. For even if what comes on the scene is only the show and imagination of what is substantive, or else mere downright perversity and pettiness, there still remains as a loftier principle the inherently firm personality which is raised in its freedom above the downfall of the whole finite sphere and is happy and assured in itself. The comic subjective personality has become the overlord of whatever appears in the real world. From that world the adequate objective presence of fundamental principle has disappeared. When what has no substance in itself has destroyed its show of existence by its own agency, the individual makes himself master of this dissolution too and remains undisturbed in himself and at ease.

(γ) In the centre between tragedy and comedy there is a third chief *genre* of dramatic poetry which yet is of less striking importance, despite the fact that it attempts to reconcile the difference between tragedy and comedy; or at least, instead of being isolated in sheer opposition to one another, these two sides meet in it and form a concrete whole.

(αα) To this category there belong for example the Greek and Roman satyric dramas. In them the main action, even if not tragic, remains serious, while the chorus of satyrs is treated comically. Tragicomedy too may be included here. An example of it is provided by Plautus in the Prologue to the *Amphitruo* [ll. 52–5, 59] where this is announced through the mouth of Mercury addressing the audience as follows:

> Quid contraxistis frontem? quia Tragoediam
> Dixi futuram hanc? Deus sum: commutavero
> Eamdem hanc, si voltis: faciam ex Tragoedia
> Comoedia ut sit omnibus iisdem versibus . . .
> Faciam ut conmista sit Tragicocomoedia.[4]

And as a reason for this mixture he adduces the fact that while on the one hand gods and kings appear as dramatis personae, there is also the comic figure of Sosia, the slave. In modern dramatic poetry, tragedy and comedy are still more intermingled, because even in modern tragedy the principle of subjectivity, free on its own account in comedy, becomes dominant from beginning to end and pushes into the background the substantive spheres of the ethical powers.

(ββ) But the deeper harmonization of tragic and comic treatment into a new whole does not consist in juxtaposing or upsetting these opposites [i.e. substance and subject] but in blunting both sides and reconciling their opposition. Instead of acting with comical perversity, the individual is filled with the seriousness characteristic of solid concerns and stable characters, while the tragic fixity of will is so far weakened, and the depth of the collisions involved so far reduced, that there can emerge a reconciliation of interests and a harmonious unification of individuals and their aims. It is in a conception like this that particularly our modern plays and dramas have the basis of their origin. The heart of this principle is the view that, despite all differences and conflicts of characters and their interests and passions, human action can nevertheless produce a really fully harmonious situation. As long ago as their day the Greeks had tragedies which did have an outcome like this, in that individuals were not sacrificed but saved: for example, in the *Eumenides* of Aeschylus the Areopagus grants to both parties, Apollo and the avenging Furies, the right to be worshipped; and in the *Philoctetes* [of Sophocles] the divine appearance and advice of Heracles settles the fight between Neoptolemus and Philoctetes, and they go off to Troy together. But in these cases the reconciliation comes from outside by command of the gods, etc., and does not have its source within the parties themselves, while in modern plays it is the individuals themselves who are led in the course of their own action to this cessation of strife and to the mutual reconciliation of their aims or characters. In this respect Goethe's *Iphigenia* is a real poetic masterpiece of a play, more so than his *Tasso*. In the latter the reconciliation with Antonio is more or less only a matter of the heart and a subjective recognition that he possesses a sense for the realities of life which is missing from Tasso's character, while the right of the ideal life to which Tasso had clung in his conflict with reality, i.e. the life of propriety and decorum, is a right principally retained as such only subjectively in the minds of the spectators and appearing objectively [in Antonio] as, at best, consideration for Tasso and sympathy with his fate.

(γγ) But on the whole the boundary lines of this intermediate kind of dramatic poetry are less firm than those of tragedy and comedy. Moreover this kind almost runs the risk of departing from the genuine type of drama altogether or of lapsing into prose. Here the conflicts are meant to proceed via their own discord to a peaceful end and therefore from the start they are not such sharp oppositions as those in tragedy. The result is that the poet is easily induced to devote the whole force of his production to the inner life of the dramatis personae and to make the course of the situations a mere means to this sketching of character; or alternatively he allows preponderating scope to externals, i.e. to situations and customs of the period. If he finds both of these procedures too difficult, he restricts himself altogether to keeping attention alive merely through the interest of complicated and thrilling events. Consequently this sphere includes a mass of modern plays which make no claim to be poetry but only to have a theatrical effect. What they aim at producing is not a genuinely poetic emotion but only one that people ordinarily feel, or else they seek to reform the public or merely to entertain it. But, in any case, for the most part they manufacture all sorts of opportunities for the actor to give a brilliant display of his accomplished virtuosity.

(b) Difference between Ancient and Modern Dramatic Poetry

The same principle which gave us the basis for the division of dramatic art into tragedy and comedy provides us with the essential turning-points in the history of their development. For the lines of this development can only consist in setting out and elaborating the chief features implicit in the nature of dramatic action, where in tragedy the whole treatment and execution presents what is *substantial* and fundamental in the characters and their aims and conflicts, while in comedy the central thing is the character's *inner* life and his *private* personality.

(α) We are not concerned here to provide a complete history of art and therefore we may start by setting aside those beginnings of dramatic art which we encounter in the East. However far Eastern poetry advanced in epic and some sorts of lyric, the whole Eastern outlook inhibits *ab initio* an adequate development of dramatic art. The reason is that truly *tragic* action necessarily presupposes either a live conception of *individual* freedom and independence or at least an individual's determination and willingness to accept freely and on his own account the responsibility for his own act and its consequences; and for the emergence of *comedy* there must have asserted itself in a still higher degree the free right of the subjective personality and its self-assured dominion. In the East these conditions are not fulfilled. Mohammedan poetry, in particular, with its grandiose sublimity is throughout far away from any attempt at dramatic expression, because in such poetry, although the independence of the individual may be vigorously asserted, the One fundamental power still more persistently dominates its every creature and decides its lot irreversibly. Dramatic art demands the vindication of (*a*) a particular element in an individual's action, and (*b*) a personality probing its own depths, and it follows from what I have said that neither of these demands can be met in Mohammedan poetry. Indeed the individual's subjection to the will of God remains, precisely in Mohammedanism, all the more abstract the more abstractly universal is the One power which dominates the whole and which in the last resort inhibits anything particular. Consequently we find the beginnings of drama only in China and India; yet even here, to judge from the few samples so far known to us, there is no question of the accomplishment of a free individual action but merely of giving life to events and feelings in specific situations presented successively on the stage.

(*β*) Therefore the real beginning of dramatic poetry must be sought in Greece where the principle of free individuality makes the perfection of the classical form of art possible for the first time. Yet within this form of art the individual can enter in connection with action only so far as is directly required by the free vitalization of the *substantive* content of human aims. Therefore what principally counts in Greek drama, whether tragedy or comedy, is the universal and essential element in the aim which the characters are realizing: in tragedy, the ethical justification of the agent's consciousness in respect of a specific action, the vindication of the act in and by itself; and, in comedy, at least in the old comedy, it is also the general public interests that are emphasized, statesmen and their way of steering the state, war and peace, the people and its ethical situation, philosophy and its corruption, and so forth. Therefore neither the various descriptions of the human heart and personal character nor particular complications and intrigues can find their place completely in Greek drama; nor does the interest turn on the fates of individuals. Sympathy is claimed above all not for these particular and personal matters but simply for the battle between the essential powers that rule human life and between the gods that dominate the human heart, and for this battle's outcome. The *tragic* heroes come on the scene as the individual representatives of these powers in much the same way as the figures of *comedy* expose the general corruption into which the fundamental tendencies of public life have been actually perverted contemporaneously with the comedy.

(*γ*) In modern, or romantic, poetry, on the other hand, the principal topic is provided by an individual's passion, which is satisfied in the pursuit of a purely subjective end, and, in general, by the fate of a single individual and his character in special circumstances.

Accordingly the poetic interest here lies in the greatness of the characters who by their imagination or disposition and aptitude display the full wealth of their heart, and their elevation over their situations and actions, as a real possibility (even if this be often impaired and destroyed solely by circumstances and complications), but at the same time they find a reconciliation in the very greatness of their nature. Therefore in this mode of treatment our interest is directed, so far as the particular matter at issue in an action is concerned, not on its ethical justification and necessity but on the individual person and his affairs. This being so, a *leitmotiv* is thus provided by love, ambition, etc.; indeed, even crime is not excluded, though this easily becomes a rock difficult to circumnavigate. For after all if a criminal, especially one like the hero in Müllner's *Guilt*, is weak and through and through base, he is only a disgusting sight. Here above all, therefore, we must demand formal greatness of character and a personality powerful enough to sustain everything negative and, without denying its acts or being inwardly wrecked, to accept its fate. – Nevertheless the substantive and fundamental ends, country, family, crown and empire, are not to be held aloof at all, even if what matters to the individual character is not the substantial nature of these ends but his own individuality; but in that case they form on the whole the specific ground on which the individual stands with his own subjective character and where he gets into a conflict, instead of providing him with the proper ultimate object of his willing and acting.

Then, further, alongside this subjective element there may come on the scene a spread of particular details concerning both the inner life and also the external circumstances and relations within which the action proceeds. Therefore we find legitimately in place here, in distinction from the simple conflicts in Greek tragedy, a variety and wealth of dramatis personae, extraordinary and always newly involved complications, labyrinths of intrigue, accidental occurrences, in short all those features which, no longer fettered by the impressive and substantive character of an essential subject-matter, are indicative of what is typical in the romantic, as distinct from the classical, form of art.

Nevertheless despite this apparently unbounded mass of particulars, even here, if the whole play is to remain dramatic and poetic, the specific character of the collision which has to be fought out must be visibly emphasized, and, on the other hand, especially in tragedy, the authority of a higher world-governor, whether Providence or fate, must be made obvious in the course and outcome of the particular action.

(c) The Concrete Development of Dramatic Poetry and its Genres

The essential differences of conception and poetic execution [in drama] have now been considered. Along with them are the different *genres* of dramatic art and they acquire their truly real perfection only when they are developed at this or that stage [in history]. Therefore, in conclusion, our consideration must be directed to this concrete manner of their evolution.

(*a*) If for the reason given above we exclude oriental beginnings, the first main sphere confronting us at once is the dramatic poetry of the Greeks because that is the stage at which tragedy proper, and comedy too, had their highest intrinsic worth. It was in that poetry that for the first time there was a clear consciousness of what the real essence of tragedy and comedy is. After these opposed ways of looking at human action had been firmly separated and strictly distinguished from one another, tragedy and comedy developed organically, and first one, and then the other, attained the summit of perfection. Still later, Roman dramatic art gives us only a pale reflection of the Greek achievement, and here the Romans did not achieve even that measure of success which later came to them in their similar efforts in epic and lyric. – In order to touch briefly on only the points of greatest import-ance, I will limit a more detailed consideration of these stages to tragedy as viewed by Aeschylus and Sophocles and comedy by Aristophanes.

(*aa*) I have said of *tragedy* already that the basic form determining its organ-ization and structure is to be found in emphasis on the substantial aspect of aims and their objects, as well as of individuals, their conflicts and their fates.

The general background of a tragic action is provided in a tragedy, as it was in epic, by that world-situation which I have previously called the 'heroic' age. In that age the universal ethical powers have not been explicitly fixed as either the law of the land or as moral precepts and duties. Con-sequently, only in heroic times can these powers enter in original freshness as the gods who either oppose one another in their own activities or appear themselves as the living heart of free human individuals. But if the ethical order is to be exhibited from the outset as the substantive foundation and general background out of which the actions of individuals grow and develop into a conflict and then are tugged back out of it into unity again, we are confronted by two different forms of the ethical order in action.

First, the naïve consciousness which wills the substantial order as a *whole*, i.e. as an undivided identity of its different aspects. This consciousness therefore remains blameless and neutral, in undisturbed peace with itself and others. But this is a purely universal consciousness, undifferentiated in its worship, faith and fortune. It therefore cannot attain to any specific action. On the contrary, it has a sort of horror of the schism implicit there. Although, inactive itself, it reverences as higher that spiritual courage which, having selected its aim, proceeds to decide and act, it is still incapable of embarking on any such course. It knows that it is but the terrain or spectator of action. Therefore, there is nothing left for it to do with the agents, whom it venerates as higher than itself, and with the energy of their decisions and struggles, but to oppose to them the object of its own wisdom, i.e. the substantive ideality of the ethical powers.

The *second* aspect is the individual 'pathos' which drives the dramatis personae, acting with an ethical justification, into opposition with others and thereby brings them into a conflict. The individuals animated by this 'pathos' are not what we all 'characters' in the modern sense of the word, but neither are they mere abstractions. They occupy a vital central position between both, because they are firm figures who simply are what they are, without any inner conflict, without any hesitating recognition of someone else's 'pathos', and therefore (the opposite of our contemporary 'irony') lofty, absolutely determinate individuals, although this determinacy of theirs is based on and is representative of a particular ethical power. Since it is only the *opposition* of such individuals, justified in their action, which constitutes the essence of tragedy, it can come into view only on the territory of actual *human* life. For it is only in that life that a particular quality can be the substance of an individual in the sense that he puts himself with his entire being and interests into such a quality and makes it an overmastering passion. On the other hand, in the case of the *blessed gods* the undifferenced divine nature is the essential thing, and, if opposition arises, there is in the last resort no seriousness about it and, as I have already pointed out in dealing with the Homeric epic, it is ultimately dissolved again ironically.[5]

Each of these two aspects is as important as the other for the whole drama. Both of them – the one and undivided consciousness of the Divine [or of the ethical powers], and the action which, resolving on ethical ends and achieving them, involves battle but comes on the scene with divine force and as a divine deed – provide the principal elements which in its works of art Greek tragedy displays as harmonized, i.e. in the chorus and the heroic agents.

In recent times the significance of the Greek *chorus* has been much discussed, and in the course of this discussion a question has been raised about whether it can or should be introduced into modern tragedy too. People have felt the need for such a substantial groundwork and yet at the same time have been unable to introduce or insert it because they have not understood or grasped deeply enough the nature of what is genuinely tragic or the necessity of the chorus in the Greek conception of tragedy. The chorus has indeed been understood to some extent by those who say that its business is tranquil reflection on the whole thing at issue while the dramatis personae remain caught in their own particular aims and situations and have now gained in the chorus and its meditations a criterion of the worth of their characters and actions, just as the public has found in the chorus an objective representative of its own judgement on what is going on in front of it in the work of art.

Upholders of this view have hit on part of the truth, because in fact the chorus confronts us as a higher consciousness,[6] aware of the substantial issues, warning against false conflicts, and weighing the outcome. Nevertheless the chorus is not at all a moralist, disengaged like a spectator, a person reflecting on the thing purely from outside, in himself uninteresting and tedious, and introduced simply for the sake of his reflections. On the contrary, the chorus is the actual substance of the ethical life and action of the heroes themselves; in contrast to these individuals it is the people as the fruitful soil out of which they grow (just as flowers and towering trees do from their own native soil) and by the existent character of which they are conditioned. Consequently the chorus is essentially appropriate in an age where ethical complications cannot yet be met by specific valid and just laws and firm religious dogmas, but where the ethical order appears only in its direct and living actuality and remains only the equilibrium of a stable life secure against the fearful collisions to which the energies of individuals in their opposing actions must lead. But what the chorus gives us is the consciousness that such a secure refuge is actually present. Therefore the chorus does not in fact encroach on the action; it does not actively exercise any right against the warring heroes but pronounces judgement purely contemplatively; it warns and sympathizes, or it appeals to divine law and those inner powers which imagination portrays to itself objectively as the group of the gods who hold sway. In so expressing itself it is lyrical, as we saw;[7] for it does nothing and has no events to relate epically. But what it says preserves at the same time the epic character of substantial universality and it does therefore move in one mode of lyric which may, in distinction from the proper form of odes, sometimes approach the paean and the dithyramb.

This position of the chorus in Greek tragedy needs essential emphasis. Just as the Greek theatre itself has its external terrain, its scene and its surroundings, so the chorus, the people, is as it were the scene of the spirit; it may be compared, in architecture, with a temple surrounding the image of the gods, for here it is an environment for the heroes in the action. In our case, however, statues stand under the open sky without such a background, and modern tragedy does not need one either, because its actions do not rest on this substantial basis but on the individual's will and character as well as on the apparently external accidents of occurrences and circumstances.

This all implies that it is an utterly false view to regard the chorus as something casually dragged in and a mere relic of the time when Greek drama originated. No doubt its external origin is to be traced to the fact that at festivals of Dionysus the chief thing, in art at any rate, was choral song, until subsequently, as a break, a narrator came on the scene, and his message was finally transformed and elevated into the actual figures of a dramatic action. But in the age of tragedy's full bloom the chorus was not retained at all merely in honour of this feature of religious festivals and Dionysus worship; on the contrary it was developed ever more beautifully and in a more measured way simply because it belongs essentially to the dramatic action itself and is so necessary to it that the decay of tragedy is especially manifested in the deterioration of the choruses which no longer remain an integral part of the whole but sink down into being an unnecessary ornament. On the other hand, the chorus is plainly unsuitable for romantic tragedy which in any case did not originate in choral songs. On the contrary, the subject-matter here is of such a kind that any introduction of choruses in the Greek sense must inevitably have misfired. For even the oldest so-called mystery-plays, moralities, and other farces from which romantic drama arose, do not present any action in the original Greek sense or any emergence from that consciousness which is unaware of division in life or the Divine. Neither does the chorus fit in with chivalry or absolute monarchy, for there the people have to obey or become partisans involved in action only in the interests of their fortune or misfortune. In general it cannot find its proper place where it is individual passions, aims, and characters that are at issue or where the play of intrigue is being pursued.

The second chief feature, contrasted with the chorus, consists of the *individuals* who act and come continually into conflict. In Greek tragedy, as I have said more than once, the occasion for collisions is produced by the ethical justification of a specific act, and not at all by an evil will, a crime, or infamy, or by mere misfortune, blindness and the like. For evil in the abstract has no truth in itself and is of no interest. But, on the other hand, it must not look as if ethical traits of character have been assigned to individuals merely by [the dramatist's] *intention*, for on the contrary their justification must be shown to lie in them *essentially*. Criminal types, like those of today, good-for-nothings, or even so-called 'morally noble' criminals with their empty chatter about fate, we therefore do not find in Greek tragedy any more than a decision or a deed resting on purely private interest and personal character, on thirst for power, lust, honour or other passions, the right of which can be rooted only in an individual's private inclination and personality. But an individual's decision, justified by the object he aims at, is carried out in a one-sided and particular way, and therefore in specific circumstances, which already carry in themselves the real possibility of conflicts, he injures another and equally ethical sphere of the human will. To this sphere another person clings as his own actual 'pathos' and in carrying out his aim opposes and reacts against the former individual. In this way the collision of equally justified powers and individuals is completely set afoot.

The range of the subject-matter here may be variously particularized but its essence is not very extensive. The chief conflict treated most beautifully by Sophocles, with Aeschylus as his predecessor, is that between the state, i.e. ethical life in its *spiritual* universality, and the family, i.e. *natural* ethical life. These are the clearest powers that are presented in tragedy, because the full reality of ethical existence consists in harmony between these two spheres and in absence of discord between what an agent has actually to do in one and what he has to do in the other. In this connection I need refer only to Aeschylus' *Seven against Thebes* and, still more appositely, Sophocles' *Antigone*. Antigone honours the bond of kinship, the gods of the underworld, while Creon honours Zeus alone, the dominating power over public life and social welfare. In [Euripides'] *Iphigenia in Aulis*, in Aeschlyus' *Agamemnon, Choephori* and *Eumenides*, and in Sophocles' *Electra* we find a similar conflict. Agamemnon, as King and commander of the army, sacrifices his daughter in the interest of the Greeks and the Trojan expedition; thereby he snaps the bond of love for his daughter and his wife. This bond Clytemnestra, his wife and Iphigenia's mother, retains in the depths of her heart, and in revenge she prepares a shameful death for her home-coming husband. Orestes, her son and the King's son, honours his mother but he has to defend the right of his father, the King, and he slays the womb that bore him.

This is a subject valid for every epoch and therefore this presentation of it, despite all national differences, continues to excite our lively human and artistic sympathy.

A second main type of collision is less concrete. The Greek tragedians are fond of portraying it especially in the fate of Oedipus. The most perfect example of this has been left to us by Sophocles in his *Oedipus Tyrannus* and *Oedipus Coloneus*. What is at issue here is the right of the wide awake consciousness, the justification of what the man has self-consciously willed and knowingly done, as contrasted with what he was fated by the gods to do and actually did unconsciously and without having willed it. Oedipus has killed his father; he has married his mother and begotten children in this incestuous alliance; and yet he has been involved in these most evil crimes without either knowing or willing them. The right of our deeper consciousness today would consist in recognizing that since he had neither intended nor known these crimes himself, they were not to be regarded as his own deeds. But the Greek, with his plasticity of consciousness, takes responsibility for what he has done as an individual and does not cut his purely subjective self-consciousness apart from what is objectively the case.

Lastly, there are other collisions depending partly on special circumstances and partly on the general relation between an individual's action and the Greek μοῖρα [fate]. For our purpose, these are of less importance.

But in considering all these tragic conflicts we must above all reject the false idea that they have anything to do with guilt or innocence. The tragic heroes are just as much innocent as guilty. On the presupposition that a man is only guilty if alternatives are open to him and he decides arbitrarily on what he does, the Greek plastic figures are innocent: they act out of this character of theirs, on *this* 'pathos', because this character, this 'pathos' is precisely what they are: their act is not preceded by either hesitation or choice. It is just the strength of the great characters that they do not choose but throughout, from start to finish, *are* what they will and accomplish. They are what they are, and never anything else, and this is their greatness. For weakness in action consists only in a cleavage between the individual and his object, in which case character, will and aim do not appear as having grown into an absolute unity; and since no fixed aim is alive in the individual's soul as the substance of his own individuality, as the 'pathos' and power animating his whole will, he may swither irresolutely from this to that and let caprice decide. From this swithering the Greek plastic figures are exempt; for them the bond between the subject and what he wills as his object remains indissoluble. What drives them to act is precisely an ethically justified 'pathos' which they assert against one another with the eloquence of their 'pathos' not in sentimental and personal rhetoric or in the sophistries of passion, but in solid and cultivated objective language. (Sophocles above everyone else was a master in the depth, measure, and plastic and living beauty of language of this kind.) At the same time, however, their 'pathos' is pregnant with collisions and it leads them to injurious and guilty acts. But they do not claim to be innocent of these at all. On the contrary, what they did, and actually had to do, is their glory. No worse insult could be given to such a hero than to say that he had acted innocently. It is the honour of these great characters to be culpable. They do not want to arouse sympathy or pity, for what arouses pity is not anything substantive, but subjective grief, the subjective depth of personality. But their firm and strong character is one with its essential 'pathos', and what excites our admiration is this indestructible harmony and not the pity and emotion that Euripides alone has slipped into expressing.

The tragic complication leads finally to no other result or denouement but this: the two sides that are in conflict with one another preserve the justification which both have, but what each upholds is one-sided, and this one-sidedness is stripped away and the inner, undisturbed harmony returns in the attitude of the chorus which clearly assigns equal honour to all the gods. The true development of the action consists solely in the cancellation of conflicts *as conflicts*, in the reconciliation of the powers animating action which struggled to destroy one another in their mutual conflict. Only in that case does finality lie not in misfortune and suffering but in the satisfaction of the spirit, because only with such a conclusion can the necessity of what happens to the individuals appear as absolute rationality, and only then can our hearts be ethically at peace: shattered by the fate of the heroes but reconciled fundamentally. Only by adherence to this view can Greek tragedy be understood.

Therefore we should not interpret such a conclusion as a purely moral [*moralisch*] outcome where evil is punished and virtue rewarded, i.e. 'when vice vomits, virtue sits at table'.[8] Here there is no question at all of an introverted personality's subjective reflection and its good and evil, but, when the collision was complete, of the vision of an affirmative reconciliation and the equal validity of both the powers that were in conflict. Neither is the necessity of the outcome a blind fate, a purely irrational and unintelligible destiny which many people call 'classical', but a rational one, although the rationality here does not appear as a self-conscious Providence whose divine end and aim becomes manifest to itself and others in the world and individuals. On the contrary, the rationality consists in the fact that the power supreme over individual gods and men cannot allow persistence either to one-sided powers that make themselves independent and thereby overstep the limits of their authority or to the conflicts that follow in consequence. Fate drives individuality back within its limits and destroys it if these are crossed. But an irrational compulsion and innocent suffering would inevitably produce in the soul of the spectator mere indignation instead of ethical peace and satisfaction.

In another way, therefore, a tragic reconciliation is nevertheless different from an epic one. If we look at Achilles and Odysseus, for example, they reach their goal, and this is proper; but they are not steadily favoured by fortune; on the contrary, they have to taste the bitter wine of a sense of finitude and to fight their way through difficulty, loss and sacrifice. For Truth demands that in the course of life and the objective sweep of events the nullity of the finite shall come into appearance too. The wrath of Achilles is appeased, he obtains from Agamemnon what he had been injured by losing, he wreaks his revenge on Hector, the funeral celebrations for Patroclus are completed, and Achilles is recognized as the most glorious of men. But his wrath and its appeasement has cost him his dearest friend, the noble Patroclus; in order to avenge his loss on Hector, he finds himself compelled to desist from his wrath and plunge once more into the battle against the Trojans, and when he is recognized as the most glorious of men he has at the same time a sense of his early death. Similarly, Odysseus does in the end arrive at Ithaca, the goal of his wishes, but asleep and alone after long years of delay and toil, after losing all his companions and all the booty from Troy. Thus both have paid their debt to finitude, and Nemesis has entered into its rights by the downfall of Troy and the fate of the Greek heroes. But Nemesis is simply the ancient justice which degrades what has risen too high only in order to restore by misfortune the mere equilibrium of good and ill fortune, and it touches and affects the realm of finitude without any further *ethical* judgement. This is epic justice in the field of events, the comprehensive reconciliation which consists in mere equalization. The more profound tragic reconciliation, on the other hand, depends on the advance of specific ethical substantive powers out of their opposition to their true harmony. But the ways in which this harmony can be brought about are very different, and I will therefore bring to your notice only the chief features at issue in this connection.

First, it needs special emphasis that if the one-sidedness of a 'pathos' is the real ground of the collisions, this can only mean that it is carried out into actually living action, and the one-sided 'pathos' has become the one and only 'pathos' of a specific individual. Now if the one-sidedness is to be cancelled, it is the individual, since he has acted solely as this *one* 'pathos', who must be got rid of and sacrificed. For the individual is only this *one* life and, if this is not to prevail on its own account as this *one*, then the individual is shattered.

This sort of development is most complete when the individuals who are at variance appear each of them in their concrete existence as a totality, so that in themselves they are in the power of what they are fighting, and therefore they violate what, if they were true to their own nature, they should be honouring. For example, Antigone lives under the political authority of Creon [the present King]; she is herself the daughter of a King [Oedipus] and the fiancée of Haemon [Creon's son], so that she ought to pay obedience to the royal command. But Creon too, as father and husband, should have respected the sacred tie of blood and not ordered anything against its pious observance. So there is immanent in both Antigone and Creon something that in their own way they attack, so that they are gripped and shattered by something intrinsic to their own actual being. Antigone suffers death before enjoying the bridal dance, but Creon too is punished by the voluntary deaths of his son and his wife, incurred, the one on account of Antigone's fate, the other because of Haemon's death. Of all the masterpieces of the classical and the modern world – and I know nearly all of them and you should and can – the *Antigone* seems to me to be the most magnificent and satisfying work of art of this kind.

But the tragic denouement need not every time require the downfall of the participating individuals in order to obliterate the one-sidedness of both sides and their equal meed of honour. We all know that the *Eumenides* of Aeschylus does not end with the death of Orestes or the discomfiture of the Eumenides. (These were the Furies, the avengers of a mother's blood and the violation of family piety, against Apollo who means to maintain the dignity and veneration of the King and the head of the family, and who provoked Orestes to kill his mother.) On the contrary, Orestes is excused punishment and both the gods are honoured. But at the same time we see clearly in this decisive conclusion what their gods meant to the Greeks when they brought them before their eyes in a combat between one another as particular individuals. To the contemporary Athenians they were only elements which were bound together into the entire harmony of ethical life. The votes of the Areopagus were equal; it is Athene, the goddess representing the whole substance of living Athenian life, who inserts the white stone which liberates Orestes, but she promises altars and worship to the Eumenides and Apollo equally.

Secondly, in contrast to this objective reconciliation, the assuaging of conflict may be of a subjective kind when the individual agent gives up the one-sidedness of his aim. But in this desertion of a substantive 'pathos' of his own he would appear as lacking in character, and this contradicts the solidity of the Greek plastic figures. In this case, therefore, the individual can only put himself at the mercy of a higher power and its advice and command, so that while he persists on his own account in his 'pathos', his obstinate will is broken by a god. In such a case the knots cannot be untied but, as in the *Philoctetes*, for example, are cut by a *deus ex machina*.

Finally, more beautiful than this rather external sort of denouement is an inner reconciliation which, because of its subjective character, already borders on our modern treatment. The most perfect classical example of this that we have before us is the eternally marvellous *Oedipus Coloneus*. Oedipus has murdered his father, taken the Theban throne, and mounted the marriage-bed with his mother. These unconsciously committed crimes do not make him unhappy; but of old he had solved a riddle and now he forcibly extracts [from the oracle] a knowledge of his own dark fate and acquires the dreadful realization that it has been accomplished in himself. With this solution of the riddle in his own person he has lost his happiness as Adam did when he came to the knowledge of good and evil [Genesis, 3]. The seer now, he blinds himself, resigns the throne, exiles himself from Thebes, just as Adam and Eve were driven from Paradise, and wanders away a helpless old man. In Colonus, sore afflicted, instead of listening to his son's request that he might return, he invokes on him his own Furies [or curse]; he expunges all his own inner discord and is purified within. Then a god himself calls him [i.e. to death]; his blind eyes are transfigured and clear; his bones become a salvation and safeguard of the state that received him as friend and guest. This transfiguration in death is for us, as for him, a visible reconciliation within his own self and personality. Attempts have been made to find a Christian tone here: the vision of a sinner whom God pardons and a fate endured in life but compensated with bliss in death. But the Christian religious reconciliation is a transfiguration of the soul which, bathed in the spring of eternal salvation, is lifted above its deeds and existence in the real world, because it makes the heart itself into the grave of the heart (yes, the spirit can do this), pays the imputations of earthly guilt with its own earthly individuality and now holds itself secure against those imputations in the certainty of its own eternal and purely spiritual bliss. On the other hand, the transfiguration of Oedipus always still remains the Greek transfer of consciousness from the strife of ethical powers, and the violations involved, into the unity and harmony of the entire ethical order itself.

What is further implied in this reconciliation is *subjective* satisfaction, and this enables us to make the transition to the sphere of comedy, the opposite of tragedy.

(*ββ*) What is comical, as we saw, is a personality or subject who makes his own actions contradictory and so brings them to nothing, while remaining tranquil and self-assured in the process. Therefore comedy has for its basis and starting-point what tragedy may end with, namely an absolutely reconciled and cheerful heart. Even if its possessor destroys by the means he uses whatever he wills and so comes to grief in himself because by his own efforts he has accomplished the very opposite of what he aimed at, he still has not lost his peace of mind on that account. But, on the other hand, this subjective self-assurance is only possible if the aims, and so with them the characters in question, either have no real substance in themselves or, if they have, then their essentiality has been made an aim and been pursued in a shape really opposed to it fundamentally and therefore in a shape without substance; and the result is that it is always only what is inherently null and indifferent that comes to grief, and the individual remains firm on his feet and undisturbed.

On the whole this is also the character of the old Greek comedy as it has been preserved for us in the plays of Aristophanes. In this matter we must be very careful to distinguish whether the dramatis personae are comical themselves or only in the eyes of the audience. The former case alone can be counted as really comical, and here Aristophanes was a master. On these lines, an individual is only portrayed as laughable when it is obvious that he is not serious at all about the seriousness of his aim and will, so that this seriousness always carries with it, in the eyes of the individual himself, its own destruction, because from beginning to end he cannot devote himself to any higher and universally valid interest which would bring him into a conflict of substance [i.e. with another such interest]. Even if he really does so devote himself, he can only exhibit a character which, owing to what it directly and presently is, has already annihilated what it apparently wanted to accomplish, and we can see at once that the substantial interest has never had a real hold on him. The comical therefore plays its part more often in people with lower views, tied to the real world and the present, i.e. among men who are what they are once and for all, who cannot be or will anything different, and, though incapable of any genuine 'pathos', have not the least doubt about what they are and what they are doing. But at the same time they reveal themselves as having something higher in them because they are not seriously tied to the finite world with which they are engaged but are raised above it and remain firm in themselves and secure in face of failure and loss. It is to this absolute freedom of spirit which is utterly consoled in advance in every human undertaking, to this world of private serenity, that Aristophanes conducts us. If you have not read him, you can scarcely realize how damn good [*sauwohl*] a human being can feel.[9]

The interests within which this kind of comedy moves need not be drawn at all from spheres opposed to ethical life, religion and art; on the contrary, the old Greek comedy keeps precisely within this objective and substantive sphere, but it is by subjective caprice, vulgar folly and absurdity that individuals bring to nought actions which had a higher aim. And here Aristophanes had available to him rich and happy material partly in the Greek gods and partly in the Athenians. For making the gods into human individuals has itself produced a contrast with the loftiness of their significance owing to their being so represented and particularized, particularized and humanized right down to detail, and their form can be portrayed as an empty pride in a subjective personality thus inappropriately given to them. But what Aristophanes especially loves is to expose to the ridicule of his fellow-citizens in the most comical and yet profound way the follies of the masses, the insanity of their orators and statesmen, the absurdity of the [Peloponnesian] war, and above all, most mercilessly, the new direction that Euripides had taken in tragedy. The persons in whom he embodies the objects of his magnificent ridicule are made into fools from the start by his inexhaustible humour, so that we can see at once that we are to get nothing but ineptitude from them. Take, for example, Strepsiades, who wants to go to the philosophers to learn how to be rid of his debts, or Socrates, who offers to teach Strepsiades and his son;[10] or Dionysus, who is made to descend into the underworld in order to bring a true tragedian up from there;[11] or Cleon,[12] the women,[13] and the Greeks who want to draw the goddess of peace from the well;[14] and so forth. The keynote resounding in all these portrayals is the self-confidence of all these figures, and it is all the more imperturbable the more incapable they obviously are of accomplishing their undertaking. The fools are such naïve fools, and even the more sensible of them also have such an air of contradiction with what they are devoted to, that they never lose this naïve personal self-assurance, no matter how things go. It is the smiling blessedness of the Olympian gods, their unimpaired equanimity which comes home in men and can put up with anything. In all this Aristophanes is obviously not a cold or malignant scoffer. On the contrary he is a man of most gifted mind, the best of citizens to whom the welfare of Athens was always a serious matter and who proved to be a true patriot throughout. Therefore, as I have said earlier, what is portrayed in his comedies is not the complete dissolution of religion and morality but both the all-pervasive corruption which plumes itself on keeping step with the fundamental powers, and also the shape of things and the appearance of individuals, which are a mask concealing the fact that real truth and substance are no longer there and can be simply and openly handed over to the unfeigned play of subjective caprice. Aristophanes presents to us the absolute contradiction between (a) the true essence of religion and political and ethical life, and (b) the subjective attitude of citizens and individuals who should give actuality to that essence. But in this very triumph of the subjective attitude, whatever its insight, there is implicit one of the greatest symptoms of Greek corruption, and thus these pictures of a naïve fundamental 'all is well with me' are the final great outcome of the poetry of this gifted, civilized and ingenious Greek people.

(β) We turn now at once to the dramatic art of the modern world, and here too I will only bring out in general some of the main differences of importance in relation to tragedy, drama and comedy.

(αα) At its plastic height in Greece, tragedy remains one-sided by making the validity of the substance and necessity of ethical life its essential basis and by leaving undeveloped the individuality of the dramatis personae and the depths of their personal life. Comedy on its side brings to view in a converse mode of plasticity, and to perfection, the subjective personality in the free expatiation of its absurdity and its absurdity's dissolution.

Modern tragedy adopts into its own sphere from the start the principle of subjectivity. Therefore it takes for its proper subject-matter and contents the subjective inner life of the character who is not, as in classical tragedy, a purely individual embodiment of ethical powers, and, keeping to this same type, it makes actions come into collision with one another as the chance of external circumstances dictates, and makes similar accidents decide, or seem to decide, the outcome. Here there are the following chief points to discuss.

(i)   The nature of the various aims which the characters have and which are to be attained;
(ii) the tragic characters themselves and the collisions to which they are subjected;
(iii) the difference from Greek tragedy in respect of the sort of denouement and the tragic reconciliation.

However far the centre of romantic tragedy is the individual's sufferings and passions (in the strict sense of that word), nevertheless in human action a basis of specific ends drawn from the concrete spheres of family, state, church, etc. is never missing. For, by acting, man, as man, enters the sphere of the real world and its particular concerns. But since now it is not the substantial element in these spheres which engrosses the interest of individuals, their aims are broadly and variously particularized and in such detail that what is truly substantial can often glimmer through them in only a very dim way; and, apart from this, these aims acquire an altogether different form. For example, in the religious sphere, the dominating subject-matter is no longer the particular ethical powers made by imagination into individual gods and displayed either in their own person or as the 'pathos' of human heroes, but instead the story of Christ, the saints, etc. In the political sphere what is brought before us in all sorts of different ways is especially the monarchy, the power of vassals, the strife between dynasties or between members of one and the same royal family. Indeed, furthermore, civil and private rights and other relationships are dealt with and, similarly, even aspects of family life arise which were not yet compatible with Greek drama. For since the principle of subjectivity itself has gained its right in the [religious, political, and social] spheres mentioned above, it follows that new features appear even in them which modern man is entitled to make the aim and guide of his action.

On the other hand, it is the right of personality as such which is firmly established as the sole subject-matter, and love, personal honour, etc., are taken as ends so exclusive that the other relationships either can only appear as the external ground on which these modern interests are played out or else stand on their own account in conflict against the demands of the individual's subjective heart. The situation is more profound when the individual character, in order to achieve his goal, does not shrink from wrong and crime, even if he has not envisaged himself as unjust and criminal in choosing his end.

But instead of having this particular and personal character the ends chosen may be extensive, universal, and comprehensive in scope, or, again, they may be adopted and pursued as having substance in themselves. (*a*) As an example of the former case I will only refer to Goethe's *Faust*, the absolute philosophical tragedy.[15] Here on the one side, dissatisfaction with learning and, on the other, the freshness of life and enjoyment in the world, in general the tragic quest for harmony between the Absolute in its essence and appearance and the individual's knowledge and will, all this provides a breadth of subject-matter which no other dramatist has ventured to compass in one and the same work. A similar example is Schiller's [*Robbers* where] Karl Moor is enraged by the entire civil order and the whole situation of the world and mankind in his day, and his *rebellion* against it has this universal significance. Wallenstein likewise adopts a great universal aim, the unity and peace of Germany. He failed in his aim partly because his forces, collected artificially and held together by purely external links, broke up and scattered just when things became serious for him, and partly because he revolted against the authority of the Emperor, a power on which he and his undertaking were bound to be shipwrecked. Universal ends, like those pursued by Karl Moor and Wallenstein, cannot be accomplished by a single individual by making others his obedient instruments; on the contrary, such ends prevail by their own force, sometimes with the will of the many, sometimes against it and without their knowledge. (*b*) As examples of the adoption of ends in virtue of their substantial character, I will mention only some tragedies of Calderón in which the rights and duties involved in love, honour, etc. are used by the dramatis personae as a sort of code of laws rigid and inflexible in themselves. Something similar occurs frequently in Schiller's characters, although their point of view is quite different; anyway this is true in the sense that these individuals adopt and fight for their aims by regarding them at the same time as universal and absolute human rights. So, for example, in *Intrigue and Love* Major Ferdinand means to defend natural rights against fashionable conventions and, above all, the Marquis Posa [in *Don Carlos*] demands freedom of thought as an inalienable possession of mankind.

But in modern tragedy it is generally the case that individuals do not act for the sake of the *substantial* nature of their end, nor is it that nature which proves to be their motive in their passion; on the contrary, what presses for satisfaction is the *subjectivity* of their heart and mind and the privacy of their own character. For consider the examples just cited: in the case of the Spanish dramas, what the heroes of love and honour aim at is in itself of such a subjective kind that the rights and duties involved in it can coincide immediately with what their own heart wishes. And, in Schiller's youthful works, bragging about nature, human rights and the reform of mankind is little more than the extravagance of a subjective enthusiasm; when in his later years Schiller tried to vindicate a more mature 'pathos', this happened simply because he had it in mind to restore in modern dramatic art the principle of Greek tragedy.

In order to exhibit in more detail the difference in this respect between Greek and modern tragedy, I will direct attention only to Shakespeare's Hamlet. His character is rooted in a collision similar to that treated by Aeschylus in the *Choephori* and Sophocles in the *Electra*. For in Hamlet's case too his father, the King, is murdered and his mother has married the murderer. But whereas in the Greek poets the King's death does have an ethical justification, in Shakespeare it is simply and solely an atrocious crime and Hamlet's mother is guiltless of it. Consequently the son has to wreak his revenge only on the fratricide King in whom he sees nothing really worthy of respect. Therefore the collision turns strictly here not on a son's pursuing an ethically justified revenge and being forced in the process to violate the ethical order, but on Hamlet's personal character. His noble soul is not made for this kind of energetic activity; and, full of disgust with the world and life, what with decision, proof, arrangements for carrying out his resolve, and being bandied from pillar to post, he eventually perishes owing to his own hesitation and a complication of external circumstances.

If we turn now, in the second place, to that aspect which is of more outstanding importance in modern tragedy, to the characters, namely, and their conflict, the first thing that we can take as a starting-point is, in brief summary, the following:

The heroes of Greek classical tragedy are confronted by circumstances in which, after firmly identifying themselves with the one ethical 'pathos' which alone corresponds to their own already established nature, they necessarily come into conflict with the opposite but equally justified ethical power. The romantic dramatis personae, on the other hand, are from the beginning in the midst of a wide field of more or less accidental circumstances and conditions within which it is possible to act either in this way or in that. Consequently the conflict, for which the external circumstances do of course provide the occasion, lies essentially in the character to which the individuals adhere in their passion, not because of any substantial justification but because they are what they are once and for all. The Greek heroes too do act in their individual capacity, but, as I have said, when Greek tragedy is at its height their individuality is itself of necessity an inherently ethical 'pathos', whereas in modern tragedy it remains a matter of chance whether the individual's character is gripped by something intrinsically justified or whether he is led into crime and wrong, and in either case he makes his decision according to his own wishes and needs, or owing to external influences, etc. It is true, therefore, that character and an ethical end *may* coincide, but since aims, passions and the subjective inner life are all particular [and not universal], this coincidence is not the *essential* foundation and objective condition of the depth and beauty of a [modern] tragedy.

Few generalizations can be made about further differences in [modern] characterization because this sphere is wide open to variations of every kind. I will therefore touch on only the following chief aspects.

A first contrast which strikes the eye quickly enough is that between (*a*) the individuals who come on the scene as living and concrete people, and (*b*) an abstract and therefore formal characterization. As an example of the latter we can cite especially the tragic figures in French and Italian drama. They originate from an imitation of classical models and may count more or less as mere personifications of specific passions – love, honour, fame, ambition, tyranny, etc. They relate the motives of their actions as well as the degree and kind of their feelings with great declamatory splendour and much rhetorical skill, but this way of explaining themselves reminds us more of Seneca's failures than of the Greek dramatic masterpieces. Spanish tragedy too borders on this abstract characterization; but in this case the passion of love, in conflict with honour, friendship, royal authority, etc., is itself of such an abstractly subjective kind, and the rights and duties involved are so sharply emphasized, that a fuller individualization of the characters is impossible, since in this as it were subjective substantiality this passion is supposed to be prominent as the real interest of the piece. Nevertheless the Spanish figures often have a solidity, even if there is little in it, and a sort of brittle personality which the French ones lack; at the same time, in contrast to the cold simplicity of the action's development in French tragedy, the Spanish, even in tragedy, can make up for a deficiency in variations of character by an acutely invented wealth of interesting situations and complications.

But in the portrayal of concretely human individuals and characters it is especially the English who are distinguished masters and above them all Shakespeare stands at an almost unapproachable height. For even if some purely single passion, like ambition in Macbeth or jealousy in Othello, becomes the entire 'pathos' of his tragic heroes, still such an abstraction does not devour their more far-reaching individuality at all, because despite this determinant they still always remain complete men. Indeed the more Shakespeare proceeds to portray on the infinite breadth of his 'world-stage' the extremes of evil and folly, all the more, as I have remarked earlier, does he precisely plunge his figures who dwell on these extremes into their restrictedness with a wealth of poetry and give them spirit and imagination;[16] by the picture in which they can contemplate and see themselves objectively like a work of art, he makes them free artists of their own selves, and thereby, with his strongly marked and faithful characterization, can interest us not only in criminals but even in the most downright and vulgar clouts and fools. The way that his tragic characters reveal themselves is of a similar kind: individual, real, directly living, extremely varied, and yet, where this emerges necessarily, of a sublimity and striking power of expression, of a depth of feeling and gift for invention in images and similes produced on the spur of the moment, of a rhetoric, not pedantic but issuing from the actual feeling and outpouring of the character – take all this into account, this combination of directly present life and inner greatness of soul, and you will scarcely find any other modern dramatist who can be compared with Shakespeare. Goethe in his youth did try to achieve a similar truth to nature and an individuality of personality but without achieving the inner force and height of passion [of Shakespeare's characters], and Schiller again has fallen into a violence which has no really solid kernel in its expansive storming.

A second difference in modern characters consists in their being either firm or inwardly hesitant and discordant. The weakness of irresolution, the swithering of reflection, perplexity about the reasons that are to guide decision – all this does occur here and there in the tragedies of Euripides, but he already abandons polished plasticity of character and action and goes over to subjective emotion. In modern tragedy such dithering figures generally appear by being themselves in the grip of a twofold passion which drives them from one decision or one deed to another simultaneously. This vacillation I have mentioned already in another context,[17] and here I will only add that, even if the tragic action must depend on a collision, to put this discord into one and the same individual must always involve much awkwardness. For mental distraction into opposed interests has its source partly in a vagueness and stupidity of mind, partly in weakness and immaturity. We have some figures of this sort even in Goethe's youthful productions: Weislingen [in *Götz*], for example, Fernando in *Stella* and Clavigo [in *Clavigo*] above all. These are men in two minds who cannot acquire a finished and therefore firm individuality. It is quite different if two opposed spheres of life or two opposite duties, etc., seem equally sacrosanct to a character [who is] already assured in himself and yet sees himself compelled to align himself with one to the exclusion of the other. In that case the vacillation is only a transitional phase and is not the nerve of the man's character itself.

Again, a different kind consists of the tragic case where someone is led astray by passion against his better judgement into opposite aims (like Joan in Schiller's *Maid of Orleans*), and now must perish unless he can rescue himself from this discord both within and in his external actions. Yet, if the lever of the tragedy is this personal tragedy of inner discord, there is about it something now sad and painful, now aggravating, and the poet does better to avoid it instead of looking for it and pre-eminently developing it.

But what is worst of all is to exhibit such indecision and vacillation of character, and of the whole man, as a sort of perverse and sophistical dialectic and then to make it the main theme of the entire drama, so that truth is supposed to consist precisely in showing that no character is inwardly firm and self-assured. The one-sided aims of particular passions and characters should certainly not come to be realized without a struggle, and in everyday life when the force of circumstances reacts against them, and other individuals oppose them, they are not spared the experience of their finitude and instability. But this outcome, which alone forms an appropriate conclusion, must not be inserted by a sort of dialectical machinery into the individual's own character, for otherwise the person as *this* personality is only an empty indeterminate form instead of growing in a living way along with determinate aims and a defined character.

It is something different again if a change in the whole man's inner condition appears itself to be a logical consequence of precisely his own peculiarities, so that what develops and emerges is something that was implicit in his character from the start. For example, in *King Lear*, Lear's original folly is intensified into madness in his old age, just as Gloucester's mental blindness is changed into actual physical blindness and only then are his eyes opened to the true difference in the love of his sons.

It is precisely Shakespeare who gives us, in contrast to this portrayal of vacillating characters inwardly divided against themselves, the finest examples of firm and consistent characters who come to ruin simply because of this decisive adherence to themselves and their aims. Without ethical justification, but upheld solely by the formal inevitability of their personality, they allow themselves to be lured to their deed by external circumstances, or they plunge blindly on and persevere by the strength of their will, even if now what they do they accomplish only from the necessity of maintaining themselves against others or because they have reached once and for all the point that they *have* reached. The passion, implicitly in keeping with the man's character, had not broken out hitherto, but now it arises and is fully developed – this progress and history of a great soul, its inner development, the picture of its self-destructive struggle against circumstances, events, and their consequences – all this is the main theme in many of Shakespeare's most interesting tragedies.

The last important point – the one we now have still to discuss – concerns the tragic denouement to which the modern characters are driven as well as the sort of tragic reconciliation with which this is compatible. In Greek tragedy it is eternal justice which, as the absolute power of fate, saves and maintains the harmony of the substance of the ethical order against the particular powers which were becoming independent and therefore colliding, and because of the inner rationality of its sway we are satisfied when we see individuals coming to ruin. If a similar justice appears in modern tragedy, then, owing to the non-universal nature of aims and characters, it is colder, more like criminal justice, owing to the greater reflectiveness of the wrong and crime into which individuals are forced when they are intent on accomplishing their ends. For example, Macbeth, Lear's elder daughters and their husbands, Richard III, the President in [Schiller's] *Intrigue and Love*, deserve for their atrocities nothing better than what happens to them. This sort of denouement is usually so presented that the individuals are shipwrecked on a power confronting them which they had deliberately defied in the pursuit of their own private ends. So, for example, Wallenstein is wrecked by the stability of the Emperor's power, but even old Piccolomini, who in [secretly] upholding the established order has become a traitor to his friend and misused the form of friendship, is punished by the death of his son who was sacrificed to the end that his father really wanted to achieve. Götz von Berlichingen too attacks an existent and firmly established political order and therefore perishes, just as Weislingen and Adelheid meet an unfortunate end owing to wrong and disloyalty, although they are on the side of this legal order and its power. This subjectivity of character immediately implies the demand that the individuals must have shown themselves inwardly reconciled to their own particular fate. This satisfaction may be religious when the heart knows that it is assured of a higher and indestructible bliss in exchange for the destruction of its mundane individuality, or alternatively it may be of a more abstract and mundane kind when the strength and equanimity of the character persists, even to destruction, without breaking, and so preserves its subjective freedom, in the face of all circumstances and misfortunes, with energy unjeopardized; or, finally, it may be more concrete owing to a recognition that its fate, however bitter, is merely the one appropriate to its action.

But on the other hand the tragic denouement is also displayed as purely the effect of unfortunate circumstances and external accidents which might have turned out otherwise and produced a happy ending. In this case the sole spectacle offered to us is that the modern individual with the non-universal nature of his character, his circumstances, and the complications in which he is involved, is necessarily surrendered to the fragility of all that is mundane and must endure the fate of finitude. But this mere affliction is empty, and, in particular, we are confronted by a purely horrible external necessity when we see fine minds, noble in themselves, perishing in such a battle against the misfortune of entirely external circumstances. Such a history may touch us acutely, and yet it seems only dreadful and we feel a pressing demand for a necessary correspondence between the external circumstances and what the inner nature of those fine characters really is. It is only from this point of view that we can feel ourselves reconciled in e.g. the fate of Hamlet or Juliet. Looked at from the outside, Hamlet's death seems to be brought about accidentally owing to the fight with Laertes and the exchange of rapiers. But death lay from the beginning in the background of Hamlet's mind. The sands of time[18] do not content him. In his melancholy and weakness, his worry, his disgust at all the affairs of life, we sense from the start that in all his terrible surroundings he is a lost man, almost consumed already by inner disgust before death comes to him from outside. The same is the case in *Romeo and Juliet*. The soil on which these tender blooms were planted is foreign to them, and we are left with nothing but to bewail the tragic transience of so beautiful a love which is shattered by the crazy calculations of a noble and well-meaning cleverness, just as a tender rose in the vale of this transitory world is withered by rude storms and tempests. But the woe that we feel is only a grievous reconciliation, an unhappy bliss in misfortune.

(ββ) Since the poets present to us the mere downfall of individuals, they can equally well give such a turn to equally accidental complications that, however little other circumstances may also seem to produce this result, a happy outcome for the situation and the characters can be produced, and this is something which may be of interest to us. A happy denouement has at least as much justification as an unhappy one, and when it is a matter of considering this difference alone, I must admit that for my part a happy denouement is to be preferred. And why not? To prefer misfortune, just because it is misfortune, instead of a happy resolution, has no other basis but a certain superior sentimentality which indulges in grief and suffering and finds more interest in them than in the painless situations that it regards as commonplace. Thus if the interests at issue are in themselves of such a kind that it is really not worthwhile for an individual to sacrifice himself for them, since without self-sacrifice he can renounce them or come to an agreement with others about them, then the conclusion need not be tragic. For the tragedy of conflicts and their resolution must in general prevail only where this is necessary for justifying them in virtue of some higher outlook. But if there is no such inevitability, mere suffering and misfortune are not justified by anything.

This is the natural reason for plays and dramas that are midway between tragedy and comedy. I have already indicated the strictly poetical element in this kind of dramatic poetry. But in Germany touching features of civil life and family circles have been all the rage or there has been preoccupation with chivalry to which an impetus has been given since the time of Goethe's *Götz*, but what has been celebrated above all in this field and most frequently is the triumph of the subjectively moral outlook. The usual topics here are money and property, class-differences, unfortunate love-affairs, mental wickedness in trifling matters and narrow social circles, and the like, and, in general, with what we see elsewhere every day, only with this difference that in these moralizing plays virtue and duty win the day and vice is put to shame and punished or is moved to repentance, so that the reconciliation is supposed to lie in this moral conclusion where both vice and virtue get their due. Thus the chief interest is made to lie in the individual's own - personal disposition and the goodness or evil of his heart. But the more the abstract moral disposition is made the kingpin, the less can it be a passionate concentration on something, on a really substantial end, that the individual is tied to, while in the last resort even a definite character cannot hold out and accomplish its aim. For once everything is shuffled into the moral disposition and the heart, there is no support any longer, given this subjectivity and strength of moral reflection, for a character otherwise firm or at least for his personal ends. The heart can break, and its dispositions may alter. Such touching plays as Kotzebue's *Menschenhass und Reue* [Misanthropy and Repentance] and many of the moral trespasses in Iffland's dramas, taken strictly, have a result which is really neither good nor bad. The chief theme usually ends in forgiveness and the promise of reform and then there appears every possibility of inner conversion and the repudiation of the old self. Here there is of course the lofty nature and the greatness of the spirit. But if the young wastrel, like most of Kotzebue's characters and like Iffland's too here and there, is a blackguard, a rascal, and now promises to reform, then in the case of such a fellow who is worthless from the start, conversion is only hypocrisy, or so superficial that it has not gripped his heart, and an end has been made of the thing in only an external way for a moment, but at bottom it can only lead to false starts when the thing is only played over and over again from the beginning.

(γγ) Finally, in modern comedy especially there is an essentially important difference on which I have touched already in connection with Greek comedy, namely whether the folly and one-sidedness of the dramatis personae appears laughable to the audience only or to themselves as well, whether therefore the characters in the comedy can be mocked solely by the audience or by themselves also. Aristophanes, the comic author par excellence, made the latter alternative the fundamental principle of his plays. But in the new comedy in Greece and later in Plautus and Terence the opposite tendency was developed, and this has acquired such universal prominence in modern comedy that a multitude of our comic productions verges more or less on what is purely prosaically laughable and even on what is bitter and repugnant. This is the attitude especially of Molière, for example, in his more subtle comedies which are not meant to be farces. There is a reason for prose here, namely that the characters are deadly serious in their aims. They pursue them therefore with all the fervour of this seriousness and when at the end they are deceived or have their aim frustrated by themselves, they cannot join in the laughter freely and with satisfaction but, duped, are the butt of the laughter of others, often mixed as it is with malice. So, for example, Molière's Tartuffe, *le faux dévot*, is unmasked as a downright villain, and this is not funny at all but a very serious matter; and the duping of the deceived Orgon leads to such painful misfortune that it can be assuaged only by a *deus ex machina*, i.e. when the police officer at the end says to him [ll. 1905–9]:

> Remettez-vous, monsieur, d'une alarme si chaude,
> Nous vivons sous un prince, ennemi de la fraude,
> Un prince dont les yeux se font jour dans les cœurs,
> Et que ne peut tromper tout l'art des imposteurs.[19]

There is nothing really comical either about the odious *idée fixe* of such rigid characters as Molière's miser whose absolutely serious involvement in his narrow passion inhibits any liberation of his mind from this restriction.

Next, as a substitute for this kind of thing, mastery in this field has the best opportunity for its cleverness by displaying its subtly developed skill in the precise portrayal of characters or the carrying out of a well-considered intrigue. The intrigue generally arises from the fact that an individual tries to achieve his aims by deceiving other people. He seems to share their interests and to further them, but this false furtherance actually produces the contradiction of falling into his own trap and so coming to grief himself. Next, on the other hand, the opposite means are commonly employed, i.e. the individual puts a false face on himself in order to put others into a similar perplexity: this coming and going makes possible in the most ingenious way endless tergiversation and complicated involvement in all sorts of situation. In inventing such intrigues and their complications the Spanish are the finest masters and have given us in this sphere much that is attractive and excellent. The subject-matter here is provided by interests such as love, honour, etc. In tragedy these lead to the most profound collisions, but in comedy (for example, the pride which will not confess a love that has been long felt and at the end is just for this reason betrayed) they are clearly without substance from the start and are annulled comically. Finally, the characters who contrive and conduct such intrigues in modern comedy are usually, like the slaves in Roman comedy, servants or chambermaids who have no respect for the aims of their masters, but further them or frustrate them as their own advantage dictates and only give us the laughable spectacle of masters being really the servants, or the servants masters, or at least they provide an occasion for other comic situations which they contrive by external means or by their own arrangements. We ourselves, as spectators, are in the secret and we can always feel assured in the face of all the cunning and every betrayal, often very seriously pursued against the most estimable fathers, uncles, etc., and now we can laugh over every contradiction implicit or obvious in such trickeries.

In this way modern comedy displays to the spectators (partly in character-sketches, partly in comical complications of situations and circumstances) private interests and characters involved in them with their casual obliquities, absurdities, unusual behaviour and follies. But such a frank joviality as pervades the comedies of Aristophanes as a constant reconciliation does not animate this kind of modern comedy at all. Indeed these comedies of intrigue may be actually repulsive when downright evil, the cunning of servants, the deceitfulness of sons and wards, gains the victory over honest masters, fathers and trustees when these older people have themselves not been actuated by bad prejudice or eccentricities which would have made them laughable in their helpless folly and put them at the mercy of the projects of other people.

Nevertheless, in contrast to this on the whole prosaic way of treating comedy, the modern world has developed a type of comedy which is truly comical and truly poetic. Here once again the keynote is good humour, assured and careless gaiety despite all failure and misfortune, exuberance and the audacity of a fundamentally happy craziness, folly and idiosyncrasy in general. Consequently there is presented here once more (in a deeper wealth and inwardness of humour), whether in wider or narrower circles of society, in a subject-matter whether important or trivial, what Aristophanes achieved to perfection in his field in Greece. As a brilliant example of this sort of thing I will name Shakespeare once again, in conclusion, but without going into detail.

Now, with the development of the kinds of comedy we have reached the real end of our philosophical inquiry. We began with symbolic art where personality struggles to find itself as form and content and to become objective to itself. We proceeded to the plastic art of Greece where the Divine, now conscious of itself, is presented to us in living individuals. We ended with the romantic art of emotion and deep feeling where absolute subjective personality moves free in itself and in the spiritual world. Satisfied in itself, it no longer unites itself with anything objective and particularized and it brings the negative side of this dissolution into consciousness in the humour of comedy. Yet on this peak comedy leads at the same time to the dissolution of art altogether. All art aims at the identity, produced by the spirit, in which eternal things, God and absolute truth are revealed in real appearance and shape to our contemplation, to our hearts and minds. But if comedy presents this unity only as its self-destruction because the Absolute, which wants to realize itself, sees its self-actualization destroyed by interests that have now become explicitly free in the real world and are directed only on what is accidental and subjective, then the presence and agency of the Absolute no longer appears positively unified with the characters and aims of the real world but asserts itself only in the negative form of cancelling everything not correspondent with it, and subjective personality alone shows itself self-confident and self-assured at the same time in this dissolution.

Now at the end we have arranged every essential category of the beautiful and every essential form of art into a philosophical garland, and weaving it is one of the worthiest tasks that philosophy is capable of completing. For in art we have to do, not with any agreeable or useful child's play, but with the liberation of the spirit from the content and forms of finitude, with the presence and reconciliation of the Absolute in what is apparent and visible, with an unfolding of the truth which is not exhausted in natural history but revealed in world-history. Art itself is the most beautiful side of that history and it is the best compensation for hard work in the world and the bitter labour for knowledge. For this reason my treatment of the subject could not consist in a mere criticism of works of art or an instruction for producing them. My one aim has been to seize in thought and to prove the fundamental nature of the beautiful and art, and to follow it through all the stages it has gone through in the course of its realization.

I hope that in this chief point my exposition has satisfied you. And now when the link forged between us generally and in relation to our common aim has been broken, it is my final wish that the higher and indestructible bond of the Idea of beauty and truth may link us and keep us firmly united now and for ever.

Notes

1 Where, as in this case, Knox translates 'sittlich' as 'moral', I have substituted the word 'ethical'. [s.h.]

2 'weder das Substantielle noch die Subjektivität'. [s.h.]

3 Knox's translation has 'what is real, i.e. the downright opposite'. The German text has simply 'dies bare Gegenteil'. [s.h.]

4 'Why have you screwed up your faces? Because I have said that this will be a tragedy? I am a god: I will change it if you like and make it a comedy, and with all the same lines too . . . I will make it a mixture, a tragicomedy'. [Translator's note.]

5 For Hegel's account of the epic, see *Aesthetics*, pp. 1040–1110 (not included in this collection). [s.h.]

6 Knox's translation has 'higher moral consciousness', although Hegel speaks only of a 'higher' (*höheres*) consciousness. [s.h.]

7 See Hegel, *Aesthetics*, p. 1151 (not included in this collection). [s.h.]

8 The last line of Schiller's poem, *Shakespeares Schatten*. [Translator's note.]

9 Knox's translation has 'how men can take things so easily'. The full German text is 'wie dem Menschen sauwohl sein kann'. [s.h.]

10 Aristophanes, *The Clouds*. [s.h.]

11 Aristophanes, *The Frogs*. [s.h.]

12 Aristophanes, *The Knights*. [S.H.]
13 Aristophanes, *Ecclesiazusae* and *Thesmophoriazusae*. [S.H.]
14 Aristophanes, *Peace*. [S.H.]
15 'die absolute philosophische Tragödie'. Knox's translation has 'the one absolutely philosophical tragedy'. [S.H.]
16 Knox's translation has '[all the more] does he precisely plunge his figures who dwell on these extremes into their restrictedness; of course he equips them with a wealth of poetry but he actually gives them spirit and imagination, and, by the picture'. The German text is '[um so mehr gerade] versenkt er selbst auf diesen äußersten Grenzen seine Figuren nicht etwa ohne den Reichtum poetischer Ausstattung in ihre Beschränktheit, sondern er gibt ihnen Geist und Phantasie; er macht sie'. [S.H.]
17 See Hegel, *Aesthetics*, pp. 242–4, 579 (not included in this collection). [S.H.]
18 'Sandbank der Endlichkeit'. See Shakespeare, *Macbeth*, Act 1, scene 7: 'this bank and shoal of time'. [S.H.]
19   Sir, all is well; rest easy and be grateful.
                We serve a Prince to whom all sham is hateful,
                A Prince who sees into our inmost hearts,
                And can't be fooled by any trickster's arts.

J. B. P. Molière, *Tartuffe*, translated into English verse by R. Wilbur (London: Faber and Faber, 1961), p. 104 (Act 5, scene 7). [S.H.]

31

Philosophy of Religion:
Preface and the
Consummate Religion

Preface

[. . .] The object is religion. This is the loftiest object that can occupy human beings; it is the absolute object. It is the region of eternal truth and eternal virtue, the region where all the riddles of thought, all contradictions, and all the sorrows of the heart should show themselves to be resolved, and the region of the eternal peace through which the human being is truly human. All the endless intricacies of human activity and pleasures arise from the determination of human being as implicitly spirit. Everything that people value and esteem, everything on which they think to base their pride and glory, all of this finds its ultimate focal point in religion, in the thought or consciousness of God and in the feeling of God. God is the beginning and end of all things. God is the sacred centre, which animates and inspires all things. Religion possesses its object within itself – and that object is God, for religion is the relation of human consciousness to God. The object of religion *is* simply through itself and on its own account; it is the absolutely final end in and for itself, the absolutely free being. Here our concern about the final end can have no other final end than this object itself. Only in this context do all other aims experience their settlement. In its concern with this object, spirit frees itself from all finitude. This concern is the true liberation of the human being and is freedom itself, true consciousness of the truth. Everything [else] drops into the past. Finite life seems like a desert. Religion is the consciousness of freedom and truth. If our concern with it is a feeling then it is bliss, and if an activity then it has to manifest God's glory and majesty. This concept of religion is universal. Religion holds this position for all peoples and persons. Everywhere this concern is regarded as the sabbath of life. Truly in this region of the spirit flow the waters of forgetfulness from which the soul drinks. All the griefs of this bank and shoal[1] of life vanish away in this ether, whether in the feeling of devotion or of hope. All of it drops into the past. In religion all cares pass away, for in it one finds oneself fortunate. All harshness of fate passes into a dream. Everything earthly dissolves into light and love, not a remote but an actually present liveliness, certainty and enjoyment. Even if [the bliss of] religion is put off into the future, it is still radiant in life here and now, or in the actuality within which this image is effective and substantial. Such is the universal content of religion among human beings; this content it is our intent to consider.

Comparison of Philosophy and Religion with Regard to Their Object

But it should be noted straightaway that the proposal to 'consider' it involves a relationship to it that is already twisted out of shape. For when we speak of 'consideration' and 'object' we are distinguishing the two as freestanding, mutually independent, fixed sides that are mutually opposed. For example, space is the object of geometry, but the spatial figures that it considers are distinct from the considering spirit, for they are only its 'object'. So if we say now that philosophy ought to consider religion, then these two are likewise set in a relationship of distinction in which they stand in opposition to one another. But on the contrary it must be said that the content of philosophy, its need and interest, is wholly in common with that of religion. The object of religion, like that of philosophy, is the eternal truth, God and nothing but God and the explication of God. Philosophy is only explicating *itself* when it explicates religion, and when it explicates itself it is explicating religion. For the *thinking* spirit is what penetrates this object, the truth; it is thinking that enjoys the truth and purifies the subjective consciousness. Thus religion and philosophy coincide in one. In fact philosophy is itself the service of God [*Gottesdienst*], as is religion. But each of them, religion as well as philosophy, is the service of God in a way peculiar to it (about which more needs to be said). They differ in the peculiar character of their concern with God. This is where the difficulties lie that impede philosophy's grasp of religion; and it often appears impossible for the two of them to be united. The apprehensive attitude of religion toward philosophy and the hostile stance of each toward the other arise from this. It seems, as the theologians frequently suggest, that philosophy works to corrupt the content of religion, destroying and profaning it. This old antipathy stands before our eyes as something admitted and acknowledged, more generally acknowledged than their unity. The time seems to have arrived, however, when philosophy can deal with religion more impartially on the one hand, and more fruitfully and auspiciously on the other.

This linkage between them is nothing new. It already obtained among the more eminent of the church fathers, who had steeped themselves particularly in Neo-Pythagorean, Neoplatonic and Neo-Aristotelian philosophy. For one thing, they themselves first passed over to Christianity from philosophy; and for another, they applied that philosophical profundity of spirit to the teachings of Christianity. The church owes to their philosophical instruction the first beginnings of Christian doctrine, the development of a *dogmatics*. [...]

The Consummate Religion: Christianity

Introduction

[...] Faith and thought have often been opposed in such a way that we say: one can be convinced of God, of the truths of religion, in no other way than by thinking. But the witness of spirit can be present in manifold and various ways; it is not required that for all of humanity the truth be brought forth in a philosophical way. The needs of human beings are different in accord with their cultivation and their free spiritual development; and this diversity in accord with the stage of development also encompasses that standpoint [we call] trust or belief on the basis of *authority*. Miracles also have their place here, but it is interesting to note that miracles have been reduced to a minimum – namely, to those recounted in the Bible.

That sympathy of which we have spoken earlier,[2] where the spirit or the soul cries out, 'Yes, that is the truth' – that sympathy is so immediate a form of certainty that it can be as secure for one person as thinking is for another. [It is] something so immediate that just for this reason it is something posited, given, or positive; [it is so immediate] that precisely this immediacy has the form of positivity and is not brought forth by means of the concept. We ought to bear in mind, however, that only human beings have religion. Religion has its seat and soil in the activity of thinking. The heart and feeling that directly sense the truth of religion are not the heart and feeling of an animal but of a thinking human being; they are a thinking heart and a thinking feeling, and whatever [measure] of religion is in this heart and feeling is a thought of this heart and feeling. But to be sure, in so far as we begin to draw conclusions, to reason, to give grounds, to advance to the categories of thought, this is invariably thinking.

Since the doctrines of the Christian religion are present in the Bible, they are thereby given in a positive fashion; and if they are subjectively appropriated, if spirit gives witness to them, this can happen in an entirely immediate fashion, with one's innermost being, one's spirit, one's thought, one's reason, being touched by them and assenting to them. Thus the Bible is for Christians the basis, the fundamental basis, which has this effect on them, which strikes a chord within them, and gives firmness to their convictions. Beyond this, however, human beings, because they are able to think, do not remain in the immediacy of assent and testimony, but also indulge in thoughts, in deliberation, in considerations concerning this immediate witness. These thoughts and considerations result in a developed religion; in its most highly developed form it is *theology* or scientific religion, whose content, as the witness of spirit, is [also] known in scientific fashion.

But here the opposing thesis perhaps comes in, for the theologians say that we ought to hold exclusively to the Bible. In one respect, this is an entirely valid principle. For there are in fact many people who are very religious and hold exclusively to the Bible, who do nothing but read the Bible, cite passages from it and in this way lead a very pious, religious life. Theologians, however, they are not; such an attitude has nothing of a scientific, theological character. But just as soon as religion is no longer simply the reading and repetition of passages, as soon as what is called explanation or interpretation begins, as soon as an attempt is made by inference and exegesis to find out the *meaning* of the words in the Bible, then we embark upon the process of reasoning, reflection, thinking; and the question then becomes how we should exercise this process of thinking, and whether our thinking is correct or not. It helps not at all to say that one's thoughts are based on the Bible. As soon as these thoughts are no longer simply the words of the Bible, their content is given a form, more specifically, a logical form. Or certain presuppositions are made with regard to this content, and with these one enters into the process of interpretation. These presuppositions are the permanent element in interpretation; one brings along representations and principles, which guide the interpretation.

The interpretation of the Bible exhibits its content, however, in the form of a particular age; the interpretation of a thousand years ago was wholly different from that of today. Among the presuppositions that one brings to the Bible today belong, for example, the views that humanity is good by nature, or that we cannot cognize God. Thus here the positive can enter again in another form: we bring with us certain propositions such as that human beings have these feelings, are constituted in this or that particular way. So everything then depends on whether this content, these views and propositions, are true; and this is no longer the Bible, but instead words that spirit comprehends internally. If spirit expresses in a different way what is expressed in the Bible, then this is already a form that spirit gives [the content], the form of thinking. The form that one gives to this content has to be investigated. Here again the positive enters, in the sense that, for example, the formal logic of inference has been presupposed, namely, finite relations of thought. In terms of the ordinary relations of inference, only the finite can be grasped and cognized, only the understandable, but not the divine. This way of thinking is not adequate to the divine content; the latter is ruined by it. In so far as theology is not a mere rehearsal of the Bible but goes beyond the words of the Bible and concerns itself with what kinds of feelings exist internally, it utilizes forms of thinking, it engages in thinking. If it uses these forms haphazardly, because one has presuppositions and prejudices, the result is something contingent and arbitrary. [What is pertinent here] can only be forms that are genuine and logically developed in terms of necessity.

But the investigation of these forms of thought falls to philosophy alone. Thus theology itself does not know what it wants when it turns against philosophy. Either it carries on unaware of the fact that it needs these forms, that it itself thinks, and that it is a question of proceeding in accord with thought; or it fosters a deception, by reserving for itself the option to think as it chooses, in contingent fashion, when it knows that the cognition of the true nature of spirit is damaging to this arbitrary sort of cognition. This contingent, arbitrary way of thinking is the positive element that enters in here. Only the *concept* on its own account liberates itself truly and thoroughly from the positive. For in philosophy and in religion there is found this highest freedom, which is thinking itself as such.

Doctrine itself, the content, also takes on the form of the positive, as noted above; it is valid, it is firmly established, it is an entity that has to be reckoned with in actual society. Everything rational, every law, has this form. But only its *form* is positive; its *content* must be that of spirit. The Bible has this form of positivity, yet according to one of its own sayings, 'The letter kills, but the Spirit gives life' [2 Cor. 3:6]. It is a question, then, as to which spirit we bring in, which spirit gives life to the positive. We must know that we bring with us a concrete spirit, a thinking, reflecting, sensing spirit; we must be aware of this spirit, which is at work, comprehending the content. This comprehension is not a passive acceptance, but since it is spirit that comprehends, it is at the same time its activity. Only in the mechanical sphere does one of the sides remain passive in the process of reception. Spirit, therefore, reaches out to, attains the positive realm; it has its representations and concepts, it is logical in essence, it is a thinking activity. This, its [own] activity, spirit must know.

This thinking can proceed in one or another of the categories of finitude. It is, however, spirit that begins in this way from the positive but is itself there essentially alongside it. It is to become the true and proper Spirit, the Holy Spirit, which comprehends the divine and knows its content to be divine. This is the witness of spirit, which, as we have shown above, may be more or less developed. In regard to positivity, the main point is that spirit conducts itself in a thinking fashion and its activity occurs within the categories or determinations of thought; here spirit is purely active, sentient or rational. But most people are not conscious of the fact that they are active in this reception. Theologians are like the Englishman who didn't know that he was speaking prose;[3] because they work exegetically and (so they believe) in a passively receptive way, [they] have no inkling of the fact that they are thereby active and reflective. But if thinking is merely contingent, it abandons itself to the categories of finite content, of finitude, of finite thinking, and is incapable of comprehending the divine in the content; it is not the divine but the finite spirit that moves in such categories. As a result of such a finite thinking and comprehending of the divine, or of what is in and for itself, as a result of this finite thinking of the absolute content, the fundamental doctrines of Christianity have for the most part disappeared from dogmatics. Philosophy is pre-eminently, though not exclusively, what is at present essentially orthodox; the propositions that have always been valid, the basic truths of Christianity, are maintained and preserved by it.

In our present consideration of this religion, we shall not set to work in *merely historical* fashion, which would entail starting with external matters, but rather we shall proceed *conceptually*. The form of activity that begins with externals appears to be [capable of] comprehension only on one side, while on the other it is independent. Our attitude here essentially takes the form of an activity such that thinking is conscious of itself, of the process involved in the categories of thought – a thinking that has tested and recognized itself, that knows how it thinks and which are the finite and which the true categories of thought. [. . .]

A. The First Element: The Idea of God In and For Itself

In accord with the first element, then, we consider God in his eternal idea, as he is in and for himself, prior to or apart from the creation of the world, so to speak. In so far as he is thus within himself, it is a matter of the eternal idea, which is not yet posited in its reality but is itself still only the abstract idea. But God is the creator of the world; it belongs to his being, his essence, to be the creator; in so far as he is not the creator, he is grasped inadequately. His creative role is not an *actus* that happened once; [rather,] what takes place in the idea is an *eternal* moment, an eternal determination of the idea.

Thus God in his eternal idea is still within the abstract element of thinking in general – the abstract idea of thinking, not of conceiving. We already know this pure idea, and therefore we need only dwell on it briefly.

Specifically, the eternal idea is expressed in terms of the holy *Trinity*: it is God himself, eternally triune. Spirit is this process, movement, life. This life is self-differentiation, self-determination, and the first differentiation is that spirit *is* as this universal idea itself. The universal contains the entire idea, although it only contains it, it is only implicitly the idea. In this primal division is found the other, the particular, what stands over against the universal – that which stands over against God as distinguished from him, but in such a way that this distinguished aspect is God's entire idea in and for itself, so that these two determinations are also one and the same for each other, an identity, the One. Not only is this distinction implicitly sublated, and not only do we know that, but also it is established that the two distinguished moments are the same, that this distinction is sublated in so far as it is precisely what posits itself as no distinction at all; hence the one remains present to itself in the other.

That this is so is the Holy Spirit itself, or, expressed in the mode of sensibility, it is eternal love: *the Holy Spirit is eternal love.*

When we say, 'God is love', we are saying something very great and true. But it would be senseless to grasp this saying in a simple-minded way as a simple definition, without analysing what love is. For love is a distinguishing of two, who nevertheless are absolutely not distinguished for each other. The consciousness or feeling of the identity of the two – to be outside of myself and in the other – this is love. I have my self-consciousness not in myself but in the other. I am satisfied and have peace with myself only in this other – and I *am* only because I have peace with myself; if I did not have it, then I would be a contradiction that falls to pieces. This other, because it likewise exists outside itself, has its self-consciousness only in me, and both the other and I are only this consciousness of being-outside-ourselves and of our identity; we are only this intuition, feeling and knowledge of our unity. This is love, and without knowing that love is both a distinguishing and the sublation of the distinction, one speaks emptily of it. This is the simple, eternal idea.

When we speak of God in order to say what he is, it is customary to make use of attributes: God is thus and so; he is defined by predicates. This is the method of representation and understanding. Predicates are determinate, particular qualities: justice, goodness, omnipotence, etc. Because they have the feeling that this is not the authentic way to express the nature of God, the Orientals say that God is πολυώνυμος [worshiped under many names] and does not admit of exhaustion by predicates[4] for names are in this sense the same as predicates. The real deficiency in this way of defining by predicates consists in the very fact that gives rise to this endless number of predicates, namely, that they designate only particular characteristics, of which there are many, and all of them are borne by the subject. Because there are particular characteristics, and because one views these particularities in their determinateness, one thinks and develops them, they fall into opposition and contradiction with each other as a result, since they are not only distinct but opposed, and these contradictions remain unresolved.

This is also evident when these predicates are taken as expressing God's relation to the world.[5] The world is something other than God. Predicates as particular characteristics are not appropriate to the nature of God. Here, then, is the occasion for the other method, which regards them as relations of God to the world: e.g., the omnipresence and omniscience of God in the world. Accordingly, the predicates do not comprise the true relation of God to himself, but rather his relation to an other, the world. So they are limited and thereby come into contradiction with each other.

We are conscious of the fact that God is not represented in living fashion when so many particular characteristics are enumerated alongside one another. Put in another way, this is the same point that was stated earlier: the contradictions among the different predicates are not resolved. The resolution of the contradiction is contained in the idea, i.e., in God's determining of himself to distinguish himself from himself while [remaining] at the same time the eternal sublation of the distinction. The distinction left as is would be a contradiction.

If we assign predicates to God in such a way as to make them particular, then we are immediately at pains to resolve their contradiction. This is an external action, a product of our reflection, and the fact that it is external and falls to us, and is not the content of the divine idea, implies that the contradictions cannot in fact be resolved. But the idea is itself the resolution of the contradictions posited by it. Its proper content, its determination, is to posit this distinction and then absolutely to sublate it; this is the vitality of the idea itself. [...]

When we say 'God', we speak of him merely as abstract; or if we say, 'God the Father', we speak of him as the universal, only abstractly, in accord with his finitude. His infinitude means precisely that he sublates this form of abstract universality and immediacy, and in this way distinction is posited; but he is precisely the sublating of the distinction. Thereby he is for the first time true actuality, the truth, infinitude.

This is the speculative idea, i.e., the rational element, in so far as it is thought, the thinking of what is rational. For the non-speculative thinking of the understanding, distinction remains as distinction, e.g., the antithesis of finite and infinite. Absoluteness is ascribed to both terms, yet each also has a relation to the other, and in this respect they are in unity; in this way contradiction is posited.

The speculative idea is opposed not merely to the sensible but also to what is understandable; for both, therefore, it is a secret or mystery. It is a μυστήριον for the sensible mode of consideration as well as for the understanding. In other words, μυστήριον is what the rational is; among the Neoplatonists, this expression already means simply speculative philosophy.[6] The nature of God is not a secret in the ordinary sense, least of all in the Christian religion. In it God has made known what he is; there he is manifest. But he is a secret or mystery for external sense perception and representation, for the sensible mode of consideration and likewise for the understanding.

The sensible in general has as its fundamental characteristic externality, the being of things outside each other. Space-time is the externality in which objects are side by side, mutually external and successive. The sensible mode of consideration is thus accustomed to have before it distinct things that are outside one another. Its basis is that distinctions remain explicit and external. In reason this is not the case. Therefore, what is in the idea is a mystery for sensible consideration. For in [the region of] the idea, the way [things are looked at], the relations [ascribed to things], and the categories [employed] are entirely different from those found in sense experience. The idea is just this distinguishing which at the same time is no distinction, and does not persist in its distinction. God intuits himself in what is distinguished, he is united with himself only in his other, and is only present to himself in it; only there does God close with himself and behold himself in the other. This is wholly repugnant to sense experience, since for it one thing is here and another there. Everything counts as independent; what counts for it is not to be the sort of thing that subsists because it possesses itself in another.

For sense experience, two things cannot be in one and the same place; they exclude each other. But in the idea, distinctions are not posited as exclusive of each other; rather they are found only in this mutual inclusion of the one with the other. This is the *truly supersensible* [realm], not that of the understanding, which is supposed to be above and beyond; for the latter is just as much a sensible [realm] where things are outside one another and indifferently self-contained.

In the same way this idea is a mystery for the understanding and beyond its ken. For the understanding holds fast to the categories of thought, persisting with them as utterly independent of each other, remaining distinct, external to each other, and fixed. The positive is not the same as the negative, the cause is not the effect, etc. But for the concept it is equally true that these distinctions are sublated. Precisely because they are distinctions, they remain finite, and the understanding persists in finitude. Indeed, even in the case of the infinite, it has the infinite on one side and finitude on the other. But the truth of the matter is that neither the finite nor the infinite standing over against it has any truth; rather both are merely transitional. To that extent this is a mystery for sensible representation and for the understanding, and both resist the rationality of the idea. [...]

B. The Second Element: Representation, Appearance

[...] The truth is [now to be] considered as posited in the second element, in the finite element. [...]

In the church Christ has been called the 'God-man'. This is a monstrous compound, which directly contradicts both representation and understanding. But what has thereby been brought into human consciousness and made a certainty for it is the unity of divine and human nature, implying that the otherness, or, as we also say, the finitude, weakness and frailty of human nature, does not damage this unity, just as otherness does not impair the unity that God is in the eternal idea. It is the appearance of a human being in sensible presence; God in sensible presence can take no other shape than that of human being. In the sensible and mundane order, only the human is spiritual; so if the spiritual is to have a sensible shape, it must be a human shape.

The historical, sensible presence of Christ

This appearance of the God-man has to be viewed from two different perspectives at once. First, he is a human being in accord with his external circumstances. This is the non-religious perspective [*die irreligiöse Betrachtung*] in which he appears as an ordinary human being. Second, there is the perspective that occurs in the Spirit or with the Spirit. Spirit presses toward its truth because it has an infinite cleavage and anguish within itself. It wills the truth; the need of the truth and the certainty thereof it will have, and must have. Here for the first time we have the religious view [*das Religiöse*].

When Christ is viewed in the same light as Socrates, then he is regarded as an ordinary human being, just as in Islam he is regarded as a messenger of God in the general sense that all great men are messengers of God. If one says no more of Christ than that he is a teacher of humanity, a martyr to the truth, one is not adopting the religious standpoint; one says no more of him than of Socrates. But there is this human side of Christ too – his appearance as a living human being – and we shall mention briefly its moments.

The first moment is that he is *immediately a human being* in all the external contingencies, in all the temporal exigencies and conditions, that this entails. He is born like every other human being, and as a human he has the needs of other human beings; only he does not share the corruption, the passions, and the evil inclinations of the others, nor is he involved in particular worldly interests, along with which integrity and teaching may also find a place. Rather he lives only for the truth, only for its proclamation; his activity consists solely in completing the higher consciousness of humanity.

Thus the second moment is that of his teaching office. The question now is this: 'How can, how must this teaching be constituted?' This original teaching cannot be constituted in a manner similar to the later doctrine of the church; it must have its own distinctive aspects, which in the church partly take on another character and are partly set aside. Once the community is established, once the kingdom of God has attained its determinate being and its actuality, these teachings are either interpreted in other ways or else they fall by the wayside.

Since what is at issue is the consciousness of absolute reconciliation, we are here in the presence of a new consciousness of humanity, or a new religion. Through it a new world is constituted, a new actuality, a different world-condition, because [humanity's] outward determinate being, [its] natural existence, now has religion as its substantiality. This is the aspect that is negative and polemical, being opposed to the subsistence of externality in the consciousness of humanity. The new religion expresses itself precisely as a new consciousness, the consciousness of a reconciliation of humanity with God. This reconciliation, expressed as a state of affairs, is the kingdom of God, an actuality. The souls and hearts [of individuals] are reconciled with God, and thus it is God who rules in the heart and has attained dominion.

This kingdom of God, the new religion, thus contains implicitly the characteristic of negating the present world. This is its polemical aspect, its revolutionary attitude toward all the determinate aspects of that outer world, [all the settled attitudes] of human consciousness and belief. So what is at issue is the drawing of those who are to achieve the consciousness of reconciliation away from present actuality, requiring of them an abstraction from it. The new religion is itself still concentrated and does not actually exist as a community, but has its vitality rather in that energy which constitutes the sole, eternal interest of its adherents who have to fight and struggle in order to achieve this for themselves, because it is not yet coherent with the world consciousness and is not yet in harmony with the condition of the world.

Hence the first emergence of this religion directly contains this polemical aspect. It poses the demand that one should remove oneself from finite things and elevate oneself to an infinite energy for which all other bonds are to become matters of indifference, for which all other bonds – indeed, all things hitherto regarded as ethical and right – are to be set aside. Thus Christ says: 'Who is my mother, who are my brothers? Whoever does the will of God is my mother, [my] sister, and [my] brother.' Or: 'Follow me! Leave the dead to bury the dead. Go forth and proclaim the kingdom of God.' 'I have not come to bring peace on earth, but rather children will leave their parents and follow me.'[7]

We see here a polemical attitude expressed against the ethical relationships that have hitherto prevailed. These are all teachings and characteristics that belong to its first appearance, when the new religion constitutes the sole interest [of its adherents], which they were bound to believe they were still in danger of losing. This is the one side.

This renunciation, surrender and setting aside of all vital interests and moral bonds is an essential characteristic of the concentrated manifestation of the truth, a characteristic that subsequently loses its importance when the truth has achieved a secure existence. Beyond that is the proclamation of the kingdom of God. Humanity must transpose itself into this kingdom in such a way as to cast itself immediately upon this truth. This is expressed with the purest, most colossal boldness, as, for example, at the beginning of the Sermon on the Mount: 'Blessed are the [poor] in spirit, for theirs is the kingdom of God. Blessed are the pure in heart, [for] they shall see God' [Matt. 5:3, 8].

Nothing is said about any mediation through which this elevation [of soul] may come to pass for humanity; rather what is spoken of is this immediate being, this immediate self-transposition into the truth, into the kingdom of God. It is to this kingdom, to this intellectual, spiritual world, that humanity ought to belong.

With respect to details, there are more specific teachings, among which the teaching about love constitutes a focal point: 'Love your neighbor as yourself' [Matt. 22:39]. But these teachings are already found in the Old Testament [cf. Deut. 6:5; Lev. 19:18]. Thus the following [distinctive] moment or determinate aspect enters into these teachings. Because the demand, 'Seek first . . .' – [i.e.,] cast yourself upon the truth – is expressed so directly, it emerges almost as a subjective declaration, and to this extent the person of the teacher comes into view. Christ speaks not merely as a teacher, who expounds on the basis of his own subjective insight and who is aware of what he is saying and doing, but rather as a prophet. He is the one who, because his demand is immediate, expresses it immediately from God, and God speaks it through him. His having this life of the Spirit in the truth, so that it is simply there without mediation, expresses itself prophetically in such a way that it is God who says it. It is a matter of the absolute, divine truth that has being in and for itself, and of its expression and intention; and the confirmation of this expression is envisaged as God's doing. It is the consciousness of the real unity of the divine will and of his harmony with it. In the form of this expression, however, the accent is laid upon the fact that the one who says this is at the same time essentially human. It is the Son of Man who speaks thus, in whom this expression, this activity of what subsists in and for itself, is essentially the work of God – not as something suprahuman that appears in the shape of an external revelation, but rather as [God's] working in a human being, so that the divine presence is essentially identical with this human being.

We still have to consider the fate of this individual, namely, that he became, humanly speaking, a martyr to the truth in a way that coheres closely with his earlier role, because the establishment of the kingdom of God stands in stark contradiction to the worldly authority [*vorhandenen Staate*], which is grounded upon another mode, a different determinate form, of religion.

These are the principal moments in the appearance of this man, upon the human view of it. But this is only one side, and it is not a religious view.

Human appearance of Christ.[8] This teacher gathered friends about him. Inasmuch as his teachings were revolutionary, Christ was accused and executed, and thus he sealed the truth of his teaching by his death. Even unbelief can go this far in [the view it takes of] this story: it is quite similar to that of Socrates, only on a different soil. Socrates, too, brought inwardness to consciousness; his δαιμόνιον is nothing other than this. He also taught that humanity must not stop short at obedience to ordinary authority but must form convictions for itself and act according to them. Here we have two similar individualities with similar fates. The inwardness of Socrates was contrary to the religious beliefs of his people as well as to their form of government, and hence he was put to death: he, too, died for the truth.

Christ happened to live among another people, and to this extent his teaching has a different hue. But the kingdom of heaven and the purity of heart contain, none the less, an infinitely greater depth than the inwardness of Socrates. This is the outward history of Christ, which is for unbelief just what the history of Socrates is for us.

With the death of Christ, however, the reversal of consciousness begins. The death of Christ is the midpoint upon which consciousness turns; and in the comprehension of it lies the difference between outward comprehension and that of faith, which entails contemplation with the Spirit, from the Spirit of truth, the Holy Spirit. According to the comparison made earlier, Christ is a human being like Socrates, a teacher who lived his life virtuously, and who brought humanity to the awareness of what the truth really is and of what must constitute the basis of human consciousness. But the higher view is that the divine nature has been revealed in Christ. This consciousness is reflected in those often-quoted passages which state that the Son knows the Father, etc. – sayings which of themselves have at the outset a certain generality about them and which exegesis can draw out into the arena of universal views, but which faith comprehends in their truth through an interpretation of the death of Christ. For faith is essentially the consciousness of absolute truth, of what God is in and for himself. But we have already seen what God is in and for himself: he is this life-process, the Trinity, in which the universal places itself over against itself and therein remains identical with itself. God, in this element of eternity, is the conjoining of himself with himself, the closure of himself with himself. Only faith comprehends and is conscious of the fact that in Christ this truth, which has being in and for itself, is envisaged in its process, and that through him this truth has been revealed for the first time.

The death of Christ and the transition to spiritual presence

It is this second view that leads us for the first time into the religious sphere as such, where the divine itself is an essential moment. Among those friends and acquaintances who were taught by Christ, there was present this presentiment, this representation, this desire for a new kingdom, a new heaven and a new earth, a new world. This hope and certainty penetrated the actuality of their hearts and became entrenched there. But the suffering and death of Christ superseded his human relationships, and it is precisely in his death that the transition into the religious sphere occurs. On the one hand it is a natural death, brought about by injustice, hatred, and violence.

But in the hearts and souls [of believers] is the firm [belief] that the issue is not a moral teaching, nor in general the thinking and willing of the subject within itself and from itself; rather what is of interest is an infinite relationship to God, to the present God, the certainty of the kingdom of God – finding satisfaction not in morality, ethics or conscience, but rather in that than which nothing is higher, the relationship to God himself. All other modes of satisfaction involve the fact that they are still qualities of a subordinate kind, and thus the relationship to God remains a relationship to something above and beyond, which in no sense lies present at hand.

The defining characteristic of this kingdom of God is the *presence of God*, which means that the members of this kingdom are expected to have not only a love for humanity but also the consciousness that God is love. This is precisely to say that God is present, that his presence must exist as one's own feeling, as self-feeling. The kingdom of God, God's presentness, *is* this determination [of one's feeling]; so the certainty of God's presentness belongs to it. But since the kingdom is on the one hand [present] in need or feeling [on the part of the subject], the latter must, on the other hand, distinguish itself from it, must establish a distinction between this presence of God and itself, but in such a way that this presence remains certain to it, and this certainty can here occur only in the mode of sensible appearance. Because this is how the content behaves, we have here the religious aspect, and the formation of the community begins here. This content is the same as what is called the outpouring of the Holy Spirit: it is the Spirit that has revealed this. The relationship [of believers] to a mere human being is changed into a relationship that is completely altered and transfigured by the Spirit, so that the nature of God discloses itself therein, and so that this truth obtains immediate certainty in its manner of appearance.

In this experience, then, Christ, who at first was regarded as a teacher, friend and martyr to the truth, assumes quite a different posture. On the one hand, the death of Christ is still the death of a human being, a friend, who has been killed by violent means; but when it is comprehended spiritually, this very death becomes the means of salvation, the focal point of reconciliation. To have before oneself the intuition of the nature of spirit and of the satisfaction of its needs in a sensible fashion is, therefore, what has been disclosed to the friends of Christ only after his death. The authentic disclosure was given to them by the Spirit, of whom Christ had said, 'He will guide you into all truth' [John 16:13]. By this he means: only that into which the Spirit will lead you will be the truth. Regarded in this respect, Christ's death assumes the character of a death that constitutes the transition to glory, but to a glorification that is only a restoration of the original glory. Death, the negative, is the mediating term through which the original majesty is posited as now achieved. The history of the resurrection and ascension of Christ to the right hand of God begins at the point where this history receives a spiritual interpretation. That is when it came about that the little community achieved the certainty that God has appeared as a human being.

But this humanity in God – and indeed the most abstract form of humanity, the greatest dependence, the ultimate weakness, the utmost fragility – is natural death. 'God himself is dead', it says in a Lutheran hymn,[9] expressing an awareness that the human, the finite, the fragile, the weak, the negative are themselves a moment of the divine, that they are within God himself, that finitude, negativity, otherness are not outside of God and do not, as otherness, hinder unity with God. Otherness, the negative, is known to be a moment of the divine nature itself. This involves the highest idea of spirit. In this way what is external and negative is converted into the internal. On the one hand, the meaning attached to death is that through death the human element is stripped away and the divine glory comes into view once more – death is a stripping away of the human, the negative. But at the same time death itself is this negative, the furthest extreme to which humanity as natural existence is exposed; God himself is [involved in] this.

The truth to which human beings have attained by means of this history, what they have become conscious of in this entire history, is the following: that the idea of God has certainty for them, that humanity has attained the certainty of unity with God, that the human is the immediately present God. Indeed, within this history as spirit comprehends it, there is the very presentation of the process of what humanity, what spirit is – implicitly both God and dead. This [is] the mediation whereby the human is stripped away and, on the other hand, what-subsists-in-itself returns to itself, first coming to be spirit thereby.

It is with the *consciousness* of the community – which thus makes the transition from mere humanity to the God-man, to the intuition, consciousness and certainty of the union and unity of divine and human nature – that the community begins; this consciousness constitutes the truth upon which the community is founded. This is the explication of reconciliation: that God is reconciled with the world, or rather that God has shown himself to be reconciled with the world, that even the human is not something alien to him, but rather that this otherness, this self-distinguishing, finitude as it is expressed, is a moment in God himself, although, to be sure, it is a disappearing moment.

For the community, this is the history of the appearance of God. This history is a divine history, whereby the community has come to the certainty of truth. From it develops the consciousness that knows that God is triune. The reconciliation in Christ, in which one believes, makes no sense if God is not known as the triune God, [if it is not recognized] that God *is*, but also is as the other, as self-distinguishing, so that this other is God himself, having implicitly the divine nature in it, and that the sublation of this difference, this otherness, and the return of love, are the Spirit.

These are the moments with which we are here concerned and which establish that humanity has become conscious of the eternal history, the eternal movement, which God himself is. Other forms such as that of sacrificial death reduce automatically to what has been said here. 'To sacrifice' means to sublate the natural, to sublate otherness. It is said: 'Christ has died for all.'[10] This is not a single act but the eternal divine history: it is a moment in the nature of God himself; it has taken place in God himself.

This is the presentation of the second [element of] the idea, the idea in appearance, the eternal idea as it has become [present] for the immediate certainty of humanity, i.e., as it has appeared. In order that it should become a certainty for humanity, it had to be a sensible certainty, which, however, at the same time passes over into spiritual consciousness, and likewise is converted into the immediately sensible – in such a way that the movement and history of God is seen in it, the life that God himself is.

We[11] have seen God as the God of free humanity, though still at first in the subjective, limited forms of the folk-spirits and in the contingent shapes of phantasy; next we saw the anguish of the world following upon the suppression of the folk-spirits. This anguish was the birthplace for the impulse of spirit to know God as spiritual, in universal form and stripped of finitude. This need was engendered by the progress of history and the progressive formation of the world-spirit. This immediate impulse, this longing, which wants and desires something determinate – this instinct, as it were, of spirit, which is impelled to seek for this – demanded such an appearance, the manifestation of God as infinite spirit in the shape of an actual human being. The faith that rests upon the witness of the Spirit then makes the life of Christ explicit for itself. The teaching and the miracles of Christ are grasped and understood in this witness of faith. The history of Christ is also narrated by those upon whom the Spirit has already been poured out. The miracles are grasped and narrated in this Spirit, and the death of Christ has been truly understood through the Spirit to mean that in Christ God is revealed together with the unity of divine and human nature. Thus the death of Christ is the touchstone, so to speak, by which faith is verified, since it is here, essentially, that its understanding of the appearance of Christ is set forth. This death means principally that Christ was the God-man, the God who at the same time had human nature, even unto death. It is the lot of human finitude to die. Death is the most complete proof of humanity, of absolute finitude; and indeed Christ has died the aggravated death of the evildoer: not merely a natural death, but rather a death of shame and humiliation on the cross. In him, humanity was carried to its furthest point.

Now, however, a further determination comes into play. *God has died, God is dead* – this is the most frightful of all thoughts, that everything eternal and true *is not*, that negation itself is found in God. The deepest anguish, the feeling of complete irretrievability, the annulling of everything that is elevated, are bound up with this thought. However, the process does not come to a halt at this point; rather, a reversal takes place: God, that is to say, maintains himself in this process, and the latter is only the death of death. God rises again to life, and thus things are reversed. The resurrection is something that belongs just as essentially to faith [as the crucifixion]. After his resurrection, Christ appeared only to his friends. This is not an external history for unbelievers; on the contrary, this appearance occurs only for faith. The resurrection is followed by the glorification of Christ, and the triumph of his ascension to the right hand of God concludes this history, which, as understood by [believing] consciousness, is the explication of the divine nature itself. If in the first sphere we grasped God in pure thought, then in this second sphere we start from the immediacy appropriate to intuition and sensible representation. The process is now such that immediate singularity is sublated: just as in the first sphere the seclusion of God came to an end, and his original immediacy as abstract universality, according to which he is the essence of essences, has been sublated, so here the abstraction of humanity, the immediacy of subsisting singularity, is sublated, and this is brought about by death. But the death of Christ is the death of this death itself, the negation of negation. We have had the same course and process of the explication of God in the kingdom of the Father, but this is where it occurs in so far as it is an object of consciousness. For at this point the urge to *see* the divine nature was present.

Concerning Christ's death, we have still finally to emphasize the aspect that it is God who has put death to death, since he comes out of the state of death. In this way, finitude, human nature and humiliation are posited of Christ – as of him who is strictly God – as something alien. It is evident that finitude is alien to him and has been taken over from an other; this other is the human beings who stand over against the divine process. It is their finitude that Christ has taken [upon himself], this finitude in all its forms, which at its furthest extreme is evil. This humanity, which is itself a moment in the divine life, is now characterized as something alien, not belonging to God. This finitude, however, on its own account (as against God), is evil, it is something alien to God. But he has taken it [upon himself] in order to put it to death by his death. As the monstrous unification of these absolute extremes, this shameful death is at the same time infinite love.

It is out of infinite love that God has made himself identical with what is alien to him in order to put it to death. This is the meaning of the death of Christ. It means that Christ has borne the sins of the world and has reconciled God [with the world (2 Cor. 5:18–19)].

Suffering and death interpreted in this way are opposed to the doctrine of moral imputation, according to which all individuals are accountable only for themselves, and all are agents of their own actions. The fate of Christ seems to contradict this imputation, but the latter only applies in the region of finitude, where the subject stands as a single person, not in the region of free spirit. It is characteristic of the region of finitude that all individuals remain what they are. If they have done evil, then they *are* evil: evil is in them as their quality. But already in the sphere of morality, and still more in that of religion, spirit is known to be free, to be affirmative within itself, so that its limitation, which extends to evil, is a nullity for the infinitude of spirit. Spirit can undo what has been done. The action certainly remains in the memory, but spirit strips it away. Imputation, therefore, does not attain to this sphere.

For the true consciousness of spirit, the finitude of humanity has been put to death in the death of Christ. This death of the natural has in this way a universal significance: finitude and evil are altogether destroyed. Thus the world has been reconciled; by this death it has been implicitly delivered from its evil. In the true understanding [*Verstehen*] of death, the relation of the subject as such [to death] comes into view in this way. Here any merely historical view comes to an end; the subject itself is drawn into the process. The subject feels the anguish of evil and of its own estrangement, which Christ has taken upon himself by putting on humanity, while at the same time destroying it by his death.

C. The Third Element: Community, Spirit

The third element is the element of the community. The first [moment of this element] is, then, the immediate origin of the community – this we have already observed. It is the outpouring of the Holy Spirit [Acts 2]. [It is] spirit that comprehends this history spiritually as it is enacted in [the sphere of] appearance, and recognizes the idea of God in it, his life, his movement. The community is made up of those single, empirical subjects who are in the Spirit of God. But at the same time this content, the history and truth of the community, is distinguished from them and stands over against them. On the one hand, faith in this history, in reconciliation, is an immediate knowledge, an act of faith; on the other hand, the nature of spirit in itself is this process, which has been viewed both in the universal idea and in the idea as [it occurs] in appearance; and this means that the subject itself becomes spirit, and thus a citizen of the kingdom of God, by virtue of the fact that the subject traverses this process in itself. It has been set forth above[12] that the human subject – the one in whom is revealed what is through the Spirit the certainty of reconciliation for humanity – has been marked out as singular, exclusive and distinct from others. Thus for the other subjects the presentation of the divine history is something that is objective for them, and they must now traverse this history, this process, in themselves. In order to do this, however, they must first presuppose that reconciliation is possible, or more precisely, that this reconciliation has happened in and for itself, that it is the truth in and for itself, and that reconciliation is certain. In and for itself, this is the universal idea of God; but the other side of the presupposition is that this is certain for humanity, and that this truth is not [valid] for it [simply] through speculative thinking. This presupposition implies the certainty that reconciliation has been accomplished, i.e., it must be represented as something historical, as something that has been accomplished on earth, in [the sphere of] appearance. This is the presupposition in which we must first of all believe.

1. The origin of the community

For the origin of faith there is necessary first a human being, a sensible human appearance, and second, spiritual comprehension, consciousness of the spiritual. The content is spiritual, involving the transformation of immediacy into what has spiritual character. Verification is spiritual, it does not lie in the sensible, and cannot be accomplished in an immediate, sensible fashion. The transformation of something immediate into a spiritual content is a transition that we have seen in the form of the proofs for the existence of God[13] – namely, that there is also a sensible world, although the truth is not the sensible, not the immediate world of finitude, but is rather the infinite.

As to the empirical mode of the appearance, and investigations concerning the conditions surrounding the appearance of Christ after his death, the church is right in so far as it refuses to acknowledge such investigations; for the latter proceed from a point of view implying that the real question concerns the sensible and historical elements in the appearance [of Christ], as though the confirmation of the Spirit depended on narratives of this kind about something represented as [merely] historical [*historisch*], in historical [*geschichtlich*] fashion. It is said that the Holy Scriptures should be treated like the writings of profane authors. One can do this with regard to what concerns the merely historical, the finite and external. But for the rest, it is a matter of comprehension by the Spirit; the profane [aspect] is not the attestation of the Spirit.

Thus the community itself is the existing Spirit, the Spirit in its existence [*Existenz*], God existing as community.

The first moment is the idea in its simple universality for itself, self-enclosed, having not yet progressed to the primal division, to otherness – the Father. The second is the particular, the idea in appearance – the Son. It is the idea in its externality, such that the external appearance is converted back to the first [moment] and is known as the divine idea, the identity of the divine and the human. The third element, then, is this consciousness – God as the Spirit. This Spirit as existing and realizing itself is the community.

The community begins with the fact that the truth is at hand; it is known, extant truth. And this truth is what God is: he is the triune God; he is life, this process of himself within himself, the determining of himself within himself. The second aspect of this truth, then, is that it has also appeared, it has a relation to the subject, and is [present] for the subject; moreover, the subject is essentially related to it, and is meant to be a citizen of the kingdom of God. That the human subject ought to be a child of God implies that reconciliation is accomplished in and for itself within the divine idea, and secondly that it has appeared too, and hence the truth is certain for humankind. The appearing is precisely this certainty, the idea as it comes to consciousness in the modality of appearance. The third aspect is the relationship of the subject to this truth, the fact that the subject, to the extent that it is related to this truth, arrives precisely at this conscious unity, deems itself worthy of this known unity, brings this unity forth within itself and is fulfilled by the divine Spirit.

The fact that the single subject is now filled by the divine Spirit is brought about by mediation in the subject itself, and the mediating factor is that the subject has this faith. For faith is the truth, the presupposition, that reconciliation is accomplished with certainty in and for itself. Only by means of this faith that reconciliation is accomplished with certainty and in and for itself is the subject able and indeed in a position to posit itself in this unity. This mediation is absolutely necessary.

In this blessedness mediated through the laying hold of the truth, the difficulty that is immediately involved in the grasping of the truth is overcome. This difficulty is that the relationship of the community to this idea is a relationship of the single, particular subject; it is removed in the truth itself. It consists in the fact that the subject is different from absolute spirit. This difference is removed, and its removal happens because God looks into the human heart, he regards the substantial will, the innermost, all-encompassing subjectivity of the human being, one's inner, true, and earnest willing. But apart from this inner will, and distinct from this inner, substantial actuality, there is still the external and deficient side of humanity: we commit errors; we can exist in a way that is not appropriate to this inward, substantial essentiality, this substantial, essential inwardness. The difficulty is removed by the fact that God looks into the heart and sees what is substantial, so that externality – otherness, finitude and imperfection in general, or however else it may be defined – does no damage to the absolute unity; finitude is reduced to an inessential status, and is known as inessential. For in the idea, the otherness of the Son is a transitory, disappearing moment, not a true, essentially enduring, absolute moment.

This is the concept of the community in general, the idea which, to this extent, is the process of the subject within and upon itself, the process of the subject that is taken up into the Spirit, is spiritual, so that the Spirit of God dwells within it. This process, which is its pure self-consciousness, is at the same time the consciousness of truth, and the pure self-consciousness that knows and wills the truth is precisely the divine Spirit within it.

2. *The subsistence of the community*

The community, whose concept we have just seen, also *realizes* itself. The real community is what we generally call the *church*. This is no longer the *emerging* [*entstehende*] but rather the *subsisting* [*bestehende*] community, which maintains itself. In the subsisting community the church is, by and large, the institution whereby [its] subjects come to the truth, appropriate the truth to themselves, so that the Holy Spirit becomes real, actual and present within them and has its abode in them, whereby the truth can be within them and they can enjoy and give active expression to the truth of the Spirit; it is the means whereby they as subjects *are* the active expression of the Spirit.

The first thing that is present in the church is its universality, which consists in the fact that the truth is here presupposed, that it exists as truth already present – not, as in the case of the emerging church, that the Holy Spirit is poured out and engendered for the first time. This is a changed relationship to the beginning [of their religion] for [its] subjects, and for the subjects in their beginnings. The presupposed, extant truth is the *doctrine* of the church, its doctrine of faith. We know the content of this doctrine: it is the doctrine of reconciliation. It is no longer the case that a person is elevated to [the sphere of] absolute meaning by the outpouring and ordaining of the Spirit, but rather that this meaning is something that is known and acknowledged. It is the absolute capability of the subject, both within itself and objectively, to share in the truth, to come to the truth, to abide in the truth, to attain to the consciousness of truth. This consciousness of doctrine is here present and presupposed.

Thus it is that doctrine is elaborated within the community itself only as something presupposed and finished. The Spirit that was shed abroad is the beginning, that which makes the beginning, which raises up. The community is the consciousness of this Spirit, the expression of what spirit has discovered and what it has been touched by, namely, that Christ is for spirit. Hence doctrine has been essentially brought forth and developed in the church. First it is [present] as intuition, faith, feeling – as the felt witness of the Spirit like a flame of fire. But it is supposed to be present and presupposed; thus it must be developed from the concentration and interiority of feeling into representation as something immediately present. Accordingly, the doctrine of faith is essentially constituted in the church first of all, and then later it is thinking, developed consciousness, which also asserts its rights in the matter, adducing the other [forms of truth] to which it has attained by way of the cultivation of thought, by way of philosophy. For these thoughts, on behalf of these thoughts, and on behalf of this otherwise known truth, thinking first develops a consciousness that is only intermixed with other, impure thoughts. Thus doctrine is developed out of other concrete contents that are intermixed with impurities. This doctrine is present to hand and must then be preserved too. This happens in the church. There, that which is doctrine must also be taught. It *is*, it exists, it is valid, it is acknowledged and immediately presupposed. But it is not present in a sensible manner, such that the comprehension of the doctrine can take place through the senses – in the way that the world, for example, is of course presupposed as a sensible entity, to which we are related externally and sensibly. Instead, spiritual truth exists only as known, and the fact that it also appears, and the mode of its appearance, is precisely this, that it is taught. The church is essentially a teaching church, by virtue of which there is a teaching office whose function is to expound doctrine.

Human beings are already born into this doctrine; they have their beginnings in this context of valid truth, already present, and in the consciousness of it. The relationship of single members to this presupposed truth that subsists in and for itself has yet a second aspect. Since individuals are born into the church, they are destined straightaway, while they are still unconscious, to participate in this truth, to become partakers of it; their vocation is for the truth. The church expresses this too, in the sacrament of *baptism*, which says that the human being, the individual, is in the fellowship of the church, where evil has been overcome, implicitly and explicitly, and God is reconciled, implicitly and explicitly. Initially, doctrine is related to this individual as something external. The child is at first spirit only implicitly, it is not yet realized spirit, is not yet actual as spirit; it has only the capability, the potentiality, to be spirit, to become actual as spirit. Thus the truth is something external to it, and comes to the subject initially as something presupposed, acknowledged and valid. This means that the truth necessarily comes to humanity at first as *authority*.

All truth, even sensible truth – although it is not truth in the proper sense – comes to people initially in the form of authority; i.e., it is something present that possesses validity and exists on its own account. That is how it comes to me – as something distinct from me. Similarly, the world comes to us in sense perception as an authority confronting us: it *is*, we find it so, we accept it as something that is really there and relate ourselves to it as such. That is how it is, and it is valid just the way it is. Doctrine, which is spiritual, is not present as a sensible authority of that kind; it must be *taught*, and it is taught as valid truth. Custom is something that is valid, an established conviction. But because it is something spiritual, we do not say, 'It is', but rather, 'It is right.' However, because it confronts us as what is real, we also say, 'It is.' And because it presents itself to us as something valid, we call its way of being 'authority'.

Just as people have to learn sensible content from authority, and to be content with the way things are just because they are so – the sun is there, and because it is there I must put up with it – so also they have to learn doctrine, the truth. What is learned in this way must be taken up by individuals into themselves in order to assimilate it, to appropriate it. As we have already said,[14] the inner spirit is the absolute possibility of this knowledge; it conforms to this content that is itself spirit. What is there in human inwardness, i.e., in one's rational spirit, is therefore brought to consciousness for the individual as something objective; or what is found within the individual is developed so that one knows it as the truth in which one abides. This is the concern of education, practice, cultivation. With such education and appropriation it is a question merely of becoming habituated to the good and the true [*Wahrhafte*]. To this extent it is not a matter of overcoming evil because evil has been overcome in and for itself. The child, inasmuch as it is born into the church, has been born in freedom and to freedom. For one who has been so born, there is no longer an absolute otherness; this otherness is posited as something overcome, as already conquered. The sole concern of such cultivation is to prevent evil from emerging, and the possibility of this does in general reside in humanity. But in so far as evil does emerge among human beings when they do evil, at the same time it is present as something implicitly null, over which spirit has power: spirit has the power to undo evil.

Repentance or *penitence* signifies that, through the elevation of human beings to the truth, which they now will, their transgression is wiped out. Because they acknowledge the truth over against their evil and will the good – through repentance, that is to say – their evil comes to naught. Thus evil is known as something that has been overcome in and for itself, having no power of its own. The undoing of what has been done cannot take place in a sensible manner; but in a spiritual manner or inwardly, what has been done can be undone. Therefore it is the concern of the church that this habituating and educating of spirit should become ever more inward, that this truth should become ever more identical with the self, with the human will, and that this truth should become one's volition, one's object, one's spirit. The battle is now over, and the consciousness arises that there is no longer a struggle, as in the Parsee religion or the Kantian philosophy, where evil is always sure to be overcome, yet it stands in and for itself over against the supreme good, so that in these views there is nothing but an unending progression.

The subsistence of the community is completed by sharing in the appropriation of God's presence [i.e., the *communion*]. It is a question precisely of the conscious presence of God, of unity with God, the *unio mystica*, [one's] self-feeling of God, the feeling of God's immediate presence within the subject. This self-feeling, however, since it exists, is also a movement, it presupposes a movement, a sublation of difference, so that a negative unity issues forth. This unity begins with the host. Concerning the latter, three kinds of view are now prevalent. According to the first, the host – this external, sensible thing – becomes by consecration the present God, God as a thing in the manner of an empirical thing.[15] The second view is the Lutheran one, according to which the movement does indeed begin with something external, which is an ordinary, common thing, but the communion, the self-feeling of the presence of God, comes about only in so far as the external thing is consumed – not merely physically but in spirit and in faith. God is present only in spirit and in faith. Here there is no transubstantiation, or at any rate only one by which externality is annulled, so that the presence of God is utterly a spiritual presence – the consecration takes place in the faith of the subject. The third view is that the present God exists only in representation, in memory, and to this extent he does not have this immediate subjective presence.[16]

The subject is expected to *appropriate* doctrine, the truth, and hence the third aspect of the community's self-maintenance is the partaking of the presence of God.

3. The realization of the spirituality of the community

The third [aspect] is the *realization* of the spirituality of the community in universal actuality. This involves the *transformation* of the community at the same time. The standpoint is this: in religion the *heart* is reconciled. This reconciliation is thus in the heart; it is spiritual. It is the pure heart that attains to this partaking [*Genuss*] of God's presence within it, and consequently reconciliation, the enjoyment [*Genuss*] of being reconciled. At the same time, however, this reconciliation is abstract and has the world as such over against it. The self that exists in this reconciliation, in this religious communion, is the pure heart, the heart as such, universal spirituality; but at the same time the self or subject constitutes that aspect of spiritual presence in accord with which there is a developed worldliness present in it, and thus the kingdom of God, the community, has a relationship to the worldly. In order that reconciliation may be real, it is required that it should be known in this development, in this totality; it should be present and brought forth [into actuality]. The principles for this worldly realm are ready to hand in the spirituality of the community; the principle, the truth, of the worldly *is* the spiritual.

The spiritual is the truth of the worldly realm in the more proximate sense that the subject, as an object of divine grace and as one who is reconciled with God, already has infinite value in virtue of its vocation; and this is made effective in the community. On the basis of this vocation, the subject is known as spirit's certainty of itself, as the eternity of spirit. The vocation to infinitude of the subject that is inwardly infinite is its *freedom*. The substantial aspect of the subject is that it is a free person, and as a free person it relates itself to the worldly and the actual as a being that is at home with itself, reconciled within itself, an utterly secure and infinite subjectivity. This vocation of the subject ought to be foundational in its relation with what is worldly. This freedom of the subject is its rationality –

the fact that as subject it is thus liberated and has attained this liberation through religion, that in accord with its religious vocation it is essentially free. This freedom, which has the impulse and determinacy to realize itself, is rationality. Slavery contradicts Christianity because it is contrary to reason. What is required, therefore, is that this reconciliation should also be accomplished in the worldly realm.

The first form of this reconciliation with worldliness is the immediate one, and just for this reason it is not the genuine mode of reconciliation. It appears as follows: at first the community contains the element of spirituality, of being reconciled with God, within itself, in abstraction from the world, so that spirituality renounces the worldly realm, placing itself in a negative relation to the world and also to itself. For the world is in the subject; it is there as the impulse toward nature, toward social life, toward art and science. What is concrete in the self, its passions etc., certainly cannot be justified *vis-à-vis* the religious aspect just because they are natural impulses; but on the other hand, monkish withdrawal means that the heart is not concretely developed, that it exists as something undeveloped, or that spirituality, the state of being reconciled and the life of reconciliation are and ought to remain concentrated within themselves and undeveloped. But the very nature of spirit is to develop itself, to differentiate itself even unto worldliness.

The second way of defining this reconciliation is that worldliness and religiosity do indeed remain external to each other, but they have to enter into relation all the same. Hence the relation in which they stand can itself only be an external one, or more precisely, a relation in which one prevails over the other, and thus there is no reconciliation at all. The religious, it is felt, should be the dominant element; what is reconciled, the *church*, ought to prevail over what is unreconciled, the worldly realm. Accordingly, this is a uniting with a worldly realm that remains unreconciled. In itself, the worldly sphere is uncultured, and as such it ought only to be dominated. But the dominating power takes this same worldliness up into itself, including all of its passions; as a result of its dominion, there emerges in the church itself a worldliness devoid of spirit just because the worldly realm is not in itself reconciled. A dominion predicated on the lack of spirit is posited, in terms of which externality is the principle and humanity in its relatedness exists at the same time outside itself – this is the relationship of *unfreedom* in general. In everything that can be called human, in all impulses, in all attitudes that have reference to the family and to activity in public life, a cleavage enters into play. The ruling principle is that humanity is not at home with itself. In all these forms, it exists in a general condition of servitude, and all these forms count for nothing, they are unholy. Inasmuch as human being subsists in them, it is essentially a finite and ruptured being which has in that form no validity; what is valid is something else. This reconciliation with the worldly realm, and with the human heart, comes about in such a way that it is precisely the opposite of [genuine] reconciliation. The further development of this condition of rupture within reconciliation itself is what appears as the corruption of the church, the absolute contradiction of the spiritual within itself.

The third way is that this contradiction is resolved in the *ethical realm*, or that the principle of freedom has penetrated into the worldly realm itself, and that the worldly, because it has been thus conformed to the concept, reason and eternal truth, is freedom that has become concrete and will that is rational. The institutions of ethical life are divine institutions – not holy in the sense that celibacy is supposed to be holy by contrast with marriage or familial love, or that voluntary poverty is supposed to be holy by contrast with active self-enrichment, or what is lawful and proper. Similarly, blind obedience is regarded as holy, whereas the ethical is an obedience in freedom, a free and rational will, an obedience of the subject toward the ethical. Thus it is in the ethical realm that the reconciliation of religion with worldliness and actuality comes about and is accomplished.[17]

Thus reconciliation has three *real* stages: the stage of immediacy [or of the heart], which is more an abstraction than it is reconciliation; the stage in which the church is dominant, a church that is outside itself; and the stage of ethical life. [. . .]

Notes

1 'Sandbank des Lebens'. See Shakespeare, *Macbeth*, Act 1, scene 7. [Editor's (i.e. P. C. Hodgson's) note.]
2 Hegel, *Lectures on the Philosophy of Religion*, p. 397 (not included in this collection). [S.H.]
3 Hegel is alluding here to the dialogue between M. Jourdain and the teacher of philosophy in Molière's *Le Bourgeois gentilhomme*, Act 2, scene 4, where the philosopher assures M. Jourdain that he is indeed speaking prose (and that one must really speak either prose or verse). Hegel erroneously ascribes M. Jourdain's lack of culture to an Englishman. [Editor's note.]
4 Hegel may be referring here to Philo, to whom Neander attributes just this expression. [Editor's note.]
5 Most likely an allusion to Schleiermacher. [Editor's note.]
6 Hegel attributes the connection between mystery and speculation to Proclus in particular. [Editor's note.]
7 Here Hegel conflates and quotes loosely from Matthew 12:48, 50; Mark 3:33–4; Luke 9:59–60; Matthew 8:21–2; and Matthew 10:34–8. The last clause ('but rather children will leave . . .') is not found in any of the Gospels but may be inferred from Matthew 10:35–8. [Editor's note.]
8 The following passage in smaller type is taken from transcripts of Hegel's 1831 lectures. [S.H.]
9 Johannes Rist, 'O Traurigkeit, O Herzeleid' (1641). [Editor's note.]
10 See 2 Cor. 5:14–15. [Editor's note.]
11 The following passage in smaller type is taken from transcripts of Hegel's 1831 lectures. [S.H.]
12 See Hegel, *Lectures on the Philosophy of Religion*, pp. 455–6 (not included in this collection. [S.H.]

13 See Hegel, *Lectures on the Philosophy of Religion*, pp. 162–89 (not included in this collection). [S.H.]
14 See Hegel, *Lectures on the Philosophy of Religion*, pp. 473–4 (above, p. 501). [S.H.]
15 Hegel is referring here (in what is held by some to be a crudely reductive way) to Catholicism. [S.H.]
16 The reference here, of course, is to the Reformed view, but it applies properly only to Zwingli, not to Calvin. [Editor's note.]
17 In Hegel's view, the transition from the medieval virtues of chastity, poverty and obedience to authority, to the modern virtues of marriage, activity (or labour) and obedience to what is ethical and rational, is brought about by Luther's Reformation. See G. W. F. Hegel, *The Philosophy of History*, translated by J. Sibree, with an introduction by C. J. Friedrich (New York: Dover Publications, 1956), pp. 380–1, 422–3. [S.H.]

32

History of Philosophy: Introduction

1. Concept and Aim of the History of Philosophy[1]

[...] The true, thus inwardly determinate, has the urge to *develop*. Only what is living and spiritual moves, bestirs itself within, and develops. Consequently the Idea, concrete in itself and developing, is an organic system, a totality including in itself a wealth of stages and features.

Philosophy is explicit knowledge of this development and, as conceptual thinking, is itself this thinking development. The further this development of thought has thriven, the more perfect philosophy is.

Further, this does not proceed outwards into the external world; on the contrary, the dispersal of the development is at the same time a movement inwards; i.e. the universal Idea still lives as its basis and remains all-embracing and unalterable.

Since the outward going of the philosophical Idea in its course of development is not an alteration, a becoming something different, but equally a movement into itself, a deeper plumbing of its own depths, its advance is an advance of a hitherto general and rather indeterminate Idea to greater determinacy in itself. The further development of the Idea is one and the same thing as its greater determinacy. Here is what is most expansive and intensive at once. The expansion, as development, is not a dispersal and a falling apart but a holding together which is all the more powerful and intensive, the richer and wider the expansion of what is held together.

These are the abstract points about the nature of the Idea and its development. Thus developed, philosophy is built up within itself. There is *one* Idea in the whole and in all its members, just as in a living individual *one* life, one pulse beats in all his limbs. All the parts arising in it, as well as their systemization, emanate from the one Idea; all these particularizations are only mirrors and copies of this one life; they have their reality only in this unity, and their differences, their different specific characters, are together themselves only the expression of and the form contained in the Idea. Thus the Idea is the centre, at the same time the periphery, the source of light which in all its expansions never leaves itself but remains present and immanent in itself. Thus it is the system of necessity, and of *its own* necessity which is thereby its own freedom too.

Thus philosophy is a system in development, and this is the history of philosophy too. This is the cardinal point, the fundamental conception which this treatment of that history will display.

To explain this, I must first bring to your notice the difference which may exist between ways of regarding this phenomenon: i.e. the emergence of the different stages in the advance of thought may occur with consciousness of the necessity whereby each following stage succeeds its predecessor and whereby *this* stage and formation, and no other, appears. Alternatively this may occur without this consciousness, in the manner of an apparently accidental emergence so that while the Concept does work *within* by its own logic, this logic is not expressed. This happens in nature: in the stages of a tree's development, trunk, branches, leaves, blossom, fruit, each of them emerges independently, but the inner Idea conducts and determines this one by one progression. In a child too the physical capacities, and especially the intellectual activities, come into being successively, simply and effortlessly, so that parents, experiencing this for the first time, are confronted by what looks like a miracle; where do all these things come from that were there within and that now appear? The whole series of these phenomena has the shape only of a succession in time.

To display the first way of regarding this emergence, i.e. the derivation of the formations, the thought-out and known necessity of the specific categories, is the task and business of philosophy itself, and since it is the pure Idea which is at issue here, not yet its further particularized formation in nature and spirit, it is principally the task and business of *Logic*.

But the other method, showing that the different stages and factors of development appear in time, as happening at these particular places, in this or that people, under these political circumstances and under these complications thence arising, in short in this empirical form, this is the spectacle afforded by the history of philosophy.

This [double method] is the only worthy way of studying philosophy. Logic is the true way because it works through the *concept* of the thing. The fact that philosophy also appears and is proved in the real world too is what emerges from the study of this history itself.

In accord with this, I maintain that the succession of philosophical systems in history is the same as their succession in the logical derivation of the categories of the Idea. I maintain that if the fundamental concepts appearing in the history of philosophy are treated purely as what they are in themselves, discarding what affects their external form, their application to particular [circumstances] etc., then we have before us the different stages in the determination of the Idea itself in their logical order and essence. Conversely, if we take the logical process by itself, then we have in its chief stages the progress of the historical facts; but of course our aim must be to discern these pure concepts within the historical form of those facts. Further, from one point of view, temporal succession in history must naturally be distinguished from logical succession. But to explain this point of view further would take us too far away from our purpose here.

I make only this further remark, that it is clear from what I have said that the study of the history of philosophy is the study of philosophy itself; it cannot be anything else. A student of the history of physics, mathematics, etc., does indeed in that way become acquainted with physics, mathematics, etc. But in order, in the empirical shape and historical appearance of philosophy, to recognize its progress as the development of the Idea, a man must of course bring with him a knowledge of the Idea, just as, for the judgement of human actions, a man must bring with him the conceptions of what is right and fitting. Otherwise, as happens in so many histories of philosophy, an eye with no notion of the Idea sees nothing displayed there, but a disorderly pile of opinions. The business of a lecturer on the history of philosophy is to apprise you of this Idea and to interpret the historical phenomena in its light. An observer must bring with him the concept of the thing from the start if he is to discern it in its appearance and expound the subject truly; so we should not be surprised that there is so much shallow philosophical history wherein the row of philosophical systems is displayed as a row of mere opinions, errors and witticisms – witticisms hatched indeed with a great expenditure of ingenuity, mental exercise, and whatever other compliments may be paid to this formal procedure. Given the lack of philosophical temper in these authors, how could we expect them to grasp and expound what rational thinking is?

From what I have said about the formal nature of the Idea, namely that it is only a history of philosophy set forth as such a system of the development of the Idea which deserves the name of a science, it is clear that a collection of facts does not constitute a science. Only as a rationally based succession of phenomena, themselves containing and revealing what reason is, does this history show itself as rational, as a rational event. How should everything happening in rational affairs not itself be rational? There must from the start be a rational belief that it is not chance which rules in human affairs. And it is precisely the business of philosophy to realize that so far as its own appearance is historical, that appearance is just to that extent determined by the Idea.

I deal now with the introductory general concepts in their closer application to the history of philosophy, an application which will bring to our notice the most significant aspects of this history. [...]

2. Application of the Categories [of Thought, Concept and Idea] to the History of Philosophy[2]

(a) *Variety of philosophies*

[...] Philosophy is the thought which comprehends itself; this thought is concrete and thus is the self-comprehending reason. This self-comprehension is a self-developing comprehension. The first mode of reason and of the existence of thought is, like the seed, wholly simple. But this simple mode of existence is the urge to give itself some further determinacy. The first self-comprehension of the spirit is universal and abstract; but reason is concrete in itself. This inherently concrete is to be brought into consciousness, and this can only happen if the single parts are made to emerge one after another – each characteristic explicitly following its predecessor – as happens in the plant. But special notice must be taken of the fact that this procession of concepts separately from one another is at the same time unified in the knowledge of the individual systems. The concrete conceptions of reason progress but the earlier ones do not perish in the intellectual system of the later ones. History is like the development of an individual man. We learn bit by bit. An ability to write, which was the great thing for us to learn as boys, we retain as men. But the elementary character of an earlier stage is united with what comes later into the whole of an education. So too in the history of philosophy what precedes is retained; nothing is discarded. The further details of this progress we will get to know more clearly in the history of philosophy. But we must presuppose that this progress has come about rationally, that a Providence presides over it. This must be presupposed in the study of history, and therefore how much more must it be presupposed in the march of philosophy because this is the holy of holies, the innermost self of the spirit!

In this way the idea that here, by accident, one man has had this opinion, and another man that one, disappears; there is here no discussion of the opinions of individuals, although of course notice is to be taken of this idea in connection with accidental knowing.

The advance of philosophy is necessary. Each philosophy must have appeared of necessity at the time of its appearance. Each philosophy has thus appeared at the right time; none has outsoared its own time; all of them have comprehended the spirit of their own time in thought. Religious ideas and categories of thought, the contents of law and philosophy, etc., all these are one and the same spirit. The philosophies have brought into consciousness what was present in their time about religion, the state, etc. Therefore it is unsound to suppose that an earlier philosophy is repeated. But this is a point to be made now in more depth.

The first inference from what has been said is that the whole of philosophy is an inherent and necessary progress; it is rational in itself, inherently free, determined by itself, by the Idea. Accident, the notion that this, that, or the other could happen is once and for all abandoned and set aside as soon as one enters upon the study of the history of philosophy. Just as the development of categories in philosophy proceeds necessarily, so the same is true in its history. This progress is more precisely defined as proceeding in accordance with the contrast of content and form. What conducts the forward development is the inner dialectic of the thought-formations. I mean that what is shaped is something determinate. It must have a character;

determinacy is necessary to its being and existing. But, if so, it is something finite, and the finite is not the truth; it is not what it ought to be. It contradicts its content, i.e. the Idea, and must perish. On the other hand, its existence of course implies that it contains the Idea in itself, but, because it is determinate, its form is finite and its existence is one-sided and restricted. The Idea, as its inmost being, must shatter this form, destroy this one-sided existence in order to give to it the absolute form which is identical with the content. What conducts the development lies in this dialectic of the inherent infinity of the Idea which exists in a one-sided form and must cancel this one-sidedness. This is the one determinate thread which has to be our guide in the history of philosophy. The progress, as a whole, is necessary. This follows from the nature of the Idea. The history of philosophy has simply to confirm this a priori, this heart of the nature of the Idea; of this nature it is simply an example.

The second, more precise, point is that every single philosophy, taken by itself, has been, and still is, necessary, so that no philosophy has perished; all are retained. Philosophies are downright necessary and so are imperishable factors of the whole, of the Idea, and therefore they are retained, but not only in memory; they are retained affirmatively. This being so, we must distinguish between the special principle of a philosophy in itself and the execution of this principle or its application to the world. The principles themselves are retained; they are necessary; they exist eternally in the Idea. [. . .]

Different philosophies have not only contradicted but have refuted one another. Therefore you may well ask: what sense this mutual refutation has? The answer is derived from what has been said already. What is refutable is only this, that some concrete mode or *form* of the Idea counts as the highest now and for every time. It has been the highest in *its* time, but since we have conceived the activity of the spirit as self-development, it ceases to be the highest, is no longer recognized to be such, and so is, as it were, degraded to being only one factor in the stage following. The *content* is not refuted. Refutation is only setting aside one determination of it and making it a subordinate one. No philosophical principle has been lost; all such principles are retained in what follows. It is only the standing which they have had which is altered.

Refutation of this kind occurs in every development e.g. the growth of a tree from its seed. The flower is a refutation of the leaves. It seems to be the highest and true existence of the tree. But the flower is refuted by the fruit. The fruit which comes last contains everything which preceded, all the forces developed earlier. It cannot become actual without the prior emergence of all the earlier stages. Now these stages, in nature, fall apart from one another, since nature as such is the Idea in the form of externality and separatedness. In the spirit this succession, this refutation, occurs too, but in such a way that the earlier stages remain unified. The latest, the most modern, philosophy must therefore contain in itself the principles of all the previous philosophies and consequently it is the highest one.

Therefore it is easier to refute than to justify, i.e. to recognize and emphasize the affirmative element in something. The history of philosophy exhibits (i) the restrictedness of the element to be negated in past principles, but also (ii) the element to be affirmed in them. Nothing is easier than to show up the negative element. We give ourselves the satisfaction of mind in finding, when we recognize the negative element, that we stand higher than what we are judging. This flatters our vanity. To refute something is to be above it. When we are away above something, we have not worked our way into it. But to find the affirmative means having worked our way into the thing and having justified it, and this is far more difficult than refuting it. So, in so far as philosophies are shown to be refuted, they must also be shown as retained.

Further we must notice in this connection that no philosophy has been refuted; and yet all of them have been. But what is refuted is not the principle of a philosophy, but only the claim of one principle to be final and absolute and, as such, to have absolute validity. The refutation is the reduction of one principle to be a specific factor in the whole. Thus the principle as such has not disappeared, but only its form, its form of being final and absolute. This is the meaning of refutation in philosophy. The atomic principle, for example, means that the atom is the absolute; it is indivisible and one – further characterized, it is the individual, and, still further characterized, the subjective. I too am one, an individual, but also a subject, and so I am spirit. But the atom is wholly abstract independence and mere unity, and atomism, by trying to comprehend the absolute in the abstract character of the one, has got to the point of defining it as many ones, as infinitely many ones. Today we are no longer atomists; the atomic principle has been refuted. True, the spirit is also one, but no longer *one* in this abstraction. Mere unity is too poor a description and definition of the spirit; such a description cannot be exhaustive. So unity does not express the absolute. Nevertheless, this principle is still retained (it has held out right down to Fichte's 'I'), though not as a full description of the absolute. Hence no philosophy, no principle of any philosophy, has been simply refuted; all principles have been retained too, and we cannot do without any of them. In a true philosophy all principles must be retained.

So there are two sides in our relation to the principle of any philosophy, one positive and one negative. The negative one is insight into the one-sidedness of a principle, while the positive or affirmative one is insight into the fact that this principle is a necessary factor in the Idea. Only if we have regard to both of these sides can we do justice to a philosophy. Every judgement must contain both of these sides. In every philosophy we must discern both its deficiency and its truth. Deficiency is easy to see. But to find the good demands deeper study and a riper age. [. . .]

In connection with the refutation of one philosophy by another, there is still a further point to make which will come before us in the history of philosophy itself and will show us what relation philosophies have to one another and how far their principles have altered their standing. Refutation, as we have seen, comprises a negation in itself. This consists in the fact that a system of philosophy, in which people have believed, will no longer do. Now this negation has a double form. One form is that when some philosophy or other is set over against its predecessor and the principle of the later one is affirmed, the later system shows the untenability of the preceding one. In itself every principle of the intellect is one-sided, and this one-sidedness is shown up when one principle is set over against another. But this other is equally one-sided. Here no totality is present as a unity comprising both principles. The totality exists completely only in the course of development. For example, Epicureanism is opposed by Stoicism, and Spinoza's substance, as absolute unity, is opposed by the unity of Leibniz's monad – concrete individuality. The self-developing spirit integrates the one-sidedness of one principle by making the other appear.

The second and higher form of negation is the uniting of different philosophies into one whole so that no philosophy remains standing in independence. On the contrary, all philosophies appear as parts of one. Their principles are united by being reduced to elements of the one Idea, or they are still present only as factors, specifications, aspects of the one Idea. And this is the concrete – i.e. what unites the others in itself and constitutes the true unity of these factors.

This concrete unity is to be distinguished from eclecticism, i.e. from a mere collection of different principles and opinions, as it were different rags making up a single garment. The concrete is the absolute and perfect identity of these differences, not an external collocation of them – just as the human soul is the concrete unity of souls in general, because the vegetable soul is included in the animal one and both of these in the human one.

Amalgamations like these, where such particular philosophies are united in one, we shall become acquainted with in the history of philosophy. One such amalgam, for example, is Platonic philosophy. If we take up Plato's Dialogues, we find that some have an Eleatic character, others Pythagorean, others again Heraclitean, and yet Plato's philosophy has united these earlier philosophies in itself and so transfigured their inadequacies. Plato's philosophy is not eclectic at all but an absolute and true penetration of all these and a unification of them. One other amalgam is Alexandrian philosophy which has been called Neoplatonic, Neo-Pythagorean, Neo-Aristotelian, and in fact it has united these opposites in itself. [. . .]

Philosophies are the forms of the *one*. Of course we see them as different from one another, but the truth in them is the ἀρχόμενον, the *one* in all of them. If we look more closely, we will see how there is an advance in their principles so that the one following is only a further determination of its predecessor; it is only in this that the difference consists. But the principles also emerge in opposition to one another, and in fact at the point when thoughtful reflection is more developed, has become more intelligent; e.g. the principles of Stoicism and Epicureanism. Stoicism makes thinking as such its principle; precisely the opposite is what Epicureanism defines as true, namely, feeling, pleasure. Thus the first is universal, the other is particular, single; the first takes man as thinking, the second as feeling. It is only both together which constitute the entirety of the Concept; man consists of both, universal and particular, thought and feeling. Truth lies in both together, but they appear one after another in opposition to one another. Then in Scepticism the negative emerges against these two principles. It cancels the one-sidedness of each of them, but it errs when it supposes that it has destroyed them, since both are necessary. Thus the essence of the history of philosophy is that one-sided principles are made into factors, concrete elements, and preserved, as it were in an amalgam. The principle of the later philosophy is higher, or, what is the same thing, deeper. [. . .]

So the essential thing is, first, to know what the principles of the philosophical systems have been and, secondly, to realize that each principle must be recognized as necessary. Because each is necessary, it emerges in its time as the highest principle. Then, when things have advanced further, the earlier principle is only an ingredient in the newer and further determined principle, but it is not discarded; it is taken up into the new one. All principles are thus retained. For example, *one*, or unity, is throughout the basis of *all*; whatever develops in Reason simply advances in Reason's unity. We cannot do without the category of unity, even if the philosophy of Democritus, which has made it its supreme principle, is, so far as we are concerned, empty. [. . .]

(b) Our concern not with history proper but with the history of thought

A third inference from what has been said up to this point is that we have not to do with the *past*, but with thinking, with our own spirit. Thus it is not history proper that we are concerned with, or rather it is a history which at the same time is no history, since the thoughts, principles, ideas confronting us are something present; they are specific characteristics in our own spirit. Past or historical material, as such, no longer exists; it is dead. The abstract historical tendency to preoccupy itself with lifeless topics has gained ground in recent times. The heart must be dead which proposes to find satisfaction in dealing with corpses and the dead. The spirit of truth and life lives only in what *is*. The living spirit says: 'Let the dead bury their dead and follow me' [Matthew 8:22] If I have only an historical knowledge of thoughts, truths and facts, they are outside my spirit; i.e. for me they are dead; my thinking and my spirit are not in them; in them my thought is not present, and my inmost being is not there either. The possession of purely historical facts is like the legal possession of things that I do not know what to do with. If someone stops at the mere knowledge of what this or that man has thought, of what has been handed down, then he has just handed himself over and renounced what has made him a man, namely his thinking. In that event he is preoccupied solely with the thinking and the spirit of others; he investigates only what has been true for others. But he ought to think for himself. If you are preoccupied with theology purely historically, perhaps by learning what Church Councils, heretics and non-heretics, have known about the nature of God, then you may well have edifying thoughts, but the real spirit of the thing will have escaped you. To acquire that spirit no theological learning is needed. When the historical trend is preponderant in a given age, then we can assume that the spirit has fallen into despair, has died, has given up the attempt to satisfy itself, for otherwise it would not have been preoccupied with matters which for it are dead.

In the history of thought, it is with thoughts that we have to do; we must consider how the spirit plumbs its own depths in order to reach conscious- ness of itself, how man renders an account to himself of the consciousness of his spirit. In order to be able to do this, man must be present in this process with *his* own spirit. Here, however, I am talking only against a *purely* historical procedure. In no way should what I have said make the study of history in general contemptible. We ourselves do wish here to take up the *history* of philosophy. But if a period of time treats everything historically, and so is always busy with nothing but a world which exists no longer and so wanders around in mausoleums, then the spirit gives up its own life which consists in the thinking of itself.

Everything is retained. Thus in the history of philosophy we are therefore concerned with the past but no less with the present, i.e. with the things which necessarily have an interest for our thinking spirit. This is like what we have to do with in political history, with great men, with the right and the true; this is human, it attracts us and moves us emotionally. It is not something abstractly historical which confronts us. We can take no interest in what is dead and gone; that is interesting only to scholars and people with empty heads.

Also connected with a purely historical treatment is the fact that a teacher of the history of philosophy is supposed not to be partisan. This demand for neutrality has generally no other meaning but that such a teacher is to act in expounding the philosophies as if he were dead, that he is to treat them as something cut off from his spirit, as something external to him, and that he is to busy himself with them in a really thoughtless way. Tennemann, for example, assumes the appearance of neutrality, but, when examined more closely, he is entirely locked up in Kant's philosophy, the fundamental pro- position of which is that truth cannot be known.[3] But in that event the history of philosophy is a miserable occupation if the author knows in advance that he must deal solely with unsuccessful enterprises. Tennemann praises the most varied philosophers for their study, their genius, etc., but he also blames them for having not yet arrived at Kant's standpoint or in other words for having philosophized. If so, we are not to be partisans of the thinking spirit. But if we are to study the history of philosophy in a worthwhile way, our neutrality consists in our not being partisans for the opinions, thoughts, concepts, of individuals. Nevertheless, we must be partisans of philosophy and must not restrict ourselves to, or content ourselves with, merely knowing the thinking of other people. Truth is only known when we are present in it with our own spirit; mere knowledge of it is no proof that we are really at home in it. [. . .]

3. Consequences for the Treatment of the History of Philosophy

It is obvious already from the start that the period of one semester is too short for me to expound completely the history of philosophy, this work of the spirit through several millennia. Our field must therefore be restricted. Two things follow, in relation to the extent of the field, from what has been said already about the kind of history which is our subject.

(a) *Our concern only for the principles of philosophies and their development*

We concern ourselves solely with the principles of the philosophies and the development of those principles. This is particularly the case with the earlier philosophies, less because of lack of time, than because in them it is only their principles which can interest us. They are the most abstract, simplest, and therefore also the vaguest principles, or rather the sort containing all the categories although none of them has yet been made explicit. These abstract principles are adequate to a certain extent and reach a certain point of interest for us still. But their development is not yet complete and therefore they are particular in character, i.e. their application extends over only one specific sphere. Take, for example, the principle of mechanism; we would be dissatisfied if we proposed to apply it, as Descartes did, to the nature of animals. Therefore our deeper conception of that nature requires a more concrete principle. Explanations of the nature of plants and animals on the basis of this principle would not satisfy us. An abstract principle has in the real world its own appropriate sphere, e.g. the principle of mechanism holds good in the inorganic sphere of nature, i.e. in a sphere of abstract existence. (Life is concrete, the inorganic is abstract.) But for a higher sphere this principle is no longer adequate. The old, abstract philosophies interpreted the universe on the principle of atomism, for example. But a principle like that is totally unsatisfactory for a higher philosophy, for life and mind. Consequently, consideration of its bearing on life and mind is of no interest to us. From this point of view, then, it is philosophical interest itself which determines us to consider here only the principles of the philosophies.

(b) *Historical and biographical details of the ancients not our concern*

The result is that in studying early Greek philosophy we have to stick to what is philosophical and not to history, biography, criticism, etc., and so not to what has been written about it or what is adventitious to it. All sorts of things have been brought into the history of philosophy, e.g. that Thales is supposed to have been the first to predict an eclipse of the sun, or that Descartes and Leibniz were skilled in mathematical analysis, and lots more of the same kind. All this we leave on one side.[4] So too we can hardly bother ourselves here with the history of the spread of philosophical systems. Our topic is purely and simply the doctrines of those systems, not their extrinsic history. For example, we can name a host of teachers of Stoicism who had great influence in their own day and even developed Stoicism in detail. We ignore this detail and pass over these men. Inasmuch as they became famous as teachers only, the history of philosophy is silent about them. [. . .]

The philosophies of subordinate principles or standpoints, we may also say, were not consistent; they have had profound glimpses of the truth but these lay outside the application of their principles. For example, Plato's *Timaeus* may be regarded as a philosophy of nature; it also enters the empirical field, but in this development, especially in physiology, it is obviously very insufficient. Its principle was not yet adequate for apprehending nature as spirit (for embracing the whole of nature). Yet it did not lack profound insights in detail. Such insights owe nothing to the principle; they exist inconsistently and wholly independently as happy thoughts. [. . .]

A further point to be noticed in this connection is directly associated with the conception of development and the concrete. [. . .]

The first stage in a development is the most abstract, the most indigent, the poorest in specifications, while the advanced stage is the richer. This at once shows us the correct relation of the stages to one another. True, this may seem to contradict our ordinary ideas because we might suppose that the first stage is the concrete one. It might be argued that the child exists in the original wholeness of his nature and is on friendly terms with the whole of the world, while the adult is no longer this totality; he restricts himself, makes his own only one specific part of the whole, gives himself *one* occupation, and thus he lives an abstract life. A similar argument is applied to the stages of intelligence and knowledge: feeling and intuition are supposed to be the first, wholly concrete, stage, while thinking is later, an activity which abstracts. But in fact the reverse is true in our subject. We must keep in view the ground on which we are standing. In the history of philosophy we are on the ground of thought. If we compare feeling with thought, it is clear that, from one point of view, feeling, like sense-perception generally, is certainly the more concrete, i.e. it is more concrete when taken generally, but it is poorer in *thoughts*. Thus we have to distinguish natural concreteness from the concreteness of thought. The natural kind is varied in contrast with the simplicity of thought. Compared with the natural variety of sense-perception, the adult consciousness is poor; but in respect of thinking, the child is the poorer and the adult more concrete because he is richer in thoughts. In our subject we are concerned with the concreteness of thought, and here scientific thinking is the more concrete in comparison with sense-perception.

Thus spirit in its beginnings is the poorer, and later it is the richer. When this is applied to the different forms of philosophy, it follows at once, in the *first* place, that the earliest philosophies are the poorest in content; in them the Idea is at its least determinate stage; they keep entirely to generalities which are left [abstract], unfilled. This we must realize so as not to require from ancient philosophies determinate contents which only a later and more concrete consciousness is in a position to provide. For example, if we ask (with Flatt: *De theismo Thaleti Milesio abjudicando*, Tübingen, 1785, p. 4) whether the philosophy of Thales was theism or not, our question is based on our own idea of God. But a deeper idea, like ours, is not yet to be found in the early Greek philosophers. Consequently, we are right enough, on the one hand, to describe the philosophy of Thales as atheism; but, on the other hand, this is to do him a great wrong because the thought of Thales, thought at its beginning, could not at that time have developed and attained the depth which we have. Depth, as intensive, seems to be opposed to the extensive; but in the spirit the greater intensiveness is at the same time the wider expansion and the greater wealth. The true intensiveness of spirit is to arrive at the strength of opposition, separation, division, and its expansion is the power to overlap opposition and to overcome separation. So too in recent times the question has been raised whether Thales asserted a personal God or a non-personal purely universal Being. Here it is a matter of the attribution of subjectivity, the conception of personality. But subjectivity, as we understand it, is a far too rich and intensive conception for it to have occurred to Thales; it is not to be sought in the earlier Greek philosophers at all.

A *second* inference from what has been said concerns, once again, the manner of treating the ancient philosophers. In them we must go to work with historical precision; we must ascribe to them only what is directly and historically reported about them. In many, indeed in most, histories of philosophy lots of things are wrong about these philosophers because we often find attributed to one or other of them a mass of metaphysical propositions of which he never knew one word. It is easy enough for us to find a philosophical argument and transform it according to our own level of reflection. But the most important thing in the history of philosophy is precisely to know whether such a proposition was already developed or not, because it is in this development that the progress of philosophy consists. In order to grasp this progress in its necessity we must treat each stage in and by itself, i.e. keep solely to the standpoint of the philosopher whom we are studying. In every proposition, every idea, there are of course other further specific propositions inherent, following from it logically, but it is a totally different matter whether they have already been made explicit or not. The entire difference in the various philosophies in the history of philosophy is the difference between thought implicit and thought being made explicit. Everything depends on setting forth explicitly what has been contained implicitly. Therefore we cannot keep too strictly to history, to the actual words of the philosophers themselves. Otherwise we easily introduce further categories which were foreign to their minds. Aristotle says [*Met.* 983ᵇ21] that Thales said: 'The principle (ἀρχή) of all things is water', but on the other hand it is asserted as historical that Anaximander was the first to use the word ἀρχή in the sense of 'principle'. Perhaps the word was current in Thales' time, possibly meaning 'beginning' (in time), but not as the thought of what is universal and the ground of everything. Thus we cannot ascribe to Thales so early the category of cause or principle; that category belongs to a further development of the intellect. Difference in culture consists only in the difference of the categories brought into the consciousness of an age. To go further with examples, we might say with Brucker[5] that Thales silently adopted the proposition *ex nihilo nihil fit*, because he treated water as an *eternal* element, as something which *is*. If so, then Thales has to be reckoned amongst the philosophers who deny creation from nothing. But this conclusion cannot be ascribed to Thales himself; looked at historically, he knew nothing whatever about any such proposition.

Professor Ritter[6] too, whose *Geschichte der ionischen Philosophie* is sedulously composed and who on the whole is moderately careful not to introduce foreign matter, has nevertheless ascribed to Thales more, perhaps, than is historically justified. He says, 'therefore we must regard the treatment of nature, which we find in Thales, as a dynamic one throughout'. This is something totally different from what Aristotle says. None of this is reported about Thales by any of the ancient authors. This inference does suggest itself, but it cannot be justified historically. By such inferences we ought not to make something different of an early Greek philosophy from what it was originally.

A *third* inference is that we must not hope to find answered for us in the early philosophers the questions arising in our minds or out of our interests. Such questions presuppose a greater development and a deeper precision of thought than was available to the early Greeks whose conceptions lacked the intensity of our thinking. Every philosophy is a philosophy of its time, is a link in the whole chain of spiritual development; thus it provides satisfaction only for those interests which are appropriate to their time.

As I have remarked before, all philosophies do live on in accordance with their principles; the stages at which they lived are also stages in *our* philosophy.[7] But our philosophy has gone beyond these stages, and consequently the earlier philosophies cannot be revived. No more can there be any Platonism or Aristotelianism. The concepts and forms which they had are no longer suited to our minds. Attempts at revival were indeed made, e.g. in the fifteenth and sixteenth centuries, when Platonic, Aristotelian, Epicurean and Stoic schools were founded. But these schools could in no way be the same as those in antiquity. A chief reason for these revivals was that it was supposed that Christianity had put an end to philosophy, and that if someone did still wish to pursue philosophy, he was told that he had better choose one of the ancient ones. But this retreat is only wandering through the earlier stages which every individual has to go through in his education.

This explains at the same time how those who study ancient philosophy alone come away from it dissatisfied. In it we can find only a certain degree of satisfaction. We can grasp the philosophies of Plato and Aristotle, but they do not answer *our* questions; they had different needs. In Plato, for example, we find unanswered our questions about the nature of freedom or the origin of evil, of wickedness, yet it is just these questions which pre-occupy us. The same is true of questions about the scope of knowledge, the opposition of subject and object, etc. The infinite demand of the subjectiv-ity, the independence, of the spirit in itself was still foreign to the Athenians. At that time man had not so turned in on himself as he has in our day. Yes, he *was* subject, but he had not yet established himself as such; he knew himself only in his essentially ethical unity[8] with his world, in his duties to the state. The Athenian and the Roman knew that his essence was to be a free citizen. That man as such is free in his essence, this neither Plato nor Aristotle knew. (Essentially, it is only in the principle of Christianity that the individual personal spirit has infinite and absolute worth.) When it comes to these questions, Plato and Aristotle do not satisfy us.

The earliest philosophies were necessarily quite simple, abstract and gen-eral. Only later do we find a mature self-consciousness, a self-knowledge of the spirit, a thinking in itself, with many categories compressed into one. But at the start no difference has been reached and we are at what is sim-plest and most abstract. This start is then further worked upon and becomes an object for the spirit which imposes a new form on what went before. Concreteness involves a one and an other and then more; consequently, only gradually is the concrete formed by concentrating all these together, by adding new categories to those of the previous principles. This must be borne in mind in judging an earlier philosophy, in order to know what to look for in it, for example, not to expect to find in Platonism everything which only our time seeks. We cannot be completely satisfied with an older philosophy, however excellent it may be. So too we cannot adopt or set up an older philosophy as the one valid now. We belong to a riper age of the spirit which does comprise the wealth of all earlier philosophies and pos-sesses them all concretely in itself. This deeper principle is alive in us, although not self-consciously. The spirit sets tasks to itself which were not yet tasks for an older philosophy, e.g. the opposition of good and evil, of freedom and necessity. These problems were neither treated nor solved by the Greeks. So it would be inept to propose to make Greek philosophy valid again. At the Renaissance it was of course necessary to become acquainted with Plato and Neo-Platonism; but we cannot abide by these philosophies. In the most recent philosophy the principles of preceding philosophies are unified. That philosophy is necessarily a developed system which contains the earlier ones as members in its organization. That philosophy is often called Pantheism, Eleaticism, etc. This is only a term used by superficial minds. These earlier standpoints are further determined later on, and thereby their one-sidedness is superseded.

What has been said up to this point comprises the conception, the meaning, of the history of philosophy. We have to consider the individual philosophies as stages in the development of the *one* Idea. Each philosophy displays itself as a necessary thought-determination, or category, of the Idea. In the succession of philosophies there is nothing arbitrary; the order in which they emerge is settled by necessity. This will be shown and characterized in more detail in the exposition of the history of philosophy.[9] Each factor in the whole comprises the totality of the Idea in a one-sided form; because of its one-sidedness it cancels itself and so, refuting its own finality, unites with what it lacked, i.e. its opposite number, and so becomes deeper and richer. This is the dialectic of these specific categories. But this movement does not end in nothing; the superseded categories have themselves an affirmative character. It is in this sense that we have to treat the history of philosophy.

Thus the history of philosophy is itself science. Philosophy in its non-historical development is the same as the history of philosophy. In a philosophy we have to begin with the simplest conceptions and proceed to more concrete ones. The same is the case with philosophy's history. In both we have a necessary progress and this is the same in both. What is interesting in the history of philosophy is therefore self-determining thought in a strictly scientific progress.

The history of philosophy is a mirror of philosophy, except that it is philosophy's complete development in time, in the realm of appearance and externality. This development is grounded indeed in the logical Idea and its development, yet we cannot conduct the exposition of our subject in its logical strictness throughout. But we must at least hint at that. [. . .]

The second point in the Introduction is the relation of philosophy to the rest of the manifestations of the spirit and the history of philosophy to the history of other subjects. [. . .]

4. Relation of the History of Philosophy to the Rest of the Manifestations of the Spirit

[. . .] We know that the history of philosophy is not on its own but has a connection with history generally, with the history of affairs as well as of religion, etc., and it is natural for us to recall the chief features of political history, the character of the age, and the whole situation of a people wherein a philosophy has arisen. But, this apart, this connection is inner, essential, necessary, not merely external or simultaneous. (Simultaneity is no relation.)

Therefore there are two things to notice: (i) the strictly historical aspect of this connection and (ii) the connection of the subject, i.e. the connection of philosophy itself with religion and the other intellectual activities related to it. These two things are to be considered more fully in order to distinguish more precisely the conception, the specific character, of philosophy.

The historical position of philosophy

The first point which must be noticed is the general relation of the philosophy of a given period to the rest of the characteristics of that period.

(*a*) It is usually said that political matters, religion, mythology, etc., are to be noticed in the history of philosophy because they have had a great influence on the philosophy of the time and vice versa. But if you are satisfied with categories like 'great influence', 'effect on one another', etc., all you have to do is to point to an external connection, i.e. you start by regarding both as on their own, independent of one another. But here we must consider this relation from a different aspect altogether: the essential category is unity, the inner connection of all these different manifestations. Here we must keep hold of the fact that it is only *one* spirit, *one* principle, which is stamped on the political situation and manifested in religion, art, moral and social life, trade and industry, so that all these different forms are but branches of one main trunk. This is the chief point of view. The spirit is *one* and one only; there is one spirit as the substance of an era, a people, an age, but it is shaped and manifested in various ways; and these different manifestations are the factors which have been adduced. Thus we must not have the idea that politics, constitutions, religions, etc., are the root or cause of philosophy, or that, conversely, philosophy is the basis of them. All these factors have *one* single character which lies at their root and runs through them all. However manifold all these different things are, there is no contradiction between them. Not one of them contains anything different in kind from their basis, no matter how much they seem to contradict one another. They are only shoots from the same root, and philosophy is one of them.

It is presupposed here that all this stands in one necessary connection so that only *this* philosophy, *this* religion, can exist along with *this* political constitution, *this* state of the sciences. There is only *one* spirit; its development is a single progress – one principle, one Idea, one character expressed in the most varied formations. This is what we call the spirit of an age. This too is nothing superficial or determined from outside; knowledge of it must be drawn, not from petty externals, but from its great formations in the world. Philosophy is one of these and it is contemporary with a specific religion, political constitution, art, morals, science, etc. [. . .]

Thus the historical shape of a philosophy stands in a necessary connection with political history. Before there can be a philosophy at all, a people must have reached a certain stage of intellectual development. The necessities of life must have been supplied [cf. Aristotle: *Met.* 982ᵇ22], the agony of desire must have vanished; the purely finite interests of men must have been worked off, and their minds must have advanced so far as to take an interest in universal matters. Philosophy is free activity (hence the need for philosophy). So it can be regarded as a luxury because luxury is the satisfaction derived from things that are not directly necessary, and from this point of view philosophy is of course dispensable. But all depends on what you call necessary. From the point of view of the thinking spirit, however, philosophy must be regarded as the most necessary thing of all. [...]

Thus philosophy as such only enters at a specific epoch in a whole civilization. But it occurs there not as philosophy simply but as a specific philosophy; and this specific character of conscious thought also constitutes the basis of everything else that exists, of every aspect of the history of the time. The laws of peoples, their morals, their social life, etc., are most intimately associated with this specific character. It is essential here to keep hold of the fact that when the spirit has reached a specific stage, it builds this principle into the entire wealth of its world, works it out into the many-sidedness of its existence, so that all the other specific characters of that world are dependent on this fundamental one. The philosophy of our time, or any philosophy necessary within Christendom, could not exist in heathen Rome because all aspects, branches, situations and relations of a whole civilization are expressions of one and the same specific character which philosophy enunciates in terms of pure thought. Therefore it cannot be said that political history is the cause of philosophy, since a branch is not the cause of a whole tree; the branch and the trunk have a common root, and the root common to philosophy and politics, etc., is the spirit of the age, i.e. the specific stage in the development of the spirit at a time which has its proximate cause (its ground) in the preceding stage but, in general terms, in one form of the Idea. To demonstrate this unity, to expound this whole growth, to comprehend it as proceeding from one root, is the task of the philosophy of world-history, which must be left aside here. We are only concerned with one branch, with the pure thought of these aspects, situations, etc., with the philosophical consciousness of each era. But we had at least to point out the connection between the principle of philosophy and the principle of the rest of history.

(β) Thus philosophy is *one aspect* of the entire formation or manifestation of the spirit – it is the consciousness of the spirit and spirit's supreme flowering, since its endeavour is to know what spirit is. In general terms, the dignity of man is to know what he is and to know this in the purest way, i.e. to rise to the thought of what he is. From this the position of philosophy among the other forms of the spirit can be inferred.

(αα) Philosophy is identical with the spirit of the age in which it appears; it does not rise above its time but is only a consciousness of the substance of its time or the thoughtful knowledge of what there is in that time. Neither does an individual transcend his time; he is a son of it; its substance is his own essence, and he only manifests it in a particular form. No one can escape from the substance of his time any more than he can jump out of his skin. Looked at fundamentally, no philosophy can overleap its own time.

(ββ) But philosophy does also stand above its time, i.e. makes it an object set over against itself, its content is the same as the content of the time, but, as knowledge of this content, it is away above it. This, however, is only formal, and in fact philosophy has no other content but that of the time.

(γγ) This very knowledge is of course the actuality of spirit – I *am* only to the extent that I know myself. So the difference of form is also a real and actual difference. Thus it is this knowledge which produces a new form in the development of spirit. Developments in this sphere are merely ways of knowing. By this self-knowledge the spirit differentiates itself from what it is; it makes itself an object to itself and develops itself within; this entails a new difference between what it is implicitly and what it is actually, and in this way a new formation of the spirit emerges. Thus philosophy in itself is already a further specific characterization of the spirit; it is its inner birthplace which appears later as actuality. The concrete character of this emerges in the history of philosophy itself. Thus we will see that what Greek philosophy had been, entered actuality in the Christian world.

So this is the second point, namely that philosophy is primarily only the thinking of what is substantive in its own time; it does not transcend its time but only brings out its content in thought.

(γ) The third point to notice in connection with philosophy and history concerns the date at which philosophy emerges in comparison with the emergence of the other formations of the spirit. Philosophy appears at a specific time, not contemporaneously with the other formations.

The spirit of an age is the substantive life of that age. That life is this immediate, living and actual spirit. For example, we descry the Greek spirit at the time when Greek life was blossoming, was fresh, forceful and young, before any corruption had broken in, or we see the Roman spirit at the time of the Republic – and so on. The spirit of the age is thus the way in which a specific spirit is present as actually living. But philosophy is the thinking of this spirit, and the thought, however much it is a priori also, is essentially the result of the spirit, because the spirit is life, the activity of self-production; its procedure is to produce itself as a result, to emerge as a result. This activity contains a negation as an essential factor. If something is to be produced, then it must be produced from something else, and this something else is precisely thereby negated. Thus thinking is the negation of the natural mode of life. For example, the child exists as a human being but still immediately, directly, in a natural way; then education is the negation of this natural way, the discipline imposed by the spirit on itself in order to rise out of its immediacy. Similarly, the thinking spirit, at the start of its movement, exists in its natural shape; then it becomes reflective and rises above that shape, i.e. negates it; and finally, it realizes itself in comprehending itself.

Thinking enters. The consequence is that the existing world, the spirit realized in the morals [*Sittlichkeit*] and force of life at that time, is negated; thought, spirit's substantive mode of existence, attacks and weakens simple ethical life, simple religion, etc., and this ushers in a period of corruption. Then the next step is that thought concentrates itself in itself, becomes concrete and so produces for itself an ideal world in opposition to this real one. Thus when philosophy is to emerge among a people, there must first have been a break in the real world. At that point philosophy is the reconciliation of the corruption which had been begun by thought. This reconciliation happens in the ideal world, in the world of the spirit into which men take flight when the earthly world satisfies them no longer. Philosophy begins with the downfall of a real world. When philosophy enters, 'paints its grey in grey',[10] disseminates its abstractions, then the fresh colour of youth and life has already perished. In that event it is a reconciliation which philosophy produces, but only in the intellectual world, not in the earthly one. So too, the Greeks when they began to think, withdrew from political life; and they began to think when everything in the world outside was stormy and wretched, i.e. at the time of the Peloponnesian war. That was when the philosophers withdrew into their world of thought. They became, what the masses called them, idlers. And so, in almost all peoples, philosophy only appears when public life no longer gives satisfaction and ceases to engross the popular interest, when the citizen can no longer take any part in government.

This is an essential point which will be proved in the history of philosophy itself. With the downfall of the states in Ionia, the Ionian philosophy arose. The spirit was no longer satisfied by the external world. Similarly in Rome, philosophy only began with the fall of the Republic when demagogues took over the government and everything was caught up in dissolution and a struggle for something new. And only with the downfall of the Roman Empire – an Empire so great, magnificent, but inwardly already dead – did the older Greek philosophies experience their lofty and supreme development through the Neo-Platonists or Alexandrians. [. . .]

In the misfortunes of the Empire political, ethical, and religious life had weakened, and this we encounter again in the fifteenth and sixteenth centuries when the Germanic life of the Middle Ages won another form, when the spirit of the peoples no longer found its satisfaction where it had been found previously. Earlier on, politics was still in unity with religion, and the Church dominated even when the state fought it. Now, however, the breach between the state–civil, ethical, political life – and the Church occurred, and at this date people began to philosophize, even if at first only in the form of learning and revivifying Greek philosophies. Not till later did philosophy have the form of independent thinking. [. . .][11]

Notes

1 This passage was written by Hegel himself in 1820. [S.H.]
2 All following passages are taken from student transcripts of Hegel's lectures. [S.H.]
3 See W. G. Tennemann, *Geschichte der Philosophie*, 11 parts (Leipzig, 1798–1819). [S.H.]
4 But Hegel did not abide by this intention. [Translator's note.]
5 J. J. Brucker, *Historia critica philosophiae* (Leipzig, 1766–7), 1: 465–78. [Translator's note.]
6 A. H. Ritter, *Geschichte der ionischen Philosophie* (Berlin, 1821), pp. 12–13. [Translator's note.]

7 Hegel, *Introduction to the Lectures on the History of Philosophy*, pp. 94, 98 (above, pp. 513, 516). [s.h.]
8 See above, p. 481, note 1. [s.h.]
9 Not included in this collection. For Hegel's detailed exposition of the history of philosophy from the Greeks to German Idealism, see G. W. F. Hegel, *Lectures on the History of Philosophy: The Lectures of 1825–1826*, edited by R. F. Brown, translated by R. F. Brown and J. M. Stewart, with the assistance of H. S. Harris, 3 vols (Berkeley: University of California Press, 1990ff).
10 See Hegel, *Elements of the Philosophy of Right*, p. 23. See above, p. 327. [s.h.]
11 One should bear in mind, however, that in 1806 Hegel saw his *own* philosophy as contemporaneous with the birth of a new era. See Hegel, *Phenomenology of Spirit*, p. 6 (above, p. 50). [s.h.]

Bibliography

Hegel in German

The following list includes the historical-critical edition of Hegel's collected works, the associated edition of selected lectures and manuscripts, the popular Suhrkamp study edition of his works, and six other texts which contain important additional material from his lectures.

G. W. F. Hegel, *Gesammelte Werke*, edited by the Rheinisch-Westfälische Akademie der Wissenschaften in association with the Deutsche Forschungsgemeinschaft, 22 vols published or planned (Hamburg: Felix Meiner, 1968ff).

G. W. F. Hegel, *Vorlesungen: Ausgewählte Nachschriften und Manuskripte*, edited by the members of the Hegel-Archiv, 13 vols published or planned (Hamburg: Felix Meiner, 1983ff).

G. W. F. Hegel, *Werke in zwanzig Bänden*, edited by E. Moldenhauer and K. M. Michel, 20 vols and Index (Frankfurt: Suhrkamp Verlag, 1969ff).

G. W. F. Hegel, *Naturphilosophie*. Vol. 1: *Die Vorlesung von 1819/20*, edited by M. Gies in association with K. -H. Ilting (Naples: Instituto Italiano per gli Studi Filosofici, 1982).

G. W. F. Hegel, *Vorlesungen über Rechtsphilosophie. 1818–1831*, edited by K. -H. Ilting, 4 vols (Stuttgart: Frommann-Holzboog, 1973–4).

G. W. F. Hegel, *Philosophie des Rechts: Die Vorlesung von 1819/20 in einer Nachschrift*, edited by D. Henrich (Frankfurt: Suhrkamp Verlag, 1983).

G. W. F. Hegel, *Vorlesungen über die Philosophie der Weltgeschichte. Erste Hälfte: Die Vernunft in der Geschichte*, edited by J. Hoffmeister (Hamburg: Felix Meiner, 1955).

G. W. F. Hegel, *Vorlesung über Ästhetik. Berlin 1820/21. Eine Nachschrift. I. Textband*, edited by H. Schneider (Frankfurt: Peter Lang, 1995).

G. W. F. Hegel, *Einleitung in die Geschichte der Philosophie*, edited by J. Hoffmeister (Hamburg: Felix Meiner, 1940).

Hegel in English

The following is a comprehensive, though not exhaustive, list of English translations of Hegel's works. Alternative translations of the whole, or of part, of the same German text are grouped together as 8, 8a, and so on. Translations which contain material from the same area of Hegel's philosophy, but which are based on different German editions (usually utilizing texts and lectures from different years), are listed as separate items.

1) *Hegel. Selections*, edited by J. Loewenberg (New York: Charles Scribner's Sons, 1929).
2) *The Philosophy of Hegel*, edited with an introduction by C. J. Friedrich (New York: Random House, 1953).
3) *Hegel: The Essential Writings*, edited and with introductions by F. G. Weiss, foreword by J. N. Findlay (New York: Harper and Row, 1974).
4) *Hegel. Selections*, edited, with introduction, notes, and bibliography by M. J. Inwood (New York: Macmillan, 1989).
5) G. W. F. Hegel, *Three Essays, 1793–1795: The Tübingen Essay, Berne Fragments, The Life of Jesus*, edited and translated with an introduction and notes by P. Fuss and J. Dobbins (Notre Dame: University of Notre Dame Press, 1984).
6) G. W. F. Hegel, *Early Theological Writings*, translated by T. M. Knox, with an introduction, and fragments translated by R. Kroner (Chicago: University of Chicago Press, 1948).
7) 'Hegel. *Philosophical Dissertation on the Orbits of the Planets* (1801). Preceded by the 12 Theses Defended on August 27, 1801', translation by P. Adler, *Graduate Faculty Philosophy Journal* 12, 1–2 (1987): 269–309.
7a) 'Hegel's *Habilitationsthesen*', translated with introduction and annotated bibliography by N. Waszek, in *Hegel and Modern Philosophy*, edited by D. Lamb (London: Croom Helm, 1987), pp. 249–60.
8) G. W. F. Hegel, *The Difference between Fichte's and Schelling's System of Philosophy*, translated by H. S. Harris and W. Cerf (Albany: SUNY Press, 1977).
8a) G. W. F. Hegel, *The Difference Between the Fichtean and Schellingian Systems of Philosophy*, translated by J. P. Surber (Reseda, CA: Ridgeview, 1978).
9) G. W. F. Hegel, *Faith and Knowledge: An English Translation of 'Glauben und Wissen'*, translated and edited by W. Cerf and H. S. Harris (Albany: SUNY Press, 1977).
10) G. W. F. Hegel, 'On the Essence of Philosophical Criticism' (with Schelling), 'How the Ordinary Human Understanding Takes Philosophy (as Displayed in the Works of Mr Krug)', and 'Relationship of Skepticism to Philosophy', translated by H. S. Harris, in *Between Kant and Hegel. Texts in the Development of German Idealism*, translated and annotated by G. di Giovanni and H. S. Harris (Albany: SUNY Press, 1985).
11) G. W. F. Hegel, *Natural Law*, translated by T. M. Knox, introduction by H. B. Acton ([Philadelphia]: University of Pennsylvania Press, 1975).
12) G. W. F. Hegel, *'System of Ethical Life' (1802/3) and 'First Philosophy of Spirit' (Part Three of the System of Speculative Philosophy 1803/4)*, edited and translated by H. S. Harris and T. M. Knox (Albany: SUNY Press, 1979).
13) G. W. F. Hegel, *Jena System of 1804–1805: Logic and Metaphysics*, translation edited by J. Burbidge and G. di Giovanni, introduction and notes by H. S. Harris (Montreal: McGill-Queen's University Press, 1986).
14) *Hegel and the Human Spirit: A Translation of the Jena Lectures on the Philosophy of Spirit (1805–6) with Commentary*, edited by L. Rauch (Detroit: Wayne State University Press, 1983).
15) *Hegel's Political Writings*, translated by T. M. Knox, with an introductory essay by Z. A. Pelczynski (Oxford: Clarendon Press, 1964).
16) G. W. F. Hegel, 'Who Thinks Abstractly', translated by W. Kaufmann, in W. Kaufmann, *Hegel. Reinterpretation, Texts, and Commentary* (London: Weidenfeld and Nicolson, 1966), pp. 460–5.
17) G. W. F. Hegel, *Phenomenology of Spirit*, translated by A. V. Miller, with analysis of the text and foreword by J. N. Findlay (Oxford: Oxford University Press, 1977).

17a) G. W. F. Hegel, *The Phenomenology of Mind*, translated, with an introduction and notes by J. B. Baillie (New York: Harper and Row, 1967).

17b) G. W. F. Hegel, *Preface and Introduction to the Phenomenology of Mind*, translated by J. B. Baillie, edited, with an introduction by L. S. Stepelevich (New York: Macmillan, 1990).

17c) G. W. F. Hegel, *Phenomenology of Spirit*, selections translated and annotated by H. P. Kainz (University Park, PA: Pennsylvania State University Press, 1994).

18) G. W. F. Hegel, *The Philosophical Propaedeutic*, translated by A. V. Miller, edited by M. George and A. Vincent (Oxford: Blackwell, 1986).

19) G. W. F. Hegel, *Science of Logic*, translated by A. V. Miller, foreword by J. N. Findlay (Atlantic Highlands, NJ: Humanities Press International, 1989).

19a) G. W. F. Hegel, *Science of Logic*, translated by W. H. Johnston and L. G. Struthers, 2 vols (London: George Allen and Unwin, 1929).

20) G. W. F. Hegel, *Encyclopedia of the Philosophical Sciences in Outline* [1817] *and Critical Writings*, edited, with introduction by E. Behler (New York: Continuum, 1990).

21) G. W. F. Hegel, *The Encyclopaedia Logic. Part 1 of the Encyclopaedia of the Philosophical Sciences with the Zusätze* [1830], translated by T. F. Geraets, W. A. Suchting and H. S. Harris (Indianapolis: Hackett Publishing, 1991).

21a) G. W. F. Hegel, *Logic. Being Part One of the Encyclopaedia of the Philosophical Sciences (1830)*, translated by W. Wallace, with foreword by J. N. Findlay (Oxford: Clarendon Press, 1975).

22) G. W. F. Hegel, *Philosophy of Nature. Being Part Two of the Encyclopaedia of the Philosophical Sciences (1830)*, translated by A. V. Miller, with foreword by J. N. Findlay (Oxford: Clarendon Press, 1970).

22a) G. W. F. Hegel, *Philosophy of Nature*, edited and translated with an introduction and explanatory notes by M. J. Petry, 3 vols (London: George Allen and Unwin, 1970).

23) G. W. F. Hegel, *Philosophy of Mind. Being Part Three of the Encyclopaedia of the Philosophical Sciences (1830)*, translated by W. Wallace, together with the *Zusätze* in Boumann's text (1845), translated by A. V. Miller, with foreword by J. N. Findlay (Oxford: Clarendon Press, 1971).

23a) G. W. F. Hegel, *Philosophy of Subjective Spirit*, edited and translated by M. J. Petry, 3 vols (Dordrecht: D Reidel, 1978).

23b) G. W. F. Hegel, *The Berlin Phenomenology* [from the *Philosophy of Subjective Spirit*], edited and translated by M. J. Petry (Dordrecht: D. Reidel, 1981).

24) G. W. F. Hegel, *Lectures on Natural Right and Political Science. The First Philosophy of Right. Heidelberg 1817–1818*, edited by the Staff of the Hegel Archives, with an introduction by O. Pöggeler, translated by J. M. Stewart and P. C. Hodgson (Berkeley: University of California Press, 1995).

25) G. W. F. Hegel, *Elements of the Philosophy of Right*, edited by A. W. Wood, translated by H. B. Nisbet (Cambridge: Cambridge University Press, 1991).

25a) G. W. F. Hegel, *Philosophy of Right*, translated with notes by T. M. Knox (Oxford: Clarendon Press, 1952).

25b) G. W. F. Hegel, *Philosophy of Right*, translated by S. W. Dyde (London: G. Bell and Sons, 1896).

26) G. W. F. Hegel, *Lectures on the Philosophy of World History. Introduction: Reason in History*, translated by H. B. Nisbet, with an introduction by D. Forbes (Cambridge: Cambridge University Press, 1975).

27) G. W. F. Hegel, *The Philosophy of History*, translated by J. Sibree, with an introduction by C. J. Friedrich (New York: Dover Publications, 1956).

27a) G. W. F. Hegel, *Reason in History: A General Introduction to the Philosophy of History*, translated with an introduction by R. S. Hartman (New York: Macmillan, 1987).

27b) G. W. F. Hegel, *Introduction to the Philosophy of History, with Selections from the Philosophy of Right,* translated with introduction by L. Rauch (Indianapolis: Hackett, 1988).

28) G. W. F. Hegel, *Aesthetics. Lectures on Fine Art,* translated by T. M. Knox (Oxford: Clarendon Press, 1975).

28a) G. W. F. Hegel, *Introduction to Aesthetics,* translated by T. M. Knox, with an interpretative essay by C. Karelis (Oxford: Clarendon Press, 1979).

28b) G. W. F. Hegel, *Introductory Lectures on Aesthetics,* translated by B. Bosanquet, edited with an introduction and commentary by M. Inwood (Harmondsworth: Penguin Classics, 1993).

28c) G. W. F. Hegel, *The Philosophy of Fine Art,* translated by F. P. B. Osmaston, 4 vols (London: G. Bell and Sons, 1920).

28d) *Hegel on Tragedy,* edited by A. and H. Paolucci (New York: Doubleday, 1960).

28e) *Hegel: On the Arts,* edited by H. Paolucci (New York: Ungar, 1978).

29) G. W. F. Hegel, *Lectures on the Philosophy of Religion,* edited by P. C. Hodgson, translated by R. F. Brown, P. C. Hodgson and J. M. Stewart, with the assistance of H. S. Harris, 3 vols (Berkeley: University of California Press, 1984–7).

29a) G. W. F. Hegel, *Lectures on the Philosophy of Religion* (One Volume Edition: The Lectures of 1827), edited by P. C. Hodgson, translated by R. F. Brown, P. C. Hodgson and J. M. Stewart, with the assistance of H. S. Harris (Berkeley: University of California Press, 1988).

29b) *G. W. F. Hegel: Theologian of the Spirit,* edited by P. C. Hodgson (Edinburgh: T. & T. Clark, 1997).

30) G. W. F. Hegel, *The Christian Religion,* edited and translated by P. Hodgson (Missoula, MT: Scholars Press, 1979).

31) G. W. F. Hegel, *Lectures on the Philosophy of Religion,* translated by E. G. Speirs and J. B. Sanderson, 3 vols (New York: Humanities Press, 1962).

32) G. W. F. Hegel, *Introduction to the Lectures on the History of Philosophy,* translated by T. M. Knox and A. V. Miller (Oxford: Clarendon Press, 1985).

32a) G. W. F. Hegel, 'Introduction to the History of Philosophy', translated by Q. Lauer, in Q. Lauer, *Hegel's Idea of Philosophy* (New York: Fordham University Press, 1971).

33) G. W. F. Hegel, *Lectures on the History of Philosophy: The Lectures of 1825–1826,* edited by R. F. Brown, translated by R. F. Brown and J. M. Stewart, with the assistance of H. S. Harris, 3 vols (Berkeley: University of California Press, 1990ff).

34) G. W. F. Hegel, *Lectures on the History of Philosophy,* translated by E. S. Haldane and F. H. Simson, 3 vols (London: Kegan Paul, Trench and Trübner, 1892–6).

35) *Hegel: The Letters,* translated by C. Butler and C. Seiler, commentary by C. Butler (Bloomington: Indiana University Press, 1984).

Secondary Works on Hegel

The following is a list of selected secondary works on Hegel in English. For further works on Hegel, see K. Steinhauer, *Hegel-Bibliographie* (Munich: K. G. Sauer, 1980) and the 'Bibliographical Essay' in Houlgate, *Freedom, Truth and History* (below). Articles on Hegel in English can also be found in *The Owl of Minerva (Journal of the Hegel Society of America),* the *Bulletin of the Hegel Society of Great Britain, Hegel-Studien, Hegel-Jahrbuch* and the *Jahrbuch für Hegelforschung.*

T. W. Adorno, *Hegel: Three Studies,* translated by S. W. Nicholsen, with an introduction by S. W. Nicholsen and J. J. Shapiro (Cambridge, MA: MIT Press, 1993).

S. Avineri, *Hegel's Theory of the Modern State* (Cambridge: Cambridge University Press, 1972).

F. Beiser, ed., *The Cambridge Companion to Hegel* (Cambridge: Cambridge University Press, 1993).

S. Bungay, *Beauty and Truth. A Study of Hegel's Aesthetics* (Oxford: Oxford University Press, 1984).

J. Burbidge, *On Hegel's Logic. Fragments of a Commentary* (Atlantic Highlands, NJ: Humanities Press, 1981).

J. Burbidge, *Real Process: How Logic and Chemistry Combine in Hegel's Philosophy of Nature* (Toronto: University of Toronto Press, 1996).

R. S. Cohen and M. Wartofsky, eds, *Hegel and the Sciences* (Boston: D. Reidel, 1984).

A. B. Collins, ed., *Hegel on the Modern World* (Albany: SUNY Press, 1995).

J. Derrida, 'From Restricted to General Economy: A Hegelianism Without Reserve', in *Writing and Difference*, translated with an introduction and additional notes by A. Bass (London: Routledge and Kegan Paul, 1978), pp. 251–77.

J. Derrida, 'The Pit and the Pyramid: Introduction to Hegel's Semiology', in *Margins of Philosophy*, translated, with additional notes, by A. Bass (Brighton: The Harvester Press, 1982), pp. 69–108.

J. Derrida, *Glas*, translated by J. P. Leavey, Jr. and R. Rand (Lincoln: University of Nebraska Press, 1986).

W. Desmond, *Art and the Absolute. A Study of Hegel's Aesthetics* (Albany: SUNY Press, 1986).

W. Desmond, ed., *Hegel and His Critics. Philosophy in the Aftermath of Hegel* (Albany: SUNY Press, 1989).

W. A. deVries, *Hegel's Theory of Mental Activity. An Introduction to Theoretical Spirit* (Ithaca: Cornell University Press, 1988).

J. D'Hondt, *Hegel in His Time: 1818–1831*, translated by J. Burbidge, with N. Roland and J. Levasseur (Peterborough, Ontario: Broadview, 1988).

L. Dickey, *Hegel. Religion, Economics, and the Politics of Spirit, 1770–1807* (Cambridge: Cambridge University Press, 1987).

E. Fackenheim, *The Religious Dimension in Hegel's Thought* (Chicago: University of Chicago Press, 1967).

J. N. Findlay, *Hegel: A Re-examination* (New York: Oxford University Press, 1958).

J. C. Flay, *Hegel's Quest for Certainty* (Albany: SUNY Press, 1984).

M. N. Forster, *Hegel and Skepticism* (Cambridge, MA: Harvard University Press, 1989).

H. -G. Gadamer, *Hegel's Dialectic. Five Hermeneutical Studies*, translated and with an introduction by P. C. Smith (New Haven: Yale University Press, 1976).

G. di Giovanni, ed., *Essays on Hegel's Logic* (Albany: SUNY Press, 1990).

E. E. Harris, *An Interpretation of the Logic of Hegel* (Lanham, MD: University Press of America, 1983).

H. S. Harris, *Hegel's Development. Towards the Sunlight. 1770–1801* (Oxford: Clarendon Press, 1972).

H. S. Harris, *Hegel's Development. Night Thoughts (Jena 1801–1806)* (Oxford: Clarendon Press, 1983).

M. Heidegger, *Hegel's Phenomenology of Spirit*, translated by P. Emad and K. Maly (Bloomington: Indiana University Press, 1988).

S. Houlgate, *Hegel, Nietzsche and the Criticism of Metaphysics* (Cambridge: Cambridge University Press, 1986).

S. Houlgate, *Freedom, Truth and History. An Introduction to Hegel's Philosophy* (London: Routledge, 1991).

S. Houlgate, ed., *Hegel and the Philosophy of Nature* (Albany: SUNY Press, 1998).

J. Hyppolite, *Genesis and Structure of Hegel's Phenomenology of Spirit*, translated by S. Cherniak and J. Heckman (Evanston, IL: Northwestern University Press, 1974).

M. Inwood, ed., *Hegel* (Oxford: Oxford University Press, 1985).

W. Jaeschke, *Reason in Religion. The Foundations of Hegel's Philosophy of Religion*, translated by J. M. Stewart and P. C. Hodgson (Berkeley: University of California Press, 1990).

J. Kaminsky, *Hegel on Art. An Interpretation of Hegel's Aesthetics* (Albany: SUNY Press, 1962).

A. Kojève, *Introduction to the Reading of Hegel: Lectures on the 'Phenomenology of Spirit'*, edited by A. Bloom, translated by J. H. Nichols, Jr. (Ithaca: Cornell University Press, 1980).

D. Kolb, *The Critique of Pure Modernity. Hegel, Heidegger, and After* (Chicago: University of Chicago Press, 1986).

Q. Lauer, *A Reading of Hegel's Phenomenology of Spirit* (New York: Fordham University Press, 1976).

A. MacIntyre, ed., *Hegel: A Collection of Critical Essays* (Garden City, NY: Doubleday, 1972).

W. Maker, *Philosophy Without Foundations. Rethinking Hegel* (Albany: SUNY Press, 1994).

J. McCumber, *The Company of Words. Hegel, Language, and Systematic Philosophy* (Evanston, IL: Northwestern University Press, 1993).

G. D. O'Brien, *Hegel on Reason and History. A Contemporary Interpretation* (Chicago: University of Chicago Press, 1975).

J. O'Neill, ed., *Hegel's Dialectic of Desire and Recognition: Texts and Commentary* (Albany: SUNY Press, 1996).

C. O'Regan, *The Heterodox Hegel* (Albany: SUNY Press, 1994).

Z. A. Pelczynski, ed., *Hegel's Political Philosophy. Problems and Perspectives* (Cambridge: Cambridge University Press, 1971).

Z. A. Pelczynski, ed., *The State and Civil Society. Studies in Hegel's Political Philosophy* (Cambridge: Cambridge University Press, 1984).

M. J. Petry, ed., *Hegel and Newtonianism* (Dordrecht: Kluwer, 1993).

T. Pinkard, *Hegel's Phenomenology. The Sociality of Reason* (Cambridge: Cambridge University Press, 1996).

R. Pippin, *Hegel's Idealism. The Satisfactions of Self-consciousness* (Cambridge: Cambridge University Press, 1989).

R. Plant, *Hegel. An Introduction* (Oxford: Blackwell, 1983).

J. Ritter, *Hegel and the French Revolution: Essays on the Philosophy of Right*, translated and with an introduction by R. D. Winfield (Cambridge, MA: MIT Press, 1982).

G. Rose, *Hegel Contra Sociology* (London: Athlone Press, 1981).

F. W. J. von Schelling, 'Hegel', in *On the History of Modern Philosophy*, translation, introduction and notes by Andrew Bowie (Cambridge: Cambridge University Press, 1994), pp. 134–63.

R. Stern, *Hegel, Kant and the Structure of the Object* (New York: Routledge, 1990).

R. Stern, ed., *G. W. F. Hegel: Critical Assessments*, 4 vols (London: Routledge, 1993).

J. Stewart, ed., *The Hegel Myths and Legends* (Evanston, IL: Northwestern University Press, 1996)

C. Taylor, *Hegel* (Cambridge: Cambridge University Press, 1975).

C. Taylor, *Hegel and Modern Society* (Cambridge: Cambridge University Press, 1979).

N. Waszek, *The Scottish Enlightenment and Hegel's Account of 'Civil Society'* (Dordrecht: Martinus Nijhoff, 1988).

K. R. Westphal, *Hegel's Epistemological Realism. A Study of the Aim and Method of Hegel's Phenomenology of Spirit* (Dordrecht: Kluwer, 1989).

A. White, *Absolute Knowledge: Hegel and the Problem of Metaphysics* (Athens, OH: Ohio University Press, 1983).

R. Williams, *Recognition. Fichte and Hegel on the Other* (Albany: SUNY Press, 1992).

R. Williams, *Hegel's Ethics of Recognition* (Berkeley: University of California Press, 1997).

R. Winfield, *Reason and Justice* (Albany: SUNY Press, 1988).

A. W. Wood, *Hegel's Ethical Thought* (Cambridge: Cambridge University Press, 1990).

Index